THE WAITE GROUP ®

POWERBUILDER 5
HOW-TO

Daryl Biberdorf, Keith Glidden, Shelley Powers

Waite Group Press™
A Division of Sams Publishing
Corte Madera, CA

Publisher: *Mitchell Waite*
Editor-in-Chief: *Charles Drucker*

Acquisitions Manager: *Jill Pisoni*

Editorial Director: *John Crudo*
Project Editor: *Andrea Rosenberg*
Content Editors: *Heidi Brumbaugh, Harry Henderson*
Copy Editor: *Deirdre Greene*
Technical Reviewer: *Andy Tauber, Team Powersoft*

Production Director: *Julianne Ososke*
Production Manager: *Cecile Kaufman*
Cover Design: *Sestina Quarequio*
Cover Illustration: *Jeff Koegel*
Design: *Karen Johnston*
Production: *Judith Levinson, Bill Romano*
Illustrations: *Larry Wilson*

© 1996 by The Waite Group, Inc.®
Published by Waite Group Press™, 200 Tamal Plaza, Corte Madera, CA 94925.

Waite Group Press™ is a division of Sams Publishing.

Printed in the United States of America
96 97 98 99 • 10 9 8 7 6 5 4 3 2 1

Library of Congress Cataloging-in-Publication Data
Biberdorf, Daryl.
   PowerBuilder 5 how-to / Daryl Biberdorf, Keith Glidden, Shelley Powers.
     p. cm.
   ISBN: 1-57169-055-7
   1. Application software--Development. 2. PowerBuilder.
I. Glidden, Keith. II. Powers, Shelley III. Title.
QA76.76.A65B52   1996
005.2--dc20
                                       96-8645
                                           CIP

DEDICATION

To my beloved wife, Dea.
—Daryl Biberdorf

To my wife and children for their unmerited patience.
—Keith Glidden

This is dedicated to Rob and Zoe for being there for me.
—Shelley Powers

Message from the
Publisher

WELCOME TO OUR NERVOUS SYSTEM

Some people say that the World Wide Web is a graphical extension of the information superhighway, just a network of humans and machines sending each other long lists of the equivalent of digital junk mail.

I think it is much more than that. To me, the Web is nothing less than the nervous system of the entire planet—not just a collection of computer brains connected together, but more like a billion silicon neurons entangled and recirculating electro-chemical signals of information and data, each contributing to the birth of another CPU and another Web site.

Think of each person's hard disk connected at once to every other hard disk on earth, driven by human navigators searching like Columbus for the New World. Seen this way the Web is more of a super entity, a growing, living thing, controlled by the universal human will to expand, to be more. Yet, unlike a purposeful business plan with rigid rules, the Web expands in a nonlinear, unpredictable, creative way that echoes natural evolution.

We created our Web site not just to extend the reach of our computer book products but to be part of this synaptic neural network, to experience, like a nerve in the body, the flow of ideas and then to pass those ideas up the food chain of the mind. Your mind. Even more, we wanted to pump some of our own creative juices into this rich wine of technology.

TASTE OUR DIGITAL WINE

And so we ask you to taste our wine by visiting the body of our business. Begin by understanding the metaphor we have created for our Web site—a universal learning center, situated in outer space in the form of a space station. A place where you can journey to study any topic from the convenience of your own screen. Right now we are focusing on computer topics, but the stars are the limit on the Web.

If you are interested in discussing this Web site or finding out more about the Waite Group, please send me e-mail with your comments, and I will be happy to respond. Being a programmer myself, I love to talk about technology and find out what our readers are looking for.

Sincerely,

Mitchell Waite

Mitchell Waite, C.E.O. and Publisher

200 Tamal Plaza
Corte Madera, CA 94925
415-924-2575
415-924-2576 fax

Website:
http://www.waite.com/waite

CREATING THE HIGHEST QUALITY COMPUTER BOOKS IN THE INDUSTRY

Waite Group Press
Waite Group New Media

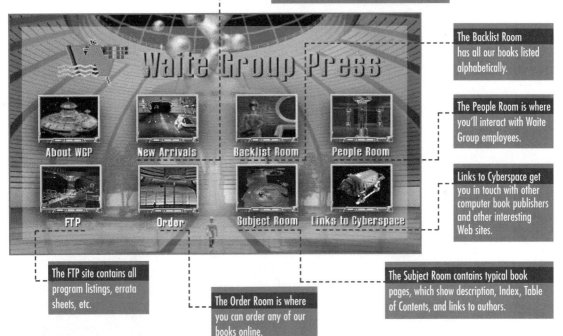

ABOUT THE AUTHORS

Daryl Biberdorf

Daryl Biberdorf is a Certified PowerBuilder Instructor and consultant, and has been using PowerBuilder since its introduction in 1991. His language background includes C, Pascal, Fortran, Basic, and several assembly languages. Daryl began programming at age 13, and first published a program, "Snake Escape", in the premier issue of *Compute!'s Gazette* in the early 1980s. He has since received his B.S. in Computer Engineering from Texas A&M University and now lives in Dallas, Texas, with his wife, Dea.

Keith Glidden

Keith Glidden is President of Object Technology Systems, a Southern California based consulting and education firm. Keith has developed custom PowerBuilder applications since the early part of 1992, starting with PowerBuilder 2.0. He is a Certified PowerBuilder Instructor and Certified PowerBuilder Developer. His firm builds custom applications in PowerBuilder, Visual Basic, and C/C++, as well as custom Web pages. He also provides educational services for many of the above development environments. He lives in Alta Loma, California, with his wife, Stephanie, and two daughters, Brittany and Devin. He enjoys jet skiing, snow skiing, and amateur radio.

Shelley Powers

Shelley Powers has worked professionally for several years in the Northwest, and for the last 2 years has been a consultant, first working for a consulting company and now as an independent with her own company, YASD. Shelley is a Microsoft Certified Product Specialist as well as a Powersoft Certified Professional-Associate Level, and is experienced with several client-server tools and relational databases. She has worked for years with Windows, including Windows 95 and NT, as well as UNIX and VAX/VMS. Currently she is working on a JavaScript book for Waite Group Press.

TABLE OF CONTENTS

CONTENTS

ACKNOWLEDGMENTS

All of the authors give a special thanks to the editors of the text: Andy Tauber of Team Powersoft for the massive amounts of technical editing done in a very short period, and Heidi Brumbaugh and Harry Henderson for their equally impressive job of content editing. Likewise, special thanks go to all the people at the Waite Group Press. Thanks to Jill Pisoni and Andrea Rosenberg for their undying work, support, and patience over the past year. It's not easy coordinating an effort of this magnitude between so many parties who are scattered all over the country. To Mitchell Waite, thank you for the opportunity to add to your already impressive library of fine technical books. To Dave Litwack of Powersoft, thanks for creating such an impressive product, allowing the rest of us to benefit.

Daryl Biberdorf would like to acknowledge his wife, Dea, for her patience, understanding, and support throughout the harder-than-expected task of creating this work. You can now retake full possession of your husband. Thanks also to Tom Parsoneault for the regularly-asked-for advice. Daryl also owes a special debt to his students for asking questions, many solutions of which appear here.

Keith Glidden would first like to thank Jesus Christ, for through Him all things are possible. Secondly, to my family, who have done without me for quite some time. My time at home has been spent in front of computer screens, with my mind a million miles away from you. It's now time for that to change. Thank you for your love, support, and encouragement. I now return my life to you. A very special thanks and much gratitude must also go to Joe Angarella of QBD Technical Services, who has contributed so much over the past year. Joe, your insight, patience, and dedication to this technology, as well as your friendship, cannot be overstated. My life is just better with you around.

Shelley Powers would like to thank her clients at Nike, the Apparel development team led by Julie Fugate, for their understanding and support during the writing process. She would also like to thank her family and friends, especially Clare and Rae Powers, Michael and Cathy Conn-Powers, Martha and Fred Gray, and Jannine and Beren Setter, for their patience and encouragement.

Daryl Biberdorf
Keith Glidden
Shelley Powers

FOREWORD

Since PowerBuilder 1.0's introduction in 1991, it has become the leading client/server development tool. Along the way, Powersoft has made numerous improvements and changes to adapt to the growing client/server market and to incorporate leading-edge technology as it has come available. The latest version, PowerBuilder 5.0, marks a significant change for the PowerBuilder development community. This newest product adds many exciting new features including native-code compiling, distributed objects, true function overloading, event parameters, and many user-interface enhancements. With this release, Powersoft has asserted its leadership in the graphical client/server tools market.

However, the book market for PowerBuilder has focused heavily on introductory coverage of the product, with only a handful of titles including coverage of intermediate and advanced topics. *PowerBuilder 5.0 How-To* is partially intended to fill this gap in advanced material. We, the authors, have accumulated years of development and instructional experience using PowerBuilder to address difficult programming problems. Our goal has been to pool our combined expertise, working with the many facets of PowerBuilder to create a book that addresses "real world" PowerBuilder problems in a readable, concise fashion. Specifically, we wanted to give developers the ability to quickly locate a fully coded and documented example to explain a topic in its entirety, including the "gotchas" that so often hamper development.

One of the difficulties we faced is the breadth of the tool. In addition to being a graphical development environment, PowerBuilder also offers a rich set of object capabilities, database tools, deployment options, and target platforms. Addressing all of these topics has been a challenge for us; we made numerous changes to our covered topics so that they were covered neither inadequately nor excessively.

We have tried to avoid including too much introductory material, but not to ignore the needs of beginning PowerBuilder developers. We also strove to achieve a balance in coverage of new and old product features. We did not want to slight valuable techniques merely because they existed in pre-5.0 versions of the tool, yet we also wanted to cover the exciting new features of PowerBuilder 5.0. We think we have achieved these goals after much hard work.

As you work with PowerBuilder 5.0 and read this work, we hope that you will find it to be a worthy addition to your development library.

PREFACE

Is there anyone today who has not heard of PowerBuilder? I'm beginning to think not. Even my mother knows about this marvelous tool. This has not always been the case, however. It's been a fast and furious growth over the past several years. I remember my first introduction to PowerBuilder. It was back in April of 1992, during the Comdex/Windows World Conference in Chicago. Microsoft was announcing Windows 3.1, and it seemed like everyone in the world had descended on Illinois for the event. At that time, I was working in the Aerospace industry, and we were just beginning the venture into graphical interfaces for our users. Up to that point, most of my development centered around DOS character-based applications written in Clipper. Prior to leaving for the affair, my boss asked me to check into this tool called "PowerBuilder." My response was "Power...what?" He told me that PowerBuilder was a Windows-based development tool for client/server applications. "Fine," I thought, "what could it hurt?". Anyway, I left for Chicago and had other things on my mind, like checking out the latest offerings from companies that I had actually heard of.

After spending several hours at the exhibits one day, it dawned on me that I had promised to check out this "Power something or other," and set out looking for the vendor. Walking through the conference hall, I was amazed at the magnitude of most vendors. There was Microsoft, of course, filling the majority of the exhibit hall. Alongside were the Borlands, Computer Associates, and other major players of that time. Just as I thought I had exhausted my search, something caught my eye. Off in the corner was a small display table, with one lone sales rep, and no one for her to talk to. Figuring that maybe, just maybe, she had some pens, mousepads, or some other free giveaway, I made my way over to the display. And, there it was—Powersoft. Yes indeed, this lone table strategically placed in the far reaches of the Windows World galaxy was the one vendor I had come so far to see.

I approached the table, gave my salutations to the Powersoft rep, and proceeded to ask for a demo of the product. She had one PC, which was acting as client and server machine, with only a monochrome display with which to work. I sort of laughed inside, figuring I was in for a future story to tell. Well, I was right, but the outcome was not nearly what I thought it would be. Suffice it to say that I left that display utterly amazed, and returned home on a serious quest to make this tool my primary development environment. This was version 2.0, which had just been released. Suffice it to say that even with the power available at the time, things have come a long way with this product.

That was over four years ago, and the time since has been riddled with astonishment, opportunity, and endless fun. I can honestly say that I have not worked a day in my life since PowerBuilder became a major part of my work day. It has been pure, unadulterated fun. I can't believe I actually get paid for working with this tool. But, enough about my past. What do you have to gain in the pages of this book? Well, I hope you have any mystery that's been troubling you unraveled, for one. I believe that your imagination will flourish, and you will embellish your career. Those are tall orders to fill in a few pages of text. This book will guide you step by step through ideas and concepts that it took many of us months to figure out on our own. I myself have spent countless hours over the past few years buried knee deep in reference manuals, user guides, and API reference books, just to solve problems that could have been accomplished in a few minutes had a book like this existed at the time.

You also have new challenges ahead of you. PowerBuilder is now a cross-platform tool, supporting Window 3.1x, Windows 95, NT, UNIX, and the Macintosh. A heterogeneous environment is the norm these days, rather than the exception. If you're reading this book, you no doubt have roots in the Windows 95 arena. Although this environment holds many of the old Windows 3.1 truths, there remains much learning to be done. PowerBuilder 5.0 brings with it new controls such as the Tab folder and Treeview objects. The corporate environment is getting tougher to develop in these days, as users become more savvy. Object orientation is a reality, as are distributed objects, OLE, and multiplatform environments. You need something to keep you on the edge, lest you fall behind and get left out in the cold. The pages of this book are filled with techniques and concepts you simply won't find anywhere else.

There is something (and I'm confident of the quantity) in here for everyone. It does not matter what your level of expertise is with PowerBuilder. If you are new to it, there are many good topics here to lay the groundwork for a solid start. Work through the examples to understand the basics of this tool. Topics such as "How do I build a DataWindow?" are just up your alley. If you're comfortable working in PowerBuilder, and have created an application or two, you'll find material in here to keep you from reaching a learning plateau. Although many of the topics are very specific, they always leave room for you to incorporate them into the application you might be building at work. Check out topics like "How do I run an application from my PowerBuilder application?" or "How do I use a Custom Class User Object?". For those of you who are seasoned veterans, check out some of the OLE, object oriented, or other advanced topics. Topics like "How do I create an OLE server application?" are well suited for your level of expertise. You'll find things in here so timely and powerful, you'll want to keep this text closer than arm's reach away.

There is one other subtle advantage you have. This book is the compilation of three authors, who come from very different backgrounds. That is three times the experience at your fingertips. We have reviewed each other's work, and I for one have also learned some things in the process. But it's not just the knowledge of multiple authors that you gain. There have been countless others who have given their input, suggestions, and criticisms, all in an attempt to make this a better text. I feel that goal has been achieved. And, keep this in mind: I've used this product for over four years, and continue to learn more about it each time I use it. It's a robust tool, and one that you will not outgrow.

— Keith Glidden

INTRODUCTION

A major new tool release can be both exciting and disappointing. You are excited about the new features and that existing problems have been fixed, but you can be disappointed when you receive the tool and it seems to demonstrate little or no difference from the previous release. PowerBuilder 5.0 will not be one of those releases that disappoints. From new styles to new controls, new functions to new event posting, and especially with the new ability to generate machine code executables, this release is a major change. Instead of disappointment you may find yourself in the middle of an unexpected learning curve, trying to absorb all of the new features, and this book will help.

Why Should You Read This Book
New PowerBuilder Version 5.0

The new release of PowerBuilder 5.0 will be of major impact to its users. Not only is there a different look and feel in the Painters but you can now compile your applications into a true machine code executable for improved performance. Additionally you have access to new controls, new DataWindow styles, and new functionality with registry access and OLE 2.0 automation and distributed PowerBuilder. The How-To's in this book were all written in PowerBuilder 5.0 and demonstrate both the 5.0 "gimmes" as well as the "gotchas". With this you can pick a topic and see how the code changed (or stayed the same) and use this information when planning the conversions of your applications. If you are new to PowerBuilder 5.0, all of the major components of PowerBuilder are covered, making it an ideal companion book to your PowerBuilder tutorial and beginning user manuals and books. For all PowerBuilder users the samples in this book will enable you to make use of the new 5.0 features quickly and easily.

New Operating System Requirements—Registry and Property Sheets

With Windows 95 and Windows NT 3.51 and now NT 4.0, you have an operating system that is very different for your users and for your applications. Instead of initialization (.ini) files, you use the registry online database. Instead of accessing object attributes in menus or in scattered dialogs, you access them in property sheets. The How-To's in this book were written and tested in Windows 95, Windows NT 3.51, and Windows NT 4.0. They provide comprehensive coverage of all the new operating system's features and provide complete code listings you can use in your own applications.

Using PowerBuilder to Add the New Windows 95 Look and Feel to Your Applications

With Windows 95 you now have more control over the operating system than ever before. You can choose the color of button faces as well as the desktop. You can access the properties of most objects just by right-clicking with your mouse on them. Sound and video are more integrated into the operating system, as can be seen by the sample video files (.avi) that came with Windows 95 install. You no longer have to access your applications from a Program Manager group; you can place it directly on the desktop itself. You have access to new controls such as ListView and TreeView controls and the Tab control, which is used for the new property sheets. In this How-To you will see examples using these new Windows 95 features and also demonstrating how these new features are used in PowerBuilder itself.

Exciting New Multimedia Features—via the API

One of the most exciting things about Windows 95 is the new multimedia enhancements. If your PC is capable, you can add sound to most events and you can play video files with little or no trouble. How-To's in this book cover how you can integrate multimedia into your applications and include enough .avi files for you to have a little fun trying this out. In addition, you will see complete code listings on accessing the Windows Application Programming Interface (API) to check system resources and find out information about tables in a database via ODBC.

Tighter Integration with New OLE 2.0 Features

With Powerbuilder 5.0 you will be able to create your own OLE 2.0 automation server, which can be used by other applications whether they are PowerBuilder-based or not. OLE 2.0 is more highly integrated with the operating system and you can drag and drop applications on icons to start them, or easily send data from your application to another, such as Microsoft Excel. You can make use of the new OLE Custom Controls (OCX's) in your user objects or directly in your window. These new features add a new level of sophistication to applications and this book provides How-To's that will enable you to apply these capabilities in your new and existing applications. With the clear instructions and complete code listings, these features will be easier to implement than you might think.

Real World Problems and Common Sense Solutions

The How-To's in this book are examples of questions that you and your co-workers are probably asking each other right now. Questions such as "How do I send parameters in an event?" or "How do I drag between windows?" or "How can I use an OLE Custom Control in a user object?" are not theoretical but real world problems and concerns you need answers to in order to build your application. And they are answers you need right away because you are working with a tight deadline. You don't want to have to read through the principles of how to do something; you just want to see the code that accomplishes it, and this book provides this information directly. Unlike other books where you start with the first chapter and progress to more difficult concepts, the chapters in this book each cover a specific component of PowerBuilder and provide examples that range in complexity from easy to advanced. Browse through the Table of Contents and go to the How-To that covers what you are most interested in at the moment. Most of the How-To's are completely independent of each other, and if they do reference another How-To, which one it is and what you need are written in detail.

What the CD Contains

The CD that comes with this book includes complete code samples for every How-To in this book. In addition, the CD also includes several .WAV and .AVI files you can use for testing and for fun, and also includes examples of registry files you can examine for copying and modifying for your own use. The CD also includes a subdirectory that contains several examples of using the new PowerSoft Window plugin that was being beta tested at the time this book was being written. Additionally, this subdirectory also contains several examples of HTML (HyperText Markup Language) that were generated using the new Saveas HTML option.

Who Should Read This Book

This book is not an introduction or tutorial style of book and is not meant to replace these types of books. This book assumes that you, the reader, have some familiarity with the tool, though you do not have to be an expert. We also do not make an assumption about the skill level of the reader when we give a rating of easy, moderate, or advanced for each How-To. These do nothing more than indicate the complexity of the example. However, if you are very inexperienced with PowerBuilder, you may want to run through a basic tutorial or beginning user manual prior to working with the more moderate and advanced How-To samples. Following the section in this introduction labeled "How This Book Is Organized" will be a section titled "Chapter Review Guidelines." Examine the "Beginning PowerBuilder Chapters" topic listing those chapters that cover more basic PowerBuilder functionality. For the experienced but not expert user, check out the section titled "Intermediate PowerBuilder Chapters." For the highly experienced user, check out the "Advanced PowerBuilder Chapters" section.

System Requirements

This book assumes that you have either the Enterprise, Desktop, or Professional version of PowerBuilder 5.0 installed. You will need disk space for each of the samples that you will copy to your disk. To work with the PowerBuilder window plugin, you must install this also from the PowerBuilder CD-ROM or from the PowerSoft Web site (www.powersoft.com), following the instructions that they provide. Your PC must have a CD-ROM player in order to access the sample code and the sample database. You should have either Windows 95 or Windows NT (3.51 and above) installed. The samples in this book have not been verified or designed to run in Windows 3.1 or 3.11. If you have enough memory to run PowerBuilder 5.0, you should have enough memory to run the book samples. The sample snapshots shown in the book were taken in VGA mode but you should set up your environment to the resolution and color system you are most comfortable with.

The Book Chapters in Detail

The book has 19 chapters. The samples in the book were fully tested with PowerBuilder beta version build 164. We will attempt to compile and test in later beta versions if we receive them in time. The chapters and an overview of what they contain follow:

Chapter 1: Controls

The power of a tool such as PowerBuilder can be found in the ease with which controls are added to windows. This chapter provides How-To's that extend the basic functionality of some of the more commonly used window controls. Additionally, this chapter demonstrates how to add controls at runtime. In addition, the chapter will also provide coverage of the more complex Windows 95 controls, the ListView, TreeView, and Tab controls.

Chapter 2: General Windows Techniques

PowerBuilder provides the Window as the main interface object for the user, and builds in the functionality to manage it. However, there are times when you will want to extend the functionality of the window and this chapter provides examples of this. The chapter demonstrates how to prevent closing of a window when the user has not saved changes and how to provide a splash screen when the window opens. Additionally, the chapter details how to build a directory file listbox, how to inherit from a window and how to adjust the controls on the window when the window resizes.

Chapter 3: Application Styles

PowerBuilder provides support and a template tool to generate MDI (Multiple Document Interface) applications, yet with the new Windows 95 user interface this application style is actually not considered the only standard, or even the most preferred. This How-To actually departs a little from the standard "standalone" format to provide an example of building a library that contains commonly used objects, which are then used elsewhere in the chapter. The other How-To's provide detailed instructions demonstrating how to build a Single Document Interface (SDI), a Workbook, and a Workspace style of application.

Chapter 4: Applications

Your application will need to communicate with the operating system and will also need to store information between application runtimes. This How-To demonstrates how to store preferences and other application settings to the Registry. In addition, the chapter also provides a demonstration of how to access environment information at runtime and how to build an error handler that is more informative than the one PowerBuilder provides.

Chapter 5: Drag and Drop

When used correctly, drag and drop can be an effective and fun-to-use tool for your application users. PowerBuilder provides the events you need to capture drag-and-drop movements, but you will need to provide the functionality. This chapter demonstrates how to provide visual cues to your user when they can or cannot drop an object. Another How-To provides an example of using drag and drop to visually display the delete buffer and to implement undo for deleting. Additionally, you will be able to work with code to allow you to drag between windows, and to even drag to an object to enable OLE 2.0 automation.

Chapter 6: Menus

No matter what other interface components you implement for your application, the menu is still the main interface component most of us are accustomed to using. This How-To demonstrates how to inherit from an existing menu and how to change menus at runtime. In PowerBuilder, the toolbar is directly related to the menu and this chapter also demonstrates how to show only one toolbar at a time and to manage toolbars. With the new Windows 95 right mouse functionality, you will need to use popup menus in your application, and this chapter provides a How-To demonstrating this.

Chapter 7: Database Objects

It is unusual to find applications in business use that do not use databases, and this How-To demonstrates what you need to know to create and manage databases and work with the new Sybase SQL Anywhere database engine. If you are new to client-server applications and are unfamiliar with what is happening at the server end, this chapter is a must read. You will start out by creating a database and then you will define a table in it. The basis of a relational database system is how the tables are related so you will implement both primary and foreign keys. Additionally, you will get a chance to try importing and exporting data, creating a view, executing a SQL script and working with formats and edit styles using the database Extended Attributes. Even if you do not use Sybase SQL Anywhere, or you have DBAs that do this work normally, you should understand these concepts in order to build a more effective database application.

Chapter 8: Database Programming

The PowerBuilder DataWindow will not solve all your database access needs, and you will need to know how to connect to a database and access data directly from it. This chapter provides How-To's that demonstrate connecting to a database and then using embedded SQL to access data from it. You will also be able to see how to use SQL when you cannot embed it, for user-defined queries and dynamic tables. Advanced topics cover accessing a blob or long varchar column and querying the system catalog at runtime.

Chapter 9: DataWindow Painter

If you ask any PowerBuilder person what the most useful component of PowerBuilder is, they will answer the DataWindow. This chapter provides demonstrations of building computed columns and computed fields, and incidentally demonstrating the new DataWindow Painter Property Sheets. The chapter also provides a How-To on the PowerBuilder Report Painter tool, a useful but highly underutilized tool. Though most updateable DataWindows are for one table only, another How-To demonstrates how to create an updateable DataWindow for a join between two tables. And the chapter would not be complete without coverage of the two new DataWindow styles introduced in PowerBuilder 5.0: the OLE 2.0 and the Rich Text style.

Chapter 10: DataWindow Controls—Updates

Once you have defined your DataWindow, you need to use it. The most important use of the DataWindow control is to update the data it represents in the database, and this chapter provides a comprehensive overview of handling updating using DataWindow controls. Techniques in the chapter discuss how to validate data and how to provide more useful database error handling. More advanced features are discussed such as preventing a user from entering data based on other values, or coordinating multiple DataWindow updates. How to use the DataWindow status flags for custom processing is also discussed. This chapter will enable you to ensure that your application provides robust and save database transactions.

Chapter 11: DataWindow Controls—General Programming

You can do just about anything with a DataWindow control, and this chapter covers most of what you can do. Demonstrations of printing a DataWindow, including a correct page count or providing a popup menu for options, are provided as well as changing the DataWindow in the DataWindow control. In addition, you will see how to cache data for dropdowns that can be shared across windows, and how to modify what the dropdowns show based on user actions. The chapter ends with a discussion of the composite DataWindow object and techniques you can use with this style.

Chapter 12: Dynamic DataWindows

You are not limited to working with DataWindows only during the design process; you can also extensively modify the DataWindow at runtime. Techniques demonstrated in this How-To detail how to create a DataWindow using a blank DataWindow control at runtime, and how to modify an existing DataWindow's SQL. This one feature more than any other is essential in most business applications that allow users to select the criteria they want and to modify the SQL accordingly. More advanced topics cover how to modify the DataWindow column attributes at runtime. Rumors to the contrary, you will still be making use of Modify in your applications, but this chapter demonstrates alternative methods of modification, including adding new objects to the DataWindow. Lastly, you can save the syntax for the DataWindow to either a PowerBuilder library or to the database for the user to access at a later time.

Chapter 13: Working with OLE 2.0

OLE 2.0 has reached a new level of integration with Windows 95 and NT and this is a technology you will want to consider starting to use in your applications. Yet this is also a technology that is, at first glance, a little intimidating. The How-To's in this chapter demonstrate some of the techniques you can use in your applications, such as using the automation functions of an OLE 2.0 automation server to extend the functionality of your application. You will also see an example of how easy it can be to use the the OLE Custom Controls (OCX's) in your applications, by making use of one that PowerBuilder is providing with its installation. A more advanced use of OLE 2.0 will be demonstrated in the last How-To wherein a PowerBuilder OLE 2.0 automation server application is created.

Chapter 14: User-Defined Functions

No matter how fancy the operating system, or how fun the new toys, you will still implement much of your code in functions. This chapter demonstrates when and how to write functions that should become part of every application's common library. The chapter starts with demonstrating how to create a global function, and how to use SQL in it. It then progresses to demonstrating object level functions, including how to hide these functions. The chapter provides techniques for closing all open MDI sheets, and for providing a simple user entry message box.

Chapter 15: External Functions

PowerBuilder provides most of the functionality you will need to meet your application needs. However, there are times when you will need to go beyond what it provides by accessing the API or other functions directly, and this chapter covers how you can do this. You can directly access the API to display memory usage. The How-To's progress to demonstrating how to pass variables, both singly and in structures, to external functions. Techniques of starting an application and determining when it is done allow your applications to work with other applications and are essential for some of the new application styles. Advanced topics cover how to access ODBC information directly, essential in a heterogeneous database environment. Demonstrations of accessing external subroutines are given, as well as how to use the API to play sound and video files, which are becoming a more important component of business applications.

Chapter 16: User Objects

If the DataWindow is the most important component PowerBuilder provides, the user object is the second most important component, and this chapter demonstrates how to build and use custom and standard user objects. User objects are one of the key components to creating re-usable code and creating a standard look and feel that makes your application present a more unified look no matter how many developers have worked on it. The chapter starts by demonstrating how to build a custom class object that is a non-visual user object. It then progresses to building a standard visual user object, a custom visual user object, and a user object that manages error handling for your application. More complex examples of objects provide techniques for modifying the standard message object, using a custom control defined in a Dynamic Link Library (DLL) as well as creating a custom transaction object. Advanced topics cover building and using C++ classes and using them in your application.

Chapter 17: Event Driven Programming

Windows applications communicate with each other, internally with events, and this chapter provides an overview of event handling in PowerBuilder. Demonstrations of triggering an event are given, as well as posting an event. With PowerBuilder 5.0 you can also pass a parameter in an event now, and this technique is described. Passing information between windows is facilitated by being able to pass information in the message object and this is described in the last How-To of the chapter.

Chapter 18: Introduction to Object Oriented Programming

Object oriented programming principles could and do fill bookcases of books, so this chapter does not attempt to instruct in the basics of OO programming. What it does provide is a demonstration of using PowerBuilder's built-in functionality to implement some OO concepts such as adding attributes (properties) and hiding them for an object, how to overload object functions, and how to communicate with the object. More advanced topics cover sharing a variable across classes and writing a script that will look for unsaved changes in all windows.

Chapter 19: Deployment Information

With PowerBuilder version 5.0, applications can now be compiled into machine code. You also have the option of compiling to the traditional pCode as before, and this chapter demonstrates both. In addition, the chapter discusses how to create a Dynamic Link Library, and how the PowerBuilder DLLs differ from standard DLLs. The chapter also discusses how to use the Registry to capture install and uninstall options. At the time this book went to press, the setup application was not yet available and setup instructions were not included with this chapter.

Chapter Review Guidelines
Beginning PowerBuilder Chapters

The chapters covering the more basic components of PowerBuilder are: Chapter 1 on Controls, Chapter 2 on General Window Techniques, Chapter 4 on Applications, Chapter 6 on Menus, Chapter 7 on Database Objects, Chapter 9 on the DataWindow Painter, Chapters 10 and 11 on DataWindow controls, Chapter 17 on Event Programming, and the first How-To's in Chapter 19.

Intermediate PowerBuilder Chapters

For more intermediate PowerBuilder concepts, the order of the chapters would be: Chapter 3 on Application Styles, Chapter 5 on Drag and Drop, Chapter 8 on Database Programming, Chapter 14 on User Defined Functions, the first How-To's in Chapter 16 on User Objects, and Chapter 18 on Object Oriented Programming.

Advanced PowerBuilder Chapters

More advanced topics in PowerBuilder are covered in: Chapter 12 on Dynamic DataWindows, Chapter 13 on OLE 2.0, Chapter 15 on External Functions, the latter How-To's in Chapter 16, Chapter 18 on Object Oriented Programming (again), and the How-To in Chapter 19.

PowerBuilder and the Web

PowerSoft will be implementing throughout 1996 several new Internet and Web-related tools and features. One new feature is the ability to use the Saveas function to save a DataWindow in the HTML (HyperText Markup Language) format that can be read and displayed by Web browsers. The second feature is a plugin that would allow the user to embed a PowerBuilder window directly into a Web page.

There was no time to add a new chapter to the book on the plugin, but we were able to create some examples to demonstrate its use. Check the Installation section to find out how to install the Web sample subdirectory.

At the time of this writing the Netscape browser was the only one capable of using plugins. These are small applications or "applets" that allow the Web writer to embed content such as .wav sound files or .avi video files and now PowerBuilder windows. With the plugin, the browser will have a tool to play or read the embedded source.

There are some limitations in using the plugins. The windows will have to be defined as child windows, and you will not have the traditional MDI (Multiple Document Interface) menu or sheet capability you are probably used to. The SDI (Single Document Interface) style of application that is regaining popularity with Windows 95 is the best approach to this type of use. You can create a right mouse button menu for use with your window and provide the functionality you need there or with buttons on the window itself.

Accessing a database using the plugin will be no different than how you access a database now. If you are in a client-server setup, you will still need to have all of the database connectivity in place that you have when accessing a standard PowerBuilder application. The plugin does open and work with the window in the client's environment.

Be cautious when using the plugin in an environment where the Web page reader will be accessing it via the modem. A complex window with several DataWindows and controls can take a while to download, especially with slower modems. One of the windows in the sample, the RETAIL.HTM sample, took nearly five minutes to download using a 14.4K modem.

To see how plugins perform in an Internet environment, the samples provided in the disk will be accessible at www.yasd.com or at www.waite.com/waite. You can also test locally by defining the plugin in your browser as a helper application. Make sure that you specify the MIME type of "application/powerbuilder" and a data type of "pbd". Leave the Action as "Unknown: prompt user".

INSTALLATION

What the CD Contains

The CD that comes with this book contains all of the source code mentioned in the book in both an executable format and in the source code format. The executable programs may be compiled using pCode or using machine code, but they are not standalone applications. You will still need to have the PowerBuilder runtime environment installed in order to run them. You will also need to install the sample database, ZOO, in addition to the sample files.

How to Install the CD Files and Run the Applications

At the time this book went to press, the PowerBuilder setup utility, PBSETUP, was not yet available. Please examine the root directory of the CD for a readme.txt file that may contain last-minute information about installing from the CD. If the setup utility does become available before the sample CD is burned (created), this will be noted in the readme.txt file.

The samples files are organized into subdirectories representing the individual chapters and How-To's. The Chapter 1 files will be located in a subdirectory called CHAP01, Chapter 2 into CHAP02, and so on. The samples are then organized into How-To's, such as HOWTO011, and so on. Each chapter may contain a readme.txt file, which you should read prior to installing the chapter. This readme file will contain last-minute instructions about setting up or running the application, such as setting up the PowerBuilder library list, running a registry file, or some other important information. The database for the book, called ZOO, is located in a separate subdirectory called DATABASE. Any registry files that must be run before all or some of the applications will work properly will be installed in a subdirectory called REGISTRY. Note that there may be other registry files located in the individual subdirectories.

Using the Explorer or the File Manager, create a subdirectory on your local disk for the book. In it, create a separate subdirectory for the database and copy the database to this subdirectory. Access the ODBC administration tool that should be located in your Control Panel to set up the database. You will need to have installed Sybase SQL Anywhere, which came with PowerBuilder, to run the database included with this book. When the ODBC administrator opens, select the Add button. From the Installed ODBC Drivers, select the Sybase SQL Anywhere 5.0 driver. In the dialog that opens up, name your Data Source Name "Zoo" and change the UserID to "DBA" and the Password to "sql". In the Database Startup section, type in the location and file for the Database file you just copied, and be sure to check the Local radiobutton. Close and save the results.

Once you have set up the database, you can now copy the source code or application executables for each chapter. For each, make a subdirectory of the same name in your book directory and copy all of the files to this subdirectory. Follow any instructions in the readme.txt file that may have come with the chapter. You should be able to run any executables at this point. If you want to work with the source code, you will need to migrate each of the source code PowerBuilder libraries as these were created with a beta release version of PowerBuilder. PowerBuilder has a built-in migration utility, so double-click on the application object for each library and follow the instructions from there. For those library's that do not have an application object, add them to any of your migrated libraries' library paths and choose Migrate from the Tools in the PowerBuilder Library painter.

Installing the Web Examples

There are several examples of using the new Powersoft Window Plug-In, and using the new Saveas HTML feature of PowerBuilder 5.0. These can be found in the subdirectory titled "Web." Install this by copying the contents to your local drive.

Powersoft will provide the Window Plug-In on the PowerBuilder 5.0 Maintenance CD or their Web site at www.powersoft.com when available. Follow the installation instructions that they provide for this tool. You will need to have a browser such as Netscape 2.x or later that is capable of working with plug-ins.

Test the HTML files (they will have an extension of .HTM) by opening them in your browser using the File...Open File menu option.

Note: Projects in this book were compiled using a late beta version of PowerBuilder 5.0. Projects on the CD-ROM were compiled using the last beta version (Build 164). It is possible that you could encounter problems opening the executable (.EXE) files on the CD using the release version of PowerBuilder 5.0. If you experience such problems, please try recompiling the projects with the provided source code on the CD.

CHAPTER 1
CONTROLS

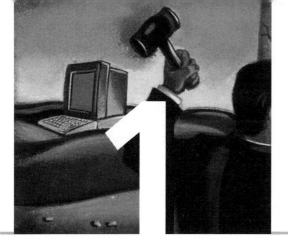

CONTROLS

How do I...

Controls are a powerful part of Windows development. Thanks to the provided controls, many of the mundane tasks involved in the user interface are handled for us without a single line of code. Examples of this are the checking and unchecking of a CheckBox or RadioButton control, how Windows allows the user to select an item from a DropDownListBox, and the placement of the focus rectangle when a control comes into focus.

However, even with all of the standard behavior, there comes a time when you want to make a control work a little differently. Either the user wants an interface that is a little different, you need to provide a better way for a particular application to work, or your creative juices are just flowing beyond the norm. That's what this chapter is all about. Certainly, many more possibilities exist than there is room for, but hopefully the samples here will get you thinking.

1.1 Perform an Exact String Search on a ListBox

ListBox controls hold lists of data available for selection. If the user clicks on an item, that item is highlighted. Quite often, it is desirable to do this under program control, such as when the program is allowing the user to search for a particular item. Most often, this occurs in ListBoxes containing many items — too many for the user to search visually. PowerBuilder provides you with functions for just this task. You can search a ListBox based on the item text contained in the control. However, the search performed is not case sensitive, nor is it an exact search. If the user enters "Cal", the ListBox will match that with "California". This is usually a positive trait, but not always. It could lead to data integrity errors if the ListBox contains many items that all begin with the same few letters. The ability to perform an exact search is presented in this How-To.

1.2 Dynamically Add Controls to a Window

Most of the time, controls are added to a window when you paint the window. But a problem arises if the number of necessary controls is not known at design time. For example, if you want to display all of the bitmap files that exist in a directory, it is impossible to determine how many Picture controls to place on the window. These controls must be added dynamically. In this How-To, we will create a custom message box function that allows you to dynamically place a variable number of buttons with custom text. This extends the power and usability provided with the MessageBox() function.

1.3 Perform an Incremental Search on a DropDownListBox

One of the standard behaviors of a DropDownListBox is that the user can search for an item by pressing the first letter of the item in question. However, if several items exist with the same starting letter, the user is forced to continue the search by repetitively pressing the same first letter. Many users find this counterintuitive, and annoying. Wouldn't it be nice to type the text of the desired item, and have the ListBox find the closest match (as with the standard Windows Help index)? That is exactly what you'll learn in this How-To.

1.4 Use a Tab Control

Over the past several years, Tab controls have gained popularity with Windows users. They provide excellent space management, as one can place much information on a window. Users select a particular tab that organizes common data. Without a Tab control, multiple windows are necessary. In order to implement this type of control, PowerBuilder developers have resorted to external controls (at additional monetary cost), or have built their own using C/C++ or the UserObject painter (at additional time cost). With Windows 95, the Tab control becomes standard fare. How-To 1.4 examines this new control, demonstrates its use, and points out its pitfalls.

1.5 Use TreeView and ListView Controls

As another new addition to the Windows 95 environment, TreeView and ListView controls also replace similar custom controls. As with the Tab control of How-To 1.4, developers turned to other tools or vendors to provide the functionality of these controls. How-To 1.5 shows you how to incorporate the new Windows 95 features into your PowerBuilder applications, without the necessity to venture outside of the native PowerBuilder environment.

COMPLEXITY
BEGINNING

1.1 How do I...
Perform an exact string search on a ListBox?

Problem

I have a ListBox control containing many different items. I am allowing the user to search for a particular item from a SingleLineEdit control. When I do the search, the item that most closely matches the entered text is selected. I don't want a ListBox item that is ten characters long to be highlighted if the user enters only the first four characters. Also, the search seems to be case insensitive. How can I perform a case sensitive exact text search in a ListBox?

Technique

The ListBox control provides the FindItem() function that searches the list of items for a particular value. This function does a case insensitive search, and matches only as much data as indicated in the argument. If the ListBox contains an item "California", the string "cal" will match. This kind of behavior is usually beneficial, but in some cases where you need to validate user input through an exact search, this is not desirable. In this How-To you will learn how to perform an exact string search in the ListBox.

Steps

Open and run the application in the LISTSRCH.PBL library. Enter a value in the SingleLineEdit control, and press ENTER or TAB. Only if you entered an exactly matching string will the entry in the ListBox be highlighted. Entering a partial string results in no match. Figure 1-1 shows the main window of the application at runtime.

1. Create a new application object called "listsrch" and store it in a .PBL called LISTSRCH.PBL.

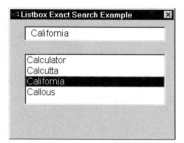

Figure 1-1 Main window of the
LISTSRCH application

2. Create a new window object and put one ListBox and one SingleLineEdit
control on the window. Set the properties of the window and its controls as
shown in Table 1-1. Use Figure 1-1 as a reference.

3. Place the following code in the Modified event of sle_value. Once the text
of sle_value has been changed, this event fires.

```
Long ll_items, ll_index
String ls_value

//Get total number of listbox items
ll_items = lb_list.TotalItems()

//Set the listbox so no items are selected
lb_list.SelectItem ( 0 )

//Loop through all items in the list box and compare it to the text value
For ll_index = 1 to ll_items
//Get the text of the item in the listbox
    ls_value = lb_list.Text ( ll_index )
    If this.text = ls_value Then
//Found it, highlight the item and exit the for loop
        lb_list.SelectItem ( ll_index )
        Exit
    End If
Next
```

4. Double-click on the ListBox to display its Style dialog box. Select the Items
tab, and insert the items from Table 1-1 into the ListBox. Once you have
inserted each item, click the Apply button to save these items in the ListBox.

OBJECT/CONTROL	PROPERTY	VALUE
Window	Name	w_listbox_search
	TitleBar	"Listbox Exact Search Example"

OBJECT/CONTROL	PROPERTY	VALUE
	Minimize Box	FALSE
	Maximize Box	FALSE
	Resizable	FALSE
SingleLineEdit	Name	sle_value
	Auto HScroll	TRUE
ListBox	Name	lb_list
	Items	California
		Calculator
		Calcutta
		Callous

Table 1-1 Properties for w_listbox_search and controls

5. Save the window as w_listbox_search.

6. Write the script for the Open event of the Application object to open the window, as shown below:

```
//Open the window
Open ( w_listbox_search )
```

7. Run the application and test your scripts.

How It Works

When the text in the SingleLineEdit control changes, the Modified event executes. The script first turns off any highlighted items by calling SelectItem(0). Then, it determines the number of items in the ListBox with the TotalItems() function. Stepping through the list with a For...Next loop, the script examines the value returned from the Text() function. This function returns the text of whichever item number was passed to it. This value is compared to the value the user entered in the SingleLineEdit control. If an exact match is found, the script highlights the entry and exits the For...Next loop. If the item cannot be found, the loop ends, and nothing is selected in the ListBox.

Comments

All standard controls supply a default behavior. It is possible to modify or completely change this behavior with a little code and some thought. In this example, the user is forced to enter all the text in question and tab out of the SingleLineEdit control before the search actually happens. A more user-friendly approach may be to perform the search on every keystroke. This is not possible with an "out-of-the-box" SingleLineEdit control. If you are interested in performing this kind of action, read the example in How-To 1.3.

COMPLEXITY
ADVANCED

1.2 How do I...
Dynamically add controls to a window?

Problem

I have been using the PowerScript MessageBox() function to provide easy and consistent communication with the user. However, this function does not always fit my needs. I would like to have a varying number of buttons, each with custom text. I need to know which button the user pressed, and I'd like to provide custom text on each button. The MessageBox() function has only a limited number of choices, and does not offer a way to customize the text on each of the buttons. I would like to write my own response window, and add buttons with appropriate text at runtime, but I don't know how to add these controls dynamically. How is this accomplished?

Technique

Adding controls at runtime is a straightforward process. The difficulty is writing the code to be generic enough to work in all cases, but specific enough to provide the necessary power. The standard user object is paramount to this process. The basic steps involve creating a standard user object which contains all the code necessary at runtime. This code must be generic, as context specific information is unavailable at design time. It must also be smart enough to know how to handle processing based upon data contained in its *instance*. Every occurrence of an object is referred to as an instance, or separate copy. Each control that you dynamically place on a window will do a job slightly different from the others. You cannot change the code at runtime, so it must be able to cope with these differences. This How-To uses many concepts such as triggering events, message handling, and object instantiation. Each button within the custom message box knows its instance "handle" (not the button's window handle, but a custom instance variable set by the scripts that open it), and uses this handle in the communication process back to the parent window. This object allows you to select a custom number of buttons, each with its own text property, as well as the default and cancel buttons (for the (ENTER) and (ESCAPE) keys respectively). The object then notifies the caller, returning the button number that the user pressed. This behavior closely models that of the MessageBox() function.

Steps

Open and run the application in MSGBOX.PBL. Using the RadioButtons, select the number of command buttons you wish to display in the upcoming message box.

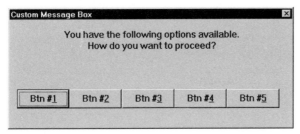

Figure 1-2 Custom message box in action

Then, click the Message... button. A custom message box object displays with the requested number of buttons, each with programmer-defined text. If you select the first button, the application displays another custom message box. The scripts demonstrate how to use the object to do decision branching, based on the button the user presses. Figure 1-2 shows the custom message box in action.

1. Create a new Application object called "msgbox", and save it in a library called MSGBOX.PBL. Do not generate an application template for this application.

2. Start the UserObject painter, and create a new standard visual user object. This object must be sub-classed from the CommandButton type. Declare the following instance variables for the object. The iw_parent property later holds a pointer to the window on which the object resides. It is used to close the associated window when the user clicks the button. The integer ii_instance holds the handle for the object.

```
Protected:
Window iw_parent
Integer ii_instance
```

3. Place the following code in the Clicked event of the object. The ii_instance property holds a value to indicate which button instance this is (as multiple button objects may potentially exist on the window). You will provide a function that allows other scripts to initially set this value.

```
Integer li_button

//When the user clicks this button, set up the information necessary
//to close the window. iw_parent has been set previously
li_button = ii_instance

//Close the window and send the button number back in the DoubleParm
CloseWithReturn ( iw_parent, li_button )
```

4. Create a public access object function called SetInstance(). Give this function the properties shown in Table 1-2. Place the following code in this function. This function sets the handle property for the object, and gets called when the object is instantiated on a window.

continued on next page

continued from previous page
```
//Set the instance number for this object
ii_instance = ai_instance

Return
```

PROPERTY	VALUE	DATATYPE
Name	SetInstance	
Returns	(None)	
Argument 1	ai_instance	Integer

Table 1-2 Function declaration for SetInstance()

5. Create one more public access function. Name this function SetParent(), using the properties in Table 1-3 in the declaration. Place the following code in the function. This function sets the iw_window instance variable to point to the parent window. Again, the function gets called as the object is instantiated. Save the object using the name suo_cb, and close the User Object painter.

```
//Set the parent window
iw_parent = aw_parent

Return
```

PROPERTY	VALUE	DATATYPE
Name	SetParent	
Returns	(None)	
Argument 1	aw_parent	Window

Table 1-3 Function declaration for SetParent()

6. Create a new window object. This window will receive instances of the suo_cb object at runtime. Place one StaticText control on the surface. This control holds the message you wish to display to the user, and is initialized later, as the dialog box opens. Don't worry about the size or the title of the window, but you will want to size the StaticText large enough to later hold the message. Give this window the properties shown in Table 1-4. Place the following instance variable declaration in the window. The first variable holds pointers to each button that you will later place on this window. The second is the default x (horizontal) coordinate for the buttons.

```
suo_cb isuo_cb[]      //array of command buttons
integer ii_x=50    //position of button
```

OBJECT/CONTROL	PROPERTY	VALUE
Window	Name	w_msgbox
	Type	Response
StaticText	Name	st_message
	Alignment	Center

Table 1-4 Properties for window object used for custom message box

7. Create a public access function for this window called CreateMessage().
Give this function the properties shown in Table 1-5, and place the following code in the function. The function is responsible for instantiating the
buttons, and setting all of the properties for the buttons. This is done
through an array that you populate before calling CreateMessage(). It then
sets the instance variable of the button (ii_instance) to indicate which window object the buttons reside on. Save the window using the name
"w_msgbox". This must be done now, since you will need to reference this
object in another script in step 11, but you are not yet done with the scripts
for this object.

```
Environment le_env
Integer li_num, li_button

//Create the buttons with their text

//First, set the title and text for the message
this.Title = as_title
st_message.text = as_message

//Find out how many buttons are needed. A string array was passed,
//so get the number of elements to find out the number of buttons
li_num = UpperBound ( as_buttons[] )

//Loop through and open the user object once for each requested button
For li_button = 1 to li_num
//Create the button
    isuo_cb [ li_button ] = Create suo_cb
//Instantiate the new object
    OpenUserObject ( isuo_cb [ li_button ] )

//Set the properties which are of interest
    isuo_cb [ li_button ].x = ii_x
    //set x
    ii_x += isuo_cb [ li_button ].width        //set width
    isuo_cb [ li_button ].y = this.Height - 300    //and height
    isuo_cb [ li_button ].text = as_buttons [ li_button ] //set text
    isuo_cb [ li_button ].TabOrder = li_button * 10 //set tab order
    isuo_cb [ li_button ].SetInstance ( li_button ) //set instance
    isuo_cb [ li_button ].SetParent ( this )    //set parent window
Next

//li_button now is one larger than necessary. Lower it to keep accuracy
li_button --
```

continued on next page

continued from previous page

```
//Set the width of the window to the width of the sum of the buttons plus
//space on either side (to center buttons on the window)
this.Width = isuo_cb [ li_button ].Width * &
        li_num + ( isuo_cb [ 1 ].x * 3 )

//Size and position the message text
st_message.width = this.Width - 100
st_message.x = 50

//Get environment info and center the messagebox within the user's
//screen coordinates.
GetEnvironment ( le_env )
this.x = PixelsToUnits ( ( le_env.ScreenWidth / 2 ), xPixelsToUnits! ) &
            - ( this.Width / 2 )

//Set the properties of the default and cancel buttons
isuo_cb [ as_default ].Default = TRUE
isuo_cb [ as_Cancel ].Cancel = TRUE
isuo_cb [ as_default ].SetFocus()
```

PROPERTY	VALUE	
Name	CreateMessage	
Returns	(None)	
Argument 1	as_buttons[ ]	String
Argument 2	as_title	String
Argument 3	as_message	String
Argument 4	as_default	Integer
Argument 5	as_cancel	Integer

Table 1-5 Function declaration for CreateMessage()

8. Place the following code in the Open event of the window. The script calls a function in another object (ccuo_msgbox, which has not yet been created). The purpose of the script is to do the instantiation of the button objects. Since you have not yet created the ccuo_msgbox object, you will not yet be able to compile this script.

```
ccuo_msgbox lccuo_msgbox

//Create a copy of the messagebox object
lccuo_msgbox = Message.PowerObjectParm

//Place the buttons on the window, using the MakeButtons function.
//Pass the window (this) to the function so it knows which window
//to place the buttons on
lccuo_msgbox.MakeButtons ( this )
```

9. You must create the MakeButton() function in a user object before you can close the above script. Start the UserObject painter, and create a new custom class object. This object manages the message box window created above. Place the following shared variable declaration in this object. These variables hold the text for each button (ss_buttons[]), the Title for the message box (ss_title), the text for the message (ss_text), and which buttons are the default and cancel buttons (if any).

```
string ss_buttons[], ss_title, ss_text
int ss_default, ss_cancel
```

10. Create a public access function called MakeButtons(). Give the function the properties shown in Table 1-6. Place the following code in this function. The function calls the CreateMessage() function of the custom message box. You created this function in step 6 above. Save this object using the name ccuo_msgbox. Do not close this painter as you'll need to come back and add one more function in step 12.

```
//ss_buttons is an array of strings containing each button text
//ss_title contains the title for the messagebox
//ss_default is the default button for new messagebox
//ss_cancel is the button to fire if user presses cancel

//Call the function in the window object to create the messagebox

aw_window.CreateMessage ( ss_buttons[], ss_title, ss_text, ss_default, &
                          ss_cancel )
Return
```

PROPERTY	VALUE	
Name	MakeButtons	
Returns	(None)	
Argument 1	aw_window	w_msgbox

Table 1-6 Function declaration for MakeButtons()

11. Return to the w_msgbox object, and compile and save the script of the Open event that you coded in step 7. Save the window object and close the Window painter.

12. Return to the UserObject painter where you have ccuo_msgbox loaded. Declare a public access function named SetUp(), and use Table 1-7 to set the function declaration. Place the following code in this function. The function performs the initial processing necessary to set up the message box. You will later call this function from the main window. The SetUp() function is responsible for starting the whole process. Notice that the function declaration is the same as the CreateMessage() function. All of the arguments declared in this function get passed along to CreateMessage(). This completes the work necessary for the message box. The remainder of the steps are needed only to set up the example.

```
//Declare a local instance of the messagebox object
w_msgbox lw_msgbox
```

continued on next page

continued from previous page

```
//Set the various info about the buttons, and pass them along to
//the messagebox
ss_buttons[] = as_buttons
ss_title = as_title
ss_text = as_text
ss_default = as_default
ss_cancel = as_cancel

//Open the message box, setting this object as the parameter. This
//is necessary in order for the w_msgbox object to call functions in
//this object.
OpenWithParm ( lw_msgbox, this )
```

PROPERTY	VALUE	
Name	SetUp	
Returns	(None)	
Argument 1	as_buttons[ ]	String
Argument 2	as_title	String
Argument 3	as_message	String
Argument 4	as_default	Integer
Argument 5	as_cancel	Integer

Table 1-7 Function declaration for SetUp()

13. Create a new window object and place six RadioButtons and a CommandButton on the surface. Figure 1-3 shows the completed window at runtime. Give this window the properties shown in Table 1-8. Declare the following instance variable for the window. This variable holds the number of buttons requested for the custom message box, and gets set in the Clicked event for each of the RadioButtons.

```
Protected:
Integer ii_buttoncount
```

OBJECT/CONTROL	PROPERTY	VALUE
Window	Name	w_main
	TitleBar	"Custom Message Box Example"
	Resizable	FALSE
RadioButton	Name	rb_one
	Text	"1"
	Checked	TRUE
	Name	rb_two
	Text	"2"
	Name	rb_three

OBJECT/CONTROL	PROPERTY	VALUE
	Text	"3"
	Name	rb_four
	Text	"4"
	Name	rb_five
	Text	"5"
	Name	rb_six
	Text	"6"
CommandButton	Name	cb_message
	Text	"&Message..."

Table 1-8 Properties for main window of message box example

14. Place the following code in the Clicked event for *each* of the RadioButtons. This sets the instance variable to indicate the number of buttons for the upcoming message box. Since this script uses the text of the RadioButton to determine the number, make sure the text property of the buttons contains only a valid number ("1" as opposed to "&1").

```
//Set the instance variable (number of buttons) based on the text of
//this radiobutton

ii_buttoncount = Integer ( this.text )
```

15. Place the following code in the Clicked event of cb_message. First, the script populates an array of strings used as the button text. Here is where you would use whatever text is appropriate for your particular application. Next, the ccuo_msgbox gets instantiated, and then calls its SetUp() function, passing the button text array, title, message, default, and cancel buttons. Since the message box is a Response window, the SetUp() function does not return until the user clicks a button. The clicked button number gets passed back in the DoubleParm property of the Message object. This script then tests for button number 1, and again displays a message box if the user pressed that button. This is just to demonstrate the technique used for opening additional message boxes.

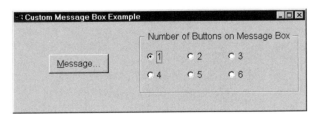

Figure 1-3 Main window at runtime

```
ccuo_msgbox lccuo_msgbox
Integer li_count
String ls_buttons[], ls_buttons1[]

//Label each of the buttons with a number using an array
For li_count = 1 to ii_ButtonCount
    ls_buttons [ li_count ] = "Btn #&" + String ( li_count )
Next

//Instantiate the messagebox
lccuo_msgbox = Create ccuo_msgbox

//Call the messagebox function responsible for setup code
lccuo_msgbox.SetUp ( ls_buttons[], "Custom Message Box", &
                    "You have the following options available.~r~n" + &
                    "How do you want to proceed?", 1, 1 )

//Since the messagebox is a response window, the next line of code
//won't execute until the user closes the messagebox
//Check the message object for the button number the user pressed.
//If they pressed the first button, we'll do one more example of using
//this object
If Message.DoubleParm = 1 then
    ls_buttons1 [ 1 ] = "&Oh Well"
    ls_buttons1 [ 2 ] = "&Help"
    lccuo_msgbox.SetUp ( ls_buttons1[], "Secondary Message", &
                        "Please choose from the following options.", 1, 1)
End If

//Release resources used by the object
Destroy lccuo_msgbox

//Tell the user what button they pressed
MessageBox ( "Test", "You pressed button #" + &
                    String ( Message.DoubleParm ) )
```

How It Works

The first time through these scripts may seem a little unnerving, as might be the second and third. Let's step through the process one piece at a time. In order to create a message box at runtime, you must first populate an array of strings that are used as the text for each button. The message box figures out the number of buttons based on the number of elements in this array. You then instantiate the non-visual object that maintains the message box (ccuo_message), passing this array, as well as the message title, message text, and a number that corresponds to the default and cancel buttons (if appropriate) to the non-visual's SetUp() function. The SetUp() function then populates its own shared variables with this information, and opens the message box window, passing itself as a reference. This reference is necessary so that the message box object is able to call functions in the non-visual later. The message box window obtains this reference, and calls the MakeButtons() function of the non-visual, passing itself back as an argument. MakeButtons() calls the CreateMessage() function of the window object that it receives (an instance of w_msgbox), passing the shared variables populated in the SetUp() function. The CreateMessage() function performs most of the work. It is here that the number of desired buttons gets determined, and instantiated using the OpenUserObject() PowerScript function. This is done in a loop, and the properties of each button (user object) are set using the arguments passed to CreateMessage(). The function then sizes the resulting window so all buttons are visible, centers the message box within the user's screen, and sets the focus to the default button.

When the user clicks a button, the User Object button closes the parent window (set during the CreateMessage() function), and passes its instance handle back (also set in CreateMessage()) using the PowerScript CloseWithReturn() function. PowerBuilder places this returned value in the DoubleParm property of the Message object, and your original calling script (Clicked event of cb_message in this case) retrieves this value to determine the next action to take.

Comments

These objects are generic enough to allow you to create custom message boxes in all of your applications. All you need to do is copy the objects (ccuo_msgbox, suo_cb, and w_msgbox) to a common library, populate a string array used for the button text, instantiate a copy of the ccuo_msgbox object, and call its SetUp() function. It is a little more work than simply using the MessageBox() function, but you now have the power to display consistent, custom messages with any number of buttons that you wish. Without these objects, you would have to create separate window objects with the appropriate number of buttons, each explicitly coded for the task at hand.

COMPLEXITY
INTERMEDIATE

1.3   How do I...
Perform an incremental search on a DropDownListBox?

Problem

I use DropDownListBoxes in my applications. Some of my users are very keyboard oriented and prefer it over the mouse. When one of these DropDownListBoxes comes into focus, they want to search for a particular item by typing the first few characters of the item in question. I've told them that a DropDownListBox does not work this way, that they must repetitively type the starting character until they find what they want. They find this counterintuitive, and I agree. I want to allow them to type the exact item (or a portion of it) and have the DropDownListBox find the closest match. How can I do this?

Technique

DropDownListBoxes have a good mouse interface, but many users don't like the way they behave with the keyboard. The example presented here changes this default behavior. What is even more interesting is the fact that the default behavior still works, in that repetitively pressing one key continues to search for consecutive items. This makes it all the better. Those users who are well grounded into the standard interface won't suffer and have to re-learn it. The basic technique used here involves telling the DropDownListBox control that it should respond to each keystroke — an event not triggered by a standard DropDownListBox. A custom user object performs this action. Each time a user presses a key, the script builds a search string and compares it to the items in the control.

Steps

Open and run the sample application stored in the DDLBSRCH.PBL file. Type in a state name and watch how the list scrolls to the appropriate item. Notice that there is a StaticText control at the bottom of the window that will display the text of what you have typed. This is for display purposes only. Also, notice that the [BACKSPACE] key works as you would expect. This takes an additional step in code that could easily get overlooked. Figure 1-4 shows the main application window at runtime.

1. Create a new Application object and call it "ddlbsrch". Save it in a library called DDLBSRCH.PBL.

2. Create a new window and place a DropDownListBox control and StaticText control on it. Set the properties of the window and the controls as shown in Table 1-9. Insert some items into the list. This example uses the names of a few of the 50 states.

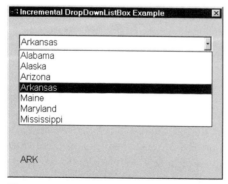

Figure 1-4 DropDownListBox search example application window

OBJECT/CONTROL	PROPERTY	VALUE
Window	Name	w_ddlb_search
	TitleBar	"Incremental DropDownListBox Example"
	Minimize Box	FALSE
	Maximize Box	FALSE
	Resizable	FALSE
DropDownListBox	Name	ddlb_list
	Items	Anything you wish

Table 1-9 Property settings for window and controls

3. In order to do the incremental search, it is necessary to obtain the text the user is typing. The first step is to map a user event to ddlb_list. Click on the DropDownListBox and select User Events from the Declare menu. Map the event shown in Table 1-10. This event fires each time the user presses a key. This event is not a part of the standard PowerBuilder events, as it is unnecessary most of the time. PowerBuilder allows you to map this event to a DropDownListBox if necessary.

CONTROL	EVENT NAME	EVENT ID
ddlb_list	ue_keydown	pbm_keydown

Table 1-10 Custom user event for ddlb_list

4. Select Instance Variables... from the Declare menu. Place the following declaration in that dialog box. Instance variables are known to every script in the window. This variable will hold the value that the user enters while the DropDownListBox has focus.

```
String is_criteria
```

5. Place the following code in the GetFocus event of ddlb_list. This is not necessary for our example, but is something you will want to include in your applications. The reason is simple - this script initializes the instance variable to the empty string so old values are not left from previous searches.

```
//Initialize the instance variable that holds the user's search
//criteria. Set it equal to the empty string.

is_criteria = ''
```

6. Place the following code in the ue_keydown event of ddlb_list. This script gets the keystroke and adds the typed character to the instance variable is_criteria. The KeyDown() function performs this task. The argument for this function is the key code that you want to test. It then returns a TRUE or FALSE value to indicate whether or not the key in question is depressed.

Notice that there is no way to have PowerBuilder directly tell you which key is down. The script must figure this out through a loop. It simply loops through all values (1-127, the standard ASCII character set) and exits the loop if it finds the corresponding key code. This looping will have little (if any) effect on system performance, given the power and speed of today's average desktop machine. The first task this script performs is to test for the BACKSPACE key, as this must be handled differently. If the BACKSPACE key is down, the script strips off the rightmost character; otherwise the loop executes and concatenates the typed character onto the end of the instance variable. Finally, the SelectItem() function highlights the item in the control. As a side task, the code sets the Text property of the StaticText control so the user can see what he or she has typed so far.

```
//Add the new character to the search criteria
Integer li_key

//Handle backspace key specially
If KeyDown ( keyBack! ) Then
    is_criteria = Left ( is_criteria, Len ( is_criteria ) - 1 )
Else
    //loop through the possible key values and see which one was pressed
    For li_key = 1 to 127
        If KeyDown ( li_key ) Then
            is_criteria = is_criteria + Char ( li_key )
            Exit
        End If
    Next
End If
st_display.text = is_criteria
this.SelectItem ( is_criteria, 1 )
```

7. Save this window as w_ddlb_search and close the painter.

8. Write the script necessary to open the window. Place the following code in the Open event of the Application object.

```
//Open the window for the user
Open ( w_ddlb_search )
```

9. Save the Application object and run the application.

How It Works

As with the SingleLineEdit control, the DropDownListBox does not provide an event that responds to each character typed. For this reason, it is necessary to map the pbm_keydown event to a custom user event. With the pbm_keydown event in place, the control responds to each keystroke. In this event, the script performs a loop to figure out which key is down and concatenates this value to the end of an instance variable. The instance variable is known throughout the window, so it's safe to use it in any script. As far as the scope of the variable is concerned, an instance variable is to a window (and its controls) what a local variable is to an event. Once the script knows what the 'current' text is that the user has entered, the script calls the SelectItem() function to highlight the closest matching item. SelectItem() takes two arguments. The first is the string that you are looking for, the second is the item number at which to begin searching. This script always searches from the first item in the list.

Comments

Some of the controls do not respond to individual keystrokes, so you must take that task on yourself with custom user events. This requires mapping an event to the pbm_ keydown or pbm_char event ID. The difference between these events is that pbm_char happens only once per keypress, regardless of how long you hold down a key. The pbm_keydown event may repeat if you hold the key down long enough. This event continues to fire until you release the key.

COMPLEXITY
ADVANCED

1.4 How do I...
Use a Tab control?

Problem

I have many windows that the user opens to manipulate various pieces of data. Sometimes, the different windows contain data dependent on each other, sometimes the data is independent. Many times, the users will open a myriad of these windows, and the screen gets very cluttered looking. They have trouble finding the particular window they need later on. I've suggested that they close unnecessary windows, but it's a suggestion that I cannot enforce. I've seen many Windows applications that use Tab Folder controls, allowing virtually unlimited selection of differing data elements. I know that I could purchase a custom Tab control, or write my own, but I'm told that PowerBuilder now supports a Tab control. I've never used one of these. Can this new control help me and my users out?

Technique

Yes! The situation you have described is just the place to use a Tab control. This type of control allows you to encapsulate many different sets of data or program options within one control, and allows the user to "flip through" the options, much as you would use file folders in a filing cabinet. The Tab control, although one control, usually contains multiple tabs. These individual tabs are called *tabpages*. These tab sheets behave much like individual window objects, in that you can place other controls within the tab sheets. As the user clicks on a tabpage, PowerBuilder automatically brings the tabpage into view, and displays the controls placed on that particular tabpage. Whichever tabpage (and associated controls within it) was displayed gets hidden behind the new current tabpage. In this How-To, you will create one window containing a Tab control and three DataWindows. Users can easily flip between each tab, displaying only the data they are interested in. This way, one window handles the job of three (or more).

Steps

Open and run the application contained in the TABCTRL.PBL library. Figure 1-5 shows this application at runtime. Click on each of the tabs, and watch how the context of the data changes depending on which tab is in the foreground. This control gives you the ability to place many configurations within one window. Each tab could present a different DataWindow, or be used to set application level settings, grouping each setting type on its own tab. Many applications use this style of interface to reduce overhead and increase the ease of use. Virtually everybody is familiar with this tab paradigm. Windows 95 itself uses tabpages in its properties, dialogs, etc.

1. Start the Application painter and create a new Application object. Call this object "tabctrl", and save it in a library named TABCTRL.PBL. When prompted, do not generate an application template.

2. Start the DataWindow painter. In step 3, you will create a window on which you will place a Tab control and several DataWindows. Create three DataWindows. The first uses a join between the guests and guests_type tables. The second comes from the employee and person tables, while the last comes from the store table. The columns you select for display are not important, so use your imagination and discretion. Save the DataWindows as d_guests, d_employees, and d_stores respectively.

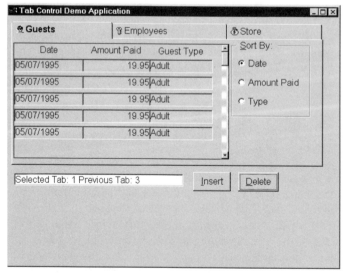

Figure 1-5 Tab folder application at runtime

3. Create a new window in the Window painter. Use the control DropDownPictureList box, and place one Tab control on the window surface. The icon for the Tab control should be obvious, but you can always let the PowerTips guide you. Then, place one StaticText box below the tab. Use Figure 1-5 as an example. Your Tab control won't look exactly like the above figure, as it will only contain one tabpage. The example application's Tab control has three tabpages. In order to add the additional tabpages, right mouse click on the Tab control (the sheet part, not the top tab), and select Insert TabPage from the popup menu. Repeat this step, thereby completing the construction of the tab. Give the window and associated controls the properties shown in Table 1-11. Note that to set the properties for the Tab control, right mouse click on the tabpage and select Properties... from the popup. To set the properties for each tabpage, right mouse click the tab portion of the tabpage.

OBJECT/CONTROL	PROPERTY	VALUE
Window	Name	w_tabs
	Title	"Tab Control Demo Application"
	Type	Popup
Tab	Name	"tab_zoo"
	Show Picture	TRUE
	Ragged Right	FALSE
Tabpage	Name	tabpage_guests
	Text	"Guests"
	Picture	Custom076!
	Name	tabpage_employees
	Text	"Employees"
	Picture	CreateIndex!
	Name	"tabpage_stores"
	Text	"Store"
	Picture	Custom048!
StaticText	Name	st_selectedtab
	Text	blank
	Border	3D Lowered
CommandButton	Name	cb_Insert
	Text	"&Insert"
	Name	cb_Delete
	Text	"&Delete"

Table 1-11 Property settings for window and controls

4. Now you'll place the controls on the surface of each of the tabpages. Click on tabpage_guests, and place a DataWindow, and a GroupBox within the tabpage. Place three RadioButtons within the GroupBox. Again, use Figure 1-5 as an example. Give these controls the properties shown in Table 1-12.

CONTROL	PROPERTY	VALUE
DataWindow	Name	dw_guests
	DataWindow Object	d_guests
	VScroll Bar	TRUE
GroupBox	Name	gb_sort
	Text	"&Sort By:"
	Border	3D Lowered
RadioButton	Name	rb_date
	Text	"Date"
	Border	3D Lowered
	Name	rb_paid
	Text	"Amount Paid"
	Border	3D Lowered
	Name	rb_type
	Text	"Type"
	Border	3D Lowered

Table 1-12 Properties for controls on tabpage_guests

5. Click on the Employees tabpage. Place one DataWindow control here. Set the properties as shown in Table 1-13.

CONTROL	PROPERTY	VALUE
DataWindow	Name	dw_employees
	DataWindow Object	d_employees
	VScroll Bar	TRUE

Table 1-13 Property settings for DataWindow control on tabpage_employees

6. Click on the Stores tabpage, and place one DataWindow control on it. Set the properties using Table 1-14.

CONTROL	PROPERTY	VALUE
DataWindow	Name	dw_stores
	DataWindow Object	d_stores
	VScroll Bar	TRUE

Table 1-14 Property settings for DataWindow control on tabpage_stores

7. Place the following script in the Open event for the window. This connects to the database, does the initial set up for the DataWindow controls, and retrieves the data for each DataWindow. Notice the syntax used to access the DataWindows on each of the tabpages. It is just standard dot notation, but is one level deeper than you may be used to in working with controls.

```
//Connect to the database
SQLCA.DBParm = "ConnectString='dsn=zoo;uid=dba;pwd=sql'"
SQLCA.DBMS = "ODBC"

Connect Using SQLCA;

//Setup the datawindow on the guest tab
Tab_Zoo.TabPage_Guests.dw_Guests.SetTransObject ( SQLCA )
Tab_Zoo.TabPage_Guests.dw_Guests.Retrieve()

//Setup the datawindow on the employee tab
Tab_Zoo.TabPage_Employees.dw_Employees.SetTransObject ( SQLCA )
Tab_Zoo.TabPage_Employees.dw_Employees.Retrieve()

//Setup the datawindow on the stores tab
Tab_Zoo.TabPage_Stores.dw_Stores.SetTransObject ( SQLCA )
Tab_Zoo.TabPage_Stores.dw_Stores.Retrieve()
```

8. Place the following script in the Close event of the window, used to disconnect from the Zoo database.

```
//Disconnect from the database

Disconnect Using SQLCA;
```

9. Place the following script in the SelectionChanged event of the Tab control. The SelectionChanged event fires after the user clicks a tabpage. In this script, PowerBuilder makes the NewIndex and OldIndex parameters available which tell you which tab now has focus, and which one just lost focus, respectively. Then, the Insert and Delete buttons are enabled if the user selects the Guests tab.

```
Boolean lb_State

//Show the user which tab they selected, and which just lost focus

st_selectedtab.Text = "Selected Tab: " + String ( NewIndex ) + &
```

continued on next page

continued from previous page

```
        " Previous Tab: " + String ( OldIndex )

//Set the state of the command buttons, based on which tab was selected
If NewIndex = 1 Then lb_State = TRUE
cb_Insert.Enabled = lb_State
cb_Delete.Enabled = lb_State
```

10. Place the following code in the Clicked event of rb_Date, located on tabpage_guests. This allows the user to sort the DataWindow based on the guest's visit date.

```
//Sort the datawindow by the visit date

dw_guests.SetSort ( "visit_date" )
dw_guests.Sort()
```

11. Open the Script painter for rb_amount, and write the following code in the Clicked event, allowing the user to sort by amount paid.

```
//Sort the datawindow by the amount paid

dw_guests.SetSort ( "amount_paid" )
dw_guests.Sort()
```

12. Finally, place the following code in the Clicked event of rb_type.

```
//Sort the datawindow by guest type

dw_guests.SetSort ( "guest_type_guest_type_desc" )
dw_guests.Sort()
```

How It Works

Tab controls contain tabpages, which behave much like window objects. You can place individual controls within a tabpage, and those controls are visible only when the associated tabpage is in the foreground. When a tabpage comes into the foreground, the control responds with the SelectionChanged event to alert you to the change in focus. Just prior to this, the SelectionChanging event fires in case you need to do some cleanup work prior to the tabpage losing focus. Such an example might include calling AcceptText() to validate DataWindow input. In this How-To, you set the Ragged Right property to FALSE. Ragged Right specifies whether or not the tab indexes fill the entire control (FALSE), or if the rightmost tab index stops partway across the control (TRUE).

Comments

Each tabpage and the Tab control itself respond to different events. The Tab control responds to far more events than does the tabpage, providing notification of mouse clicks, double-clicks, right mouse clicks, right mouse double-clicks, and keypresses. The tabpage responds to the "standard" events such as the Constructor, Destructor, and drag and drop events. The addition of the Tab control opens the door to all PowerDevelopers, giving them access to this popular interface style. Up until

PowerBuilder 5.0, this kind of functionality was reserved to those who could build or buy their own. While this would not be a difficult affair, it would add yet another level of complexity. For example, buying a control requires the additional purchase. And, you now have one more vendor to deal with (not optimal when problems arise). Building one requires the time and/or technical knowledge necessary to correctly implement it.

COMPLEXITY
ADVANCED

1.5 How do I...
Use TreeView and ListView controls?

Problem

Many popular Windows applications display data in a hierarchical list. This type of list allows the user to drag and drop from one place to another. Once such example is the Windows 95 Explorer. Explorer displays drives, directories, and other desktop resources on the one side, while displaying a detail list on the right. This would be of great use in allowing for drill down type operations. Drill downs allow a user to gain more and more detail about a topic, starting from a high level view. How can I provide this kind of capability in my PowerBuilder application?

Technique

What you have described is known as a *TreeView* and *ListView*. Since you're familiar with Explorer, let's take its behavior as an example. On the left side of Explorer's window is a TreeView, which displays items one below the other. Clicking on one *branch* of the view causes Explorer to display the files, directories, shortcuts, etc. from that branch in a ListView on the right hand side. Providing this kind of operation requires two separate controls. In this How-To, you will build a simple application that demonstrates the power (and complexity) of these two new PowerBuilder controls. Let's first cover some of the terminology surrounding these controls.

TreeView and ListView controls contain *items*. An item is a collection of data properties that make up what the user sees in the control. For example, an item consists of a *label* (the text that the user sees), a *handle* which identifies the item, and *data* which can be anything you want, but usually provides a logical means for locating the item. The data property of the item is similar to the tag property of a control — it's just additional storage for the item. Items reside on *levels*. Using the Explorer example, all directories in the root would constitute level 1. For TreeView controls, each item can have *child items*, similar to how directories can contain other directories. Additionally, both controls support pictures next to the items in the list. These pictures are under your control. In this How-To, the TreeView contains a list of all the departments from the database. Clicking on a department results in the ListView displaying all of the employees from that department. Double-clicking causes the TreeView to expand the item, showing all employees underneath that item. If the user clicks on an employee from the TreeView, pertinent information about the employee shows in the ListView. Finally, the user can drag an employee from the ListView to another department in the TreeView.

Steps

Run the application in the TREELIST.PBL library. The TreeView (on the left) shows all departments, and the ListView (on the right) shows any employees in the first department. If employees exist within a department, the TreeView shows a + sign next to the department. Click on each department, and watch the ListView respond by showing all employees. Now, double-click on a department. The TreeView expands to show a hierarchal view. Click on an employee in the TreeView. The employee name, address, and phone number appear in the ListView. Finally, click on a department, and, from the ListView, drag an employee to a different department. This sample demonstrates many of the functions and properties of these new controls. Figure 1-6 shows the completed application, with a drag and drop operation in progress.

1. Create a new Application object called "treelist", and store it in a library named TREELIST.PBL. Do not generate an application template for this application.

2. Create a new window object with one TreeView, one ListView, and one CommandButton on the surface. Use Figure 1-6 as a reference. Table 1-15 shows the property settings for the controls.

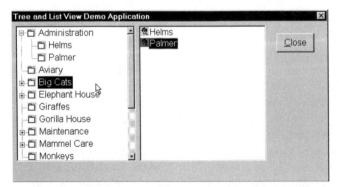

Figure 1-6 TreeList application during a drag and drop

OBJECT/CONTROL	PROPERTY	VALUE
Window	Name	w_treeview
	Title	"Tree and List View Demo Application"
	Type	Response
TreeView	Name	tv_items
	Lines at Root	TRUE
	Border	3D Lowered
ListView	Name	lv_list
	Show Header	FALSE
	Border	3D Lowered
	View	Small Icon
	Drag Icon	DRAGFLDR.ICO
CommandButton	Name	cb_close
	Text	"&Close"

Table 1-15 Properties for w_TreeView window

3. Set the pictures for the tv_items. Double-click on the TreeView control, and select the Pictures tab. This control only uses one picture. Set Picture Name 1 to Custom039!.

4. The ListView control uses several pictures. Double-click on lv_list, and select the Small Picture tab. Set the pictures as shown in Table 1-16.

PICTURE NUMBER	PICTURE NAME
1	Custom076!
2	LibraryList!
3	LibraryList!
4	Custom002!
5	Custom020!

Table 1-16 Pictures for lv_list ListView control

5. The Open event of the window initially populates the TreeView control from the database. To do this, it must declare two database cursors, and retrieve the data one row at a time. First, it retrieves a department. Then, a second cursor retrieves the employees from that department. As the database returns each data element, the Open event places them into the TreeView control using the InsertItemSort() function. InsertItemSort() takes three arguments. The first is the level in which to insert. This script sets that value to 0 (root level). Second is the label of the item. This is a string value, and is what the user sees in the control. The last argument is the picture index. InsertItemSort() results in a TreeView with all the items sorted. If this is not what you want, the InsertItem() function would also do the job. In Step 3 you set one picture, which is index number 1. After obtaining a department, a *dynamic cursor* retrieves the employees. You use a dynamic cursor anytime you don't know (at design time) what parameters must be used in the statement. In this example, you don't know what the department ID will be, as it varies each time you retrieve a department. This department ID is necessary in order to find each employee within that department. Finally, since you will work with employees, you'll need to know the employee ID. The script sets the Data property of the item to this value, and stores it in the TreeView. The key to doing this is understanding how TreeViewItems work. The TreeViewItem data type contains all of the properties for the individual items. To modify one, you must first call GetItem() to populate the TreeViewItem variable, change the property you are interested in, and finally put the item back in the TreeView using the SetItem() function. Table 1-17 lists the properties for a TreeViewItem.

```
String ls_Dept, ls_Select, ls_Name
Integer li_ID, li_Count = 1
Long ll_Handle, ll_Item
TreeViewItem ltv_Item

//Populate the tree control with all department info
DECLARE dept_cur CURSOR For
    SELECT dept_dsc, dept_id
      FROM department;


//Open the cursor
Open dept_cur;

//Fetch each row, placing it into the tree
Fetch dept_cur Into :ls_Dept, :li_ID;
Do While SQLCA.SQLCode = 0
    ll_Handle = tv_Items.InsertItemSort ( 0, ls_Dept, 1 )
    li_Count ++

//Now that we have a department, select all the employees from that
//department. We need a dynamic cursor since we don't know the
//input parameters (department ID)
    ls_Select = "SELECT person.last_name, employee.person_id " + &
                "FROM person, employee, department " +&
                "WHERE person.person_id=employee.person_id " + &
                "AND employee.person_id=person.person_id " + &
                "AND department.dept_id=employee.dept_id " + &
                "AND department.dept_id = '" + String ( li_ID ) + "'"

    DECLARE emp_cur DYNAMIC CURSOR FOR SQLSA;
    PREPARE SQLSA FROM :ls_select;
    OPEN DYNAMIC emp_cur;
    FETCH emp_cur INTO :ls_name, :li_ID;

//Get all the employees from the selected department and put them
```

```
//in the TreeView
    Do While SQLCA.SQLCode = 0
        ll_Item = tv_Items.InsertItemSort ( ll_Handle, ls_name, 1 )
        tv_Items.GetItem ( ll_Item, ltv_Item )
        ltv_Item.Data = li_ID
        tv_Items.SetItem ( ll_Item, ltv_Item )
        FETCH emp_cur INTO :ls_name, :li_ID;
    Loop

//Close the cursor, or it won't open next time
    Close emp_cur;
    Fetch dept_cur Into :ls_Dept, :li_ID;
Loop

//Close the cursor
Close dept_cur;
```

PROPERTY NAME	DATA TYPE	USE
Data	Any	User specific data
Bold	Boolean	If item is displayed in bold
Children	Boolean	If the item has child items
CutHighlighted	Boolean	
DropHighlighted	Boolean	If the item highlights when it's a valid drop target
Expanded	Boolean	If the item has been expanded
ExpandOnce	Boolean	
HasFocus	Boolean	If the item has focus
Selected	Boolean	If the item has been selected
Level	Integer	Level number of the item
OverlayPictureIndex	Integer	
PictureIndex	Integer	Index of the picture array in use
SelectedPictureIndex	Integer	Index of picture for a selected item
StatePictureIndex	Integer	
ItemHandle	Long	Unique identifier of the item
Label	String	String that displays in the control

Table 1-17 Properties for TreeViewItem data type

6. Declare the following instance variable for the window. This value holds the item that the user clicks on in tv_Item. You will use this value later when you code the drag and drop events.

```
Long il_Handle
```

7. As the user clicks on items in tv_Items, you'll want to display all of the child items in the ListView control. The following script for the SelectionChanged event of tv_Items accomplishes this task. When this event fires, PowerBuilder supplies you with the *NewHandle* and *OldHandle* arguments. These values indicate the specific item the user clicked on (NewHandle), as well as the previously selected item (OldHandle). First, the script stores the NewHandle in the instance variable you created above. The next step is to clear the contents of the ListView control, accomplished by the call to DeleteItems(). This must be done so that only information about the current TreeViewItem displays. So, once the ListView is empty, the script populates it with the child items from the current item. The key to this step is the GetItem() function. GetItem() obtains the details of an item. Remember, a TreeView item contains many properties, not just the label that is visible. GetItem() passes the NewHandle variable, along with a local variable of type TreeViewItem. You can think of a TreeViewItem as a structure containing fields for each of the properties. Next, the script checks the Level property of the item. Since this TreeView control contains different data elements (departments and employees), you must know what level the user selected. If it is level 1, they clicked on a department, so you populate the ListView with all of the employees. Otherwise, you know they clicked on an employee, so you populate the ListView with data specific to that employee. If this is a department, the script sets the ListView control's DragAuto property to TRUE, thus allowing drag and drop. This example only allows the user to drag and drop employees, not employee data. Therefore, DragAuto is disabled if the ListView contains employee data.

```
Long ll_Handle
TreeViewItem ltv_Item
String ls_Select, ls_fn, ls_ln, ls_a1, ls_a2, ls_city, ls_st, ls_ph

//Set the instance variable used later if the user drags and drops
il_Handle = NewHandle

//Delete all items from the list
lv_List.DeleteItems()

//Get this item, and find the info
This.GetItem ( NewHandle, ltv_Item )

If ltv_Item.Level = 1 Then                //It's a department
//Populate with all employees from this department
    lv_List.DragAuto = TRUE
    ll_Handle = This.FindItem ( ChildTreeItem!, NewHandle )
    Do While ll_Handle <> -1
        This.GetItem ( ll_Handle, ltv_Item )
        lv_List.AddItem ( ltv_Item.Label, 1 )
        ll_Handle = This.FindItem ( NextTreeItem!, ll_Handle )
    Loop

Else
    lv_List.DragAuto = FALSE
//Get the employee ID, and populate with employee data
//We need a dynamic cursor, since the input parameter can vary
    ls_Select = "SELECT first_name, last_name, address_one, " + &
```

```
                    "address_two, city, state_cd, phone_nbr FROM person" + &
                    " WHERE person_id = " + String ( ltv_Item.data )
      DECLARE emp_cur DYNAMIC CURSOR FOR SQLSA;
      PREPARE SQLSA FROM :ls_select;
      OPEN DYNAMIC emp_cur;
      Fetch emp_cur INTO :ls_fn, :ls_ln, :ls_a1, :ls_a2, :ls_city, :ls_st,
                         :ls_ph;
      If SQLCA.SQLCode = 0 Then
          lv_List.AddItem ( ls_fn + " " + ls_ln, 1 )
          lv_List.AddItem ( ls_a1, 2 )
          lv_List.AddItem ( ls_a2, 3 )
          lv_List.AddItem ( ls_city + ", " + ls_st, 4 )
          lv_List.AddItem ( ls_ph, 5 )
      Else
          MessageBox ( "Database", SQLCA.SQLErrText )
      End If
      Close emp_cur;
  End If
```

8. Place the following code in the DragWithin event of tv_Items. If the user is currently dragging an employee, it is good design to show them what item of the TreeView control would receive the drop. That's what the SetDropHighlight() function does. This event makes the current handle available (the handle of the item the mouse is over), so it simply sets the drop highlight to that row. However, it is possible that the user has the mouse over an employee in the expanded tree. Clearly, dropping one employee on another does not make sense. Therefore, this script tests the level of the item that the mouse is over. If it is 1, the script knows that it is a department, and therefore sets the highlight.

```
TreeViewItem ltv_Item

//The user is dragging an employee. Make sure we're over a department
//and not another employee. The user cannot drop one employee
//onto another

This.GetItem ( Handle, ltv_Item )
If ltv_Item.Level = 1 Then
    This.SetDropHighlight ( Handle )
End If
```

9. The following code goes in the DragDrop event. You may want to read it over several times, or even trace through the debugger and watch what happens. This is probably the most complex script to understand. The intent here is to move an employee from one department to another. The user selects a department, thereby displaying the employees in the ListView control. At that time, the SelectionChanged event stores the item handle in the instance variable. Here is where you'll use this information. From the ListView control, the user drags an employee, and drops it on a department. This script must do several things. First, it must delete the employee from the original department item. This is why you stored the handle to the original item in the instance variable. In order to accomplish this, the script must get all the child items of the original item in turn, and compare the label with the label of the dropped item. This happens with the help of the FindItem() function. FindItem() takes two arguments. The first is the navigation method to use (i.e., find a child, find the root, find next, etc.), followed by the handle of the item on which to start. This continues in a loop until a match is found, or it runs out of child items (this should never occur, as a match will always exist at this point). When it finds a match, it obtains the Data property of the item. This property holds the employee ID, and must be maintained. Then, the script inserts the employee as a child of the department on which it was dropped, and sets this new item's Data property to that of the old item. Finally, it deletes the old item, and selects the new department for display in the ListView.

```
Integer li_Index, li_Handle, li_HandleNew
ListView llv_Control
ListViewItem lvi_Item
TreeViewItem ltv_Item, ltv_ItemNew

//Only ListViews can be dropped, otherwise we must figure out what
//control type got dropped
llv_Control = GetFocus()
li_Index = llv_Control.SelectedIndex()

//See if the user dropped on a department (level 1)
This.GetItem ( Handle, ltv_Item )
If ltv_Item.Level = 1 Then        //OK
    llv_Control.GetItem ( li_Index, lvi_Item )
    li_HandleNew = This.InsertItemSort ( Handle, lvi_Item.Label, 1 )
    This.GetItem ( li_HandleNew, ltv_ItemNew )

//Delete the item from the old department item that matches
    li_Handle = This.FindItem ( ChildTreeItem!, il_Handle )
    This.GetItem ( li_Handle, ltv_Item )
//Loop through each item in the dragged 'from' item, looking
//for the same label. When found, it must be deleted
    Do While ltv_Item.Label <> lvi_Item.Label
        Yield()
        li_Handle = This.FindItem ( NextTreeItem!, li_Handle )
        This.GetItem ( li_Handle, ltv_Item )
    Loop

//Since the data property of the item holds the employee id, we
//must transfer that over to the newly inserted item
    ltv_ItemNew.Data = ltv_Item.Data
    This.SetItem ( li_HandleNew, ltv_ItemNew )
    This.DeleteItem ( li_Handle )
    llv_Control.DeleteItem ( li_Index )

//Turn off the hightlight on the dropped item, and select it to show the
//new items in that department
    This.SetDropHighlight ( 0 )
    This.SelectItem ( Handle )
End If
```

10. Place the following code in the BeginDrag event of lv_List. If you look back at the DragDrop event of the TreeView control, you'll notice that the first thing it does is to assign the control having focus to a variable of type ListView. If the dropped control were not a ListView, a runtime error results. Since the ListView control has its AutoDrag property set to TRUE, it will not receive focus if you simply click and drag. Therefore, this script manually sets the focus when the drag begins.

```
//Since the control is in AutoDrag mode, we must set the focus.
//This is so a runtime error does not occur in the dragdrop event
//of the TreeView.

This.SetFocus()
```

11. Place the following code in the Clicked event of cb_Close, in order to shut the application down.

```
//Close the application
Close ( Parent )
```

12. You'll want to disconnect from the database. Do this in the Close event of the window. Save the window and close the painter.

```
//Disconnect from the database
Disconnect Using SQLCA;
```

13. Finally, place the following code in the Open event of the Application object. This connects to the database, and opens the window if the connect was successful. Save the Application object and run the program.

```
//Connect to the database
SQLCA.DBMS = "ODBC"
SQLCA.DBParm = "ConnectString='DSN=zoo;UID=dba;PWD=sql'"
Connect Using SQLCA;

//Check if connect worked
If SQLCA.SQLCode <> 0 Then
    MessageBox ( "Database", SQLCA.SQLErrText )
Else
    Open ( w_TreeView )
End If
```

How It Works

The key to understanding these controls lies in the TreeViewItem and ListViewItem data types. These controls behave a little like a DataWindow, in that you must use functions to obtain or modify the data in them. Tables 1-18 and 1-19 list some of the common functions and their uses. Note that "common" here refers to functions that are frequently used, not ones that are shared between the two controls (although many of the function names are the same). TreeView and ListView controls are nothing more than sets of items. Each item contains many properties. Remember that a handle uniquely identifies an item, and many of the events for each control supply this handle to you.

FUNCTION NAME	ARGUMENT(S)	PURPOSE
AddPicture()	Picture Name	Add picture to index
DeletePicture()	Index	Delete from control
DeletePictures()	*none*	Delete all items
CollapseItem()	ItemHandle	Collapse one branch
DeleteItem()	ItemHandle	Delete one item
ExpandItem()	ItemHandle	Expand one branch
ExpandAll()	ItemHandle	Expand all sub-branches
GetItem()	ItemHandle {, Item}	Get item data
InsertItem()	ParentHandle, HandleAfter, Item	Insert one item
InsertItemSort()	ParentHandle, Label, PictureIndex	Insert one item and sort
SetItem()	ItemHandle, Item	Set item data
Sort()	SortType	Sort one branch
SortAll()	ItemHandle, SortType	Sort all branches

Table 1-18 Common functions for TreeView control

FUNCTION NAME	ARGUMENT(S)	PURPOSE
AddColumn()	Label, Alignment, Width	Add one column to view
AddItem()	Label, PictureIndex	Add an item
DeleteColumn()	Index	Delete one item
DeleteColumns()	*none*	Delete all items
GetColumn()	Index, Label, Alignment, Width	Gets the current column
GetItem()	Index, Column, Label	Get item data
FindItem()	Start, LabelPartial, Wrap	Find item based on label
InsertItem()	Index, Label, PictureIndex	Insert item in view
SelectedIndex()	*none*	Get current selected item
SetColumn()	Index	Make column current
SetItem()	Index, Item	Set the item data
Sort()	SortType	Sort the view
TotalColumns()	*none*	Get number of columns
TotalItems()	*none*	Get number of items

Table 1-19 Common functions for ListView control

Comments

TreeView and ListView controls contain many functions and events, only a few of which were demonstrated in this How-To. Many more functions exist, as well as a healthy number of events. It is not the focus here to fully document each of these controls, but instead to make you aware of some of their operations and abilities. You may also have noticed that the example does not update the database if you move an employee from one department to another. This is left for you as an exercise. Both the TreeView and ListView controls provide a plethora of capabilities, and can get quite complex for robust applications. The function interface for them allows virtually unlimited flexibility, if you are willing to write some code.

CHAPTER 2

GENERAL WINDOW TECHNIQUES

GENERAL WINDOW TECHNIQUES

How do I...

From your user's point of view, the "little things" in an application are what make the difference between an application that is fun to use and one that is merely adequate. Similarly, the programming techniques you use in your application make the difference between an easily maintainable program and one that is less easily maintained. PowerBuilder offers several facilities to embellish your program's appearance as well as its extensibility. The techniques presented in this chapter allow you to polish your applications while simplifying the eventual modifications and corrections you may have to make.

2.1   Check for Unsaved Changes Before Closing a Window

When the user closes a window, you should check for unsaved work within the window, giving the user the opportunity to save and exit, exit only, or cancel the close operation. This task is simple enough if a script is what closes the window (using the Close() function) but becomes impossible if the user closes the window via the control menu or the window Close button. PowerBuilder's CloseQuery event lets you deal with such "ungraceful" exits. This How-To contains all the steps to make it work.

2.2   Inherit a Window

Inheritance is the object oriented programming technique that allows you to construct program components with functionality that can later be shared ("inherited") by other components of the same type. This technique goes beyond simple cut-and-paste techniques by making the relationship between the original objects (ancestors) and those derived from the original objects (descendants) dynamic. Changes to the functionality in the ancestor automatically propagate to the descendants in most cases. Inheritance allows you to write much-needed processing, such as checking for unsaved changes in the window or coordinating master-detail updates, so that that functionality will be incorporated into all the windows that you construct. This How-To builds two windows that inherit common processing from a third window to demonstrate the power of this technique.

2.3   Open a Splash Window During Application Startup

Most commercial programs show a window containing an application logo to the user as the programs perform time-consuming tasks during program startup. This How-To shows how to create a popup window to perform this task.

2.4   Animate a Picture on a login Screen

As your program prompts the user for his or her ID and password, an animated picture on the login screen adds flair to an otherwise dull aspect of your program. This How-To demonstrates how easy it is to add this feature.

2.5   Pass Parameters Between Windows

Many windows in your application may need to communicate with each other, as in passing a customer ID from a selection window to a detail window. For example, your user could pick a customer from a list of customers in one window and then view that customer's account information in another window. Using global variables for this purpose is both error prone and inelegant. This How-To demonstrates how to use the PowerBuilder Message object to pass data between windows in your application.

2.6   Adjust a Window's Controls When the Window is Resized

When the user resizes a window, we normally want to adjust the size and positioning of controls on the window to maintain the window's "balanced" look. The concepts involved in this technique are simple, although the calculations may be complex. This How-To provides an example of adjusting a particular window's controls in response to a resize.

COMPLEXITY
BEGINNING

2.1 How do I...
Check for unsaved changes before closing a window?

Problem

I have created a window that lets the user enter data into my program. However, I would like to prevent the user from accidentally losing work if he or she exits the window without saving. I am able to do this if I look for unsaved changes when the user exits by clicking a CommandButton (such as Done or Exit), but I can't do this if the user accesses the window's system Close button (in the top right corner of the window) or control menu (in the top left corner of the window) to leave instead. I am also unable to give the user the ability to cancel the accidental closing of a window. How can I always check for unsaved changes and implement the cancel capability I need for my application?

Technique

PowerBuilder offers a window event called CloseQuery that will allow you to look for unsaved changes and cancel the close operation. The CloseQuery event is triggered regardless of how the user closes the window. If any unsaved changes are found, your code will ask the user if he or she wants to save the changes. You will allow the user to answer Yes, No, or Cancel. While Yes and No are easy to implement, Cancel requires special handling. You must tell Windows to abort the close operation by returning a value of 1 from the CloseQuery event.

Steps

The completed application for this How-To can be found on the accompanying CD-ROM in the file CLOSEQRY.PBL and in executable form in CLOSEQRY.EXE. Access the application (through PowerBuilder or by running CLOSEQRY.EXE). Change the contents of the SingleLineEdit and attempt to close the window using the control menu in the upper left corner of the window. The application will tell you that you have unsaved changes and give you several options. If you click Cancel, the window will not close. Choosing Yes (save changes) or No (do not save changes) both cause the window to close. (This example does not actually save data even if you choose Yes.)

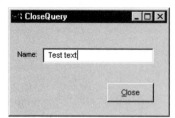

Figure 2-1 The w_closeqry window

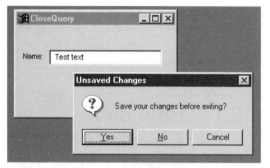

Figure 2-2 The CLOSEQRY application asking the user to save unsaved changes

Steps

1. Create a new .PBL and Application object called CLOSEQRY.PBL and a_closeqry, respectively. Answer "No" when prompted to generate an application template.

2. Create a new window called w_closeqry. Use the property settings shown in Table 2-1. Your result should resemble the window shown in Figure 2-1.

WINDOW/CONTROL NAME	PROPERTY	VALUE
Window		
w_closeqry	Title	"CloseQuery"
CommandButton	Name	cb_close
	Text	"&Close"
SingleLineEdit	Name	sle_name
	Auto HScroll	TRUE
	Accelerator	"n"
	Border	3D Lowered
StaticText	Name	st_name
	Text	"&Name:"
	Alignment	Left

Table 2-1 Window and control settings for w_closeqry

3. Make the following instance variable declaration using the Declare/Instance Variables… menu item.

```
// flag that indicates if anything has been modified on the window
boolean ib_modified
```

4. Place the following script in the CloseQuery event of w_closeqry.

```
integer li_ret

// look for unsaved changes
IF ib_modified THEN
    li_ret = MessageBox("Unsaved Changes", &
                "Save your changes before exiting?", Question!,
YesNoCancel!)
    CHOOSE CASE li_ret
        CASE 1 // Yes
            // save their changes here
        CASE 2 // No
            // do nothing
        CASE 3 // Cancel

            RETURN 1
            // use the following 2 lines for PowerBuilder 4.0
            // Message.ReturnValue = 1
            // RETURN
    END CHOOSE
END IF
```

5. Code the following script in the Clicked event for cb_close.

```
// Close the window that contains this button
Close( parent )
```

6. Open the Script painter for the sle_name SingleLineEdit. Using the Declare/User Events menu item, declare a custom user event called ue_modified. Map this event to the PowerBuilder event pbm_keydown. This procedure causes the SingleLineEdit to receive a ue_modified event every time the user presses a key while sle_name has focus. Using the Select Event dropdown at the top of the painter, switch to the ue_modified event, and code the following script.

```
ib_modified = TRUE
```

7. Save the w_closeqry window and exit the painter for w_closeqry (see Figure 2-2.)

8. Code the following script in the Application object's Open event.

```
Open( w_closeqry )
```

9. Run the application. Try typing something into the sle_name SingleLineEdit. Attempt to exit the window via the Close button (in the top right corner). Notice that you receive a message box informing you of your unsaved changes. Click Cancel and observe that the window does not close. Try using the Close CommandButton (on the window surface). Again observe that you can abort the close operation by clicking Cancel.

How It Works

Unlike the window Close event, a window's CloseQuery event gives your program the opportunity to detect unsaved changes and prompt the user to save them and exit, to discard them and exit, or to cancel the close operation. It is possible to code these first two processes in the Close event. However, the Close event will not allow you to stop the closing of the window. The CloseQuery event occurs before the Close event, while your program still has time to stop the close process. To stop the close, your program must inform Windows to stop closing the window by returning a value of 1. Doing so will abort the close operation and allow the window to remain open.

Comments

While the basic technique to abort the closing of a window is simple, as is demonstrated by this How-To, a good CloseQuery event script is usually moderately to highly complex in order to properly deal with errors encountered while attempting to save data. How-Tos in Chapter 11, *DataWindow Controls–General Programming*, will assist you in writing these more complex scripts.

Using return values to abort a close operation is new to PowerBuilder 5.0. If you are using PowerBuilder 4.0, you can use the Message object to perform the same task. The comments in the script for step 4 show the programming steps needed for step 4.

COMPLEXITY
INTERMEDIATE

2.2 How do I...
Inherit a window?

Problem

I find that coding the same types of processing on every window I build is extremely tedious. In addition, when I find problems, I must correct the problem in every window rather than relying on a centrally located script. I have heard of a technique called inheritance that is available in an object-oriented programming environment, but I don't know much about it. How do I inherit a window?

Technique

Inheritance is a feature of object-oriented programming that allows one window, called the descendant, to derive its processing from another window, called the ancestor. Strictly speaking, PowerBuilder does not restrict inheritance to windows; menus and user objects can also be inherited. When you create the descendant window, all events, scripts, controls, control events, control scripts, functions, and variables defined on the ancestor are available in the descendant, unless you instruct PowerBuilder otherwise. The actual process of inheriting a window is quite simple. The real issues are determining which scripts should be inherited and where to place those scripts in the inheritance "chain."

This How-To will concentrate on the basic mechanics of inheriting a window along with demonstrations of the various inheritance options. For more information on inheritance as it relates to object-oriented programming, refer to Chapter 18, *Introduction to Object-Oriented Programming.*

Steps

The demonstration application for this How-To can be found in the file INHERIT1.PBL on the included CD-ROM. Using the procedure in step 2, you must add a library to the Application object's search path in order to explore this application. Unlike most of the other How-Tos there is no finished application to run. The focus here will be on exploring inheritance and how PowerBuilder supports this technique. Follow along using the steps below to explore PowerBuilder inheritance.

1. Create a new .PBL and Application object called INHERIT1.PBL and a_inherit, respectively. You will not want an application template for this application.

2. Choose the Properties button from the toolbar and click on the Libraries tab. Use the Browse... CommandButton to add CLOSEQRY.PBL (originally used in How-To 2.1) to the library list. At this point, both INHERIT1.PBL and CLOSEQRY.PBL should be in your library search path. The Libraries tab is pictured in Figure 2-3. You are performing this step to make the window you created in How-To 2.1 available to the a_inherit application. Click OK to close the property sheets and choose File/Save to save this Application object.

3. Code the following script in the Application object's Open event.

```
Open( w_closeqry )
```

4. Run the application. Change the contents of the SingleLineEdit. Verify that the Close button results in your being prompted for unsaved changes. This is the same window created in How-To 2.1. Exit the application.

5. Open a Window painter by clicking the proper icon in the PowerBar. When the Select Window window appears, click the Inherit button (instead of the New button you have been using all along). A new window, the Inherit From window, will appear as shown in Figure 2-4. This window allows you to specify the ancestor window that should be used to create the descendant window. Change the current library to CLOSEQRY.PBL, select w_closeqry from the list, and click OK.

6. At this point, a new window identical to w_closeqry has appeared in the Window painter. Using the File/Save menu item, save this window as w_descendant.

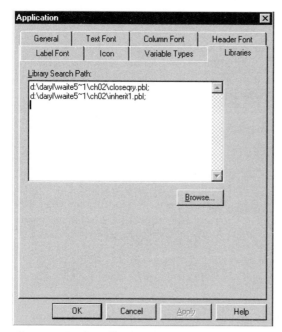

Figure 2-3 The Libraries tab within the Application painter

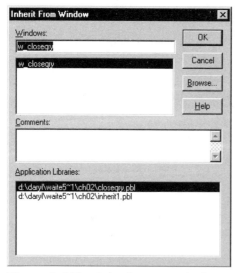

Figure 2-4 The Inherit From window

7. Change the window properties and add the controls listed in Table 2-2 to the w_descendant window.

WINDOW/CONTROL NAME	PROPERTY	VALUE
Window		
w_descendant	Title	"Descendant"
CommandButton	Name	cb_message
	Text	"&Message"

Table 2-2 Window and control settings for w_descendant

8. Save the w_descendant window and close the painter.

9. Code the following script in the Open event of the Application object (replacing the script that you coded previously).

```
Open( w_descendant )
```

10. Run the application. Type something into the sle_name SingleLineEdit and click the Close button. Notice that the message we coded in the CloseQuery event of w_closeqry appears as a result. Even though processing was not placed on this event on the descendant, it is available because w_descendant was inherited from w_closeqry. Answer No to the question and cause the window to close.

11. Open the w_closeqry window. Change the CloseQuery event script by altering the text displayed by the MessageBox() function call. The following script provides an example.

```
integer li_ret

// look for unsaved changes
IF ib_modified THEN
    li_ret = MessageBox("Unsaved Changes", &
             "You have unsaved changes. Click OK to continue closing "+&
             "or Cancel to abort the close.", Question!, OKCancel!)
    IF li_ret = 2 THEN   // OK -- cancel the close
        Message.ReturnValue = 1
        RETURN
    END IF
END IF
```

12. Exit the Script painter, save w_closeqry, and exit the Window painter.

13. Without opening w_descendant, run the application. Again type something into the sle_name SingleLineEdit and click the Close button. Notice that the message displayed has changed even without opening w_descendant. The change made in w_closeqry was automatically propagated to the w_descendant window. Exit the application.

14. Open the w_descendant window in the Window painter.

15. Open the Script painter for the window. Click the Select Event dropdown at the top of the painter and notice that the CloseQuery event has a purple script icon next to it. The purple color indicates that the CloseQuery event script is inherited. Switch to the CloseQuery event. Notice that there is no script for this event. You can view the ancestor script by selecting the Compile/Display Ancestor Script menu item. The window that appears has buttons to allow you to view scripts at multiple levels in the inheritance chain, to select all of the ancestor script (for copying purposes), to copy the script to the clipboard, and to cancel the window. You may not edit the ancestor script on this window. Click the Cancel button and close the window.

16. Place the following script on the CloseQuery event for w_descendant.

```
// show a simple messagebox to demonstrate an extended script
MessageBox( "Descendant", "This is a descendant message!" )
```

17. Close the Script painter and save the window.

18. Run the application. Edit the SingleLineEdit and click the Close button. Observe that your ancestor message appears first. Click OK or Yes (so that the window will continue closing) and observe that the descendant message appears next. By placing a script at the descendant level, you have *extended* the ancestor script. Inherited scripts are executed starting at the highest level ancestor. Exit the application.

19. Enter the Script painter for the w_descendant window. Click on the Declare menu item and notice that the Extend Ancestor Script menu item is checked. This setting is the default and explains the behavior you saw in the preceding step. Select the Override Ancestor Script option. Leave the Script painter and save the window.

20. Run the application. Edit the SingleLineEdit and attempt to close the window. Notice that you only see the descendant window's message now. This occurs because you instructed PowerBuilder to override *all* ancestor scripts in the preceding step. Click the Close button to end the application.

21. Enter the Script painter for the w_descendant window, and add the following line of code at the very end of the CloseQuery event script.

```
CALL w_closeqry::closequery
```

22. Leave the Script painter and save the window.

23. Run the application again. Change the contents of the SingleLineEdit, attempt to close the window, and verify that the descendant's message appears *before* the ancestor's. The behavior occurs because the descendant script has overridden the ancestor script (due to the setting of the Declare/Override Ancestor Script menu item) only to programmatically invoke the ancestor script later on. Click the Close button to end the application.

24. Close the Window painter for w_descendant.

25. Open the w_closeqry window. Move the cb_close CommandButton to the left side of the screen. Save the window and exit the painter.

26. Run the application and notice that the descendant window's Close button has also moved to the left side of the screen. This behavior occurs because properties (including x and y) are inherited. Close the application by clicking the Close button.

27. Open w_descendant in the Window painter. You are free to move the cb_close CommandButton wherever you wish. However, doing so will break the inheritance link between the ancestor and descendant *for the changed properties only*. If you make further changes to cb_message on the ancestor window, w_closeqry, those changes will not be propagated to w_descendant. To reestablish the link, select cb_close (by clicking on it), and select the Edit/Reset Properties menu item. When this action is completed, cb_close's properties will revert to those on w_closeqry. Note that this action synchronizes *all* properties; there is no way to reestablish links on individual properties.

28. Attempt to delete cb_close. Observe that PowerBuilder prohibits this action. You cannot delete inherited controls. You can, however, *hide* inherited controls by setting their Visible property to FALSE.

29. Add the following script to cb_message's Clicked event.

```
MessageBox( "Message", "This is a message coded only on the descendant.")
```

30. Save the window and run the application. Verify that the cb_message CommandButton displays the message coded in the preceding step. Exit the application.

How It Works

The preceding exercise demonstrates the basic features of inheritance in a programming environment. In simple terms inheritance allows you to build dynamic relationships between the components of your application. Unlike a simple copy and paste operation that is common to traditional programming languages, the dynamic relationship allows changes made in the ancestor to automatically propagate to the descendant. You experimented with the different facets of inheritance in this How-To. You constructed an ancestor window, w_closeqry, and coded some basic functionality for it (w_closeqry::CloseQuery, cb_close::Clicked, and sle_name::ue_modified). You then inherited a descendant window, w_descendant, and saw that the functionality defined for the ancestor was automatically present. Using the scripts, you were able to experiment with the settings for Override Ancestor Script and Extend Ancestor Script to see the relationship between ancestor and descendant. Finally, you saw the effects of changing properties on a descendant control versus changing them on the ancestor.

An inherited window in PowerBuilder receives all of the following from the ancestor: window events and scripts, window properties, window functions, window structures, window variables, control events and scripts, and control properties. You cannot delete an inherited control.

The adding, deleting, or renaming of a control on the ancestor is considered a structural change by PowerBuilder. Unlike the non-structural changes explored in this How-To, structural changes do not automatically propagate. Descendant objects should be *regenerated* following structural changes in ancestor objects. You may regenerate an object by opening it in the correct painter or by using the Regenerate toolbar icon in the Library painter. If the structural change is due to a deleted or renamed control on the ancestor *and* there were extended scripts on the old controls in the descendant objects, you must regenerate the objects by opening them in the painter to allow PowerBuilder to remove references to the deleted controls. Structural changes should generally be avoided, as they can cause descendant scripts on deleted controls to be lost.

Comments

Inheritance is one of the single most powerful features of an object-oriented programming environment. By allowing you to build on other application components, you significantly reduce the overall amount of programming required to perform a task. The code itself also tends to be of higher quality because more reuse results in more debugging. Inherited scripts must also be very flexible in order for them to adapt to the changing requirements of descendant objects.

While not demonstrated in this How-To, it is also possible to have multiple levels of inheritance. That is, you can create a window that is inherited from a window that is already a descendant. You can try this yourself in this example by inheriting a window from w_descendant. Scripts and controls added at the w_descendant level will then be propagated to your new window as they were between w_closeqry and w_descendant.

Inheritance is also the feature that allows for the use of frameworks, a special type of class library that provides you with "building block" objects you can use to build your own programs. Instead of writing scripts to prompt for unsaved changes, to adjust for a resized window, to check for errors, and so forth, you can inherit from a pre-built object that already includes this functionality. You also get the benefit of other developers' having tested (and debugged) the objects and scripts you inherit. Frameworks are an excellent way to dramatically reduce the amount of new code required to build a system.

COMPLEXITY
BEGINNING

2.3 How do I...
Open a splash screen during application startup?

Problem

Most commercial applications that I have seen display a nice window showing the application logo and other information during the occasionally long startup process. I would like to show the same kind of window to my users. How do I open a splash screen during application startup?

Technique

The core of this technique is a *popup* window, an infrequently used window type with some interesting capabilities for this application. A popup window is helpful in this instance because popup windows do not require title bars and borders, features which will detract from our splash screen. You will place the controls you need on the window surface and arrange for the window to close either automatically (via a Timer event) or manually (by calling the Close() function). In this example you will place a single PictureButton (for a nice three-dimensional look) on the window surface. The picture on the button will be a bitmap containing our application logo and any other information that the user should see. Rather than sizing the window and button manually, you will set the OriginalSize property of the PictureButton to TRUE and use the Resize event on the window to fit the window to the PictureButton.

Steps

This sample is contained in the files SPLASH.PBL and SPLASH.EXE on the included CD-ROM. Access this application from PowerBuilder or by starting the executable. Run the program and you will see the main window open to fill the display with a smaller splash window on top as shown in Figure 2-5. The splash window contains the application logo and is displayed while the application sets itself up. When you are satisfied with the splash window display, use the Close button on the main window (in the upper right corner) to end the application. To construct this program, follow the steps on the next page.

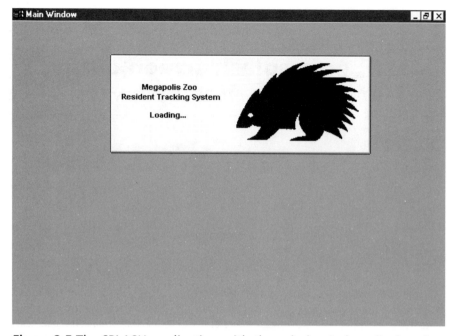

Figure 2-5 The SPLASH application with the splash window displayed

1. Using the Application painter, create a new .PBL and Application object called SPLASH.PBL and a_splash, respectively.

2. Create the splash window itself, called w_splash, using the Window painter along with the settings shown in Table 2-3. Note that when creating the window, you must first set the WindowType property to Popup! before you can set TitleBar, Resizable, and Border to FALSE. Be careful to avoid altering the size of the PictureButton, or you will override the OriginalSize property. For convenience in coding window scripts, leave some extra space around the PictureButton for access to the window surface. Your result (in the Window painter) should resemble Figure 2-6.

WINDOW/CONTROL NAME	PROPERTY	VALUE
Window		
w_splash	Window Type	Popup
	Title Bar	FALSE
	Resizable	FALSE
	Border	FALSE
PictureButton	Name	pb_logo

WINDOW/CONTROL NAME	PROPERTY	VALUE
	Disabled File Name	"PORC.BMP"
	Enabled	TRUE
	Original Size	TRUE

Table 2-3 Window and control settings for the w_splash window

3. This program is structured so that the splash window remains open for a maximum of ten seconds. As is also done in How-To 2.4, the program can request that Windows send the window a Timer event. To do so, place the following code in the Open event of w_splash.

```
// Tell this window when 10 seconds have gone by
Timer( 10, this )
```

4. When the window actually receives a Timer event, it should terminate the splash window. Note that the program will wait to turn off the timers until the window is really closed. Use the following code in the Timer event of the w_splash to let this happen.

```
// Close this window (timer is turned off in the Close event)
Close( this )
```

5. Here we actually turn off the Timer events when the window closes by placing the following script in the Close event of w_splash.

```
// Turn off any running timer events
Timer( 0, this)
```

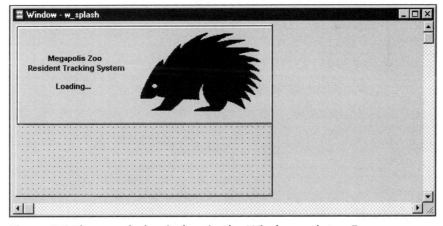

Figure 2-6 The w_splash window in the Window painter. Excess window area simplifies access to scripts.

6. Because the w_splash window has *lots* of excess space surrounding the PictureButton, your program should adjust the window dimensions to fit the PictureButton itself. This will have the effect of leaving only the PictureButton visible, giving this program an attractive three-dimensional look. To handle the adjustments, code the following statements in the Resize event of the w_splash.

```
// Adjust the window size to that of the picturebutton.
// This event will only be received when the window opens.
pb_logo.Move( 0, 0 )
this.Resize( pb_logo.width, pb_logo.height )
```

7. Save w_splash.

8. Using the Window painter create a new window called w_main with the properties shown in Table 2-4. This window will serve as our application's main window. However, it does not do anything in this example except to serve as a backdrop for the splash window.

WINDOW NAME	PROPERTY	VALUE
Window		
w_main	Title	"Main Window"
	Initial State	Maximized (on the Position tab)

Table 2-4 Window settings for the w_main window

9. When the application starts, it should open the main window (giving the application a backdrop) and then open the splash window. To perform these tasks, place the following code in the Application object Open event.

```
// Open the main window
Open( w_main )

// Open the splash window and use a parent of w_main to force the
// popup to remain on top where it can be seen
Open( w_splash, w_main )

// Perform the initialization processing
// In this case, just take some time looping for a while
integer li_index, li_tally
FOR li_index = 1 TO 25000
    li_tally = li_tally + li_index
NEXT

// If the splash window should be closed down immediately following
// initialization, uncomment the following line of script
//IF IsValid( w_splash ) THEN Close( w_splash )
```

10. Save and run the application.

How It Works

When the Splash application starts, the Open event in the Application object opens the main window. Because the main window has a WindowType value of Main, the application's Open script continues executing immediately following the Open (w_main) function call. Following the opening of the main window, the script opens the splash screen, w_splash, which is also an asynchronous process in that the Application script continues immediately. At this point the script can begin the initialization process, represented in the coded script with a loop to cause a visible delay in time. However, w_splash sets up a Windows timer in the Open event. When w_splash receives a Timer event, it automatically closes itself. As a result, the w_splash window can be opened and forgotten.

The Resize event on the w_splash window is interesting as well. It can be very difficult to size controls and windows in the Window painter so that the controls exactly fill the space. Once sized this way, it is a challenge to code scripts on the window surface itself. You can circumvent this problem by coding the Resize event. In w_splash's case the script adjusts the window's dimensions to that of the PictureButton and repositions the PictureButton in the upper left corner of the window, causing the PictureButton to fill the window. The Resize event will be revisited later in this chapter.

Comments

This application makes use of a PictureButton solely to achieve a nice three-dimensional effect on the logo. It is possible to use a bitmap editor to place the necessary "etching" into the bitmap itself. If you use this latter method, you should place a Picture control instead of a PictureButton control on the window surface and make the appropriate changes to the Resize event on the w_splash window. It is also possible that your program will finish initializing before the splash screen's timer interval expires. To remove the splash screen prematurely, use the Timer() function to set the timer interval for the splash window to zero (0) and then close the window with the Close() function.

COMPLEXITY
BEGINNING

2.4 How do I...
Animate a picture on a login screen?

Problem

I have a window that prompts the user to login to the database. While it is functional, I would like it capture a user's attention. How do I add a *moving* picture to this login window?

Technique

To begin with, you must place a Picture control on the login window using the appropriate icon in the Window painter. You will also need a standard bitmap picture (.BMP format) for each stage in the animation sequence. Microsoft Windows will, on request, send you an event at regular time intervals. Using PowerBuilder's Timer() function, you can turn on this timer so that your window receives a Timer event at each interval. When your window receives the event, you will alter the Picture control's properties to display a different frame in the animation sequence. When the window is closed, you will need to tell Windows to stop sending Timer events.

Steps

The completed application for this How-To can be found on the accompanying CD-ROM in the file ANIMATE.PBL and in executable form in ANIMATE.EXE. Access the application through PowerBuilder or by running CLOSEQRY.EXE. Observe the moving picture on the login window as shown in Figure 2-7. Remember that you can alter the rate at which the picture changes to suit your particular animated sequence by changing the timer interval.

1. Using the Application painter, create a new .PBL and Application object called ANIMATE.PBL and a_animate, respectively. Click No when prompted to generate an application template. Use File/Update to save the new Application object and close the Application painter.

2. Use the Window painter to create a new window called w_login. Set the window properties as shown in Table 2-5. This window should be a response window to prevent the user from working with any other part of the application until he or she has logged in.

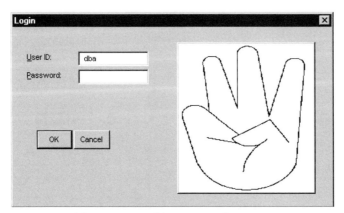

Figure 2-7 The animated login window

WINDOW/CONTROL NAME	PROPERTY	VALUE
Window		
w_login	Title	"Login"
	Window Type	Response
StaticText	Name	st_userid
	Text	&User ID:
StaticText	Name	st_password
	Text	&Password:
SingleLineEdit	Name	sle_userid
	Accelerator	"u"
SingleLineEdit	Name	sle_password
	Password	TRUE
	Accelerator	"p"
Picture	Name	p_1
	File Name	"HAND1.BMP"
CommandButton	Name	cb_ok
	Text	"OK"
	Default	TRUE
CommandButton	Name	cb_cancel
	Text	"Cancel"
	Cancel	TRUE

Table 2-5 Window and control settings for the w_login window

3. Add the controls listed in Table 2-5 to the window so that the result resembles Figure 2-7.

4. Using the Declare/Instance Variables menu item, make the following variable declarations. These declarations will provide the window with a list of bitmaps to cycle through as well as indicators for the current bitmap number and the highest bitmap number available.

```
// array containing the list of bitmaps to display, in order
string  is_bitmaps[] = { "hand1.bmp", "hand2.bmp", "hand3.bmp",
"hand4.bmp", "hand5.bmp"}

// declare array indexes needed for cycling through the bitmaps
integer ii_picture = 1, ii_maxpicture
```

5. As part of the window's initialization, the window must get the number of bitmaps to cycle through, set the first bitmap to display, and arrange for the Timer event to occur. To perform these tasks, place the following code in the window Open event.

```
// get the number of bitmaps
ii_maxpicture = UpperBound( is_bitmaps )

// set the initial bitmap
p_1.picturename = is_bitmaps[ ii_picture ]

// set the timer to send the window an event every second
Timer( 1, this )
```

6. When the window receives a Timer event, it should advance to the next picture in the sequence. Code the following script on the Timer event to make this happen.

```
// advance the picture to the next frame
IF ii_picture = ii_maxpicture THEN
    ii_picture = 1
ELSE
    ii_picture = ii_picture + 1
END IF

p_1.picturename = is_bitmaps[ ii_picture ]
```

7. Place the following code in the window Close event to turn off the Timer events when the window is closed.

```
// turn off the timer
Timer( 0, this )
```

8. Using the Application painter, place the following code in the application Open event.

```
// Open the login window
Open( w_login )
```

9. Save and run the application.

How It Works

The instance variables declared for the w_login window allow your program to preserve values between script executions. In this case one of our variables, ii_bitmaps, is an array that contains the names of each of the bitmap files that will be displayed to animate the picture. Two other variables, ii_picture and ii_maxpicture, track the current picture number and the highest picture number. When the window first opens, the Open event script establishes a value for ii_maxpicture, sets the initial picture in the animation sequence, and uses the Timer() function to have Windows send the window a Timer event once every second.

When the window receives a Timer event, the script advances the picture counter, ii_picture, to the next picture in sequence and changes the displayed picture in the picture control. This cycle continues until the window is closed, which generates a Close event. The Close event script turns off the Timer events by calling Timer() with an interval value of 0.

Comments

Windows is capable of sending Timer events as frequently as 18 times per second and can support up to 16 timers running simultaneously. It is good practice to turn off timers when they are no longer needed; the login window in this application turns the timer off in the window Close event.

For best performance when displaying bitmaps, set the OriginalSize property of the picture control to TRUE, which will prevent PowerBuilder from scaling the picture to the size of the picture control. Many bitmap editors will allow you to scale a bitmap and to save the scaled bitmap with its new dimensions.

COMPLEXITY
INTERMEDIATE

2.5 How do I...
Pass parameters between windows?

Problem

I would like to open a window that receives incoming information from the calling script. Additionally, I would like this window to be able to communicate information back to the calling script when the window closes. I know that I can use global variables to accomplish this task, but there must be a better way. How do I pass parameters between windows?

Technique

The heart of this technique is PowerBuilder's Message object, used in conjunction with one of three functions: OpenWithParm(), OpenSheetWithParm(), and CloseWithReturn(). The functions allow for the passing of a single parameter, which is placed into the Message object when the function is called. The receiving window copies the contents of one of three Message object properties into a variable in order to use the incoming information. It is possible to bypass the single parameter limitation of the Message object by passing a structure, a data type composed of more than one variable.

PowerBuilder provides a single global Message object, called Message, to each PowerBuilder application. The Message object is used for two things: to pass parameters between windows and to communicate information to the Windows operating system. This How-To concentrates on the first use, while an example of the second use is presented in How-To 2.1, "How do I check for unsaved changes before closing a window?"

Information sent using the Message object is contained in one of three properties: DoubleParm, StringParm, or PowerObjectParm. The data types passed in each property are listed in Table 2-6. Even though three properties are available, only one may be used at a time.

PROPERTY	DATA TYPES PASSED	COMMENTS
DoubleParm	all numeric types	integer, real, decimal
StringParm	string	
PowerObjectParm	all other types	structures, window and control references

Table 2-6 Message object properties and their uses

This How-To demonstrates the passing both of a simple string and of a structure. While not shown, the passing of a numeric value is similar, requiring only a code modification to access Message.DoubleParm instead of the other properties.

Steps

The application for this How-To is stored on the included CD-ROM in the files PARAM.PBL and PARAM.EXE. Start the program from PowerBuilder or by running the executable (from Windows Explorer). When the program starts, a simple Changer window will appear as shown in Figure 2-8. This window gives you the opportunity to change its title, size, and color by choosing one of the buttons shown. Click the Change title… button and the New Title window will appear as shown in Figure 2-9. Enter a new title name ("New Changer Title" is good) and click OK; the title you just entered appears in the title of the original Changer window. Now click the Change color and size… button to see the color and size specification window, w_newcolor_and_size, as pictured in Figure 2-10. Change the values for color and size and click OK. Once again your changes are propagated back to the first Changer window. Choose Close to end the PARAM application. To construct this application, follow the steps below.

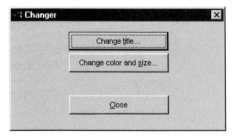

Figure 2-8 The w_changer window in the PARAM application

Figure 2-9 The w_newtitle window in the PARAM application

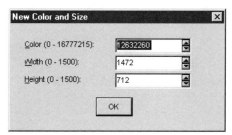

Figure 2-10 The w_newcolor_and_size window in the PARAM application

1. Using the Application painter, create a new .PBL and Application object called PARAM.PBL and a_param, respectively. Click No when prompted to generate an application template. Save the Application object and exit the painter.

2. Start the Window painter and create a new window called w_newtitle. Set the window's properties and add controls as shown in Table 2-7. Your window should resemble the window in Figure 2-9.

OBJECT/CONTROL NAME	PROPERTY	VALUE
Window		
w_newtitle	Title	"Changer"
	Window Type	Response
StaticText	Name	st_title
	Text	"&Title:"
SingleLineEdit	Name	sle_title
	Auto Hscroll	TRUE
	Accelerator	"t"
CommandButton	Name	cb_ok
	Text	"OK"
	Default	TRUE

Table 2-7 Window and control settings for the w_newtitle window

3. When the w_newtitle window is opened from the main Changer window (not yet created), it needs to accept an incoming value indicating the current title of the Changer window. This value will be found in the StringParm property of the Message object. To handle this step, add the following script to w_newtitle's Open event.

```
// Receive the incoming data and show it to the user
sle_title.text = Message.StringParm
```

4. When the user has finished entering a new title, he or she will want to press OK to apply this change to the main Changer window's title. A special function, CloseWithReturn() allows the w_newtitle window to close while passing back the altered window title. Use the following script for the Clicked event of cb_ok.

```
// Close this window, returning the new title
CloseWithReturn( parent, sle_title.text )
```

5. You are now ready to begin construction of the w_newcolor_and_size window which allows the user to alter the color and size of the Changer window. However, this window will be passing back multiple values (color, width, and height). The Message object will allow you to pass multiple values by using a structure, which is simply a custom data type composed of other variables. Using the Structure painter, create a new global structure. Create variables within this structure as shown in Table 2-8. When you have entered these variables, use the File/Save menu item to save this structure under the name s_color_size.

VARIABLE NAME	DATA TYPE
l_color	long
i_width	integer
i_height	integer

Table 2-8 Definition for structure s_color_size

6. Using the Window painter, create a new window called w_newcolor_and_size. Set the window properties and add controls as shown in Table 2-9. Your window should resemble the window in Figure 2-10.

OBJECT/CONTROL NAME	PROPERTY	VALUE
Window		
w_newcolor_and_size	Title	"New Color and Size"
	Window Type	Response
StaticText	Name	st_color
	Text	"&Color (0 - 16777215):"
StaticText	Name	st_width
	Text	"&Width (0 - 1500):"
StaticText	Name	st_height
	Text	"&Height (0 - 1500):"

OBJECT/CONTROL NAME	PROPERTY	VALUE
EditMask	Name	em_color
	Mask	"#######"
	Accelerator	"c"
	Spin Control	TRUE
	Min	0
	Max	16777215
EditMask	Name	em_width
	Mask	"####"
	Accelerator	"w"
	Spin Control	TRUE
	Min	0
	Max	1500
EditMask	Name	em_height
	Mask	"####"
	Accelerator	"h"
	Spin Control	TRUE
	Min	0
	Max	1500
CommandButton	Name	cb_ok
	Text	"OK"
	Default	TRUE

Table 2-9 Window and control settings for the w_newcolor_and_size window

7. As with the w_newtitle window above, the w_newcolor_and_size window must accept incoming values for the Changer window's current size and color. The incoming values will be contained in the Message object's PowerObjectParm property. By assigning this property to a variable of type s_color_size (the structure you created), your program can accept these incoming values. To handle these steps, add the following script to w_newcolor_and_size's Open event.

```
// declare a structure
s_color_size lstr_colorsize

// get the incoming structure
lstr_colorsize = Message.PowerObjectParm

// copy this information to the window
em_color.text = String( lstr_colorsize.l_color )
em_width.text = String( lstr_colorsize.i_width )
em_height.text = String( lstr_colorsize.i_height)
```

8. The OK CommandButton should send back the new color and size values given by the user. For this the program must declare a structure, populate it with the values from the window, and send it back, again using CloseWithReturn(). The following script for the Close event on cb_ok will accomplish this step.

```
// declare a structure
s_color_size lstr_colorsize

// copy the current settings to the structure
lstr_colorsize.l_color = Long( em_color.text )
lstr_colorsize.i_width = Integer( em_width.text )
lstr_colorsize.i_height = Integer( em_height.text )

// Return these new values while closing the window
CloseWithReturn( parent, lstr_colorsize )
```

9. You are finally ready to create the master window, w_changer. Use the settings shown in Table 2-10 in conjunction with Figure 2-8 to construct the w_changer window.

OBJECT/CONTROL NAME	PROPERTY	VALUE
Window		
w_changer	Title	"Changer"
	Resizable	FALSE
	Window Type	Main
CommandButton	Name	cb_title
	Text	"Change &title..."
CommandButton	Name	cb_colorsize
	Text	"Change color and &size..."
CommandButton	Name	cb_close
	Text	"&Close"
	Default	TRUE
	Cancel	TRUE

Table 2-10 Window and control settings for the w_changer window

10. In response to the user clicking the Change title... CommandButton, your program should invoke the w_newtitle window, passing it the current title of the Changer window. The OpenWithParm() function handles the passing of the parameter; simply indicate the value to pass as the second parameter to the function. PowerBuilder will automatically examine the data type of that parameter and store it in the correct property of the Message object. When the OpenWithParm() function returns, the script can examine the appropriate property of the Message object (StringParm in this case) and assign it to the title. The code for the Clicked event of cb_title looks like the following.

```
// Prompt the user for a new title, passing the current title
OpenWithParm( w_newtitle, parent.title )

// Copy the returned value into the title
Parent.title = Message.StringParm
```

11. The script for the Clicked event of cb_colorsize resembles the script in step 10, except that it has a little more work to do. It must create a structure and populate it with the values to pass before it calls OpenWithParm(). When OpenWithParm() returns, it must take out the component pieces of the structure and assign them appropriately in the window. Place the following code in the Clicked event for cb_colorsize.

```
// declare a variable of type s_color_size
s_color_size lstr_colorsize

// copy the information into the structure
lstr_colorsize.l_color = parent.backcolor
lstr_colorsize.i_width = parent.width
lstr_colorsize.i_height = parent.height

// Prompt the user for new information, sending the structure
OpenWithParm( w_newcolor_and_size, lstr_colorsize)

// Receive the new information
lstr_colorsize = Message.PowerObjectParm

// If we get something back from that window, use it.
IF IsValid( lstr_colorsize) THEN
    // Copy this information to the window
    parent.backcolor = lstr_colorsize.l_color
    parent.width = lstr_colorsize.i_width
    parent.height = lstr_colorsize.i_height
END IF
```

12. Add the following script to the cb_close button's Clicked event.

```
// Close the parent window
Close( parent )
```

13. Complete the code for this application by placing the following code in the application Open event. It needs only to open the Changer window.

```
Open( w_changer )
```

14. Save and run the application.

How It Works

When the user clicks the Change title button (cb_title), the Clicked event script uses OpenWithParm() to open the New Title window, sending the current title along in the Message object. In the New Title window Open event, the script copies the incoming parameter, stored in Message.StringParm, to the window title. When the user clicks Close, the Clicked event script uses CloseWithReturn() to send the specified title back. The original Clicked event script on cb_title receives the data in the incoming Message object and copies it to the current window.

The Change color and size button works similarly, but with the added twist of sending a structure to communicate more than one item of data to the w_newcolor_size window. The only real difference is in the use of the PowerObjectParm property of the Message object to obtain the structure reference.

To assist you in understanding the Message object, the flow of processing with the Message object is represented pictorially in Figure 2-11.

Comments

The Message object offers you an elegant, powerful way of sending data between windows. However, there are a few precautions to take when using it. Because the Message object is a global object and because it serves as an interface to Windows, it is extremely volatile. It is *imperative* that your script copy the incoming Message object properties into variables (or window properties) as soon as possible in the Open event of the receiving window. This step should be the very first line of the script. Otherwise, your own programmatic actions may overwrite the contents of the Message object, giving your application invalid values.

CloseWithReturn() also deserves special mention. CloseWithReturn() should be used *exclusively* with *response* windows. The reason for this requirement is that response windows are *synchronous*. When a script opens a response window, that script is suspended until the response window closes. This synchronous behavior allows the calling script to examine the Message object, which will contain valid data, following the response window's closing. If the script opens any other kind of window, the calling script will immediately continue execution following the Open() call instead of waiting for a response.

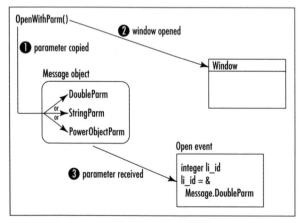

Figure 2-11 A summary of Message object processing

If you study the Message object in PowerBuilder's help library, you will notice that there are several additional properties other than those discussed here. In spite of their names, the WordParm and LongParm properties are not used for parameter passing using the methods discussed in this How-To. However, they *can* be used with events to pass parameters; these techniques are explored more fully in the How-To's in Chapter 18.

COMPLEXITY
INTERMEDIATE

2.6   How do I...
Adjust a window's controls when the window is resized?

Problem

I have a window with several controls that looks great when I lay it out in the Window painter. But whenever my user resizes the window, either the window has too much empty space around the edges or some of the controls are cropped or do not display. How do I adjust the controls on the window to maintain their nice appearance when the user resizes the window?

Technique

The Resize event on a window allows your program to react when the user resizes that window. Based on your application requirements, you can code a script for this event that will adjust the size and positioning of the window's controls based on the new size of the window. The calculations in the Resize event script range from extremely simple to very complex, depending on how many controls are affected and how sophisticated your processing is. Note that the Resize event is issued when the window initially opens as well as when the user resizes the window. This last fact can simplify your work in the Window painter, since in some cases you can depend on the dynamic positioning in the Resize event to arrange the window controls properly instead of arranging them exactly from the Window painter.

This How-To shows two examples of Resize processing. The first window, w_simple_resize, resizes a single MultiLineEdit control so that it exactly fills the window area. The second window, w_complex_resize, positions several controls as the window dimensions are altered.

Steps

The complete working Resize application can be found in RESIZE.PBL and the corresponding .EXE on the included CD-ROM. Access the application and run it. When it starts, two windows will appear. One window, titled Simple Resize, contains a

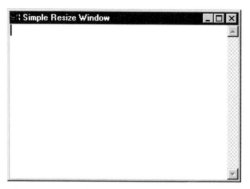

Figure 2-12 The Simple Resize window

Figure 2-13
The Complex Resize
window

MultiLineEdit control that exactly fills the window as shown in Figure 2-12; it looks like a MultiLineEdit control that has a title bar. Alter the window's dimensions and observe that the MultiLineEdit is continuously readjusted.

The second window, titled Complex Resize Window and shown in Figure 2-13, has several controls. Try making the window larger, first in one dimension, then the other, then both. Observe that the StaticText and MultiLineEdit controls get wider or taller as needed while the CommandButtons maintain their relative positions. Try making the window very small in one dimension. Notice that the window "bounces back" to its original size for that dimension. All of these techniques are demonstrated in this How-To. To construct this application for yourself, follow the steps below:

1. Create a new PBL and Application object called RESIZE.PBL and a_resize, respectively, using the Application painter. You will not need a PowerBuilder-generated template for this demonstration. Save the new Application object.

2. Using the Window painter, create a new window called w_simple_resize using the settings shown in Table 2-11. As shown in Figure 2-14, it is not necessary to position or size the MultiLineEdit in the Window painter.

WINDOW/CONTROL NAME	PROPERTY	VALUE
Window		
w_simple_resize	Title	"Simple Resize Window"
MultiLineEdit	Name	mle_resize
	VScroll Bar	TRUE
	Border	None

Table 2-11 Window and control settings for w_simple_resize

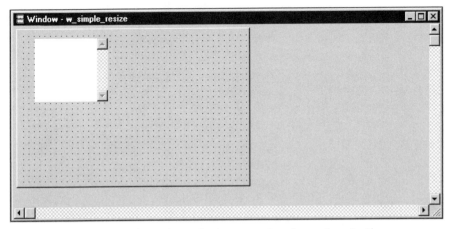

Figure 2-14 The simple resize window, w_simple_resize, in the Window painter

3. Place the following code in the Resize event on w_simple_resize. This script will be responsible for adjusting the MultiLineEdit's dimensions and position whenever the window is "resized" (when it opens and when the user alters its dimensions).

```
// move the MultiLineEdit to the upper left corner of the window
mle_resize.Move( 0, 0 )

// size the mle to fill the window
mle_resize.Resize( this.workspacewidth(), this.workspaceheight() )
```

4. Save the w_simple_resize window.

5. Create a new window, w_complex_resize, using the Window painter. Use the names, controls, and properties shown in Table 2-12. Unlike w_simple_resize, positioning on this window is very important. The resize processing will attempt to maintain the relative positioning and sizes of the controls, and it bases its calculations on the original positions and sizes. Your window should resemble the one shown in Figure 2-13.

WINDOW/CONTROL NAME	PROPERTY	VALUE
Window		
w_complex_resize	Title	"Complex Resize Window"
StaticText	Name	st_comments
	Text	"Enter &comments below:"
	Border	3D Raised

continued on next page

continued from previous page

WINDOW/CONTROL NAME	PROPERTY	VALUE
MultiLineEdit	Name	mle_comments
	VScroll Bar	TRUE
	Border	3D Lowered
CommandButton	Name	cb_ok
	Text	"OK"
	Default	TRUE
CommandButton	Name	cb_cancel
	Text	"Cancel"
	Cancel	TRUE

Table 2-12 Window and control settings for w_complex_resize

6. Make the following instance variable declarations using the Declare/Instance Variables... menu item. These variables will allow the w_complex_resize window to "remember" the original dimensions and spacings that were set in the Window painter (you did lay out this window carefully, didn't you?).

```
// flag to track the first entry into the Resize event
boolean ib_firsttime = TRUE

// original dimensions of the window
integer ii_origwidth, ii_origheight

// gap between buttons
integer ii_buttongap

// gap between buttons and window, buttons and mle
integer ii_button_bottom, ii_button_mle
```

7. When the window receives a Resize event for the first time (when the window opens), it must set the values for the instance variables declared in step 6. For all Resize events after the first, it should readjust the control placement and size to accommodate those new dimensions. Place the following code in the script for the w_complex_resize Resize event to perform these calculations.

```
// declare variables for the current window dimensions
integer li_windowwidth, li_windowheight

// declare variables for the current workspace dimensions
integer li_workwidth, li_workheight

// declare temporary variables
integer li_x, li_y, li_width, li_height

// get the dimensions of the window
li_windowwidth = this.width
li_windowheight = this.height
```

```
// get the dimensions of the window's *work* area
li_workwidth = this.WorkSpaceWidth()
li_workheight = this.WorkSpaceHeight()

// If this is not the first time through this script, make sure
// the user hasn't resized things too small
IF ib_firsttime = FALSE THEN
    // we won't let the window get smaller than it was originally
    IF li_windowwidth < ii_origwidth OR li_windowheight < ii_origheight
THEN
        // Adjust the dimensions. Watch out! This causes another Resize
event.
        this.Resize( ii_origwidth, ii_origheight )
        RETURN
    END IF

ELSE  // this is the first time through this script
    // preserve the original dimensions and some relative positioning info
    ib_firsttime = FALSE

    // original height and width
    ii_origwidth = li_windowwidth
    ii_origheight = li_windowheight

    // the gap between the OK and Cancel buttons
    ii_buttongap = cb_cancel.x - ( cb_ok.x + cb_ok.width )

    // the gap between the buttons and the bottom of the window
    ii_button_bottom = li_workheight - ( cb_ok.y + cb_ok.height )

    // the gap between the mle and the buttons
    ii_button_mle  = cb_ok.y -  mle_comments.y - mle_comments.height

END IF

// adjust the width of the statictext
st_comments.width = li_workwidth - ( 2 * st_comments.x )

// adjust the positioning of the OK button
li_x = (li_workwidth - cb_ok.width - cb_cancel.width - ii_buttongap) / 2
li_y = li_workheight - ( ii_button_bottom + cb_ok.height )
cb_ok.Move( li_x, li_y )

// adjust the positioning of the Cancel button
li_x = cb_ok.x + cb_ok.width + ii_buttongap
li_y = li_workheight - ( ii_button_bottom + cb_cancel.height )
cb_cancel.Move( li_x, li_y )

// Adjust the height of the mle
li_width = li_workwidth - ( 2 * mle_comments.x )
li_height = cb_ok.y - mle_comments.y - ii_button_mle
mle_comments.Resize( li_width, li_height )
```

8. Save the w_complex_resize window.

9. Finally, your program should open both of these windows when it starts. Code the following script in the Application object's Open event.

```
// Open both windows
Open( w_simple_resize )
Open( w_complex_resize )
```

10. Save the Application object and run the application.

How It Works

Both of the example windows in the Resize application make use of the Resize event to size and position the controls on the window. The Resize event occurs once when the window opens as well as whenever the window is resized (by the user or programmatically). The Resize event for the simple window, w_simple_resize, simply positions the MultiLineEdit at the upper left corner of the window and sizes the MultiLineEdit to match the dimensions of the window work area. This technique can be easily adapted to adjust a DataWindow control so that it always fills an MDI sheet.

The other window, w_complex_resize, performs significantly more advanced processing than that performed by w_simple_resize. The Resize event on w_complex_resize was built on the assumption that the MultiLineEdit, mle_comments, is the one that the user would most want to adjust. On a Resize event, the script adjusts the width of st_comments to keep it centered at the top of the window. Additionally, the script keeps the two CommandButtons a fixed distance from the bottom of the window and centered horizontally. The MultiLineEdit, mle_comments, has its dimensions adjusted to shrink or grow based on the resize action. Finally, the Resize event script will prevent the window from being made smaller than when it started. All of these tasks are accomplished via several *instance variables* that store the initial settings for the various distances and a script that calculates all of the new dimensions and positions based on these stored positions and the current positions and dimensions. This script requires careful study for full understanding.

Comments

No single Resize event script will fulfill all potential application requirements. The two examples shown here are merely representative of two common types of processing that occur on a resize action. Also, the processing becomes more complex as the number of controls on a window increases. Most of the complexities will arise from the situation that occurs when a window is made smaller than the designer intended. What do you do when controls overlap? For this reason the w_complex_resize window's code to prevent the window from being made too small is a requirement for most applications. Finally, because of the arithmetic involved in these computations, you may find it helpful to draw diagrams of the particular window in order to derive the calculations needed.

CHAPTER 3
APPLICATION STYLES

APPLICATION STYLES

How do I...

3.1   Make use of a common object library for logging in and accessing database and application information?

3.2   Build and use an SDI application?

3.3   Build a dynamic item catalog using the workbook application style?

3.4   Access application components based on object type using the workspace style of application?

Probably the most common application style in use for business application building is the Multiple Document Interface (MDI) application style. However, there are other application styles that are available for use that could be very productive for your applications. The Single Document Interface (SDI) application style is a viable option for simpler applications, the workbook style is effective when you need the same view of different data or different views of the same data, and the workspace and project application styles focus on your application's data object(s) rather than the functionality that manipulates them. With the different styles you can create applications that are more responsive to the needs of your users and be able to customize what a specific group has access to with a minimum of additional code.

No matter what style of application you choose, necessary additions to your development environment would include framework libraries to inherit from and common usage libraries providing objects used as is across all your applications.

This chapter will provide four fairly complex How-Tos that will demonstrate creating PowerBuilder libraries and applications that fall outside of the traditional MDI style.

3.1 Make Use of a Common Object Library for Logging In and Accessing Database and Application Information

Regardless of the style of your application you will need to provide some common functionality such as gathering database information for connecting, accessing application specific information such as the default path, and getting information from the person using your application such as his or her password and userid. This How-To provides some basic functions and windows for this type of information access.

3.2 Build and use an SDI application

A common misunderstanding with the advent of Windows 95 and other new technology is that the Single Document Interface (SDI) is now obsolete. This How-To demonstrates, by building a simple standalone report viewer, that this application style is not only effective but easy to implement using PowerBuilder.

3.3 Build a dynamic item catalog using the workbook application style

A simple online catalog application that shows a different company or object on each 'page' of a window could be an invaluable tool for most companies, for their own use or for distribution to their clients. This How-To demonstrates a simple example of this type of application using the workbook application style.

3.4 Access application components based on object type using the workspace style of application

In this How-To you will build a small application that focuses on what is being viewed or manipulated, rather than how this is occurring . Steps will demonstrate how you can have several very easy-to-access reports and data entry screens, all focused around specific data objects, and yet only have one main window.

COMPLEXITY
INTERMEDIATE/ADVANCED

3.1 How do I...
Make use of a common object library for logging in and accessing database and application information?

Problem

No matter what application I work on, and no matter what style or how it looks, I usually need to get login information from the user, and get database connection and application specific information such as the default path. How can I create a common PowerBuilder library that contains these types of functions and that can be used regardless of application style?

Technique

PowerBuilder allows you to set more than one library file (.PBL) into your development path. This technique lends itself to separating out common functions and objects into one or more PowerBuilder libraries for use by multiple applications. This How-To demonstrates the steps necessary to create a function that will access database connection information from the registry, create a function that will access application specific information from the registry, and create a window that will process login information and access database security information.

Steps

Access the DATAWINDOW.EXE application from the samples included with this book. You will login to the application via a login window that asks for your userid and your password, if any, as shown in Figure 3-1. What does not show is that when the application first opens, the database connection and application path information is accessed from the registry before this login window is called. After you type in a userid and password such as "spalmer" and "zoorusone1" the application verifies your userid and accesses your database permissions from the database.

To create your own common PowerBuilder library, follow the steps below.

1. You will need to create a new library. Access the Library painter and select the Library menu option and then the Create... menu item.

2. Type "MYCOMMON" into the Library Name field and "Common Application Objects" into the Comments section. Save your library.

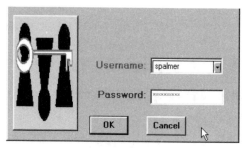

Figure 3-1 Login window

3. You will not need an Application object for this library as you will never run anything directly from it. However, you will need to have access to some Application object for testing and setting of global values. Locate the WORKSPC.PBL library and remove the reference to COMMON.PBL in the library list.

4. Access the property sheets for the object and add MYCOMMON.PBL to the front of your library list.

5. The first common component you create will be an application structure. Access the Structure painter.

6. Create a structure with data values. The first is "path" and it is of type string. The second is "userid" and is also of type string. The last is "permission" and it is of type integer.

7. Close the structure and save it as app_structure. Make sure you save this in MYCOMMON.PBL.

8. The next component you will create will be the function to get the database connection information from the registry. Create a new function and call it f_set_database with a single argument of type TRANSACTION and passed by reference. The function will return an integer.

9. Type in the code that will access information for the transaction structure.

```
// access registry keys for
// at_trans transaction data
String  ls_Database_key
Integer li_return

ls_Database_key =
"HKEY_LOCAL_MACHINE\SOFTWARE\PB5HOWTO\CurrentVersion\Database"

// access transaction data
// access direct values rather than all
// and set directly to transaction object
```

```
li_return = RegistryGet(ls_Database_Key, "PARM", at_trans.dbparm)
li_return = RegistryGet(ls_Database_Key, "Database", at_trans.database)
li_return = RegistryGet(ls_Database_Key, "PWD", at_trans.dbpass)
li_return = RegistryGet(ls_Database_Key, "UID", at_trans.userid)
li_return = RegistryGet(ls_Database_Key, "DBMS", at_trans.DBMS)

return li_return
```

10. The registration values were entered when the "PowerBuilder 5.0 How-To" samples were installed but you can see a sample registry file in Figure 3-2. Registry files have a ".REG" file extension and can be created with any ASCII editor such as Notepad. See Chapter 19, *Deployment Information*, and the third How-To (19.3) for information about setting database connection information into the registry.

11. Close and save the user defined global function.

12. In your Application object, access the Open script. Access the global variables and define two variables. The first is a global variable for your new application structure, and the second is an environment variable.

```
// application object
app_structure gstr_application

// environment object
Environment ge_environment
```

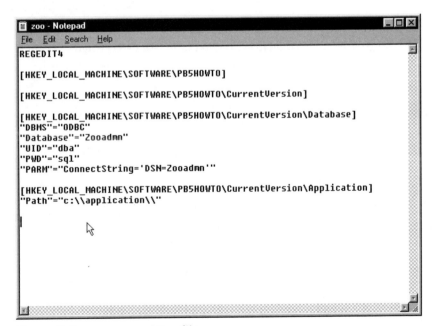

Figure 3-2 zoo.reg registry file

13. Close and save the Application object.

14. The next common component you create will be the f_set_application function. This function takes no arguments and returns an integer value.

15. Type in code that will access the application-specific data from the registry. At this time the only value it will get will be the application path. The path can be used to read or write to files and access graphical or other objects at runtime.

```
// access application specific data

String  ls_Application_key
Integer li_return

ls_Application_Key
="HKEY_LOCAL_MACHINE\SOFTWARE\PB5HOWTO\CurrentVersion\Application"

// access application data
li_return = registryGet(ls_Application_key, "Path", gstr_application.path)

return li_return
```

16. Close and save the function. Notice how the path information was loaded into the global application structure variable. Again, see How-To 19.3 for information about setting this type of value when the application is installed.

17. The last component you will create will be the login window. From the DataWindow painter create a new DataWindow using Quick Select as the data source and Tabular as the format.

18. Select the app_user table and the usernm column. Go to the Design view.

19. Change the background on the DataWindow to Silver. Delete the column title and move the Header band to the top. Change the font color to dark red.

20. Save your DataWindow as "dd_username".

21. Create a second DataWindow using an external data source, and Tabular formatting.

22. Create a column named "username" of type string and 8 characters in length.

23. Remove the column header, move the Header band to the top, and change the font color to dark red and the font style to Bold.

24. Access the field property sheet and change the Border to None. Access the Edit tab, and change the Edit Style to DropDownDW.

25. Choose the new dd_username DataWindow you just created. The usernm field is both the display and data value.

26. Check the Always Display Arrow option and the VScroll Bar.

27. Close and save the DataWindow as d_empl_username.

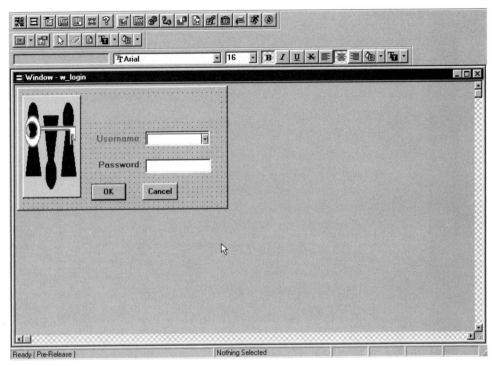

Figure 3-3 w_login window

28. Create a new window from the Window painter. To match the picture in Figure 3-1, place a bitmap control in the left side of the window and access the "login.bmp" that came with the CD-ROM for this book. Size the control to match the picture.

29. Modify the window properties and add the controls as defined in Table 3-1 and as shown in Figure 3-3.

CONTROL NAME	CONTROL TYPE	ATTRIBUTE	VALUE
w_login	Window	Window_color	Silver
		Window_type	Response
p_1	Picture	File_Name	"login.bmp"
		Width	440
		Height	660
		Border	3D Raised
st_title	StaticText	Text	None
		Name	"st_title"

continued on next page

continued from previous page

CONTROL NAME	CONTROL TYPE	ATTRIBUTE	VALUE
dw_1	DataWindow	Object Name	"d_empl_username"
		Border	3D Lowered
sle_1	SingleLineEdit	Border	3D Lowered
st_1	StaticText	Text	"Username:"
		Text Color	Dark Green
st_2	StaticText	Text	"Password:"
		Text Color	Maroon/Dark Red
cb_1	CommandButton	Text	"OK"
		default	checked
cb_2	CommandButton	Text	"Cancel"

Table 3-1 w_login controls and their attributes

30. Access the Open event for the w_login window. Type in code that will set the StaticText control text field to the title that is passed to the window and that will populate the username DropDownDataWindow.

```
// get title
String ls_Title

ls_title = Message.StringParm

st_title.text=ls_title

// load child datawindow with
// user names from database
DataWindowChild dwcChild

dw_1.InsertRow(0)
dw_1.GetChild("username", dwcChild)

dwcChild.SetTransObject(sqlca)
dwcChild.Retrieve()
```

31. Access the Clicked event for cb_1, the "OK" CommandButton. In this event type code that will get the username the user picks and access the app_user table for the password and permissions. The password and username are verified. The permission value is loaded into the global application structure variable.

```
// get password and check against user table
String  ls_password, ls_dbpassword
String  ls_username
Long    ll_row
Integer li_permission

// verify that user picked username
ll_row = dw_1.GetRow()
IF ll_row <= 0 THEN
```

```
        MessageBox("Login", "You must choose an employee name to login.")
        return
END IF

ls_username = dw_1.GetItemString(ll_row, "username")
if ls_username = "" then
        MessageBox("Login", "You must choose an employee name to login.")
        return
END IF

// access password
ls_password = sle_1.Text

// verify password
SELECT password, permission_id into :ls_dbpassword, :li_permission
 from
   app_user where usernm = :ls_username;

if UPPER(ls_dbpassword) <> UPPER(ls_password) then
        MessageBox("Login", "Incorrect password.  Please re-enter.")
        return
end if

// capture user name and database permission
gstr_application.userid = ls_username
gstr_application.permission=li_permission

CloseWithReturn(parent, 1)
```

32. Access the Clicked event for the Cancel CommandButton. Type in code to close the parent window and return a value of 0 to tell the calling program that the user requested a Cancel.

```
CloseWithReturn(parent, 0)
```

33. Close and save the window.

34. In order to use the new common objects, you will need to add the following code to the application Open script for the application using them.

```
Integer li_Return

// set application object
f_set _application()

// set sqlca transaction object
f_set_database(sqlca)

// connect to database
connect using sqlca;

if sqlca.sqlcode <> 0 then
        MessageBox ("Cannot Connect to Database", sqlca.sqlerrtext)
        return
end if

// access login information
```

continued on next page

continued from previous page

```
Open(w_login)

li_return = Message.DoubleParm

if li_return <= 0 then
    return
end if
```

35. The purpose of this code is to access database connection information from the registry, access application information from the registry, connect to the database, and open a Login window.

How It Works

A common library would contain objects that all of your objects will need to access directly. This would not necessarily include anything you would inherit from, which should go into one or more framework libraries. Frameworks usually contain objects that you will inherit from such as a common sheet or menu ancestor object. A common or utility library will contain objects you will use directly such as a login window or a function to set the database as shown in this How-To. You will usually want to keep your inheritable objects separate from those you use directly.

To use these objects, always make sure the common library is the first library in your library path.

Comments

There is always discussion as to whether it is better to use non-visual user objects and user functions, or to use global user functions as was demostrated here. A good rule of thumb is to use a non-visual user object to capture several like functions that are generally accessed together, and to use a global function when the processing is unique to the function.

COMPLEXITY
INTERMEDIATE

3.2   How do I...
Build and use an SDI application?

Problem

Most of my users need to have access to the full functionality of my application, but I do have some users such as managers that only need to access pre-defined reports. Is SDI an effective windows management style for this type of application, and how do I create a standalone report viewer?

Technique

A Single Document Interface (SDI) application only requires one primary or main window. Creating an application using this style can easily be done by creating a separate PowerBuilder library (.PBL) with its own Application object, creating a window, and opening the window from the Application object. Child and popup windows and controls provide the functionality.

Steps

Access the SINGLE.PBL library and run the application. The application opens to one window that contains a Tab control with three tabpages and a separate DataWindow as shown in Figure 3-4. Double-click on one of the reports listed in the top DataWindow of the first tab and the data report is listed in the DataWindow at the bottom of the window as shown in Figure 3-5. The syntax for the DataWindow for this report is stored in an external PowerBuilder library labeled USER.PBL. Do the same with the DataWindow report listed in the control labeled "Database" and the results will look similar to that shown in Figure 3-6. Click on the third tab; PowerBuilder Stored Report (PSR) and the application will bring up a dialog box prompting you to select a file with the .PSR extension, a PowerBuilder Stored Report, as shown in Figure 3-7. Select the file called "Train.PSR" and the application will display the stored report as shown in Figure 3-8. The interesting thing about this last report is that the data shown in the report isn't from the database you are currently attached to. A PowerBuilder Stored Report stores the data from the DataWindow as well as its formatting.

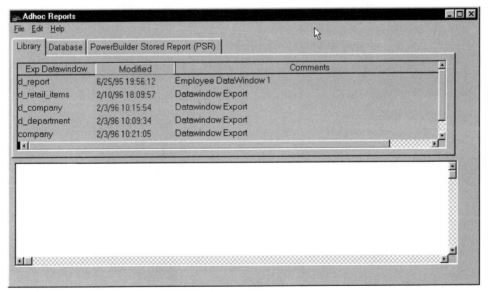

Figure 3-4 The Single application on opening

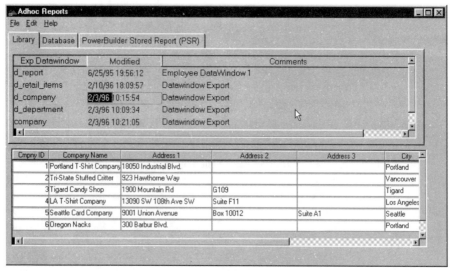

Figure 3-5 The Single application displaying DataWindow stored in a PowerBuilder library

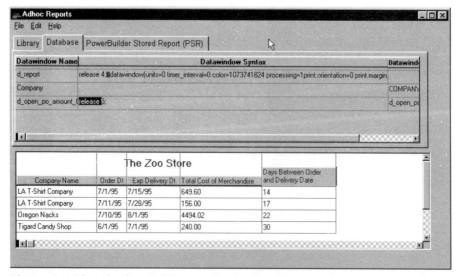

Figure 3-6 The Single application displaying DataWindow stored in the database

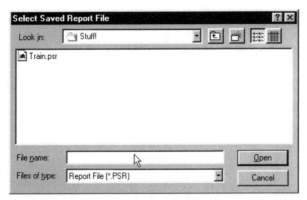

Figure 3-7 The Single application with the prompt for a PowerBuilder Stored Report (PSR) file

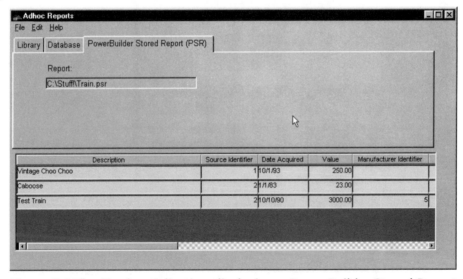

Figure 3-8 The Single application displaying a PowerBuilder Stored Report

One window provides the functionality to allow you to display DataWindows stored in a library, the database, and a stored file. The steps to create this application are outlined below.

1. Create a new application library and call it MYAPP.PBL.

2. Create a new Application object in this library by going to the Application painter and selecting New... from the File menu. A dialog prompting you to

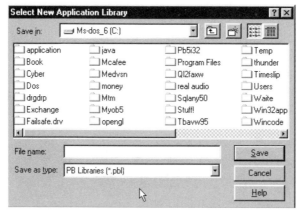

Figure 3-9 Select New Application Library
dialog box

choose the PowerBuilder library will open as shown in Figure 3-9. Select
your new MYAPP.pbl.

3. Another dialog will appear prompting you to name your new application
object as shown in Figure 3-10. Name your new application object "myapp".

4. PowerBuilder will display a MessageBox asking you whether you want
PowerBuilder to generate an application template. Select No by pressing the
[ENTER] key.

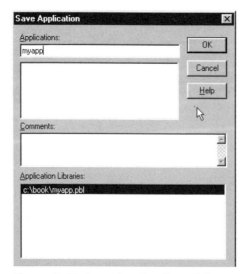

Figure 3-10 Save Application dialog
box

5. Access the library list from the property sheet for the Application object and add the COMMON.PBL library and then add your new library. You can create a common PowerBuilder library following the steps in the first How-To for this chapter.

6. Add code to the Application object Open script to access the database object for the ZOOADMN database and to connect to the database. The function f_set_database can be found in COMMON.PBL. This function accesses the information for the ZOOADMN database from the system registry and loads the appropriate values into the transaction object.

```
// set application object
f_set_application()

// set sqlca transaction object
f_set_database(sqlca)

connect using sqlca;

if sqlca.sqlcode <> 0 then
    MessageBox ("Cannot Connect to Database", sqlca.sqlerrtext)
    return
end if
```

7. Create a new menu in the Menu painter.

8. Type in "File" for the first main menu item and underneath this add the menu item "&Print", a menu separator "-" and then the menu item "E&xit".

9. Next to the File main menu item type in "&Edit" with no menu items. This will act as a placeholder for any later work.

10. At the end type in "&Help" for the Help main menu item. Underneath this type in "&About".

11. Close and save the menu as "m_single_menu".

12. Next, create a single window using the Window painter. To match the pictures shown in Figures 3-4 through 3-7 set the properties for the window using Table 3-2. Define the properties for the window by double-clicking anywhere in the window.

CONTROL NAME	CONTROL TYPE	ATTRIBUTE	VALUE
w_adhoc_reports	Window	Title	"Adhoc Reports"
		Type	Main
		Background Color	ButtonFace
		Menu	m_single_menu
tab_1	tabpage_1	Name	"Library"
	tabpage_2	Name	"Database"

continued on next page

continued from previous page

CONTROL NAME	CONTROL TYPE	ATTRIBUTE	VALUE
	tabpage_3	Name	"PowerBuilder Stored
			Report (PSR)"
dw_library	DataWindow Control	DataWindow	d_datawindow
		Name	dw_library
dw_database	DataWindow Control	DataWindow	d_dbdatawindow
st_1	StaticText	Text	"Report:"
		Background Color	ButtonFace
		Border	3D Lowered
st_2	StaticText	Text	None
		Name	st_report
		Border	3D Lowered

Table 3-2 w_adhoc_reports window and control properties

13. Close the property sheet and save the window as w_adhoc_reports.

14. Place a Tab control in the top part of the window, and place a DataWindow control named dw_library into the tabpage that is created with the Tab control

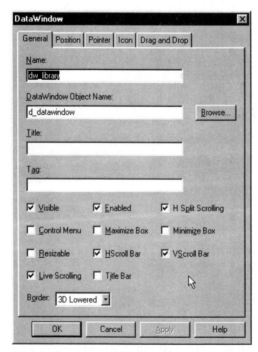

Figure 3-11 Datawindow control
dw_library property sheet

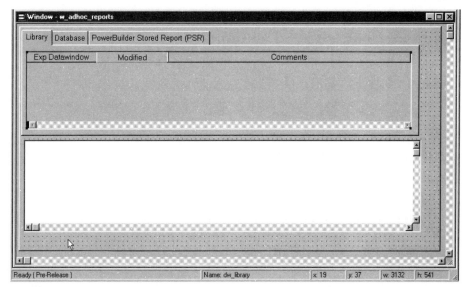

Figure 3-12 Report view window after adding tab and tabpages

and define it using Table 3-2. The sheet should look similar to that shown in Figure 3-11.

15. Insert a new tabpage by placing the mouse anywhere in the Tab control and selecting Insert TabPage from the popup menu.

16. Place a DataWindow control into the second tabpage and call it dw_database with properties as defined in Table 3-2.

17. Create a third tabpage and place two StaticText controls, one on top of the other and defined as shown in Table 3-2. Your window should look similar to that shown in Figure 3-12.

18. Save the window. Access the Open event for the window and type in code to access the Library directory for the first tab, and the database for the second. Populate both of the DataWindows for these two tabs.

```
string ls_datawindows

dw_1.InsertRow(0)

// access library directory for stored datawindows
// from user.pbl
ls_datawindows = LibraryDirectory(gstr_application.path + "user.pbl",
DirDataWindow!)
tab_1.tabpage_1.dw_library.ImportString(ls_datawindows)
```

continued on next page

continued from previous page
```
// access stored datawindow in
// datawindow table
tab_1.tabpage_2.dw_database.SetTransObject(sqlca)
tab_1.tabpage_2.dw_database.Retrieve()
ls_datawindows = LibraryDirectory("user.pbl", DirDataWindow!)
```

19. Access the DoubleClicked event for the DataWindow in the first tab. Type in the following code that will access the DataWindow listed in the row the user clicked on and use the CREATE PowerBuilder function to re-create the stored DataWindow in the display DataWindow.

```
// Export datawindow from library, set trans object and run
String ls_dwsyn, ls_errors
String ls_datawindowname
String ls_File

ls_datawindowname = GetItemString(row, 1)
ls_File = gstr_application.Path + "user.pbl"

ls_dwsyn = LibraryExport(ls_file, &
    ls_datawindowname, ExportDataWindow!)

// create datawindow
dw_1.Create(ls_dwsyn, ls_errors)

//set transaction object and retrieve
dw_1.SetTransObject(sqlca)
dw_1.Retrieve()
```

20. Save your changes to this DataWindow control. Access the Script painter for the DataWindow control, dw_database, located in the second tabpage. Type the following code into the DoubleClicked event for this control.

```
// access syntax and create datawindow
String ls_dwsyn, ls_errors

ls_dwsyn = this.Object.Data[row, 2]

// create datawindow
dw_1.Create(ls_dwsyn, ls_errors)

//set transaction object and retrieve
dw_1.SetTransObject(sqlca)
dw_1.Retrieve()
```

21. The code to implement the third tabpage, and to select a PowerBuilder Stored Report, will be placed in the SelectionChanged event for the Tab control itself. This code will open the common FileOpen and assign the .PSR file to the display DataWindow.

```
int li_rc
string ls_path, ls_file

if newindex = 3 then
```

```
//
//This will open the standard file open dialog box with PSR extensions
li_rc = GetFileOpenName("Select Saved Report File", &
    ls_path,ls_file,"psr","Report File (*.PSR),*.PSR")

If li_rc = 0 Then
    Return
End If

tab_1.tabpage_3.st_report.text = ls_path
//assign the filename (.psr) to the datawindow dataobject.
dw_1.dataobject = ls_path
end if
```

22. To allow your users to print any of the reports, create a user event for the window and call it "ue_print". Type the following into this event.

```
dw_1.Print()
```

23. Save your window and open the Application object. Access the Open script for the application and place code to open your new window at the end.

```
Open(w_adhoc_reports)
```

24. Open your menu again and access the Print menu item from the File main menu. Type the following into the Clicked event.

```
w_adhoc_reports.TriggerEvent("ue_print")
```

25. In the Clicked event for the Exit menu item type the following.

```
close(w_adhoc_reports)
```

26. In the About menu item under the Help main menu, type the following into the Clicked event. This code will open the generic About box located in COMMON.PBL and set the title on the window to the application name.

```
OpenWithParm(w_about, "Viewer Application")
```

27. Save your application. From PowerBuilder run your new application and try out some of the reports. There are some reports already stored in the sample database that came with this book, and there is a USER.PBL library containing several canned reports. Additionally there are .PSR files also located in the subdirectory where the samples were installed.

How It Works

As stated in the introduction, a Single Document Interface (SDI) style of application requires only one main window. With the addition of more sophisticated controls such as the Tab control you can provide considerable functionality that is also easily accessible without having to build a large framework around it.

Comments

An SDI application is usually one that is fairly simple and provides one basic functionality. You will not want to use this application style with a more complex application as you will either have to make extensive use of popup menus or you will have a window that is highly complex and not very intuitive. A rule to go by is to keep the standard Notepad application in mind when you use this style. If the functionality of your application does not exceed the functionality provided by Notepad, then use this style. Otherwise consider some of the others that are detailed elsewhere in this chapter.

COMPLEXITY
INTERMEDIATE/ADVANCED

3.3   How do I...
Build a dynamic item catalog using the workbook application style?

Problem

My company orders items from several other companies and wants an application that allows the user to access items for sale by any one company easily and quickly. What would be an effective approach for this type of application?

Technique

The workbook application style is the style used by applications such as Microsoft Excel. The application functionality is duplicated across pages, with each page accessing a different dataset, or a different view of the same data. This How-To will present a different dataset on each page, with all of the datasets derived from one DataStore object. You will make use of the Tab control and the ability to dynamically add user objects as tabpages based on some factor determined at runtime.

Steps

Access the WRKBOOK.PBL library and run the application. The window that opens has a Tab control with a company name on each tab, as shown in Figure 3-13. Click on any of the tabs and the DataWindow displayed shows only those retail items for that specific company. Insert, delete, or modify any of the retail items and save the result.

Follow the steps on the following page to create your own Retail Items Catalog using the workbook application style.

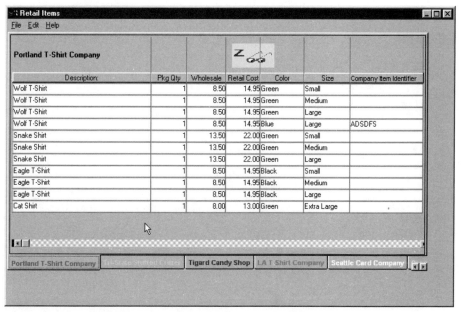

Figure 3-13 Retail Items catalog

1. Create a new PowerBuilder library and application object. Call each RETAIL. For a refresher on how to create a library and Application object, follow steps 1-7 in How-To 3.2 on building an SDI application.

2. Create a new Datawindow using Quick Select as the data source and Grid as the format. Pick the company table and select the company_id and company_name columns.

3. Close and save the DataWindow as "d_company". Don't worry about what it looks like as this DataWindow will not be seen.

4. Create a second DataWindow using SQL Select and Grid style. From the tables pick retail_item and company.

5. Select all of the columns from the retail_item table and the company_name column from the company table.

6. Sort the DataWindow on item_desc. Go to the DataWindow Design view.

7. Set the background color to Silver, and change the border style of the column headers to 3D Raised. Change the column colors to the default window's background color.

8. Move the company_name column to the Header band by accessing its property sheet and then choosing Background from the Layer option on the Postion tab-page. This will let you move the column. Delete the column header.

9. Add a Picture control to the Header band and change the File Name to "logoc.BMP".

10. Access the Rows menu item and then select Update. In the Specify Update Characteristics dialog choose all of the retail_item columns.

11. Specifiy the primary key for the table and close the dialog.

12. Your DataWindow should look similar to that shown in Figure 3-14. Close and save the DataWindow as "d_retail_item_entry".

13. Create a new user object of type Custom Visual. The user object must be of this type to use in a Tab control.

14. On this object place a DataWindow control and change the DataWindow Object Name to "d_retail_item_entry". Change the border on the control to None.

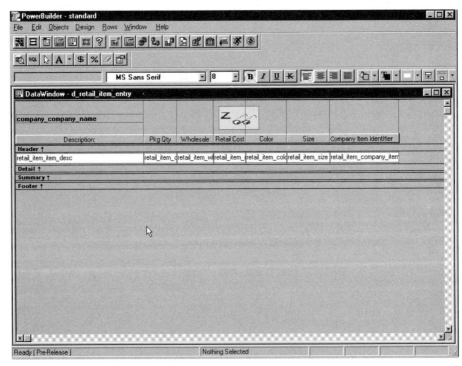

Figure 3-14 d_retail_item_entry DataWindow

15. Create an instance variable of type integer and call it i_MyCompanyID. This value will be set in a later step.

16. Create a user function called uf_filter_data with no arguments and no return value and type in code that will filter the DataWindow based on the company id.

```
// Filter on company id
String ls_Filter

ls_Filter = "retail_item_company_id = " + string(i_mycompanyid)

dw_1.SetFilter(ls_Filter)
dw_1.Filter()
```

17. Save the function and access the constructor for the user object. In this event type in the code that will set the company instance variable from the Message object.

```
i_mycompanyid = Message.DoubleParm
```

18. Close the user object and name it "uo_datawindows".

19. Create a new window and name it "w_retail_item_sheets". Access the WRKSPACE.PBL that came with the CD-ROM with this book. Copy the menu m_retail_sheets from that library to your new one.

20. Open the property sheet for the window and change the title of the window to "Retail Items", select "m_retail_sheets" from the menu list, and select "Main" as the window type. Use your own preferences for the window color, but to match the example choose the default ButtonFace color. Save your changes.

21. Create three instance variables for the window that will hold the current DataWindow (the DataWindow from the tabpage that is displayed), the retail item DataStore which you will create later, and an unbounded array of user objects.

```
// current datawindow
DataWindow idw_Current

// retail datastore
DataStore ids_Retail

// array of user objects
uo_datawindows i_uoDataWindows[]
```

22. Add a Tab control to your window and size it to fit the window, leaving a narrow border. You can adjust it and the window after running the application if you find it is too small or too large.

23. The Tab control automatically generates the first tabpage. Do nothing with this page, as you will hide it at runtime. Access the script for the Tab control and type the following into the SelectionChanging event.

```
// access datawindow object matching
// tab just clicked
// Filter datastore and assign
// instance variable to datawindow in user object

uo_datawindows u_this

u_this = i_uoDataWindows[newindex]
u_this.uf_Filter_Data()

idw_Current = u_this.dw_1
```

24. Next, you will add code to the Open event for the window. This code will create an array of long values that will hold several colors which will be used for the tabs.

```
// create datastore
// set to base datawindow
//
// setup each datawindow to share this object
//
// each datawindow will filter object to company
Long            ll_Count, ll_RowCount, ll_CurrentColor
DataStore       lds_company
String          ls_CompanyName
Integer         li_CompanyID
Long            ll_ColorArray[8]

// hide tabpage - placeholder only
tab_1.tabpage_1.visible=FALSE

// assign colors to color array
ll_ColorArray[1] = RGB(255,255,255)
ll_ColorArray[2] = RGB(255,0,0)
ll_ColorArray[3] = RGB(0,255,0)
ll_ColorArray[4] = RGB(0,0,255)
ll_ColorArray[5] = RGB(255,0,255)
ll_ColorArray[6] = RGB(255,255,0)
ll_ColorArray[7] = RGB(0,255,255)
ll_ColorArray[8] = RGB(0,0,0)
```

25. Type the following code that will create two DataStores: one for the retail item DataWindow, d_retail_item_entry, and a local one for the company DataWindow, d_company. Data is retrieved into both DataStores.

```
// create retail items datastore
ids_Retail = Create DataStore
ids_Retail.DataObject = "d_retail_item_entry"

ids_Retail.SetTransObject(sqlca)
```

```
ids_Retail.Retrieve()

// create company datastore
lds_company = Create DataStore
lds_company.DataObject = "d_company"

lds_company.SetTransObject(sqlca)
lds_company.Retrieve()
```

26. Type in code that will open the tabpages. The company DataStore is used as
one would use a cursor, to provide the company name and company id
used to create the user object for the tab. As each row from the company
table is accessed, a matching tabpage is created from the uo_datawindow
user object. The user object just opened will be loaded into the instance
array, and the DataWindow associated with the user object will be shared
with the DataStore using the ShareData PowerBuilder function. Next the
tab color is chosen from the array using the modulus function Mod
PowerBuilder function. This function will return the remainder when one
number is divided by another. Using this with the size of the array will
allow us to access the colors based on the tab count. The tab text color is
changed, and the company name is assigned to the tab text.

```
// access company store for company name and id
// using datastore in place of cursor
ll_RowCount = lds_company.RowCount()
if ll_RowCount <= 0 then
    MessageBox(this.title, "Could not access company table.")
    PostEvent(Close!)
    return
end if

FOR ll_Count = 1 to ll_RowCount

    // access company name and id
    ls_CompanyName = lds_company.Object.Data[ll_Count, 2]
    li_CompanyID = lds_company.Object.Data[ll_Count, 1]

    // open user object and load into instance array
    tab_1.OpenTabWithParm(i_uoDataWindows[ll_Count], li_CompanyID,
li_CompanyID)

    // share data  with datastore
    ids_Retail.ShareData(i_uoDataWindows[ll_Count].dw_1)

    // access tab color and assign company name to tab
    ll_CurrentColor = Mod(ll_Count, 8) + 1
    i_uoDataWindows[ll_Count].TabTextColor = ll_ColorArray[ll_CurrentColor]
    i_uoDataWindows[ll_Count].Text = ls_CompanyName
NEXT
```

27. Finish the Open event by typing in code that will set the first tab as the
selected one, assign the first tab user object DataWindow as the current
object, and filter the data based on the company.

```
tab_1.SelectTab(1)

// filter for first datawindow
i_uoDataWindows[1].uf_filter_data()
idw_Current = i_uoDataWindows[1].dw_1


// cleanup
destroy lds_company
```

28. The next code you type will be in the SelectionChanging event for the Tab control. This code will access the user object from the instance array based on the index of the tab that was clicked. This index is an event argument, newindex. The DataWindow for the user object is filtered and assigned to the current DataWindow instance variable.

```
// access datawindow object matching
// tab just clicked
// Filter datastore and assign
// instance variable to datawindow in user object

uo_datawindows u_this

u_this = i_uoDataWindows[newindex]
u_this.uf_Filter_Data()

idw_Current = u_this.dw_1
```

29. In the Close event for the window, type code that will destroy the retail item DataStore you created in the Open event.

```
// Clean Up

destroy ids_Retail
```

30. You will create several user events to handle deleting, inserting, and saving to the DataWindow that has control at the time the activity occurs. In the Declare user event dialog, use the following.

```
ue_insert        pbm_custom30
ue_delete        pbm_custom31
ue_save          pbm_custom32
```

31. In the ue_delete event, type code to delete the current row for the current DataWindow.

```
Long ll_Row

ll_Row = idw_Current.GetRow()

if ll_Row > 0 then
    idw_Current.DeleteRow(ll_Row)
end if
```

32. In the ue_insert event, type code to create a new row for the current DataWindow, get the next available retail number for the company, and set this and the company ID into the row.

```
// access next retail item for company
// and set it and company id into row
Integer li_CompanyID, li_ItemID
String  ls_CompanyName
Long    ll_Row

// modify datawindow to set tabs on color and size
idw_Current.SetTabOrder(8, 60)
idw_Current.SetTabOrder(9, 70)

// set company to row
if idw_Current.RowCount() > 0 then
    li_CompanyID = idw_Current.GetItemNumber(1, "retail_item_company_id")

    // get next id
    Select MAX(item_nbr) into :li_ItemID from
        retail_item where company_id = :li_CompanyID;

    if IsNull(li_ItemID) then
        li_ItemID = 0
    end if

    li_ItemID++

    idw_Current.SetItem(ll_Row, "retail_item_item_nbr", li_ItemID)
    ls_CompanyName = idw_Current.GetItemString(1, "company_company_name")
    ll_Row=idw_Current.InsertRow(0)
    idw_Current.SetItem(ll_Row,"retail_item_company_id", li_CompanyID)
    idw_Current.SetItem(ll_Row, "company_company_name", ls_CompanyName)
    idw_Current.AcceptText()
end if
```

33. In the ue_save event, update the database and set the tabs on the color and size fields. These fields cannot be changed once a row has been saved.

```
// save changes
if idw_Current.Update() > 0 then
    COMMIT;
else
    ROLLBACK;
end if


// modify datawindow to set tabs on color and size
idw_Current.SetTabOrder(8, 0)
idw_Current.SetTabOrder(9, 0)
```

34. To finish you will create two more user_events, ue_print and ue_save-datawindow, using pbm_custom33 and pbm_custom34 respectively.

35. Type the following in the ue_print event.

```
idw_Current.Print()
```

36. Type in a call to w_savesource in the ue_savedatawindow. This is a window in COMMON.PBL that came with the samples for this book, and that will save your DataWindow to the USER.PBL file or to the database. With this you can then access the DataWindow as it is at a later time. See the SDI How-To 3.2 for directions in building a viewer that can access these stored objects.

```
OpenWithParm(w_savesource, idw_Current)
```

37. Your new window should look similar to that shown in Figure 3-15. Save the window and open your Application object and add code to open your new window. Save your application.

```
Open(w_retail_item_sheets)
```

38. Run your new application, testing your changes by selecting serveral tabs and viewing the results.

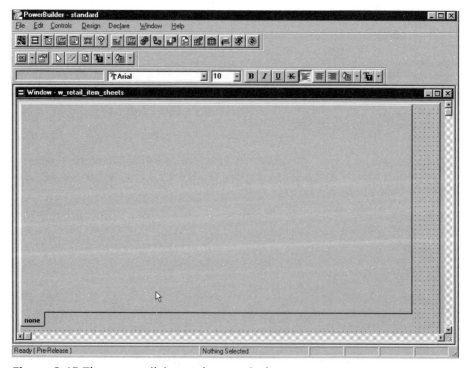

Figure 3-15 The w_retail_item_sheets window

How It Works

The concept of a catalog implies different datasets derived from one data source and accessed independently with little or no effort on the part of the user. The workbook application style is ideal for this type of application. The PowerBuilder Tab object is what makes this application style possible, and fairly easy to implement.

The real key to making this type of application work is the ability to drive the number of pages from the data, rather than hard code the pages at design time. With the concept of adding a user object as a tabpage, your application can add a new dataset and your application will not need any modifications. Test this by adding a new company to the ZOOADMN database. You can do this through the ADMIN application.

Comments

The workbook application style works best with an application that needs to provide different views of the same data object, or a separate view of different data sets again derived from the same data object. If you need to provide different functionality for more than one data object, you should probably use the Multiple Document Interface (MDI) application style.

COMPLEXITY

INTERMEDIATE/ADVANCED

3.4   How do I...

Access application components based on object type using the workspace style of application?

Problem

My application has several distinct but related data entities such as company and retail items. However, I will be accessing all of the objects based on the values of just one. I would like to try creating this application as a workspace style application based on this one defining value. How can I use PowerBuilder to create a workspace style of application?

Technique

When you have a small predefined set of related data objects and you are accessing the application for a specific subset of the data for these objects, you could use the project or workspace style of application. If the data will be accessed from several very distinct looking tools, use the project style which is not discussed in this book. However, if the tools and the access are similar and you want a more cohesive look, use the workspace style. This How-To will create a workspace style of application.

Steps

You will be creating a workspace style of application but, in the interests of brevity, many of the components will be copied from an existing application, as the details of creating these objects are not necessary to demonstrate using this style of application. Access the WRKSPACE.PBL library and run the application. At the login type in "jtower" as the user with no password.When the application opens as shown in Figure 3-16, you will be prompted to provide a company name or to provide part of the name as shown in Figure 3-16. You will accept the "%" value, which means you will get all companies. The application will use the wildcard character '%' to search for a group of companies. You will be presented with three main options: Reports, Data Entry, or running the Report Viewer, as can be seen in Figure 3-17. Select the Reports button and a different window will show with a report in it as shown in Figure 3-18. From the DropDownListBox at the top, select the "PO by Company - graph" report option and the report changes as shown in Figure 3-19. Click the Main menu button, return to the Main menu, and select the Data Entry option. The Data Entry window appears, with Company Id as the first data entry field, as shown in Figure 3-20. As with the Reports Window you could select Purchase Order or Retail Item from the DropDownListBox at the top.

The steps to create this rather colorful application follow.

1. Create a new library and Application object. For details, see steps 1-7 in How-To 3.2 on building an SDI application . Call your application library MYWORK and your Application object mywrk_app.

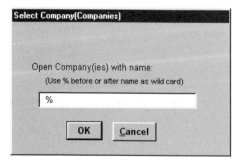

Figure 3-16 Company Selection dialog for WRKSPACE

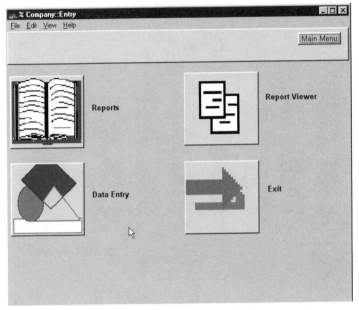

Figure 3-17 WRKSPACE main menu window

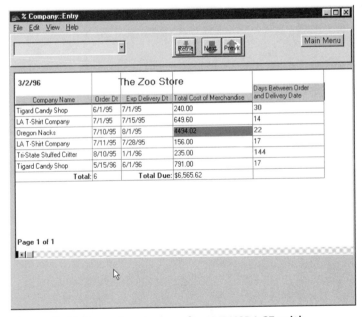

Figure 3-18 Reports window for WRKSPACE with
Purchase Order report

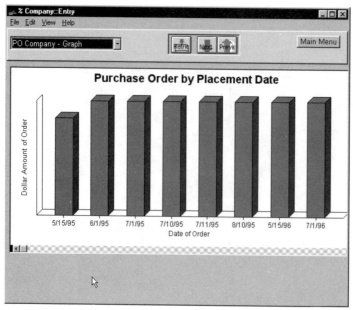

Figure 3-19 PO by Company-graph report for WRKSPACE

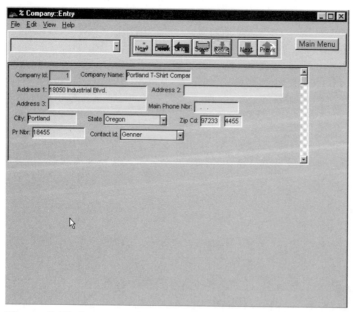

Figure 3-20 Customer Data Entry window for WRKSPACE

2. The first action you will do will be to copy all of the DataWindows you need from the WRKDW.PBL that came on the CD-ROM with this book or you can add this library to your library list.

```
d_company
d_open_po_amount
d_po_company_graph
d_po_graph
d_po_status
d_purchase_order
d_retail_item_entry
d_retail_items
dd_company
dd_dept
dd_emp_name
dd_person
dd_po_status
dd_position
dd_state
```

3. You will also copy the menu to your application. Access the FRAMEWRK.PBL and copy the m_app_menu to your library, or add FRAMEWRK.PBL to your library list.

4. Create a new window which will be the main window for your application. Change the background color to Silver for your window and change the title to "Company".

5. At the top of the window place a Picture control. Change the File Name of the bitmap to "bar.BMP" which comes on the CD-ROM and modify it as shown in Figure 3-21 and defined in Table 3-3.

6. Next add four more Picture controls to serve as buttons and four static text controls as their labels. In addition, add two DropDownListBoxes to the toolbar picture placing one on top of the other. Place a command button in the right side of the toolbar area as shown in Figure 3-22. The properties for all the controls are listed in Table 3-3.

CONTROL NAME	CONTROL TYPE	ATTRIBUTE	VALUE
p_bar	Picture	Border	3D Raised
		File Name	bar.bmp
		Width, Height	2750,230
		X, Y Postion	1,1
p_2	Picture	Border	3D Raised
		File Name	book32.bmp
		Width, Height	600,500
		X, Y Position	20, 305

continued on next page

continued from previous page

CONTROL NAME	CONTROL TYPE	ATTRIBUTE	VALUE
p_3	Picture	Border	3D Raised
		File Name	book.bmp
		Width, Height	600, 500
		X, Y Position	20, 905
p_4	Picture	Border	3D Raised
		File Name	rpt.bmp
		Width, Height	600,500
		X, Y Position	1425, 305
p_5	Picture	Border	3D Raised
		File Name	bye.bmp
		Width, Height	600, 500
		X, Y Position	1425, 905
ddlb_entry	DropDownListBox	Border	3D Lowered
		Width, Height	915, 530
		X, Y Position	20, 60
		Visible	unchecked
ddlb_report	DropDownListBox	Border	3D Lowered
		Width, Height	915, 530
		X, Y Position	20, 60
		Visible	unchecked
cb_1	CommandButton	Text	"Main Menu"
		Width, Height	350, 85
		X, Y Position	2345, 35

Table 3-3 Controls for w_company window

7. Save the window as "w_company" but do not close it. Create an instance variable called "idw_current" of type DataWindow.

8. Create several user events for this new window as shown in Table 3-4 below.

USER EVENT	EVENT NUMBER
ue_print	pbm_custom30
ue_printpreview	pbm_custom31
ue_savedatawindow	pbm_custom32
ue_copydatawindow	pbm_custom33
ue_increasezoom	pbm_custom34

USER EVENT	EVENT NUMBER
ue_descreasezoom	pbm_custom35
ue_showruler	pbm_custom36
ue_save	pbm_custom37
ue_delete	pbm_custom38
ue_new	pbm_custom39
ue_undo	pbm_custom40
ue_retrieve	pbm_custom41
ue_next	pbm_custom42
ue_prev	pbm_custom43
ue_postopen	pbm_custom44

Table 3-4 User events for new workspace window w_company

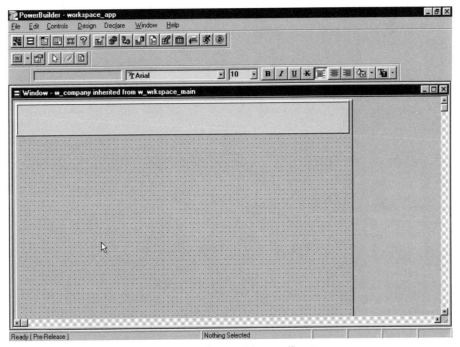

Figure 3-21 Basic workspace window with 'toolbar'

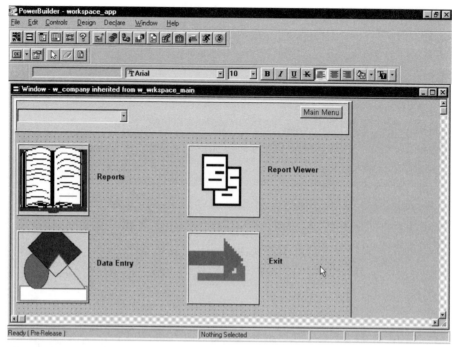

Figure 3-22 Workspace with controls

9. You will add code for all of your new events. Each event and the associated code is listed below.

ue_copydatawindow
```
idw_Current.SaveAs()
```

ue_decreasezoom
```
// access current value
// if not smaller or equal to 25% decrement by 25%
Integer li_zoom

li_zoom=Integer(idw_Current.Object.Datawindow.Zoom)

if li_zoom > 25 then
    li_zoom -= 25
    idw_Current.Object.Datawindow.Zoom=li_zoom
end if
```

ue_increasezoom
```
// access current value
// if not larger then 200% increment by 25%
Integer li_zoom
```

```
li_zoom=Integer(idw_Current.Object.Datawindow.Zoom)

if li_zoom < 200 then
    li_zoom += 25
    idw_Current.Object.Datawindow.Zoom=li_zoom
end if
```

ue_delete
```
// delete row
Long ll_row

ll_row = idw_Current.GetRow()
if ll_row <= 0 then return

idw_Current.DeleteRow(ll_row)
```

ue_new
```
//new row
Long ll_row

ll_row=idw_Current.InsertRow(0)
idw_Current.ScrollToRow(ll_row)
```

ue_next
```
// scroll to next row if not at end
Long ll_row, ll_row_count

ll_row_count = idw_current.RowCount()
ll_row = idw_current.GetRow()
ll_row++

if ll_row <= ll_row_count then
    idw_current.SetRow(ll_row)
    idw_current.ScrollToRow(ll_row)
end if
```

ue_prev
```
// scroll to next row if not at end
Long ll_row

ll_row = idw_current.GetRow()
ll_row =- 1

if ll_row > 0 then
    idw_current.SetRow(ll_row)
    idw_current.ScrollToRow(ll_row)
end if
```

ue_print
```
idw_Current.Print()
```

ue_printpreview
```
// access menu
// if preview checked
//      turn off and uncheck
// else check and turn on print preview
//
```

continued on next page

continued from previous page

```
m_app_main m_this
m_this = this.menuid

if m_this.m_file.m_printpreview.checked=TRUE then
    idw_Current.Object.Datawindow.Print.Preview='NO'
    m_this.m_file.m_printpreview.checked=FALSE
else
    idw_Current.Object.Datawindow.Print.Preview='YES'
    m_this.m_file.m_printpreview.checked=TRUE
end if
```

ue_retrieve
```
// retrieve data
idw_Current.Retrieve(gs_lookup)
```

ue_save
```
if idw_current.Update() > 0 then
    COMMIT;
    MessageBox(this.title, "Changes have been saved.")
else
    ROLLBACK;
    MessageBox(this.title, "An error has occured and changes rolled back.")
end if
```

ue_savedatawindow
```
OpenWithParm(w_savesource, idw_Current)
```

ue_showruler
```
// access menu
// if ruler checked
//      turn off and uncheck
// else check and turn on print preview
//
m_app_main m_this
m_this = this.menuid

if m_this.m_view.m_showrulers.checked=TRUE then
    idw_Current.Object.Datawindow.ruler='NO'
    m_this.m_view.m_showrulers.checked=FALSE
else
    idw_Current.Object.Datawindow.ruler='YES'
    m_this.m_view.m_showrulers.checked=TRUE
end if
```

ue_undo
```
// check to see if deleted rows
// if so, undelete last row
Long ll_row

ll_row = idw_current.DeletedCount()
if ll_row > 0 then
    idw_current.RowsMove(ll_row, ll_row, Delete!, idw_current, 1, Primary!)
end if
```

10. Close the window and save your results.

11. Create a new window and change its style to Response. Place two StaticText controls on the window. Type "Open Company(ies) with name:" in one of the controls and "(Use % before or after name as wild card)" in the other.

12. Place a SingleLineEditBox control underneath the two StaticText controls, and change the text in this to "%". Change the style on this to 3D Lowered.

13. Underneath the SingleLineEdit control place two CommandButtons, one labeled "OK" and set to default, and the other labeled "Cancel". Your window should look similar to that shown in Figure 3-23.

14. Access the Clicked event for the OK CommandButton and type in code to get the company search string.

```
String ls_company

ls_company = sle_1.Text

CloseWithReturn(parent, ls_company)
```

15. Access the Clicked event for the Cancel CommandButton and type in code to return an empty string.

```
CloseWithReturn(parent, "")
```

16. Close the window and save it as w_get_company. Open the w_company window.

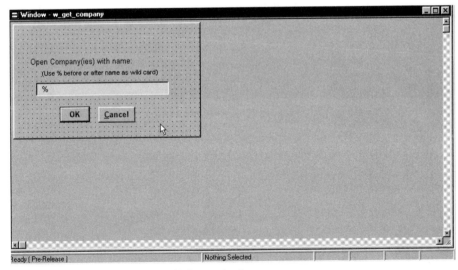

Figure 3-23 Get Company dialog window

17. Create a new global variable called "gs_lookup" of type string and two global variables of type integer called "gi_entry" and "gi_report".

18. Access the Open event for the window and type code to post to the ue_postopen event.

```
this.PostEvent("ue_postopen")
```

19. Access the ue_postopen event and open the new w_get_company window. Type in code that will also assign the return value to the global variable gs_lookup.

```
// get company name string

Open(w_get_company)
gs_lookup = Message.StringParm

if gs_lookup = "" then
    Close(this)
end if
```

20. You will next create a child window called "w_company_entry". Change the title to "::Entry". Create a DataWindow control on the window.

21. Change the border style on the DataWindow to 3D Lowered.

22. Create a function called wf_set_datawindow. The function will take no arguments and will have no return value.

23. Type the function code that will change the DataWindow based on the current data entry DataWindow chosen.

```
// change dataobject based on
// dw choice
CHOOSE CASE gi_entry
    CASE 1
        dw_1.DataObject = "d_company"
    CASE 2
        dw_1.DataObject = "d_purchase_order"
    CASE 3
        dw_1.DataObject = "d_retail_item_entry"
END CHOOSE

// as entry - set to new
idw_Current = dw_1
idw_Current.SetTransObject(sqlca)
this.TriggerEvent("ue_new")
```

24. Close and save the function. Access the Open event for the window and type in code to size the window and to call the new function. The code will also move the window to fit under the toolbar of the parent window (which is 230 PowerBuilder units in height).

```
this.Move(0,230)


wf_set_datawindow()
```

25. Create a user event for the window called "ue_change". This event will be a custom user event and will be defined with an integer parameter "ai_datawindow".

26. In the new event, type code that will call the new wf_set_datawindow function.

```
SetPointer(HourGlass!)

wf_set_datawindow()

SetPointer(Arrow!)
```

27. Close and save the new window.

28. To save time you will create another window very similar to the one you just created by re-opening w_company_entry and saving it as w_company_report.

29. Open the wf_set_datawindow function and replace the code in this function with the code listed below.

```
CHOOSE CASE gi_report
    CASE 1
        dw_1.DataObject = "d_open_po_amount"
    CASE 2
        dw_1.DataObject = "d_po_company_graph"
    CASE 3
        dw_1.DataObject = "d_po_graph"
    CASE 4
        dw_1.DataObject = "d_po_status"
    CASE 5
        String ls_syntax
        dw_1.DataObject = "d_retail_items"
        ls_syntax = dw_1.Object.DataWindow.Syntax
        ls_syntax=f_standard_report(ls_syntax)
        dw_1.Create(ls_syntax)
END CHOOSE

idw_Current = dw_1

idw_Current.SetTransObject(sqlca)

this.TriggerEvent("ue_retrieve")
```

30. Change the title on the window to "::Report" and close and save the new child window.

31. Open the w_company main workspace window. Create two instance variables to hold the report and entry windows.

```
// current child window for entry
w_company_entry iw_entry_child

// current child window for report
w_company_report iw_report_child
```

32. Access the ddlb_entry DropDownListBox and add the items in Table 3-5.

ITEM NUMBER	ITEM
1	Company
2	Purchase Order
3	Retail Items

Table 3-5 Titles for data entry DataWindows

33. Access the SelectionChanged event for the ListBox and type in code that will trigger a ue_change event for the entry child window.

```
if IsValid(iw_entry_child) then
    gi_entry = index
    iw_entry_child.Trigger Event ue_change(index)
end if
```

34. Access the ddlb_report DropDownListBox and type into the Items titles for each of the report DataWindows as shown in Table 3-6.

ITEM NUMBER	ITEM
1	Open Purchase Amount
2	PO By Company - Microsoft Graph
3	PO Company - graph
4	Purchase Order Status
5	Retail Items

Table 3-6 Titles for report DataWindows

35. Access the SelectionChanged event for the ListBox and type in code that will trigger a ue_change event for the report child window.

```
if IsValid(iw_report_child) then
    gi_entry = index
    iw_report_child.Trigger Event ue_change(index)
end if
```

36. Place one ListBox control over the other as shown in Figure 3-24. Remove the check for the visibility option for both of the controls.

37. Next you will copy two other objects into your library. Access the FRAMEWRK.PBL and select the u_entry_toolbar and the u_report_toolbar objects. Copy them to your library. These user objects will provide the button toolbars you will use for accessing the report and entry DataWindows. Each of the buttons on the toolbars triggers an event in the parent window, which you have already created and already added code for.

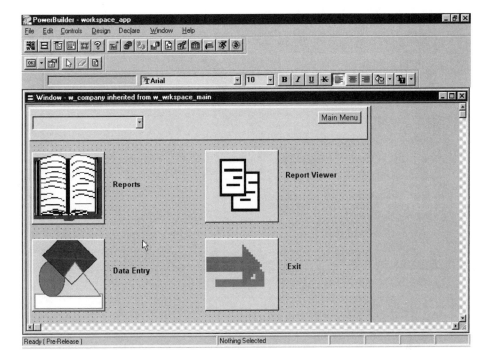

Figure 3-24 w_company with ListBox controls for DataWindow titles

38. Select the user object from the controls and place a user control for the u_entry_toolbar and the u_report_toolbar user objects on the Picture toolbar as shown in Figure 3-25 and in Figure 3-26. Remove the visible check from both of these user objects.

39. Close the window, saving your work to this point. Open your Application object and access the library list for the window. Add in the SINGLE.PBL just before your library. Close and save the application.

40. Only a little more code and you'll be done. Open the w_company window again and access the Clicked event for the Picture control for the Reports option. In the Clicked event for this control, type code to open the w_report_company child window. This window will display in the client area of the main window. Accessing the DataWindow of the child window will enable the main window, w_company, to perform the actions the user requests, such as changing the report DataWindow or accessing the next or previous row.

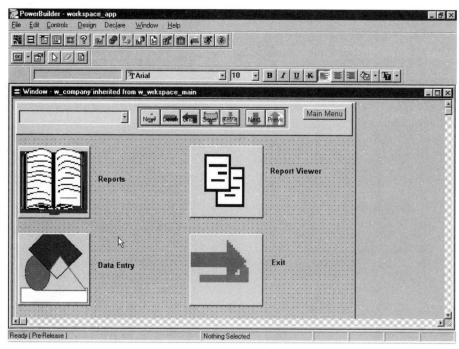

Figure 3-25 w_company with data entry toolbar

```
// make toolbar and listbox visible
SetPointer(HourGlass!)
ddlb_report.Visible=TRUE
uo_report.Visible=TRUE

// open report window
Open(iw_report_child,"w_company_report", parent)

idw_current = iw_report_child.idw_current

SetPointer(Arrow!)
```

41. Access the Clicked event for the Picture control for the Data Entry option. Type in code similar to that in the last step except you will be accessing the w_entry_company child window. Note that the child DataWindow you accessed above is for the report child DataWindow

```
// make toolbar and listbox visible
SetPointer(HourGlass!)
ddlb_entry.Visible=TRUE
uo_entry.Visible=TRUE

// open report window
Open(iw_entry_child,"w_company_entry", parent)
```

```
idw_current = iw_entry_child.idw_current
```

```
SetPointer(Arrow!)
```

42. Access the Clicked event for the Picture control for the Report Viewer and type in code that will open the w_adhoc_reports window.

```
Open (w_adhoc_reports)
```

43. Access the Clicked event for the Picture control for the Exit button and type in code to close the parent window.

```
Close(parent)
```

44. At long last you are ready to code your last event. Access the Main menu CommandButton and in the Clicked event type in code that will close any open child windows, and hide any of the ListBox controls or the toolbar user objects.

```
if IsValid (iw_entry_child) then
    Close(iw_entry_child)
    ddlb_entry.Visible=FALSE
    uo_entry.Visible=FALSE
end if

if IsValid (iw_report_child) then
    Close(iw_report_child)
    ddlb_report.Visible=FALSE
    uo_report.Visible=FALSE
end if
```

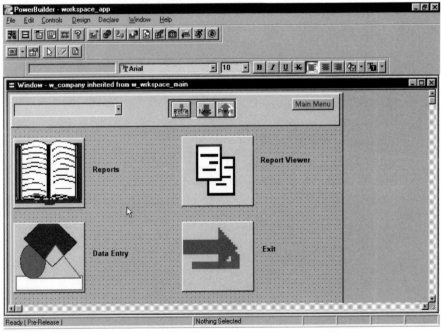

Figure 3-26 w_company with report toolbar

45. That's it! Close your window and save the results. Place a call to this window and the w_login window in your Application object Open script.

```
// get login info
OpenWithParm(w_login, "Company")

if Message.DoubleParm = 0 then return

// open main window
Open(w_company)
```

46. Save your application and run it. Again, login as "jtower" with no password. Try out different search strings and try out each of the reports and data entry DataWindows.

How It Works

A workspace application can be one main window with child windows used for other functionality or to display other views. These child windows display in the same client area as the main window, and are closed when the parent closes. We closed the windows primarily to free up the resource use of the DataWindow. You could combine the functionality of a workspace style application and an MDI style application by designing the application to center its functionality around the data rather than around the functions. The main difference between an MDI application and a workspace one is that the workspace references an object. This is usually an object stored or mapped to a file, but we mapped our object to database storage rather than file storage.

You could make use of a framework to develop workspace style applications. Open the WRKSPACE.PBL library and notice how most of the functionality for the application is inherited from objects in FRAMEWRK.PBL. In fact, FRAMEWRK.PBL contains objects that could be used for every type of application.

Comments

A project style application would be very similar to the workspace application, except that each tool that accesses the data would be in a different window and each window would have its own entry in the window taskbar. Additionally, minimizing or restoring the main window object would minimize or return to normal size all of the tools currently tied to it. To see an example of a project style application, check out the Anchor Bay application that comes with PowerBuilder 5.0.

CHAPTER 4
GENERAL APPLICATION TECHNIQUES

GENERAL APPLICATION TECHNIQUES

How do I...

This chapter includes a variety of simple techniques that allow you to place more functionality into your Application objects and the application as a whole. These techniques include preserving application configuration and user settings from the registry, obtaining a complete description of the computer your application is running on, and replacing the standard system error handler with one of your own design. The result of applying these techniques is an application with a higher level of polish along with technical features that simplify debugging and porting.

4.1   Preserve My Application Settings in the Registry

One of the nicest features you can add to any application is the ability for the application to "remember" the settings in use the last time the program was run. Microsoft Windows 95 and Windows NT make use of a special database called the registry to store these kinds of settings. This How-To will explore the PowerBuilder functions that allow you to save and retrieve values in the registry.

4.2 Get a Description of the Environment at Runtime

It is frequently helpful and sometimes necessary for your PowerBuilder application to know the specific configuration of the computer that is running the program, including the operating system, PowerBuilder version, and display capabilities. This How-To introduces the GetEnvironment() function and shows the different pieces of information contained in the PowerBuilder Environment object.

4.3 Write a System-Level Error Handler to Replace the Standard PowerBuilder One

One of the common problems faced by PowerBuilder developers is addressing fatal runtime errors that occur while testing an application. By default PowerBuilder shows an informative error message under these circumstances, but there is no convenient way to preserve this information in a way that simplifies defect logging and debugging. This How-To demonstrates a simple method you can use to trap and preserve system-level errors for later review.

COMPLEXITY
BEGINNING

4.1 How do I...
Preserve my application settings in the registry?

Problem

When I run my application, my user is always forced to re-specify various application settings such as database connection information and window sizes and positions. I would like to be able to save these settings at the close of a session and restore them at the start of the next session. How do I accomplish this?

Technique

Microsoft Windows 95 and NT already offer a standard repository for saving this type of information. This repository, called the *registry,* is maintained by the operating system. By using several standard functions, including RegistrySet() and RegistryGet(), your program can manipulate the contents of the registry to save and retrieve your application settings.

Steps

The sample application for this How-To can be found in SETTINGS.PBL on the included CD-ROM. Run the application and you will see the windows shown in Figure 4-1. Notice that the Login window appears with information already populated in its fields. Change some of these fields and click Login (it does not actually login).

Figure 4-1 The Settings application

Notice the original size and position of the main window that appears. Alter the main window's size and position and exit the application. Run the application again and observe that the changes you made to the Login window now appear instead of the original values. Click Login and then observe that the main window is also using the settings you gave it during the previous session. To implement this application, follow the steps below.

1. Using the Application painter, create a new PowerBuilder library and Application object called SETTINGS.PBL and a_settings, respectively. You will not need an application template for this application. Save the Application object.

2. Using the Window painter, create a new window called w_login using the controls and property settings shown in Table 4-1. Your end result should resemble Figure 4-2.

WINDOW/CONTROL NAME	PROPERTY	VALUE
Window		
w_login	Title	"Login"
	Window Type	Response
StaticText	Name	st_userid
	Text	"&User ID:"
	Alignment	Left
StaticText	Name	st_password
	Text	"&Password:"

continued on next page

continued from previous page

WINDOW/CONTROL NAME	PROPERTY	VALUE
	Alignment	Left
StaticText	Name	st_database
	Text	"&Database:"
	Alignment	Left
SingleLineEdit	Name	sle_userid
	Accelerator	"u"
	Border	3D Lowered
	Auto HScroll	TRUE
SingleLineEdit	Name	sle_password
	Password	TRUE
	Accelerator	"p"
	Border	3D Lowered
	Auto HScroll	TRUE
SingleLineEdit	Name	sle_database
	Accelerator	"d"
	Border	3D Lowered
	Auto HScroll	TRUE
CommandButton	Name	cb_login
	Text	"&Login"
	Default	TRUE
CommandButton	Name	cb_cancel
	Text	"Cancel"
	Cancel	TRUE

Table 4-1 Window and control settings for w_login

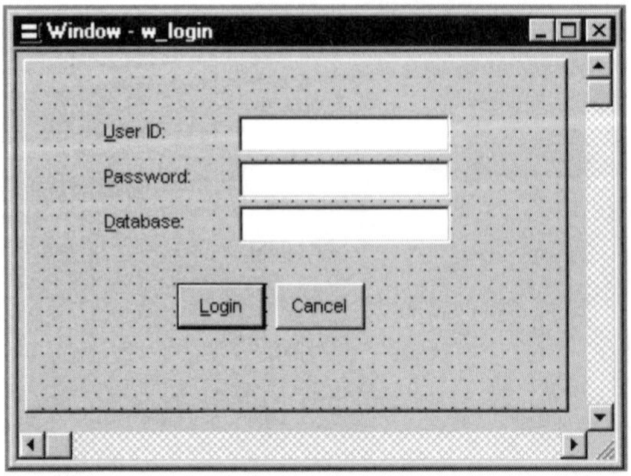

Figure 4-2 The w_login window

3. When the Login window opens, it should access the registry and retrieve the userid and database that were last used by the window (or default values if there are no previous values). To find this information, the following script accesses the settings for the RegistrySettings program (this application); this information is stored in a hierarchy beginning at HKEY_CURRENT_USER (representing the current user's configuration for all programs) and working down through Software (the settings category), RegistrySettings (this application), and Database (application database parameters). Enter this script on the Open event of w_login.

```
string ls_userid, ls_database

// establish the default values in case we don't find the information
// in the registry
ls_userid = "dba"
ls_database = "Orders"

// Lookup the RegistrySettings application's userid and database
RegistryGet( "HKEY_CURRENT_USER\Software\RegistrySettings\Database", &
        "Userid", ls_userid)
RegistryGet( "HKEY_CURRENT_USER\Software\RegistrySettings\Database",&
        "Database", ls_database )

// copy these settings into the singlelineedits
sle_userid.text = ls_userid
sle_database.text = ls_database

// place focus on the userid field and select all of the text in it
// so that the user can easily replace the entire contents
sle_userid.SetFocus()
sle_userid.SelectText( 1, Len( sle_userid.text) )
```

4. When the user logs in by clicking the Login CommandButton, it should preserve the currently specified userid and password in the registry. Place the following script in the Clicked event of cb_login to save these settings.

```
// write the userid and database values into the registry

RegistrySet( "HKEY_CURRENT_USER\Software\RegistrySettings\Database", &
        "Userid", sle_userid.text )
RegistrySet( "HKEY_CURRENT_USER\Software\RegistrySettings\Database",&
        "Database", sle_database.text )


Close( parent )
```

5. The Cancel CommandButton needs only to close the Login window. Use the following script for the Clicked event of cb_cancel.

```
Close( parent )
```

6. Using the Window painter create a main window called w_main using the settings shown in Table 4-2.

WINDOW/CONTROL NAME	PROPERTY	VALUE	
Window			
w_main	Title	"Settings Application"	
	Window Type	Main	
	Initial State	Normal	
	Width	1715	*(approximately)*
	Height	1101	*(approximately)*

Table 4-2 Window and control settings for w_main

7. As with the Login window, w_login, the w_main window should also retrieve its configuration from the registry. However, the script must translate a string value representing the window's state (normal or maximized) to the corresponding enumerated WindowState value. Additionally, our programs might want to store window size and position information for many windows, so we need a way to differentiate the different windows in the registry. The ClassName() function which returns the name of the window class (w_main in this case) will be used at the lowest level of the registry naming hierarchy. Use the following script for the Open event of w_login to accomplish these tasks.

```
integer li_winwidth, li_winheight
integer li_x, li_y
string ls_temp, ls_class, ls_winstate

// this group of settings is grouped under the name of the window
// class name, so we need to obtain it now
ls_class = this.ClassName()

// find out the window state and size
ls_winstate = "Maximized"
RegistryGet( "HKEY_CURRENT_USER\Software\RegistrySettings\"+&
        ls_class,"WindowState", ls_winstate )

ls_temp = "100"
RegistryGet( "HKEY_CURRENT_USER\Software\RegistrySettings\"+&
        ls_class, "Width", ls_temp )
li_winwidth = Integer( ls_temp )

ls_temp = "100"
RegistryGet( "HKEY_CURRENT_USER\Software\RegistrySettings\"+&
        ls_class, "Height", ls_temp )
li_winheight = Integer( ls_temp )

ls_temp = "0"
RegistryGet( "HKEY_CURRENT_USER\Software\RegistrySettings\"+&
        ls_class, "X", ls_temp )
li_x = Integer( ls_temp )

ls_temp = "0"
```

```
RegistryGet( "HKEY_CURRENT_USER\Software\RegistrySettings\"+&
        ls_class, "Y", ls_temp )
li_y = Integer( ls_temp )


// adjust the window state, size, and position
IF ls_winstate <> "Maximized" THEN
    this.WindowState = Normal!
    this.Resize( li_winwidth, li_winheight )
ELSE
    this.WindowState = Maximized!
END IF

this.Move( li_x, li_y)


// Due to a PowerBuilder anomaly, we must force PowerBuilder to accept
// any changes in the WindowState property. Without this, it won't work.
this.Show()
```

8. The w_main window must also save its settings when it closes. Code a
Close event script for w_main using the following script. Save the window
when you are done.

```
// Save the current window settings to the .INI file
string ls_winstate
string ls_class

// We'll identify this group of settings in the registry
// according to the name of this window class, so get it now.
ls_class = this.ClassName()

// should this setting be recorded as maximized/normal
IF this.WindowState = Maximized! THEN
    ls_winstate = "Maximized"
ELSE
    ls_winstate = "Normal"
END IF

// write the settings into the registry
RegistrySet( "HKEY_CURRENT_USER\Software\RegistrySettings\" + &
        ls_class, "WindowState", ls_winstate)

RegistrySet( "HKEY_CURRENT_USER\Software\RegistrySettings\" + &
        ls_class, "Width", String( this.width ) )

RegistrySet( "HKEY_CURRENT_USER\Software\RegistrySettings\" + &
        ls_class, "Height", String( this.height ) )

RegistrySet( "HKEY_CURRENT_USER\Software\RegistrySettings\" + &
        ls_class, "X", String( this.x ) )

RegistrySet( "HKEY_CURRENT_USER\Software\RegistrySettings\" + &
        ls_class, "Y", String( this.y ) )
```

9. Using the Application painter, code a script for the Application object's Open event as follows.

```
Open( w_main )
Open( w_login )
```

10. Save and run the application. Observe that the w_login window appears using the default userid and password values coded as parameters to the RegistryGet() function calls in w_login's Open event. Change these values and click Login. Now alter the size and position of the w_main window and exit the application. If you run the application again you will notice that w_login appears using the changed userid and password values and that w_main appears with the changed size and position.

11. After performing step 10, you now have additional settings stored in your system's registry. You can examine the registry using the Registry Editor provided with the operating system. To invoke the Registry Editor, use the Run... command to invoke the program REGEDIT.EXE. You can find the Run... command in the Start menu (Windows 95 or Windows NT with the Explorer shell) or in the File menu (Windows NT without the Explorer shell). Expand the TreeView control to examine the hierarchy HKEY_CURRENT_USER/Software/RegistrySettings. You should have a display that resembles the one shown in Figure 4-3.

How It Works

A pair of functions, RegistryGet() and RegistrySet(), provide the basis for this How-To. The Open events of each of the two windows, w_main and w_login, use

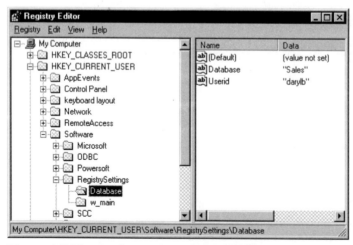

Figure 4-3 The Registry Editor (REGEDIT.EXE) showing the RegistrySettings saved configuration

RegistryGet() to read the saved settings from the registry. The program has been structured to use defaults, so that meaningful values are still available even if the registry entries the program needs do not exist.

When the user clicks the Login button on w_main, the RegistrySet() function saves the current values for userid and password to the registry. A similar action occurs when the w_main window closes (via user action or the Close() function). Note that RegistrySet() only writes string values; numeric values must be converted to strings before calling this function.

There are three other PowerBuilder functions that manipulate the registry: RegistryKeys() to obtain a list of keys at a given level, RegistryValues() to obtain a list of values for a particular key, and RegistryDelete() which removes registry entries from the system. The two functions presented in this How-To, RegistryGet() and RegistrySet(), along with RegistryDelete() are the most commonly needed registry functions.

Comments

Saving program settings to the registry is one of the best ways to improve the level of polish of your application. For consistency purposes, it is a good idea to place scripts like those in w_main's Open and Close events in an ancestor window, allowing inherited descendants of this window to automatically obtain this functionality. In order to generalize this script for use in the ancestor, you may utilize the ClassName() function as was done in this How-To, which allows your program to determine the name of a particular window. Your script can use window names obtained with this function as key names in the registry.

The registry also plays an important role in application installation. For more information on this role, please refer to How-To 19.3, "How do I install a PowerBuilder application using the registry?"

COMPLEXITY
BEGINNING

4.2 How do I...
Get a description of the environment at runtime?

Problem

I would like my PowerBuilder application to be able to check that the user is using the correct version of PowerBuilder. Additionally, I have some screen calculations that need to be altered if the user is running on a higher resolution display than the one I used to develop my application. Is there any way for my application to obtain information about my user's machine configuration?

Technique

PowerBuilder offers a function called GetEnvironment() that returns the information you require. A system structure, called the Environment object, will contain system configuration information following a call to GetEnvironment(). Using this information, your program can adjust its behavior appropriately.

Steps

This sample application can be found on the accompanying CD-ROM under the name ENVIRON.PBL. If you run this application, it will present a simple window (shown in Figure 4-4) giving you details of your current machine configuration. Your program can make use of this information as appropriate.

1. Using the Application painter, create a new PowerBuilder library and Application object called ENVIRON.PBL and a_environment, respectively. You will not need an application template for this How-To.

2. Create a new global function called f_cputypetostring using the specifications show in Table 4-3. Place the following script in the body of the function and save the function when done. This function will be called to translate a variable of type cputype (which can't be displayed) to a string (which can).

```
// Evaluate CPU type and return it as a string
string ls_type

CHOOSE CASE a_cputype
    CASE i286!
        ls_type = "i286"
    CASE i386!
        ls_type = "i386"
    CASE i486!
        ls_type = "i486"
    CASE Pentium!
        ls_type = "Pentium"
    CASE m68000!
        ls_type = "m68000"
    CASE m68020!
        ls_type = "m68020"
    CASE m68030!
        ls_type = "m68030"
    CASE m68040!
        ls_type = "m68040"
    CASE alpha!
        ls_type = "Alpha"
    CASE hppa!
        ls_type = "HPPA"
    CASE Mips!
        ls_type = "MIPS"
    CASE PowerPC!
        ls_type = "PowerPC"
    CASE Sparc!
        ls_type = "SPARC"
    CASE RS6000!
```

```
        ls_type = "RS6000"
END CHOOSE

RETURN ls_type
```

FUNCTION SPECIFICATIONS

Function	Name	f_cputypetostring
	Access	Public
	Returns	string
Arguments	a_cputype	cputypes *(must be typed in)* Value

Table 4-3 Function specifications for f_cputypetostring()

3. Create a global function called f_ostypetostring using the specifications shown in Table 4-4. Use the following script as the body of the function and save the function when done. This function is similar to f_cputypetostring in that it translates an enumerated value (of type ostype in this case) to a string.

```
// Evaluate the ostype and return it as a string
string ls_type

CHOOSE CASE a_ostype
    CASE aix!
        ls_type = "AIX"
    CASE hpux!
        ls_type = "HP/UX"
    CASE macintosh!
        ls_type = "Macintosh"
    CASE osf1!
        ls_type = "OSF/1"
    CASE sol2!
        ls_type = "Solaris"
    CASE windows!
        ls_type = "Windows"
    CASE windowsnt!
        ls_type = "Windows NT"
END CHOOSE

RETURN ls_type
```

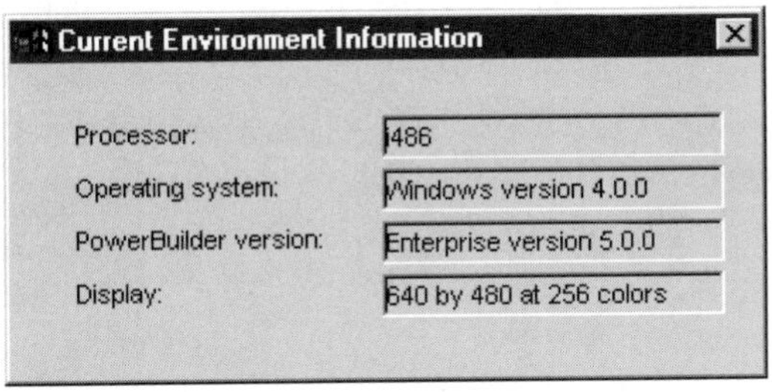

Figure 4-4 The Environment application

FUNCTION SPECIFICATIONS

Function	Name	f_ostypetostring	
	Access	Public	
	Returns	string	
Arguments	a_ostype	ostypes *(must be typed in)*	Value

Table 4-4 Function specifications for f_ostypetostring()

4. Create a global function called f_pbtypetostring using the specifications show in Table 4-5. Use the following script as the body of the function. Save the function when done.

```
// Evaluate the pbtype and return it as a string
string ls_type

CHOOSE CASE a_pbtype
    CASE desktop!
        ls_type = "Desktop"
    CASE enterprise!
        ls_type = "Enterprise"
END CHOOSE

RETURN ls_type
```

FUNCTION SPECIFICATIONS

Function	Name	f_pbtypetostring	
	Access	Public	
	Returns	string	
Arguments	a_pbtype	pbtypes *(must be typed in)*	Value

Table 4-5 Function specifications for f_pbtypetostring()

5. Create a main window called w_environment using the specifications listed in Table 4-6. Your end result should resemble the window shown in Figure 4-5. Note that the figure shows text properties of st_cpu, st_os, etc., in order to assist you in placing the "empty" StaticText controls. You do not need to specify these properties when building the window.

WINDOW/CONTROL NAME	PROPERTY	VALUE
Window		
w_environment	Title	"Current Environment Settings"
	Maximize Box	FALSE
	Minimize Box	FALSE
	Resizable	FALSE

WINDOW/CONTROL NAME	PROPERTY	VALUE
StaticText	Name	st_cpulabel
	Text	"Processor:"
	Alignment	Left
StaticText	Name	st_oslabel
	Text	"Operating system:"
	Alignment	Left
StaticText	Name	st_pblabel
	Text	"PowerBuilder version:"
	Alignment	Left
StaticText	Name	st_screenlabel
	Text	"Display:"
	Alignment	Left
StaticText	Name	st_cpu
	Text	"" (empty)
	Border	3D Lowered
	Alignment	Left
StaticText	Name	st_os
	Text	"" (empty)
	Border	3D Lowered
	Alignment	Left
StaticText	Name	st_cpu
	Text	"" (empty)
	Border	3D Lowered
	Alignment	Left
StaticText	Name	st_pb
	Text	"" (empty)
	Border	3D Lowered
	Alignment	Left
StaticText	Name	st_screen
	Text	"" (empty)
	Border	3D Lowered
	Alignment	Left

Table 4-6 Specifications for the w_environment window

6. Code the following script in the Open event of the w_environment window.
This script declares a variable of type environment, which will hold all of
the environment information. It then calls GetEnvironment() to obtain this
information, which is then displayed.

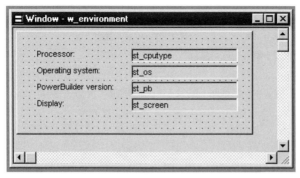

Figure 4-5 The w_environment window

```
// declare the environment structure
environment l_environment

// get the specifics of our environment. If it doesn't work,
// tell the user
IF GetEnvironment( l_environment ) < 0 THEN
    MessageBox( "Error", "Could not get environment information.",
Exclamation! )
    RETURN
END IF

// display all of the various things we got back
st_cputype.text = f_CPUTypeToString( l_environment.cputype )
st_os.text  = f_OSTypeToString( l_environment.ostype ) + " version " + &
         String( l_environment.osmajorrevision ) + "." + &
         String( l_environment.osminorrevision ) + "." + &
         String( l_environment.osfixesrevision )
st_pb.text = f_PBTypeToString( l_environment.pbtype ) + " version " +&
         String( l_environment.pbmajorrevision )+ "." + &
         String( l_environment.pbminorrevision ) + "." + &
         String( l_environment.pbfixesrevision )

st_screen.text = String( l_environment.screenwidth ) + " by " + &
         String( l_environment.screenheight ) + " at " + &
         String( l_environment.numberofcolors ) + " colors"
```

7. Save the w_environment window.

8. In the Application painter, place the following script in the Open event of the Application object.

```
Open( w_environment)
```

9. Run the application. Observe that the displayed window (w_environment) shows you the specifics of your current configuration.

How It Works

The GetEnvironment() function and the corresponding Environment structure are the keys to this application. By calling GetEnvironment() your program can obtain all of the details about your machine configuration. Observe the use of the f_pbtypetostring(), f_cputypetostring(), and f_ostypetostring() functions that convert the enumerated values contained in the environment structure to string values which can be displayed.

Comments

This application only demonstrates how to call the function and view the results, but your programs do not need to be as limited. A few suggested uses of the environment information include adjusting window sizes depending on the user's screen resolution (indicated by the ScreenWidth and ScreenHeight properties), taking advantage of version-specific features of your operating system, and calling external functions based on the processor type and operating system.

COMPLEXITY
INTERMEDIATE

4.3 How do I...
Write a system-level error handler to replace the standard PowerBuilder one?

Problem

When I am debugging an application, I occasionally encounter a PowerBuilder runtime error due to a programming mistake. When this happens PowerBuilder generates an error message telling me the nature of the problem, but there is no convenient way to record this information. I want the capability to save these error messages to a file or to print them on a printer. How do I write my own error handler to implement these features?

Technique

The Application object in PowerBuilder has a standard event called SystemError that is received any time the application encounters a runtime error. These errors include conditions such as dividing a number by zero, referencing a null object (one that has not yet been created), and exceeding array boundaries. When the SystemError event occurs, your program can display, print, and save the exact error conditions by examining the Error object. This How-To demonstrates the usage of a custom error handler window that allows the user to print the error or to save it. Note that there is no perfect method for handling system errors as some of them affect system integrity and will make the system unstable, which may prevent printing the error message or saving it to disk.

Steps

The completed application for this How-To is stored in ERRORHND.PBL on the included CD-ROM. Access the application (from PowerBuilder or by running ERRORHND.EXE). When the Errors Galore window appears (shown in Figure 4-6), click one of the CommandButtons other than Exit to generate a system error. Notice that the System Error window (shown in Figure 4-7) appears showing you the error condition. You may print this information by clicking Print or save it to a file by clicking Save.... Clicking Continue will close the second window and allow the program to continue. Clicking Halt will end the program.

1. Using the Application painter, create a new library and Application object called ERRORHND.PBL and a_error_handler, respectively. Click No when prompted to use an application template.

2. Create the w_error_generator window pictured in Figure 4-6 using the window and control settings depicted in Table 4-7. Save the window without closing the painter when you have completed this step.

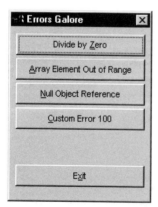

Figure 4-6 The error generating window for the Error Handler application

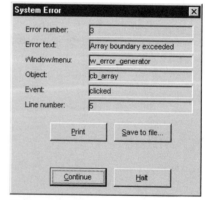

Figure 4-7 The error handler window for the Error Handler application

WINDOW/CONTROL NAME	PROPERTY	VALUE
Window		
w_error_generator	Title	"Errors Galore"
	Maximize Box	FALSE
	Minimize Box	FALSE
	Resizable	FALSE
CommandButton	Name	cb_zero
	Text	"Divide by &Zero"
CommandButton	Name	cb_array
	Text	"&Array Element Out of Range"
CommandButton	Name	cb_nullobject
	Text	"&Null Object Reference"
CommandButton	Name	cb_custom
	Text	"&Custom Error 100"
CommandButton	Name	cb_exit
	Text	"E&xit"

Table 4-7 Specifications for the w_error_generator window

3. Enter the following script for the Clicked event on the cb_zero CommandButton to have a division by zero error appear on demand.

```
// generate a division by zero error
real lr_temp

lr_temp = 5.3 / 0
```

4. Place the following script on the Clicked event for the cb_array CommandButton to reference an array element outside the array's declared boundaries.

```
// generate an array index out of bounds error
integer li_temp[10], li_index

FOR li_index = 1 TO 11
    li_temp[li_index] = li_index
NEXT
```

5. Code a script for the Clicked event for the cb_nullobject CommandButton. This script causes an error by referencing properties of an object that has not been instantiated.

```
window lw_temp

// at this point, lw_temp does not refer to a valid window (it does
// not point to valid memory), and will generate an error

lw_temp.title = "Boom!"
```

6. In addition to the "real" errors coded in previous steps, PowerBuilder also offers the ability to create custom errors for testing (to make sure your error handler really works!) and for application-specific fatal errors. To implement this error, we need to populate the Error object and use SignalError() to cause the SystemError event to occur. Place the following script on the Clicked event for cb_custom to make this happen.

```
// This button generates an application-specific error condition
// using error code 100.

// Populate the Error object with specifics of the error
Error.Number = 100
Error.Text = "This is a test error code."
Error.Windowmenu = parent.ClassName()
Error.Object = this.ClassName()
Error.ObjectEvent = "clicked"
Error.Line = 11
SignalError()
```

7. Code the following script on the Clicked event for cb_exit to provide a way to end the program.

```
Close( parent )
```

8. Save the w_error_generator window.

9. In the Application painter, enter the following script for the Application object Open event.

```
Open( w_error_generator )
```

10. Save and run the application. Click on one of the error buttons and observe PowerBuilder's standard error message. One of these messages is shown in Figure 4-8.

11. Using the Window painter, create a window called w_error_handler using the specifications shown in Table 4-8. This window is shown in Figure 4-9. Note that the figure shows text properties of st_number, st_text, etc., in order to assist you in placing the "empty" StaticText controls. You do not need to specify these properties when building the window.

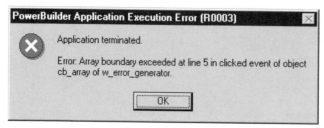

Figure 4-8 An example of PowerBuilder's default error message

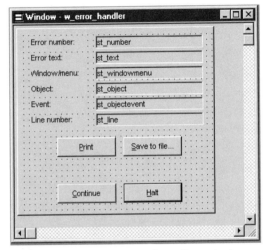

Figure 4-9 The w_error_handler window during design

WINDOW/CONTROL NAME	PROPERTY	VALUE
Window		
w_error_handler	Title	"System Error"
	Window Type	Response
StaticText	Name	st_numberlabel
	Text	"Error number:"
	Alignment	Left
StaticText	Name	st_textlabel
	Text	"Error text:"
	Alignment	Left
StaticText	Name	st_windowmenulabel
	Text	"Window/menu:"
	Alignment	Left
StaticText	Name	st_objectlabel
	Text	"Object:"
	Alignment	Left
StaticText	Name	st_objecteventlabel
	Text	"Event:"
	Alignment	Left
StaticText	Name	st_linelabel
	Text	"Line:"
	Alignment	Left

continued on next page

continued from previous page

WINDOW/CONTROL NAME	PROPERTY	VALUE
StaticText	Name	st_number
	Text	"" (empty)
	Border	3D Lowered
	Alignment	Left
StaticText	Name	st_text
	Text	"" (empty)
	Border	3D Lowered
	Alignment	Left
StaticText	Name	st_windowmenu
	Text	"" (empty)
	Border	3D Lowered
	Alignment	Left
StaticText	Name	st_object
	Text	"" (empty)
	Border	3D Lowered
	Alignment	Left
StaticText	Name	st_objectevent
	Text	"" (empty)
	Border	3D Lowered
	Alignment	Left
StaticText	Name	st_line
	Text	"" (empty)
	Border	3D Lowered
	Alignment	Left
CommandButton	Name	cb_print
	Text	"&Print"
CommandButton	Name	cb_savetofile
	Text	"&Save to file..."
CommandButton	Name	cb_continue
	Text	"&Continue"
CommandButton	Name	cb_halt
	Text	"&Halt"
	Default	TRUE

Table 4-8 Specifications for the w_error_handler window

12. Place the following script in the Open event of w_error_handler. This event
script will obtain the contents of the Error object and copy them into the
appropriate fields on the display.

```
// Copy the contents of the Error object into the display
st_number.text = String( error.Number )
st_text.Text = error.Text
st_windowmenu.text = error.WindowMenu
st_object.text = error.Object
st_objectevent.text = error.ObjectEvent
st_line.text = String( error.Line )
```

13. To print the error contents, our program will use PowerBuilder's basic printing capabilities to produce a simple report of the error. To do so, code the following script in the Clicked event of cb_print.

```
long ll_job

// This may take a moment, so turn on the hourglass
SetPointer(Hourglass!)

// open up the print job. Terminate the script if we can't
ll_job = PrintOpen( "PowerBuilder Error Report" )
IF ll_job < 0 THEN
    SetPointer(Arrow!)
    MessageBox("Print", "Print failed.", StopSign! )
    RETURN
END IF

// Print everything
Print( ll_job, "Error number: " + st_number.text)
Print( ll_job, "Error text:    " + st_text.text)
Print( ll_job, "Window/menu:   " + st_windowmenu.text)
Print( ll_job, "Object:        " + st_object.text)
Print( ll_job, "Event:         " + st_objectevent.text)
Print( ll_job, "Line:          " + st_line.text)

PrintClose( ll_job )
SetPointer(Arrow!)
```

14. To save the error to a file, the program must use PowerBuilder's file functions to write an ASCII file. The following script for the Clicked event of cb_savetofile will perform this task.

```
string ls_pathfile, ls_filename
integer li_file

// Prompt the user for a filename
CHOOSE CASE GetFileSaveName( "Record Error to File", &
        ls_pathfile, ls_filename, "err", "Error files (*.err),*.err" )
    CASE 1  // Good -- write the error
        li_file = FileOpen( ls_pathfile, LineMode!, Write!, &
                    LockReadWrite!, Append! )
        IF li_file <> -1 THEN
            FileWrite( li_file, "----" )
            FileWrite( li_file, "Error number: " + st_number.text)
            FileWrite( li_file, "Error text:    " + st_text.text)
            FileWrite( li_file, "Window/menu:   " + st_windowmenu.text)
            FileWrite( li_file, "Object:        " + st_object.text)
            FileWrite( li_file, "Event:         " + st_objectevent.text)
```

continued on next page

continued from previous page

```
            FileWrite( li_file, "Line:           " + st_line.text)
            FileWrite( li_file, "----" )
            FileClose( li_file )
        ELSE
            MessageBox( "Save", "Save failed.", StopSign! )
        END IF
    CASE 0  // Cancel -- ignore
    CASE -1 // Error
            MessageBox( "Save", "Save failed.", StopSign! )
END CHOOSE
```

15. If the user clicks Continue, the program should continue running. The error handler window can communicate this information back by using CloseWithReturn() as is done in the following script for the Clicked event of cb_continue.

```
// Return to the calling script, telling it to continue execution
CloseWithReturn( parent, 1 )
```

16. If the user wants to end the application, you can use a similar method. Place the following script on the Clicked event for cb_halt.

```
// Return to the calling script, telling it to halt
CloseWithReturn( parent, 0 )
```

17. Save the w_error_handler window.

18. The one big step that's still missing is to have the w_error_handler window appear when an error occurs. From the Application painter, enter the following script on the Application object SystemError event.

```
// In the event of an error, open the error handler window
Open( w_error_handler )
```

```
// halt the program if the user presses Halt on w_error_handler
IF Message.DoubleParm = 0 THEN HALT
```

19. Save and run the application. Verify that the error handler window, w_error_handler, allows you to print the error message to your default printer or to save the error to a file. Click Continue to continue experimenting or click Halt to terminate the program.

How It Works

When PowerBuilder encounters a runtime error, it populates the Error object with the details of the error and dispatches a SystemError event to the Application object for the program. If nothing has been coded on this event, PowerBuilder displays its own standard error message and terminates the program. You examined this behavior in step 10. When you elect to write a script for the SystemError event, you have the opportunity to use a more sophisticated handler than the default one.

In this How-To, you created an error handler window called w_error_handler that displays the contents of the Error object, including the error number and message as well as the exact location of the error. This window improves on the default error handler by allowing the user to print or save the error message for later reference. The single Open(w_error_handler) line in the SystemError event instructs PowerBuilder to use your extended error handler instead of the default one. In addition, the replacement error handler allows the user to continue execution or to stop the program. Note that continuing the program may result in other anomalies caused by the earlier error.

Comments

The application for this How-To makes use of PowerBuilder's text printing capabilities using the PrintOpen(), Print(), and PrintClose() functions (in the Clicked event of cb_print). Additionally, if the user elects to save the error message, the Clicked event script on cb_save is written to *append* the new error to the specified file if it already exists. This last feature allows you to maintain a log of errors as you are debugging.

CHAPTER 5
DRAG AND DROP

5

DRAG AND DROP

How do I...

Drag and drop does not in itself add to the functionality of your application. It does, however, provide an intuitive and easy-to-use interface for your users. Dragging a data row from one DataWindow to another, or dragging a row to a trashcan to delete it are useful implementations of drag and drop, as these activities imply moving an object from one position or state to another. In addition, drag and drop is an effective way to give your user the ability to undo the previous action. If you implement deleting a row by moving it to a trashcan, you can also implement an undo for this activity by allowing the user to drag the row back to the DataWindow.

Drag and drop is a built-in feature for PowerBuilder but you need to perform some maintenance, such as changing the icon when it's over a part of the application that does not participate in this functionality in this particular case. You'll learn how to do that in this chapter as well as how to implement a drag and drop recycling bin, how to let the user drag and drop data between DataWindows, and how to find out where in the DataWindow the drop occurred. You will also learn how to drag between windows by using the MDI frame's clock to timestamp a DataWindow row. Lastly, you will use drag and drop to send data to Microsoft Word using OLE 2.0 automation services. All the examples for this chapter can be found in the PowerBuilder library DRGDRP.PBL.

5.1 Change the Drag Icon to a "No" Symbol When It's Dragged over a Non-Target

Your users will need some form of communication from your application when they are in a "no drop" zone on the window. In this How-To you will learn the basics of determining which icon to display and at what time.

5.2 Drag Entries from One DataWindow to Another

One of the more popular uses of drag and drop in a PowerBuilder application is to drag a data row or field from one DataWindow to another. In this How-To you will learn how to drag and drop fields and entire rows. In addition you will learn how to implement a dragable DataWindow list that will trigger a data retrieve when dropped in a second window.

5.3 Drag Between Windows

Your users may want to drag an object from one window in your application to another. This How-To will demonstrate the technique of accessing data from a DataWindow in one window to use in a DataWindow in another application.

5.4 Use Drag and Drop to Interact with Another Application Using OLE 2.0

You can use a combination of drag and drop and OLE 2.0 automation services to send specific DataWindow rows to another application and this How-To will demonstrate this technique.

COMPLEXITY
INTERMEDIATE

5.1 How do I...

Change the Drag icon to a "No" symbol when it's dragged over a non-target?

Problem

I want to implement drag and drop in my application but how do I let my application's user know what's okay to drag and where it's okay to drop? How can I change the drag icon based on what object it's over?

Technique

PowerBuilder has built in drag and drop capability in all its controls and the window object. Each of these objects can be set to drag mode automatically or in response to certain events. In addition, each of these objects trigger events when a dragged object is over it, when it is dropped, and when the dragged object is no longer over it. You can set the drag icon for the control during development and change the icon at runtime based on whether the object can be dropped at its current position. If you do not specify an icon, the outline of the control will represent the dragged object, a less than ideal icon if the object is larger, such as a DataWindow control.

This How-To will demonstrate the steps necessary to set a control to drag automatically, and to manually implement drag mode. In addition, you will learn the basics of changing the drag icon based on position and how to determine what is being dragged. Finally, you will see several different techniques of using drag and drop that just may be a little out of the ordinary.

Steps

Run DRGDRP.EXE, and select Dragging Objects from the Drag and Drop menu. From the menu items displayed, select Dragging Objects. Figure 5-1 shows the window. Using the right mouse button menu, type or paste something into the SingleLineEdit control located in the upper left corner. Click on the object with the left mouse button and, without releasing the button, drag it into any of the controls below. Notice that when the object is over the ListBox and SingleLineEdit controls, the icon changes from an 'X' to an 'O' as can be seen in Figure 5-2. The icon change shows

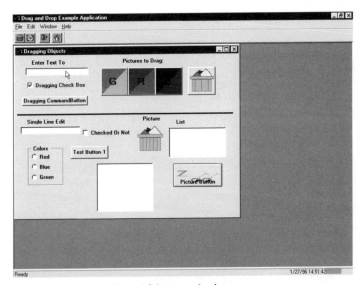

Figure 5-1 Dragging Objects window

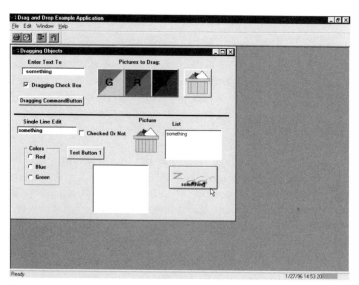

Figure 5-2 Dragging Objects window with drag in progress

that the object you are dragging can be dropped at that point. Drop the object into one of these and view the results. Try dragging the object and dropping it into any of the other controls. Now try the same with the other objects in the top part of the window, dragging them to the controls in the bottom part of the window, and observe the results. Particularly try dragging one of the color Picture controls to the RadioButtons and the ListView below.

To create this application follow the steps below:

1. Create a new window, inheriting from w_genapp_sheet. Set the window title to "Dragging Objects" and set the background color to light gray.

2. Next, create the controls that are shown in Figure 5-1. To match the demonstration window use the Line drawing tool to create a line separating the two halves of the window. The controls in the top are a SingleLineEdit box, a CheckBox, a CommandButton, and four Picture controls, each labeled with a StaticText control. The controls in the bottom half of the window are a SingleEditLine, with a StaticText label, a ListBox, again with StaticText label, a GroupBox, three RadioButtons, a CheckBox, a Picture, a CommandButton, a PictureButton, and a ListView control. Change the attributes of these controls as shown in Table 5-1.

CONTROL NAME	ATTRIBUTE	VALUE
sle_text	Border	3D Lowered
	Background.Color	Standard window color
st_1	Text	"Enter text to drag:"

CONTROL NAME	ATTRIBUTE	VALUE
cbx_drag	Border	3D Lowered
	Text	"Dragging Text Box"
cb_drag	Text	"Dragging CommandButton"
p_green	File Name	"green.bmp"
	Border	3D Raised
	Tag	"Green"
p_red	File Name	"red.bmp"
	Border	3D Raised
	Tag	"Red"
p_blue	File Name	"blue.bmp"
	Border	3D Raised
	Tag	"Blue
p_full	File Name	"full.bmp"
	Border	3D Raised
	Tag	"Full"
st_2	Text	"Pictures to Drag"
sle_drag	Border	3D Lowered
	Background.Color	Standard window color
st_3	Text	"Single Line Edit Field"
gb_colors	Text	"Colors"
	Border	3D Lowered
rb_red	Text	"Red"
	Border	3D Lowered
rb_green	Text	"Green"
	Border	3D Lowered
rb_blue	Text	"Blue"
	Border	3D Lowered
cbx_drop	Text	"Checked or Not"
	Border	3D Lowered
p_drop	PictureName	"tutdel.bmp"
st_4	Text	"Picture"
lb_drop	Border	3D Lowered
st_5	Text	"List Box"
pb_drop	Text	"Picture Button"
	Enabled File	"logo.bmp"
cb_drop	Text	"Text Button 1"
lv_1	View	Small Icon

continued on next page

continued from previous page

CONTROL NAME	ATTRIBUTE	VALUE
	Scrolling	Checked
	Edit Labels	Checked
	Delete Items	Checked
	Auto Arrange	Checked

Table 5-1 Attributes for Controls in w_01

3. Next, set the controls to Autodrag. Do this by selecting the control, and then clicking the right mouse button to pull up the object popup menu. Select the Properties option and then select the Drag and Drop tab. Check the Drag Auto CheckBox.

4. Next, set DragIcon for sle_text by selecting an icon in the Drag Icon Name edit box or by selecting the Browse... button to select an icon file. This will bring up a dialog box as shown in Figure 5-3 which will allow you to select an icon file. If you do not set the icon, the control outline will be the default drag icon. From the list of icons that show up, choose the NO.ICO file and press OK. This icon will symbolize that the control cannot be dropped. By default you will be setting the icon to display this "No" icon, changing only in those areas where you can drop the control. This follows the assumption that there are more areas in your window where you can't drop the object than there are where you can.

5. Do the same for the cbx_drag, cb_drag, p_green, p_red, p_blue, and p_full controls.

6. Next, you will add PowerScript to three events for each of the objects that will accept dropped objects. Each control will accept certain controls only.

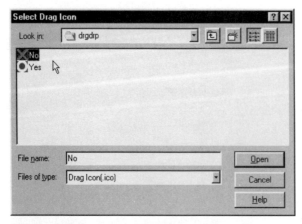

Figure 5-3 Choosing DragIcon using Select Drag Icon dialog

This means that you will code the DragEnter event to check to see the type of object being dragged, and if it is one that the control will process, the Drag icon will change to the "O" or "Yes" icon. Code the DragEnter event for sle_drop first.

```
IF TypeOf(source) = SingleLineEdit! THEN
    ldo_Control.DragIcon = "yes.ico"
END IF
```

7. The variable *source* is an argument for the DragDrop event and is of type dragobject. This script will check to see if the type of dragged object is a SingleLineEdit control, and if so, will change the icon to the "Yes" icon. The ListBox lb_drop will also accept a SingleLineEdit control, so you will add the same code to the ListBox DragEnter event.

8. Code the DragEnter event of the Picture control, p_drop, to accept dragged objects of type Picture; the CommandButton, cb_drop, to accept an object of type CommandButton; the CheckBox control, cbx_drop, to accept the CheckBox type; and the RadioButton controls, rb_green, rb_red, and rb_blue, to accept the Picture control (more on this later). Lastly, code the ListView control, lv_1, to accept a Picture control.

Picture Control

```
CHOOSE CASE TypeOf(source)
CASE Picture!
  source.DragIcon = "no.ico"
END CHOOSE
```

CommandButton

```
CHOOSE CASE TypeOf(source)
CASE Picture!
CASE CommandButton!
  source.DragIcon="yes.ico"
CASE SingleLineEdit!
  source.DragIcon="yes.ico"
END CHOOSE
```

CheckBox

```
IF TypeOf(source) = CheckBox! THEN
    source.DragIcon = "yes.ico"
END IF
```

RadioButton

```
CHOOSE CASE TypeOf(source)
CASE Picture!
  ldo_Control.DragIcon="yes.ico"
```

ListView

```
IF TypeOf(source) = Picture! THEN
    source.DragIcon = "yes.ico"
END IF
```

9. The PictureButton control will accept three types of controls, a Picture control, a SingleLineEdit control and a CommandButton control.

```
CHOOSE CASE TypeOf(source)
CASE Picture!
  source.DragIcon="yes.ico"
CASE CommandButton!
  source.DragIcon="yes.ico"
CASE SingleLineEdit!
  source.DragIcon="yes.ico"
END CHOOSE
```

10. The next event to code is the DragLeave event. In order for the dragged object icon to return to the "No" icon if it is no longer over the object, place code to change it back in the DragLeave event for the control. The easiest way to do this is just to code the change to the "No" icon, regardless of whether it had been changed to the "No" icon or not. Type the following into all of the drag and drop target controls, in the DragLeave event:

```
source.DragIcon = "yes.ico"
```

11. The DragDrop events will access the type of control being dragged. If it is a type it can accept, it will *cast* the object to the specific type of control. Casting a generic object will allow you to access the attributes and functions of that object as long as the casting is appropriate to the object. Casting a dragged object of type SingleLineEdit to one that is Picture will result in a runtime error. Once you have cast the object, access the properties of the dragged object that you want to use. The DragDrop event for the SingleLineEdit sle_drop contains the following code:

```
SingleLineEdit lsle_Control

IF TypeOf(source) = SingleLineEdit! THEN
  lsle_Control = source
  this.Text = lsle_Control.Text
  source.DragIcon = "no.ico"
END IF
```

12. Type the code for the DragDrop events for the other controls, except the RadioButtons, the PictureButton, and the ListView controls as follows:

CommandButton

```
SingleLineEdit lsle_which
CommandButton lcb_which
Picture lp_which

CHOOSE CASE TypeOf(source)
CASE Picture!
  lp_which = source
  this.PictureName = lp_which.PictureName
CASE CommandButton!
    lcb_which = source
    This.Text = lcb_which.Text
```

```
CASE SingleLineEdit!
    lsle_which = source
    this.Text = lsle_which.Text
END CHOOSE
source.DragIcon = "no.ico"
```
        Picture

```
Picture lp_Control

CHOOSE CASE TypeOf(source)
CASE Picture!
  lp_Control = source
  this.PictureName = lp_Control.PictureName
  source.DragIcon = "no.ico"
END CHOOSE
```
        ListBox

```
SingleLineEdit lsle_Control

CHOOSE CASE TypeOf(source)
CASE SingleLineEdit!
  lsle_Control = source
  this.AddItem(lsle_Control.Text)
  source.DragIcon = "no.ico"
END CHOOSE
```
        CheckBox

```
CheckBox     lcbx_Control

CHOOSE CASE TypeOf(source)
CASE CheckBox!
    lcbx_Control = source
   this.Checked=lcbx_Control.Checked
    source.DragIcon = "no.ico"
END CHOOSE
```

13. The RadioButtons will accept a drop from the Picture control and will check the RadioButton that matches the 'color' of the Picture. As the exact file path could change for the bitmap in the Picture control, the tag attribute of the Picture controls is used to see which one is being dropped.

```
IF TypeOf(source) = Picture! THEN
  CHOOSE CASE Lower(source.Tag)
      CASE "red"
         rb_red.Checked=TRUE
      CASE "green"
         rb_green.Checked=TRUE
      CASE "blue"
         rb_blue.Checked=TRUE
    END CHOOSE
    source.DragIcon = "no.ico"
END IF
```

14. The next object to code for DragDrop is the PictureButton. If the dragged object is a Picture, pb_drop will pull out the PictureName. If the dropped object was a CommandButton, the Text attribute is accessed.

```
SingleLineEdit lsle_which
CommandButton lcb_which
Picture lp_which

CHOOSE CASE TypeOf(source)
CASE Picture!
  lp_which = source
  this.PictureName = lp_which.PictureName
CASE CommandButton!
    lcb_which = source
    This.Text = lcb_which.Text
CASE SingleLineEdit!
    lsle_which = source
    this.Text = lsle_which.Text
END CHOOSE
source.DragIcon = "no.ico"
```

15. All that's left is to code the ListView control. The picture from the Picture control is accessed and inserted into the ListView control. This returns the index for the picture which is then used to add the ListView label and the picture tag. Figure 5-4 shows the Dragging Objects window with several of the Picture controls dragged into the ListView control.

```
Picture lp_which
integer iItem

if TypeOf(source) = Picture! then
    lp_which = source
    iItem=this.AddSmallPicture(lp_which.PictureName)
    this.AddItem(lp_which.tag, iItem)
end if
source.DragIcon = "no.ico"
```

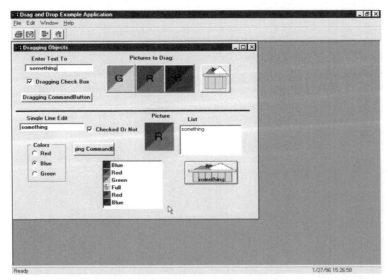

Figure 5-4 Dragging Objects after experimenting with several of the controls

How It Works

Automatic drag-and-drop clicking on the control with the active mouse button (as defined in the Control Panel) starts the drag process. The Drag icon will be the control outline if the DragIcon attribute is not set. Due to the size of some controls, you should change the icon for your objects. Signal the user when he or she is over an object that can be dropped on by coding the DragEnter event to check the type of control and to change the icon accordingly. When the dragged object leaves the control, coding in the DragLeave event changes the icon back. When you are over areas that the operating system does not allow drops on, Windows itself will change your icon to its equivalent of the "No" icon.

During the DragDrop event, your code can access any part of the dragged object that you wish. For a CheckBox you can access the Text, or the Checked value, or even the Border. You can accept more than one type of control and access the attributes accordingly. Note that you will be *casting* the object to the specific control type in order to access the appropriate attributes.

Lastly, any PowerBuilder control, and the Window object itself, are drag and drop objects, which means that they all have the four drag and drop events, DragEnter, DragLeave, DragDrop, and DragWithin.

Comments

Be creative in the use of drag and drop. Note the use of dropping on the RadioButtons to click them using a Picture object. Another effective use of this technique is accessing a toolbar made up of pictures and dragging them into a control such as the ListView control, or a list of bitmaps onto a PictureButton. However, use this technique in a meaningful manner and always have your users test innovative implementations of drag and drop for usability.

COMPLEXITY
INTERMEDIATE

5.2 How do I...
Drag entries from one DataWindow to another?

Problem

I have a DataWindow that contains data that is really the combination of two other DataWindows. The other DataWindows have already been created. I would like to let the user "grab" the data from the two DataWindows and place it into the third, and have this DataWindow be smart enough to know what data to grab. What would be a nice visual way to let the user grab data from one or more DataWindows and drop it into another DataWindow?

Technique

DataWindow controls have the four drag and drop events necessary for this project: DragEnter, DragLeave, DragWithin, and DragDrop. The data movement will be simulated by accessing the row number and DataWindow of the control where the drag begins and accessing the appropriate data when the drop occurs.

Steps

Run the DRGDRP.EXE application and select the Drag and Drop menu. Then choose Dragging DataWindows. The window that opens contains two DataWindow controls, both of which have the same type of DataWindow. Notice from Figure 5-5 that the bottom DataWindow has a "Deleted Row" label, and right below it a Delete Row SingleLineEdit control which will hold the count for deleted rows. Click on any of the rows in the top DataWindow and drag it to the second DataWindow. Notice that in this window, the Drag icon is the control itself. The dragged row shows up in the second window, which represents the DataWindow control's deleted buffer. Do this a few more times, and then click on the Deleted Rows DataWindow control and drag it to the top DataWindow. This is equivalent to an "undo" operation, and will undelete that row. The deleted row counter changes accordingly. Figure 5-6 shows the window with some of the rows deleted.

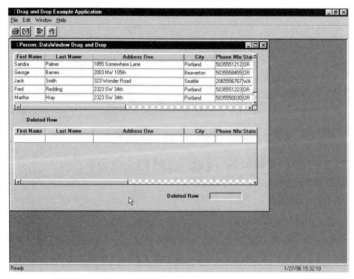

Figure 5-5 Dragging DataWindows window from drgdrp

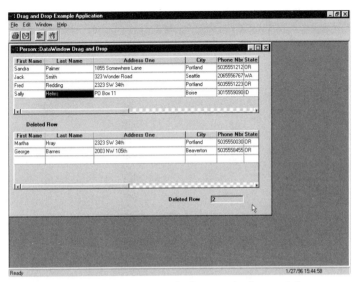

Figure 5-6 Dragging DataWindows window with deleted rows

The steps to create a window similar to this are below:

1. Access the DRGDRP.PBL library. Back up the existing window, w_03, by opening it and saving it as w_03_bak.

2. Create a new window by inheriting from the w_genapp_sheet. In this window, place two DataWindow controls, one positioned in the top half of the window and named "dw_persons", the other in the bottom half of the window and named "dw_deleted".

3. Change the DataWindow for each of the controls to d_emp_pers_pos.

4. Size the controls approximately to the size of the ones in the original window as shown in Figure 5-5.

5. In the Open event for the Window, type the following code to set the transaction object for both windows, and to retrieve in the top DataWindow and insert a blank row in the bottom DataWindow.

```
// set transaction objects
// and retrieve from person and position

dw_person.SetTransObject(sqlca)
dw_deleted.SetTransObject(sqlca)

dw_person.Retrieve()

dw_deleted.InsertRow(1)
```

6. Open the Save event for the window and enter the code to save the results.

```
// update window, and if no error, commit changes
Integer    li_Result

li_Result = dw_person.Update()

IF li_Result <> -1 THEN
    COMMIT;
ELSE
    ROLLBACK;
END IF

// 'clear' out deleted buffer
dw_deleted.Reset()

dw_deleted.InsertRow(0)
```

7. Only the top DataWindow is saved as the other is acting as a visual Delete buffer. Next create an instance variable for the window of type Long and call it "il_DraggedRow".

8. Access the Clicked event in the top DataWindow control, dw_person, and type the following code which will get the clicked row from the event argument list. Check to see if it is valid, and assign this value to the new instance variable. The last line item of the code will put the control into drag mode.

```
// get clicked row and start drag process
Long    ll_Row

ll_Row = row      //access row from event arguments
if ll_Row <= 0 then return

il_DraggedRow = ll_Row

Drag(Begin!)
```

9. Next, access the DragDrop event for the same DataWindow control. In this event, type code to delete the dragged row from the dw_deleted DataWindow, using the PowerBuilder function RowsMove to move the row from the deleted buffer in dw_person, and place it back into the primary buffer. The first part of the code you type will test to ensure that a row is being dragged, that the type of dragged object is a DataWindow, and that the object being dragged is not the same as the one receiving the drop. Lastly, decrement the deleted row count and write out to the SingleLineEdit control.

```
// delete dropped row, and then 'copy' it into this window.
Long    ll_RowCount
DataWindow ldw_which

// do not process if no row is being dragged
IF il_DraggedRow <= 0 then return

// do not process if dropped object is not datawindow
if TypeOf(source) <> DataWindow! then return
```

```
ldw_which = source

// do not process if datawindow object being dragged
// is same as one receiving drop
if ldw_which = this then return

dw_Deleted.DeleteRow(il_DraggedRow)
dw_person.RowsMove(il_DraggedRow, il_DraggedRow, Delete!, dw_person, 1,
Primary!)

ll_RowCount = dw_person.DeletedCount()

sle_1.Text = String(ll_RowCount)
```

10. Go to the next DataWindow control, dw_deleted. Access the Clicked event
for this control and type code identical to the code you placed in the
Clicked event of dw_person.

```
// get clicked row and start drag process
Long      ll_Row

ll_Row = row    //clicked row from event arguments
if ll_Row <= 0 then return

il_DraggedRow = ll_Row

Drag(Begin!)
```

11. In the DragDrop event for this same control, type code that will copy the
row from the dw_person DataWindow into the dw_deleted DataWindow
and move the row into the dw_person deleted buffer after first checking to
see if the drop is a valid drop. Lastly, type code that will increment the
deleted counter and redisplay it in the SingleLineEdit control.

```
// delete dropped row, and then 'copy' it into this window.
Long      ll_RowCount
DataWindow ldw_which

// do not process if no row is being dragged
IF il_DraggedRow <= 0 then return

// do not process if dropped object is not datawindow
if TypeOf(source) <> DataWindow! then return
ldw_which = source

// do not process if datawindow object being dragged
// is same as one receiving drop
if ldw_which = this then return

dw_Deleted.DeleteRow(il_DraggedRow)
dw_person.RowsMove(il_DraggedRow, il_DraggedRow, Delete!, dw_person, 1,
Primary!)

ll_RowCount = dw_person.DeletedCount()

sle_1.Text = String(ll_RowCount)
```

12. Close and save the window, and run the application again. Note that when you drag the DataWindow controls, the control outline shows up, as shown faintly in Figure 5-7. This is because you did not specify another Drag and Drop icon for the controls and the default of the control outline was used.

How it Works

Drag and drop combined with the RowsCopy and RowsMove PowerBuilder functions will enable you to visually implement dragging a row into the deleted buffer for the DataWindow. This will enable your users to inspect the deleted rows at any time until they save. In addition, you can also use this to emulate the filter buffer by creating a DataWindow for this and using RowsCopy to copy from the filter buffer after every filter operation.

You can drag between different DataWindow types. In the DragDrop event of the target window you can access the fields from the source DataWindow that are appropriate for the target. Use this to create rows for an associative (many-to-many) table type.

Comments

As can be seen from the application, you will usually want to use an icon for dragging and dropping as the default of the control outline can be rather large. Create

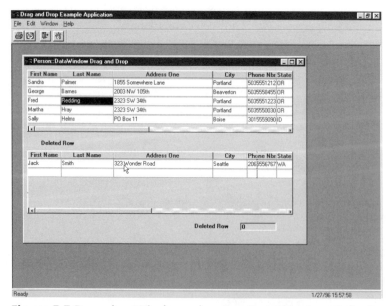

Figure 5-7 Dragging Windows showing DataWindow default drag icon

one that is the same for the entire application and use it for each dragable control. Create another one that represents "no drop" zones, and use this to prevent ambiguity.

Additionally, always check the validity of the dragged object. If you open the original Dragging Window, w_03_bak, you will find that the SingleLineEdit control is set to drag automatically. If this is dropped into one of the DataWindows, you may have undesirable results, such as an incorrectly deleted row.

Lastly, another approach to using drag and drop and a 'delete' buffer is shown in Figure 5-8 and Figure 5-9, which show a Window that implements deletion and deletion undo with a Picture control that is changed based on whether there are deleted rows or not. You can examine the code for this in the w_02 window.

COMPLEXITY
INTERMEDIATE

5.3 How do I...
Drag between windows?

Problem

I want to give my users the ability to access information from one DataWindow to use when they are updating or creating a row in another DataWindow, but I don't want to have to duplicate the DataWindow. How can I access data using drag and drop from another window?

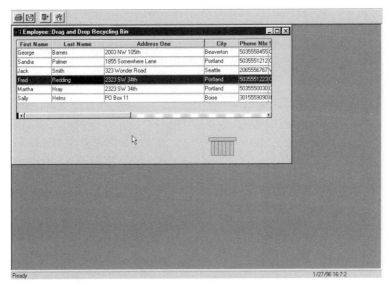

Figure 5-8 DataWindow with no deleted rows

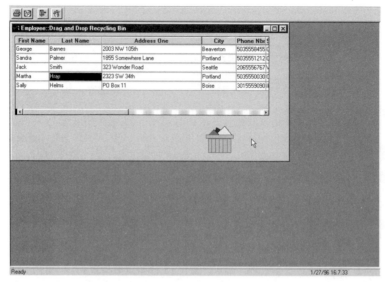

Figure 5-9 DataWindow with deleted rows

Technique

This How-To demonstrates setting a DataWindow to drag when the user clicks on a valid row. In the target DataWindow, the DragDrop event is coded to verify that the object being dragged is a DataWindow, cast it to a DataWindow type, and then access the data using normal DataWindow data accessing techniques.

Steps

Run DRGDRP.EXE and select the Drag and Drop menu, and then choose the Dragging Between Windows menu option. Two windows open, one for Person and one for Employee with the Employee window on top. The DataWindow control for the employee contains fields from the person table. Select a person in the Person window by using the arrow keys. Click on the Employee window to set focus to this. Click on the Person window DataWindow and drag the data to the Employee window and drop over the DataWindow. Notice, as shown in Figure 5-10, that the person's first and last name and phone number have been copied to the Employee DataWindow.

The steps necessary to do this follow.

1. Back up the existing timestamping window, w_04, to w_04_bak.

2. Create a new window inheriting from w_genapp_sheet and naming it "w_04".

3. On this new window place a DataWindow control and size it to fit the window, leaving a thin border. Anchor the d_employee DataWindow to the

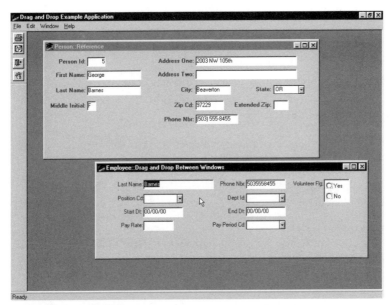

Figure 5-10 Dragging data from DataWindow in Person window to DataWindow in Employee window

control, and name it "dw_employee". Lastly, set the border style on the control to 3D Lowered.

4. In the Open event of the window, type code to set the transaction object and insert a new row and enable several menu items.

```
// set trans object and retrieve
m_genapp_sheet m_this

dw_employee.SetTransObject(sqlca)
dw_employee.InsertRow(0)

m_this = this.menuid

m_this.m_edit.m_query.enabled=TRUE
m_this.m_edit.m_savewindow.enabled=TRUE
m_this.m_edit.m_insert.enabled=TRUE
m_this.m_edit.m_delete.enabled=TRUE
```

5. In the ue_savedatawindow event, type code to trigger the Save event.

```
this.TriggerEvent(Save!)
```

6. In the Save event of the window, type the following code to update and commit any changes.

```
Integer li_return
// update and commit
li_return=dw_employee.Update()
```

continued on next page

continued from previous page

```
IF li_return = -1 THEN
    ROLLBACK;
ELSE
    COMMIT;
END IF
```

7. In the ue_insert event, type in code to create a new row.

```
Long ll_row
ll_row=dw_employee.InsertRow(0)
dw_employee.ScrollToRow(ll_row)
```

8. In the ue_delete event, type in code to delete the current row.

```
Long lRow

lRow = dw_employee.GetRow()
if lRow <= 0 then return

dw_employee.DeleteRow(lRow)
```

9. The last code for the window events will be to retrieve to the DataWindow in the ue_retrieve event.

```
dw_employee.Retrieve()
```

10. Close and save the window. Open the m_genapp_frame menu and examine the code for the Dragging Between Windows menu item, located under the Drag and Drop main menu.

```
// increment counter and open sheet, placing ref into
// sheet array

// open person sheet also
ii_SheetCount++
OpenSheet(iw_OpenSheets[ii_SheetCount],"w_person", w_genapp_frame, &
          0, Original!)

// open employee last so shows on top
ii_SheetCount++
OpenSheet(iw_OpenSheets[ii_SheetCount],"w_04", w_genapp_frame, &
          0, Original!)
```

11. Two windows are opened. One, the Person window, provides the data that will be dropped into the other, the Employee window. An alternative approach could be to have the Person window as another menu option. Close the menu and reopen your new w_04 window.

12. In the DragDrop event for the DataWindow control, dw_employee, type in the following code that will verify that the dragged object is of the DataWindow type. Once verified, the code will access the pertinent fields from the Person DataWindow and place the data into the matching fields for the Employee DataWindow.

```
DataWindow dw_draggedobject
Long lRow

// not dropping in valid row
```

```
if row <= 0 then return

// only accepting drop from datawindow
if TypeOf(source) = DataWindow! then
   dw_draggedobject = source

   lRow = dw_draggedobject.GetRow()
   this.Object.Data[row,1] = dw_draggedobject.Object.Data[lRow,2]
   this.Object.Data[row,2] = dw_draggedobject.Object.Data[lRow,3]
   this.Object.Data[row,3] = dw_draggedobject.Object.Data[lRow,11]
   this.Object.Data[row,10] = dw_draggedobject.Object.Data[lRow,1]
end if
```

13. Close and save your new window and run the DRGDRP application from PowerBuilder.

How It Works

As stated previously, you can drag any window control including DataWindow Controls. In addition, you can drag a control from one window into another without necessarily knowing the window you are dragging from.

Comments

In this example, you assume that the DataWindow being dragged is the Person DataWindow and access its data without verification. In your application you will want to verify your source prior to accessing a component directly.

COMPLEXITY
ADVANCED

5.4   How do I...
Use drag and drop to interact with another application using OLE 2.0?

Problem

My users have access to several applications and they want to be able to send data from my application to others interactively. How can I implement this using drag and drop?

Technique

You can use drag and drop combined with OLE 2.0 to allow your users to interactively send data from your PowerBuilder application to the target application using the other application's automation functions. The method described in this section will open a generic Microsoft Word document after the data has been retrieved into a DataWindow control in the window. The user will be able to drag any of the rows from the DataWindow to a Picture control. This will trigger a DragDrop event which uses automation functions to send the data in a formatted string to the Word document that is currently opened. When the window is closed the user will be prompted to save the Word document if he or she wishes.

Steps

Run the Drag and Drop application, DRGDRP.EXE, and select the Drag and Drop and OLE 2.0 menu item from the Drag and Drop main menu. The window will open, retrieve data into the DataWindow control, and then use OLE 2.0 automation to open a generic Word document. Drag one of the DataWindow rows and drop it on the Picture button that symbolizes the Word icon as shown in Figure 5-11. The row count shown in the SingleLineEdit box next to the Picture control will increase to show the number of rows that have been moved to the Word document. If Word is open when the data drop occurs, a new document is created and the rows are written to this as shown in Figure 5-12. If Word is not open, the application is started and a document is created. When you close the window, the document closes and you are prompted to save it as shown in Figure 5-13. At this point, you can save the document or not.

How to do this in your application is outlined in the steps that follow.

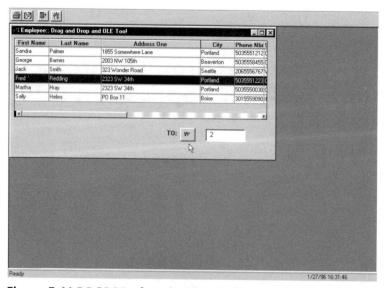

Figure 5-11 DRGDRP after dropping a row of data on Word icon

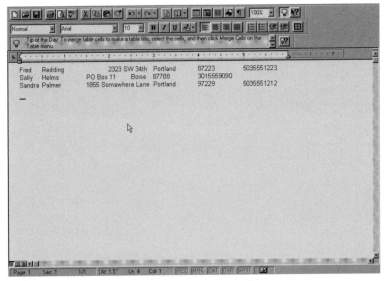

Figure 5-12 Rows being written to Word

1. Backup the existing window w_05 by renaming it to w_05_backup. Create a new window by inheriting from w_genapp_sheet.

2. On this new window place a DataWindow control and set the DataWindow Object Name property to the d_emp_pers_pos DataWindow.

3. Below the DataWindow control place a Picture control and set the bitmap by typing in "word.bmp" as the bitmap for the control. Label the control by placing a StaticText control to the left and typing "TO:" in the Text property of this control.

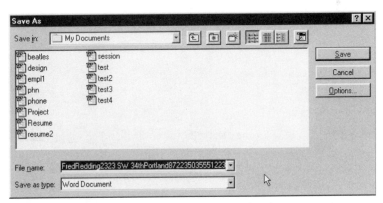

Figure 5-13 Word prompt asking user whether to save changes

4. Lastly, place a SingleLineEdit control to the right of the Picture control.

5. Declare an instance variable of type OLEObject and call it ole_employee. This object will be instantiated in a couple of steps.

6. Declare an instance variable of type Long and call this il_DraggedRow. This variable will be set to the row currently being dragged.

7. Next, type the following code into the Open event for the window. This code will set the database transaction for the DataWindow, retrieve the data, set the SingleLineEdit control to display "0", and post to the ue_init user event.

```
// set transaction object
// and retrieve
dw_1.SetTransObject(sqlca)
dw_1.Retrieve()

sle_1.Text = "0"
this.PostEvent("ue_init")
```

8. In the ue_init event, type in code that will instantiate the OLE object and connect it to Microsoft Word. Once the connection has been established, issue a FileNew server function call to create a new document and go to the first line with the editgoto command. These functions are provided by the Microsoft Word application using its Word Basic command language.

```
Integer iResult
String sFileName

w_genapp_frame.SetMicroHelp("Opening Word Document...")
SetPointer(HourGlass!)

// instantiate the OLE object to a Word Object
ole_employee = create OLEObject
iResult=ole_employee.ConnectToNewObject("Word.Basic")

if iResult < 0 then
    MessageBox(this.title, "Could not Connect to Microsoft Word.")
end if

SetPointer(Arrow!)
w_genapp_frame.SetMicroHelp("Ready")

ole_employee.FileNew()
ole_employee.editgoto("1")
```

9. Open the Script window for the DataWindow control and go to the Clicked event. Type the following code that will access the selected row and start the drag and drop process by using the Drag function:

```
// highlight row, assign it to instance
// variable, and start drag operation
Long ll_row
```

```
this.SelectRow(0, FALSE)
ll_row = row
il_DraggedRow = ll_row
this.SelectRow(ll_row, TRUE)

this.Drag(Begin!)
```

10. Next, open the Script window for the Picture control and access the
DragDrop event. In this event, you will type code that will access the fields
from the dragged row and form a string by concatenating the field values
you want to access. Separate the values with the Tab control character preceded by the tilde, "~t".

```
String sText, sFirstName, sLastName, sPhone
String sCity, sZip, sAddress
Integer iResult
Integer lRow

if il_draggedrow <= 0 then return
lRow = il_draggedrow
if TypeOf(source) <> DataWindow! then return

w_genapp_frame.SetMicroHelp("Copying employee...")
SetPointer(HourGlass!)

iResult = Integer(sle_1.Text)
iResult++

// access dragged row, format a string
// and pass to Word Document
sFirstName     = dw_1.Object.Data[lRow, 1]
sLastName      = dw_1.Object.Data[lRow, 2]
sAddress       = dw_1.Object.Data[lRow, 3]
sCity          = dw_1.Object.Data[lRow, 4]
sZip           = dw_1.Object.Data[lRow, 8]
sPhone         = dw_1.Object.Data[lRow, 5]

//format string
sText   = sFirstName + "~t" + sLastName + "~t~t"
sText   = sText + sAddress + "~t" + sCity + "~t" + sZip + "~t~t" + sPhone
+ "~r"

// insert into the Word document using the Insert function call
ole_employee.insert(sText)

// Update the rows dragged counter
sle_1.Text = String(iResult)
SetPointer(Arrow!)
w_genapp_frame.SetMicroHelp("Ready")
```

11. The code you just typed will validate that the drop is a valid drop operation
for this control. You also typed a carriage return at the end of the string to
have Word place a new line between each of the entries. Lastly, in the Close
event for the window, type code to have Microsoft Word prompt the user to

save the document if he or she wishes, and to disconnect the OLE object
and then destroy it.

```
//close and save document
ole_employee.FileClose(1)

ole_employee.DisconnectObject()
Destroy ole_employee
```

How It Works

Using a combination of drag and drop and OLE 2.0 automation can allow you to
build an application that is integrated with the other OLE 2.0 compliant applications your user might use. This allows you to concentrate on building only the functionality
you need while accessing other functionality from other applications.

Drag and drop with OLE 2.0 usually implies dragging a file or object of the application type into a control of the application type and that OLE 2.0 control being activated.
You can try this by placing a Microsoft Word OLE 2.0 control on a window and dragging a Word document file from the Explorer or File Manager onto this control. When
the drop occurs, the OLE 2.0 control is activated and the document dropped
shows in the application.

Using drag and drop gives your users the ability to interact with the application
and allows them to define what does or does not get communicated to the other application and when the communication occurs. In the chapter on PowerBuilder and
OLE 2.0, Chapter 13, you will see an example similar to this, but which sends all
the data to the Word Application with no interaction from the user.

Comments

When OLE 2.0 automation services are in use, the fact that the application is being
accessed may not be noticeable to the user. You should provide a visual cue when
you connect to the server and especially when your user interacts with the other application, unless such communication is being deliberately hidden from the user.

CHAPTER 6
MENU BASICS

MENU BASICS

How do I...

In many applications, menus are the primary method used to invoke the features of your application. While not difficult to construct, it requires a bit of effort on the part of the developer to offer a menu that works well within an application. Fortunately, well-defined menu standards exist that dictate the requirements for the most common menu operations such as opening a document, printing a document, or invoking help. Adhering to these standards will result in an application that is significantly easier for the users of your programs to master. The best source for menu standards in the Windows 95 and Windows NT environments is the book *Windows Interface Guidelines for Software Design,* available from the Microsoft Press; see the bibliography of this text for more details.

This chapter will cover all aspects of building a menu in PowerBuilder, including constructing a menu and inheriting others from it, managing toolbars, controlling menu options at runtime, and working with popup menus.

6.1   Build a Menu and Inherit from It

Because menus are expected to play such an important role in your application, PowerBuilder developers should plan on spending time developing a menu structure that is useful by itself as well as being useful as an ancestor of other menu objects. This How-To focuses on the construction of a basic menu for an MDI frame window and proceeds to demonstrate how to derive sheet menus from it using inheritance. Additionally, this How-To shows how to use the new dropdown toolbar feature of PowerBuilder 5.0.

6.2   Change Menus at Runtime

Since the menu is just a property of a window object, the menu can be changed at runtime. In this How-To, we'll examine the reasons for doing this, and how it is accomplished. Our example centers around an example that is common in today's robust applications. This is a technique of giving the user the ability to use "short" or "full" menus. Often, applications are so feature rich that the new user becomes overwhelmed by the sheer number of options. Displaying a short menu is one way of overcoming this problem.

6.3   Manage Toolbars in My Application

One of the common problems facing developers writing applications in the MDI style is how to manage all aspects of a toolbar. This How-To will show you how to control the toolbar from a menu as well as how to detect when your user moves the toolbars. You'll also learn how to prevent the user from making any toolbar changes from the toolbar popup menu.

6.4   Use Popup Menus

As your users work with other applications in the Windows environment, they may come to ask why *your* application does not provide the "floating" menus that appear when you right-click an object on the display. These menus are called popup menus. Popup menus aren't inherently difficult, but there are other application concerns that have to be addressed when using them. This How-To explores these concerns so that you can use popup menus with ease.

COMPLEXITY
BEGINNING

6.1   How do I...
Build a menu and inherit from it?

Problem

I am attempting to construct an MDI application, but I have encountered a hurdle when it comes to menus. I am unsure of how to integrate menus into my program, especially since my efforts so far have resulted in menus that are inefficient, unwieldy, or too specialized. How do I create a generic menu and inherit from it so that I can develop menus in an orderly fashion?

Technique

In order to master the construction of a menu in PowerBuilder, you must have a clear understanding of how to navigate the Menu painter and of the relationships between menus and windows and between ancestor menus and descendant menus. The painter itself is straightforward, but the relationships can be more challenging. This How-To focuses on the techniques required to build a menu so that it is generic enough to be reusable without being clumsy and difficult to use.

Steps

To experiment with the program for this How-To, access the Menu Basics application by running MENUBSC.EXE from Windows or MENUBSC.PBL from PowerBuilder. When the program starts, a simple frame window will appear as shown in Figure 6-1. Without releasing the left mouse button, browse the two menus at the top of the frame and observe the MicroHelp text that appears in the status line at the bottom left corner of the frame window, as shown in Figure 6-2.

Press the <ESC> key twice to completely close any open menus. Place your mouse pointer over the buttons on the toolbar without pressing a mouse button. After a short delay, a small box, called a PowerTip, will appear showing you a label indicating the button's function, as shown in Figure 6-3. Choose the New toolbar button (or the File/New menu item), and a single sheet will open as depicted in Figure 6-4. Additionally, you will notice that the number of menu choices has expanded (because another menu has been loaded) and that a second toolbar has appeared on the display. This second toolbar is specific to the newly opened sheet and has options

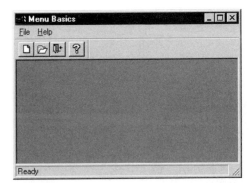

Figure 6-1 The Menu Basics application when started

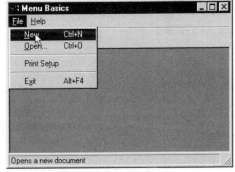

Figure 6-2 The status line displaying MicroHelp in the Menu Basics application

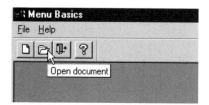

Figure 6-3 A PowerTip at work

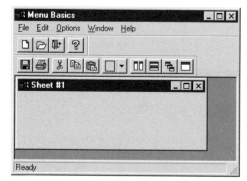

Figure 6-4 An open sheet after choosing the File/New menu item

corresponding to the expanded menu choices. You can browse the menus and tool-bar buttons as done previously to verify that they work as the frame menu's did. In fact, you will notice that the frame's toolbar is still displayed and that you can invoke the New toolbar button to create a second sheet. After doing so, select the Window menu item and notice that a list of all open sheets is displayed at the bottom of that dropdown menu.

You can use the cascaded menu items for the Options/Colors menu item to alter the color of each of the sheets. Experiment with these settings to verify that the sheet windows change colors in response to these options. You can also invoke these options from the dropdown item in the sheet toolbar.

When you are satisfied with the basic workings of this application, choose the Exit toolbar button (or the File/Exit menu item) and end the program. To construct this application, follow the steps below.

1. Use the Application painter to create a new .PBL and Application object called MENUBSC.PBL and a_menubasics, respectively. Answer No when prompted to construct an application template.

2. Start the Menu painter by choosing the Menu toolbar button from the PowerBar. Choose New on the Select Menu window to begin construction of the frame menu in this application.

3. When the painter first opens, you will be looking at a fairly complex dis-play. In the edit field that has appeared at the top of the painter (see Figure 6-5), enter the first top-level menu item, "&File". (The top-level menu items are the ones that will appear in the menu bar when you run the pro-gram.) As you type in this menu item, notice that the Menu Item Name field on the General tab indicates that this menu item name (for program-ming purposes) will be m_file. These names will be completed automatically as you enter each menu item text.

4. Go ahead and complete the top level menu items. However, entering the top-level menu items can be tricky. You must place your mouse pointer in

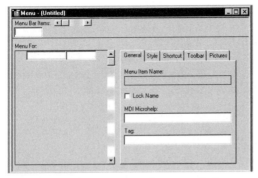

Figure 6-5 The Menu painter and the
first edit field

the gray area to the right of the newly entered "&File" menu item and click
once. If you did so correctly, a new edit field will appear under your mouse
pointer, and you can proceed. Add top-level menu items for "&Edit",
"&Window", and "&Help".

5. To prevent losing any work, choose the File/Save menu item from the Menu
painter and save this menu as m_frame.

6. At this point you are ready to enter the dropdown menu items for each of
the top-level menus. Click once on the "&File" entry you made previously
and then click to enter the field to the right of the hand icon on the display,
as shown in Figure 6-6. Type in "&New" as the menu item text and notice
that the Menu Item Name field shows m_new as you expected from what
you saw in step 3.

7. Now cursor down once and enter the "&Open..." menu item.

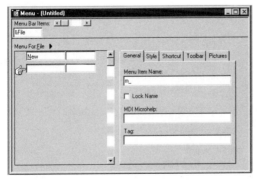

Figure 6-6 The entry area for dropdown
menu items

8. You need a menu separator bar at this point. To enter one, cursor into the field below the Open menu item you just entered and type in "-" (yes, a single hyphen). You will notice that the Menu Item Name for the separator bar is m_-, which is a valid PowerBuilder object name. However, you will be entering more separator bars as you go on, which will have names that conflict with this one. PowerBuilder will suggest a unique name as this occurs; you can accept these values in this exercise.

9. You are now ready to complete the rest of m_frame. Using the information listed in Table 6-1, complete the menu. Most of the properties on the tabs are self-explanatory. Some of these will be discussed more fully in the "How It Works" section later in this How-To. Of special note are the Shift Over/Down properties of the Help and Window menu items. Setting this property to TRUE will cause the menus to shift to the right to make room for new menu items added in the descendant created later. Be sure to save your work periodically.

TOP-LEVEL MENU ITEM TEXT	SUB-MENU ITEM TEXT	PROPERTY	VALUE
"&File"		Name	m_file
	"&New"	Name	m_new
		MDI Microhelp	"Opens a new document"
		Shortcut	Ctrl+N
		Toolbar Text	"New,New document"
		Picture Name	"ScriptNo!"
	"&Open"	Name	m_open
		MDI Microhelp	"Opens an existing document"
		Shortcut	Ctrl+O
		Toolbar Text	"Open,Open document"
		Picture Name	"Custom050!"
	"-"	Name	m_-
	"&Save"	Name	m_save
		MDI Microhelp	"Save the current document"
		Visible	FALSE
		Shortcut	Ctrl+S

TOP-LEVEL MENU ITEM TEXT	SUB-MENU ITEM TEXT	PROPERTY	VALUE
		Toolbar Text	"Save,Save document"
		Toolbar Visible	FALSE
		Picture Name	"Save!"
	"Save &As..."	Name	m_saveas
		MDI Microhelp	"Save the current document under a new name"
		Visible	FALSE
	"-"	Name	m_-1
	"&Close"	Name	m_close
		MDI Microhelp	"Close the current document"
		Visible	FALSE
		Shortcut	Ctrl+F4
	"-"	Name	m_-2
	"&Print"	Name	m_print
		MDI Microhelp	"Print the current document"
		Visible	FALSE
		Shortcut	Ctrl+P
		Toolbar Text	"Print"
		Picture Name	"Print!"
	"Print Se&tup"	Name	m_printsetup
		MDI Microhelp	"Set the default printer"
	"-"	Name	m_-3
	"E&xit"	Name	m_exit
		MDI Microhelp	"Exit Menu Basics"
		Type Option	Exit
		Shortcut	Alt+F4
		Toolbar Text	"Exit"
		Picture Name	"Exit!"

continued on next page

continued from previous page

TOP-LEVEL MENU ITEM TEXT	SUB-MENU ITEM TEXT	PROPERTY	VALUE
"&Edit"		Name	m_edit
		Visible	FALSE
	"Cu&t"	Name	m_cut
		MDI Microhelp	"Cut"
		Shortcut	Ctrl+X
		Toolbar text	"Cut"
		Space Before	1
		Picture Name	"Cut!"
	"&Copy"	Name	m_copy
		MDI Microhelp	"Copy"
		Shortcut	Ctrl+C
		Toolbar text	"Copy"
		Picture Name	"Copy!"
	"&Paste"	Name	m_paste
		MDI Microhelp	"Paste"
		Shortcut	Ctrl+V
		Toolbar text	"Paste"
		Picture Name	"Paste!"
"&Window"		Name	m_window
		Visible	FALSE
		Shift Over/Down	TRUE
	"&Tile Vertical"	Name	m_tilevertical
		MDI Microhelp	"Tile sheets vertically"
		Toolbar Text	"Vert,Tile vertically"
		Space Before	1
		Picture Name	"Tile!"
	"Tile &Horizontal"	Name	m_tilehorizontal
		MDI Microhelp	"Tile sheets horizontally"
		Toolbar Text	"Horz,Tile horizontally"
		Picture Name	"Horizontal!"

TOP-LEVEL MENU ITEM TEXT	SUB-MENU ITEM TEXT	PROPERTY	VALUE
	"Cascade"	Name	m_cascade
		MDI Microhelp	"Cascade sheets"
		Toolbar Text	"Cascade"
		Picture Name	"Cascade!"
	"&Layer"	Name	m_layer
		MDI Microhelp	"Layer sheets"
		Toolbar Text	"Layer"
		Picture Name	"Layer!"
	"-"	Name	m_-4
	"Arrange &Icons"	Name	m_arrangeicons
		MDI Microhelp	"Arrange icons"
"Help"		Name	m_help
		Shift Over/Down	TRUE
	"Help &Contents"	Name	m_helpcontents
		MDI Microhelp	"Help"
		Shortcut	F1
		Toolbar Text	"Help"
		Space Before	1
		Picture Name	"Help!"
	"-"	Name	m_-5
	"&About..."	Name	m_about
		MDI Microhelp	"Display information about Menu Basics"
		Type Option	About

Table 6-1 Menu settings for m_frame

10. To prevent losing all the work done so far, be sure to save the m_frame menu at this time.

11. You are now ready to begin placing scripts on some of these menu items. Many of them will not have scripts at this time because they are options that do not really apply to a frame window. Most of those inapplicable options were marked as invisible (Visible = FALSE) when you were constructing this menu object. Many of the scripts coded on a menu will need a reference to the frame window. To make this menu object generic, we will arrange to provide a frame window reference to the menu whenever it is created at runtime and use that value throughout. Use the Declare/Instance Variables... menu item to make the following variable declaration. This variable will hold the frame window reference.

```
private window iw_frame
```

12. Because iw_frame was declared as private, your menu should provide a function to initialize this value. Now use the Declare/Menu Functions... menu item to create a function with the specifications listed in Table 6-2. The following script should be used for the body of this function.

```
// Set our internal frame reference to the passed value
iw_frame = aw_frame
```

FUNCTION SPECIFICATIONS

Function	Name	mf_init	
	Access	Public	
	Returns	(None)	
Arguments	aw_frame	window	value

Table 6-2 Specifications for the mf_init() function

13. After saving the menu, code the following script on the Exit menu item's Clicked event. This script should terminate the application by closing the frame window.

```
// if we've been initialized properly (indicated by
// a valid frame window in this case), close the frame

IF IsValid( iw_frame ) THEN
    Close( iw_frame )
END IF
```

14. Place the following code on the Clicked event for m_about (the About... menu item under the Help menu). This script is responsible for displaying the About box, which normally contains the application icon, name, and copyright information. In this case, we'll show a fake one to avoid having to create a response window for this purpose.

```
// show a basic About box; a "real" about box is a
// response window rather than a messagebox

MessageBox( "About Menu Basics", "About box information goes here" )
```

15. Save the m_frame menu.

16. Using the Window painter, create a new window called w_frame. This window will serve as the frame window for our application. As a foundation the frame window sets the context for the sheets in the application and is the anchor for the menus, toolbars, and microhelp within the application. Use the settings in Table 6-3 to configure this window.

WINDOW/CONTROL NAME	PROPERTY	VALUE
Window		
w_frame	Title	"Menu Basics"
	Menu Name	"m_frame"
	Window Type	MDI Frame with Microhelp
	Initial State	Maximized

Table 6-3 Window and control settings for w_frame

17. Save the w_frame window.

18. Use the Application painter to enter the following script for the Open event of the Application object. This script simply opens the frame window.

```
Open( w_frame )
```

19. Run the application using the Run toolbar button. You should verify that the frame window appears with its simple menu and toolbar and that the Exit menu item properly terminates the program. If you need to make any adjustment to the m_frame menu, you should recheck Table 6-1 and make appropriate corrections.

20. You are now ready to create a descendant of m_frame called m_sheet. If you still have m_frame open (check the list of open painters under the Window menu), close that object now. Choose the Menu painter, and click Inherit... when the Select Menu window appears. When the Inherit From Menu window appears, choose m_frame and click OK.

21. At this point you should be looking at what appears to be m_frame all over again. You are going to customize this descendant of m_frame to enable the options that were disabled when m_frame was created and to make additions to m_sheet so that it will work properly with the sheet windows. Begin by making the property changes listed in Table 6-4.

TOP-LEVEL MENU ITEM TEXT	SUB-MENU ITEM TEXT	PROPERTY	VALUE
"&File"			
	"&New"	Toolbar Visible	FALSE
	"&Open..."	Toolbar Visible	FALSE
	"&Save"	Visible	TRUE
		Toolbar Visible	TRUE
	"Save &As"	Visible	TRUE
	"&Close"	Visible	TRUE
	"&Print"	Visible	TRUE
		Toolbar Visible	TRUE
	"E&xit"	Toolbar Visible	FALSE
"&Edit"		Visible	TRUE
"&Window"		Visible	TRUE
"&Help"			
	"Help &Contents"	Toolbar Visible	FALSE

Table 6-4 Changes to the m_sheet menu

22. Save the m_sheet menu.

23. Code the Clicked event for the File/Close menu item m_close as follows. This script simply closes the owner of the menu, represented by ParentWindow.

```
// Close the window that owns this sheet
Close( ParentWindow )
```

24. You should now add an Options top-level menu item to the m_sheet menu. To perform this step, click once in the gray area to the right of the Help menu item in *your* menu (not PowerBuilder's!). A new edit field should appear. Enter "&Options" for the menu text of this new menu item. Even though this menu item appears to the right of Help, it will appear between

Edit and Window. This occurs because you enabled the Shift Over/Down property for both the Window and Help menu items in step 9. Complete this new menu using the specifications in Table 6-5.

TOP-LEVEL MENU ITEM TEXT	SUB-MENU ITEM TEXT	PROPERTY	VALUE
"&Options"			
	"&Filter..."	Name	m_filter
		MDI Microhelp	"Enter a filter for the document"
	"&Sort..."	Name	m_sort
		MDI Microhelp	"Sort the document"
	"&Auto Save"	Name	m_autosave
		MDI Microhelp	"Enable automatic saving"
		Checked	TRUE
	"&Colors"	Name	m_colors
		MDI Microhelp	"Color options"
		Space Before	1
		Toolbar Object Type	MenuCascade
		Columns	2

Table 6-5 The Options menu for the m_sheet menu

25. Save the m_sheet menu without closing the painter.

26. You also need to add four cascaded menu items to the m_colors menu item. These options will allow the user to alter the background color of the corresponding sheet window. We will make it possible to change the color using a dropdown toolbar. To create these items, first click on the m_colors menu item and then choose the Next Level toolbar button. When you have done so, the dropdown menu area will change to show you an empty field to begin adding these new options. Add the options listed in Table 6-6.

CASCADED MENU ITEM TEXT	PROPERTY	VALUE
"&Gray"	Name	m_gray
	Checked	TRUE
	Picture Name	"gray.bmp"

continued on next page

continued from previous page

CASCADED MENU ITEM TEXT	PROPERTY	VALUE
"&Red"	Name	m_red
	Picture Name	"red.bmp"
"&White"	Name	m_white
	Picture Name	"white.bmp"
"&Blue"	Name	m_blue
	Picture Name	"blue.bmp"

Table 6-6 The cascaded menu items for the Colors menu item

27. You now need to write a function that will tell the window to change color and will check the correct menu item to indicate the current color selection. While this function is straightforward, note the use of the Item[] array to loop over the cascaded menus for a passed menu item am_parent. To create this mf_setcolor() function, use the function specifications listed in Table 6-7 and the script shown below.

```
long ll_upper, ll_temp

// send a color change message to the parent window
ParentWindow.PostEvent( "ue_color", al_color, 0 )

// get the number of cascading/dropdown items for a menu item
ll_upper = UpperBound(am_parent.item[])

// work through them all. If the item is the one to check
// then check it, otherwise uncheck it
FOR ll_temp = 1 TO ll_upper
    IF am_parent.item[ll_temp] = am_checked THEN
        am_checked.checked = TRUE
    ELSE
        am_parent.item[ll_temp].checked = FALSE
    END IF
NEXT
```

FUNCTION SPECIFICATION			
Function	Name	mf_setcolor	
	Access	private	
	Returns	(None)	
Arguments	al_color	long	value
	am_parent	menu	value
	am_checked	menu	value

Table 6-7 Function specification for mf_setcolor()

28. You now need to code the scripts for each of these cascaded menu items. These scripts all call the mf_setcolor() function created in step 27. The only difference is in the color value they specify. You may want to use the clipboard to assist you during these next four steps. Begin by coding the Clicked event of m_gray as follows.

```
mf_setcolor( 12632256, parent, this )   // 12632256 is gray
```

29. Use the following script for the Clicked event of m_red.

```
mf_setcolor( 255, parent, this ) // 255 is red
```

30. For the Clicked event of m_white, use the script below.

```
mf_setcolor( 16777215, parent, this ) // 16777215 is white
```

31. To complete the cascaded menu items, use the following script for m_blue's Clicked event.

```
mf_setcolor( 16711680, parent, this ) // 16711680 is blue
```

32. Save the m_sheet menu and close the Menu painter.

33. Using the Window painter again, create a new window called w_sheet using the specifications listed in Table 6-8. This window is a simple sheet to use in this application. Save the window without closing the painter when you are done.

WINDOW/CONTROL NAME	PROPERTY	VALUE
Window		
w_sheet	Title	"Sheet"
	Menu Name	"m_sheet"
	Window Type	Main

Table 6-8 Window and control settings for w_sheet

34. To easily differentiate the sheets as they are opened, we want to place a counter value in the window title. The easiest way to implement this is by using a shared variable. Using the Declare/Shared Variables... menu item, make the following declaration.

```
integer si_sheetcount
```

35. The w_sheet window should increment this sheet counter, add it to the title, and call the mf_init() menu initialization function you created in step 12. Use the following script for the Open event of w_sheet. Save the window and close the Window painter when you are done.

```
// get a reference to this window's menu
m_frame lm_sheet
lm_sheet = this.menuid
```

continued on next page

continued from previous page

```
// initialize it so that it knows which frame to use
lm_sheet.mf_init( w_frame )

// increment the sheet counter and put it in the title
si_sheetcount ++
this.title = this.title + " #" + string( si_sheetcount )
```

36. In order to change the window color, the window needs to respond to the ue_color event being sent from the m_sheet color menu items. To create this custom event, use the Declare/User Events... menu item to declare a user event called ue_color mapped to the PowerBuilder event pbm_custom01.

37. Use the following script for w_sheet's newly created ue_color event to alter the background color of the window.

```
// accept the incoming parameter and alter the background color
long ll_color
this.backcolor = Message.WordParm
```

38. You are now ready to finish hooking the pieces together for this application. Use the Menu painter to reopen the m_frame menu created previously. Use the following script for the Clicked event for the File/New (m_new) and File/Open (m_open) menu items. Strictly speaking, these scripts should not be identical; the Open option should prompt the user for a "document" to open whereas New should create a new "document" from scratch. In our case, we'll let them do the same thing.

```
w_sheet lw_sheet

IF IsValid( iw_frame ) THEN
    OpenSheet( lw_sheet, iw_frame )
END IF
```

39. You should also allow the user to arrange the sheets on the frame. This and the following four steps contain the code needed to arrange these sheets. Because they are so similar you may want to use the clipboard to copy and paste these scripts. To begin, code the Clicked event for m_tilevertical (Window/Tile Vertical) using the following script.

```
// arrange sheets for the frame

IF IsValid( iw_frame ) THEN
    iw_frame.ArrangeSheets( Tile! )
END IF
```

40. Use the following script for the Clicked event of m_tilehorizontal (Window/Tile Horizontal).

```
// arrange sheets for the frame

IF IsValid( iw_frame ) THEN
    iw_frame.ArrangeSheets( TileHorizontal! )
END IF
```

41. Use the following script for the Clicked event of m_cascade (Window/Cascade).

```
// arrange sheets for the frame

IF IsValid( iw_frame ) THEN
    iw_frame.ArrangeSheets( Cascade! )
END IF
```

42. Enter the script below for the Clicked event of m_layer (Window/Layer).

```
// arrange sheets for the frame

IF IsValid( iw_frame ) THEN
    iw_frame.ArrangeSheets( Layer! )
END IF
```

43. Also provide a script to arrange the minimized windows within the frame using the following script for the Clicked event of m_arrangeicons (Window/Arrange Icons).

```
// arrange sheets for the frame

IF IsValid( iw_frame ) THEN
    iw_frame.ArrangeSheets( Icons! )
END IF
```

44. Save the m_frame window.

45. Save and run the application.

How It Works

The menu object itself is a straightforward part of the PowerBuilder application. Using a menu consists of creating the menu object class as an entry in a .PBL and of specifying that class as the menu for a particular window (in the properties for the window in the Window painter). The real trick is to construct a menu that is sufficiently generic to be useful in a variety of situations. Much of this How-To was spent constructing a frame menu, m_frame, that contained the essential menu items needed in many places in the application; most of these items were hidden (Visible = FALSE) because they were not immediately needed at the frame menu level. In the descendant sheet menu, m_sheet, you made these items visible and added some scripts appropriate for use at the sheet level (such as Close).

The chief difficulty in constructing a generic menu in PowerBuilder is in creating an interface between a menu and the window that "owns" it at runtime. Because PowerBuilder treats menus and windows as separate objects, they have very little knowledge of each other's structure and capabilities. The temptation is to construct a menu that explicitly refers to windows by name (e.g., w_frame) rather than with the *ParentWindow* pronoun, which refers to the owner window and should usually be used for generality. However, the ParentWindow pronoun is not satisfactory in all situations. Consider the Exit menu item. In order to terminate the application, the Exit menu item must close the *frame* window. However, if you had coded the Exit menu item on m_sheet to close the ParentWindow, you would have only closed the sheet. In this case a reference to the frame window is appropriate. To allow your menu to access the frame window without giving an actual frame window name (which would compromise the reusability of the menu), this menu has an instance variable, iw_frame, defined to reference the window for the menu. You coded an mf_init() function to set this value. Every window will need to invoke this function, but it can generally be coded in a window ancestor. It also alleviates the need to edit menu scripts if you decide to use this menu in other applications.

We also need to discuss the behavior of menus and toolbars in an MDI application. When you constructed this application, you created two distinct menu classes, m_frame and m_sheet, attached to two distinct window classes, w_frame and w_sheet. When you initially opened the frame window from the Open event of the Application object, PowerBuilder automatically instantiated a copy of the m_frame class. Each time you open a sheet (using the OpenSheet() function in the New menu item), PowerBuilder instantiates a copy of the m_sheet class for *each* sheet that is opened. As an example, if there are two sheets open, *three* menus have been instantiated by your program: two copies of m_sheet for the sheet windows and one copy of m_frame for the frame window. As you move from window to window, PowerBuilder automatically switches the menus at the top of the frame window so that the menu belonging to the active sheet is the one displayed. Toolbars behave a bit differently, however, in that PowerBuilder will allow *two* toolbars to be displayed at once: one for the frame menu, m_frame, and one for the sheet menu, m_sheet. While the frame toolbar is always displayed, the sheet toolbar is switched to match the active sheet. PowerBuilder thus supports the display of up to two toolbars at a time: one for the frame menu and one for the active sheet's menu. Also, the fact that both toolbars are displayed is why a number of sheet toolbar items were marked as invisible; it is confusing for the user to see the same toolbar actions in different locations.

Comments

We often think of menu and window objects as being tightly coupled, but this is not the case. As this How-To demonstrates, thinking ahead is an important part of designing a usable menu structure. To increase your mastery of this topic, you might try adding a ue_print user event to the w_sheet window class that can be triggered from the m_sheet menu object.

COMPLEXITY
INTERMEDIATE

6.2   How do I...
Change menus at runtime?

Problem

I am building an MDI application. I have the frame window and several sheets that I open. However, this application will be used by power users and novices alike. I'd like to give the power users some additional capabilities that the novices do not need.

If I create the menu with the power user in mind, and include all the options, it could overwhelm the novice. If I create a menu geared towards the novice, the power users won't have enough capabilities. I have seen Windows applications that include an option for full menus and short menus. If I want to do the same thing, do I have to create one menu with many hidden items and make them visible at runtime? This seems like a lot of work as the full menu option I have will require many options. Can I create two menus and change the menu in use at runtime instead?

Technique

We've seen the use of objects and properties. Properties control what an object looks like. A menu, although an object in its own right, is also a property of a window. We set this property at design time while in the Window painter. It is also possible to change the properties of objects at runtime using PowerBuilder's dot notation. It seems logical, then, that it is possible to alter the menu associated with a window by modifying the window's menuid property. While you might be tempted to try this technique to change the menu-window association, that is not how it is done. In order to change menus we need to use a function provided by PowerBuilder that exists just for this purpose. In the process, we will use many of the techniques discussed up to this point in this chapter.

Steps

This example is a single document interface. In fact, the application doesn't do anything except allow you to change the menu. Open and run the sample application in CHNGMENU.PBL. This application starts in "short" menu mode as shown in Figure 6-7. In fact, there are only two menu bar items, each with one option. The File menu contains an Exit item, while the Options menu contains an item to switch to full menus. Select Full Menus from the Options menu and look at what happens. The window with a "full" menu is shown in Figure 6-8. We will keep the example simple in order to concentrate on the technique.

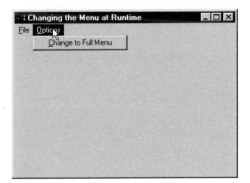

Figure 6-7 The CHNGMENU application in "short" menu mode

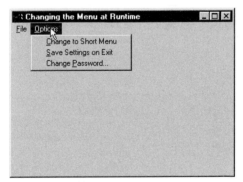

Figure 6-8 The CHNGMENU application in "full" menu mode

1. Using the Application painter, create a new Application object called a_chngmenu in a new library called CHNGMENU.PBL. You will not need an application template for this application.

2. Create a new menu object called m_short using the Menu painter. The structure and property settings of this menu are shown in Table 6-9. After completing this step be sure to save the menu.

TOP-LEVEL MENU ITEM TEXT	SUB-MENU ITEM TEXT	PROPERTY	VALUE
"&File"		Name	m_file
	"E&xit"	Name	m_exit
		Shift Over/Down	TRUE
"&Options"		Name	m_options
	"&Change to Full Menu"	Name	m_menutype

Table 6-9 Structure and property settings for the m_short menu object

3. Place the following code in the Clicked event of m_exit.

```
//Exit the application by closing the window
Close ( ParentWindow )
```

4. To create the "full" version of this menu, we will use inheritance as described in How-To 6.1. After ensuring that you have exited the Menu painter for m_short, invoke the Menu painter from the toolbar and choose the Inherit... CommandButton. When the Inherit From window appears, choose m_short and click OK. Add items for New, Open, and Save to the end of the File menu; at runtime, these options will appear above the Exit menu item due to m_exit's Shift Over/Down setting. Also change the text of m_menutype to indicate short menus instead of full menus. Add items for Save Settings on Exit and Change Password to the Options menu. These changes are summarized in Table 6-10.

TOP-LEVEL MENU ITEM TEXT	SUB-MENU ITEM TEXT	PROPERTY	VALUE
"&File"			
	"&New"	Name	m_new
	"&Open"	Name	m_open
	"&Save"	Name	m_save

TOP-LEVEL MENU ITEM TEXT	SUB-MENU ITEM TEXT	PROPERTY	VALUE
"&Options"			
	"&Change to Short Menu"	DLBName	m_menutype
	"&Save Settings on Exit"	Name	m_savesettingsonexit
	"Change &Password"	Name	m_changepassword

Table 6-10 Changes and additions required to create the m_full menu object

5. You need to add the script to switch to the short menu by coding the m_menutype menu item (under the Options top-level menu item). Once the Script painter is active for m_menutype, choose the Override Ancestor Script option from the Design menu. This may seem odd since there is no ancestor script to override at this point. You will be coding the ancestor script shortly. Use the following code for the Clicked event of the m_menutype menu item.

```
//Change the menu of the window using the appropriate function call
ParentWindow.ChangeMenu ( m_short )
```

6. Save the m_full menu object.

7. Use the File/Open... menu item to open the m_short menu object created previously. Place the following script on the Clicked event of m_menutype. This script has the same effect as the previous step, except that it puts the full menu on the window.

```
//Change the menu of the window using the appropriate function call
ParentWindow.ChangeMenu ( m_full )
```

8. Start the Window painter and create a new window called w_change using the specifications shown in Table 6-11. The most important step here is to associate m_short with the w_change window. Save the window when done.

WINDOW/CONTROL NAME	PROPERTY	VALUE
Window		
w_change	Title	"Changing the Menu at Runtime"
	Menu Name	"m_short"

Table 6-11 Window settings for the w_change window

9. Write the code for the Open event of the Application object so that the window will open. You can use the following script.

```
//Open the window
Open ( w_change )
```

10. Save the Application object and run the application.

How It Works

The menu that is displayed on a window is just a property of the window. Like nearly all properties, it is possible to change the menu associated with a window at runtime. However, PowerBuilder does not allow us to do this using standard dot notation, because the menu is considered a protected property. Protected properties must be manipulated exclusively through function calls which serve as the interface to the object. This access method is used for certain properties to prevent invalid modifications by ensuring the correctness of the new property value. Additionally, these property changes may require other internal changes which the function performs. In this case, the ChangeMenu() function may be called against the window object to alter the menu associated with the window.

Comments

Many Windows applications support this concept of full menus and short menus, and this is one easy way to provide the same capacity to our users. If you are creating a complex application, it may be confusing to the new user to see a wealth of menu options. Keep it simple, with basic functionality, but allow the more advanced user to have all the options they need to complete the job.

Changing the menu is also a good choice if you need to indicate that the application is in a different mode. For example, PowerBuilder allows us to change the tab order of the controls on a window. Once you select Tab Order from the Design menu, you must complete the setting of the tab order. While in this "Tab Order" mode, all the items on the menu are disabled. If you need this kind of interface, it may be easier to create two menus. One would be the standard menu, while the other would be a descendant of it with all appropriate menu items disabled. Changing menus at runtime is much easier than manually setting all the enabled properties for the appropriate menu items.

COMPLEXITY
INTERMEDIATE

6.3 How do I...
Manage toolbars in my application?

Problem

I know how to define and use toolbars in my application, but I only have a vague idea of how to manage those toolbars. The features I'm talking about include giving the user a menu item with which to turn toolbars on and off, preventing my user from moving the toolbar, knowing when the user moves the toolbar, and displaying only one toolbar. How do I manage toolbars in my application?

Technique

The methods for managing the aspects of the toolbar just described are actually quite simple, but they require a little bit of setup to work (hence the "Intermediate" rating for this How-To). To allow the user to turn the toolbar on and off from a menu item, you'll need to control a window property called *ToolbarVisible*. However, you'll have to make use of the Selected event on a menu item in order to get the checkmark to display properly. To prevent the user from relocating the toolbars, you can set the *ToolbarUserControl* property of the Application object. Finally, the windows in your application get a *ToolbarMoved* event when a toolbar is moved, but you have to know how to decipher the details passed to that event.

Steps

To sample this How-To, access the Toolbars application library on the included CD-ROM. You may run this application from within PowerBuilder or by executing TOOLBARS.EXE. Once it starts, you'll see an empty frame window with a simple menu along with a toolbar as shown in Figure 6-9. Click the Window top-level menu item so that the toolbar menu items will appear. Note that the Show Toolbar menu item is checked, which correctly indicates that the toolbar is visible. Press <ESC> to close that window. Right-click on the toolbar and choose FrameBar, which will cause the displayed frame toolbar to disappear. Choose the Window menu item again and note that the Show Toolbar menu item is no longer checked, which still correctly indicates the state of the toolbar. Choose the Show Toolbar menu item to cause the toolbar to reappear. Now choose the Window/Tell Me menu item. Right-click the toolbar again and choose one of the location options: Top, Bottom, Left, Right, or Floating. Notice that the machine beeps at you (an annoyance in a production application, but this is a demo, right?) and uses the MicroHelp line at the bottom of the frame to tell you where the toolbar was moved.

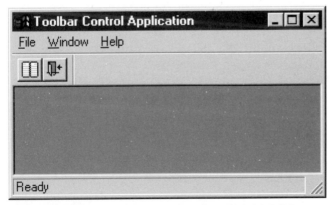

Figure 6-9 The Toolbars application F06-09.PCX

Now pick the File/Open sheet menu item to open a test sheet window. Again choose Window/Show Toolbar and verify that it works properly. Specifically, note that only the sheet's toolbar was affected. Also turn on the Window/Tell Me option. Relocate either of the two toolbars that are now displayed; notice that the MicroHelp tells you not just *where* the toolbar was moved, but also *which* toolbar was moved. Finally, choose the Window/Lock Toolbars menu item. With this option turned on, you will not be able to manipulate your toolbars by right-clicking. You can, however, use the Window/Show Toolbar menu item. Note that locking the toolbar is a *global* option; it is set for all toolbars. There is no way to lock a single toolbar. Choose File/Exit to end this application. To construct this program, follow the steps below.

1. Use the Application painter's File/New menu item to create a new .PBL and Application object called TOOLBARS.PBL and a_toolbars, respectively. Answer "No" when prompted to generate an application template.

2. Use the Window painter to create a new window. Once the painter opens, use the File/Save menu item to save the window under the name w_frame. We actually want w_frame to be a frame window, but we have a problem here. We can't make w_frame a frame window unless we have a menu. Our menu, on the other hand, will need to make a couple of references to w_frame. It's so hard to keep everyone happy here. For now, we'll create the w_frame window and do everything *but* give it a menu and its frame window status.

3. Using the Declare/User Events... menu item, create a custom user event for w_frame called ue_showhidetoolbar and map it to the internal PowerBuilder event pbm_custom01.

4. Use the following script for the ue_showhidetoolbar event (just declared). This script will allow the menus created later to tell the window when to show or hide the toolbar.

```
long ll_val

// capture the incoming parameter from TriggerEvent()/PostEvent()
ll_val = Message.WordParm

CHOOSE CASE ll_val
    CASE 0
        this.toolbarvisible = FALSE
    CASE 1
        this.toolbarvisible = TRUE

END CHOOSE
```

5. The w_frame requires custom properties to indicate whether it should tell you when the toolbar moves and whether a single sheet toolbar is being displayed. Use the Declare/Instance Variables... menu to make the following property declaration.

```
private boolean ib_tell, ib_singletoolbar
```

6. The w_frame window will need a function to turn toolbar notification on and off. We'll provide a function interface for this feature. Use the Declare/Window Functions... menu item to declare a new window function with the specifications listed in Table 6-12. Use the following script for the body of the function. Save the w_frame window when done.

```
ib_tell = ab_notify
```

FUNCTION SPECIFICATIONS

Function	Name	wf_settoolbarnotify	
	Access	public	
	Returns	(None)	
Arguments	ab_notify	Boolean	value

Table 6-12 Specifications for the wf_settoolbarnotify() function

7. Declare a function for the w_frame window so that those objects outside the frame window can determine if toolbar notification is turned on or not. Use the Declare/Window Functions... menu item along with the declaration listed in Table 6-13 to make this declaration. The code for the body of this function appears below. Again save the frame window when done.

```
RETURN ib_tell
```

FUNCTION SPECIFICATIONS

Function	Name	wf_gettoolbarnotify
	Access	public
	Returns	boolean
Arguments	(None)	

Table 6-13 Specifications for the wf_gettoolbarnotify() function

8. You also need to create the sheet window for this application. Use the Window painter to create this new window and save it under the name w_sheet. As with w_frame, we'll complete the property settings for this window later.

9. Declare a custom user event for w_sheet using the Declare/User Events... menu item. Call the event ue_showhidetoolbar and map it to pbm_custom01.

10. Use the following script as the body for ue_showhidetoolbar. This is the same script from step 4 above.

```
long ll_val

// capture the incoming parameter from TriggerEvent()/PostEvent()
ll_val = Message.WordParm

CHOOSE CASE ll_val
    CASE 0
        this.toolbarvisible = FALSE
    CASE 1
        this.toolbarvisible = TRUE

END CHOOSE
```

11. Save the w_sheet window. We're now done with building windows for the time being. Let's turn our attentions to the construction of the menus.

12. Using the Menu painter, begin work on a new menu with the property settings shown in Table 6-14. Save this menu under the name m_frame, but don't close the painter just yet.

TOP-LEVEL MENU ITEM TEXT	SUB-MENU ITEM TEXT	PROPERTY	VALUE
"&File"		Name	m_file
	"&Open Sheet"	Name	m_opensheet
		Toolbar Item/Picture	"Custom017!"
		Toolbar Item/Text	"Open sheet"
		MDI Microhelp	"Open a test sheet"
	"E&xit"	Name	m_exit
		Toolbar Item/Picture	"Exit!"
		Toolbar Item/Text	"Exit"
		MDI Microhelp	"Exit the application"
		Shift Over/Down	TRUE
"&Window"		Name	m_window
	"Show &Toolbar"	Name	m_showtoolbar
		MDI Microhelp	"Turns the toolbar on and off"
	"&Lock Toolbars"	Name	m_locktoolbars
		MDI Microhelp	"Turns user control of toolbars on and off"
	"Tell &Me"	Name	m_tellme

TOP-LEVEL MENU ITEM TEXT	SUB-MENU ITEM TEXT	PROPERTY	VALUE
		MDI Microhelp	"Turn on notification of toolbar moves"
"&Help"		Name	m_help
	"&About..."	Name	m_about

Table 6-14 Menu property settings for m_frame

13. Your program will need a simple script to end the application. Use the following script on the Clicked event of m_exit to accomplish this task.

```
Close( w_frame )
```

14. You can use the following script on the Clicked event of m_opensheet to cause a sheet to open when the Open Sheet menu item is chosen.

```
OpenSheet( w_sheet, w_frame, 0, Original! )
```

15. We don't have a real About box for this program, but you can place the next line of code on the Clicked event of m_about to say *something*.

```
MessageBox( "About", "This is an oversimplified About Box." )
```

16. Now for the fun stuff. The Window/Show Toolbar menu item should handle turning the toolbar on and off. The following script performs this function by activating an event on the menu's parent window (the menu's owner window) and passing it a value, ll_val, indicating what to do.

```
long ll_val

// if the menu item is CURRENTLY not checked, we want to SHOW the toolbar
// (indicated by ll_val = 1) and vice versa

IF this.checked=FALSE THEN ll_val = 1 ELSE ll_val = 0

ParentWindow.PostEvent( "ue_showhidetoolbar", ll_val, 0 )
```

17. To prevent the user from moving the toolbars, place the following script on the m_locktoolbars menu item Clicked event.

```
application la_1

la_1 = GetApplication()
la_1.ToolBarUserControl = This.checked
```

18. What the preceding scripts do *not* do, however, is properly handle the checking of the Show Toolbar and Lock Toolbars menu items. We cannot place the script to handle Show Toolbar on the m_showtoolbar menu item, because the user might turn off the toolbar by right-clicking on it rather than by using the Show Toolbar menu item. We cannot place the script for

Lock Toolbars on the m_locktoolbars menu item because it is a *global* setting which could have been turned on when a *different* menu was displayed. To fix these problems, we can use the Selected event on m_window. That's odd; it's rare that we code anything on top-level menu items. However, the Selected event will occur as the user is dropping down the Window menu, allowing us to determine the state of the checkmarks. Use the following code on that event to make this magic happen.

```
m_showtoolbar.checked = parentwindow.toolbarvisible
m_locktoolbars.checked = NOT GetApplication().ToolBarUserControl
m_tellme.checked = w_frame.wf_gettoolbarnotify()
```

19. Complete this menu by placing the following script on the Clicked event of the m_tellme menu item. This script tells the frame window (which gets the actual notification when the toolbar is moved) to inform you of changes.

```
w_frame.wf_settoolbarnotify( NOT this.checked )
```

20. Save the m_frame menu and close the Menu painter.

21. Now use the Menu painter to *inherit* from the m_frame window you just created. To do so, start the Menu painter and choose the Inherit... button when prompted for a menu to open. Choose m_frame as the ancestor window and click OK.

22. You should now be in the Menu painter looking at the menu structure you created for m_frame (but you're actually working on m_sheet, remember). We are inheriting here to avoid re-coding all the scripts already entered. All we want to do here is to make changes to this menu to make it appropriate for use with a sheet. Make the menu structure and property changes listed in Table 6-15 below to begin.

TOP-LEVEL MENU ITEM TEXT	SUB-MENU ITEM TEXT	PROPERTY	VALUE
"&File"			
		Name	m_file
	"&Open Sheet"	*(change)*	
		Toolbar Item/Visible	FALSE
	"E&xit"	*(change)*	
		Toolbar Item/Visible	FALSE
	"&Save"	*(new menu item; add at the end)*	
		Name	m_save

TOP-LEVEL MENU ITEM TEXT	SUB-MENU ITEM TEXT	PROPERTY	VALUE
		Toolbar Item/Picture	"Custom008!"
		Toolbar Item/Text	"Save"
		MDI Microhelp	"Save document (not really implemented)"
	"&Close"	(new menu item; add at the end)	
		Name	m_close
		MDI Microhelp	"Close this sheet"

Table 6-15 Menu property settings for m_sheet

23. Save the m_sheet menu.

24. Place the following script in the Clicked event of m_save.

```
MessageBox( "Save", "Pretend a save just took place." )
```

25. Also enter a script for the Close menu item's Clicked event to close the sheet window.

```
Close( ParentWindow)
```

26. To implement displaying a single toolbar, the inherited sheet menu must be able to display those toolbar items that are normally found on the frame's toolbar. m_sheet needs a function that can be called from the w_frame window to handle this task. Use the Declare/Menu Functions... menu item to create a function called mf_showsheettoolbaritems() using the function specification listed in Table 6-16. The body of the function appears below. Save the m_sheet menu when you are done.

```
m_file.m_exit.toolbaritemvisible = ab_show
m_file.m_opensheet.toolbaritemvisible = ab_show
```

FUNCTION SPECIFICATIONS			
Function	Name	mf_showsheettoolbaritems	
	Access	public	
	Returns	(None)	
Arguments	ab_show	Boolean	value

Table 6-16 Specifications for the mf_showsheettoolbaritems function

27. Use the Window painter to reopen the w_frame window created previously. Configure the window using the property settings in Table 6-17.

WINDOW/CONTROL NAME	PROPERTY	VALUE
Window		
w_frame	Title	"Toolbar Control Application"
	Menu	TRUE
	Menu name	m_frame
	Window Type	MDI Frame with Microhelp

Table 6-17 Window property settings for the w_frame window

28. To handle the single toolbar option, the frame window w_frame will require a function to examine all open sheets, turning their toolbar items on and off as appropriate. The function wf_setsheettoolbars() will perform this task. Use the Declare/Window Functions… menu item to make the function declaration listed in Table 6-18. The body of the function appears below. Observe the use of GetFirstSheet() and GetNextSheet() to loop over the open sheets.

```
m_sheet lm_sheet
window lw_sheet

// reduce the amount of flicker as we make adjustments to the toolbars
this.SetRedraw( FALSE )

// get a reference to the first sheet
lw_sheet = this.GetFirstSheet()

// if a sheet is open, set the frame's toolbar to visible or not visible
// based on whether or not a single toolbar has been chosen.
// if no sheets are open, the frame toolbar should be visible regardless
IF IsValid(lw_sheet) THEN
    this.toolbarvisible = NOT ib_singletoolbar
ELSE
    this.toolbarvisible = TRUE
END IF

// loop over all of the sheets, setting their toolbar items to visible or not
// based on whether we are showing a single toolbar
DO WHILE IsValid( lw_sheet)
    lm_sheet = lw_sheet.menuid
    lm_sheet.mf_showsheettoolbaritems( ib_singletoolbar )
    lw_sheet = this.GetNextSheet( lw_sheet )
LOOP

this.SetRedraw( TRUE )
```

FUNCTION SPECIFICATIONS		
Function	Name	wf_setsheettoolbars
	Access	public
	Returns	(None)

FUNCTION SPECIFICATIONS

Arguments	*(None)*

Table 6-18 Specifications for the wf_setsheettoolbars() function

29. The frame needs a function to obtain the value of ib_singletoolbar (whether or not a single toolbar is being displayed). Create a wf_setsingletoolbar() function using the Declare/Window Functions... menu item. The function declaration is listed in Table 6-19. The body of the script appears below.

```
// accept the new value into the internal ib_singletoolbar property
ib_singletoolbar = ab_set

// ensure that the toolbars are set to conform to this new setting
this.wf_setsheettoolbars()
```

FUNCTION SPECIFICATIONS

Function	Name	wf_setsingletoolbar	
	Access	public	
	Returns	(None)	
Arguments	ab_set	boolean	value

Table 6-19 Specifications for the wf_setsingletoolbar() function

30. A function to obtain the value of ib_singletoolbar would also be valuable. Declare a wf_getsingletoolbar() function by choosing Declare/Window Functions.... Use the function declaration shown in Table 6-20 and the script below.

```
RETURN ib_singletoolbar
```

FUNCTION SPECIFICATIONS

Function	Name	wf_getsingletoolbar
	Access	public
	Returns	boolean
Arguments	*(None)*	

Table 6-20 Specifications for the wf_setsingletoolbar() function

31. Use the File/Open... menu item to open the w_sheet window, also created previously. Set up the properties for this window as listed in Table 6-21.

WINDOW/CONTROL NAME		PROPERTY	VALUE
Window			
w_sheet		Title	"Sheet"
		Menu	TRUE
		Menu name	m_sheet

Table 6-21 Window property settings for the w_sheet window

32. To assist with the management of the single toolbar option, it will be helpful to know how many sheets are open at a time. Declare a shared variable for this purpose by choosing the Declare/Shared Variables… menu item and making the following declaration.

```
integer si_sheetcount
```

33. When an instance of w_sheet opens with the single toolbar option set, the sheet may need to tell the frame window to adjust the toolbar display for this new sheet. Place the following code on the Open event to implement this.

```
si_sheetcount = si_sheetcount + 1

// if we're showing only one toolbar, tell the frame to handle that.
IF w_frame.wf_getsingletoolbar() THEN
    w_frame.wf_setsheettoolbars()
END IF
```

34. When the sheet closes, it should adjust the sheet counter. A complication arises, however, if the single toolbar option is turned on and this is the last open sheet. If these conditions occur, the frame needs to redisplay its own toolbar. The wf_setsheettoolbars() function on w_frame will perform this task, but it will not work correctly until the sheet is *completely* closed. We'll need to *post* the wf_setsheettoolbars() function so that its execution will be delayed until after the sheet is completely closed. Use the following script for the Close event of w_sheet to accomplish this task. Save the window when you are done.

```
si_sheetcount --

// if this is the last open sheet and we're showing a single toolbar,
// we need to have the frame re-display its own toolbar (which is
// currently hidden). However, we'll need to post the wf_setsheettoolbars
// function so that its execution is delayed until after the
// actual closing of this sheet.
IF si_sheetcount = 0 AND w_frame.wf_getsingletoolbar() THEN
    w_frame.function post wf_setsheettoolbars()
END IF
```

35. Using the Application painter, code the Open event of the Application object as follows.

```
Open( w_frame )
```

How It Works

The actions performed by this application, in simplest form, are quite easy to implement. The difficulties are caused by two chief considerations: how to handle communication between menus and windows (which are completely separate objects in PowerBuilder) and how to make the menu correctly reflect the toolbar settings.

This application handles communication using three different methods. Events provide one means, as was done on the Show Toolbar menu item. We declared a custom user event, ue_showhidetoolbar, on both the windows in this application. This event is activated from the m_showtoolbar menu item. Notice the use of parameter passing in conjunction with the event mechanism. This method is fully covered in How-To 17.3. The second method used was a function method. Two functions, wf_settoolbarnotify() and wf_gettoolbarnotify(), were declared on the frame window to provide an interface to the toolbar notification capabilities of the frame window. These functions are called from the Window and Window/Tell Me menu items to get and set the toolbar notification state. Functions were chosen here because it is easy to return values (in the case of wf_gettoolbarnotify()). Finally, the Lock Toolbars menu item directly accesses the ToolbarUserControl property of the Application object. Generally, direct manipulation should be avoided because it makes objects quite dependent on each others' internal structure. However, the Application object is a special case because there is no way to declare custom events for an Application object. Functions will not solve the problem because attempts to invoke a custom function against a variable of type Application will not work. In short, the Application object's limited interface forces us to use a less-than-ideal method.

The last thing of interest to us here is the use of the Selected event on the Window menu item. The application receives this event when the user "highlights" a menu item. When this happens in this application, the program quickly establishes the status of the checkmarks before the dropdown menu below Window is drawn. This method is also quite reliable, which is necessary here because the scripts for the Show Toolbar, Lock Toolbars, and Tell Me menu items use their checked or unchecked status to make their changes to the toolbars.

COMPLEXITY
INTERMEDIATE

6.4 How do I...
Use popup menus?

Problem

I am interested in using popup menus in my application, the kind that appear when you right-click on something, but I am having some difficulty. I am particularly interested in knowing how to use a popup menu with features that are not duplicated on the window's menu. I'm also searching for a *good* way to pass parameters between my popup menu and its corresponding window; so far I've been using global and instance variables. There has to be a better way than that! How do I use popup menus?

Technique

The core of any PowerBuilder program that uses popup menus is the PopMenu() function, which is used here. Certain difficulties arise in dealing with displaying a menu that is not currently "in use" in the application (i.e., is not instantiated by being attached to an open window). To circumvent this problem, our program will instantiate (create) a popup-only menu, show it to the user with PopMenu(), and destroy it when it's done. Finally, we have to deal with the communication issue. In this application, the menu will pass parameters to the invoking window when the user makes a selection from the popup menu.

Steps

You can begin testing this application by opening the a_popup Application object in the POPUP.PBL library found on the included CD-ROM. Once the application is run-

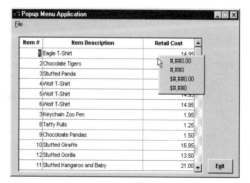

Figure 6-10 The Popup menu application showing the sorting popup menu

Figure 6-11 The Popup menu application showing the formatting popup menu

ning, you will see a simple DataWindow showing a list of retail items sold in the Zoo store. Place your pointer in either the Item number or Item Description columns and click the right mouse button. When you do, a popup menu will appear as shown in Figure 6-10. This menu allows you to sort on either item number or item description. Choose Sort by Description from that popup menu. The menu will disappear and the contents of the DataWindow will re-sort. Now try right-clicking on the Retail Cost column. Notice that a popup menu containing a list of display formats appears as indicated in Figure 6-11. Choose a format such as "$#,##0.00" from the popup menu and notice the corresponding change in the formatting of the retail cost values. Finally, look at the window's menu displayed at the top of that menu. That menu does not contain any of the items seen in either of the popup menus. Choose the Exit CommandButton to end this application. You can construct this program by following the steps below.

1. Use the Application painter to create a new .PBL and Application object called POPUP.PBL and a_popup, respectively. Do not accept an application template when offered.

2. Create the simple DataWindow object required by this application. It is a simple grid display of three columns from the retail_item table. Use the specifications listed in Table 6-22 when constructing this DataWindow. Save this object under the name d_retail_item_list.

WINDOW	OPTION	VALUE
New DataWindow		
	Data Source	Quick Select
	Presentation Style	Grid
Quick Select		
	Table	retail_item
	Columns	item_nbr, item_desc, retail_cost

Table 6-22 The d_retail_item_list DataWindow object

3. Use the Menu painter to create the popup menu structure as listed in Table 6-23. Save this menu as m_popup. You will code the scripts for the menu items in the steps that follow.

TOP-LEVEL MENU ITEM TEXT	SUB-MENU ITEM TEXT	PROPERTY	VALUE
"&Sort"		Name	m_sort
	"Sort by &Number"	Name	m_sortbynumber
	"Sort by &Description"	Name	m_sortbydescription
"&Format"		Name	m_format
	"#,##0.00"	Name	m_###000
	"#,##0"	Name	m_###0
	"$#,##0.00"	Name	m_$###000
	"$#,##0"	Name	m_$###0

Table 6-23 Menu property settings for m_popup

4. Place the following script on the m_sortbynumber menu item's Clicked event. This script tells the window to sort based on item number.

```
ParentWindow.PostEvent( "ue_sort", 0, "item_nbr A" )
```

5. Code a script similar to the one you just typed in for the Clicked event of the m_sortbydescription menu item. Use the following code.

```
ParentWindow.PostEvent( "ue_sort", 0, "item_desc A" )
```

6. We now turn our attention to the formatting menu items. Interestingly, our program can use the text properties of the menu items (containing a valid PowerBuilder format) directly. Because of this, you should place the following script on the Clicked event of each of the four formatting menu items. The Windows clipboard will be helpful here.

```
// tell the window that the user wants to format.  The expression this.text
specifies the display
// format
ParentWindow.PostEvent( "ue_format", 0, this.text )
```

7. Save the m_popup menu.

8. You should now create the main window's menu, m_main. This is a very simple menu, containing only File and Exit menu items as listed in Table 6-24.

TOP-LEVEL MENU ITEM TEXT	SUB-MENU ITEM TEXT	PROPERTY	VALUE
"&File"		Name	m_file
	"E&xit"	Name	m_exit

Table 6-24 Menu property settings for m_main

9. Code the Exit menu item's Clicked event using the following script.

```
Close( parentwindow )
```

10. Save the m_main menu.

11. Create the main window for this application using the Window painter. The specifications are listed in Table 6-25. Save this window as w_main.

WINDOW/CONTROL NAME	PROPERTY	VALUE
Window		
w_main	Title	"Popup Menu Application"
	Menu name	"m_main"
	MaximizeBox	FALSE
	Resizable	FALSE
CommandButton	Name	"cb_exit"
	Text	"E&xit"
DataWindow control	Name	dw_1
	DataWindow object name	"d_retail_item_list"
	HScrollBar	TRUE
	VScrollBar	TRUE
	Border	3D Lowered

Table 6-25 Window and control settings for the w_main window

12. Click on the background of the w_main window. Then use the Declare/User Events... menu item to declare two custom user events. Call one ue_sort and map it to pbm_custom01. Call the second one ue_format and map it to pbm_custom02. These events will be used by the popup menu to communicate with the main window.

13. Also declare an instance variable on the window to contain a reference to the column the user has pointed to when right-clicking. Use the Declare/Instance Variables... menu item to make this declaration. The declaration is shown on the next line.

```
string is_colatpointer
```

14. Place the following script in the Open event of w_main. This script connects to the database, and retrieves data into the DataWindow set up on the window.

```
sqlca.dbms = 'ODBC'

sqlca.dbparm = "ConnectString='DSN=Zoo;UID=dba;PWD=sql',DisableBind=1"

CONNECT USING sqlca;

IF sqlca.sqlcode < 0 THEN
    MessageBox("Connect Error", sqlca.sqlerrtext )
    Close( this )
    RETURN
END IF

dw_1.SetTransObject( sqlca )

dw_1.Retrieve()
```

15. We should be sure to disconnect from the database. To do so, place the following code on the Close event of w_main.

```
// if the transaction object is connected, disconnect it.
IF sqlca.dbhandle() > 0 THEN
    DISCONNECT USING sqlca;
END IF
```

16. Save the w_main window to preserve your work.

17. Your program now needs to cause the appropriate submenu within m_popup to appear when the user right-clicks on the DataWindow control. To present the proper submenu, the script will need to determine which column the user is clicking. The GetObjectAtPointer() will do this. From there, the program will need to instantiate the popup menu since it does not exist in memory. PopMenu() can then be called to display the appropriate submenu, either sorting options or formatting options. The script destroys the instantiated menu when the popup is complete. Use the following script on the RButtonDown event of the DataWindow control.

```
string ls_atpointer
m_popup lm_temp

// find out where we're pointing
ls_atpointer = this.GetObjectAtPointer()

// extract just the column (the row number isn't needed)
ls_atpointer = Left( ls_atpointer, Pos( ls_atpointer, '~t' ) - 1 )

// if we didn't get an error, proceed
IF ls_atpointer<> "" THEN
    is_colatpointer = ls_atpointer
    lm_temp = CREATE m_popup

    CHOOSE CASE is_colatpointer
```

```
        CASE "retail_cost"
            lm_temp.m_format.PopMenu( parent.pointerx(), parent.pointery())
        CASE ELSE
            lm_temp.m_sort.PopMenu( parent.PointerX(), parent.PointerY() )
    END CHOOSE

    DESTROY lm_temp
ELSE
    Beep(2)
END IF
```

18. Save the w_main window to preserve your work.

19. The popup menu's sorting options activate the ue_sort event on the window. You need to code this event on w_main. The script is shown below.

```
string ls_sortexp

// capture the incoming parameter, which contains a sort expression
ls_sortexp = String( Message.LongParm, "address" )

// now do the sort
IF ls_sortexp <> "" THEN
    dw_1.SetSort( ls_sortexp)
    dw_1.Sort()
END IF
```

20. As you did with ue_sort, you will also need to code the ue_format event on w_main to react to the formatting options. Use the following script to make this happen.

```
string ls_formatexp

ls_formatexp = String( Message.LongParm, "address" )

IF ls_formatexp <> "" THEN
    dw_1.SetFormat( is_colatpointer, ls_formatexp )
END IF
```

21. Finally, you should code the Exit CommandButton's Clicked event to close the window as follows.

```
Close( parent )
```

22. Save the w_main window.

23. To complete the application, place the following script on the Open event of the Application object.

```
Open( w_main )
```

24. Save the Application object and run the program.

How It Works

You will probably find this application to be surprisingly simple once it is all put together. As briefly introduced in the Technique section above, this How-To utilizes a menu that is used solely for popup purposes. Because of this, the script must instantiate and destroy this menu before it can be accessed with PopMenu(). These steps are performed by the CREATE and DESTROY commands in the RButtonDown event of the DataWindow control. PopMenu() itself is called against a particular top-level menu item within the menu structure. In this case, we specify the Sort or Format menus when calling PopMenu(). PointerX() and PointerY() return the current location of the pointer, which tells the popup menu where to appear. Note that if you are using an MDI application (this application is SDI), PointerX() and PointerY() should be called against the *frame* window (e.g., w_frame.PointerX()) for the menu to appear in the proper location.

The popup menu itself communicates the user's selection back to the calling window through the use of PostEvent() in conjunction with parameter passing. In the case of formatting, the menu item text itself is passed back since it is a valid format string. The is_colatpointer instance variable contains the desired column for the ue_format event.

Comments

Popup menus are an excellent way to add that last bit of polish and finesse to your application. The problem most programmers encounter is how to communicate between the popup menu and its calling window. A common mistake is to use global variables for this type of communication, which makes it difficult to reuse the popup menu. Using the techniques presented in this application, your program will be significantly easier to modify and maintain.

CHAPTER 7
DATABASE
OBJECTS

DATABASE OBJECTS

How do I...

PowerBuilder provides the developer with just about every tool necessary to take a project from cradle to grave. Therefore, it makes sense that a database interface has been provided. The Database painter is this interface, and it allows the completion of many back end-related tasks. Most of the topics presented here apply to the database administrator (DBA), but are covered for several reasons. First, many PowerBuilder developers act as the DBA, especially in small shops. Also, the discussion of PowerBuilder would not be complete without it. Additionally, even if you do not perform DBA tasks, you probably work closely with the individual who does. Lastly, even though these topics are traditionally back end-related, the Database painter provides some powerful utilities on the front end as well. These front end issues are the *extended attributes*.

7.1   Create a Database

PowerBuilder is completely back end-independent. When a database is created through PowerBuilder, you are really working on the back end. Just which back end that is is a function of how you have set your preferences in the Preference painter. This How-To explores these issues, and demonstrates the techniques for creating a new database. Specifically, our database will use the SQL AnyWhere engine, the DBMS supplied with PowerBuilder. This is an ODBC type database called ZOO.DB. This database has been provided on the accompanying CD-ROM, and is used through-out the examples in this book. The extended services provided by PowerBuilder are also discussed. These are called the extended attributes.

7.2   Define a Table and Primary and Foreign Keys

Once the database exists, you'll no doubt want to add tables in which to store the data. Since the ZOO database is provided for you, we'll only create one of the tables that make up that file. We will also add a primary key and a foreign key to the table. The primary key is required before rows can be added. The foreign key is option-al as far as the database goes, but gives us a lot of power. All of these issues are covered in this How-To. Later, you'll create another table using a different technique than the one presented here.

7.3   Preview the Data

Once you have populated the tables of the database, or created a view, you'll want to preview that data. This is one area of concentration when manipulating the extend-ed attributes of a column. PowerBuilder allows us to create a DataWindow (of sorts) that is used to show us not only the data in the table, but also our display formats, edit styles, and validation rules as well. Display formats, edit styles, and validation rules are covered later in this chapter.

7.4   Import and Export Data

It is not necessary to enter table data by hand. It can be imported into the table from many sources. Usually, this is a tab delimited text file. Additionally, rows can be stored in any number of formats including tab delimited, .XLS, .DBF, or SQL Syntax. How-To 7.4 shows how to move data into and out of your tables.

7.5   Create a View

Views provide an easy mechanism for the developer to encapsulate difficult queries. The DBA is (or should be!) an expert in creating and manipulating SQL statements. Often, we as developers must craft a very complex Select statement involving many tables. We could instead ask the DBA to create a view based on our needs. Also, some back end databases allow for updatable views (one such is Oracle) which provides the developer with an easy way to update many tables at one time. In How-To 7.4 you will create a complex view for the developer.

7.6   Save Changes to a Change Log

When changes are made to a table such as modifying the column names, adding columns, or changing the primary or foreign keys, PowerBuilder gives us the option to postpone the actual table modification, and instead write the changes to a file. This way, it is possible to do database modifications when users are no longer connected to the database and without affecting their work. It is also a good way to document all changes made to the tables. We'll do just that in How-To 7.6.

7.7   Execute an SQL Script

SQL script execution is yet another PowerBuilder facility. What kinds of scripts would you want to execute? Well, how about the change log that you create in How-To 7.6? That's one good use for this capability. Additionally, if you are a SQL guru, you may write SQL statements that use data description language (DDL) such as CREATE TABLE statements, or data manipulation language (DML) such as INSERT or DELETE. The change log created above is loaded into the Database painter's Administration tool and executed at the back end.

7.8   Create Display Formats

Part of the PowerBuilder repository gives you the ability to create display formats. This allows you to tell PowerBuilder how to display the data on a column by column basis. For example, if the table stores phone numbers, it makes sense to only store the ten digits of area code, prefix, and number. However, a format such as (909) 555-1212 makes for a pleasing and intuitive user interface. There are many display formats built in, and you have the option to create your own. These are then assigned to the table on a column by column basis. You only create them once, and can reuse them for any number of tables or columns.

7.9   Create Edit Styles

Edit styles are to user input what display formats are to data output. Again, they allow you to indicate the style used for editing data. Using the same example above, you will tell PowerBuilder to give the user an edit mask that *looks* like a phone number. This increases our user's efficiency, as well as decreasing the possibility for input error.

7.10   Create Validation Rules

One more repository facility is the validation rule. This is a custom client side rule that PowerBuilder imposes on any data input or modified by the user. You could, for example, create a rule indicating that a number must be less than 100,000 and apply that to a salary column for an employee. It is here that you can impose your business rules. If the user tried to modify a salary greater than the validation rule allows, an error is generated. The validation rules can be overridden in script, based on some criteria. They can provide a basis for common business rules, or to ensure that any data that eventually gets sent to the database is consistent with what the database is expecting. This How-To creates a rule to ensure that a particular date is not in the future.

COMPLEXITY
BEGINNING

7.1 How do I...
Create a database?

Problem

I am acting as the database administrator for my company. Since PowerBuilder is a client/server development tool, I need a database to which my application will connect. I like PowerBuilder's graphical environment and would like to use it to do all of the work on the back end. I know there is a Database painter. How can I use this tool to create a database?

Technique

You are right — almost. PowerBuilder comes with a database painter that allows the developer or database administrator to do all necessary back end work. However, you cannot create a remote database. The only database PowerBuilder allows you to create is a local one, using the SQL AnyWhere engine. In this How-To you will create the ZOO database that accompanies this book. The complete database is provided for you on the CD-ROM. This database uses the Open Database Connectivity (ODBC) driver to communicate with an application. ODBC is a standard from Microsoft used for connectivity. It is a standard application programming interface (API) function library. In this How-To, you will create that database on your local computer.

Steps

In order to create the database from this example, you must have the ODBC driver loaded. If PowerBuilder was installed with the sample database, you're all set. Before proceeding you may wish to ensure that you have the proper drivers available. This is accomplished using the Preference painter. There are surprisingly few steps required to create a database, but a lot of ancillary information to absorb along the way.

1. Start the Database painter. This can be done using the appropriate toolbar button. If toolbar text is turned on, the button is labeled "Database".

2. PowerBuilder connects to the current database and displays the Select Tables dialog box. Press Cancel to close this window. If PowerBuilder failed to connect to a database, either your preferences are incorrectly set or you do not have the database drivers installed.

3. Select Create Database from the File menu. PowerBuilder opens the Create Local Database dialog box. Here, you enter information regarding the database you wish to create. Click on the More>> button. The dialog box is expanded to show additional information. Figure 7-1 shows the Create Local Database dialog box, with this expanded view. Let's briefly look at the information that this dialog box uses.

● Database Name is the name of the database. In the case of a local database, this is the name of the file that will be created. Note that the extension ".DB" will be appended to the name you specify.

● User ID is the name of the database administrator. For a local database, the default is "DBA".

● Password is the DBA password and is displayed as asterisks. The default for a local database is "SQL".

● Start Command is the name of the executable file that starts the database engine. By default, this is "dbeng50w".

● Prompt for password during connect. This option specifies not to use the password supplied in the dialog box, but instead to ask the user at the time the connection is established. Note that "user" refers to you, not the end users of your applications.

Most of the items in the Database Options box are self-explanatory. The Use ANSI blank behavior CheckBox specifies whether trailing spaces are significant for comparison purposes. The default is unchecked, meaning that

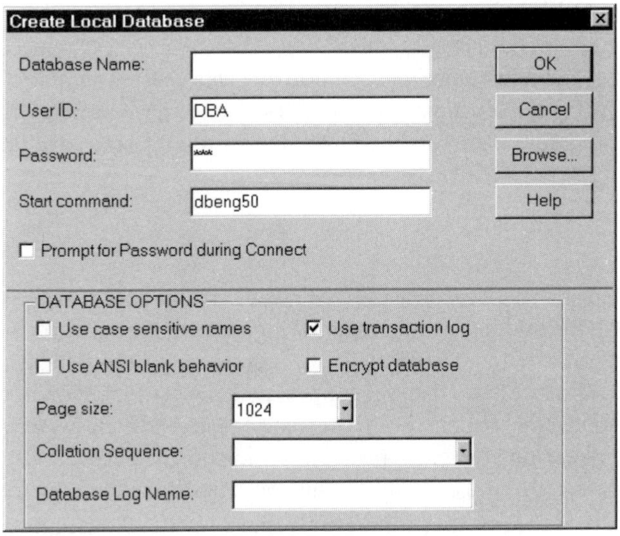

Figure 7-1 Create Local Database dialog box

blanks are significant. Page Size can be 512, 1024, 2048, or 4096 bytes. A large database should have a large page size. The default is 1024. Collation Sequence dictates how the upper 128 characters of the ASCII set are sorted. Database Log Name is the name of the transaction log file. These last two items are blank by default.

The only thing we will enter here is the database name in the first edit box. Type in "zoo2" and press the OK button. When creating a database, PowerBuilder allows you to enter the full file specification. That is, the name can consist of a valid drive and directory path. PowerBuilder will now create the requested database using the name you specified. After a few moments, you are returned to the Database painter window, and the TitleBar now displays the database name.

How It Works

When PowerBuilder needs to connect to a database, it must know which driver to load. The DBMS attribute from the Preference painter is responsible for this information. When a connection is required, PowerBuilder reads the value of DBMS and strips off all but the first three characters. It then appends the string "PB" to the front and concatenates "0x0.DLL" to the end. The "x" in the example above represents the version number of PowerBuilder. This builds a filename that PowerBuilder uses as the driver name. Therefore, if you are connecting to an ODBC database under PowerBuilder 5.0, PowerBuilder loads the driver name "PBODB050.DLL". The driver contains all necessary functions for database communication.

At the time of creation, some information is written to the ODBC.INI and PB.INI files in order to save the parameters just created. Once database creation is complete, PowerBuilder connects to that database and creates a profile entry. Profiles point to the entries in the above .INI files. To see this entry, select Connect from the File menu. You will now notice a list of available data sources (profiles), with ZOO2 checked. This checkmark indicates the database profile that PowerBuilder is currently connected to. Profiles are used by PowerBuilder to indicate a specific database setup.

Comments

When using ODBC, there is an additional layer (driver) loaded. This driver is called ODBC.DLL. ODBC.DLL is a middle layer driver allowing for vendor-independent operation. Your applications communicate with PowerBuilder's .DLL, which in turn talks to the ODBC.DLL library. Most databases support the ODBC API, but do not require it. It is used for portability reasons. For more information on the ODBC API, you are encouraged to read How-To 15.6. This How-To demonstrates how to use the API to obtain database, table, and column information. These function calls are only necessary if you intend to do very specific tasks that are not required for normal transaction processing.

COMPLEXITY
INTERMEDIATE

7.2 How do I...
Define a table and primary and foreign keys?

Problem

I have a database that my application will use and I need to create a table within that database. PowerBuilder only allows me to create a local database, but our Database Administrator set one up remotely. I am able to connect to that database. Now I just need to populate it with tables and data. I will also need to create a primary key and some foreign keys. Does PowerBuilder let me create tables in a remote database and, if so, how do I do it?

Technique

Unlike creating a database, PowerBuilder does allow you to create tables, primary keys, foreign keys, and all other table attributes for any database, whether remotely or locally installed. All of these tasks can be accomplished within the PowerBuilder environment, providing for an easy-to-use and intuitive interface. As with creating a local database, it is the job of the Database painter to fulfill these tasks.

Steps

In this How-To, an additional table is added to the ZOO database that you created in How-To 7-1. This table will track all the guests that spend their day at the zoo. It tracks the guest number, date and time of admission, the type of guest (i.e. adult, child, senior etc...), and the price they paid for admission. This table uses the data stored in the guest_type table, using the primary/foreign key relationship. Note that if you have installed the database from the CD, these tables already exist. You will either want to drop them first, create a separate database (see How-To 7.1), or create the tables presented here using a different name.

1. There are two ways to bring up the New Table interface. Regardless of the mechanism used, the interface is the same. One way is to start the Database painter and select New/Table from the Objects menu. The other way is to click on the Table toolbar icon and click New in the Select Table dialog box. Use whichever method you prefer.

2. PowerBuilder displays the Create Table sheet. Here you define each row for this table. PowerBuilder provides a scrollable window that contains six columns. These columns give you edit controls for the column name, column datatype, column width, decimal width (for numeric columns), null support, and the default column value. You can move through each edit box using the mouse or the (TAB) key. Enter the columns and related information as shown in Table 7-1.

COLUMN NAME	DATATYPE	WIDTH	DEC	NULL ALLOWED
guest_id	Numeric	5	0	No
visit_date	Date			No
visit_time	Time			No
guest_type_id	Numeric	1	0	No
amount_paid	Numeric	5	2	No

Table 7-1 Columns, data types, width, and null support for database table guests

3. Create the primary key for this table. Primary keys define the columns used to maintain uniqueness within a table. Select Table Properties... from the Edit menu and click on the Primary Key tab. This tab folder dialog box contains a horizontally scrollable control at the top of the folder showing the columns which make up the primary key. These should be empty at this point. Also on this folder is a control showing all the rows within the table. You set or modify the primary key by selecting or deselecting the columns from this control. Click on the guest_id column. This column name is displayed in the upper control. You could continue defining additional columns for the primary key by selecting them from this list. This table contains only one such column, so press the Apply button.

4. Create the foreign key for this table. Foreign keys provide referential integrity for the tables. Assume for example that a table contains information on employees. One column holds the department_id for the employee. A second table lists all of the departments within the company. If the department_id column in the employee table was a foreign key that pointed back to the department_id of the department table, the user would not be able to assign an employee to a department that was not a part of the company. It must exist in the department table first. Additionally, if the user *deletes* a department from the department table, what happens to the rows in the employee table whose value is the deleted department? The answer depends on the DBMS in use, and how PowerBuilder was instructed to handle this situation when the foreign key was established.

Click the Foreign Keys tab. This displays all foreign keys established for this table and should be blank. Press the New button to create a new foreign key. On the Foreign Key Definition dialog box that opens, enter "guest_type" in the Foreign Key Name edit box. Select the guest_type_id from the Select Columns list of columns at the bottom of the window. This specifies the column to which we want to assign a foreign key. Finally, from the Primary Key Table DropDownListBox, select table guest_type. PowerBuilder reads the primary key from that table and displays it in the Primary Key Columns list.

Some DBMSs offer support for deleting primary key columns. If your particular back end provides this support, a GroupBox labeled "On Delete Of Primary Table Row" will be visible. This GroupBox offers three RadioButtons for various options. You have the opportunity to disallow the delete, delete all dependent rows, or set the affected foreign key columns to NULL. The default is to disallow the primary key delete, which is fine. Press the OK button when you are through, followed by the OK button on the Table Properties sheet.

The remainder of the Create Table window deals with the PowerBuilder extended attributes. These attributes allow you to configure column information (on a column by column basis) when a DataWindow is created. You can, for instance, tell PowerBuilder how wide a column should be, what the default text for headers and labels are, and what the column justification should be. This information is stored in the repository. The repository is a set of five PowerBuilder system tables that are created when you create the local database, or at the time you connect to a remote database (the first time) under PowerBuilder. These attributes are read in when a DataWindow is created and stored in the DataWindow object. Therefore, once you have painted the DataWindow and some extended attributes change, the DataWindow does not reflect these changes. The real power of the extended attributes lies in the Format, Edit, and Valid DropDownListBoxes. We will explore creating these items fully in respective How-Tos later in this chapter. For now let's set some values.

5. Formats specify how the data looks on output. Several built-in choices exist. Edits dictate the style used for data input. Again, several Edit Styles are built in. Validate allows you to select a validation rule previously created. Validation rules give you the opportunity to do client side validation. How-To 7.10 explores validation rules. Notice that all of the extended attributes displayed depend on which column has been selected. To set the extended attributes, click on a column in the column list and set the various attributes accordingly. For now, refer to Table 7-2 for the columns in the guests table.

COLUMN	FORMAT	EDIT	INITIAL VALUE
guest_id	[General]	[None]	
visit_date	[None]	MM/DD/YYYY	Set To Today
visit_time	[None]	HH:MM:SS	Set To Today
guest_type_id	[General]	[None]	1
amount_paid	$#,##0.00;($#,##0.00)	###,###.00	19.95

Table 7-2 Extended attributes for guests table

6. With all of the work performed so far, the database has done absolutely *nothing*. The table and all of the attributes have been defined, but the table has not yet been created. In order to finally create the table, select Save... from the File menu. Enter a table name and press OK. After pressing the OK button on the Create New Table dialog box, PowerBuilder sends the commands to the database, which then creates the table. You are returned to the Database painter workspace and should have a table displayed as shown in Figure 7-2.

How It Works

When you create a table, PowerBuilder requires considerable work up front before it builds the actual table. All columns must be defined with a column name, datatype, width, decimal width (if appropriate), and given null value support. Any column that makes up the primary key must never support nulls. Then, you build the primary key along with any foreign key information. This table contains information to store park visitor information. Since the visit_date column tracks the date the visitor came to the park, the initial value (part of the extended attributes) was Set To Today. This tells PowerBuilder to set the value of this column to the current date. The same was done to the visit_time column, by selecting Set To Today as well. This stores the current time, since this is of type time. Since this table would be populated at the front gate as visitors arrive, applying these extended attribute values to the columns reduces user input, eliminates mistakes, and alleviates the developer from doing the same action in code. Finally, the guest_type_id is set to an initial value of 1 (indicating adult admission—our business default) and the amount paid set to $19.95 (admission price for an adult). Nothing happens with all of these settings until you save the information entered.

Comments

PowerBuilder allows for much intelligence to be built into a table, and ultimately the DataWindow. Once these extended attributes are defined and a DataWindow

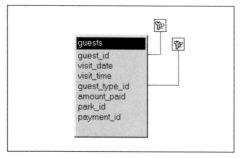

Figure 7-2 The newly created guests table with primary and foreign keys

subsequently built, all the intelligence resides locally in the DataWindow. If any extended attribute changes, you must modify the DataWindow object yourself. PowerBuilder does provide a utility to assist you in this task. The DataWindow Extended Attribute Synchronizer is this tool. You will find it installed in the PowerBuilder directory under the name DWEAS.EXE.

COMPLEXITY
BEGINNING

7.3 How do I...
Preview the data?

Problem

I would like to use the Database painter to manipulate data from some tables. I have created some tables and have been working with the extended attributes. I'd like to make sure that the primary and foreign keys are set correctly, check the initial values of new rows, verify the widths of columns, and just confirm that the data and tables are correctly set. How can I use the Database painter to preview the data?

Technique

The Database painter provides data manipulation tools that allow you to do all of the above and more. When you preview the data, the data manipulation tool retrieves all of the rows of a table into a runtime DataWindow, providing for a development time view of data. In addition, there are facilities for importing (see How-To 7.4), filtering, sorting, insertion, and deletion of data table rows. The Database painter gives you the ability to select a table and view the data stored within it.

Steps

1. Start the Database painter. When PowerBuilder displays the Select Tables dialog box, click on the table(s) you wish to preview. Select the employee and guests tables. Once the tables have been selected, press the Open button.

2. Select the table you wish to view by clicking on it. For now, select the employee table. To display the data, select Data Manipulation from the Objects menu. This is a cascading menu and allows you to select one of several presentation styles. These are the same as the DataWindow presentation styles chosen when you paint a DataWindow. To give you a better view of the data, the Grid or Tabular styles are a better choice than Freeform. Freeform displays the rows one per page, while the others display many rows, allowing for a more complete display of data. PowerBuilder builds a DataWindow and displays all of the columns and rows in the table. There is no way to limit the columns that display, but you are able to limit the rows, as outlined in the next step. If the retrieval is lengthy, you may press the Cancel button on the Database painter's toolbar. This button is a picture of a red hand and is only active while the retrieval is in process.

3. Once the retrieval is complete (either a full retrieval or the retrieval has been canceled), you can sort or filter the data presented. The Rows menu provides these capabilities. This data now resides on the client. In other words, all rows sent now exist on the client workstation, and any manipulation is done on the client machine. From the Rows menu, select Sort. PowerBuilder displays the Specify Sort Columns dialog box as shown in Figure 7-3. To specify a sort criteria, drag a column from the left hand ListBox to the right hand ListBox. Optionally, you can define a descending sort by turning off the associated CheckBox. Indicate a descending sort on the start_dt column.

4. PowerBuilder also allows the data to be filtered. Again from the Rows menu, select Filter. The Specify Filter dialog displays. Filter criteria takes the form *column RelationalOperator value* such as emp_salary > 30000. This criteria can be typed in or painted using the various ListBoxes in this dialog. Functions are also available for specialized filtering. Provide a filter to show only employees whose start date is less than 90 days ago using the following expression. The completed dialog box is shown in Figure 7-4. This shows just the employees who are still under the company's probationary time period.

```
daysafter(  start_dt , today() ) <= 90
```

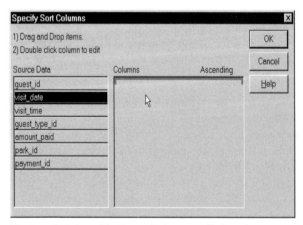

Figure 7-3 Specify Sort Columns dialog box
with drag in progress

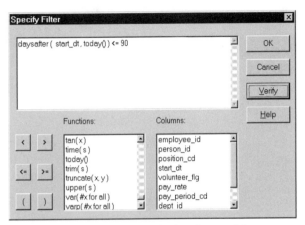

Figure 7-4 Specify Filter dialog box with completed filter criteria

5. The previewed rows may be deleted. Click on a row and select Delete from the Rows menu.

6. Finally, you can insert rows to this DataWindow by selecting Insert from the Rows menu. If any of the columns have an initial value assigned to them (as discussed in How-To 7.2), you will see those columns automatically populate with that data as the new row is inserted.

7. Update the table by selecting Save Changes to Database from the File menu.

How It Works

When previewing data, PowerBuilder displays a DataWindow that is used to manipulate that data. Previewing submits a SELECT * from *tablename* to the database and retrieves all of the rows and columns from that table. Filtering, sorting, inserts, deletes, and imports (as discussed in How-To 7.4) are all performed on the client machine. Any changes made to the DataWindow are then submitted to the database if desired.

Comments

The grid presentation style is the best choice for previewing data, as the user is allowed to size columns, move columns, and split the DataWindow horizontally. It gives you flexibility not offered in the other presentation styles. PowerBuilder also provides the developer with a great number of functions for filtering this data. All of the techniques and options available here are also available in PowerScript at runtime, affording you the ability to pass these features on to your users.

COMPLEXITY
BEGINNING

7.4   How do I...
Import and export data?

Problem

I have a table in my database and some text files with data from other sources. I would like to import that data into my database table. Also, my database contains data that I would like to use in other applications; I'd like to export that data. How can I import and export the data, and what file types are supported for each?

Technique

The Database painter provides the capability for data import and export. It is also possible to do import and export through PowerScript code for modifying tables at runtime. However, since this chapter deals with the Database painter, the PowerScript equivalents are not examined here. For import, only two file types are supported. These are tab delimited text (.TXT) and DBase II or III (.DBF) file types. However, 12 different export formats are supported, including .TXT, .DBF, .XLS, as well as SQL Syntax. In this How-To, you will import data into the guests table created in How-To 7.2, modify the data in the Database painter, and export it to various file types.

Steps

1. Start the Database painter. Be sure you connect to the sample ZOO database that accompanies this book. If this is not the current database, connect to it using the profile in the File/Connect menu item.

2. Once PowerBuilder connects, the Select Tables dialog box displays. Select the guests table and press the Open button to open the table and close the dialog box. If you have not completed How-To 7-2, you won't have this table in your database.

3. Data import and export is controlled by the Data Manipulation tool. Click on the Preview button from the toolbar or select Data Manipulation from the Objects menu. PowerBuilder creates a window, retrieves the data from the table, and displays the data in a DataWindow.

4. Import a text file by selecting Import from the Rows menu. By default, PowerBuilder lists all the .TXT files in the current directory. You can change this list to .DBF files from the List Files of Type dropdown on the Select Import File dialog box. One tab delimited file called GUESTS.TXT is provided. Click on this file and press the OK button. PowerBuilder loads the text file into the DataWindow.

5. Save the changes back to the database by selecting Save Changes to Database from the File menu.

6. Now, modify some values, or insert or delete some rows. While doing this, verify that the guest_id column remains unique as this is the primary key for this table.

7. 7. Save the changes again to the database.

8. Now, let's export the data to another file type. Select Save Rows As... from the File menu. PowerBuilder displays the Save Rows As... dialog box. Twelve file types are supported. Click on the appropriate RadioButton to set the file type and type the desired file name into the edit box. When entering the filename, ensure the proper file extension is maintained. One option of note on this window is the SQL Syntax option. This will save the data in a SQL script with the necessary insert and update statements. This script may later be utilized to build the data set. The Include Headers Checkbox is required for files with the .DBF extension, since this file type has a header used to describe the file. Select Text, name the file GUESTS2.TXT and press the OK button. PowerBuilder creates the file and exports the data to it.

How It Works

The Database painter acts as a graphical tool with which you can manipulate the back end data. When previewing the data, PowerBuilder creates a runtime DataWindow that retrieves data and allows for manipulation of that data. When the retrieval is performed, it selects every column and every row from the table. From the Rows menu you can filter data based on specified criteria. This option was examined in How-To 7.3. When you import data, the file must be of the same structure as the table. Importing and exporting is done on a table by table basis. Joins are not allowed and exporting from or importing to multiple tables is not supported.

Comments

Import and export capabilities provide an easy way to populate tables with data from other applications and provide users of other applications with data from your database. This is useful when porting from older systems to a new PowerBuilder application and for allowing users to manipulate data in a tool with which they are familiar. For example, users may wish to take data from the database, import it into a spreadsheet program, and perform what-if analysis. PowerBuilder supports a wide variety of export file types and two common import types. The tab delimited ASCII file type is supported by virtually every tool that allows exports and, therefore, is a common thread in data exchange.

7.5 How do I...
Create a view?

Problem

I have a large, complex query that I would like to create and use in several DataWindows. This query joins several tables and I don't want to worry about the structure of these underlying tables. Can I create one simple view based on a complex combination of tables? This would make data access simpler.

Technique

A *view* is a technique where several tables are combined logically into one unit that appears to be another table. This allows the various tables to be combined and seen as a whole. If your underlying SQL statement is complex, there are many tables involved, or you need to abstract the physical appearance of the data, you can create a view to simplify data access.

Steps

The Zoo database contains four tables that are of interest in creating a view. These four tables contain information pertaining to employees, departments, positions, and persons. The tables are normalized into third normal form. The view that you will build here combines these tables into one, allowing for selection of data relative to an employee, his or her department name, salary, starting date, and position. This gives you one place to go for important employee-related information instead of creating a four-table join each time the information is needed.

1. Start the Database painter. When PowerBuilder displays the Select Tables dialog box, press Cancel.

2. From the Objects menu, select New. This is a cascading menu. From the second level menu, select View. PowerBuilder starts a painter that looks very much like the DataWindow painter and displays the Select Tables dialog box again. From this dialog, select the four tables department, employee, person, and position, and press the Open button. PowerBuilder opens these tables and allows you to select columns, a sort order, a where clause, groups, a having clause, and computed columns. Select the columns from the respective tables as shown in Table 7-3. The order in which you select the columns is important, as this order will match the order in which the columns are presented when the data is previewed. Select any order that makes sense to you.

TABLE	COLUMN
department	dept_desc
employee	start_dt
	pay_rate
person	first_name
	last_name
	phone_nbr
position	postion_desc

Table 7-3 Tables and columns in the person_view view entity

3. Click on the Sort tab from the toolbox. Drag the employee.start_dt column to the sort box on the right hand side. Click the Ascending Checkbox to turn it off and make a descending sort. Just as in the DataWindow painter, you can include an Order by, Where, computed columns, Group by, and Having clauses. This view does not implement those options.

4. Select Return to Database painter from the File menu. At this time, PowerBuilder opens the Save View Definition dialog box. Here, you must give the view a name. This name will show up along with the table names later when you open tables (either from the Database painter or DataWindow painter). Name this view "person_view" and press Create. You now have a view of the employee information sorted by the employee's starting date. This view shows the most recent employees first (descending sort). PowerBuilder generates the following SQL statement and submits to the database.

```
CREATE VIEW "person_view"
    ( "first_name",
      "last_name",
      "phone_nbr",
      "start_dt",
      "pay_rate",
      "position_desc",
      "dept_dsc" ) AS
  SELECT   "person"."first_name",
           "person"."last_name",
           "person"."phone_nbr",
           "employee"."start_dt",
           "employee"."pay_rate",
           "position"."position_desc",
           "department"."dept_dsc"
    FROM   "department",
           "employee",
           "person",
           "position"
   WHERE   ( "person"."person_id" = "employee"."person_id" ) and
           ( "position"."position_cd" = "employee"."position_cd" ) and
           ( "department"."dept_id" = "position"."dept_id" )
```

5. Preview the data and notice that it looks as if the data is coming from one table.

How It Works

A view is another database entity, like a table, that is maintained at the back end. When you define a view, you are creating this entity on the database and formulating the SELECT statement necessary to access those particular columns or rows. When you select data from the view, the database handles the details required to access the various tables and columns in the view definition. This makes it easy to extract typically difficult result sets. Creation of views is usually the responsibility of the database administrator. They are a tool that can be utilized to abstract the details of the database or make complex selects easier on the developer.

Comments

There are several uses for a view and simplified data access is only one of them. Views allow for data abstraction (you need not care what the underlying structure of the tables are), provide a security mechanism, and can limit access to particular columns of a table. But, there is another powerful use for them if you are fortunate enough to be using a database that supports this last concept. DataWindows only allow you to update a single table. If multiple tables require updating from the same DataWindow, you must play some tricks with the update characteristics of the DataWindow object. At times, this requires considerable code. Some DBMS's support views that may be updated. SQL AnyWhere is not one of them. Check the documentation for your particular database. If your database supports this concept, it is a powerful way to allow multiple table updates from a DataWindow. Using this technique, build a view and use this view as the basis for the data source when creating a DataWindow. Then, using the Update dialog box within the DataWindow painter indicate which columns in the view to update. PowerBuilder will take care of the rest.

COMPLEXITY
INTERMEDIATE

7.6 How do I...
Save changes to a change log?

Problem

I have a table whose structure I need to change and I would like to document the changes that are necessary. Additionally, I don't want the changes to occur immediately as they need to be put off until a time when all of the users or developers have logged off the database. Can I indicate my changes now and actually perform the changes at a later time?

Technique

PowerBuilder supplies an activity log capable of recording all change activity to a table or view. This activity log will also record the syntax of a table, thereby allowing you to save the table syntax to a log file. This log file is a standard SQL script that you can later submit to the database or to another database for table or data replication. As far as table replication is concerned, PowerBuilder provides the *data pipeline*, which is a more suitable tool for this purpose. You can use the activity log to document changes made over time.

Steps

In this How-To, you will modify a table, adding two additional columns. This How-To does not change the table immediately, but will instead save the indicated modifications to the activity log. This log will later be used to perform the actual modification to the table.

1. Start the Database painter and open the guests table. Once the table displays in the painter workspace, double-click on it to open the Create/Alter Table painter.

2. The Create/Alter Table painter is identical to that seen in How-To 7.2, with a couple of exceptions. Of note is the fact that datatype and null value DropDown boxes are disabled. These are the only parts of the database that may not be changed. In addition, any new columns you add must allow null values. Use this painter to add two columns to the guests table. These columns and their settings are shown in Table 7-4.

COLUMN NAME	TYPE	WIDTH	DEC	NULL
park_id	numeric	1	0	Yes
payment_id	numeric	1	0	Yes

Table 7-4 New columns, types and widths for guests table

3. Modify the foreign key to set dependent rows to null. Select Table Properties... from the Edit menu and click on the Foreign Keys tab in the resulting dialog box. Select the guest_type key and click Edit. Once the Foreign Key Definition dialog appears, click on the Delete any Dependent Rows (CASCADE) RadioButton in the On Delete of Primary Table Row GroupBox. Press OK to close this dialog box and choose the Apply button, followed by the OK button in the Table Properties dialog.

4. From the Create/Alter Table painter, select Syntax from the View menu. PowerBuilder converts the changes made thus far to an SQL statement. This SQL statement is shown below. Notice that PowerBuilder will not only makes changes to the table in question, but also to the repository (PBCATxxx) tables.

```
ALTER TABLE "dba"."guests" ADD "park_id" numeric(1,0),
        ADD "payment_id" numeric(1,0);

ALTER TABLE "dba"."guests"
        DELETE FOREIGN KEY guest_type;

ALTER TABLE "dba"."guests"
        ADD FOREIGN KEY guest_type ("guest_type_id"
        ) REFERENCES "dba"."guest_type"
        ON DELETE  CASCADE;


update   "dba".pbcattbl set
        pbd_fhgt = -10,pbd_fwgt = 400 ,pbd_fitl = 'N',pbd_funl = 'N',
        pbd_fchr = 0,pbd_fptc = 34,pbd_ffce = 'Arial',pbh_fhgt = -10,
        pbh_fwgt = 400 ,pbh_fitl = 'N',pbh_funl = 'N',pbh_fchr = 0,
        pbh_fptc = 34,pbh_ffce = 'Arial',pbl_fhgt = -10,pbl_fwgt = 400 ,
        pbl_fitl = 'N',pbl_funl = 'N',pbl_fchr = 0,pbl_fptc = 34,
        pbl_ffce = 'Arial',pbt_cmnt = NULL
        where pbt_tnam = 'guests'  and pbt_ownr = 'dba';

insert into "dba".pbcatcol
        (pbc_tnam,pbc_ownr,pbc_cnam,pbc_labl,pbc_lpos,pbc_hdr,pbc_hpos,
        pbc_jtfy,pbc_case,pbc_hght,pbc_wdth,pbc_bmap)
        values
        ('guests','dba','park_id','Park Id:',23 ,'Park Id',25,
        24 ,26 ,65 ,275 ,'N');

insert into "dba".pbcatcol

(pbc_tnam,pbc_ownr,pbc_cnam,pbc_labl,pbc_lpos,pbc_hdr,pbc_hpos,pbc_jtfy,
        pbc_case,pbc_hght,pbc_wdth,pbc_bmap)
        values
        ('guests','dba','payment_id','Payment Id:',23 ,'Payment Id',25,24
,26 ,65 ,275 ,'N');
```

5. Save the log file. Select Save As from the File menu and save it using the name GUESTLOG.SQL. This file can later be executed, which you will see in the next How-To.

How It Works

As modifications are made to a table, PowerBuilder tracks these changes in a log and will not perform any action until you save those changes. At this point, any changes made are submitted to the database and the changes take effect. If you want to capture the SQL statement created, you must convert the changes to SQL format and save this statement in a log file.

Comments

If you want to make the changes online and capture the SQL statement, you can turn on the log before opening the Create/Alter Table painter. This option is available under Start/Stop Log from the Options menu of the Database painter. Once the log has been started, all modifications are written to it. To stop the logging choose Start/Stop Log again. It is a toggle, as the log is either on or off. You may clear the log contents using the Clear Log option from the Options menu. Log files are particularly useful if you wish to document the changes that have been made to the database or you need to perform some alterations to the tables and want to delay the implementation to a later time.

COMPLEXITY
BEGINNING

7.7 How do I...
Execute an SQL script?

Problem

I have saved modifications of a table to a change log and would like to execute that SQL script to actually modify the tables. How do I do this and what else can I do with SQL statements in PowerBuilder?

Technique

Among the other tools provided in the Database painter is the Administration tool or DBA Notepad. This tool affords the ability to submit virtually any SQL statement to the database. These statements include data description language (DDL) or data manipulation language (DML) statements and may be typed in directly or loaded from an existing file. Most SQL statements are supported. One thing that cannot be performed is creating a remote database.

Steps

In this How-To, you will load and execute the change log created in How-To 7-6. This change log is a modification to the guests table and includes the addition of two columns and a change to the foreign key to delete dependent columns. Other SQL statements are also explored.

1. Start the Database painter. When the Select Tables dialog box appears, press Cancel.

2. Start the DBA Notepad. This is accomplished either through the appropriate toolbar button or by selecting Database Administration from the Objects menu.

3. Using the Open item from the File menu, load the GUESTLOG.SQL file created in How-To 7.6. PowerBuilder displays the file in the painter's workspace. If you have not done How-To 7.6, you can still load the file from the accompanying CD-ROM.

4. Execute the current statement. This is done in one of three ways, each producing the same results. Select Execute SQL from the Objects menu. Pressing CTRL-U or using the toolbar item labeled Execute are the other methods. The table is altered based on the statements in the change log.

5. From the File menu, select New to clear the Administrator notepad. Type in the following SQL statement and execute it. This SQL statement lists the amount received by date for each of the different guest types.

```
SELECT visit_date, guest_type_desc, sum(amount_paid)
FROM guests, guest_type
WHERE guests.guest_type_id = guest_type.guest_type_id
GROUP BY visit_date, guest_type_desc;
```

6. Now, instead of typing in an SQL statement, let's graphically paint one. Again, clear the Notepad workspace. PowerBuilder asks if you want to save changes to the script. Feel free to save the statement if you want, but it will no longer be used in this How-To. Select Paste SQL from the Edit menu (or press CTRL-Q). The SQL Statement Type dialog shown in Figure 7-5 displays. Choose Select by double-clicking on the appropriate icon.

PowerBuilder opens a painter that resembles that of the View painter seen in How-To 7.5 and displays the Select Table dialog box. Click on the employee and person tables and press Open. The tables open and display just as in the View painter. From the tables, click on the first name, last name, city, state, and pay rate columns. Provide a descending sort order by selecting the Sort tab and dragging the pay_rate column to the sort list. Return to the Administrator by selecting Return to Database Administration from the File menu. PowerBuilder pastes the resulting SQL statement into the Notepad as shown below. Execute this script and close the Administration tool.

```
SELECT "person"."first_name",
       "person"."last_name",
       "person"."city",
       "person"."state_cd",
       "person"."zip_cd",
       "employee"."pay_rate"
  FROM "employee",
       "person"
 WHERE ( "person"."person_id" = "employee"."person_id" )
ORDER BY "employee"."pay_rate" DESC  ;
```

Figure 7-5 Statement Type dialog box

How It Works

The Administration tool is simply a buffer that holds text. When you select the Execute option, PowerBuilder submits the text to the database and displays the result set. Once the database returns the result set, PowerBuilder displays the rows in a DataWindow, as shown in How-To 7.3 where you learned how to preview data. These examples have dealt with both DML and DDL statements. In the first example, the script contained ALTER TABLE statements that modify the underlying properties of a table. CREATE TABLE, DROP KEY, or CREATE INDEX are all examples of data description language (DDL) statements that you could execute from the Administration tool. The last two examples used SELECT statements to manipulate the data within those tables. Additionally, INSERT, UPDATE, and DELETE statements could be sent to the table as well. These are examples of data manipulation language (DML).

Comments

Notice that each of the statements ends with a semi-colon (;). This is the standard SQL termination character and is required by the Administration tool. Leaving it off causes an error when you submit the statement to the database. You can change this termination character using the Preference painter under the Database section. PowerBuilder makes things as simple as possible by allowing you to enter statements by hand, load them from an existing script, or paint them, depending on which technique you are most comfortable with.

COMPLEXITY
BEGINNING

7.8 How do I...
Create display formats?

Problem

When I preview the data in my tables, some columns don't display the way I want them to. My tables store phone numbers, social security numbers, salaries, and other types of data that the user is accustomed to seeing in a special format. I don't want to store these special characters with the data as this seems an inefficient use of disk space and retrieval time. How can I tell PowerBuilder to display these columns in a particular format?

Technique

What you've described is the purpose of a display format. PowerBuilder has many display formats available right out of the box that are useful for formatting certain types of data. It also provides the option of creating your own display formats as well. Once a format exists, you tell the table to use it whenever it displays a certain column. Display formats are created once and used for any column with the data type that the format supports.

Steps

This How-To describes the process of creating a display format for a phone number column. Then the format is linked with a column in the employee table. Since display formats are not specific to any one column, you can use this anywhere you wish to display phone numbers in this format. Creating display formats is the responsibility of the Database painter.

1. Start the Database painter but do not open any tables.

2. Select Display Format Maintenance from the Objects menu. PowerBuilder opens the Display Formats dialog box shown in Figure 7-6. This lists all available formats for all data types. Click on the New button to create a user defined format. The Display Format Definition dialog of Figure 7-7 opens.

3. The new format requires a name. Since this new format will be used for phone numbers, type "phone" (without the quote marks) in the Name edit

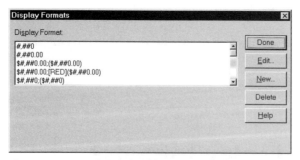

Figure 7-6 Display Formats dialog box

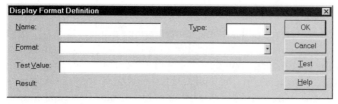

Figure 7-7 Display Format Definition dialog box

box. In the zoo database, phone numbers are a character data type, so select String from the Type DropDownListBox.

4. In the Format edit box, enter @@@-@@@@. This specifies the format string used to display the data. The format depends on the data type of the column. In general, the formats are specified in pieces, with each piece separated by semicolons. This allows formats to behave differently depending on the value. For example, formats for a number can vary depending on the sign of the number. The first piece of the format is required, other pieces are optional. Table 7-5 shows the construction of the pieces of the format for the various data types. Items within braces ({}) are optional. Table 7-6 shows the various formatting characters based on data type.

DATA TYPE	GENERAL FORMAT STRING
String	string{; null_format}
Number	positive {; negative_format {; zero_format{; null_format }}}
Date	date {;null_format}
Time	time {; null_format }

Table 7-5 Format strings for Display Formats

DATA TYPE	CHARACTER	MEANING
String	@	Replaces any character
	' '(quotes)	Display items between quotes
	\	Special character. \[displays [
Number	#	Number
	0	Zero if number does not exist. Used for trailing zeros
	$, . %, space	Literal character
	\	Special character
Date	-, \, space	Literal character
	d	Day number without leading zero
	dd	Day number with leading zero if necessary
	ddd	Three character day name abbreviation
	dddd	Full day name
	m	Month number without leading zero
	mm	Month number with leading zero if necessary
	mmm	Three character month name abbreviation
	mmmm	Full month name
	yy	Two digit year
	yyyy	Four digit year

continued on next page

continued from previous page

DATA TYPE	CHARACTER	MEANING
Time	:, /, space	Literal character
	" (quotes)	Any string between quotes
	\	Special character
	h	Hour with no leading zero
	hh	Hour with leading zero if necessary
	m	Minute without leading zero
	mm	Minute with leading zero if necessary
	s	Second without leading zero
	ss	Second with leading zero
	f, ff, fff, ffff, fffff, ffffff	Fractions of a second. Must follow s format
	AM, am, PM, pm	AM or PM (in specified case) depending on time
	A, a, P, p	A or P (in specified case) depending on time

Table 7-6 Format characters of different data types

5. Enter a sample phone number in the Test Value edit box and press the Test button to verify the format. Press OK when the format is complete and then click Done from the Display Formats dialog. Table 7-7 lists some common display formats.

FORMAT	MEANING	EXAMPLE	DATA TYPE
###-##-####	Social Security Number	123-45-6789	Number
$#,##0.00;($#,##0.00)	Dollar value w/ trailing 0	$4.00 or ($4.00) if neg	Number
(###) ##-####	Phone with area code	(800) 555-8289	Number
dddd, mmm dd, yyyy	Full spelled out date	Monday, Jan 01, 1999	Date
h:mm AM/PM	Time with AM/PM	10:24 PM	Time
mm/dd/yy hh:mm	Date and time	01/24/1999 01:52	DateTime

Table 7-7 Common display formats

6. Alter a table to use this new display format. Select Tables from the Objects menu. Open the person table. Double-click on the table and select the phone_nbr column. Use this format in the format for a column by selecting it from the Format DropDownListBox.

How It Works

The information about the display format is stored in the PowerBuilder repository table pbcatfmt. When data is retrieved from the Database painter, PowerBuilder reads this repository table (along with others) and formats the data accordingly. Additionally, when you build a DataWindow, PowerBuilder also reads this repository table, and its information becomes part of the DataWindow syntax. In other words, display format information is built into any subsequently built DataWindow. Doing so speeds up retrieval, since the format information does not need to be read from the database each time the DataWindow is accessed.

Comments

Any DataWindow that you create from this point forward will use this display format on that column. If the format is changed later, or the table is altered in the future, any existing DataWindow will not change. You can either rebuild the DataWindow or use the Synchronize PB Attributes option from the Options menu. Formats for DateTime are just an extension of the Data and Time data types.

COMPLEXITY
INTERMEDIATE

7.9 How do I...
Create edit styles

Problem

My DataWindows look flat and I'd like to spice up their appearance. I have created format styles that I have tied to my tables. When the data is retrieved, everything looks fine. However, when I click on a column that is using a format, the format goes away and the data in the current column appears as though there is no format style. What is going on and how can I correct this?

Technique

To spice up its appearance, your data requires an edit style. While a display format controls the look of data output, an edit style controls the input of data. Edit styles come in six different varieties depending on the specifics of your data. You may choose to present data to the user as a DropDownListBox, CheckBox, RadioButtons, Edits, EditMasks, or DropDownDataWindows. If a column contains a TRUE/FALSE, Yes/No or other Boolean type, a CheckBox would be an appropriate choice. If it can only be one of several predefined values, RadioButtons or a ListBox might be used. Most of these choices are for static data; that is, data that is known at development time and is not likely to change. If the column value is dynamic, where valid choices for the user may come and go, the DropDownDataWindow makes the most sense. This How-To describes the process necessary for creating any kind of edit style.

Steps

In How-To 7.7, you modified the guests table to include park_id and payment_id columns. These were both numeric types, one digit wide. The idea here is to store single digits to represent various park locations or payment methods. If the design called for payment_id to be a 1 for cash; 2, 3, 4, or 5 for various credit cards, and 6 for free pass, the user would be required to enter those values upon inserting a new row. This is certainly not a friendly interface. In this How-To, two different edit styles are used to make the interface more intuitive.

1. Start the Database painter. Open the guests table when the Select Tables dialog appears. Although it is not required for you to open a table to create an edit style, you will modify the guests table later in order to use the new edit styles created here.

2. Select Edit Style Maintenance from the Objects menu. PowerBuilder displays the Edit Styles dialog box shown in Figure 7-8. All existing edit styles are listed, showing the name and style type icon. The first edit style you will create will be a DropDownListBox. To do this, click the New... button. PowerBuilder opens the Edit Style dialog box. Select DropDownListBox from the Style dropdown.

3. Give this edit style the name payment_type. The dialog box lists all the properties available for an edit style. The most important aspect of this style

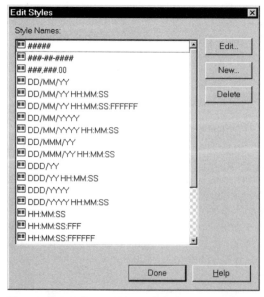

Figure 7-8 Edit Styles dialog box showing available edit styles

is what's called a *code table*. Code tables allow you to display one thing to the user, while storing something different in the database table. The code table for a DropDownListBox is shown with the double column edit boxes at the bottom of this dialog. Give this edit style the properties shown in Table 7-8, and the code table shown in Table 7-9. Press the OK button upon completion. Figure 7-9 shows the completed dialog box.

PROPERTY	VALUE
Name	payment_type
Sorted	TRUE
Vert Scroll Bar	TRUE
Always Show Arrow	TRUE

Table 7-8 Properties for Edit Style payment_type

DISPLAY VALUE	DATA VALUE
Cash	1
Visa	2
MasterCard	3
American Express	4
Discover	5
Complimentary Pass	6

Table 7-9 Code table for payment_type

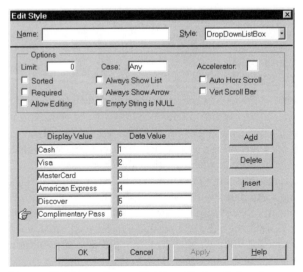

Figure 7-9 DropDownListBox Style dialog box

4. PowerBuilder adds the new edit style to the list. Notice the icon displayed to the left to indicate the type of edit style. Create a second edit style. This time use the RadioButton style with the properties of Table 7-10 and provide a code table as shown in Table 7-11.

ATTRIBUTE	VALUE
Name	parks
Columns Across	2

Table 7-10 Attributes for parks

DISPLAY VALUE	DATA VALUE
Los Angeles	1
Boston	2
Orlando	3
Dallas	4

Table 7-11 Code table for parks Edit Style

5. Open the Create/Alter Table painter for the guests table by double-clicking on that table. Using the extended attributes at the bottom of the painter, assign the edit style payment_type to the payment_id column and parks to the park_id column. Since the data will be displayed differently than before, it is necessary to change the size of the columns. For the payment_id column, make the width 1.5. The park_id column should have a height of 0.35 and a width of 2. Alter the table by selecting Save from the File menu and preview the data.

How It Works

Edit styles are used to determine the look of the data for input. When an edit style is placed on a column, PowerBuilder inserts a reference into the pbcatedt repository table. Then, as a column comes into focus for which an edit style is defined, the associated code table is presented to the user. When the user indicates a value, the code table uses the data value from that table for the value in the associated column. This allows you to create tables whose columns are based on numeric data, but which present something meaningful to the user. In cases where you have a format mask (such as the phone number example in How-To 7.8), you will probably want to create an edit style as well, since the edit mask overrides the format when the column has focus. Any time the user will type data from the keyboard, the edit style should be an edit mask (one of the six edit styles). Edit masks are like format masks in the type of data they will accept.

Comments

Edit styles come in any of six varieties. In the examples given here, the associated code tables are fairly static. It is unlikely that other parks or payment methods would be added on a continual basis. If, however, the data in the code table may change frequently, an edit style of DropDownDataWindow may be more appropriate. DropDownDataWindows look and work just like DropDownListBoxes, but the data is populated from a database table instead of being hard coded into the style. This type of edit style is crucial in applications where changes to table data are paramount.

COMPLEXITY
INTERMEDIATE

7.10 How do I...
Create validation rules?

Problem

My users will be entering data and I must validate it before the database sees it. I want to do some "on the fly" validation and prevent the user from continuing if he or she enters incorrect data. Since PowerBuilder is a client/server environment and all the data exists locally on the user's machine, how can I perform this type of client sided data validation?

Technique

Along with format and edit styles, PowerBuilder supplies capabilities to do client sided validation. Though no predefined validation rules are supplied with PowerBuilder, the Database painter makes it easy to create your own. These rules are stored in the pbcatvld repository tables, which provide a place in which to put some basic business rules. While in the Database painter preview mode, or DataWindow, the validation rules will fire as the user modifies data in a column to which it is bound.

Steps

This How-To shows you how to create two validation rules. One ensures that a numeric value must be less than 100,000; the other verifies that a date must not be in the future. The first of these would be handy for employee salary, if your company policy states that no one is allowed to make more than that amount. In the second case, the date rule will be bound to our guests table to ensure that the visit_date column is never in the future. (It will allow past dates to be entered.)

1. Start the Database painter. Connect to the Zoo database. This database has been provided on the accompanying CD-ROM and should be installed on your hard drive. Open the employee and guests tables. Although not required at this point, these tables will be used later to attach the validation rules to.

2. Select Validation Maintenance from the Objects menu. PowerBuilder displays the Validation Rules dialog which is probably empty. Press the New button to start building a new rule.

3. The Validation Rule dialog box is where you define the specifics of the rule. Figure 7-10 shows the completed salary rule definition. Give this rule the settings shown in Table 7-12. Validation rules must have a name by which they are referred. The Rule Definition here specifies that the value must be less than or equal to 100,000. The @col identifier is a placeholder that means "the value in the current column". Finally, the error message is a string that PowerBuilder will display if the rule is violated. The quotation marks are required, since this is a string value. Press OK to close the dialog box.

PROPERTY	VALUE
Name	salary
Type	number
Rule Definition	@col <= 100000
Validation Error Message	"Values for this column must be less than or equal to $100,000."
Name	future_date
Type	date
Rule Definition	@col <= Today()
Validation Error Message	"Future dates are not allowed."

Table 7-12 Properties for the salary and date validation rules

4. Create a new rule for the date. Give the new rule the properties shown in Table 7-12. This rule verifies that a date is not in the future.

5. Attach these new validation rules to a database column. Double-click on the guests table. From the Create/Alter Table painter, click on the visit_date column and select future_date from the Validation DropDownListBox. Select Save from the File menu to modify the table. Do the same for the employee table, using pay_rate as the column and the salary validation rule.

6. Preview the data and enter an invalid value for both of the columns. PowerBuilder will not let the user enter bad data into a DataWindow column that uses a validation rule.

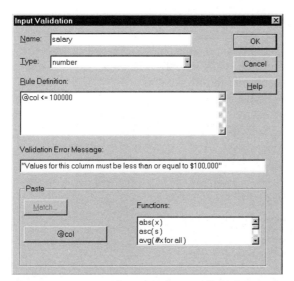

Figure 7-10 Completed Salary Validation Rule definition

How It Works

The validation rules are stored in the pbcatvld repository table. This table is used when new data is entered in a column that has a bound validation rule. When a DataWindow is created, these validation rules are read in and stored with the DataWindow object. When data is entered into a column containing a validation rule, that rule is applied to the newly entered data. If it fails, the developer-entered error message is displayed to the user. As with any setting in your applications, PowerBuilder allows the developer to override any validation rule supplied by the database. This is done on a column by column basis in PowerScript, through the ItemError event of a DataWindow control. Validation rules are meant to handle the majority of column value errors. However, rules were meant to be broken and PowerScript allows you to do just that.

Comments

There are two basic lines of defense in regards to data validation. The first is through the use of edit styles. Using various styles such as DropDownListBoxes or RadioButtons eliminates much of the potential for error. However, there are times when this is not enough, as the user must enter data by hand. When this is the case, validation rules extend the ability to the next level. Validation rules are not perfect. They are a front line means of defense. All data entered on the client must pass these rules if the database defines them. It gives the application the ability to ensure that data in a DataWindow is as close to valid as can be reasonably assumed. Validation rules can become far more complex than presented here. In the rule definition, the statement must evaluate to a Boolean (TRUE/FALSE) value. It is possible to create a validation rule that is based on the return value of a user defined function. Chapter 14 covers user defined functions, so don't limit yourself to the examples provided here. As with many areas in PowerBuilder development, the only limit is that of your imagination.

CHAPTER 8

DATABASE PROGRAMMING

8

DATABASE PROGRAMMING

How do I...

8.1 **Connect my application to a database?**

8.2 **Use embedded SQL?**

8.3 **Use dynamic SQL?**

8.4 **Query the system catalog at runtime regardless of the DBMS?**

PowerBuilder's extensive database capabilities set it apart from other graphically-based development tools. In addition to providing you with easy-to-use database management features (which are covered in Chapter 7), PowerBuilder also offers a wide variety of programming mechanisms to interact with the database. This chapter concentrates on the essentials of PowerBuilder database programming by introducing the basics of connecting to one or more databases and using some of the more advanced features of your server. PowerBuilder's abilities do not end with these topics, however. For more information on PowerBuilder's other database component, the DataWindow, refer to Chapters 9 through 12.

8.1 Connect My Application to a Database

In order for your application to obtain data from a database, it must first be able to communicate with the database. This How-To demonstrates the essential concept of connecting to a database and discusses the available connection options. Information on connecting to multiple databases simultaneously is also provided.

8.2 Use Embedded SQL

One of the methods available for manipulating a database is embedded SQL, a PowerBuilder mechanism for placing SQL statements directly into your scripts. This How-To shows you how to read and write data that is in your database using embedded SQL. As part of this exercise, you will learn how to make use of cursors to transmit multiple database rows to your application.

8.3 Use Dynamic SQL

While embedded SQL is one method of manipulating a database, it has limitations in several areas. Specifically, embedded SQL cannot modify database structures, manipulate user permissions, or issue queries that are not fully known at design time. To bypass these restrictions, PowerBuilder offers a more complex variant of embedded SQL called *dynamic SQL*. This How-To contains several examples of dynamic SQL that illustrate the major uses of this PowerBuilder feature.

8.4 Query the System Catalog at Runtime Regardless of the DBMS

Many applications have the need to query the database's system catalog at runtime to obtain descriptions of the current database configuration. The catalog describes all database objects including tables, columns, keys, and indexes. However, DBMSs vary in their system catalog structure which makes obtaining catalog information difficult. This How-To introduces techniques that allow you to query the PowerBuilder repository to obtain the needed information. By avoiding the DBMS system catalog, your program will easily adapt to the different DBMSs it might use.

COMPLEXITY
INTERMEDIATE

8.1 How do I...
Connect my application to a database?

Problem

I need my PowerBuilder application to communicate with a database, but I can't figure out how. I read the manuals, but I'm still unclear as to what my program should do to initiate communication. How do I connect my application to the database?

Technique

PowerBuilder's mechanism for communicating with a database is based on a nonvisual *transaction object*. The transaction object contains properties, listed in Table 8-1, that allow you to specify all of the information needed to establish a link with the database server. The difficulty at this point is in identifying which properties are needed by *your* application, since not all properties are needed for every application. PowerBuilder's help library contains the information you need. Once the transaction object is populated, your program should then attempt to connect to the database using the information in the object.

To inform you of the status of your database operation, the transaction object has five properties that contain information about the most recent database operation. These properties are listed in Table 8-2. The SQLCode is by far the most important of these properties because it uses only three values to categorize potentially hundreds of database responses into one of three areas: good, bad, or not found.

PowerBuilder offers you a single predefined transaction object called SQLCA which will be used for the bulk of this How-To. However, you may create your own transaction objects to establish communications with more than one server at a time.

PROPERTY	DATA TYPE	PURPOSE	EXAMPLE
DBMS	string	Name of DBMS vendor	"SYB", "OR7"
Server	string	Name of database server	"Server1"
Database	string	Name of database within server	"Customer"
UserID	string	Database user's userid	"john"
DBPass	string	Database user's password	"hello"
LogID	string	Server user's userid	"johnp"
LogPass	string	Server user's password	"serverpass"
DBParm	string	DBMS specific information	
Lock	string	Isolation level	*DBMS specific*
AutoCommit	Boolean	Automatically commit operations	FALSE

Table 8-1 Transaction object properties used to identify a database connection

PROPERTY	DATA TYPE	PURPOSE	VALUES
SQLCode	long	General status	Error (-1)
			Success (0)
			Not found (100)
SQLDBCode	long	Vendor-specific error code	
SQLErrText	long	Vendor-specific error message	
SQLNRows	long	Number of rows affected by last operation	
SQLReturnData	long	DBMS-specific information	

Table 8-2 Transaction object properties used for status information

Steps

The completed application for this How-To may be found in CONNECT.PBL on the included CD-ROM. Before starting the application, you should ensure that PowerBuilder itself was connected to the Zoo database in the Database painter. For more information on setting up the Zoo database, please refer to the introduction of this book. Run the application from PowerBuilder or by invoking CON-NECT.EXE. The Login window should appear as shown in Figure 8-1, showing the parameters used by PowerBuilder for its own database connection. Click Connect to connect to the database using these parameters. The Transaction Object Contents window, pictured in Figure 8-2, will appear showing you the results of the connection. An SQLCode value of 0 indicates that the connection was successful. Click Close and return to the Login window. Click Disconnect to terminate the database connection. Close the Transaction Object Contents dialog when it appears. Now change the DBParm SingleLineEdit to read

```
ConnectString='DSN=Zoo;UID=dba;PWD=sl'
```

(Note that the password value is deliberately misspelled.) Click Connect again. Observe the error indicators displayed on the Transaction Object Contents window. Click Close. On the Login window, click Close to end the program. To build this program, complete the steps below.

1. Create a new .PBL and Application object called CONNECT.PBL and a_connect, respectively, using the Application painter. Answer "No" when prompted for an application template.

2. Create a new window called w_show_transaction_contents using the Window painter in conjunction with the settings shown in Table 8-3.

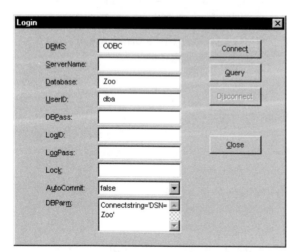

Figure 8-1 The Login window (w_login) for the Connect application

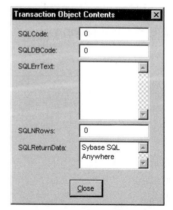

Figure 8-2 The Transaction Object Contents window (w_show_transaction_object) for the Connect application

Figure 8-3 is provided to help you in placing the controls on the dialog. You do not need to specify the text properties of the SingleLineEdit and MultiLineEdit controls on the window.

WINDOW/CONTROL NAME	PROPERTY	VALUE
Window		
w_show_transaction_object		
	Title	"Transaction Object Contents"
	WindowType	Response!
StaticText	Name	st_sqlcode
	Text	"SQLCode:"
StaticText	Name	st_sqldbcode
	Text	"SQLDBCode:"
StaticText	Name	st_sqlerrtext
	Text	"SQLErrText:"
StaticText	Name	st_sqlnrows
	Text	"SQLNRows:"
StaticText	Name	st_sqlreturndata
	Text	"SQLReturnData:"
SingleLineEdit	Name	sle_sqlcode
	DisplayOnly	TRUE
SingleLineEdit	Name	sle_sqldbcode
	DisplayOnly	TRUE
SingleLineEdit	Name	sle_sqlnrows
	DisplayOnly	TRUE
MultiLineEdit	Name	mle_sqlerrtext
	DisplayOnly	TRUE
MultiLineEdit	Name	mle_sqlreturndata
	DisplayOnly	TRUE

continued on next page

continued from previous page

WINDOW/CONTROL NAME	PROPERTY	VALUE
CommandButton	Name	cb_close
	Text	"&Close"
	Default	TRUE

Table 8-3 Window and control settings for the w_show_transaction_object window

3. Allow the Close CommandButton to exit the Transaction Object Contents window by placing the following script in the Clicked event for cb_close.

```
Close( parent )
```

4. Code the following script in the Open event for the w_show_transaction_object window. This script accepts an incoming transaction object parameter and displays the five properties that indicate the results of the last database operation. For more information on passing parameters between windows, please refer to How-To 2.3, "How do I pass parameters between windows?"

```
// declare a local transaction object
transaction lto_1

// grab the incoming parameter
lto_1 = Message.PowerObjectParm

// copy the relevant properties to the window controls
sle_sqlcode.text          = String( lto_1.sqlcode )
sle_sqldbcode.text        = String( lto_1.sqldbcode )
mle_sqlerrtext.text       = lto_1.sqlerrtext
sle_sqlnrows.text         = String( lto_1.sqlnrows )
mle_sqlreturndata.text    = lto_1.sqlreturndata
```

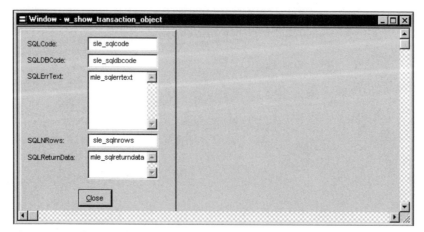

Figure 8-3 The w_show_transaction_object window with placement aids

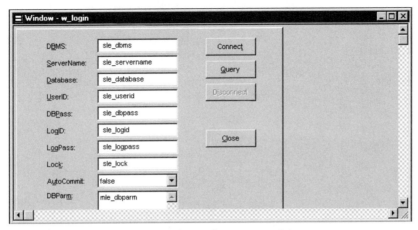

Figure 8-4 The w_login window placement aid

5. Save this window under the name w_show_transaction_object.

6. Using the Window painter, create a new window called w_login using the controls and settings shown in Table 8-4. This window is shown in Figure 8-4 to assist you in placing the window controls. You do not need to specify the text properties of the SingleLineEdit, DropDownListBox, or MultiLineEdit controls.

WINDOW/CONTROL NAME	PROPERTY	VALUE
Window		
w_login	Title	"Login"
	WindowType	Main!
StaticText	Name	st_dbms
	Text	"D&BMS:"
StaticText	Name	st_servername
	Text	"&ServerName:"
StaticText	Name	st_database
	Text	"&Database:"
StaticText	Name	st_userid
	Text	"&UserID:"

continued on next page

continued from previous page

WINDOW/CONTROL NAME	PROPERTY	VALUE
StaticText	Name	st_dbpass
	Text	"DB&Pass:"
StaticText	Name	st_logid
	Text	"Lo&gID:"
StaticText	Name	st_logpass
	Text	"L&ogPass:"
StaticText	Name	st_lock
	Text	"Loc&k:"
StaticText	Name	st_autocommit
	Text	"A&utoCommit:"
StaticText	Name	st_dbparm
	Text	"DBPar&m:"
SingleLineEdit	Name	sle_dbms
	Accelerator	"b"
SingleLineEdit	Name	sle_servername
	Accelerator	"s"
SingleLineEdit	Name	sle_database
	Accelerator	"d"
SingleLineEdit	Name	sle_userid
	Accelerator	"u"
SingleLineEdit	Name	sle_dbpass
	Accelerator	"p"
SingleLineEdit	Name	sle_logid
	Accelerator	"g"
SingleLineEdit	Name	sle_logpass
	Accelerator	"o"

WINDOW/CONTROL NAME	PROPERTY	VALUE
SingleLineEdit	Name	sle_lock
	Accelerator	"k"
DropDownListBox	Name	ddlb_autocommit
	Text	"false"
	Accelerator	"u"
	Items	false
		true
MultiLineEdit	Name	mle_dbparm
	VScroll Bar	TRUE
	Accelerator	"m"
CommandButton	Name	cb_connect
	Text	"Connec&t"
CommandButton	Name	cb_query
	Text	"&Query"
CommandButton	Name	cb_disconnect
	Text	"D&isconnect"
	Enabled	FALSE
CommandButton	Name	cb_close
	Text	"&Close"
	Cancel	TRUE

Table 8-4 Window and control settings for w_login

7. Place the following script in the Open event of w_login. This script reads the current database parameters from your PowerBuilder initialization file, PB.INI, and copies them onto the display. When running this application, you should ensure that PowerBuilder is connected to the Zoo database because PowerBuilder's connection parameters are being used by this application.

```
// The following lines read in the database settings from
// PB.INI.

sle_dbms.text      =ProfileString("PB.INI","Database","DBMS", " ")
sle_database.text  =ProfileString("PB.INI","Database","DataBase"," ")
```

continued on next page

continued from previous page

```
sle_logid.text       =ProfileString("PB.INI","Database","LogID"," ")
sle_logpass.text     =ProfileString("PB.INI","Database","LogPassword"," ")
sle_servername.text =ProfileString("PB.INI","Database","ServerName"," ")
sle_userid.text      =ProfileString("PB.INI","Database","UserID"," "  )
sle_dbpass.text =ProfileString("PB.INI","Database","DatabasePassword"," ")
sle_lock.text   =ProfileString("PB.INI","Database","Lock"," ")
mle_dbparm.text      =ProfileString("PB.INI","Database","DbParm"," ")

ddlb_autocommit.text = Lower( ProfileString("PB.INI","Database",&
        "AutoCommit","false" ))
```

8. Code the following script in the Close event of w_login. This script ensures that your program disconnects from the database properly. The DBHandle() function is used to ensure that PowerBuilder does not attempt to disconnect an already-disconnected transaction object (which is an error).

```
IF sqlca.DBHandle() <> 0 THEN
    DISCONNECT USING sqlca;
END IF
```

9. Place the following script in the Clicked event of cb_connect. This script uses the information specified on the window to connect to the database. The CONNECT statement is actually embedded SQL, which is why the semicolon (;) at the end of the statement is necessary. Following a successful connect, the script enables the Disconnect button and disables the Connect button.

```
pointer le_oldpointer

// Copy the contents of the controls to the default
// transaction object, sqlca.
sqlca.dbms = sle_dbms.text
sqlca.database = sle_database.text
sqlca.servername = sle_servername.text
sqlca.userid = sle_userid.text
sqlca.dbpass = sle_dbpass.text
sqlca.logid = sle_logid.text
sqlca.logpass = sle_logpass.text
sqlca.lock = sle_lock.text
sqlca.dbparm = mle_dbparm.text

// getting the Boolean value for autocommit is a little trickier...
IF Lower( ddlb_autocommit.text ) = "true" THEN
    sqlca.autocommit = TRUE
ELSE
    sqlca.autocommit = FALSE
END IF

// turn on the hourglass so that our user expects the slight delay here
le_oldpointer = SetPointer( HourGlass! )

// Connect to the database
CONNECT USING sqlca;

// if the connect was successful, enable Disconnect button,
```

```
// and disable this button.
IF sqlca.sqlcode = 0 THEN
    cb_disconnect.enabled = TRUE
    this.enabled = FALSE
END IF

// revert the pointer back to the original one
SetPointer( le_oldpointer )

// display the results
OpenWithParm( w_show_transaction_object, sqlca, parent )
```

10. Code the following script in the Clicked event for cb_query. This is a very simple line of embedded SQL to demonstrate how the transaction object can be examined following any embedded SQL operation. Embedded SQL is explored more fully in How-To 8.2.

```
long ll_count

SELECT count(*) INTO :ll_count FROM "company" USING sqlca;

OpenWithParm( w_show_transaction_object, sqlca, parent )
```

11. Code the script to disconnect from the database on the Clicked event of cb_disconnect as follows.

```
DISCONNECT USING sqlca;
OpenWithParm( w_show_transaction_object, sqlca, parent )
cb_connect.enabled = TRUE
this.enabled = FALSE
```

12. Place the following script that closes the Login window in the Clicked event of cb_close.

```
Close( parent )
```

13. Save the w_login window.

14. Using the Application painter, place the following script in the Open event of the Application object.

```
Open( w_login )
```

15. Save the Application object and run the application.

How It Works

PowerBuilder uses what is known as the transaction object to connect to the database. Like other objects, transaction objects have properties. Some of these properties are used to identify a connection to the database; these are listed in Table 8-1. The five remaining properties are used to indicate return status information from the database; these are listed in Table 8-2. Of the properties used for identifying a connection, DBMS is the most important. This value is used by PowerBuilder to determine the correct database driver for making a connection. If this value is incorrect or not specified, PowerBuilder will be unable to make a connection, regardless of the contents of the other properties.

The large number of connection properties, ten, is intended to allow PowerBuilder to connect to a wide variety of database products. Therefore, PowerBuilder does not use all of these properties to connect to any single database. To determine the combination of settings required for your database, access the topic "Powersoft database interfaces" in PowerBuilder's help. This topic covers the settings required for each possible combination of client operating system and database. For an ODBC database, such as Sybase SQL Anywhere, only two properties, DBMS and DBParm, are required. DBMS must be set to the value "ODBC" and DBParm must contain a valid ODBC connect string.

Once the properties of the transaction object have been initialized, your program can connect to the database by issuing the CONNECT statement. CONNECT is an embedded SQL statement that tells PowerBuilder to use the transaction object properties to attempt to establish a connection to the database. Initializing the transaction object properties can thus be compared to writing down a phone number, while CONNECTing the transaction object can be compared to making the phone call using that phone number. Once connected, your program can examine the return status properties to determine the success or failure of the connection as described below. Following the connection, your program can use the transaction object to request database services, as indicated by the embedded SQL query contained in the Query CommandButton. When your program has no further use for the database, it should issue a DISCONNECT to inform the database that the connection is no longer needed. Your application should always disconnect from the database. Unneeded connections may linger as idle processes on your database server, consuming available "seats" on your server license.

Of the five return status properties, the SQLCode value is the one PowerBuilder programmers use most often. Following an embedded SQL operation, the SQLCode contains one of three values. An error condition is indicated by -1, success by 0, and "not found" by 100. PowerBuilder uses the SQLCode value to categorize all possible error conditions from all possible database products. After using the SQLCode to determine that an error has occurred, your program can use the SQLDBCode and SQLErrText values to display or log the actual DBMS-generated error condition. *Note that the return status properties of a transaction object are only valid following an embedded SQL operation. Your program should not attempt to use these properties following a DataWindow operation.*

Some applications may require more than the single database connection allowed by the default transaction object SQLCA. To create additional transaction objects for additional database connections, you must first declare an object of type transaction and then create the object as shown in this example.

```
transaction lto_mytrans
lto_mytrans = CREATE transaction
```

These statements declare lto_mytrans as a transaction object and then allocate the memory required to hold a transaction object. At this point, you may treat lto_mytrans in the same manner as SQLCA, initializing its properties, connecting it to the database, using it, and disconnecting it from the database. When you are done with your custom transaction object, you should deallocate the memory it uses by invoking DESTROY as follows.

```
DESTROY lto_mytrans
```

With the capability to declare additional transaction objects, your program can make multiple connections to the same or different database servers.

Comments

The actual time required for a connect may range between one or two seconds to perhaps 30 seconds. Because of this noticeable delay, your program should give the user visible feedback while the connection is taking place. For shorter waits, change the pointer to an hourglass by calling SetPointer(). For waits of longer duration you can display a progress indicator window (indicating that the program is trying to connect) or use the MicroHelp line by calling SetMicroHelp().

Database connections should be regarded as scarce resources because your database server license typically restricts the number of allowable connections. An application that uses multiple connections will reduce the total capacity of your database server.

COMPLEXITY
INTERMEDIATE

8.2   How do I...
Use embedded SQL?

Problem

I have a PowerBuilder application that needs to retrieve database information and store it in an array. I know a few basic operations that can be performed with embedded SQL, but I'm unsure of how to use a stored procedure to obtain database results. I would also like to know if it is possible to open multiple cursors so that I can obtain additional result sets based on the individual row values in the first result set. How do I use embedded SQL in my program?

Technique

PowerBuilder offers a rich set of embedded SQL features that allow you to place common SQL operations in your script directly, with very little supporting code in your program. This How-To offers three examples of using embedded SQL to perform queries against a database.

The essential concept in using embedded SQL to perform queries is the *cursor*. Relational databases are quite comfortable working with sets of rows. In fact queries may be viewed as requests for the set of rows that match the criteria given in the WHERE clause. The result of a query is given a special name, the *result set*. In contrast to the set-oriented relational database, iterative languages like PowerScript must deal with one piece of information at a time. To solve this issue, database products provide an interface called a cursor that allows the result set to be constructed on the server and then accessed one row at a time by the client application. As the application fetches rows from the cursor, the cursor pointer is advanced until it reaches the end of the result set. At this time the application typically closes (releases) the cursor, freeing the server resources that had been devoted to storing the rows in the result set. This How-To focuses on cursor manipulation, as it is the most difficult aspect of embedded SQL.

The first query is a simple single-cursor example that obtains a list of all departments and their department heads' names from the database. The second query uses a stored procedure to obtain the employees in a specific department. The third query opens two result sets simultaneously to allow the program to retrieve a list of departments and then to retrieve the employees for each of the departments originally obtained. These three examples demonstrate the query capabilities of embedded SQL.

Steps

The complete solution to this How-To may be found in the file EMBED.PBL on the included CD-ROM. Before running the program, you must define the Zoo ODBC data source as described in the Setup section of this book. You may run the program in executable form or from the PowerBuilder development environment.

Once the program is running, it presents you with the window shown in Figure 8-5. The three CommandButtons on the window allow you to invoke queries of the type described in the Technique section above. Clicking the Cursor Query button will show you a list of departments and their department heads' names.

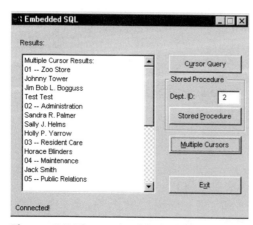

Figure 8-5 The embedded SQL application

Enter a department ID value of 2 in the Dept. ID SingleLineEdit. Click the Stored Procedure CommandButton to retrieve a list of employees for department 2. You can try other values to see which departments have employees. Finally, click the Multiple Cursors button to perform a retrieval that requires cursors for two separate result sets to be open simultaneously. When you are satisfied with the application's functionality, click the Exit button to end the program. To build this application, follow the steps below.

1. Using the Database painter or the DB Profile PowerBar button, connect to the Zoo database. PowerBuilder will require that the Zoo database be the current database in order to verify the correctness of the embedded SQL statements coded in this application.

2. Using the Application painter, create a new library and Application object for this application, called EMBED.PBL and a_embedded, respectively. You will not need an application template for this application.

3. Use the Window painter to create a window called w_embedded with the controls and property settings shown in Table 8-5. The window under development is shown in Figure 8-6 to assist you with placing the controls.

WINDOW/CONTROL NAME	PROPERTY	VALUE
Window		
w_embedded	Title	"Embedded SQL"
	MaximizeBox	FALSE
	Resizable	FALSE
	WindowType	Main
StaticText	Name	st_results
	Text	"Results:"
StaticText	Name	st_message
	Text	""
StaticText	Name	st_deptid
	Text	"Dept. &ID"
MultiLineEdit	Name	mle_results
	DisplayOnly	TRUE
	VScrollBar	TRUE
	AutoHScroll	TRUE
	Border	3D Lowered

continued on next page

continued from previous page

WINDOW/CONTROL NAME	PROPERTY	VALUE
CommandButton	Name	cb_cursor
	Text	"C&ursor Query"
CommandButton	Name	cb_storedproc
	Text	"Stored &Procedure"
CommandButton	Name	cb_multiple
	Text	"&Multiple Cursors"
CommandButton	Name	cb_exit
	Text	"E&xit"
GroupBox	Name	gb_storedproc
	Text	"Stored Procedure"

Table 8-5 Window and control settings for w_embedded

4. Define a window function called wf_error_handler on the w_embedded window as shown in Table 8-6. The wf_error_handler() function will be used repeatedly to examine the contents of a passed transaction object and to display an error message if needed.

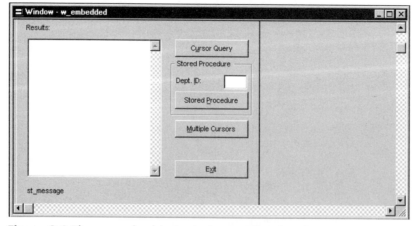

Figure 8-6 The w_embedded window under development (placement aid)

FUNCTION SPECIFICATIONS

Function	Name	wf_error_handler	
	Access	Public	
	Returns	integer	
Arguments			
	a_to	Transaction	Value
	as_title	String	Value
	as_message	String	Value

Table 8-6 Function specifications for wf_error_handler()

5. Place the following script in the body of wf_error_handler(). This script examines the SQLCode property of the passed transaction object, a_to, to determine if an error occurred. If it did, it will display an error message using the title and message strings passed to the function along with the exact database error condition.

```
string ls_errtext, ls_dbcode
integer li_sqlcode

// Preserve the original sqlcode (which may be affected by ROLLBACK later
on)
li_sqlcode = sqlca.sqlcode

IF li_sqlcode < 0 THEN
    ls_errtext = a_to.sqlerrtext
    ls_dbcode = String( a_to.sqldbcode )
    ROLLBACK USING a_to;
    MessageBox( as_title, as_message + "~r~n" +&
            "(" +ls_dbcode + ") " + ls_errtext, Exclamation! )
END IF

// Return the original value of the SQLCode
RETURN li_sqlcode
```

6. Return to the Window painter and save the window.

7. Place the following code in w_embedded's Open event. This script connects to the Zoo database, while changing the status indicator, st_message, to inform the user of the program's progress.

```
SetPointer( Hourglass! )

st_message.text = "Connecting to database..."

// set the transaction object to refer to the Zoo database
sqlca.dbms = "ODBC"
sqlca.dbparm = "ConnectString='DSN=Zoo;UID=dba;PWD=SQL'"

CONNECT USING sqlca;

IF sqlca.sqlcode < 0 THEN // unsuccessful connect
```

continued on next page

continued from previous page

```
    st_message.text = "Unsuccessful connect."
    MessageBox("Connection Error", "Could not connect to database.~r~n"+&
            "(" + string( sqlca.sqldbcode) + ") " + sqlca.sqlerrtext, &
            Exclamation! )
ELSE
    st_message.text = "Connected!"
END IF
```

8. Place a script to disconnect from the database in w_embedded's Close event as follows.

```
// If we're connected to the database, disconnect from it
IF sqlca.DBHandle() <> 0 THEN
    DISCONNECT USING sqlca;

    IF sqlca.sqlcode < 0 THEN   // couldn't disconnect
        MessageBox("Disconnection Error", &
            "Could not disconnect from database.~r~n"+&
            "(" + string(sqlca.sqldbcode) + ") " + &
            sqlca.sqlerrtext, Exclamation! )
    END IF
END IF
```

9. Code the script to perform the single cursor query in the Clicked event of cb_cursor as follows. This script issues the query to the database and processes its results. Because this result set consists of more than one row, this script must declare a cursor, open it, read through the rows one at a time, and then close the cursor.

```
string ls_dept_id, ls_dept_dsc, ls_last_name, ls_first_name,
ls_middle_initial

SetPointer( Hourglass! )

mle_results.text = "Query Results:"

// Step 1, get ready for the query
DECLARE dept_listing CURSOR FOR
   SELECT "department"."dept_id",
            "department"."dept_dsc",
            "person"."last_name",
            "person"."first_name",
            "person"."middle_initial"
      FROM "department",
            "employee",
            "person"
     WHERE ( "person"."person_id" = "employee"."person_id" ) and
           ( "department"."dept_mgr" = "employee"."employee_id" )
       ORDER BY Cast( "department"."dept_id"  as integer )
     USING sqlca;

// Step 2, tell the server to execute the query
OPEN dept_listing;

// If we're successful opening the cursor, proceed.
IF wf_error_handler( sqlca, "Open Error", "Could not open query" ) = 0 THEN
```

```
      DO WHILE sqlca.sqlcode = 0
          FETCH dept_listing INTO :ls_dept_id, :ls_dept_dsc,
              :ls_last_name, :ls_first_name, :ls_middle_initial;
          IF wf_error_handler( sqlca, "Fetch Error", "Could not fetch row" ) &
                  = 0 THEN
              // middle initials can be null, which result in null strings
              // when concatenated. Prevent this from occurring by checking it.
              IF IsNull( ls_middle_initial ) THEN
                  ls_middle_initial = ""
              ELSE
                  ls_middle_initial = ls_middle_initial + ". "
              END IF
              mle_results.text = mle_results.text + "~r~n" + &
                  string( Integer(ls_dept_id), "00" ) + "," + &
                  ls_dept_dsc + "," + ls_first_name + " " + ls_middle_initial + &
                  ls_last_name
          END IF
      LOOP

      CLOSE dept_listing;

      wf_error_handler( sqlca, "Close Error", "Could not close cursor" )

      COMMIT USING sqlca;

END IF
```

10. Code the script to perform the stored procedure retrieval on cb_stored-
proc's Clicked event as follows. Observe that the overall structure of this
script is highly similar to the script coded in step 9.

```
string ls_deptid, ls_last_name, ls_first_name, ls_middle_initial
long ll_emp_id

SetPointer( Hourglass! )

mle_results.text = "Stored Procedure Results:"


// declare the stored procedure to PB (design time)
DECLARE empsindept PROCEDURE FOR "DBA"."sp_emps_in_dept"
        deptid = :ls_deptid USING sqlca ;

ls_deptid = sle_deptid.text

// tell the database to execute the stored procedure with
// the current input values (ls_deptid in this case)
EXECUTE empsindept;

// If the stored proc opened OK, proceed
IF wf_error_handler( sqlca, "Execute Error", &
        "Could not execute stored procedure." ) = 0 THEN

    // loop through the result set normally
    DO WHILE sqlca.sqlcode = 0
        FETCH empsindept INTO :ll_emp_id, :ls_last_name, :ls_first_name,
```

continued on next page

continued from previous page

```
                    :ls_middle_initial;
        IF wf_error_handler( sqlca, "Fetch Error", "Could not fetch row" ) &
                = 0 THEN
            // middle initials can be null, which result in null strings
            // when concatenated. Prevent this from occurring by checking it.
            IF IsNull( ls_middle_initial ) THEN
                ls_middle_initial = ""
            ELSE
                ls_middle_initial = ls_middle_initial + ". "
            END IF
            mle_results.text = mle_results.text + "~r~n" + &
                string( ll_emp_id, "00000" ) + "," + &
                ls_first_name + " " + ls_middle_initial + ls_last_name
        END IF
    LOOP

    // close the stored procedure
    CLOSE empsindept;

    wf_error_handler( sqlca, "Close Error", "Could not close procedure")

    // release any locks we're holding
    COMMIT USING sqlca;
END IF
```

11. Place the script to perform the multiple cursor retrieval in the Clicked event of cb_multiple as follows. Notice that the complexity required to support two cursors is mostly caused by the need to distinguish an error condition (SQLCode = -1) from the end of the result set (SQLCode = 100).

```
string ls_dept_id, ls_dept_dsc, ls_last_name, ls_first_name, ls_middle_initial
boolean lb_stop

SetPointer( Hourglass! )

mle_results.text = "Multiple Cursor Results:"

// declare the first cursor to retrieve a listing of all departments
DECLARE dept_listing CURSOR FOR
    SELECT  "department"."dept_id",
            "department"."dept_dsc"
      FROM  "department"
      ORDER BY Cast( "department"."dept_id"  as integer )
    USING sqlca;

// declare the second cursor to retrieve employees for a specific department
DECLARE emp_listing CURSOR FOR
    SELECT  "person"."last_name",
            "person"."first_name",
            "person"."middle_initial"
      FROM  "employee", "person"
     WHERE  ( "person"."person_id" = "employee"."person_id" ) and
            ( "employee"."dept_id" = :ls_dept_id )
      ORDER BY "employee"."employee_id"
    USING sqlca;
```

```
// execute the dept_listing query
OPEN dept_listing;

// if we get an error, don't let the loop begin below
IF wf_error_handler( sqlca, "Open Error", "Could not open query" ) &
        <> 0 THEN lb_stop = TRUE

DO WHILE lb_stop = FALSE
    // get a department
    FETCH dept_listing INTO :ls_dept_id, :ls_dept_dsc;

    // if there's a problem, stop the department loop; otherwise, get
    // employees
    IF wf_error_handler( sqlca, "Fetch Error", "Could not fetch
department" ) &
            <> 0 THEN
        lb_stop = TRUE
    ELSE
        // add the department to the output
        mle_results.text = mle_results.text + "~r~n" + &
            string( Integer( ls_Dept_id), "00" ) + " -- " + ls_dept_dsc

        // execute the employee listing with the current department
        OPEN emp_listing;

        // if we encounter an error, stop the department loop; otherwise
        // get employees
        IF wf_error_handler( sqlca, "Open Error", &
                "Could not open employees" ) = -1 THEN
            lb_stop = TRUE
        ELSE
            DO WHILE sqlca.sqlcode = 0
                FETCH emp_listing INTO :ls_last_name, :ls_first_name,
                    :ls_middle_initial;
                CHOOSE CASE wf_error_handler( sqlca, "Fetch Error", &
                        "Could not fetch employee" )
                    CASE 0
                        IF IsNull( ls_middle_initial ) THEN
                                ls_middle_initial = ""
                        ELSE
                                ls_middle_initial = ls_middle_initial + ". "
                        END IF
                        mle_results.text = mle_results.text + "~r~n" + &
                            ls_first_name + " " + ls_middle_initial + &
                            ls_last_name
                    CASE 100
                        EXIT // stop the employee loop
                    CASE IS < 0
                        lb_stop = TRUE // stop the department loop
                END CHOOSE
            LOOP
            CLOSE emp_listing;
            wf_error_handler( sqlca, "Close Error", &
                    "Could not close employee cursor" )
            // COMMIT USING sqlca;    // Don't! The pending department
                                      //listing will be lost!
```

continued on next page

continued from previous page
```
        END IF
    END IF
LOOP // departments

// close the department listing
CLOSE dept_listing;

wf_error_handler( sqlca, "Close Error", "Could not close department cursor" )

COMMIT USING sqlca;    // release our locks
```
12. Code the following script on the Clicked event of cb_exit.

```
Close( parent )
```

13. Save the window.

14. Place the following script in the Open event of the Application object, a_embedded.

```
Open( w_embedded )
```

15. Save and run the application.

How It Works

The scripts in this application require only a few bits of explanation. First of all, in all three query CommandButtons, observe the use of host variables in the queries, indicated with colons preceding the variable names. The colons enable PowerBuilder to distinguish program variables (which should be substituted for at runtime) from database columns. The host variables can be used for both input (on the DECLARE) and output (on the FETCH). Also observe the comment in the multiple cursor script that warns you to avoid issuing a COMMIT before the script is done with the "outer" cursor. A COMMIT issued from a script causes *all open cursors* to be committed, resulting in all pending result sets being lost. However, many applications need the ability to COMMIT the cursors separately. To meet this requirement, your application will need to create additional transaction objects (one per "independent" cursor) as presented in the How It Works section of How-To 8.1, "How do I connect my application to a database?" By using separate transaction objects for each cursor, your program will be able to COMMIT against one transaction object without affecting the pending cursors on the other. Don't forget that additional database connections use more server resources!

Comments

If you are interested, you may change the Open event of w_embedded to set the DBMS property of SQLCA to "TRACE ODBC". This will create a log file that describes all database activity PowerBuilder generates on your program's behalf. PowerBuilder displays a message telling you that a PBTRACE.LOG file is being created when you run a program with tracing turned on.

You may also be curious about the stored procedure used in this application. You can view the stored procedure directly via the Objects/Procedure Syntax... menu item from the Database painter's database administration tool. The stored procedure has also been provided in ASCII format on the included CD-ROM under the file name SPEMPS.SQL. Note that if you want to experiment with this stored procedure, you must change PowerBuilder's terminator character from the default semicolon (";") to something else ("\" is a good choice). You may make this change by adding or changing the following line in the [Database] section of your PB.INI file.

```
TerminatorCharacter=\
```

You must make this change because Sybase SQL Anywhere uses a semicolon to delineate the commands within a stored procedure, which conflicts with PowerBuilder's usage of the semicolon.

COMPLEXITY
ADVANCED

8.3   How do I...
Use dynamic SQL?

Problem

My PowerBuilder program needs to execute some database queries that are not fully specified at runtime. I haven't been able to use embedded SQL to perform these queries because embedded SQL requires that I know all the result set columns when I code the query. I have heard some other PowerBuilder developers mention *dynamic SQL* and I think it might help me here. What exactly is dynamic SQL and how do I use it?

Technique

PowerBuilder offers embedded SQL as a highly simplified means of sending most SQL statements to the database. Even though the coding effort is higher than that required for DataWindows (see Chapters 9 through 12), PowerBuilder's embedded SQL implementation is *much* simpler than that provided by other development tools currently available.

However, in order to use embedded SQL, your SQL statements must be fully defined at compile time with known result set columns and WHERE clause criteria. PowerBuilder offers a more complex interface called dynamic SQL to allow you to perform SQL commands that do not conform to these requirements. Dynamic SQL will allow your program to send any query to the database. Additionally, some types of operations, especially Data Definition Language (DDL) statements such as CREATE and DROP, are not available at all with embedded SQL. Dynamic SQL will allow you to send DDL and Data Access Language (DAL) statements to the database as well as queries. To fully support dynamic SQL, PowerBuilder uses two new object types, the DynamicStagingArea and the DynamicDescriptionArea, in addition to the transaction object. Just as PowerBuilder provides a pre-defined global transaction object, SQLCA, PowerBuilder also provides a predefined staging area called SQLSA and a predefined description area called SQLDA. You will see these global objects referenced in the scripts that make up this How-To.

To accommodate all possible SQL statements, PowerBuilder divides dynamic SQL into four different formats, depending on the type of statement and the number of unknowns. This How-To demonstrates dynamic SQL formats 1, 2, and 4.

Steps

This How-To is contained on the included CD-ROM under the name DYNSQL.PBL and DYNSQL.EXE for the library and executable, respectively. You may run the application from the PowerBuilder development environment or standalone. If you choose to run the executable, you will be able to use PowerBuilder's Database painter by switching between PowerBuilder and this application. Doing so will allow you to see the results of DDL statements you issue from the application. Once the application is running, observe the three distinct regions on the Dynamic SQL window as shown in Figure 8-7. These regions allow you to execute dynamic SQL using formats 1,2, and 4, as described in the Technique section above.

Accept the default text in the MultiLineEdit for Format 1 and click the Execute button. This statement creates a table called bogus. You may see this table by starting

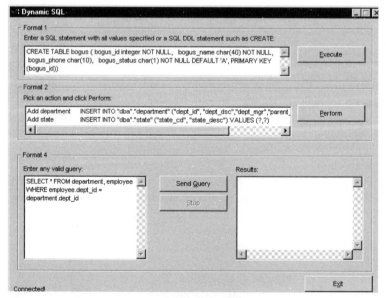

Figure 8-7 The Dynamic SQL application

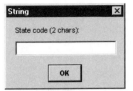

Figure 8-8 The
w_response window

PowerBuilder's Database painter and observing the list of tables. (If you were already connected to the Zoo database, you may have to connect to a different database, such as the Powersoft Demo DB, and reconnect to the Zoo database to see the table.) You can drop the bogus table by entering "DROP TABLE bogus" (without quotes). If you are comfortable with DDL statements such as CREATE, ALTER, and DROP, you may enter these commands into the Format 1 MultiLineEdit and click Execute.

Next, highlight one of the two actions in the ListBox for Format 2 and click the Perform button. The Dynamic SQL application will prompt you for the required parameters and perform the listed INSERT statement. Observe that your entries are substituted for the question marks (?) in the ListBox's SQL statements. For adding a department, you can try '95', 'Groundskeeping', 3, and '1' (all without quotes) for department ID, department description, manager ID, and parent department. For adding a state, try 'OH' and 'Ohio' or 'HI' and 'Hawaii' (again, without quotes) for state code and state description.

Finally, try entering a valid query of your choosing into the Format 4 query MultiLineEdit. You may specify any number of columns along with any WHERE criteria of your own choosing. However, this sample was not written to implement the use of question mark placeholders in the WHERE clause; see the How It Works and Comments sections of this How-To for more details on this omission. Once you have entered a query (or accepted the default), click the Send Query button and observe the results in the Results MultiLineEdit.

When you are satisfied with the operation of the program, click the Exit button to end the application. To construct this application, perform the steps below.

1. Using the Application painter create a new .PBL and Application object called DYNSQL.PBL and a_dynsql, respectively. You will not require an application template for this application.

2. Create a new window called w_response using the Window painter. Refer to Table 8-7 and Figure 8-8 for the controls and property settings for the w_response window.

WINDOW/CONTROL NAME	PROPERTY	VALUE
Window		
w_response	WindowType	Response

continued on next page

continued from previous page

WINDOW/CONTROL NAME	PROPERTY	VALUE
StaticText	Name	st_prompt
	Border	None
	Alignment	Left
SingleLineEdit	Name	sle_response
	AutoHScroll	TRUE
	Border	3D Lowered
CommandButton	Name	cb_ok
	Text	"OK"
	Default	TRUE

Table 8-7 Window and control settings for the w_response window

3. Place the following script in the Open event of w_response. This script accepts an incoming string parameter which contains the title of the window and the text to be displayed in st_prompt. These two values are contained in a single string where they are separated by a tab character (represented as '~t' in a script).

```
string ls_prompt

ls_prompt = Message.StringParm

this.title = Mid( ls_prompt, 1, Pos( ls_prompt, "~t" ) - 1)

st_prompt.text = Mid( ls_prompt, Pos( ls_prompt, "~t" ) + 1 )
```

4. Place the following script in the Clicked event of cb_ok. This script returns the user's entry in the sle_response SingleLineEdit to the calling program.

```
CloseWithReturn( parent, sle_response.text )
```

5. Save the window under the name w_response.

6. Using the File/New menu item, begin work on a new window called w_dynsql. Create this window using the settings shown in Table 8-8.

WINDOW/CONTROL NAME	PROPERTY	VALUE
Window		
w_dynsql	Title	"Dynamic SQL"
	MinimizeBox	TRUE
	MaximizeBox	FALSE
	Resizable	FALSE
	InitialState	Normal

WINDOW/CONTROL NAME	PROPERTY	VALUE
	Width	2945
	Height	1937
GroupBox	Name	gb_format1
	Text	"Format 1"
GroupBox	Name	gb_format2
	Text	"Format 2"
GroupBox	Name	gb_format4
	Text	"Format 4"
StaticText	Name	st_format1
	Alignment	Left
	Border	None
	Text	"Enter a SQL statement with all values specified or a SQL DDL statement such as CREATE:"
StaticText	Name	st_format2
	Alignment	Left
	Border	None
	Text	"Pick an action and click Perform:"
StaticText	Name	st_query
	Alignment	Left
	Border	None
	Text	"Enter any valid &query:"
StaticText	Name	st_results
	Alignment	Left
	Border	None
	Text	"Results:"
StaticText	Name	st_message
	Alignment	Left
	Border	None

continued on next page

continued from previous page

WINDOW/CONTROL NAME	PROPERTY	VALUE
MultiLineEdit	Name	mle_format1
	HScrollBar	FALSE
	VScrollBar	TRUE
	AutoHScroll	FALSE
	AutoVScroll	TRUE
	Border	3D Lowered
	Text	*(enter the following string very carefully)*
		"CREATE TABLE
		bogus (bogus_id integer NOT NULL,
		bogus_name char(40) NOT NULL,
		bogus_phone char(10),
		bogus_status char(1) NOT NULL DEFAULT 'A',
		PRIMARY KEY (bogus_id))"
MultiLineEdit	Name	mle_query
	HScrollBar	FALSE
	VScrollBar	TRUE
	AutoHScroll	FALSE
	AutoVScroll	TRUE
	Border	3D Lowered
	Text	*(enter the following string very carefully)*
		"SELECT * FROM department, employee
		WHERE employee.dept_id = department.dept_id"
MultiLineEdit	Name	mle_results
	HScrollBar	TRUE
	VScrollBar	TRUE
	AutoHScroll	FALSE
	AutoVScroll	TRUE
	DisplayOnly	TRUE
	Border	3D Lowered
CommandButton	Name	cb_execute
	Text	"&Execute"
CommandButton	Name	cb_perform
	Text	"&Perform"

WINDOW/CONTROL NAME	PROPERTY	VALUE
CommandButton	Name	cb_sendquery
	Text	"Send &Query"
CommandButton	Name	cb_stop
	Text	"&Stop"
	Enabled	FALSE
CommandButton	Name	cb_exit
	Text	"E&xit"
ListBox	Name	lb_actions
	VScrollBar	TRUE
	HScrollBar	TRUE
	Items	"Add department<Ctrl><Tab>INSERT INTO "dba"."department" ("dept_id", "dept_dsc","dept_mgr","parent_dept") VALUES (?,?,?,?)<Ctrl><Enter> Add state<Ctrl><Tab>INSERT INTO "dba"."state" ("state_cd", "state_desc") VALUES (?,?)"

Table 8-8 Window and control settings for the w_dynsql window

7. To prevent accidentally losing your work, save this window under the name w_dynsql at this time.

8. Define a function called wf_error_handler on the w_dynsql window as shown in Table 8-9. This function provides basic error handling capabilities throughout this application. Note that this function was coded in step 4 of How-To 8.2; you may copy it over if you wish. If you copy it, resume this How-To at step 11.

FUNCTION SPECIFICATIONS			
Function	Name	wf_error_handler	
	Access	Public	
	Returns	integer	
Arguments	a_to	Transaction	Value
	as_title	String	Value
	as_message	String	Value

Table 8-9 Function specifications for wf_error_handler()

9. Place the following script in the body of wf_error_handler(). This script examines the SQLCode property of the passed transaction object, a_to, to determine if an error occurred. In the event of an error this function displays an appropriate message.

```
string ls_errtext, ls_dbcode
integer li_sqlcode

// Preserve the original sqlcode (which may be affected by ROLLBACK later
on)
li_sqlcode = sqlca.sqlcode

IF li_sqlcode < 0 THEN
    ls_errtext = a_to.sqlerrtext
    ls_dbcode = String( a_to.sqldbcode )
    ROLLBACK USING a_to;
    MessageBox( as_title, as_message + "~r~n" +&
            "(" +ls_dbcode + ") " + ls_errtext, Exclamation! )
END IF

// Return the original value of the SQLCode
RETURN li_sqlcode
```

10. Return to the Window painter and save the window.

11. Using the Declare/User Events... menu item, define a window event called ue_postopen mapped to the PowerBuilder event pbm_custom01.

12. Place the following script in the Open event of w_dynsql. This event posts the custom event ue_postopen to the window, which will delay connecting to the database until the window is drawn for the first time.

```
this.PostEvent( "ue_postopen" )
```

13. Place the following script in the ue_postopen event of the w_dynsql window. This script will connect your application to the Zoo database. Note that ue_postopen is the custom event defined in step 11.

```
SetPointer( Hourglass! )

st_message.text = "Connecting to database..."

// set the transaction object to refer to the Zoo database
sqlca.dbms = "ODBC"
sqlca.dbparm = "DisableBind=1,ConnectString='DSN=Zoo;UID=dba;PWD=SQL'"

CONNECT USING sqlca;

IF sqlca.sqlcode < 0 THEN // unsuccessful connect
    st_message.text = "Unsuccessful connect."
    MessageBox("Connection Error", "Could not connect to database.~r~n"+&
            "(" + string( sqlca.sqldbcode) + ") " + sqlca.sqlerrtext, &
            Exclamation! )
ELSE
    st_message.text = "Connected!"
END IF
```

14. Place the following script in the Close event of the w_dynsql window. This script disconnects from the database.

```
// if we're connected to the database, disconnect now
IF sqlca.DBHandle() <> 0 THEN
    DISCONNECT USING sqlca;

    IF sqlca.sqlcode < 0 THEN  // couldn't disconnect
        MessageBox("Disconnection Error", &
            "Could not disconnect from database.~r~n"+&
            "(" + string(sqlca.sqldbcode) + ") " + &
            sqlca.sqlerrtext, Exclamation! )
    END IF
END IF
```

15. Save the window.

16. Place the following script in the Clicked event of cb_format1. This script captures the SQL statement entered in mle_format1 and issues it to the database.

```
string ls_sql

// most DDL statements will require autocommit to be turned on
sqlca.autocommit = TRUE

ls_sql = mle_format1.text

EXECUTE IMMEDIATE :ls_sql USING sqlca;

IF wf_error_handler( sqlca, "Create Table", "Could not create table" ) &
        = 0 THEN
    st_message.text = "Operation successful!"
ELSE
    st_message.text = "Operation failed"
END IF

sqlca.autocommit = FALSE
```

17. Code the following script in the Clicked event of cb_format2. This script analyzes the action chosen in the lb_actions listbox and prompts for the required parameters. It then sends the SQL to the database and notifies the user, via st_message, of the success or failure of the operation.

```
string ls_action, ls_sql, ls_deptid, ls_deptdsc, ls_parentdept, ls_statecd,
ls_statedesc
long ll_tab, ll_space, ll_numparms, ll_mgrid

// get the item the user picked
ls_action = lb_actions.SelectedItem()

// Locate the first space and the tab character to help us perform an
// extraction below
ll_tab = Pos( ls_action, "~t" )
ll_space = Pos(ls_action, " " )
```

continued on next page

continued from previous page

```
// extract the SQL from the action
ls_sql = Mid( ls_action, ll_tab + 1 )
ls_action = Mid( ls_action, ll_space + 1, ll_tab - ll_space - 1 )

PREPARE sqlsa FROM :ls_sql USING sqlca;
IF wf_error_handler (sqlca, "Prepare", "Could not prepare SQL" ) = 0 THEN
    // based on the option the user selected, prompt for each item. Note
    // that this is hardcoded information -- a production application would need
    // to store some means of identifying the data items and datatypes needed
    CHOOSE CASE lower( ls_action )
        CASE "department"
            OpenWithParm( w_response, "String~tDept ID:" , parent)
            ls_deptid = Message.StringParm
            OpenWithParm( w_response, "String~tDept Description:", parent )
            ls_deptdsc = Message.StringParm
            OpenWithParm( w_response, "Integer~tManager ID:" , parent)
            ll_mgrid = Long(Message.StringParm)
            OpenWithParm( w_response, "String~tDept Parent:", parent )
            ls_parentdept = Message.StringParm

            // issue this sql to the database using the information given
            // by the user
            EXECUTE sqlsa USING :ls_deptid, :ls_deptdsc, :ll_mgrid,
                :ls_parentdept;
            IF wf_error_handler(sqlca, "Execute", &
                    "Could not execute SQL") = 0 THEN
                COMMIT USING sqlca;
                st_message.text = "Department added!"
            ELSE
                ROLLBACK USING sqlca;
                st_message.text = "Department add failed"
            END IF
        CASE "state"
            OpenWithParm( w_response, "String~tState code (2 chars):" ,
parent)
            ls_statecd =Left(Trim(upper( Message.StringParm)),2)
            OpenWithParm( w_response, "String~tState name:", parent )
            ls_statedesc = Message.StringParm
            PREPARE sqlsa FROM :ls_sql USING sqlca;
            IF wf_error_handler (sqlca, "Prepare", &
                    "Could not prepare SQL" ) = 0 THEN
                EXECUTE sqlsa USING :ls_statecd, :ls_statedesc;
                IF wf_error_handler(sqlca, "Execute", &
                        "Could not execute SQL") = 0 THEN
                    COMMIT USING sqlca;
                    st_message.text = "State added!"
                ELSE
                    ROLLBACK USING sqlca;
                    st_message.text = "State add failed"
                END IF
            END IF
    END CHOOSE
END IF
```

18. Save the w_dynsql window.

19. Using the Declare/Instance Variables... menu item, declare an instance variable as follows.

```
boolean ib_stop = FALSE
```

20. Place the following code on the Clicked event of cb_sendquery. This script is significantly more complex than the others written so far. It accepts the user's query, prepares it to be sent to the database, sends it, and then processes each row one column at a time. For more details on this processing, see the How It Works section. The results are displayed in mle_results.

```
string ls_query, ls_val, ls_row
integer li_index, li_boolean

// make stopping the query an option
cb_stop.enabled = TRUE

// get the user's query and prep it for further processing
ls_query = mle_query.text

IF Trim( ls_query ) = "" THEN
    MessageBox("Query", "Please enter a query first." )
    RETURN
END IF

mle_results.text = "Query results:"

DECLARE dyncursor DYNAMIC CURSOR FOR SQLSA;

// let PowerBuilder construct an execution-capable version of the
// dynamic query
PREPARE SQLSA FROM :ls_query USING sqlca;

wf_error_handler( sqlca, "Prepare", "Could not prepare query" )

// let PB get an idea of the parameters and columns involved
DESCRIBE sqlsa INTO sqlda;
wf_error_handler( sqlca, "Describe", "Could not describe query" )

OPEN DYNAMIC dyncursor USING DESCRIPTOR sqlda;
IF wf_error_handler( sqlca, "Open", "Unable to open query" ) = 0 THEN
DO WHILE sqlca.sqlcode = 0 and ib_stop = FALSE
    // give the Stop button the opportunity to work
    Yield()

    // for each row coming out of the database, we'll have to examine the
    // data type of each column, and get it using the appropriate
    // GetDynamicxxx() function.
    FETCH dyncursor USING DESCRIPTOR sqlda;
    IF wf_error_handler( sqlca, "Fetch Dynamic Cursor", &
            "Could not fetch" ) = 0 THEN
        FOR li_index = 1 TO sqlda.numoutputs
            CHOOSE CASE   sqlda.outparmtype[ li_index]
                CASE TypeString!
                    ls_val = sqlda.GetDynamicString( li_index )
                CASE TypeDate!
```

continued on next page

continued from previous page

```
                            ls_val = string( sqlda.GetDynamicDate( li_index ), &
                                'dd mmm yyyy' )
                        CASE TypeTime!
                            ls_val = string( sqlda.GetDynamicTime( li_index ), &
                                'hh:mm:ss' )
                        CASE TypeDateTime!
                            ls_val = string( sqlda.GetDynamicDateTime( li_index ), &
                                'dd mmm yyyy hh:mm:ss' )
                        CASE TypeInteger!, TypeLong!, TypeDecimal!, TypeDouble!,&
                            TypeReal!
                            ls_val = string( sqlda.GetDynamicNumber( li_index ) )
                        CASE TypeBoolean!
                            li_boolean = sqlda.GetDynamicNumber( li_index )
                            IF IsNull( li_boolean ) THEN
                                SetNull( ls_val )
                            ELSE
                                IF li_boolean = 1 THEN ls_val = "TRUE" ELSE &
                                    ls_val = "FALSE"
                            END IF
                    END CHOOSE
                    // make sure our value isn't null; if it is, it will nullify
                    // ls_row when concatenated
                    IF IsNull(ls_val) THEN ls_Val = "(null)"
                    ls_row = ls_row + "," + ls_val
                NEXT
                ls_row = Mid( ls_row, 2 )
                mle_results.text = mle_results.text + "~r~n" + ls_row
                ls_row = ""
        END IF
LOOP
END IF

CLOSE dyncursor;

wf_error_handler( sqlca, "Close Cursor", "Could not close dyncursor" )

COMMIT USING sqlca;
wf_error_handler( sqlca, "Commit", "Could not commit")

ib_stop = FALSE
cb_stop.enabled = FALSE
```

21. Save your window.

22. Place the following script in the Clicked event of cb_stop. This button allows the user to stop a long-running query by clicking the Stop button. Observe the use of the Yield() function coded in step 20. This function allows the Stop button to be recognized.

```
ib_stop = TRUE
```

23. Code a script for the Clicked event of cb_exit as follows:

```
Close( parent )
```

24. Save your window.

25. Using the Application painter, code a script for the Open event of the a_dynsql Application object as follows.

```
Open( w_dynsql )
```

26. Save the application and run it.

How It Works

As you can tell from the scripts coded above, dynamic SQL ranges in complexity from simple to extremely complex. Examining Format 1 SQL as can be seen in the script for cb_format1 reveals that the single instruction is EXECUTE IMMEDIATE. The only requirement for EXECUTE IMMEDIATE is that it be a completely specified SQL statement; that is, with no parameters that require substitution later on. It does not have to be restricted to DDL (CREATE/ALTER/DROP) as indicated in this example; any fully specified SQL statement other than SELECT will work.

Format 2 dynamic SQL extends format 1 by allowing you to code question marks (?) as placeholders in the SQL statement. To use format 2, you must PREPARE the SQL statement into the DynamicStagingArea (SQLSA in this example) which will then contain a compiled version of the SQL statement along with information on the number of parameters. Following the PREPARE, you must EXECUTE the staging area (SQLSA) specifying variables that should be substituted in order for the question marks in the original statement. Observe that, like format 1, format 2 has no provision for retrieving data from the database. It is restricted to non-query statements. However, format 2 will execute more quickly than format 1 when the same statement is issued multiple times with different values because the PREPARE step is not repeated (as is implicitly done by EXECUTE IMMEDIATE).

Format 4 dynamic SQL is the most dynamic of all dynamic SQL. Format 4 is used when the exact columns returned by the query and the exact WHERE clause needed by the query cannot be determined at runtime. To support this type of processing, PowerBuilder offers the DynamicDescriptionArea, represented by SQLDA in this application. Once the SQL statement has been PREPAREd, as in format 2, PowerBuilder must analyze the statement to determine how many columns and their data types will be returned by the database along with how many placeholders and their data types are in use in the WHERE clause. To perform this operation, the program must DESCRIBE the staging area, SQLSA, into the DynamicDescriptionArea, SQLDA.

Internally, the SQLDA is quite complex, but it has four properties that are of interest to you: numinputs, inparmtype[], numoutputs, and outparmtype[]. Following the DESCRIBE statement, numoutputs contains a number indicating how many result set columns are being returned by the query. There are a corresponding number of elements in outparmtype[] indicating the data types of these columns. Similarly, numinputs contains a number indicating the number of placeholders used in the WHERE clause, while inparmtype[] should contain the data types of those placeholders. Unfortunately, as of this writing, inparmtype[] is not yet implemented with any database that PowerBuilder supports. This means that your program will have to find another means of determining the input parameter data types for your dynamic SQL statements. For this reason, this How-To does not support the question mark placeholders in the Format 4 WHERE clause.

Returning to the Format 4 script coded on cb_cursor's Clicked event, you can see the steps involved in processing the query. First, the script PREPAREs the DynamicStagingArea, SQLSA, from the query and DESCRIBEs it into the DynamicDescriptionArea, SQLDA. If this script supported placeholders in the query, your script could then call SetDynamicParm() on SQLDA to set the values for each of those placeholders. Following the DESCRIBE, the script OPENs the dynamic cursor and begins to FETCH the rows.

However, FETCHing the rows is no longer trivial, since the script does not know how many columns are in each row. For each row retrieved, there are a number of columns equal to the value of the numoutputs property of SQLDA. The datatype of each column can be found by accessing the appropriate element of outparmtype[]. Based on the value of a particular outparmtype[] element, the script calls the appropriate GetDynamicxxx() function and converts it to a string for display purposes. This process continues until all columns and all rows have been processed.

Comments

Dynamic SQL can be a complex but very essential part of your PowerBuilder programs. In general, most PowerBuilder programmers will avoid dynamic SQL because of complexity and speed concerns. However, as this How-To demonstrates, there are a number of tasks that only dynamic SQL can perform.

COMPLEXITY
INTERMEDIATE

8.4   How do I...
Query the system catalog at runtime regardless of the DBMS?

Problem

I would like my application to allow the user to pick a table from a list of tables in my database and to pick from a list of columns for that particular table. However, in the interest of making my application more portable between different database products, I am reluctant to code DBMS-specific queries that access the various DBMS catalog structures. Is there any way I can determine the tables and columns in my database at runtime regardless of the DBMS I'm using?

Technique

PowerBuilder maintains a set of five tables, collectively known as the *PowerBuilder repository*, that store numerous pieces of information about your database, including the tables and columns present in that database. These tables exist primarily to support DataWindow processing and contain information called *extended properties* that define default column widths, fonts, formatting, validation rules, edit styles, and so forth. However, your application can access these tables to determine the tables and columns available in your database. Note that in order for your program to obtain repository information, the repository must exist in your target database. This repository is created as part of the PowerBuilder installation process; it is generally constructed when a system-level user connects to the database for the first time. If you are interested in using a database other than Sybase SQL Anywhere, please refer to the PowerBuilder installation instructions for details on establishing the repository in your desired database.

Steps

The application for this How-To can be found in the library CATALOG.PBL and in the executable CATALOG.EXE. Start the application. After it connects to the database, the window shown in Figure 8-9 will appear. Observe the list of tables in the Tables ListBox. This listing of available tables was obtained from the PowerBuilder repository. Click on a table and observe the list of columns for the chosen table that appears in the Columns ListBox. This list is also obtained from the PowerBuilder repository. To create this application, follow the steps below.

1. Create a new application library and Application object using the Application painter. Name the library CATALOG.PBL and the Application object a_catalog. You will not need an application template for this application.

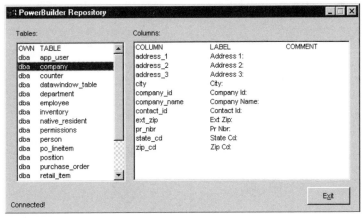

Figure 8-9 The Catalog application

2. Create a new window called w_catalog using the Window painter in conjunction with the window and control settings listed in Table 8-10 and shown in Figure 8-10.

WINDOW/CONTROL NAME	PROPERTY	VALUE
Window		
w_catalog	Title	"PowerBuilder Repository"
	MinimizeBox	TRUE
	MaximizeBox	FALSE
	Resizable	FALSE
StaticText	Name	st_tables
	Text	"&Tables:"
	Border	None
	Alignment	Left
StaticText	Name	st_columns
	Text	"&Columns:"
	Border	None
	Alignment	Left
StaticText	Name	st_message
	Text	""
	Border	None
	Alignment	Left
ListBox	Name	lb_tables
	VScrollBar	TRUE
	HScrollBar	TRUE
	Tabs	"3"
	Accelerator	"t"
	Border	3D Lowered
ListBox	Name	lb_columns
	VScrollBar	TRUE
	HScrollBar	TRUE
	Tabs	"20 40"
	Accelerator	"c"
	Border	3DLowered

WINDOW/CONTROL NAME	PROPERTY	VALUE
CommandButton	Name	cb_exit
	Text	"E&xit"

Table 8-10 Window and control settings for the w_catalog window

3. As you did in previous How-Tos in this chapter (e.g., step 4 of How-To 8.2), define a function called wf_error_handler on the w_catalog window as shown in Table 8-11. This function provides basic error handling capabilities throughout this application. You may copy this function from w_embedded in EMBED.PBL if you like.

FUNCTION SPECIFICATIONS			
Function	Name	wf_error_handler	
	Access	Public	
	Returns	integer	
Arguments	a_to	Transaction	Value
	as_title	String	Value
	as_message	String	Value

Table 8-11 Function specifications for wf_error_handler()

4. Place the following script in the body of wf_error_handler() to examine the SQLCode property of the passed transaction object, a_to. In the event of an error, this function displays an appropriate message.

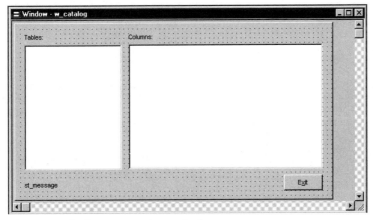

Figure 8-10 The w_catalog window

```
string ls_errtext, ls_dbcode
integer li_sqlcode

// Preserve the original sqlcode (which may be affected by ROLLBACK later
on)
li_sqlcode = sqlca.sqlcode

IF li_sqlcode < 0 THEN
    ls_errtext = a_to.sqlerrtext
    ls_dbcode = String( a_to.sqldbcode )
    ROLLBACK USING a_to;
    MessageBox( as_title, as_message + "~r~n" +&
            "(" +ls_dbcode + ") " + ls_errtext, Exclamation! )
END IF

// Return the original value of the SQLCode
RETURN li_sqlcode
```

5. Return to the Window painter and save the window.

6. Use the Declare/User Events... menu item to declare a custom user event ue_postopen mapped to pbm_custom01.

7. Place the following script in the Open event of w_catalog. This script posts to the ue_postopen custom user event to allow the window to be drawn before connecting to the database.

```
this.PostEvent( "ue_postopen" )
```

8. Code a script for the ue_postopen event on w_catalog as follows. This event connects the application to the database and retrieves the initial list of tables from the PowerBuilder repository.

```
string ls_owner, ls_table
SetPointer( Hourglass! )

st_message.text = "Connecting to database..."

// set the transaction object to refer to the Zoo database
sqlca.dbms = "ODBC"
sqlca.dbparm = "ConnectString='DSN=Zoo;UID=dba;PWD=SQL'"

CONNECT USING sqlca;

IF sqlca.sqlcode < 0 THEN // unsuccessful connect
    st_message.text = "Unsuccessful connect."
    MessageBox("Connection Error", "Could not connect to database.~r~n"+&
            "(" + string( sqlca.sqldbcode) + ") " + sqlca.sqlerrtext, &
            Exclamation! )
ELSE
    st_message.text = "Connected!"
    lb_tables.AddItem( "OWN~tTABLE" )

    // get a list of tables

    DECLARE tbllist CURSOR FOR
```

```
        SELECT "pbcattbl"."pbt_ownr",   "pbcattbl"."pbt_tnam"
        FROM "pbcattbl"
        ORDER BY 1, 2 USING sqlca;

    OPEN tbllist;

    IF wf_error_handler( sqlca, "Open", &
                "Could not open table listing" ) = 0 THEN
        DO WHILE sqlca.sqlcode = 0
            FETCH tbllist INTO :ls_owner, :ls_table;
            IF wf_error_handler (sqlca, "Fetch", &
                    "Could not fetch table") = 0 THEN
                lb_tables.AddItem( ls_owner + "~t" + ls_table)
            END IF
        LOOP

        CLOSE tbllist;

        wf_error_handler( sqlca, "Close", "Could not close table listing" )

        COMMIT USING sqlca;
    END IF
END IF
```

9. Code a script to disconnect from the database in the Close event of w_catalog as follows.

```
// if we're connected to the database, disconnect
IF sqlca.DBHandle() <> 0 THEN
    DISCONNECT USING sqlca;

    IF sqlca.sqlcode < 0 THEN   // couldn't disconnect
        MessageBox("Disconnection Error", &
            "Could not disconnect from database.~r~n"+&
            "(" + string(sqlca.sqldbcode) + ") " + &
            sqlca.sqlerrtext, Exclamation! )
    END IF
END IF
```

10. Save your window.

11. Place a script on the SelectionChanged event of lb_tables as follows. This script detects the user's click to select a table and retrieves a list of columns for that table into lb_tables.

```
string ls_table, ls_owner, ls_column, ls_temp, ls_comment, ls_label

SetPointer( hourglass! )
lb_columns.Reset()

// Don't let the user select the header line that labels the columns
IF this.SelectedIndex() = 1 THEN
    this.SelectItem( 0 )
    RETURN
ELSE
    lb_columns.AddItem( "COLUMN~tLABEL~tCOMMENT" )
    DECLARE collist CURSOR FOR
```

continued on next page

continued from previous page

```
        SELECT "pbcatcol"."pbc_cnam", "pbcatcol"."pbc_labl",
            "pbcatcol"."pbc_cmnt"
    FROM "pbcatcol"
    WHERE ( "pbcatcol"."pbc_ownr" = :ls_owner ) AND
        ( "pbcatcol"."pbc_tnam" = :ls_table ) USING sqlca;

    ls_temp = this.SelectedItem()
    ls_owner = Mid( ls_temp, 1, Pos( ls_temp, "~t" ) - 1)
    ls_table = Mid( ls_temp, Pos(ls_temp, "~t") + 1 )

    OPEN collist;

    IF wf_error_handler( sqlca, "Open", &
            "Could not open column listing" ) = 0 THEN
        DO WHILE sqlca.sqlcode = 0
            FETCH collist INTO :ls_column, :ls_label, :ls_comment;
            IF wf_error_handler (sqlca, "Fetch", &
                    "Could not fetch column") = 0 THEN
                IF IsNull( ls_label ) THEN ls_label = ""
                IF IsNull( ls_comment ) THEN ls_comment = ""
                lb_columns.AddItem( ls_column +"~t"  + ls_label + "~t" + &
                    ls_comment)
            END IF
        LOOP
    END IF
    CLOSE collist;

    wf_error_handler( sqlca, "Close", "Could not close column listing" )

    COMMIT USING sqlca;
END IF
```

12. Code the Clicked event of cb_exit to close the window as follows:

```
Close( parent )
```

13. Save the w_catalog window.

14. Using the Application painter, write a script to open the w_catalog window as follows.

```
Open( w_catalog )
```

15. Save and run the application.

How It Works

The catalog application itself is surprisingly simple. The bulk of the application resides in two scripts: the Open event of w_catalog and the SelectionChanged event on lb_tables. In response to these two events, these scripts perform some simple embedded SQL cursor statements to retrieve a list of tables and columns, respectively, from the database.

Of more importance are the contents of the PowerBuilder repository tables themselves. These tables contain information that is used primarily by the DataWindow painter which is explored more fully in Chapters 9 through 12. In simplest terms the repository is responsible for storing information that tells PowerBuilder how to display, validate, and edit the various columns and tables in a database. This How-To does not make extensive use of this information, instead extracting the table owners, table names, column names, column labels, and column comments for the tables and columns of interest. Your application can then use this information to construct custom queries (see How-To 8.3 on Dynamic SQL) or DataWindows at runtime. Because the repository structure is identical regardless of DBMS, your application does not need different DBMS-specific queries to retrieve this information.

CHAPTER 9

THE DATAWINDOW AND REPORT PAINTERS

THE DATAWINDOW AND REPORT PAINTERS

How do I...

If PowerBuilder is famous for any one item it is for the DataWindow object. This one component ensures that not only will your application look and work in a consistent manner, but also that it will take little or no time unless you want to do something beyond the standard. However, this object also has the power to allow you to provide a high level of sophistication to your application by providing edit masks for your dollar columns and validation edits for your user columns, and by providing filtering and sorting on the database server and on the client. The DataWindow columns themselves can map directly to a database table field, a computed field, or even a computed column.

In this chapter you will explore some of the components of the DataWindow. You will create both computed columns and computed fields. You will use the Expression capability in the Object Attributes property sheet to modify a field's color and font, based on the value you will use in the nested report object to create a master/detail report. Lastly, you will create two reports using the new DataWindow styles of Rich Text Format (RTF) and OLE 2.0.

9.1   Create a Computed Column

Your users will want summary information, such as the count of occurences, or the sum of two fields, or the sum of a column when grouped by other columns.You will learn how to use the DataWindow painter to modify your SQL to include computed fields.

9.2   Use the Report Painter for One-Time Reports

The Report painter is an effective tool for creating one-time reports and for use in DataWindow prototyping. In this How-To you will modify a DataWindow to create a stored report.

9.3   Create a Computed Field

In PowerBuilder you can create computed columns that will add two database fields together or that will print out the date or the page count.This How-To will provide examples of the more common types of computed columns.

9.4   Set DataWindow Attributes Conditionally

Your users would sometimes like to have numbers that are over a certain value highlighted in a different color, or change the displayed value itself based on other factors. This How-To gives some detail on conditionally changing attributes based on the data values.

9.5   Create an Updatable DataWindow Based on Two Tables

This How-To will demonstrate how to create a DataWindow from two different tables. It will also demonstrate how to set the appropriate Update characteristics to insure the appropriate fields are updated for the appropriate table. In addition, you will learn how to verify your SQL Syntax.

9.6   Use the Rich Text Format (RTF) Style to Create a Form Letter

With this DataWindow style introduced with PowerBuilder version 5.0, you can create a form letter using standard word processing capability and integrated directly with your data. This How-To demonstrates how to create a form letter directly in the DataWindow using this style.

9.7   Use the OLE 2.0 Style to Create a Microsoft Graph

Also with version 5.0 of PowerBuilder, you can use this style to connect to another application that is OLE 2.0 compliant to merge your data with that application's formatting and functionality. You do not need to worry about communicating the data from your application as this is handled using Uniform Data Transfer. This How-To demonstrates this using Microsoft Graph.

COMPLEXITY
BEGINNING

9.1   How do I...
Create a computed column?

Problem Statement

In my application's reports, I need to see things like the sum of a column when it is grouped by another column, or the difference between two columns. How can I generate SQL to do this?

Technique

This How-To will demonstrate how to create computed columns in the SQL statement by creating one that will display the difference in days between two dates, and one that will display the sum of a column when the data rows are grouped. In order to display the sum of a grouped column, you will also learn how to group the rows returned.

Steps

Run the DATAWINDOW.PBL application and login as "jtower" with no password. The DataWindow you will be creating will be in the first tabpage labeled "PO with Computed Columns". Note from this and Figure 9-1 the two columns at the end which show the sum of the purchase orders for the company for a specific order and delivery date, and the number of days between when the order was placed and when it was expected.

To create these two computed columns, follow the steps listed below.

1. Access the DATAWINDOW.PBL library.

2. From the DataWindow painter create a new DataWindow of type Grid with an SQL Select as data source.

3. From the tables that display choose purchase_order and company, select the order_dt, exp_delivery_dt, and company_name columns.

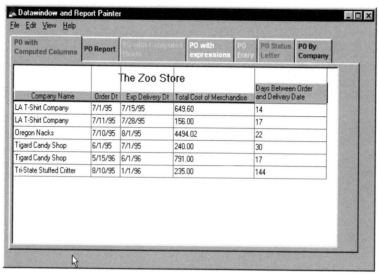

Figure 9-1 PO with Computed Columns report from the DATAWINDOW application

4. Group the rows by selecting the Group tab and dragging the company_name, order_dt, and exp_delivery_dt columns from the left to the right side of the Tab control.

5. Create the first computed column by accessing the Compute tab at the bottom of the painter and typing the following into the first blank line.

```
sum(po_amount)
```

6. The above field will create a computed column displaying the purchase order sum for the grouping just created.

7. Create the second computed column just under the first.

```
Days(order_dt, exp_delivery_dt)
```

8. Before leaving the SQL painter, access the Sort tab and drag the company_name column from the left to the right side of the control to sort on this column.

9. Access the DataWindow painter Design window.

10. Change the background color of the DataWindow to white, change the column headers to gray, and change the border on the column headers to 3D raised.

11. Add a text field in the middle of the DataWindow and type "The Zoo Store" into the text field.

12. Change the Sum Computed column header to "Total Cost of Merchandise" and change the Days Computed column header to "Days Between Order and Delivery Date".

13. Test your DataWindow in Preview. Notice the new computed column values.

14. Save the DataWindow as d_open_po_amount_01.

How It Works

The SQL painter allows you to create computed columns using the Compute tab option. You can create an aggregate computed column such as the Sum column but you will need to place all non-aggregate columns in the selection list in the Group By statement. You can use database columns to create a computed column, but note that these are database specific. Once you create the computed column, you should always change the column heading to display a more meaningful label for the column.

Comments

As noted in the steps in this How-To, the functions that can be used in a computed column are database specific. You should always set up your working environment to point to the same type of database your application will be running in when you do any work in either the Database painter or the DataWindow painter. Check with your Database Administrator for the location of a development database.

COMPLEXITY
BEGINNING

9.2 How do I...
Use the Report painter for one-time reports?

Problem Statement

I occasionally generate one-time-only reports for my clients using the Preview mode of the DataWindow painter and either copying the data to something like Microsoft Excel or generating a hard copy or printing the report. The problem with this is that many of these DataWindows are updateable and all I want is a read-only view. What is an alternative to using the Preview mode of the DataWindow painter for ad-hoc reporting?

Technique

PowerBuilder provides two painters: the Report painter and the Report Run Only tool. This How-To will access a pre-defined DataWindow and use Sort and Filter to modify the results. In addition, once the report looks the way you want, you will see that you can send this report via electronic mail or save the report in a variety of formats.

Steps

Access the DATAWINDOW.PBL library and run the application. Use "jtower" to login. Access the PO Report tab which is tab 2. Notice that unlike the PO with Computed Columns DataWindow, those purchase orders for LA T-Shirt Company are not displaying as shown in Figure 9-2. Close the application and open d_open_po_amount_report from the Report (Run Only) tool and access the Filter item from the Rows menu. If you examine the filter for this DataWindow you will notice that a filter has already been set for the result set as shown in Figure 9-3. When this report was created a filter was defined, and the filter was saved when the report was saved. If you examine the Sort for the report, you will notice that it too was defined when the report was created as shown in Figure 9-4.

The steps for using the Report painter and Report (Run Only) tool follow.

1. Access the DATAWINDOW.PBL library and backup the existing d_open_po_amount_report report by renaming it as d_open_po_amount_report_bak.

2. Open the d_open_po_amount DataWindow in the Report painter and save as d_open_po_amount_report.

3. Run the report in Preview mode. At this time all fields are displayed and the rows are sorted on company name.

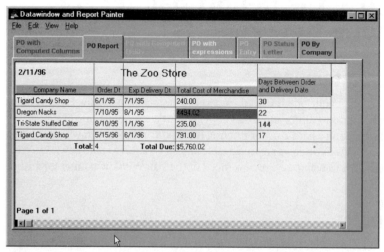

Figure 9-2 PO Report from DATAWINDOW application

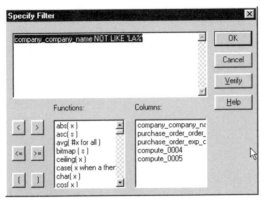

Figure 9-3 Filter dialog for
d_open_po_amount_report with
pre-defined filter

4. Filter the rows by selecting Filter from the Rows menu. The dialog box that
appears lists the columns in a ListBox in the lower right, lists the available
functions in a ListBox in the lower left, and contains a workspace on top.
You will filter out all rows that begin with "LA" as the first two characters.
You will use the new NOT LIKE operator to do this.

```
company_company_name NOT LIKE 'LA%'
```

5. Sort the rows by selecting Sort from the Rows menu. The dialog box
that appears lists the columns in the left, which you can drag to the
column in the right. The sort order is ascending by default. Drag the
purchase_order_order_dt column and drop into the columns column.
Accept the default order. Close the dialog and save the new sort order.

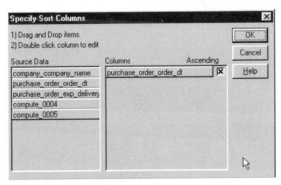

Figure 9-4 Sort dialog for
d_open_po_amount_report with pre-defined
sort

6. At this time you can save the report and run it again with the Report (Run Only) tool, or you can save the results in some form, or you can send the results using electronic mail.

7. For this How-To, save the results into a PowerBuilder Stored Report (PSR). Select the Save Rows As... menu option from the File menu. The dialog that displays provides several formats that you can save the data in as shown in Figure 9-5.

8. Select the Report RadioButton, and check the Include Headers box. Save the report as openpo.PSR.

9. To send the report select the Send option from the File menu. You will be prompted as to which Exchange setting to use.

10. You can check the results of your efforts by running the VIEWER.EXE standalone report viewer included on the CD-ROM. Run the tool and select the PowerBuilder Stored Report tab option. When the File browser opens, select your newly created stored report. Your results should look similar to the report shown in Figure 9-6.

How It Works

The Report painter differs from the DataWindow painter in that the data in the report is not updateable. This makes it ideal for experimenting with formatting changes without worrying about accidental changes to the data.

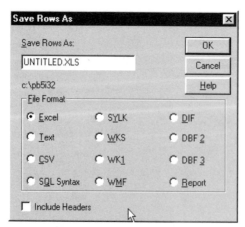

Figure 9-5 Save Rows As dialog for saving the d_open_po_amount_report report

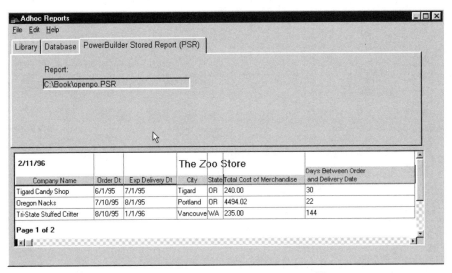

Figure 9-6 Viewer application running openpo.psr file

Comments

The Report painter is a very effective method for prototyping your DataWindows. It will allow you to define the underlying data source for the window, specify the presentation type, and then work with the user to try out different formats. The user can sit with you as you work and see results immediately, or you can hardcopy it to a file or print the result.

COMPLEXITY
INTERMEDIATE

9.3 How do I...
Create a computed field?

Problem Statement

I need to be able to display column and row totals, or averages or other calculations for a report. In addition, I need to place a date and page count on these reports. How can I do this?

Technique

The PowerBuilder DataWindow painter provides the ability to place computed fields on the DataWindow. Additionally it provides some predefined fields for Page count, Date, and a Sum. These fields operate on the data rows once they are returned to the client and they operate only on those rows that are not sorted and filtered (visible rows only).

Steps

Open the d_open_po_amount_01 DataWindow and add a Total count computed field, a Sum computed field for the Total Cost of Merchandise column, a Page field, and a Date field. How to create and place these computed fields is detailed in the following steps.

1. Access the DATAWINDOW.PBL library and backup the existing d_open_po_amount_02 DataWindow by saving it as d_open_po_amount_02_bak.

2. Open the d_open_po_amount_01 DataWindow. To create this DataWindow follow the steps in How-To 9.1.

3. The first computed field you will create will be the Total Count field. Click on the Summary band and move it down to create room for placing the field in the Summary band.

4. Select the Computed Field object button from the painter Bar dropdown as shown in Figure 9-7 or choose it from the Objects menu. Click in the

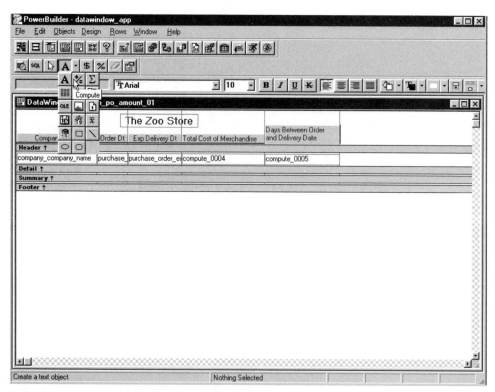

Figure 9-7 Computed Field object from dropdown on painter ToolBar

Summary band in the Order Dt column and the Computed Object property sheet will open.

5. In the sheet select the More... button to bring up the Modify Expression dialog.

6. In this dialog select the "count (#x for all)" summary function, listed in the lower left ListBox, which will place this function in the workspace at the top of the dialog.

7. Next highlight the "#X for all" part of the function call, and select the column to use for counting. In this case we will count the company name, so select this item. This will overwrite the text we have highlighted in the workspace, as shown in Figure 9-8.

8. Verify the function call and, if it verifies correctly, close the dialog, accepting the computed field definition.

9. This field will be placed in the column and in the band. To position and size this correctly change the layering of the field to layer to the background. Do this in the property sheet for the object by selecting the Postition tab and selecting "background" from the Layer DropDownListBox as shown in Figure 9-9.

10. Position the field and size it to fit within the column. Change the text color to fit the colors for the other text fields and the column header, and make sure the background of the field is the correct color. Once you have set up the field the way you wish, again select Layer from the Property sheet and set it back to the band.

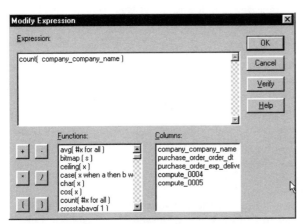

Figure 9-8 Modify Expression with expression for new computed field

Figure 9-9 Computed Object Position
Property tab with Layer changed to
Background

11. This computed field does not have a label and you will need to create one
using a text field. Select Text from the Objects menu or the letter "A" from
the dropdown toolbar and click in the Company Name field. As with the
computed field, size and reposition this field after setting it to layer to the
background, and once positioned correctly, layer it back to the band. For
the text, type in "Total:" and justify the text to the right.

12. Run the DataWindow in Preview mode and notice that your new field is
now picking up the calculated count of company name rows.

13. Return to the design tool and create the computed field to sum all of the
Total Cost of Merchandise computed column. Select the column by clicking
on it in the detail band and then select the Sum toolbar icon. The
DataWindow painter will place a computed field with the appropriate function and column in the summary band for the column. If you wish you can
now reposition the field using the techniques mentioned in previous steps.
In addition, format the field by selecting Format from the right mouse button popup menu and format it to show up as a monetary value.

```
$#,##0.00;[RED]($#,##0.00)
```

14. Run the DataWindow in Preview mode and your new summary computed
field is showing in the correct format. Return to the Design window and
create a label for this column titled "Total Due:".

15. The next computed field you will place will be the Page computed field. Make room in the Footer band by dragging down the band. Select the "Page n of n" Computed field, either from the Objects menu or from the toolbar dropdown. Click in the company name column in the Footer band. This will place a page count field at the bottom of every page if the DataWindow prints out, or the bottom of the DataWindow when it is displayed. Move this field until you are satisfied with the location, and modify the font and text colors until they are appropriate for your application needs.

16. The last computed field you will place will be one for the date. Select the Today() computed field from the Objects menu or from the toolbar and place this in the upper left hand corner of the DataWindow.

17. Preview the DataWindow. Try filtering out some of the rows and notice that the computed fields for the Total and Sum fields adjust accordingly.

18. Move the computed fields until you are satisfied with their placement and look and save the DataWindow in the name of d_open_po_amount_03.

19. Run the DATAWINDOW application from PowerBuilder and login as "jtower". Click on the third tab to display your new DataWindow as shown in Figure 9-10.

How It Works

Computed fields are fields that work on the data after it is returned from the database, or predefined fields that show the page numbers and the date. Think of a

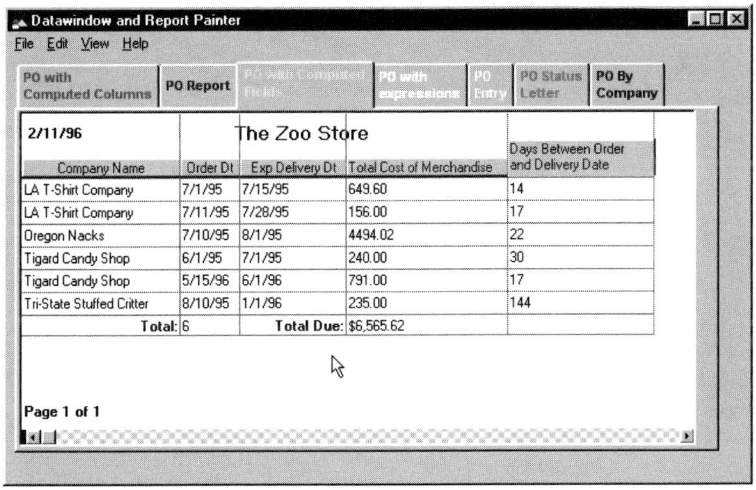

Figure 9-10 PO with computed fields from the
DATAWINDOW application

DataWindow as two objects: the data that it contains and the syntax of the presentation. Computed fields are additional syntactic objects that work with the data contained in the DataWindow without any regard as to the data source or how the data is obtained. The computed fields are generated after the data is returned and before the field is displayed.

Comments

Computed fields can also be created dynamically as will be seen in Chapter 12.

COMPLEXITY
INTERMEDIATE

9.4   How do I...
Set DataWindow column attributes conditionally?

Problem Statement

In my application some of the reports contain certain data values that are very important and my users would like these to be highlighted in some way. A case would be to set the field of a negative value to red, or, if another field is over a certain limit, to set it to green. How can I change the appearance of a field based on the data value in it?

Technique

Most DataWindow attributes can be changed dynamically at runtime. You can use the Modify function or the DataWindow Object in your script to change them, or with some of the attributes, you can set up a condition for the column to change that attribute if a certain condition is met.

This How-To will demonstrate changing the background color of a DataWindow "cell" based on the value of the data contained in it.

Steps

Run the DATAWINDOW application and login as "jtower". Select the fourth tab, labeled "PO with Expressions". When you run the application notice that the background color for the Total Cost of Merchandise changes if the value is greater than $2000. Additionally, also notice that the font color and weight changes for the Days column when the difference between the order date and the expected delivery date is greater than 20 as shown in Figure 9-11. Additionally, if you were to move your mouse cursor over this field you would find that the pointer itself changes.

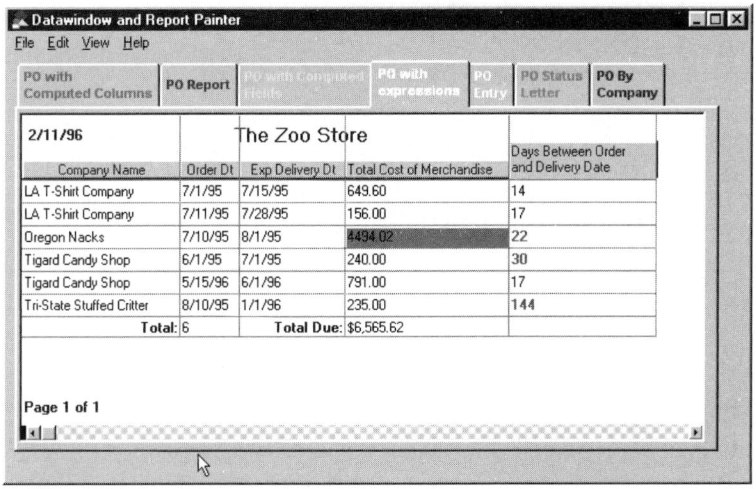

Figure 9-11 PO with Expressions from DATAWINDOW application

The steps to dynamically change the display attributes for a DataWindow column based on the data value are provided below.

1. Access the DATAWINDOW.PBL and backup the d_open_po_amount DataWindow by saving it as d_open_po_amount_bak.

2. Open the d_open_po_amount_03 DataWindow. This DataWindow was created in How-To 9.3.

3. The first modification you will make will be to the Total Cost of Merchandise computed column. Double-click on this field to bring up the Column Object property sheet. Select the Expressions tab.

4. This property sheet has a list of column attributes and a space to the right for typing a conditional expression that can change the attribute as shown in Figure 9-12. Double-click on the background color attribute.

5. The Modify Expression dialog will appear. You can use this to build an expression or you can type your expression in directly. You will type the following expression into the MultiLineEdit control.

```
if ( compute_0004 > 2000.00, RGB(255,0,0), RGB(255,255,255))
```

6. The conditional expression instructs the application to test the value for this column. If the value is over 2000.00, then it changes the attribute. In this case it changes the color to red, which is RGB(255,0,0). If the condition fails, it changes the color to RGB(255,255,255), which is white.

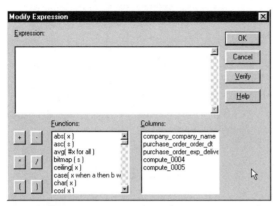

Figure 9-12 Expressions Property sheet for
the Column object

7. When the data is retrieved from the database, the above condition will be
applied to this column for each row, and the column attribute will be modified based on how the expression evaluates.

8. Verify the expression and, if it is correct, accept the expression and close the
property sheet.

9. Next you will change the column attributes for the second computed column, the Days between Order and Expected Delivery Date column. Select
this column and bring up the Attribute Conditional Expression dialog.

10. The first attribute you change will be the color attribute, which is the text
color. This time don't switch to the Modify Expression dialog, but type the
line below in the space next to the color attribute.

```
if ( compute_0005 > 20, RGB(0,127,0) , RGB(0,0,0))
```

11. If this expression evaluates to TRUE, the day count is greater than 20, and
the font color will be changed to RGB(0,127,0). If FALSE, the color will
stay as black, RGB(0,0,0), which is the color of the text elsewhere in the
report. The next two attributes will change the weight of the font and the
pointer of the mouse cursor respectively, as shown in the code below. The
property sheet should look like the one shown in Figure 9-13.

Font.weight

```
if ( compute_0005 > 20, 700, 400)
```

Pointer

```
if ( compute_0005 < 20, 'Cross!' ,' Arrow!')
```

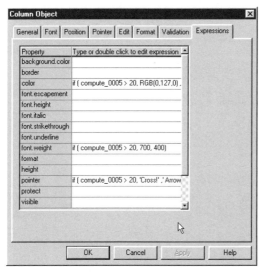

Figure 9-13 Column Object Expressions property sheet with expressions for color, font weight, and pointer

12. The first expression will alter the font to Bold if the day count is greater than 20, and the second conditional expression will change the pointer (mouse cursor) to a cross shape if TRUE.

13. Test your DataWindow in the Preview view.

14. Close and save the DataWindow as d_open_po_amount. Run the DATAWINDOW application and again login as "jtower". Select the fourth tab to view your DataWindow.

How It Works

The attribute conditional expressions allow you to code for a TRUE and a FALSE expression evaluation. You can code an additional expression by enclosing it within parentheses and placing it into one of the parameters of the conditional expression. However, this can get very cumbersome very quickly so use this approach sparingly and only when needed.

Comments

Allowable attribute values can be found in PowerBuilder help and by using the Object Browser found in the Library painter under menu item Utilities.

COMPLEXITY
INTERMEDIATE

9.5 How do I...
Create an updatable DataWindow based on two tables?

Problem Statement

I want to create a data entry DataWindow, but I need to show values from another table. How can I create this DataWindow and define which fields to update when the user wants to save?

Technique

PowerBuilder will allow a multiple table join for a DataWindow. You specify which table and fields are being updated. When the user saves data in this DataWindow, only those fields designed to be modifiable are updated. In this How-To you will create a DataWindow that joins two tables, but updates only one of them.

Steps

Access DYNAMIC.PBL and choose Employee. Login as "jtower" with no password. When the Employee window appears, add or change rows to see how the updates are occuring. You will completely recreate this DataWindow in this How-To by following the steps listed below.

1. Access DATAWINDOW.PBL. From the DataWindow painter create a new DataWindow.

2. When the New DataWindow Style dialog appears, select SQL Select as the data source, and Freeform as the presentation style.

3. The next dialog that will appear will provide a listing of tables. You will select two tables: employee and person. PowerBuilder will automatically join these tables on the foreign key if one is defined. The SQL painter should look similar to the one in Figure 9-14.

4. Select the display columns next. Select the phone_nbr column from the person table and all the columns from the employee table. Select the columns in the order you would like the DataWindow painter to display them.

5. Select a field for sorting by clicking on the Sort tab and dragging the employee.person_id column from the list on the left to the right side of the tabbed window.

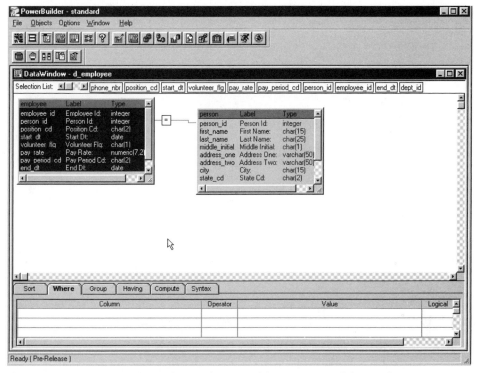

Figure 9-14 SQL painter with employee table, person table, and join

6. At this time you can check out the SQL syntax for the window by converting the SQL painter graphics to syntax. Do this by selecting the Convert to Syntax selection from the Options menu. Notice the join that was created for you by PowerBuilder, which now shows up as a Where clause in this window as shown in Figure 9-15. Convert the syntax back to graphics by selecting the Convert to Graphics selection from the Option menu.

7. You are now ready to lay out your DataWindow. Select the Design painter for the DataWindow painter. If your syntax was incorrect, it is at this point that syntactic errors would be captured and you would be notified of them.

8. In the DataWindow painter your rows will be displayed in one vertical line, with whatever defaults you have defined for the DataWindow painter. Open up the d_employee DataWindow and, using this as a template, modify your new DataWindow until it looks similar to the d_employee DataWindow.

9. For those columns that the user can modify, set the tab order to something other than 0, in the order you want the user to access.

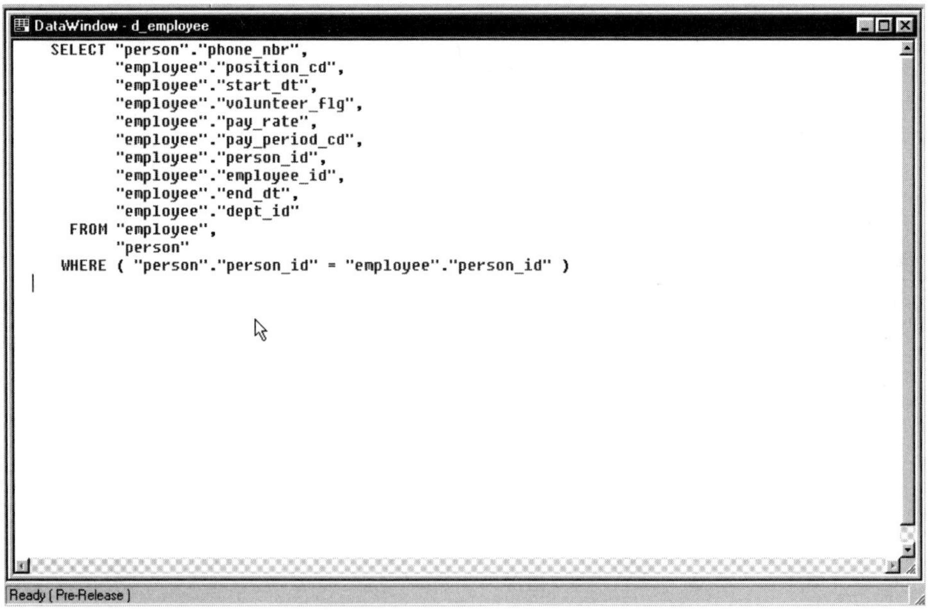

```
DataWindow - d_employee                                          _ □ X
    SELECT  "person"."phone_nbr",
            "employee"."position_cd",
            "employee"."start_dt",
            "employee"."volunteer_flg",
            "employee"."pay_rate",
            "employee"."pay_period_cd",
            "employee"."person_id",
            "employee"."employee_id",
            "employee"."end_dt",
            "employee"."dept_id"
      FROM "employee",
            "person"
     WHERE ( "person"."person_id" = "employee"."person_id" )

Ready ( Pre-Release )
```

Figure 9-15 Employee and Person join converted to Syntax

10. The last change you will make to this DataWindow before saving it will be to set the updateable fields. In the Rows menu, select the Update option. The Specify Update Characteristics dialog will appear.

11. Check the Allow Updates CheckBox.

12. Select all those columns that are updateable, in this case all the employee columns except the employee_id column and none of the person columns. The employee_id column is updated using default autoincrement by the database engine.

13. Both of these tables will appear in the Table to Update DropDownListBox in the upper right. Select employee. For the Unique Key Columns, choose the Primary Key button, which will highlight the primary key for this table, which is employee_id.

14. You can choose to update by deleting and then updating, or by just applying an update. For now select the Use Update RadioButton.

15. You can choose how restrictive the Where clause will be in an update or deletion by checking one of the RadioButtons in the Where clause for the Update/Delete GroupBox. The first choice will update or delete by the primary key field only, the second will combine this with querying on the updateable columns, and the third will query on the primary key fields and those fields that are modified. Choose the Key and Updateable Columns button.

16. Save the update choices and save the DataWindow as d_employee, responding Yes when you are prompted about overwriting the existing table.

17. Run the Admin application from PowerBuilder and test your new DataWindow.

How It Works

PowerBuilder will always attempt to join tables when you specify more than one in the SQL painter. You may want to doublecheck the results of this, as the painter does the best it can but cannot replace human judgment.

When two or more tables are specified in the SQL painter, PowerBuilder will set all tabs to 0 and set all fields to Not Updateable. You must manually change the tab order and the updateable fields and table. You can only update one of the tables. To update more than one at a time, you will need to use embedded SQL, or update the first table and then use Modify to change the updateable table from the original to the other—not the easiest of tasks.

Comments

Rarely are you going to need to specify more than one table when you are creating a data entry DataWindow. Usually when specifying more than one table you are creating a reporting DataWindow.

COMPLEXITY
INTERMEDIATE

9.6 How do I...
Use the Rich Text Format (RTF) style to create a form letter?

Problem

I need to create a form letter for my application and integrate it with data from a table. I can create the letter in a word processing application and then use OLE 2.0 to send the data to the document, but I would like to use the RTF DataWindow style to do this. How can I use this style to create a form letter?

Technique

The Rich Text Format (RTF) style will allow you to create a form letter directly in the DataWindow, or to pull in an RTF document for use as a template. All you need to do is position the data columns for the letter where the data should be located when the letter is printed.

Steps

Access DATAWINDOW.PBL and run the application, logging in as "jtower" with no password. Select the PO Status Letter option on tab 6. The DataWindow in this window is an RTF format form letter based on the purchase order and company tables. Select Print Preview from the File menu, and the full letter including headers and footers becomes visible as shown in Figure 9-16.

1. Access the DATAWINDOW.PBL and backup the existing d_po_status_letter DataWindow.

2. Create a new DataWindow using SQL Select as the data source and selecting the Rich Text DataWindow style.

3. The person table is joined to both the purchase_order and company table. Delete the join between the purchase_order and person tables.

4. Select the company, person, and purchase_order tables.

5. Select the company_name, address_1, address_2, address_3, city, state_cd, and zip_cd columns from the company table.

6. Select the first_name and last_name from the person table.

7. Select the po_nbr, order_dt, exp_delivery_dt, and po_amount columns from the purchase_order table.

8. Save the SQL you just generated and go to the Design view.

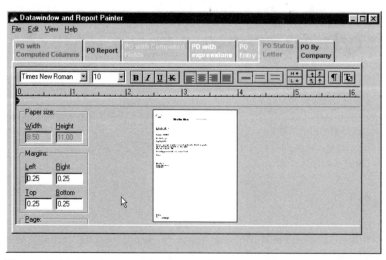

Figure 9-16 Purchase order status letter in Print Preview mode

9. The Rich Text Definition dialog will open as shown in Figure 9-17. You can select a Rich Text file, or choose to use default, which will allow you to create the form letter directly in the painter. Keep the default choice, and select the Header/Footer, Word Wrap, and Popup Menu options, as well as all of the toolbar options. Close and save the definition.

10. In the header for the form letter, place a bitmap control and the color bitmap "logoc.bmp".

11. Towards the center of the form type the header "The Zoo Store". Change the font size on this text to 16. Towards the left side of the letter, embed a date computed column.

12. In the body of the letter remove the column headings from the Company Name and Address fields and move the State and Zip Code fields to the same line as the City field.

13. Place a space between the company columns and the name columns. Type "TO:" in front of the first_name column and move the last_name column next to the first_name column.

14. Place a blank line using the <ENTER> key between the name and the purchase order number. In front of the purchase_order_po_nbr field type "Regarding:".

15. Create another blank line between the subject line and the body of the letter. In front of the remaining fields type "We are writing to request an update in status on this purchase order. The order was placed on". Move the purchase_order_order_dt field to this point in the letter and remove its column header. After this column, continue typing the letter's body with "and we have

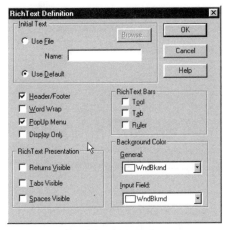

Figure 9-17 RichText Definition dialog

an expected delivery date of". Move the purchase_order_exp_delivery_dt column to this place in the letter and continue typing with "The amount of the order is". Move the last column, the purchase_order_po_amount, to this position and end the body of the letter with ".".

16. Insert a blank line and type "We would appreciate any and all information on this order."

17. Insert a blank line and the closing "Sincerely".

18. End the letter with "Sharon Callins/Account Representative/503.555.2334" with a new line in place of the slashes. You letter should look similar to the one in Figure 9-18.

19. Close and save your DataWindow as d_po_status_letter. Run the application from PowerBuilder and select Purchase Order Status Letter from the Misc menu. Modify the letter to personalize it for the person it is going to. One of the main advantages to using this style is that you can type into the DataWindow at runtime to modify it. There will also be a toolbar in the DataWindow to allow you to change the font, the font color, or other physical features.

How It Works

The Rich Text dialog style allows you to create a form letter and interface it directly with your data. With this you no longer need to use OLE 2.0 as the only way to get the results you would expect from a word processing system. The most powerful

Figure 9-18 d_po_status_letter after modifications

feature of this style is that you can dynamically alter the results using traditional word processing techniques at runtime.

COMPLEXITY
ADVANCED

9.7 How do I...
Use the OLE 2.0 style to create a Microsoft Graph?

Problem

I want to be able to use a Microsoft Graph for one of my reports. How can I use the OLE 2.0 DataWindow style to create this graph?

Technique

The OLE 2.0 DataWindow style integrates the data from the DataWindow with the functionality of the OLE 2.0 application by using Uniform Data Transfer. With this you create the OLE 2.0 object directly, run the DataWindow, and the data is automatically passed to the OLE 2.0 server application.

Steps

Run the DATAWINDOW.EXE application and select the Purchase Order by Company - Graph report. The report contains a Microsoft Graph embedded into the DataWindow as shown in Figure 9-19. Double-click on the graph and the OLE 2.0 object will activate as can be seen from the changing toolbar and background in Figure 9-20. Right mouse click on the graph and you will get a Graph popup menu as shown in Figure 9-21.

The steps to create this report follow.

1. Access the DATAWINDOW.PBL and backup the existing d_po_company_graph DataWindow.

2. Create a new DataWindow using the OLE 2.0 style and the standard SQL Select as the data source.

3. From the tables, pick company and purchase_order. Select the company_name column from company and all the columns in purchase_order.

4. Go to the painter. When you enter the painter, you will be presented with a list of OLE 2.0 objects that you can embed in your DataWindow as shown in Figure 9-22. Select the Microsoft Graph 5.0 object type. A graph with generic data will show. Click anywhere in the area surrounding the graph to continue.

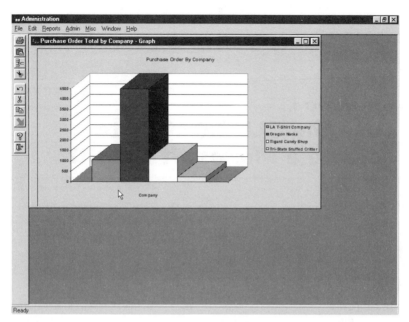

Figure 9-19 Purchase Order Total by Company with embedded
Excel Graph

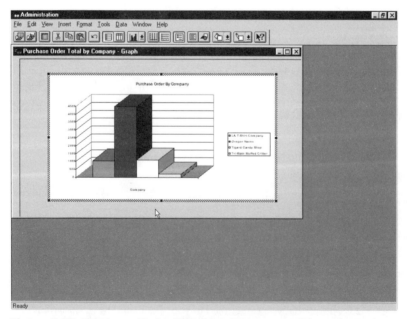

Figure 9-20 Purchase Order Total by Company with activated
Excel Graph

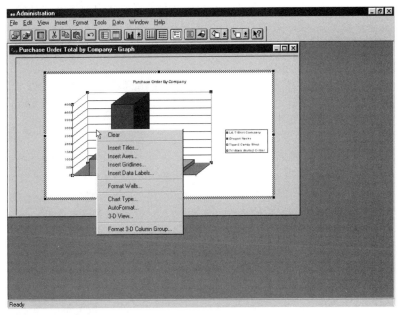

Figure 9-21 Purchase Order Total by Company with activated Excel Graph and Graph popup menu

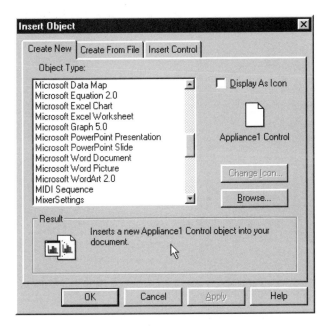

Figure 9-22 OLE 2.0 objects for the OLE 2.0 DataWindow style

5. The OLE Object property sheet will pop up. You will want to group your data on the company so drag and drop the Company Name column to the Group By column.

6. The data you will display will be the company name and the sum of the purchase order for the company. Drag and drop the Company Name column to the Target Data column. If the column shows any functions with it, double-click on the column and replace the expression with the column name in the Expression painter.

7. Drag and drop the Purchase Order Amount column to the Target Data column. The painter will automatically place the sum function around this column. The property sheet should look like the one in Figure 9-23.

8. To define the titles and labels for the graph, double-click on the graph to activate the OLE object.

9. Click the right mouse button somewhere in the area outside of the graph to access the graph properties. Select the Insert Titles option and then check the Chart Title and Category (X) Axis title.

10. Click on the title areas the graph just created and change the title of the graph to "Purchase Order by Company" and the X Axis title to "Company". The graph should look like the one shown in Figure 9-24.

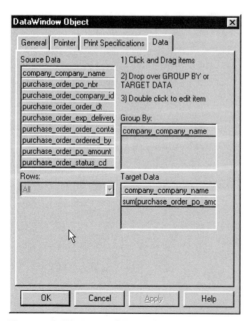

Figure 9-23 OLE Object Data property sheet

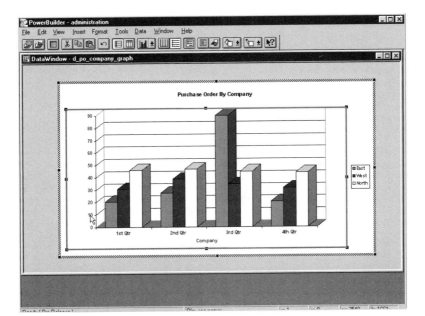

Figure 9-24 Finished Graph object

11. Test the DataWindow in Preview mode. Save the DataWindow as d_po_company_graph.

12. Run DATAWINDOW from PowerBuilder and test your new DataWindow.

How It Works

OLE 2.0 implements a standard data object and a standard interface for that object. With this standardization, each application can treat data in a common manner using Uniform Data Transfer. PowerBuilder provides this capability with the OLE 2.0 DataWindow style.

Comments

With OLE 2.0 you should review your application and examine the functionality you are offering. In those cases where another application provides the same type of functionality but in an improved manner, consider using OLE 2.0 to take advantage of this functionality. The only caution you should exercise when using this technology is to make sure your application users also have access to the same functionality. You can find out more information about implementing OLE 2.0 with PowerBuilder in Chapter 13, *Working with OLE 2.0*.

DATAWINDOW BASICS

DATAWINDOW BASICS

How do I...

Of all PowerBuilder features that receive attention, the DataWindow is one of the single most important capabilities to master. The DataWindow offers you the ability to use a single program object with a common set of integrated functions to perform data retrieval, data modification, and data reporting tasks. This chapter emphasizes the data retrieval and reporting tasks. Updates are covered in Chapter 11. In addition to constructing a couple of basic applications which demonstrate the core capabilities of the DataWindow, you will also build programs to demonstrate reporting and printing techniques. You also have the opportunity to construct dropdown ListBoxes whose contents change based on the values in other fields. All of these techniques will be valuable in your production applications.

10.1   Use a DataWindow in My Application

The purpose of this How-To is to review essential DataWindow operations, such as constructing a DataWindow object, placing it on a window surface, retrieving data into it, modifying it, and saving its contents. This How-To is intended primarily as an overview of basic DataWindow programming.

10.2   Show a List of Options When the User Double-Clicks a Field

One way to assist your users in working with your application is to provide them with a list of choices for columns (fields) that normally contain hard-to-remember coded values. A DropDownListBox or other code table edit style may be used to provide the user with this list of choices. In many cases, however, the number of choices is too large to be effectively presented in a DropDownListBox. This How-To presents a technique whereby the user can double-click on a coded column, causing a separate window containing a list of choices to appear. After making a choice, the user may click OK and return this value to the starting DataWindow. In addition to presenting the basic processing, this How-To also makes practical use of the ability to view different DataWindow objects from within the same DataWindow control.

10.3   Use a DataWindow for Reporting

In addition to its other strengths, the DataWindow makes an excellent reporting tool. This How-To allows the user to pick a report from a list, preview that report, and alter its other printing specifications, including paper size, orientation, and margins. Several valuable window functions are provided that may assist you in your own programs.

10.4   Modify the Contents of a Dropdown Based on Other Fields

To implement a dropdown control that is populated from a database, PowerBuilder offers the DropDownDataWindow. One of the most frequently asked questions about these DropDownDataWindows is, "How can I alter what dropdown B displays based on the contents of field A or dropdown A?" This How-To presents the basic mechanics of establishing a DropDownDataWindow and then addresses this question.

10.5   Sort and Filter a DataWindow

Many situations arise in which your users will want to sort or condense data brought back from the database. However, resubmitting an SQL statement to the database not only involves a delay, but system and network resources as well. This How-To presents a simple technique to allow the user to sort or filter locally (on the client) to avoid overusing precious system resources and to avoid transmitting excessive amounts of data between the client and the server computers. These options have the added benefit of being faster than the server's equivalents in most cases.

COMPLEXITY
BEGINNING

10.1 How do I...
Use a DataWindow in my application?

Problem

I am interested in using DataWindows in my application, but I am having difficulty performing all the steps required to do so. How do I incorporate a DataWindow in my program, and how do I retrieve, modify, and save data using one?

Technique

The DataWindow is PowerBuilder's primary program component for database access. The DataWindow greatly simplifies database access by giving you a graphical mechanism for creating SQL queries and formatting the resulting data for display or printing. Additionally, the DataWindow comes with programming support that makes it easy to retrieve and update data.

In order to use a DataWindow in an application, several structural components must be in place. After creating a DataWindow *object* using the DataWindow painter, you must place a DataWindow *control* on the surface of a window using the Window painter. Scripts then have to be written to establish a connection to the database and to inform the DataWindow of which transaction object to use. Finally, the DataWindow object must retrieve its data using its embedded query.

The DataWindow object itself is a complex PowerBuilder component that specifies both a data source (usually a query against a relational database) and a presentation style. PowerBuilder offers an impressive number of presentation styles, including forms, tabular listings, grids, and graphs. In order to use this object in an application, a "viewer" called a DataWindow control is placed on the surface of a window (in the Window painter). The DataWindow control is directed to view a specific DataWindow object through a process called *association*. Scrollbars can be enabled on the DataWindow control to allow the user to pan around the DataWindow object by scrolling different regions into view. The DataWindow control is especially significant because it serves as the programmatic interface to the DataWindow object. All DataWindow operations are performed in the context of a particular DataWindow control; the DataWindow object is never accessed without its corresponding control.

Steps

The working solution for this How-To may be found in the file DWBASICS.PBL on the included CD-ROM. Start the application from PowerBuilder or by running

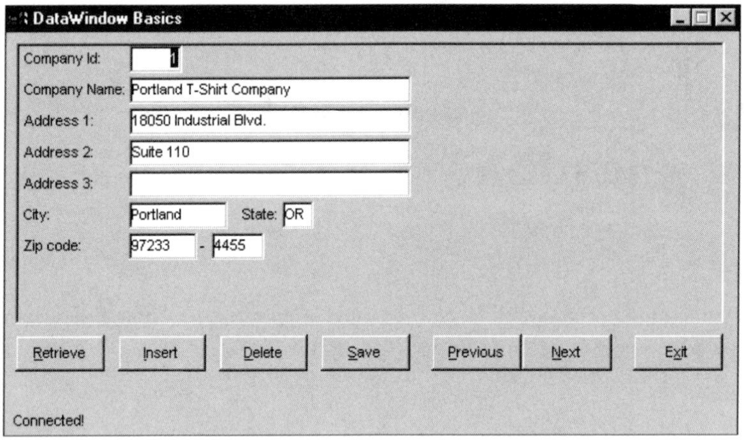

Figure 10-1 The DataWindow Basics application

DWBASICS.EXE. The DataWindow Basics window should appear as shown in Figure 10-1, displaying company information.

Change the Address 2 field to "Suite 110" and click the Save CommandButton. Click the Retrieve CommandButton and observe that the changed field has indeed been written to the database. Click the Insert CommandButton, which will add a new company row to the DataWindow and place the cursor on the Company ID column. Enter company information of your choice, using a Company ID value larger than 100 to avoid conflicts with existing companies in the Zoo database. Click Save to save your new company and again click Retrieve to verify that the company was saved properly. You may need to use the Previous or Next CommandButtons to locate the company.

Click the Delete CommandButton followed by the Save CommandButton to delete this new company. Use the Retrieve CommandButton to verify that the deletion was performed properly. When you have completed your exploration of the DWBASICS application, click Exit to end the program. To construct this application, complete the steps that follow.

1. Using the Application painter, create a new PowerBuilder Library and Application object called DWBASICS.PBL and a_dwbasics, respectively. You will not require an application template for this program.

2. Create a new DataWindow object called d_company_freeform using the DataWindow painter and the specifications shown in Table 10-1. The layout of d_company_freeform is shown in Figure 10-2.

WINDOW	OPTION	VALUE
New DataWindow		
	Data Source	Quick Select
	Presentation Style	Freeform
	Generation Options	Background color: Silver
		Text border: none
		Text color: WndText
		Column border: 3D Lowered
		Column color: WndText
		Wrap height: 3 inches
Quick Select		
	Table	company
	Columns	*all*

Table 10-1 Specifications for the d_company_freeform DataWindow object

3. Using the Window painter, create a window called w_dwbasics using the specifications shown in Table 10-2. The completed window is presented in Figure 10-3. Note that some of the StaticText objects are shown with their names in the figure to aid in their placement; you do not need to specify these as text properties.

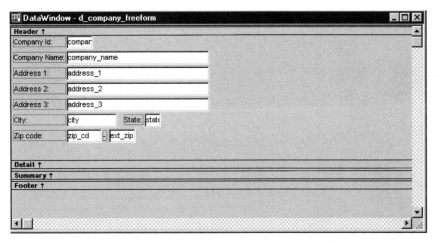

Figure 10-2 The d_company_freeform DataWindow object in design mode

WINDOW/CONTROL NAME	PROPERTY	VALUE
Window		
w_dwbasics	WindowType	Main
	Title	"DataWindow Basics"
	MaximizeBox	FALSE
	Resizable	FALSE
DataWindow control	Name	dw_1
	Border	3D Lowered
	DataWindow object name	"d_company_freeform"
StaticText	Name	st_message
	Border	None
CommandButton	Name	cb_retrieve
	Text	"&Retrieve"
CommandButton	Name	cb_insert
	Text	"&Insert"
CommandButton	Name	cb_delete
	Text	"&Delete"
CommandButton	Name	cb_save
	Text	"&Save"
CommandButton	Name	cb_previous
	Text	"&Previous"
CommandButton	Name	cb_next
	Text	"&Next"
CommandButton	Name	cb_exit
	Text	"E&xit"

Table 10-2 Window and control settings for the w_show_transaction_object
window

4. Declare a window function called wf_error_handler using the
Declare/Window Functions... menu item. The specifications for this function

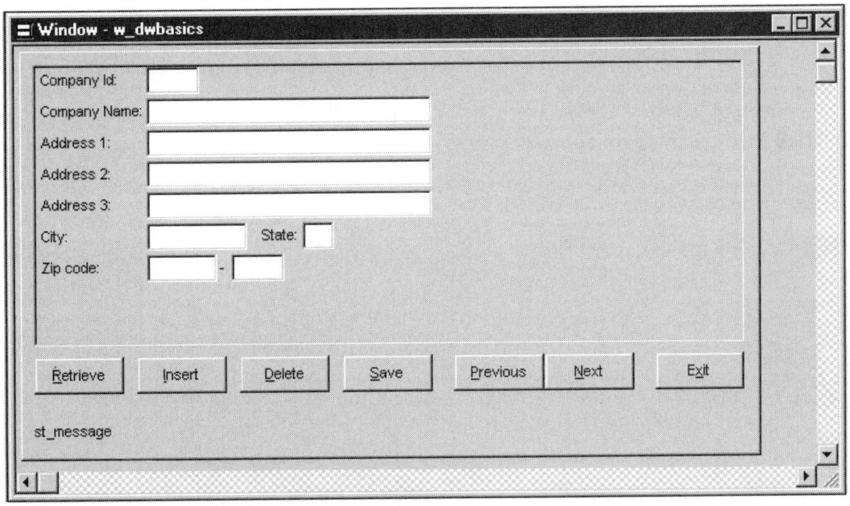

Figure 10-3 The w_dwbasics window with placement aids

are listed in Table 10-3. Place the following script in the body of the function. Note that you may copy this function from EMBED.PBL, presented in How-To 8.2.

```
string ls_errtext, ls_dbcode
integer li_sqlcode

// Preserve the original sqlcode (which may be affected by ROLLBACK
// later on)
li_sqlcode = sqlca.sqlcode

IF li_sqlcode < 0 THEN
    ls_errtext = a_to.sqlerrtext
    ls_dbcode = String( a_to.sqldbcode )
    ROLLBACK USING a_to;
    MessageBox( as_title, as_message + "~r~n" +&
        "(" +ls_dbcode + ") " + ls_errtext, Exclamation! )
END IF

// Return the original value of the SQLCode
RETURN li_sqlcode
```

FUNCTION SPECIFICATIONS			
Function	Name	wf_error_handler	
	Access	Public	
	Returns	integer	
Arguments			
	a_to	Transaction	Value

continued on next page

continued from previous page

FUNCTION SPECIFICATIONS

as_title	String	Value
as_message	String	Value

Table 10-3 Function specifications for wf_error_handler()

5. As a precaution, save the w_dwbasics window.

6. Declare a user event for w_dwbasics using the Declare/User Events menu item. The event should be called ue_postopen. Leave the event ID value for this new event blank and be sure to specify a return data type of "(None)" by pressing the Args CommandButton for this event.

7. To improve the apparent performance of the application, we want to delay retrieving data until the window is drawn. We can accomplish this by posting the custom event created in step 6. Place the following code in the Open event of w_dwbasics to accomplish this task.

this.event post ue_postopen()8. Enter the following script in the ue_postopen event (created in step 6) of w_dwbasics. This script connects to the database, and, following a successful connection, establishes the transaction object to be used by the DataWindow object (associated with the DataWindow *control* dw_1) by calling SetTransObject(). Following this, the script retrieves data into the DataWindow object by calling Retrieve().

```
string ls_owner, ls_table
SetPointer( Hourglass! )

st_message.text = "Connecting to database..."

// set the transaction object to refer to the Zoo database
sqlca.dbms = "ODBC"
sqlca.dbparm = "ConnectString='DSN=Zoo;UID=dba;PWD=SQL'"

CONNECT USING sqlca;

IF sqlca.sqlcode < 0 THEN // unsuccessful connect
    st_message.text = "Unsuccessful connect."
    wf_error_handler( sqlca, "Connection Error", &
            "Could not connect to database" )
ELSE
    st_message.text = "Connected!"
    dw_1.SetTransObject( sqlca )
    dw_1.Retrieve()
END IF
```

8. Place the following script in the Clicked event of cb_retrieve. This script examines the DataWindow object for unsaved changes, and prompts the user regarding those changes. Depending on the existence of unsaved changes and the user's response, it retrieves data into the DataWindow. Observe the use of AcceptText() to ensure that the most recently entered data has been copied into the DataWindow object's buffers where it can be detected by ModifiedCount(). Following the retrieval, the script sets the current DataWindow column (where the cursor will be located) to company_id and places focus on dw_1.

```
// refresh the contents of the DataWindow Object by
// re-retrieving. This will flush all rows currently in
// memory, and then perform the retrieve.
boolean  lb_retrieve = TRUE

IF dw_1.AcceptText() = -1 THEN
    IF  MessageBox( "Retrieve", "Flush rows and retrieve anyway?", &
        Question!, YesNo!, 2 ) = 2 THEN lb_retrieve = FALSE
ELSE
    IF ( dw_1.ModifiedCount() + dw_1.DeletedCount() ) > 0 THEN
        IF MessageBox( "Retrieve", "You have unsaved changes.~r~n" + &
            "Do you want to preserve your changes?~r~n~r~n " +&
            "Answering No will discard changes and retrieve fresh data.", &
            Question!, YesNo!, 1 ) =1 THEN lb_retrieve = FALSE
    END IF
END IF

IF lb_retrieve = TRUE THEN dw_1.Retrieve()

dw_1.SetColumn( "company_id" )
dw_1.SetFocus()
```

9. Code the following script on the Clicked event of cb_insert. This script adds a new row to the DataWindow object (via the control dw_1) and completes the processing to prepare for user data entry.

```
long ll_curr, ll_new

// determine the current row
ll_curr = dw_1.GetRow()
// insert ahead of that row
ll_new = dw_1.InsertRow( ll_curr )

// force the new row to be in view
dw_1.ScrollToRow( ll_curr )

// place the cursor on company_id
dw_1.SetColumn( "company_id" )

// transfer focus to dw_1
dw_1.SetFocus()
```

10. The following script should be placed on the Clicked event of cb_delete. This script handles the prompting and deletion process.

```
long ll_curr, ll_compid
integer li_response
string ls_company

// get the current row
ll_curr = dw_1.GetRow()
```

continued on next page

continued from previous page

```
// if we don't have one, bail out
IF ll_curr < 1 THEN RETURN

li_response = 1

// if the row already exists or the user has entered data into a
// brand new row, prompt the user for deletion
IF dw_1.GetItemStatus( ll_curr, 0, Primary! ) <> New! THEN
    ll_compid = dw_1.GetItemNumber( ll_curr, "company_id" )
    ls_company = dw_1.GetItemString( ll_curr, "company_name" )
    li_response = MessageBox( "Delete Company", "Delete company ID " + &
        string( ll_compid) + " - " + ls_company + "?", &
        Question!, YesNo!, 2 )
END IF

IF li_response = 1 THEN dw_1.DeleteRow( ll_curr )

dw_1.SetColumn( "company_id" )
dw_1.SetFocus()
```

11. The script to save any pending changes to the database can be placed on the Clicked event of cb_save as follows.

```
IF dw_1.Update() = 1 THEN
    COMMIT USING sqlca;
    IF wf_error_handler( sqlca, "Commit Error", &
            "Could not commit data." ) = 0 THEN
        st_message.text = "Data saved successfully."
    ELSE
        st_message.text = "Error saving data."
    END IF
ELSE
    MessageBox("Save", "Could not save data.", Exclamation! )
    ROLLBACK USING sqlca;
    IF wf_error_handler( sqlca, "Rollback Error", &
            "Could not rollback data." ) = 0 THEN
        st_message.text = "Rollback successful."
    ELSE
        st_message.text = "Error rolling back changes."
    END IF
END IF

dw_1.SetColumn( "company_id" )
dw_1.SetFocus()
```

12. Place the following line of script on the Clicked event of cb_previous to scroll to the previous row.

```
dw_1.ScrollPriorRow()
```

13. Place a similar line of script on the Clicked event of cb_next as indicated below to handle scrolling to the next row.

```
dw_1.ScrollNextRow()
```

14. The DataWindow Basics application should disconnect from the database when it terminates. To perform the disconnect, code the following script on

the Close event of the w_dwbasics window. Note the use of the DBHandle()
function to ensure that the application only disconnects if it has connected
successfully.

```
// if we're connected to the database, disconnect
IF sqlca.DBHandle() <> 0 THEN
    DISCONNECT USING sqlca;

    IF sqlca.sqlcode < 0 THEN  // couldn't disconnect
        wf_error_handler( sqlca, "Disconnection Error", "Could not discon-
nect from database.")
    END IF
END IF
```

15. Code the script to terminate the application on the Clicked event of
cb_exit.

```
Close( parent )
```

16. Save the w_dwbasics window.

17. Using the Application painter, code a script for the Open event of the
Application object a_dwbasics as follows.

```
Open( w_dwbasics )
```

18. Save the Application object and run the application.

How It Works

The creation of a DataWindow-capable application requires several discrete steps:
creating the DataWindow object; creating the window which will display the data;
placing a DataWindow control on the window; and writing scripts to connect to the
database, establish a transaction object for the DataWindow object, and retrieve data.

The Open event of the w_dwbasics application establishes a connection to the
database using the techniques presented in How-To 8.1. Once the window has established a connection, the SetTransObject() function is used to instruct the DataWindow
object to utilize the recently connected transaction object for all database communication. After establishing the transaction object-DataWindow object relationship,
the Retrieve() function is invoked to retrieve data using the query embedded in the
DataWindow object.

The Clicked event of the cb_retrieve CommandButton allows the user to retrieve
fresh data into the DataWindow object on demand. Before performing the retrieval,
the script examines the DataWindow object for unsaved changes. To ensure an accurate count, the script calls AcceptText() to place the most recently entered data item
into the DataWindow object's buffers. If the script determines that there are unsaved
changes (by calling DeletedCount() and ModifiedCount()) it asks for confirmation
before proceeding (which will flush the contents of the DataWindow object buffers
as a side effect).

The Clicked event of cb_insert performs the basic steps required to add a new row of data to the DataWindow. Observe the use of ScrollToRow(), SetColumn(), and SetFocus() to implement an easy-to-use interface. The Clicked event of cb_delete examines the current row, and, if it has not been newly inserted and left unmodified, prompts the user for confirmation before deleting the row. Note that neither InsertRow() nor DeleteRow() used in these two scripts cause any database operations to be performed. Both functions operate purely on the client to move rows in memory.

The cb_save CommandButton allows the user to save all pending changes to the database. Notice the use of the return code from the Update() function to check the success or failure of the operation. As explained in How-To 8.2, transaction object properties may not be used to check the success or failure of anything other than embedded SQL operations. Following the Update(), a COMMIT or ROLLBACK is executed as appropriate. The transaction object can be examined following these operations by calling the wf_error_handler() window function. Note that the transaction object properties work here because COMMIT and ROLLBACK are embedded SQL commands.

Comments

Mastery of DataWindow programming is vital to becoming an efficient, effective PowerBuilder developer. You should become intimately familiar with the techniques and functions presented in this How-To, as they form the core of all DataWindow processing.

COMPLEXITY
INTERMEDIATE

10.2 How do I...
Show a list of options when the user double-clicks a field?

Problem

I would like to present my user with a list of choices for a number of columns in my DataWindows. I would use the normal code table edit styles such as DropDownListBox or DropDownDataWindow, but I have too many choices for these methods to be effective. I want to allow the user to double-click on a field resulting in a window that displays a list of the valid choices for the field. How do I show a list of options when the user double-clicks a field?

Technique

To implement this behavior, your program must respond to the DoubleClicked event on the DataWindow control used to display the entry DataWindow object. This script must examine the column that was clicked and open a window presenting a list of choices for that field.

This application requires a single response window to display the choices along with a DataWindow object for *each* of the fields for which a choices list is desired. The DataWindow objects used for this purpose should contain columns for both the coded value (what is stored in the database) and the display value (what is shown to the user). In responding to the DoubleClicked event, the script determines if the clicked column has a list of choices available, and, if so, opens the response window. When opening the response window, the script passes a parameter indicating which of the previously mentioned DataWindow objects to use for the list of choices, which column to use for the data value, and which column to use for the display value. The response window accepts a user response and transmits the coded data value back to the original window.

Steps

The solution for this How-To may be found in the library called DBLCLICK.PBL. You may run this application from within PowerBuilder or by starting DBLCLICK.EXE. Once the program starts, it presents you with the window shown in Figure 10-4. Click the Insert CommandButton, adding a new row to the DataWindow. After specifying a new employee ID of 101, double-click the Person ID column to look up a person to assign to that employee ID. When the selection window shown in Figure 10-5 appears, click on a person, and click OK. Notice that the person ID was sent back to the original DataWindow. This same behavior exists for Position, Pay Period, and Department. Verify that all three work in the same manner. When you are satisfied with the application, click Exit. To build this program, follow the steps presented below.

Figure 10-4 The DBLCLICK application main window

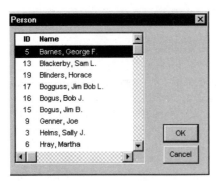

Figure 10-5 The selection window
displaying a list of choices

1. Create a new library and Application object called DBLCLICK.PBL and
a_dblclick, respectively, using the Application painter. You will not require
an application template for this How-To.

2. Create a DataWindow object called d_person_list using the settings shown
in Table 10-4. The layout of this DataWindow object is shown in Figure 10-
6. When previewed, this DataWindow object should resemble the contents
of any standard ListBox used in an application.

WINDOW	OPTION	VALUE
New DataWindow		
	Data Source	Quick Select
	Presentation Style	Tabular
	Generation Options	Background color: white
		Text border: none
		Text color: WndText
		Column border: none
		Column color: WndText
Quick Select		
	Table	person
	Columns	person_id, last_name, first_name, middle_initial

WINDOW	OPTION	VALUE
Design		
	Computed field	full_name
	Expression	"last_name +"," + first_name + " " + if(
		IsNull(middle_initial), "", middle_initial + ".")"

Table 10-4 Specifications for the d_person_list DataWindow object

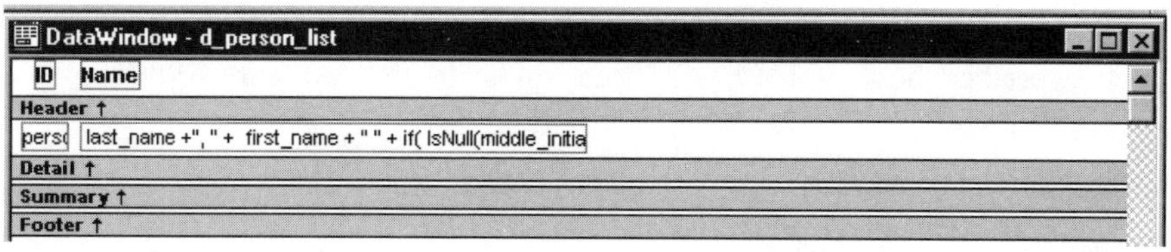

Figure 10-6 The d_person_list DataWindow object in layout mode

3. Create a DataWindow object called d_position_list. The specifications for this object are listed in Table 10-5. The object is shown in Figure 10-7. Again note that this DataWindow object should resemble the contents of a ListBox.

WINDOW	OPTION	VALUE
New DataWindow		
	Data Source	Quick Select
	Presentation Style	Tabular
	Generation Options	Background color: white
		Text border: none
		Text color: WndText
		Column border: none
		Column color: WndText
Quick Select		
	Table	position
	Columns	position_cd, position_desc, volunteer_fill_flg, constraints

Table 10-5 Specifications for the d_position_list DataWindow object

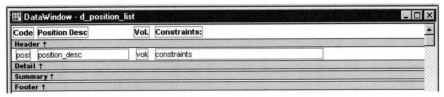

Figure 10-7 The d_position_list object in layout mode

4. Create another DataWindow object called d_department_list using the specifications in Table 10-6. The layout is pictured in Figure 10-8.

WINDOW	OPTION	VALUE
New DataWindow		
	Data Source	Quick Select
	Presentation Style	Tabular
	Generation Options	Background color: white
		Text border: none
		Text color: WndText
		Column border: none
		Column color: WndText
Quick Select		
	Table	department
	Columns	dept_id, dept_dsc

Table 10-6 Specifications for the d_department_list DataWindow object

5. Create a DataWindow object to display a list of state abbreviations and state names called d_state_list. The specifications are listed in Table 10-7; the layout is shown in Figure 10-9.

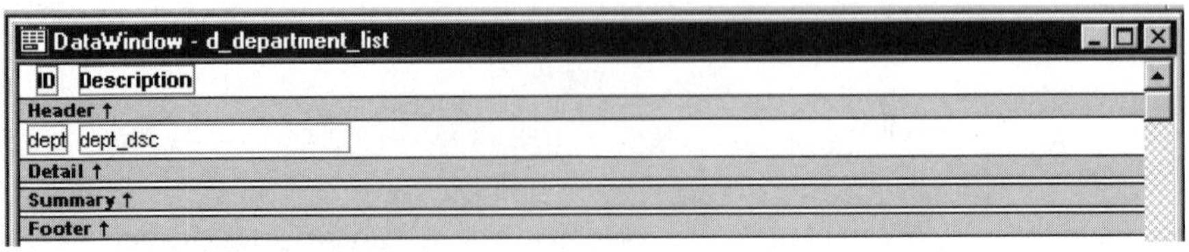

Figure 10-8 The d_department_list DataWindow object in layout mode

WINDOW	OPTION	VALUE
New DataWindow		
	Data Source	Quick Select
	Presentation Style	Tabular
	Generation Options	Background color: white
		Text border: none
		Text color: WndText
		Column border: none
		Column color: WndText
Quick Select		
	Table	state
	Columns	state_cd, state_desc

Table 10-7 Specifications for the d_state_list DataWindow object

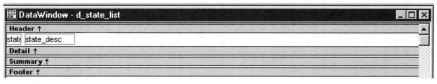

Figure 10-9 The d_state_list DataWindow object in layout mode

6. Using the settings listed in Table 10-8, create a DataWindow object called d_timeper_list to display a list of pay periods. The completed DataWindow object is shown in Figure 10-10.

WINDOW	OPTION	VALUE
New DataWindow		
	Data Source	Quick Select
	Presentation Style	Tabular
	Generation Options	Background color: white
		Text border: none
		Text color: WndText
		Column border: none

continued on next page

continued from previous page

WINDOW	OPTION	VALUE
		Column color: WndText
Quick Select		
	Table	time_period
	Columns	period_cd, period_desc

Table 10-8 Specifications for the d_timeper_list DataWindow object

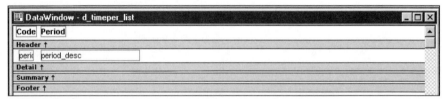

Figure 10-10 The d_timeper_list DataWindow object in layout mode

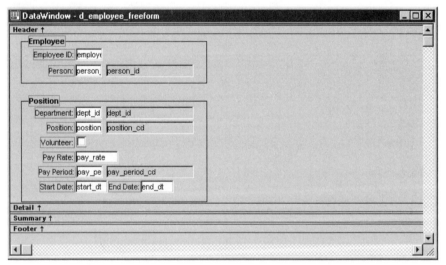

Figure 10-11 The d_timeper_list DataWindow object in layout mode

7. Using the DataWindow painter, construct a DataWindow object called d_employee_freeform using the specifications shown in Table 10-9. The layout of this DataWindow object is shown in Figure 10-11. Observe that the group box effect is achieved by using a rectangle drawing object in conjunction with a text object that has an opaque background. Also note that the layout of the DataWindow object includes four columns (person_id, dept_id, position_cd, and pay_period_cd) that are placed twice. You can place the duplicate columns by choosing the Column button on the painterBar. You will also need to modify some edit styles as explained in the next step.

WINDOW	OPTION	VALUE
New DataWindow		
	Data Source	Quick Select
	Presentation Style	Freeform
	Generation Options	Background color: Silver
		Text border: none
		Text color: WndText
		Column border: 3D Lowered
		Column color: WndText
		Wrap height: 4 inches
Quick Select		
	Table	employee
	Columns	employee_id, person_id, dept_id, position_cd,
		volunteer_flg, pay_rate, pay_period_cd,
		start_dt, end_dt

Table 10-9 Specifications for the d_employee_freeform DataWindow object

8. Alter the edit style of the duplicate person_id column in d_employee_freeform to be DropDownDataWindow by choosing the Edit tab on the properties sheet for the column and selecting a Style of DropDownDataWindow. Complete the DropDownDataWindow specification as shown in Table 10-10.

WINDOW	PROPERTY	VALUE
DropDownDataWindow Edit Style		
	DataWindow	d_person_list
	Display Column	full_name
	Data Column	person_id
	Always Show List	FALSE
	Always Show Arrow	FALSE

Table 10-10 Specifications for the DDDW edit style for person_id

9. Using the procedure listed in step 8, alter the edit style on the dept_id, position_cd, and pay_period_cd duplicate columns within d_employee_freeform to be DropDownDataWindows as listed in Table 10-11, Table 10-12, and Table 10-13.

WINDOW	PROPERTY	VALUE
DropDownDataWindow Edit Style		
	DataWindow	d_department_list
	Display Column	dept_dsc
	Data Column	dept_id
	Always Show List	FALSE
	Always Show Arrow	FALSE

Table 10-11 Specifications for the DDDW edit style for dept_id

WINDOW	PROPERTY	VALUE
DropDownDataWindow Edit Style		
	DataWindow	d_position_list
	Display Column	position_desc
	Data Column	position_cd
	Always Show List	FALSE
	Always Show Arrow	FALSE

Table 10-12 Specifications for the DDDW edit style for position_cd

WINDOW	PROPERTY	VALUE
DropDownDataWindow Edit Style		
	DataWindow	d_timeper_list
	Display Column	period_desc
	Data Column	period_cd
	Always Show List	FALSE
	Always Show Arrow	FALSE

Table 10-13 Specifications for the DDDW edit style for pay_period_cd

10. Save the d_employee_freeform DataWindow object.

11. In the Window painter, create a new window called w_getval. This window will present the user with a list of choices based on their double-click location on the main window. Specifications for this window are listed in Table 10-14. The window is shown in Figure 10-12.

WINDOW/CONTROL NAME	PROPERTY	VALUE
Window		
w_getval	WindowType	Response

WINDOW/CONTROL NAME	PROPERTY	VALUE
CommandButton	Name	cb_ok
	Text	"OK"
	Default	TRUE
CommandButton	Name	cb_cancel
	Text	"Cancel"
	Cancel	TRUE
DataWindow control	Name	dw_1
	DataWindow object name	""
	HScrollBar	TRUE
	VScrollBar	TRUE
	Border	3D Lowered

Table 10-14 Specifications for the w_getval window

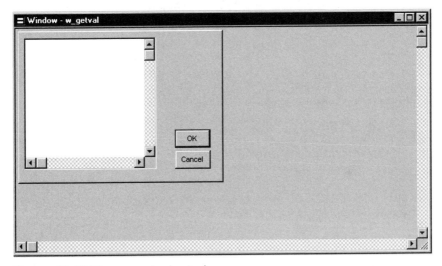

Figure 10-12 The w_getval window

12. Declare an instance variable to hold the data column name as follows.

```
string is_codecol
```

13. Place the following script on the Open event of w_getval. This script will accept the incoming parameter (which contains the title for the w_getval window, the DataWindow object to be used for the selection, and the name of the coded value column within that DataWindow). These values are then used to complete the initialization of the window.

```
string ls_parm
long ll_firsttab, ll_secondtab, ll_thirdtab
integer li_x

ls_parm = Message.StringParm

// locate the tab characters in the incoming string
ll_firsttab = Pos( ls_parm, "~t" )
ll_secondtab = Pos( ls_parm, "~t", ll_firsttab + 1 )
ll_thirdtab = Pos( ls_parm, "~t", ll_secondtab + 1 )

// extract the title from the incoming string
this.title = Mid( ls_parm, 1, ll_firsttab - 1 )

// extract the DataWindow object name to use
dw_1.dataobject = Mid( ls_parm, ll_firsttab + 1, ll_secondtab - &
        ll_firsttab - 1 )

// extract the data value column name
is_codecol = Mid( ls_parm, ll_secondtab + 1, ll_thirdtab - &
        ll_secondtab - 1 )

// extract the position of the pointer when the user double-clicked
li_x = Integer( Mid( ls_parm, ll_thirdtab + 1 ))

// position this window just to the right of the pointer
this.Move( li_x, this.y )

// complete the retrieval
dw_1.SetTransObject( sqlca )
IF dw_1.Retrieve() < 1 THEN
    cb_ok.enabled = FALSE
END IF
```

14. Code the OK button Clicked event to obtain the user's selection and return that value to the calling script.

```
string ls_ret

// first column of the pick list data value is always
// the returned code. It must be number or character to be supported
// by this code. Additional datatypes are easy to add; just follow the
// structure below.

ls_ret = dw_1.Describe( is_codecol + ".coltype" )

CHOOSE CASE Lower( Left( ls_ret, 4 ))
    CASE "char"
        ls_ret = dw_1.GetItemString( dw_1.GetRow(), is_codecol )
    CASE "numb"
        ls_ret = String( dw_1.GetItemNumber( dw_1.GetRow() , is_codecol ) )
END CHOOSE

CloseWithReturn( parent, ls_ret )
```

15. Code the Cancel button Clicked event using the following script.

```
CloseWithReturn( parent, "" )
```

16. Place the following script on the DoubleClicked event for the dw_1 DataWindow control. This script responds to double-clicking as if the user had clicked the OK CommandButton.

```
IF row > 0 THEN
    cb_ok.TriggerEvent( Clicked! )
END IF
```

17. Our program also needs to handle highlighting of the rows as the user clicks on them. Place the following script on the RowFocusChanged event of the dw_1 DataWindow control to accomplish this task.

```
IF currentrow < 1 THEN RETURN

this.SelectRow( 0, FALSE)
this.SelectRow( currentrow, TRUE)
```

18. Save the w_getval window.

19. Again using the Window painter, create a new window called w_doubleclick as specified in Table 10-15 and shown in Figure 10-13.

WINDOW/CONTROL NAME	PROPERTY	VALUE
Window		
w_doubleclick	WindowType	Main
	Title	"Options by DoubleClicking"
	MaximizeBox	FALSE
	MinimizeBox	TRUE
	Resizable	FALSE
DataWindow control	Name	dw_1
	DataWindow object name	"d_employee_freeform"
	HScrollBar	FALSE
	VScrollBar	TRUE
	Border	3D Lowered
StaticText	Name	st_message
	Text	""
CommandButton	Name	cb_retrieve
	Text	"&Retrieve"
CommandButton	Name	cb_insert
	Text	"&Insert"

continued on next page

continued from previous page

WINDOW/CONTROL NAME	PROPERTY	VALUE
CommandButton	Name	cb_delete
	Text	"&Delete"
CommandButton	Name	cb_save
	Text	"&Save"
CommandButton	Name	cb_exit
	Text	"E&xit"

Table 10-15 Specifications for the w_doubleclick window

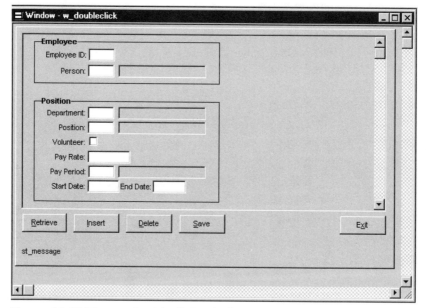

Figure 10-13 The w_doubleclick window

20. Save the w_doubleclick window.

21. Create a window function called wf_error_handler to perform embedded SQL error handling. The function specification is shown in Table 10-16. The body of the function should be as follows. Note that this is the same wf_error_handler() function that was presented in How-To 10.1.

```
string ls_errtext, ls_dbcode
integer li_sqlcode

// Preserve the original sqlcode (which may be affected by ROLLBACK later
// on)
li_sqlcode = sqlca.sqlcode

IF li_sqlcode < 0 THEN
```

```
    ls_errtext = a_to.sqlerrtext
    ls_dbcode = String( a_to.sqldbcode )
    ROLLBACK USING a_to;
    MessageBox( as_title, as_message + "~r~n" +&
            "(" +ls_dbcode + ") " + ls_errtext, Exclamation! )
END IF

// Return the original value of the SQLCode
RETURN li_sqlcode
```

FUNCTION SPECIFICATIONS

Function	Name	wf_error_handler	
	Access	Public	
	Returns	integer	
Arguments			
	a_to	Transaction	Value
	as_title	String	Value
	as_message	String	Value

Table 10-16 Function specifications for wf_error_handler()

22. Using the Declare/User Events... menu item, declare a custom user event called ue_postopen mapped to the PowerBuilder event pbm_custom01.

23. Enter a script for the Open event of w_doubleclick as indicated below. This script will delay retrieving data until the window has been drawn for the first time.

```
this.PostEvent( "ue_postopen" )
```

24. Also place a script for the ue_postopen event on w_doubleclick as follows.

```
string ls_owner, ls_table
SetPointer( Hourglass! )

st_message.text = "Connecting to database..."

// set the transaction object to refer to the Zoo database
sqlca.dbms = "ODBC"
sqlca.dbparm = "ConnectString='DSN=Zoo;UID=dba;PWD=SQL'"

CONNECT USING sqlca;

IF sqlca.sqlcode < 0 THEN // unsuccessful connect
    st_message.text = "Unsuccessful connect."
    wf_error_handler( sqlca, "Connection Error", &
            "Could not connect to database" )
ELSE
    st_message.text = "Connected!"
    dw_1.SetTransObject( sqlca )
    dw_1.Retrieve()
```

continued on next page

continued from previous page
```
END IF
```

25. Code a script to disconnect from the database in the Close event of the window.

```
// If we're actually connected to the database, attempt to
// disconnect
IF sqlca.DBHandle() <> 0 THEN
    DISCONNECT USING sqlca;

    IF sqlca.sqlcode < 0 THEN  // couldn't disconnect
        wf_error_handler( sqlca, "Disconnection Error", &
                    "Could not disconnect from database.")
    END IF
END IF
```

26. Place a script to retrieve data on the Clicked event of cb_retrieve as follows. Note that this is a less sophisticated version of the retrieve script used in How-To 10.1.

```
dw_1.Retrieve()

dw_1.SetColumn( "employee_id" )
dw_1.SetFocus()
```

27. Also code a script to Insert rows into the DataWindow. Use the following script on the Clicked event of cb_insert.

```
long ll_curr, ll_new

ll_curr = dw_1.GetRow()
ll_new = dw_1.InsertRow( ll_curr )

dw_1.ScrollToRow( ll_new )
dw_1.SetColumn( "employee_id" )
dw_1.SetFocus()
```

28. Place a script to delete rows on the Clicked event of cb_delete as follows. This is a simplified version of the deletion script from How-To 10.1.

```
dw_1.DeleteRow( 0 )

dw_1.SetColumn( "employee_id" )
dw_1.SetFocus()
```

29. Allow the DataWindow to save its changes by placing a save script on the Clicked event of cb_save.

```
IF dw_1.Update() = 1 THEN
    COMMIT USING sqlca;
    IF wf_error_handler( sqlca, "Commit Error", &
            "Could not commit data." ) = 0 THEN
        st_message.text = "Data saved successfully."
    ELSE
        st_message.text = "Error saving data."
    END IF
```

```
ELSE
    MessageBox("Save", "Could not save data.", Exclamation! )
    ROLLBACK USING sqlca;
    IF wf_error_handler( sqlca, "Rollback Error", &
            "Could not rollback data." ) = 0 THEN
        st_message.text = "Rollback successful."
    ELSE
        st_message.text = "Error rolling back changes."
    END IF
END IF
```

```
dw_1.SetColumn( "employee_id" )
dw_1.SetFocus()
```

30. Place the standard line of code in the cb_exit CommandButton Clicked event.

```
Close( parent )
```

31. Finally, code the essential DoubleClicked event script for the DataWindow control dw_1.

```
string ls_parm, ls_obj, ls_col, ls_datatype
integer li_x, li_col

// determine that the user clicked on a row
IF row < 1 THEN RETURN

// get the name of that column
li_col = this.GetClickedColumn()
ls_col = this.Describe( "#" + string( li_col ) + ".name" )

// figure out where the choices window should appear
li_x = parent.PointerX() + parent.x + 75

// build the parameter string containing, in order, the title of
// the choices window, the DataWindow object to use for presenting the
// choices, the data value column, and the position of the choices window
CHOOSE CASE Lower( ls_col )
    CASE "person_id"   // Person ID
        ls_parm = "Person~td_person_list~tperson_id~t" + string(li_x)
    CASE "position_cd"
        ls_parm = "Position~td_position_list~tposition_cd~t" + string(li_x)
    CASE "pay_period_cd"
        ls_parm = "Pay Period~td_timeper_list~tperiod_cd~t" + string( li_x
)
    CASE "dept_id"
        ls_parm = "Department~td_department_list~tdept_id~t" + string( li_x
)
END CHOOSE

// accept the return value and place it in the local DataWindow object.
IF ls_parm <> "" THEN
    OpenWithParm( w_getval, ls_parm, parent)
    ls_parm = Message.StringParm
    IF ls_parm <> "" THEN
```

continued on next page

continued from previous page

```
        ls_datatype = this.Describe ( ls_col + ".ColType" )
        CHOOSE CASE Lower( Left( ls_datatype, 4 ) )
            CASE "char"
                this.SetItem( this.GetRow(), ls_col, ls_parm )
            CASE "numb"
                this.SetItem( this.GetRow(), ls_col, Integer( ls_parm ))
        END CHOOSE
    END IF
ELSE
    MessageBox( "Selection", "No selection list available." )
END IF
```

32. Save the w_doubleclick window.

33. Connect this window to the Application object by coding the following script for the Open event of that object.

```
Open( w_doubleclick )
```

34 Save and run the application.

How It Works

The core of this application is the DoubleClicked event script on w_doubleclick::dw_1 as well as the scripts on w_getval. Based on the user's double-click on the employee display on w_doubleclick, the script evaluates the clicked column and passes the required information to the choices window w_getval. The Open event of the w_getval window uses the first two parameters inside the passed string to set the title of the window and to read in the DataWindow object required to present a list of choices. The column name used to obtain the data value is saved into an instance variable for later use. The final parameter is used to place the choices window in an appropriate location near the pointer. When the user selects an item and clicks OK, the button script uses the passed data column name to obtain the key value and returns it to the calling script.

Comments

This application demonstrates more of the flexibility that DataWindows offer your PowerBuilder applications. A single choices window is capable of presenting choices for nearly any field as long as a DataWindow object has been created to present a list of choices. This DataWindow must include the coded values for each row; one of the parameters passed to the window indicates which column is used for this purpose.

Also make note that the DropDownDataWindow edit style on the duplicate columns in d_employee_freeform allows the DataWindow object to perform quick lookups to display the actual name corresponding to a coded value.

COMPLEXITY
INTERMEDIATE

10.3 How do I...
Use a DataWindow for reporting?

Problem

I am interested in using DataWindows for reporting purposes, but I don't know what capabilities are available to me. I would like to be able to provide the ability to print a DataWindow, to perform printer setup, to preview and zoom before printing, and to tell the user in advance how many pages will be required to print the DataWindow. How do I use a DataWindow for reporting?

Technique

This application uses a variety of techniques to allow the DataWindow to be used for reporting purposes. The program alters the dataobject property of the DataWindow control so that the user can pick from a list of reports to view without switching to multiple windows. The application also utilitizes the dynamic DataWindow interface to enable Print Preview and Print Preview zoom along with the ability to alter page size, orientation, and margins. A final dynamic DataWindow technique allows the application to compute the number of printed pages for the report.

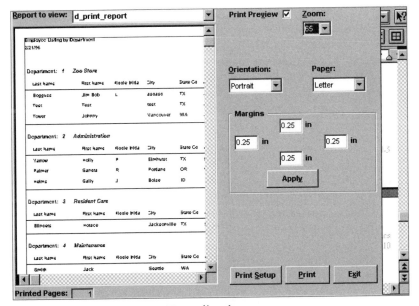

Figure 10-14 The DWPRINT application

Steps

To experiment with the reporting application, run the program DWPRINT.PBL from PowerBuilder or DWPRINT.EXE from Windows. Once started, the window shown in Figure 10-14 will appear. Notice initially that the DataWindow control appears with the default DataWindow object listed in the Report to view DropDownListBox. Choose another report (DataWindow object) from the Report to view DropDownListBox and observe that the displayed DataWindow changes below. The actual *printed* page count appears in the bottom left corner of the window. This value is quite different from any page value displayed on the report (which may indicate numbers significantly larger than the printed page value).

Choose the Print preview CheckBox to place the report into Print Preview mode. If you have a printer driver installed on your computer, blue print margin lines will appear to indicate the printable area location on a printed page. Any page numbers appearing in the report also change from the original large values (described in the preceding paragraph) to the actual page numbers for the printed report; the highest numbered page will now correspond to the printed pages value displayed in the lower left corner of the window. Try changing the values for Paper size and Paper orientation and observing the effect on the previewed report as well as on the printed page count.

You will also notice that the margins are indicated in terms of the units used to create the DataWindow object (report): PowerBuilder units (PBU), pixels (pxl), inches (in), or centimeters (cm). Experiment with changing these values and clicking Apply to alter them on the report. Again observe the effects on the page count.

You can also alter the default printer on the system (where PowerBuilder will print) by clicking the Print Setup CommandButton. If you have a printer driver installed, you can click Print to print your report. Click Exit when you are satisfied with this application. To construct this program, complete the steps below.

1. Use the Application painter to create a new library DWPRINT.PBL and Application object a_dwprint. Answer "No" when prompted for an application template.

2. Using the DataWindow painter, create two or three DataWindow objects using different presentation styles (grid, tabular, and freeform are good). The data source should be SQL Select or Quick Select and can access any tables; suggested tables to use include employee, person, and department. Alter the DataWindow units on one or two of these DataWindow objects to inches or centimeters using the General tab after choosing Properties for the DataWindow background. Alter the page size and orientation on one or two of them using the Print Specifications tab. Add page numbers to your DataWindow objects using the Page Computed Field toolbar button. Feel free to improvise. Experimenting will allow you to see the capabilities of this application.

3. Create a window called w_dwprint using the Window painter in conjunction with the specifications shown in Table 10-17. The window itself is shown in Figure 10-15.

WINDOW/CONTROL NAME	PROPERTY	VALUE
Window		
w_dwprint	Title	"DataWindow Reporting"
	WindowType	Main
	Maximize Box	FALSE
	Minimize Box	TRUE
DataWindow control	Name	dw_1
	DataWindow object name	""
	HScrollBar	TRUE
	VScrollBar	TRUE
	HSplitScrolling	TRUE
	Border	3D Lowered
StaticText	Name	st_reporttoview
	Text	"&Report to view:"
StaticText	Name	st_zoom
	Text	"&Zoom:"
StaticText	Name	st_orientation
	Text	"&Orientation"
StaticText	Name	st_papersize
	Text	"Pap&er:"
StaticText	Name	st_printedpages
	Text	"Printed pages:"
StaticText	Name	st_pagecount
	Text	""
	Border	3D Lowered
	Alignment	Right
StaticText	Name	st_leftunit

continued on next page

continued from previous page

WINDOW/CONTROL NAME	PROPERTY	VALUE
	Text	"in"
StaticText	Name	st_rightunit
	Text	"in"
StaticText	Name	st_topunit
	Text	"in"
StaticText	Name	st_bottomunit
	Text	"in"
DropDownListBox	Name	ddlb_dw
	VScrollBar	TRUE
	Border	3D Lowered
	Accelerator	"r"
DropDownListBox	Name	ddlb_zoom
	Text	"100"
	Sorted	FALSE
	VScrollBar	TRUE
	Accelerator	"z"
	Enabled	FALSE
	Border	3D Lowered
	Items	35, 65, 100, 200 *(add others as desired)*
DropDownListBox	Name	ddlb_orientation
	Text	"Landscape" *(watch capitalization)*
	Sorted	FALSE
	VScrollBar	TRUE
	Accelerator	"o"
	Items	Landscape, Portrait, Default *(watch capitalization)*
DropDownListBox	Name	ddlb_papersize
	Text	"Letter" *(watch capitalization)*
	Sorted	TRUE
	VScrollBar	TRUE
	Accelerator	"e"
	Items	Letter, Legal, A4, Default

WINDOW/CONTROL NAME	PROPERTY	VALUE
CheckBox	Name	cbx_printpreview
	Text	"Print pre&view"
	Left Text	TRUE
	Border	3D Lowered
SingleLineEdit	Name	sle_top
	AutoHScroll	TRUE
	Border	3D Lowered
SingleLineEdit	Name	sle_bottom
	AutoHScroll	TRUE
	Border	3D Lowered
SingleLineEdit	Name	sle_left
	AutoHScroll	TRUE
	Border	3D Lowered
SingleLineEdit	Name	sle_right
	AutoHScroll	TRUE
	Border	3D Lowered
GroupBox	Name	gb_margins
	Text	"Margins"
CommandButton	Name	cb_apply
	Text	"Appl&y"
CommandButton	Name	cb_printsetup
	Text	"Print &Setup..."
CommandButton	Name	cb_print
	Text	"&Print"
CommandButton	Name	cb_exit
	Text	"E&xit"

Table 10-17 Window and control settings for the w_dwprint window

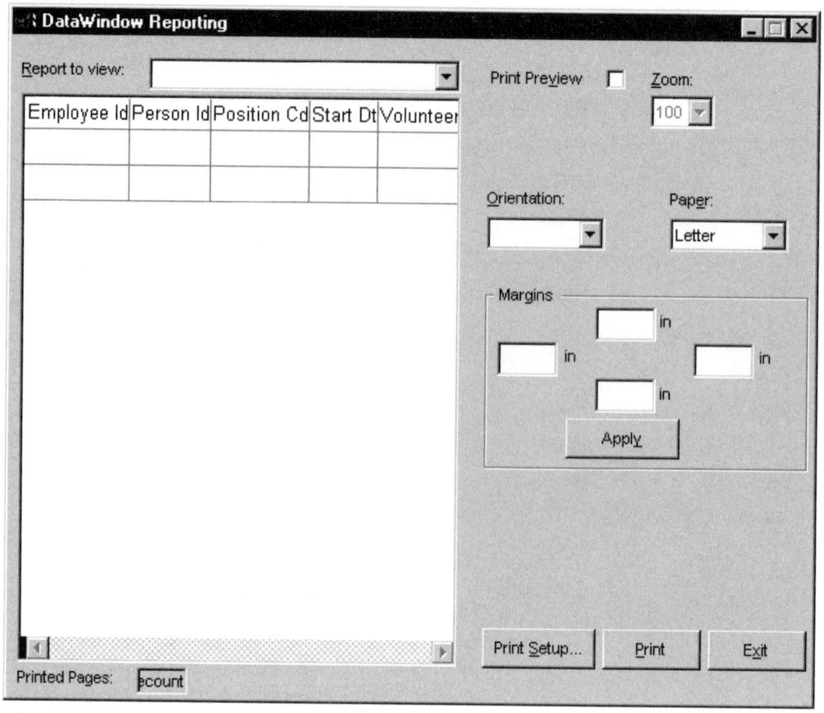

Figure 10-15 The w_dwprint window

4. Using the Declare/Instance Variables... menu item, declare an instance variable called is_units to preserve the current units for the displayed report.

```
string  is_units
```

5. Using the Declare/User Events... menu item declare a user event called ue_postopen mapped to the pbm_custom01 PowerBuilder event.

6. Save your window as w_dwprint to preserve your work so far.

7. Write a window function called wf_error_handler to perform SQL error handling. The function specification is shown in Table 10-18. The body of the function should be as follows. This is the same wf_error_handler() function that was presented in How-To 10.1.

```
string ls_errtext, ls_dbcode
integer li_sqlcode

// Preserve the original sqlcode (which may be affected by ROLLBACK later
on)
li_sqlcode = sqlca.sqlcode

IF li_sqlcode < 0 THEN
    ls_errtext = a_to.sqlerrtext
    ls_dbcode = String( a_to.sqldbcode )
    ROLLBACK USING a_to;
```

```
MessageBox( as_title, as_message + "~r~n" +&
        "(" +ls_dbcode + ") " + ls_errtext, Exclamation! )
END IF

// Return the original value of the SQLCode
RETURN li_sqlcode
```

FUNCTION SPECIFICATIONS

Function	Name	wf_error_handler	
	Access	public	
	Returns	integer	
Arguments			
	a_to	transaction	Value
	as_title	string	Value
	as_message	string	Value

Table 10-18 Function specifications for wf_error_handler()

8. Declare a window function called wf_getmargins by selecting the Declare/Window Functions... menu item. The function specification is shown in Table 10-19. Use the following script for the body of the function.

```
// this script gets the current margins for the DW and copies
// them into the singlelineedits that allow the user to change
// them. It also adjusts the displayed units correctly.

string ls_top, ls_bottom, ls_right, ls_left

is_units = dw_1.object.datawindow.units
ls_top = dw_1.object.datawindow.print.margin.top
ls_bottom = dw_1.object.datawindow.print.margin.bottom
ls_right = dw_1.object.datawindow.print.margin.right
ls_left = dw_1.object.datawindow.print.margin.left
CHOOSE CASE is_units
    CASE "0"        // PowerBuilder units
        st_leftunit.text = "PBU"
        st_rightunit.text = "PBU"
        st_topunit.text = "PBU"
        st_bottomunit.text = "PBU"
    CASE "1"        // Pixels
        st_leftunit.text = "pxl"
        st_rightunit.text = "pxl"
        st_topunit.text = "pxl"
        st_bottomunit.text = "pxl"
    CASE "2"        // 1/1000 inch
        st_leftunit.text = "in"
        st_rightunit.text = "in"
        st_topunit.text = "in"
        st_bottomunit.text = "in"
    CASE "3"        // 1/1000 centimeter
        st_leftunit.text = "cm"
        st_rightunit.text = "cm"
```

continued on next page

continued from previous page

```
            st_topunit.text = "cm"
            st_bottomunit.text = "cm"
END CHOOSE

CHOOSE CASE is_units
    CASE "0","1"        // PowerBuilder units
        sle_left.text = ls_left
        sle_right.text = ls_right
        sle_top.text = ls_top
        sle_bottom.text = ls_bottom
    CASE "2","3"        // 1/1000 of a whatever
        sle_left.text = String( Integer(ls_left) / 1000, "#0.00" )
        sle_right.text = String( Integer(ls_right) / 1000, "#0.00" )
        sle_top.text = String( Integer(ls_top) / 1000, "#0.00" )
        sle_bottom.text = String( Integer(ls_bottom) / 1000, "#0.00" )
END CHOOSE
```

FUNCTION SPECIFICATIONS

Function	Name	wf_getmargins
	Access	Private
	Returns	(None)
Arguments	*(none)*	

Table 10-19 Function specifications for wf_getmargins()

9. Create a window function called wf_getorientation by selecting the Declare/Window Functions... menu item. The body of the function is presented below. The function specifications are listed in Table 10-20.

```
// Obtain the orientation of the datawindow and update the ddlb
// on the window. Note that the ls_orient values (Landscape, etc)
// must be capitalized properly to allow the lookup in the ddlb
// to happen correctly. A more sophisticated solution would take
// advantage of Lower(), Trim(), and SelectItem()
string ls_orient

ls_orient =  dw_1.object.datawindow.print.orientation

CHOOSE CASE ls_orient
    CASE "1"
        ls_orient = "Landscape"
    CASE "2"
        ls_orient = "Portrait"
    CASE ELSE
        ls_orient = "Default"
END CHOOSE

ddlb_orientation.text = ls_orient
```

FUNCTION SPECIFICATIONS

Function	Name	wf_getorientation
	Access	Private
	Returns	(None)
Arguments	*(none)*	

Table 10-20 Function specifications for wf_getorientation()

10. Write the function called wf_getpagecount to compute the printed page count by first choosing the Declare/Window Functions... menu item. The function specification is shown in Table 10-21. The body of the script is listed below.

```
// script obtains the actual printed page count for a DataWindow.
// to do so, it turns off redraw on the DWC, places the DataWindow object
// into print preview, uses the Evaluate() dynamic datawindow command to
// compute the page count, and then undoes the earlier actions.

string ls_count, ls_temp

ls_temp = dw_1.Describe( "datawindow.print.preview" )
IF Lower( ls_temp) = "no" THEN
    dw_1.SetRedraw( FALSE )
    dw_1.Modify( "datawindow.print.preview=yes" )
END IF

ls_count = dw_1.Describe( "Evaluate('PageCount()',0) " )
st_pagecount.text = ls_count

IF Lower( ls_temp) = "no" THEN
    dw_1.Modify( "datawindow.print.preview=no" )
    dw_1.SetRedraw( TRUE )
END IF

RETURN Integer( ls_count )
```

FUNCTION SPECIFICATIONS

Function	Name	wf_getpagecount
	Access	Private
	Returns	(None)
Arguments	*(none)*	

Table 10-21 Function specifications for wf_getpagecount()

11. For the final function required for this window, use the Declare/Window Functions... menu item to create a function called wf_getpapersize using the specifications listed in Table 10-22 and the script shown below. This function obtains the paper size (e.g., letter, legal, A4, etc.) and sets the paper size DropDownListBox appropriately. As written here, this function only recognizes four paper sizes, even though the DataWindow supports more than twenty. You may expand this function along with the ddlb_papersize control to incorporate other paper sizes.

```
string ls_size

ls_size = dw_1.Describe( "datawindow.print.paper.size" )

CHOOSE CASE ls_size
    CASE "1"
        ls_size = "Letter"
    CASE "5"
        ls_size = "Legal"
    CASE "9"
        ls_size = "A4"
    CASE "0"
        ls_size = "Default"
    CASE ELSE
        MessageBox( this.title, "Unknown paper size.~r~n "+&
                    "Expand the CHOOSE CASE in wf_getpapersize()", &
                    Exclamation! )
        RETURN
END CHOOSE

ddlb_papersize.text = ls_size
```

FUNCTION SPECIFICATIONS		
Function	Name	wf_getpagecount
	Access	Private
	Returns	(None)
Arguments	(none)	

Table 10-22 Function specifications for wf_getpapersize()

12. Save the w_dwprint window now as a precaution.

13. Place the following script in the Open event of w_dwprint. This script populates the Report to view DropDownListBox with all DataWindows found in the current library.

```
// get a list of DataWindow objects from this library and put them
// in the list for ddlb_dw.
string ls_dw
long ll_pos
```

```
ls_dw = LibraryDirectory( "dwprint.pbl", DirDataWindow! )

DO WHILE ls_dw <> ""
    ll_pos = Pos( ls_dw, "~t" )
    IF ll_pos = 0 THENll_pos =Len( ls_dw) + 1
    ddlb_dw.AddItem( Left( ls_dw, ll_pos - 1 ) )
    ll_pos = Pos( ls_dw, "~n" )
    ls_dw = Mid( ls_dw, ll_pos + 1 )
LOOP

// select the first DataWindow object...
ddlb_dw.SelectItem( 1 )

// ...and show it in the DataWindow control
dw_1.dataobject = ddlb_dw.text

// complete our open processing by posting to the ue_postopen event
this.PostEvent( "ue_postopen" )
```

14. Code a script in the ue_postopen event to connect to the database and perform a DataWindow retrieval.

```
string ls_owner, ls_table, ls_objects, ls_top, ls_bottom, ls_right, ls_left
long ll_nexttab

SetPointer( Hourglass! )

// set the transaction object to refer to the Zoo database
sqlca.dbms = "ODBC"
sqlca.dbparm = "ConnectString='DSN=Zoo;UID=dba;PWD=SQL'"

CONNECT USING sqlca;

IF sqlca.sqlcode < 0 THEN // unsuccessful connect
    wf_error_handler( sqlca, "Connection Error", &
            "Could not connect to database" )
ELSE
    dw_1.SetTransObject( sqlca )
    this.wf_getorientation()
    this.wf_getpapersize()
    dw_1.Retrieve()
    this.wf_getpagecount( )
    this.wf_getmargins()
END IF
```

15. Disconnect your program from the database by entering the script shown below for the Close event on w_dwprint.

```
// If we're connected to the database, attempt to
// disconnect
IF sqlca.DBHandle() <> 0 THEN
    DISCONNECT USING sqlca;

    IF sqlca.sqlcode < 0 THEN   // couldn't disconnect
        wf_error_handler( sqlca, "Disconnection Error", &
                "Could not disconnect from database.")
```

continued on next page

continued from previous page

```
      END IF
END IF
```

16. Allow the user to change reports by coding the SelectionChanged event on ddlb_dw as follows.

```
// change the datawindow object-datawindow control relationship based on
the
// specified DataWindow object and then set up the remainder of the display
string ls_top, ls_bottom, ls_right, ls_left, ls_preview

dw_1.dataobject =this.text
IF cbx_printpreview.checked THEN ls_preview = "Yes" ELSE ls_preview = "no"

dw_1.SetTransObject( sqlca )

parent.wf_getorientation()
parent.wf_getpapersize()
parent.wf_getmargins()

dw_1.Modify( "datawindow.print.preview="+ls_preview+"~t" +&
             "datawindow.print.preview.zoom="+ddlb_zoom.text )

dw_1.Retrieve()
parent.wf_getpagecount( )
```

17. Allow the user to switch to Print Preview mode by placing the following script on the Clicked event of cbx_printpreview.

```
string ls_count

IF this.checked THEN
    dw_1.Modify( "datawindow.print.preview = Yes" )
    ddlb_zoom.enabled = TRUE
ELSE
    dw_1.Modify( "datawindow.print.preview = No" )
    ddlb_zoom.enabled = FALSE
END IF
```

18. Add the Print Preview zoom capability to the application using the script below for the SelectionChanged event of ddlb_zoom.

```
dw_1.Modify( "datawindow.print.preview.zoom=" + this.text )
```

19. Enter the following script to change the page orientation on the SelectionChanged event of ddlb_orientation.

```
string ls_orient

CHOOSE CASE Lower( Trim( this.text ))
    CASE "landscape"
        ls_orient = "1"
    CASE "portrait"
        ls_orient="2"
    CASE "default"
        ls_orient="0"
END CHOOSE
```

```
dw_1.Modify( "datawindow.print.orientation="+ ls_orient )

parent.wf_getpagecount( )
```

20. Add a script to change the page size to the SelectionChanged event of ddlb_papersize as follows.

```
string ls_paper="0"

CHOOSE CASE Lower( Trim( this.text ) )
    CASE "letter"
        ls_paper = "1"
    CASE "legal"
        ls_paper = "5"
    CASE "A4"
        ls_paper = "9"
END CHOOSE

dw_1.Modify( "DataWindow.Print.Paper.Size=" + ls_paper )
parent.wf_getpagecount( )
```

21. Margin changes can be supported by coding the following script on the Clicked event of cb_apply. This script reads the current values for each of the margin dimensions and issues an appropriate DataWindow Modify() command to alter them. Notice that this script assumes that the user has entered correct numerical values. EditMask controls may be a better solution in situations such as these.

```
string ls_top, ls_bottom, ls_left, ls_right

CHOOSE CASE is_units
    CASE "0", "1"    // PBU, Pixels
        dw_1.Modify( "datawindow.print.margin.top="+sle_top.text+ &
                " datawindow.print.margin.bottom="+sle_bottom.text+&
                " datawindow.print.margin.right="+sle_right.text+&
                " datawindow.print.margin.left="+sle_left.text )
    CASE "1","2"    // 1/1000 inch or 1/1000 cm
        ls_top =String( Int( Real( sle_top.text ) * 1000) )
        ls_bottom = String( Int( Real( sle_top.text) * 1000 ))
        ls_right = String( Int( Real( sle_right.text) * 1000 ))
        ls_left = String( Int( Real( sle_left.text ) * 1000 ))
        dw_1.Modify( "datawindow.print.margin.top="+ls_top+ &
                " datawindow.print.margin.bottom="+ls_bottom+&
                " datawindow.print.margin.right="+ls_right+&
                " datawindow.print.margin.left="+ls_left )

END CHOOSE

parent.wf_getpagecount( )
```

22. Implement the print setup capability by coding the following simple script on the Clicked event of cb_printsetup. This script invokes a Print Setup dialog box which alters the default printer for all Windows applications.

```
// allow the user to change the current printer
// this may alter the page count
```

continued on next page

continued from previous page
```
PrintSetup()
parent.wf_getpagecount()
```

23. Allow the user to print the DataWindow by coding the Clicked event of cb_print as indicated below.

```
dw_1.Print()
```

24. Enter the following script for the Clicked event of cb_exit.

```
Close( parent )
```

25. Save the w_dwprint window.

26. Using the Application painter, place the following script on the Open event of the Application object.

```
Open( w_dwprint )
```

27. Save and run the application.

How It Works

The DWPRINT application utilitizes a variety of separate techniques to provide the overall reporting functionality demonstrated in this How-To. The functions wf_getmargins(), wf_getorientation(),and wf_getpapersize() all retrieve the relevant print settings for the DataWindow object by calling the Modify() function on the appropriate DataWindow object properties. The Print Preview CheckBox uses the Describe() function to place the DataWindow object into Print Preview mode, which displays the DataWindow object so that you can see the effects of the print margin, paper size, and orientation values.

The margins' functionality deserves special mention here. Because the DataWindow object can be based on PowerBuilder units (PBUs), pixels, centimeters, or inches, this application must know what the units are in order to display the units on the window. Additionally, the DataWindow object actually uses 1/1000 inch and 1/1000 centimeter instead of the base inch and centimeter units; this prevents the DataWindow from having to deal with fractional numbers for dimensions internally. However, our user will not want to deal with such large values, so this application scales the values in both directions to show them as whole inches and centimeters and to store them as 1/1000 inch or 1/1000 centimeter. Examine the window function wf_getmargins() and the Clicked event of cb_apply to see how these conversions are performed.

The wf_getpagecount() function also requires some examination. This function computes the printed page count so that the user can know how long a given report will be. This capability requires a special implementation because the PageCount() function in the DataWindow object shows the page count for the current display device. If the DataWindow is not in Print Preview mode, the current display device is a DataWindow control. Because the DataWindow control cannot show very much data, the PageCount() values are normally inflated compared to the page numbers when actually printing. The wf_getpagecount() function overcomes this limitation by performing the following steps: turn off redraw on the DataWindow control, place the DataWindow object into Print Preview mode, obtain the page count by asking the DataWindow engine to execute the PageCount() function, turn off Print Preview mode, turn on redraw. Notice the use of the DataWindow Evaluate() function sent to the DataWindow engine using the Describe() function. Evaluate() allows your program to obtain the results of any DataWindow object function. This function works because once the DataWindow object is in Print Preview mode, the PageCount() function returns the correct values.

Finally, the application needs to allow the user to change the current printer and to print the report. The cb_printsetup CommandButton invokes the PrintSetup() function to perform the first task, and cb_print calls Print() to perform the second. Note that PrintSetup() actually alters the default printer in Windows. The Print() function sends the report to the default printer.

Comments

This How-To demonstrates the core set of DataWindow printing capabilities. You can search on the topic "Print.property" in PowerBuilder's help library to see some of the other printing properties that can be accessed by using the Modify() function. Some of these options include altering the document name (Print.document), printing the report to a file instead of to a printer (Print.filename), and printing only a few pages out of the report (Print.range).

COMPLEXITY
INTERMEDIATE

10.4 How do I...
Modify the contents of a dropdown based on other fields?

Problem

I have an application where I want the user to be able to pick from a list of choices. This is simple if I use a DropDownDataWindow. However, the list of choices should actually be limited based on the value of another field in the DataWindow. How do I modify the contents of a DropDownDataWindow based on other fields?

Technique

Setting up a DropDownDataWindow actually involves two DataWindow objects. One of the DataWindow objects should include the column for which a value is *desired*. The values themselves are usually coded; that is, they store a code instead of the textual data represented by the code. As an example, department IDs (coded values) are usually stored in the tables that reference department values instead of department names (display values). Returning to the DataWindow object, the application needs a way to provide a list of choices (in display form) that return a coded value when a value is selected. DropDownListBox, CheckBox, RadioButton, Edit Mask, and Edit edit styles in the DataWindow all provide a way of doing this. All of these methods are limited, however, in that their code table (containing coded value-display value pairs) is static.

The DropDownDataWindow allows you to bypass this static code table. Your application will need a second DataWindow object which will retrieve the list of choices from the table that contains all available values. This DataWindow object should contain a column to be used as the display value and a column to be used as the coded value. They may even be the same column (i.e., when you simply show the user a list of coded choices that require no textual explanation). The second DataWindow object will be associated with the coded column on the first DataWindow object as a DropDownDataWindow edit style, where you designate which column is used for coded values and which is used for display values. The second DataWindow object is referred to as a *child DataWindow*.

The child DataWindow has the capability to be manipulated much like a normal DataWindow. These manipulations include setting transaction objects, retrieving data, filtering rows, and sorting rows. At runtime the program simply needs to obtain a reference to the "virtual" DataWindow control corresponding to the child DataWindow object. This virtual control has a data type of DataWindowChild. This program will alter the contents of the child DataWindow based on selections in another column on the first DataWindow.

Steps

To start this application, run DDDW.PBL from PowerBuilder or by executing DDDW.EXE. The first thing you will notice is that both the department and employee dropdowns are populated as shown in Figure 10-16. Try changing the department value; the employee list will change as the department changes to show only those employees in that department. When you pick an employee, the employee information displayed in the middle of the window will change as well. To build this application, complete the steps below.

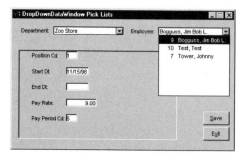

Figure 10-16 The DDDW application

1. Use the Application painter to create a new library and Application object called DDDW.PBL and a_dddw, respectively. Answer "No" when prompted to create an application template.

2. Create a DataWindow object, using the DataWindow painter, that will display a list of departments. The DataWindow object specifications are shown in Table 10-23 while the object is shown in the layout stage in Figure 10-17. Save the object as d_dept_list.

WINDOW	OPTION	VALUE
New DataWindow		
	Data Source	Quick Select
	Presentation Style	Tabular
	Generation Options	Background color: white
		Text border: none
		Text color: WndText
		Column border: none
		Column color: WndText
Quick Select		
	Table	department
	Columns	dept_id, dept_dsc

Table 10-23 Specifications for the d_dept_list DataWindow object

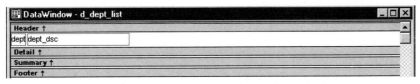

Figure 10-17 The d_dept_list DataWindow object in layout

3. Create another DataWindow object called d_employee_list that shows a list of employees. This DataWindow object should have a retrieval argument called an_dept_id that will be passed when a department is specified at runtime. The specifications for this DataWindow object are listed in Table 10-24. It is shown in layout in Figure 10-18.

WINDOW	OPTION	VALUE
New DataWindow		
	Data Source	SQL Select
	Presentation Style	Tabular
	Generation Options	Background color: white
		Text border: none
		Text color: WndText
		Column border: none
		Column color: WndText
SQL Select		
	Tables	employee, person
	Join	employee.person_id = person.person_id
	Columns	employee: employee_id
		person: last_name, first_name, middle_initial
	Retrieval Arguments	an_dept_id
Number		
	Where	employee.dept_id = :an_dept_id
Design		
	Computed field	employee_name
	Expression	"person_last_name + ", " + person_first_name +
		if(Not IsNull(person_middle_initial)," " +
		person_middle_initial + ".", "")"

Table 10-24 Specifications for the d_employee_list DataWindow object

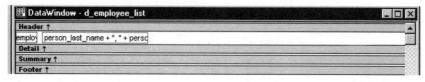

Figure 10-18 The d_employee_list DataWindow object in layout mode

4. Create a DataWindow object to display employee information and call it d_employee_info. The DataWindow object specifications are shown in Table 10-25. The layout is shown in Figure 10-19.

WINDOW	OPTION	VALUE
New DataWindow		
	Data Source	SQL Select
	Presentation Style	Freeform
	Generation Options	Background color: Silver
		Text border: none
		Text color: WndText
		Column border: 3DLowered
		Column color: WndText
SQL Select		
	Tables	employee
	Columns	*all*
	Retrieval Arguments	an_emp_id
Number		
	Where	employee.employee_id = :an_emp_id
Design		
	Computed field	no_record_found
	Expression	"if(RowCount() > 0, "", "No employee record.")"

Table 10-25 Specifications for the d_employee_info DataWindow object

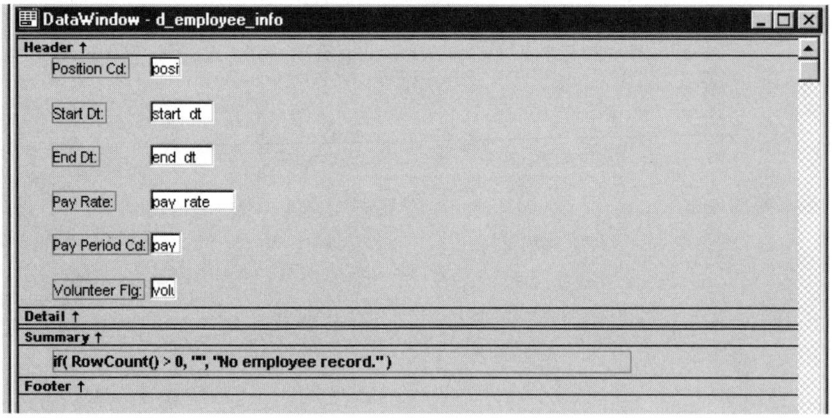

Figure 10-19 The d_employee_info DataWindow object in layout mode

5. Construct a simple DataWindow object called d_dept_emp_picklist to serve as the "front-end" for picking departments and employees. This DataWindow object is required mostly for structural reasons; no updates are used with this DataWindow. The specifications for this DataWindow object are shown in Table 10-26. This DataWindow object will be completed in step 6.

WINDOW	OPTION	VALUE
New DataWindow		
	Data Source	External
	Presentation Style	Freeform
	Generation Options	Background color: Silver
		Text border: none
		Text color: WndText
		Column border: 3DLowered
		Column color: WndText
Result Set Description		
	dept_id	Number
	emp_id	Number

Table 10-26 Specifications for the d_dept_emp_picklist DataWindow object

6. Arrange this DataWindow object as shown in Figure 10-20. Define DropDownDataWindow edit styles for the dept_id and emp_id columns as indicated in Table 10-27 and Table 10-28. Recall that the edit style may be set using the Style option on the Edit tab of the properties for the column.

WINDOW	PROPERTY	VALUE
DropDownDataWindow Edit Style		
	DataWindow	d_dept_list
	Display Column	dept_dsc
	Data Column	dept_id
	Always Show List	FALSE
	Always Show Arrow	TRUE
	VScrollBar	TRUE

Table 10-27 Specifications for the DDDW edit style for dept_id

WINDOW	PROPERTY	VALUE
DropDownDataWindow Edit Style		
	DataWindow	d_emp_list
	Display Column	employee_name
	Data Column	emp_id
	Always Show List	FALSE
	Always Show Arrow	TRUE
	VScrollBar	TRUE

Table 10-28 Specifications for the DDDW edit style for emp_id

Figure 10-20 The d_dept_emp_picklist DataWindow object when completed

7. Complete this DataWindow object by storing a single empty row of data with the object. To do so, pick the Rows/Data... menu item, choose Add, and choose OK. This single row of data will simplify the coding process later on. Save this object as d_dept_emp_picklist.

8. Using the Window painter, create a window object called w_dddw. The specifications for this window are listed in Table 10-29. The completed window is pictured in Figure 10-21.

WINDOW/CONTROL NAME	PROPERTY	VALUE
Window		
w_dddw	Title	"DropDownDataWindow Pick Lists"
	WindowType	Main
	MaximizeBox	FALSE
	MinimizeBox	TRUE
	Resizable	FALSE
DataWindow control	Name	dw_1 *(positioned at top of window)*
	DataWindow object name	d_dept_emp_picklist
	HscrollBar	FALSE
	VScrollBar	FALSE
	Border	None
DataWindow control	Name	dw_2
	Dataobject	d_employee_info
	HScrollBar	FALSE
	VScrollBar	FALSE
	Border	3DLowered
CommandButton	Name	cb_save
	Text	"&Save"
CommandButton	Name	cb_exit
	Text	"E&xit"

Table 10-29 Window and control settings for the w_dddw window

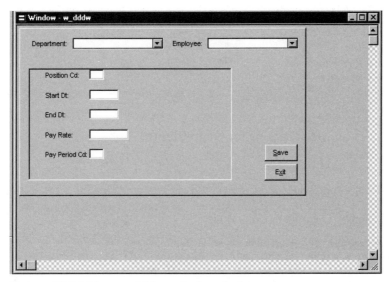

Figure 10-21 The w_dddw window in layout

9. Use the Declare/Instance Variables... menu item to declare the two child DataWindow instance variables as follows.

```
datawindowchild idwc_dept, idwc_emp
```

10. Declare a window function called wf_getdepts using the Declare/Window Functions... menu item. The function specification is shown in Table 10-30. The body of the function is shown below.

```
// retrieve departments and pull the first department retrieved
// into the base (external datawindow)

// function returns the first department ID in the list
long ll_firstdept


CHOOSE CASE  idwc_dept.Retrieve()
    CASE IS > 0
        ll_firstdept = idwc_dept.GetItemNumber( 1, "dept_id" )
        dw_1.SetItem( 1, "dept_id" , ll_firstdept )
    CASE 0
        SetNull( ll_firstdept )
        dw_1.SetItem( 1, "dept_id", ll_firstdept )
    CASE IS < 0
        MessageBox( "DataWindow Error", "Error on retrieve.", Exclamation!
)
        ll_firstdept = -1
END CHOOSE

RETURN ll_firstdept
```

FUNCTION SPECIFICATIONS

Function	Name	wf_getdepts
	Access	Private
	Returns	Long
Arguments	(none)	

Table 10-30 Function specifications for wf_getdepts()

11. Save the w_dddw window now as a precaution.

12. Declare a second window function called wf_getemps using the Declare/Window Functions... menu item. The function specification is listed in Table 10-31. The function contents are shown below.

```
// function retrieves the employees for a department. If there are no
// employees for a given department, it places a null in the emp_id
// column of the base datawindow to show it as empty.

// function returns the ID of the first employee in the list
long ll_firstemp

SetNull( ll_firstemp )

IF IsNull( al_dept_id ) THEN
    idwc_emp.Reset()
    dw_1.SetItem( 1, "emp_id", ll_firstemp )
ELSE
    CHOOSE CASE idwc_emp.Retrieve( al_dept_id )
        CASE IS > 0
            ll_firstemp = idwc_emp.GetItemNumber( 1, "employee_employee_id"
)
            dw_1.SetItem( 1, "emp_id", ll_firstemp )
        CASE 0
            dw_1.SetItem( 1, "emp_id", ll_firstemp )
        CASE IS < 0
            MessageBox( "DataWindow Error", "Error retrieving employees.", &
                Exclamation! )
            ll_firstemp = -1
    END CHOOSE
END IF

RETURN ll_firstemp
```

FUNCTION SPECIFICATIONS

Function	Name	wf_getemps
	Access	Private
	Returns	Long

FUNCTION SPECIFICATIONS

Arguments		
an_dept_id	Long	Value

Table 10-31 Function specifications for wf_getemps()

13. Save the window.

14. Code the following script on the Open event of the w_dddw window. This
script connects to the database and performs some initialization steps.

```
long ll_id

// connect to the database
sqlca.dbms = 'ODBC'
sqlca.DBParm = "ConnectString='DSN=Zoo;UID=dba;PWD=sql'"

CONNECT USING sqlca;
IF sqlca.sqlcode < 0 THEN
    MessageBox( "Connect Error", "Could not connect.~r~n" + &
            sqlca.sqlerrtext, Exclamation! )
    Close( this )
    RETURN
END IF

// get the child datawindow references for employee and department
IF dw_1.GetChild( "dept_id", idwc_dept ) < 1 THEN
    MessageBox( "DataWindow Child", "No child datawindow for department.", &
        Exclamation!)
    Close(this)
    RETURN
END IF

IF dw_1.GetChild( "emp_id", idwc_emp ) < 1 THEN
    MessageBox( "DataWindow Child", "No child datawindow for employee.", &
            Exclamation! )
    Close( this )
    RETURN
END IF

// set the child datawindows' transaction objects
idwc_emp.SetTransObject( sqlca )
idwc_dept.SetTransObject( sqlca )
// set the transaction object for the employee info datawindow
dw_2.SetTransObject(sqlca)

// obtain the departments and employees dropdowns
ll_id = this.wf_getdepts()
ll_id = this.wf_getemps(ll_id)

dw_2.Retrieve( ll_id )
```

15. Code another script on the Close event of the w_dddw window to disconnect from the database.

```
IF sqlca.dbhandle() <> 0 THEN   // it *is* connected
    DISCONNECT USING sqlca;
    IF sqlca.sqlcode < 0 THEN
        MessageBox( "Disconnect Error", "Could not disconnect~r~n" +&
            sqlca.sqlerrtext, Exclamation! )
    END IF
END IF
```

16. Place the following code on the ItemChanged event on dw_1. This script
allows the program to update the list of employees and the employee information as the department and employee values change.

```
string ls_col
long ll_id

ls_col = this.GetColumnName()

CHOOSE CASE ls_col
    CASE "dept_id"
        ll_id = Long( data )
        ll_id = parent.wf_getemps(ll_id)
    CASE "emp_id"
        ll_id = Long( data )
END CHOOSE

dw_2.Retrieve( ll_id )
```

17. Enter a simple save script for the Clicked event of cb_save as follows.

```
IF dw_2.Update() < 0 THEN
    ROLLBACK USING sqlca;
    IF sqlca.sqlcode < 0 THEN
        MessageBox("Database Error", "Rollback failed.", Exclamation! )
    END IF
ELSE
    COMMIT USING sqlca;
    IF sqlca.sqlcode < 0 THEN
        MessageBox("Database Error", "Commit failed.", Exclamation! )
    END IF
END IF
```

18. Code the cb_exit CommandButton's Clicked event script as follows.

```
Close( parent )
```

19. Save the window.

20. Using the Application painter, enter the following line of PowerScript on
the Application object Open event.

```
Open( w_dddw )
```

21. Save the Application object and run the application.

How It Works

The child DataWindow is the single most important concept in this How-To. The two list DataWindows, d_dept_list and d_employee_list, are used as the source for DropDownDataWindows on the d_dept_emp_picklist DataWindow object. The d_dept_emp_picklist serves as a user interface for choosing department and employee values.

The program obtains the DataWindow control references to the child DataWindow objects (d_dept_list and d_employee_list) and uses the child DataWindow references to set the transaction objects, and to retrieve and manipulate the child DataWindow objects. The wf_getdepts() and wf_getemps() functions each obtain the appropriate list of values and cause them to display on the d_dept_emp_picklist DataWindow object. This latter capability is implemented by obtaining the first value in the child DataWindow and using it as the value for the column on the d_dept_emp_picklist DataWindow object, forcing a desirable code table lookup.

The ItemChanged event on dw_1 responds to changing values of department and employee to retrieve an employee's appropriate value in d_employee_info. Observe that the data argument is used to obtain the changing value.

Comments

DropDownDataWindows are an immensely valuable addition to your PowerBuilder toolkit. They provide a user-friendly method of picking values and require no validation (because the user can only pick valid values). Experiment with this How-To to see the effects of altering the code flow.

COMPLEXITY
BEGINNING

10.5 How do I...
Sort and filter a DataWindow?

Problem

I am interested in being able to sort the contents of a DataWindow on my client machine without having to re-retrieve data from the server. Additionally I want my users to be able to condense the data already retrieved to assist them in viewing the data that is important to them. How do I sort and filter a DataWindow?

Technique

In a client/server environment you have the capability to perform certain functions on both the server (database) and the client. PowerBuilder allows you to sort data on the client, which avoids unnecessary database traffic and usage of server resources to construct a query and retransmit it. PowerBuilder also allows you to indicate which of the retrieved rows are shown to the user. When rows are initially retrieved, they are placed in a DataWindow object memory region called the *primary buffer*, which can be thought of as the set of rows which can ultimately be viewed by the user. When you establish a filter, PowerBuilder applies an expression to all rows in the primary buffer and a second region called the *filter buffer*. Any row that causes the expression to return TRUE is placed in the primary buffer; any row that does not match is moved to the filter buffer. No database communication takes place, and the rows are not affected in any other way.

Steps

To demonstrate this application, run the program FILTSORT.PBL from PowerBuilder or FILTSORT.EXE from Windows. When the application starts up, person information appears in the middle of the display as shown in Figure 10-22. Notice that there are currently no rows in the filter buffer. As a first step, specify a sort expression of "first_name A" (without quotes) in the Expression MultiLineEdit. Click Sort... and notice that the sort order of the DataWindow changes. Try a sort expression "city D, last_name A" and notice that the DataWindow sorts on city in descending order, and on last_name in ascending order within city. You can click the PB Sort... button to invoke the standard PowerBuilder Sort dialog instead of the raw expression mechanism implemented here.

For filters, enter a filter expression of "city = 'Portland'" and click the Filter button. Notice that the number of displayed rows decreases and that the primary and filter row counts change. Try a more complex filter of "Match(Lower(last_name), '.*e.*') and Match(Lower(first_name), '.*e.*')"; this filter shows those persons with last names and first names both containing the letter "e." As with sorting, you can

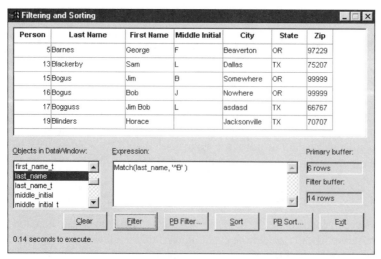

Figure 10-22 The sorting and filtering application

click the PB Filter... button to invoke PowerBuilder's Filter dialog. Click Exit to end the program.

To construct this example, follow the steps below.

1. Create a new library and Application object called FILTSORT.PBL and a_filter_sort, respectively, using the Application painter. You will not require an application template for this program.

2. Using the DataWindow painter create a DataWindow object called d_person_list. The specifications are shown in Table 10-32. The layout of this object is unimportant.

WINDOW	OPTION	VALUE
New DataWindow		
	Data Source	Quick Select
	Presentation Style	Grid
	Generation Options	Background color: white
		Text border: none
		Text color: WndText
		Column border: none
		Column color: WndText
Quick Select		
	Table	person
	Columns	person_id, last_name, first_name, middle_initial, city, state_cd, zip_cd

Table 10-32 Specifications for the d_person_list DataWindow object

3. Use the Window painter to create a window called w_filter_sort using the specifications listed in Table 10-33.

WINDOW/CONTROL NAME	PROPERTY	VALUE
Window		
w_filter_sort	Title	"Filtering and Sorting"
	WindowType	Main
	MaximizeBox	FALSE
	MinimizeBox	TRUE
	Resizable	FALSE

continued on next page

continued from previous page

WINDOW/CONTROL NAME	PROPERTY	VALUE
DataWindow control	Name	dw_1
	DataWindow object name	"d_person_list"
	HScrollBar	TRUE
	VScrollBar	TRUE
	Border	3D Lowered
StaticText	Name	st_objectsindw
	Text	"&Objects in DataWindow:"
StaticText	Name	st_expression
	Text	"&Expression:"
StaticText	Name	st_primary_label
	Text	"Primary buffer:"
StaticText	Name	st_primary
	Text	""
	Border	3D Lowered
StaticText	Name	st_filter_label
	Text	"Filter buffer:"
StaticText	Name	st_filter
	Text	""
	Border	3D Lowered
StaticText	Name	st_message
	Text	""
ListBox	Name	lb_object_list
	Sorted	TRUE
	VScrollBar	TRUE
	Accelerator	"o"
MultiLineEdit	Name	mle_expression
	VScrollBar	TRUE
	AutoHScroll	FALSE

WINDOW/CONTROL NAME	PROPERTY	VALUE
	Accelerator	"e"
CommandButton	Name	cb_clear
	Text	"&Clear"
CommandButton	Name	cb_filter
	Text	"&Filter"
CommandButton	Name	cb_pbfilter
	Text	"&PB Filter..."
CommandButton	Name	cb_sort
	Text	"&Sort"
CommandButton	Name	cb_pbsort
	Text	"P&B Sort..."
CommandButton	Name	cb_exit
	Text	"E&xit"

Table 10-33 Window and control settings for the w_filter_sort window

4. Declare a custom user event for the window by choosing the Declare/User Events... menu item. Call the event ue_postopen and map it to the PowerBuilder event pbm_custom01.

5. Save the window.

6. Place the following script on the Open event of the window to delay retrieving data until the window has been drawn initially.

```
this.PostEvent( "ue_postopen" )
```

7. Place a script on the ue_postopen event on the window as shown below.

```
string ls_owner, ls_table, ls_objects
long ll_nexttab

SetPointer( Hourglass! )

st_message.text = "Connecting to database..."

// set the transaction object to refer to the Zoo database
sqlca.dbms = "ODBC"
sqlca.dbparm = "ConnectString='DSN=Zoo;UID=dba;PWD=SQL'"
```

continued on next page

continued from previous page
```
CONNECT USING sqlca;

IF sqlca.sqlcode < 0 THEN // unsuccessful connect
    st_message.text = "Unsuccessful connect."
    MessageBox("Connect Error", "Could not connect to database.~r~n"+&
        sqlca.sqlerrtext, Exclamation!)
ELSE
    st_message.text = "Connected!"
    dw_1.SetTransObject( sqlca )
    dw_1.Retrieve()
    // Place a list of objects in the Objects ListBox
    ls_objects = dw_1.Describe( "datawindow.objects" )
    DO WHILE ls_objects <> ""
        Yield()
        ll_nexttab = Pos(ls_objects, "~t" )
        IF ll_nexttab = 0 THEN ll_nexttab = Len( ls_objects ) + 1
        lb_object_list.AddItem( Left( ls_objects, ll_nexttab - 1 ) )
        ls_objects = Mid( ls_objects, ll_nexttab + 1 )
    LOOP
        st_primary.text = string(dw_1.RowCount()) + " rows"
        st_filter.text = "0 rows"
END IF
```

8. Disconnect from the database by coding the Close event on the window.

```
IF sqlca.dbhandle() > 0 THEN
    DISCONNECT USING sqlca;

    IF sqlca.sqlcode < 0 THEN  // couldn't disconnect
        MessageBox( "Disconnect Error",  &
            "Could not disconnect from database.~r~n" + sqlca.sqlerrtext )
    END IF
END IF
```

9. When the user chooses an object in the object list, it should be inserted into the current filter expression at the insertion point. Place the following script on the SelectionChanged event of lb_object_list to use the Windows Clipboard to implement this behavior.

```
ClipBoard( this.SelectedItem() )

mle_expression.Paste()

mle_expression.SetFocus()
```

10. Code the Clicked event of cb_clear using the script below.

```
// clear out the expression mle
mle_expression.text = ""
```

11. Place a script on the Clicked event of the cb_filter CommandButton as listed below. This script applies the entered filter expression to the DataWindow and returns statistics on how many rows were affected by the operation.

```
// accept a filter expression for the dw
long ll_start, ll_end

IF dw_1.SetFilter( mle_expression.text ) < 0 THEN
    MessageBox( parent.title, "Invalid filter.", Exclamation! )
    mle_expression.SetFocus()
    st_message.text = ""
ELSE
    ll_start = CPU()
    dw_1.Filter()
    ll_end = CPU()
    st_primary.text = string(dw_1.RowCount()) + " rows"
    st_filter.text = string(dw_1.FilteredCount()) + " rows"
    st_message.text = String( (ll_end - ll_start) / 1000, "#0.00" ) + &
            " seconds to execute."
END IF
```

12. Enter the following script for the Clicked event of cb_pbfilter to invoke the internal PowerBuilder Filter Expression dialog.

```
long ll_start, ll_end
string ls_filter

SetNull(ls_filter)
IF dw_1.SetFilter( ls_filter ) > 0 THEN
    ll_start = CPU()
    dw_1.Filter()
    ll_end = CPU()
    st_primary.text = string(dw_1.RowCount()) + " rows"
    st_filter.text = string(dw_1.FilteredCount()) + " rows"
    st_message.text = String( (ll_end - ll_start) / 1000, "#0.00" ) + &
            " seconds to execute."
    mle_expression.text = "<filter specified via PowerBuilder dialog>"
ELSE
    st_message.text = "Operation canceled."
END IF
```

13. Code a script for the Clicked event of cb_sort as follows to apply the entered sort to the DataWindow.

```
long ll_start, ll_end

IF dw_1.SetSort( mle_expression.text ) < 0 THEN
    MessageBox( parent.title, "Invalid sort.", Exclamation! )
    mle_expression.SetFocus()
    st_message.text = ""
ELSE
    ll_start = CPU()
    dw_1.Sort()
    ll_end = CPU()
    st_message.text = String( (ll_end - ll_start) / 1000, "#0.00" ) +&
            " seconds to sort."
END IF
```

14. Your program can invoke the built-in PowerBuilder Sort dialog by using the script shown below for the Clicked event of the cb_pbsort CommandButton.

```
long ll_start, ll_end

IF dw_1.SetSort( mle_expression.text ) < 0 THEN
    MessageBox( parent.title, "Invalid sort.", Exclamation! )
    mle_expression.SetFocus()
    st_message.text = ""
ELSE
    ll_start = CPU()
    dw_1.Sort()
    ll_end = CPU()
    st_message.text = String( (ll_end - ll_start) / 1000, "#0.00" ) + &
        " seconds to sort."
END IF
```

15. Code the Exit CommandButton to close the window.

```
Close( parent )
```

16. Save the window.

17. Using the Application painter, enter a script for the Open event of the Application object as shown below.

```
Open( w_filter_sort )
```

18. Save the Application object and run the application.

How It Works

Filters are implemented using two functions, SetFilter() and Filter(). SetFilter() establishes the expression, while Filter() applies the expression to the DataWindow to perform the filtering operation. As the cb_pbfilter CommandButton shows, passing a NULL value to the function invokes PowerBuilder's built-in Filter dialog box. You can utilize this feature in your own applications (provided your users can figure it out, of course!). The filter expression can be any Boolean PowerScript expression. As mentioned in the Technique section above, no database traffic is generated; rows are merely rearranged in memory.

Sorting is similar to filtering in that two functions, SetSort() and Sort(), are required to establish the sorting expression and to perform the sort operation. As with SetFilter(), passing a NULL value to SetSort() displays PowerBuilder's built-in Sort dialog. Sort expressions take the form "*column_name A|D*". Multiple levels of sorting can be established by concatenating multiple sort expressions together with commas separating each expression.

Comments

In addition to implementing filters and sorts dynamically, you can also enter these statically for a given DataWindow object by selecting the Rows/Filter... and Rows/Sort... menu items when the DataWindow object is in design mode. Specifying a static filter is generally not useful, since it *always* restricts the data you bring back from the server. If your program does not need the data, your program will perform better if you implement your filter criteria in the WHERE clause of the SQL statement to limit the data coming from the server. Specifying a static sort, however, is quite useful. In general, client-side sorting as shown in this How-To is faster than performing it on the server. Exceptions to this guideline can be made for extremely large result sets that may overextend client resources such as memory.

DATAWINDOW UPDATES

DATAWINDOW UPDATES

How do I...

DataWindows offer much more than the reporting and data retrieval capabilities presented in Chapter 10, *DataWindow Basics*. DataWindows also make it easy for users to enter data and for your program to save those changes to the database. This chapter presents techniques that go beyond the simple Update() function call. You will learn how to code a sophisticated DataWindow error handler, how to properly coordinate the updating of two DataWindows, and how to use embedded SQL to save DataWindow changes.

11.1 Provide Custom Error Handling on a DataWindow

When an error occurs during a DataWindow-database interaction, a DBError event is triggered on the DataWindow control. This How-To teaches you how to use the DBError event to display, log, or print DataWindow errors when they occur, giving you more options than the simple dberror processing provided by default.

11.2   Coordinate Multiple DataWindow Updates

For single DataWindows, the Update() function is generally sufficient to perform updates. Applications that perform master/detail updates, such as employees in a department or line items on an order, require multiple DataWindows. The simple Update() no longer works in this situation without some special handling. This How-To demonstrates the necessary programming to properly coordinate multiple DataWindow updates.

11.3   Write Custom DataWindow Updates with Embedded SQL

The DataWindow Update() function works well enough when the DataWindow accesses a single table. In many cases though, you want your user to be able to edit related data from multiple tables simultaneously. Alternatively, you may have a poorly designed "legacy" database that requires more than the simple update. This How-To shows you how to use embedded SQL to perform your update.

COMPLEXITY
BEGINNING

11.1   How do I...
Provide custom error handling on a DataWindow?

Problem

When my DataWindow encounters an error on a Retrieve(), Update(), or similar operation, my program displays an unattractive error message. On top of that, I have to manually write down the contents of this message if I want it while I'm debugging. How do I provide an improved error handler for a DataWindow?

Technique

When the DataWindow encounters an error on any function that involves the database (e.g., Retrieve(), Update(), ReselectRow()), PowerBuilder triggers a DBError event on the DataWindow control involved. Inside this event your program can determine the exact nature of the error and the row causing the error, along with handling the ROLLBACK needed to undo any changes already applied to the database.

   This application uses a custom window and an external DataWindow object to display the error information for a DBError event. The window allows the user to view the error, print the error, or save it to a file. The external DataWindow object is used to simplify the printing of the error, which would be tedious except for the DataWindow object's extensive reporting capabilities.

Steps

To try out the program for this How-To, access the DBERROR.PBL library from PowerBuilder or run DBERROR.EXE. Once the program is running you will see a simple window that allows you to view and modify important person information; this window is shown in Figure 11-1. What we want to do now is cause an error. Change the first person's person ID to "2", an ID assigned to another person in the system. Choose the Save button, which will cause an error due to the duplicate primary key value you just entered. The custom error handler window pictured in Figure 11-2 will appear.

You can click the Print CommandButton to print the contents of the error message (nicely formatted in boxes, etc.). The Print Setup... CommandButton allows you to alter the default printer used for printing the error. Clicking Save saves the contents of the error to a file you specify. Clicking Close will terminate the error display.

To construct this application, follow the steps below.

1. Create a new library and Application object called DBERROR.PBL and a_dberror, respectively, using the Application painter. You will not require an application template for this How-To.

2. This program will need a structure to pass information between the person entry window and the error handler. In this case, the program will send a title for the error window, the application's error message, and the DataWindow control and transaction object used on the person entry window. Use the Structure painter to declare a structure called s_dberror, using the fields and data types shown in Table 11-1.

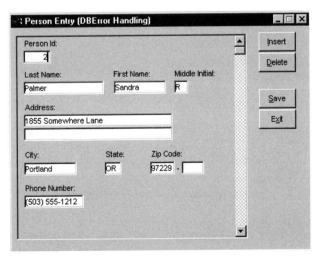

Figure 11-1 The person entry window
(w_person_entry) for the DBError application

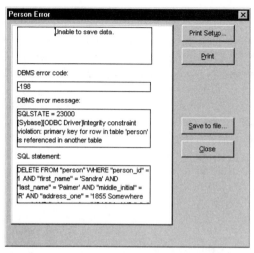

Figure 11-2 The error handler window
(w_dberror) for the DBError application

VARIABLE NAME	TYPE
s_title	string
s_message	string
to_1	transaction
s_sqlerrtext	string
l_sqldbcode	long
s_sqlsyntax	string
e_buffer	dwbuffer
l_row	long

Table 11-1 Specifications for the s_dberror structure

3. Create a freeform DataWindow object called d_person_entry using the
DataWindow painter. This is a simple DataWindow object that will allow
the user to view and change person information in the database. The exact
layout is unimportant. The specifications for the DataWindow object are
shown in Table 11-2. The DataWindow object is shown in Figure 11-3.

WINDOW	OPTION	VALUE
New DataWindow		
	Data Source	Quick Select
	Presentation Style	Freeform

WINDOW	OPTION	VALUE
	Generation Options	Background color: Silver
		Text border: none
		Text color: WndText
		Column border: 3D Lowered
		Column color: WndText
Quick Select		
	Table	person
	Columns	*(all)*
Design		
	Sort	person_id *(use the Rows/Sort... menu item)*

Table 11-2 Specifications for the d_person_entry DataWindow object

4. To make it easier to print and view the contents of the error, this application uses a DataWindow object instead of discrete window controls. To provide all the basic capabilities, you will need to create a freeform DataWindow object with an external data source. You will need to make several changes in design mode to allow the user to scroll the information, among other capabilities. Create this DataWindow object, called d_dberror, using the specifications listed in Table 11-3. The d_dberror DataWindow object is shown in Figure 11-4.

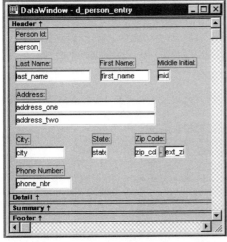

Figure 11-3 A suggested layout for the d_person_entry DataWindow object

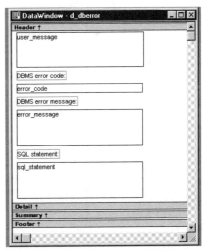

Figure 11-4 The d_dberror DataWindow object in design

WINDOW	OPTION	VALUE
New DataWindow		
	Data Source	External
	Presentation Style	Freeform
	Generation Options	Background color: White
		Text border: none
		Text color: WndText
		Column border: none
		Column color: WndText
		Wrap height: None
Result Set Description		
	Name	user_message
	Type	string
	Length	2000
	Name	error_code
	Type	number
	Name	error_message
	Type	string
	Length	32767
	Name	sql_statement
	Type	string
	Length	32767
Design		
	Column	user_message
	Border	Box
	Column	error_code
	Border	Box
	Autosize Height	TRUE
	Column	error_message

WINDOW	OPTION	VALUE
	Border	Box
	Autosize Height	TRUE
	Auto HScroll	FALSE
	AutoVScroll	FALSE
	HScrollBar	FALSE
	VScrollBar	TRUE
	Column	sql_statement
	Border	Box
	Autosize Height	TRUE
	Auto HScroll	FALSE
	Auto VScroll	FALSE
	HScrollBar	FALSE
	VScrollBar	TRUE
	Text object	dbms_error_code_t
	Text	"DBMS error code:"
	Text object	dbms_error_message_t
	Text	"DBMS error message:"
	Text object	sql_statement_t
	Text	"SQL statement:"

Table 11-3 Specifications for the d_dberror DataWindow object

5. Create the error handler window itself using the Window painter. The property settings for the window are listed in Table 11-4. The window itself is shown in Figure 11-5. Save this window under the name w_dberror.

WINDOW/CONTROL NAME	PROPERTY	VALUE
Window		
w_dberror	Title	""
	WindowType	Response
DataWindow control	Name	dw_1
	DataWindow Object name	"d_dberror"
	HScrollBar	FALSE
	VScrollBar	TRUE

continued on next page

continued from previous page

WINDOW/CONTROL NAME	PROPERTY	VALUE
	Border	3D Raised
CommandButton	Name	cb_printsetup
	Text	"Print Set&up..."
CommandButton	Name	cb_print
	Text	"&Print"
CommandButton	Name	cb_savetofile
	Text	"&Save to file..."
CommandButton	Name	cb_close
	Text	"&Close"

Table 11-4 Specifications for the w_dberror window

6. One feature this window provides is the ability to save the error information to a file. However, long text strings will require special formatting to make them easier to read. Create a function called wf_format_string that will format a long string by breaking at or near spaces and commas. (This isn't a very sophisticated formatter.) The function declaration is shown in Table 11-5. The body of the function is listed below.

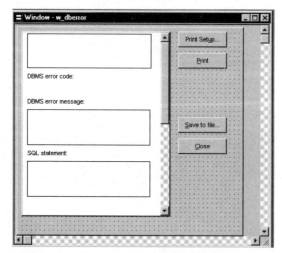

Figure 11-5 The w_dberror window

```
string ls_output, ls_char
long ll_loc, ll_len, ll_linebreak

// break things at close to 50 characters (adjust to suit your taste)
ll_linebreak = 50

// get the length of the input
ll_len = Len(as_input)

// if the input is shorter than the break length, use it "as-is"
IF ll_len <= ll_linebreak THEN
    ls_output = as_input + "~r~n"
ELSE
    // while there is more to format, evaluate each 50th character, and
    // single step through the string beyond that character to locate a
    // space or comma
    DO WHILE as_input <> ""
        ll_loc = ll_linebreak
        ls_char = Mid(as_input, ll_loc, 1 )
        DO UNTIL ls_char = " " or ls_char = "," OR ll_loc > ll_len
            ll_loc ++
            ls_char = Mid(as_input, ll_loc, 1 )
        LOOP

        ls_output = ls_output + Left( as_input, ll_loc - 1 ) + "~r~n"
        as_input = Mid( as_input, ll_loc + 1 )
    LOOP
END IF
RETURN ls_output
```

FUNCTION SPECIFICATIONS

Function	Name	wf_format_string	
	Access	private	
	Returns	string	
Arguments	as_input	string	value

Table 11-5 Function specifications for wf_format_string()

7. When the window opens, it should accept the incoming s_dberror structure and place its contents into the DataWindow. Very importantly, the window must ROLLBACK the transaction that caused the error *before* the window is displayed to prevent database locks from being held longer than necessary. Place the following script in the Open event of the window to accomplish these tasks. Save your window when done.

```
s_dberror lstr_dberror
long ll_new

// pick up the incoming structure
lstr_dberror = Message.PowerObjectParm
```

continued on next page

continued from previous page

```
// if there is not a row stored in the DataWindow object
// (which would be a normal thing in this situation), add
// one to the DWO buffer
IF dw_1.RowCount() < 1 THEN
    ll_new = dw_1.InsertRow( 0 )
    dw_1.ScrollToRow( ll_new )
END IF

// copy the dberror structure information into the DWO
dw_1.SetItem(1, "error_code", lstr_dberror.l_sqldbcode )
dw_1.SetItem( 1, "error_message", lstr_dberror.s_sqlerrtext )
dw_1.SetItem(1,"sql_statement", lstr_dberror.s_sqlsyntax )
dw_1.SetItem( 1, "user_message", lstr_dberror.s_message )

// modify the title
this.title = lstr_dberror.s_title

ROLLBACK USING lstr_dberror.to_1;
```

8. Allow the user to change the default printer by placing the following script on the Clicked event of cb_printsetup.

```
// invoke the print setup dialog
PrintSetup()
```

9. The user should also be allowed to print the error information. However, several modifications should be made to the DataWindow object to allow it to print without scrollbars (you can't scroll on paper) and to allow the individual fields to move based on their height. These changes are undone following the printing process. The script for the Clicked event of cb_print is shown below.

```
// turn off redraw so the user can't see what we're doing
dw_1.SetRedraw( FALSE )

// this script needs to modify the DWO so that the fields containing
// what might have been scrollable edit boxes expand in size when printed
// to display the entire error without scroll bars (since you can't scroll
// a piece of paper). We'll also set up several fields to slide so that
// they
// can move as the other fields change size.
dw_1.object.datawindow.detail.height.autosize = "Yes"
dw_1.object.user_message.height.autosize = "Yes"
dw_1.object.sql_statement.height.autosize = "Yes"
dw_1.object.error_message.height.autosize = "Yes"
dw_1.object.dbms_error_code_t.slideup = "DirectlyAbove"
dw_1.object.dbms_error_message_t.slideup = "DirectlyAbove"
dw_1.object.sql_statement_t.slideup = "DirectlyAbove"
dw_1.object.sql_statement.slideup = "DirectlyAbove"
dw_1.object.error_message.slideup = "DirectlyAbove"
dw_1.object.error_code.slideup = "DirectlyAbove"

dw_1.Print()

dw_1.object.datawindow.detail.height.autosize = "No"
dw_1.object.user_message.height.autosize = "No"
```

```
dw_1.object.sql_statement.height.autosize = "No"
dw_1.object.error_message.height.autosize = "No"
dw_1.object.dbms_error_code_t.slideup = "No"
dw_1.object.dbms_error_message_t.slideup = "No"
dw_1.object.sql_statement_t.slideup = "No"
dw_1.object.sql_statement.slideup = "No"
dw_1.object.error_message.slideup = "No"
dw_1.object.error_code.slideup = "No"

dw_1.SetRedraw( TRUE )

RETURN
```

10. The save capability can be coded on the Clicked event of cb_save as follows.

```
string ls_pathfile, ls_file
integer li_fileid
boolean lb_failed = FALSE

IF GetFileSaveName( "Save Error", ls_pathfile, ls_file, "err", &
      "Error files (*.err),*.err,All files (*.*),*.*") > 0 THEN
   li_fileid = FileOpen( ls_pathfile, LineMode!, Write!, &
                         LockReadWrite!, Append! )
   IF li_fileid >= 0 THEN // file has been opened successfully

      IF FileWrite( li_fileid, "----- begin error -----" ) < 0 THEN &
            lb_failed = TRUE
      IF lb_failed = FALSE THEN
         IF FileWrite( li_fileid, &
                parent.wf_format_string( dw_1.GetItemString(&
                dw_1.GetRow(), "user_message") )) < 0 THEN &
             lb_failed = TRUE
      END IF
      IF lb_failed = FALSE THEN
         IF FileWrite( li_fileid, "DBMS Error Code:~r~n"+ &
             string(dw_1.GetItemNumber(dw_1.GetRow(), &
             "error_code" ))) < 0 THEN  lb_failed = TRUE
      END IF
      IF lb_failed = FALSE THEN
         IF FileWrite( li_fileid, "DBMS ErrorText:~r~n"+ &
             parent.wf_format_string(dw_1.GetItemString(dw_1.GetRow(), &
             "error_message") )) < 0 THEN lb_failed = TRUE
      END IF
      IF lb_failed = FALSE THEN
         IF FileWrite( li_fileid, "SQL Statement:~r~n"+ &
             parent.wf_format_string(dw_1.GetItemString(dw_1.GetRow(), &
             "sql_statement" ))) < 0 THEN   lb_failed = TRUE
      END IF
      IF lb_failed = FALSE THEN
         IF FileWrite( li_fileid, "----- end error -----" ) < 0 THEN &
            lb_failed = TRUE
      END IF
      IF lb_failed = FALSE THEN
         IF FileClose( li_fileid) < 0 THEN lb_failed = TRUE
      END IF

   ELSE
```

continued on next page

continued from previous page
```
        lb_failed = TRUE
    END IF
END IF

IF lb_failed THEN MessageBox( "Save", "Save failed.", Exclamation! )
```

11. Complete the w_dberror window by coding the Clicked event of cb_close as follows. Save the window, and close the painter when you are done.

```
Close( parent )
```

12. Create another window, w_person_entry, using the Window painter. The window and control settings are shown in Table 11-6. The window itself is displayed in Figure 11-6.

WINDOW/CONTROL NAME	PROPERTY	VALUE
Window		
w_person_entry	Title	"Person Entry (DBError Handling)"
	WindowType	Main
	MaximizeBox	FALSE
	Resizable	FALSE
DataWindow control	Name	dw_1
	DataWindow Object name	"d_person_entry"
	HScrollBar	TRUE
	VScrollBar	TRUE
	Border	3D Lowered
CommandButton	Name	cb_insert
	Text	"&Insert"
CommandButton	Name	cb_delete
	Text	"&Delete"
CommandButton	Name	cb_save
	Text	"&Save"
CommandButton	Name	cb_exit
	Text	"E&xit"

Table 11-6 Window and control settings for the w_person_entry window

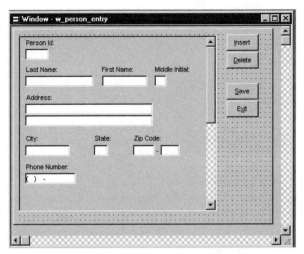

Figure 11-6 The w_person_entry window

13. Place the following code on the Open event of w_person_entry to connect to the database and perform a DataWindow retrieval.

```
sqlca.dbms = "ODBC"

// we'll also be sure to turn bind variables off so that we can
// see the contents of the SQL statements being sent to the database
sqlca.dbparm = "DisableBind=1,ConnectString='DSN=Zoo;UID=dba;PWD=sql'"

CONNECT USING sqlca;
IF sqlca.sqlcode < 0 THEN
    MessageBox("Connection Error", &
            "Could not connect to database.", Exclamation! )
    Close( this )
ELSE
    dw_1.SetTransObject( sqlca )
    dw_1.Retrieve()
END IF
```

14. Also provide a script to disconnect from the database on the Close event of w_person_entry as indicated below.

```
IF sqlca.dbhandle() > 0 THEN
    DISCONNECT USING sqlca;
    IF sqlca.sqlcode < 0 THEN
        MessageBox("Disconnect Error", &
            "Could not disconnect from database.", Exclamation! )
    END IF
END IF
```

15. Allow the user to insert a new person entry by coding the Clicked event of cb_insert using the script that follows.

```
long ll_new

ll_new = dw_1.InsertRow(0)
dw_1.ScrollToRow( ll_new )
dw_1.SetColumn( "person_id")
dw_1.SetFocus()
```

16. The user can delete a person by coding the Clicked event of cb_delete using
the following script.

```
string ls_first, ls_last, ls_middle
long ll_curr

ll_curr = dw_1.GetRow()

// if we're on a valid row, obtain the identifying information for
// that row and confirm that the user wants to delete
IF ll_curr > 0 THEN
    // if this is a new, unmodified row, delete it without prompting,
    // otherwise ask first
    IF dw_1.GetItemStatus( ll_curr, 0, Primary! ) = New! THEN
        dw_1.DeleteRow( ll_curr )
    ELSE
        ls_first = dw_1.GetItemString( ll_curr, "first_name" )
        ls_last = dw_1.GetItemString( ll_curr, "last_name" )
        ls_middle = dw_1.GetItemString( ll_curr, "middle_initial" )
        IF IsNull(ls_middle) THEN ls_middle = "" ELSE &
            ls_middle = ls_middle + ". "
        IF IsNull(ls_first) THEN ls_first = ""
        IF IsNull(ls_last) THEN ls_last = ""
        IF MessageBox( "Delete Person", "Are you sure you want to "+&
                "delete " + ls_first + " " + ls_middle + ls_last + "?", &
                Question!, YesNo! ) = 1 THEN
            dw_1.DeleteRow( ll_curr )
            dw_1.SetFocus()
        END IF
    END IF
END IF
```

17. Code the save functionality by placing the following script on the Clicked
event of cb_save.

```
IF dw_1.Update() > 0 THEN
    COMMIT USING sqlca;
END IF
```

18. The user can end the application by clicking on cb_exit. Use the following
script for the Clicked event of cb_exit.

```
Close( parent )
```

19. Most importantly, the application should respond to DataWindow-database
errors by showing the user the w_dberror error handling window.
Complete the link to this window by using the script below for the DBError
event of dw_1.

```
s_dberror lstr_dberror

// populate the dberror structure with the pertinent information,
```

```
// including the title of the error window, message to the user,
// and transaction object and datawindow control references
lstr_dberror.s_title = "Person Error"
lstr_dberror.s_message = "Unable to save data."
lstr_dberror.to_1 = sqlca
lstr_dberror.dw_1 = this

// open the error handler window, passing this information
OpenWithParm( w_dberror, lstr_dberror, parent )

 // don't display standard error
this.SetActionCode( 1 )
```

20. Save the w_person_entry window.

21. Complete the application by switching to the Application painter and coding the Clicked event of the Application object as follows.

```
Open( w_person_entry )
```

22. Save the Application object and run the program.

How It Works

The basic concepts behind this application are surprisingly simple. Whenever the DataWindow encounters a database error (on Retrieve(), Update(), etc.), the DataWindow control receives a DBError event. During the DBError event, you have the opportunity to examine the database error code and error text by examining the event parameters, sqldbcode and sqlerrtext respectively, and to see the SQL statement that caused the problem by accessing sqlsyntax. Because the actual error handler in this application is provided by w_dberror instead of the w_person_entry window itself, w_dberror must have some means of obtaining the error information. This example populates a structure variable, lstr_dberror of type s_dberror, with the information about the error and passes that structure to the w_dberror window. The w_dberror window's Open event accepts this incoming information and uses it accordingly.

However, one database consideration is commonly overlooked in handling the DBError event. Most databases will grant your application locks on the affected rows (or pages, depending on your database server) that will prevent other users from writing (shared locks) or reading (exclusive locks) those rows or pages. These locks may have a serious effect on *concurrency,* the number of simultaneous users your database can support. The ROLLBACK and COMMIT SQL commands release all held locks as part of their operation. Application programmers make a mistake, however, when they fail to perform the ROLLBACK until after the user responds to the error. Thus, the duration of the locks is determined by the user, not by the application. The w_dberror Open event performs a ROLLBACK at the end of the script, before the window is drawn on the screen, reducing the amount of time the locks are held.

A DataWindow was used instead of discrete controls (such as MultiLineEdits and SingleLineEdits) to simplify the printing process. Using the DataWindow reduces printing to a series of DataWindow modifications to remove the scrollbars on the DataWindow columns and to allow the DataWindow columns to "slide" (move) based on the other columns' sizes. The DataWindow Print() function sends the error information to the printer. Redrawing is turned off for the DataWindow while these modifications are taking place so that the user does not notice the changes.

The Save CommandButton utilizes some of the PowerBuilder file functions, including FileOpen(), FileWrite(), and FileClose(), to save the information to a file. This is a simple process except that many database error messages will be lengthy. The w_dberror window includes a wf_format_string() function to break these messages into manageable "chunks" so that they can be read more easily.

Comments

Custom DBError event handling should be a standard part of all but your "test" programs. The easiest way to achieve this level of consistency is to create a standard user object DataWindow control that includes a script for the DBError event. Use descendants of this standard user object instead of the standard DataWindow control, and your program will automatically incorporate the standard functionality.

The row and buffer arguments for the DBError event are also highly valuable, although they are not used in this How-To. These parameters allow your program to determine the row number of the row causing the error along with the buffer containing the row. You can use this information to inform the user of the exact item of data causing the problem and to position the user's cursor on the offending row or column. If you use this function, remember that the user cannot view the contents of the filter or delete buffers without your program's assistance.

COMPLEXITY
BEGINNING

11.2 How do I...
Coordinate multiple DataWindow updates?

Problem

I have an application with two DataWindows that supports a master-detail/relationship in my database, where one "master" row is related to multiple "detail" rows. Everything works perfectly if the save is successful, but the program has problems whenever an error occurs. The problem is that the database is OK, but the user can't attempt to save again after correcting the problem. How do I coordinate multiple DataWindow updates?

Technique

As the user makes changes in a DataWindow, the DataWindow engine maintains flags to allow it to generate the correct SQL to be sent to the database. Upon successful completion, the DataWindow engine automatically resets the flags, indicating that the DataWindow data is in agreement with the data in the database. The difficulty arises when more than one DataWindow is involved, because the flags now depend on updates in other DataWindows. This How-To demonstrates the proper management of the flags to properly coordinate the multiple DataWindow updates.

Steps

To start this How-To, access the MULTUPDT.PBL application or run MULTUPDT.EXE. When the program starts, it shows companies (the master records) with the products our zoo offers from each company (the detail records). Notice that as you scroll through the companies, the detail records change to match the currently displayed master. (This is deliberately programmed into the application.) This application is pictured in Figure 11-7.

To begin with, see what happens when the multiple DataWindow update is performed incorrectly. Using the currently displayed company (whatever it is), make a change to the company address by typing into the appropriate field. Add a detail line for this company by clicking the Add Detail CommandButton. Specify an item number of "1", which will cause a database error when the update is performed (because that item number is already used). Complete the rest of the detail line with appropriate information. Click the Bad Update CommandButton. You should receive a database error indicating that the item number value is not unique. Correct the item number on the new line to a value such as "500", which is not used. Click Bad Update again. You should not receive an error. Now click the Refresh button and observe that even though the new detail line is there, the address change on the company is not.

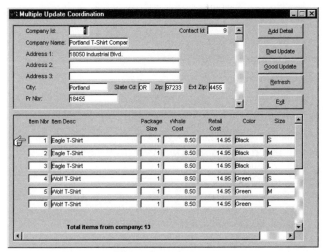

Figure 11-7 The Multiple Update application

Again make a change to the company address and add a detail line with an item number of "1". This time click Good Update. Once again you will receive the error. Correct the problem by changing the item number to "501" and click Good Update again. Clicking the Refresh CommandButton will reveal that all changes were now applied to the database.

To construct this program perform the steps below.

1. Using the Application painter, create a PowerBuilder library and Application object called MULTUPDT.PBL and a_multupdt, respectively. You will not need an application template for this program.

2. Create the "master" DataWindow object to allow for editing company information. Call it d_company and use the specifications listed in Table 11-7. The DataWindow object itself is pictured in Figure 11-8.

WINDOW	OPTION	VALUE
New DataWindow		
	Data Source	Quick Select
	Presentation Style	Freeform
	Generation Options	Background color: Silver
		Text border: none
		Text color: WndText
		Column border: 3D Lowered
		Column color: WndText
Quick Select		
	Table	company
	Columns	(all)
Design		
	Sort	company_id (use the Rows/Sort... menu item)

Table 11-7 Specifications for the d_company DataWindow object

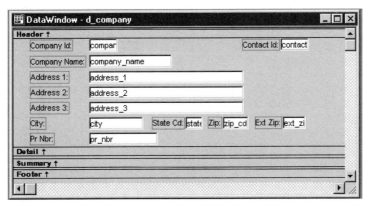

Figure 11-8 The d_company DataWindow object in layout

3. You will also need a DataWindow object to deal with the product "detail" items. In order for this DataWindow to be synchronized with the "master" DataWindow, d_company, you must also declare and use a retrieval argument on this new DataWindow. This retrieval argument will be set to the current company value as the user moves through the list of companies. Call this new DataWindow object d_retail_item. Use the specifications listed in Table 11-8, laying it out as shown in Figure 11-9. Be sure to remove the company_id column from the display; it will be populated programmatically.

WINDOW	OPTION	VALUE
New DataWindow		
	Data Source	SQL Select
	Presentation Style	Tabular
	Generation Options	Background color: Silver
		Text border: none
		Text color: WndText
		Column border: 3D Lowered
		Column color: WndText
Quick Select		
	Table	retail_item
	Columns	(all)
	Retrieval Argument	an_company_id Number
		(use the Objects/Retrieval Arguments... menu item)

continued on next page

continued from previous page

WINDOW	OPTION	VALUE
	Where clause	"retail_item"."company_id" = :an_company_id
Design		
	Sort	item_nbr *(use the Rows/Sort... menu item)*
	Computed field	total_items
	Expression	"'Total items from company: ' +
		count(item_nbr for all)"
	Band	Footer

Table 11-8 Specifications for the d_retail_item DataWindow object

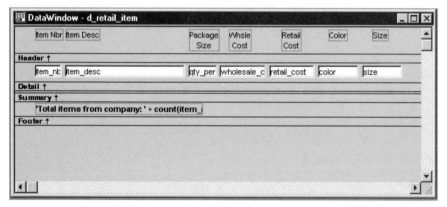

Figure 11-9 The d_retail_item DataWindow object in layout mode

4. Use the Window painter to create the window to serve as the program's primary interface. Name the window w_multupdt. The specifications are shown in Table 11-9. The layout is shown in Figure 11-10.

WINDOW/CONTROL NAME	PROPERTY	VALUE
Window		
w_multupdt	Title	"Multiple Update Coordination"
	WindowType	Main
	MaximizeBox	FALSE
	Resizable	FALSE
DataWindow control	Name	dw_master
	DataWindow object name	"d_company"
	HScrollBar	TRUE

WINDOW/CONTROL NAME	PROPERTY	VALUE
	VScrollBar	TRUE
	Border	3D Lowered
DataWindow control	Name	dw_detail
	DataWindow object name	"d_retail_item"
	HScrollBar	TRUE
	VScrollBar	TRUE
	Border	3D Lowered
CommandButton	Name	cb_adddetail
	Text	"&Add Detail"
CommandButton	Name	cb_badupdate
	Text	"&Bad Update"
CommandButton	Name	cb_goodupdate
	Text	"&Good Update"
CommandButton	Name	cb_refresh
	Text	"&Refresh"
CommandButton	Name	cb_exit
	Text	"E&xit"

Table 11-9 Window and control settings for w_multupdt

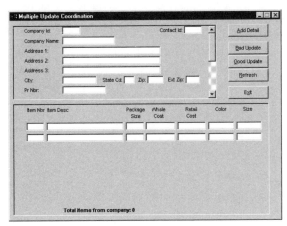

Figure 11-10 The w_multupdt window

5. Declare an instance variable on the window to hold the currently displayed company ID. To do so, use the Declare/Instance Variables... menu item to make the following variable declaration.

```
long il_company_id
```

6. The window will need to establish a connection to the database and populate the master DataWindow. Code the Open event on the w_multupdt window as follows.

```
sqlca.dbms = "ODBC"
sqlca.dbparm = "DisableBind=1,ConnectString='DSN=Zoo;UID=dba;PWD=sql'"

CONNECT USING sqlca;
IF sqlca.sqlcode < 0 THEN
    MessageBox("Connection Error", &
            "Could not connect to database.", Exclamation! )
    Close( this )
ELSE
    dw_master.SetTransObject( sqlca )
    dw_detail.SetTransObject( sqlca )
    dw_detail.SetRowFocusIndicator( Hand! )
    dw_master.Retrieve()
END IF
```

7. The window should also terminate its database connection when it is closed. To do so, place the following script on the Close event of the window.

```
IF sqlca.dbhandle() > 0 THEN
    DISCONNECT USING sqlca;
    IF sqlca.sqlcode < 0 THEN
        MessageBox("Disconnect Error", &
            "Could not disconnect from database.", Exclamation! )
    END IF
END IF
```

8. Because the master DataWindow control, dw_master, is designed to show a single company at a time, it makes good user interface sense to refresh the detail DataWindow, dw_detail, as the user scrolls through companies. This behavior does not happen by default. To accomplish this task, the following script obtains the first row displayed on a page and makes that row current by calling SetRow(). SetRow() causes a RowFocusChanged event to occur. The RowFocusChanged event, coded later, is the event responsible for performing the actual retrieval against the detail DataWindow.

```
// force the current row to change as the user scrolls
string ls_displayed
long ll_curr

ls_displayed = this.object.datawindow.firstrowonpage

ll_curr = Long( ls_displayed )

// make the displayed row current
// (which will cause a rowfocuschanged event, synching the dw's)
this.SetRow( ll_curr )
```

9. If the user scrolls through the companies using the cursor keys, the detail should also change. Place the following script on the RowFocusChanged event on dw_master to make this behavior happen.

```
il_company_id = this.object.data[ currentrow, 1 ] // company_id column

dw_detail.Retrieve( il_company_id )
```

10. To add detail lines, the Clicked event of cb_add detail should add a new detail item, populate the company ID field, force the new row into view, and position the user's cursor on it. Use the following script for this event to make these things occur.

```
long ll_new, ll_masterrow, ll_company

ll_new = dw_detail.InsertRow( 0 )

dw_detail.object.data[ ll_new, 1 ] = il_company_id  // company_id column

dw_detail.ScrollToRow( ll_new )
dw_detail.SetColumn( "item_nbr" )
dw_detail.SetFocus()
```

11. To peform the "bad" update, the program should perform the DataWindow updates as usual using the following script for the Clicked event of cb_badupdate.

```
IF dw_master.Update() > 0 THEN
    IF dw_detail.Update() > 0 THEN
        COMMIT USING sqlca;
    ELSE
        ROLLBACK USING sqlca;
        MessageBox( "Bad Update", "Update failed.", StopSign! )
    END IF
ELSE
    ROLLBACK USING sqlca;
    MessageBox( "Bad Update", "Update failed.", StopSign! )
END IF
```

12. The "good" update code is surprisingly similar to the bad update code. There are only two significant differences. First, the Update() function is called with an optional second parameter of FALSE, which prevents the DataWindow engine from clearing the DataWindow flags, even if the Update() is successful. Second, the script uses ResetUpdate() to clear the flags if and only if both updates were performed properly. The following code will accomplish the good update on the Clicked event of cb_goodupdate.

```
IF dw_master.Update(TRUE, FALSE) > 0 THEN
    IF dw_detail.Update( TRUE, FALSE) > 0 THEN
        COMMIT USING sqlca;
        dw_master.ResetUpdate()
        dw_detail.ResetUpdate()
    ELSE
        ROLLBACK USING sqlca;
```

continued on next page

continued from previous page
```
        MessageBox( "Bad Update", "Update failed.", StopSign! )
    END IF
ELSE
    ROLLBACK USING sqlca;
    MessageBox( "Bad Update", "Update failed.", StopSign! )
END IF
```

13. The Refresh CommandButton should allow you to reset the application without having to exit. Place the following simple script on the Clicked event of cb_refresh.

```
dw_master.Retrieve()
```

14. The cb_exit CommandButton should terminate the window. Enter the following script on the Clicked event of cb_exit.

```
Close(parent)
```

15. Save the w_multupdt window.

16. To complete the program, the Application object must open the w_multupdt window when the program starts. Place the following script on the Open event of the Application object.

```
Open( w_multupdt )
```

17. Save the Application object and run the application.

How It Works

The central concept to coordinating multiple DataWindow updates properly is to manage the DataWindow flags. As you can see by examining the script for cb_badupdate's Clicked event, no special steps are taken. When you tried the demonstration steps, PowerBuilder was sucessfully updating the master DataWindow (with a minor address change), which resulted in the clearing of the flags. When PowerBuilder continued that script and updated the detail DataWindow, the operation failed, resulting in a ROLLBACK on the server. At this point in the program the detail DataWindow's flags are preserved, but the master's are not. The database has correct information, of course, but it is out of sync with the status of the flags on the master DataWindow. After correcting the problem and re-saving, you saw the anomaly where the address change was not taken; this is but a minor error. More significant errors can be seen if you add a script to add new master entries.

The solution to this problem is quite simple. By specifying the optional second parameter to the Update() function, you told PowerBuilder to *preserve* all flag statuses until your program says otherwise. In this fashion, only a successful update on both the master and the detail will allow the flags to be reset (following a COMMIT operation). In all error circumstances, the program performs a database ROLLBACK, and the DataWindow flags correctly reflect that situation.

Comments

To see more severe consequences of failing to coordinate a multiple DataWindow update properly, add a CommandButton to add *master* rows to the database. Create a master row that incorporates a primary key value used by another master row. Add detail lines to the master and click Save. You will receive a database error, which you expect. If you then correct the problem by assigning the company a unique ID and click Save again, you will receive a referential integrity violation, however, because the detail rows reference a company *that was never actually added*. It was never added because a ROLLBACK was performed.

COMPLEXITY
ADVANCED

11.3 How do I...
Write custom DataWindow updates with embedded SQL?

Problem

I have a DataWindow that joins two tables to obtain its data. I want my user to view and edit the information this way because it is more natural for the user. (After all, from their perspective, the data structures are irrelevant.) I am having difficulty because the DataWindow only wants to update one table at a time. How do I write a custom DataWindow update that uses embedded SQL?

Technique

One way to solve this problem is to make use of the flags that the DataWindow engine maintains about the contents of a DataWindow. As the user makes changes, or adds or deletes rows from the DataWindow, the DataWindow engine flags these changes so that it can generate correct SQL using the Update() function. Even though the Update() function is not sufficient for this scenario, your program can use the flags to generate SQL on its own. Instead of performing a normal Update(), your program can examine the rows in the DataWindow buffers and issue its own SQL commands to the database.

Before proceeding, note that this is but one way to solve this particular problem. The techniques presented here are best used when the DataWindow requires complex manipulations such as accessing a denormalized database table.

Steps

To try out this How-To, open the library EMBEDDW.PBL and run the application. When the program starts, the program allows you to enter employee information as shown in Figure 11-11. However, some of the employee information, such as

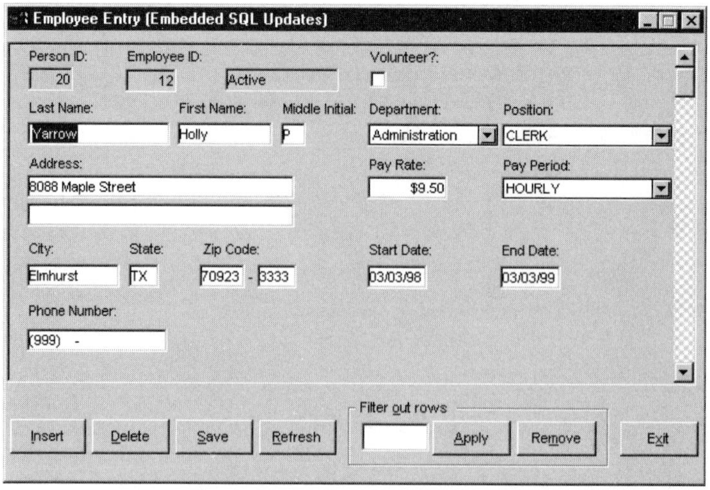

Figure 11-11 The Employee Entry (Embedded SQL Updates)
application

addresses and phone numbers, is stored in the person table while other information
such as pay rates and positions is stored in the employee table. The DataWindow object
used for this How-To uses a join operation in its query to pull data from two tables.
By default a DataWindow object cannot update the result set from a joined query.

Make changes to an employee's address and choose Save to write this changed
information to the database. Click Refresh to re-retrieve this data and observe that
the alteration was indeed made. Choose the Insert button to add a new employee.
Observe that the Person ID and Employee ID columns are empty; they will be set
when the data is added to the database. Complete all fields for this new employee.
As you do so, notice that checking the Volunteer CheckBox makes the pay rate and
pay period columns unavailable; clearing the box makes them available again. Enter
the last name you typed in for the employee in the Filter out rows SingleLineEdit.
Click Apply and notice that the newly entered row is no longer visible; it has been
placed into the DataWindow object's filter buffer. Choose Save to save this information.
You can click Refresh to prove to yourself that the new row was written, even though
it had been filtered out; this capability has been added to the application.

You may choose Exit to end the application. All actions just demonstrated have
been implemented using embedded SQL instead of the normal DataWindow
Update() function. To construct this program follow the steps listed below.

1. Use the Application painter to create a new Application object called
a_embedded_dw and a new PBL called EMBEDDW.PBL. Answer No when
prompted to build an application template.

2. Create a DataWindow object to provide the code table for a
DropDownDataWindow for departments. Use the name d_department_list
for this DataWindow object. The specifications for this DataWindow object

are listed in Table 11-10. The object is shown in design mode in Figure 11-12. Be sure to remove the header text in the Header band along with the dept_id column from the display.

WINDOW	OPTION	VALUE
New DataWindow		
	Data Source	Quick Select
	Presentation Style	Tabular
	Generation Options	Background color: white
		Text border: none
		Text color: WndText
		Column border: none
		Column color: WndText
Quick Select		
	Table	department
	Columns	dept_id, dept_dsc
Design		
	Sort	dept_dsc *(use the Rows/Sort... menu item)*

Table 11-10 Specifications for the d_department_list DataWindow object

Figure 11-12 The d_department_list object in design mode

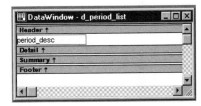

Figure 11-13 The d_period_list object in design mode

3. You will need to create a second DataWindow object, d_period_list, to provide the code table for a DropDownDataWindow for time periods. This DataWindow should be similar in appearance to the one created in step 2. Use the specifications in Table 11-11 and the picture in Figure 11-13 to guide you.

WINDOW	OPTION	VALUE
New DataWindow		
	Data Source	Quick Select

continued on next page

continued from previous page

WINDOW	OPTION	VALUE
	Presentation Style	Tabular
	Generation Options	Background color: white
		Text border: none
		Text color: WndText
		Column border: none
		Column color: WndText
Quick Select		
	Table	time_period
	Columns	period_desc, period_cd
Design		
	Sort	period_desc *(use the Rows/Sort... menu item)*

Table 11-11 Specifications for the d_period_list DataWindow object

4. One other code table DataWindow object is required in this application to provide for a position listing. Give this DataWindow object the name d_position_list. The specifications and layout are shown in Table 11-12 and Figure 11-14.

WINDOW	OPTION	VALUE
New DataWindow		
	Data Source	Quick Select
	Presentation Style	Tabular
	Generation Options	Background color: white
		Text border: none
		Text color: WndText
		Column border: none
		Column color: WndText
Quick Select		
	Table	position

WINDOW	OPTION	VALUE
	Columns	position_desc, position_cd
Design		
	Sort	position_desc *(use the Rows/Sort... menu item)*

Table 11-12 Specifications for the d_position_list DataWindow object

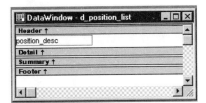

Figure 11-14 The
d_position_list object in
design mode

5. You should now begin work on the d_person_employee_entry
DataWindow object which serves as the foundation DataWindow object in
this application. Work on this object will take a couple of steps. First, construct the basic DataWindow object according to the settings listed in Table
11-13. To guide you in establishing the basic layout, refer to Figure 11-15.
Figure 11-15 will be used in later steps as you refine this object.

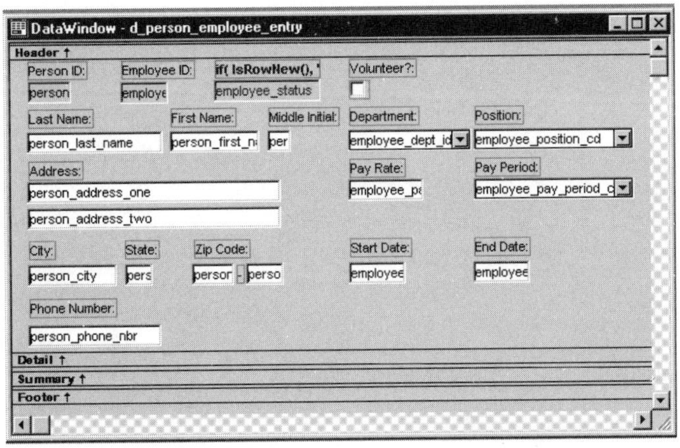

Figure 11-15 The d_person_employee_entry object in
design mode

WINDOW	OPTION	VALUE
New DataWindow		
	Data Source	SQL Select
	Presentation Style	Freeform
	Generation Options	Background color: Silver
		Text border: none
		Text color: WndText
		Column border: 3D Lowered
		Column color: WndText
		Wrap height: 3 inches
SQL Select	Tables	person, employee
	Join	"person"."person_id" = "employee"."person_id"
	Columns	employee: *(all)*
		person: *(all)*
	Where clause	"employee"."status" = 'A'
Design	Sort	person_id *(use the Rows/Sort... menu item)*
	Column	person_id
	Background color	light gray
	Column	employee_id
	Background color	Silver
	Column	phone_nbr
	Edit style	Edit Mask
	Mask	"###-####"
	Column	volunteer_flg
	Border	None
	Edit style	Check Box

WINDOW	OPTION	VALUE
	Text	""
	3D	TRUE
	On	"Y"
	Off	"N"
	Column	employee_department_id
	Edit style	DropDownDataWindow
	DataWindow	d_department_list
	Display column	dept_dsc
	Data column	dept_id
	Always show arrow	TRUE
	VScrollBar	TRUE
	HScrollBar	FALSE
	Column	employee_position_cd
	Edit style	DropDownDataWindow
	DataWindow	d_position_list
	Display column	position_desc
	Data column	position_cd
	Always show arrow	TRUE
	VScrollBar	TRUE
	HScrollBar	FALSE
	Column	employee_pay_period_cd
	Edit style	DropDownDataWindow
	Display column	d_period_list
	Display column	period_desc
	Data column	period_cd
	Always show arrow	TRUE
	VScrollBar	TRUE
	HScrollBar	FALSE
	Column	employee_start_dt
	Edit style	Edit Mask
	Mask	"mm/dd/yy"

continued on next page

continued from previous page

WINDOW	OPTION	VALUE
	Column	employee_end_dt
	Edit style	Edit Mask
	Mask	"mm/dd/yy"
	Computed field	new_employee_message
	Expression	if(IsRowNew(), 'New employee', '')
	Color	dark blue

Table 11-13 Specifications for the d_person_employee_entry DataWindow object

6. Save the d_person_employee_entry object to preserve your work.

7. The employee_pay_rate and employee_pay_period columns need to be configured so that they are disabled and have a light gray background when the volunteer CheckBox is checked. This can be accomplished through the use of a conditional property setting. Right-click on employee_pay_rate and choose Properties... from the popup menu. Choose the Expressions tab on the Column Object window that appears, as shown in Figure 11-16. Use the properties and expressions shown in Table 11-14 to configure employee_pay_rate. Perform the same set of steps to employee_pay_period. In this case 12632256 is a 24-bit color value representing white, while 16777215 represents light gray.

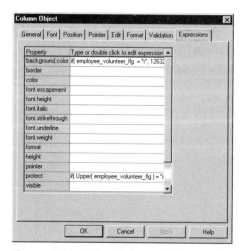

Figure 11-16 The Column Object properties dialog showing the Expressions tab

PROPERTY	VALUE
background.color	if(Upper(employee_volunteer_flg) = 'Y', 12632256, 16777215)
protect	if(Upper(employee_volunteer_flg) = 'Y', 1, 0)

Table 11-14 Property settings for employee_pay_rate and employee_pay_period columns

8. This application will ultimately use the DeleteRow() functions to remove rows from the DataWindow object primary buffer and to place them in the delete buffer. However, to save memory, PowerBuilder does not maintain the delete buffer if the DataWindow does not have update capability. Because this DataWindow object was created from a joined result set, it will not have update capability by default. Use the Rows/Update Properties... menu item to make the DataWindow updateable. In this case, the exact update characteristics don't matter; much of this step is a technicality. A set of suitable specifications for the Specify Update Properties window is listed in Table 11-15. This window is shown in Figure 11-17.

SETTING	VALUE
Allow updates	TRUE
Table to update	employee
Where Clause for Update/Delete	Key Columns
Key Modification	Use Delete then Insert
Updateable Columns	person_person_id
Unique Key Column(s)	employee_employee_id
Identity Column	(None)

Table 11-15 Update characteristics for d_person_employee_entry

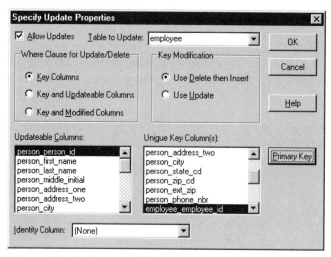

Figure 11-17 The Specify Update Properties window

9. Save the d_person_employee_entry DataWindow object.

10. Use the Window painter to create the w_employee_entry window as shown in Figure 11-18. The window and control settings are shown in Table 11-16.

WINDOW/CONTROL NAME	PROPERTY	VALUE
Window		
w_employee_entry	Title	"Employee Entry (Embedded SQL Updates)"
	WindowType	Main
	MaximizeBox	FALSE
	Reiszable	FALSE
DataWindow control	Name	dw_1
	DataWindow object name	"d_person_employee_entry"
	HScrollBar	TRUE
	VScrollBar	TRUE
	Border	3D Lowered
CommandButton	Name	cb_insert
	Text	"&Insert"
CommandButton	Name	cb_delete
	Text	"&Delete"

WINDOW/CONTROL NAME	PROPERTY	VALUE
CommandButton	Name	cb_save
	Text	"&Save"
CommandButton	Name	cb_refresh
	Text	"&Refresh"
CommandButton	Name	cb_apply
	Text	"&Apply"
CommandButton	Name	cb_removefilter
	Text	"Re&move"
CommandButton	Name	cb_exit
	Text	"E&xit"
SingleLineEdit	Name	sle_filterout
	AutoHScroll	TRUE
	Accelerator	"o"
	Case	Lower
GroupBox	Name	gb_filteroutrows
	Text	"Filter &out rows"

Table 11-16 Window and control settings for the w_employee_entry window

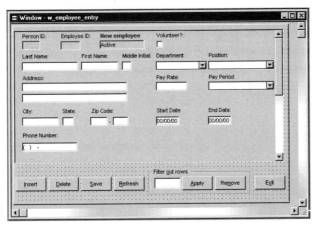

Figure 11-18 The w_employee_entry window

11. When this application assigns new person and employee IDs, it relies on a counters table in the database to obtain needed values. The program must make sure the values are correct before it can rely on the counters table. Create a function called wf_fixcounters that can be called to correct any problems. The function declaration is listed in Table 11-17. Use the following script for the body of the function.

```
// script ensures that the counter table has correct values so that
// attempts
// to use wf_getpersonid() and wf_getemployeeid() do not cause problems


UPDATE counter SET employee_id = (SELECT MAX( employee_id ) FROM employee
),
                         person_id = (SELECT MAX (person_id ) FROM person
) USING sqlca;

IF sqlca.sqlcode = 0 THEN
    COMMIT USING sqlca;
    IF sqlca.sqlcode = 0 THEN
        RETURN 1
    ELSE
        MessageBox("Database Error", "Could not fix counters.~r~n"+&
            sqlca.sqlerrtext, Exclamation! )
        RETURN -1
    END IF
ELSE
    ROLLBACK USING sqlca;
    MessageBox("Database Error", "Could not fix counters.~r~n"+&
        sqlca.sqlerrtext, Exclamation! )
    RETURN -1
END IF

RETURN -2
```

FUNCTION SPECIFICATIONS		
Function	Name	wf_fixcounters
	Access	private
	Returns	integer
Arguments	(none)	

Table 11-17 Function declaration for wf_fixcounters()

12. Another function will be needed to obtain a new employee ID from the counters table. Declare a function wf_getemployeeid as indicated in Table 11-18. Use the script shown below for the function body.

```
// this function requests the next available employee_id value
// from the database and will prevent two users from
// getting the same employee_id.

long ll_employeeid
```

```
UPDATE "counter"
SET "employee_id" = employee_id + 1 USING sqlca ;
IF sqlca.sqlcode = 0 THEN
        SELECT "counter"."employee_id"
            INTO :ll_employeeid  FROM "counter"  USING sqlca;
    IF sqlca.sqlcode = 0 THEN RETURN ll_employeeid
ELSE
    MessageBox( "employee", "Could not get a employee ID.~r~n"+&
        sqlca.sqlerrtext, Exclamation! )
END IF

RETURN -1
```

FUNCTION SPECIFICATIONS

Function	Name	wf_getemployeeid
	Access	private
	Returns	long
Arguments	(none)	

Table 11-18 Function declaration for wf_getemployeeid()

13. Another function, wf_getpersonid, should obtain a new person ID value, similar to wf_getemployeeid(). The function declaration for wf_getpersonid() is shown in Table 11-19. The body of the function is shown below.

```
// this function requests the next available person_id value
// from the database and will prevent two users from
// getting the same person_id.

long ll_personid

UPDATE "counter"
SET "person_id" = person_id + 1 USING sqlca ;
IF sqlca.sqlcode = 0 THEN
        SELECT "counter"."person_id"
            INTO :ll_personid  FROM "counter"  USING sqlca;
    IF sqlca.sqlcode = 0 THEN RETURN ll_personid
ELSE
    MessageBox( "Person", "Could not get a person ID.~r~n"+&
        sqlca.sqlerrtext, Exclamation! )
END IF

RETURN -1
```

FUNCTION SPECIFICATIONS

Function	Name	wf_getpersonid
	Access	private
	Returns	long

continued on next page

continued from previous page

Arguments	*(none)*

Table 11-19 Function declaration for wf_getpersonid()

14. To "delete" employees, create a function called wf_delete_personemp using the declaration listed in Table 11-20. This script really doesn't delete rows from the database, which would cause referential integrity problems in those tables that have foreign key relationships with the employee table. Instead this script marks those employees as inactive by setting their status column to "T". The body of this function follows.

```
// "Deletion" doesn't really mean deleting, because that would remove all
// inventories or other tasks that were performed by the "deleted"
// employee. We'll simply mark the employee as inactive

long ll_empid

ll_empid = dw_1.GetItemNumber( al_row, "employee_employee_id", Delete!, &
        TRUE )

UPDATE "employee"     SET "status" = 'T'
WHERE "employee"."employee_id" = :ll_empid USING sqlca  ;

IF sqlca.sqlcode = 0 THEN
    RETURN 1
ELSE
    RETURN -1
END IF
```

FUNCTION SPECIFICATIONS

Function	Name	wf_delete_personemp	
	Access	private	
	Returns	long	
Arguments	al_row	long	value

Table 11-20 Function declaration for wf_delete_personemp()

15. Save the w_employee_entry window to preserve your work.

16. Create another function to change existing employee information. This function must access the values for the columns in the proper buffer (filter or primary) and update the appropriate tables. Call this function wf_update_personemp. The function specifications are listed in Table 11-21. The code appears below.

```
long ll_empid, ll_personid, ll_deptid, ll_return =-1
string ls_addr1, ls_addr2, ls_city, ls_extzip, ls_fname, ls_lname, ls_middle
string ls_phone, ls_state, ls_zip
string ls_payperiod, ls_position, ls_volunteer
```

```
date ld_end, ld_start
dec{2} lc_pay

ll_personid = dw_1.GetItemNumber( al_row, "employee_person_id" , &
    ae_buffer, TRUE )
ll_empid = dw_1.GetItemNumber( al_row, "employee_employee_id",&
    ae_buffer, TRUE )

ls_addr1 = dw_1.GetItemString( al_row, "person_address_one", &
    ae_buffer, FALSE )
ls_addr2 = dw_1.GetItemString( al_row,"person_address_two", &
    ae_buffer, FALSE)
ls_city = dw_1.GetItemString( al_row, "person_city", &
    ae_buffer, FALSE )
ls_extzip = dw_1.GetItemString( al_row, "person_ext_zip", &
    ae_buffer, FALSE )
ls_fname = dw_1.GetItemString( al_row, "person_first_name", &
    ae_buffer, FALSE)
ls_lname = dw_1.GetItemString(al_row, "person_last_name", &
    ae_buffer, FALSE)
ls_middle = dw_1.GetItemString(al_row, "person_middle_initial", &
    ae_buffer, FALSE )
ls_phone = dw_1.GetItemString( al_row, "person_phone_nbr", &
    ae_buffer, FALSE )
ls_state = dw_1.GetItemString( al_row, "person_state_cd", &
    ae_buffer, FALSE )
ls_zip = dw_1.GetItemString( al_row, "person_zip_cd", &
    ae_buffer, FALSE)

ll_deptid = dw_1.GetItemNumber(al_row, "employee_dept_id", &
    ae_buffer, FALSE )
ld_end = dw_1.GetItemDate( al_row, "employee_end_dt", &
    ae_buffer, FALSE )
ls_payperiod = dw_1.Getitemstring( al_row, "employee_pay_period_cd", &
    ae_buffer, FALSE )
lc_pay= dw_1.GetItemNumber( al_row, "employee_pay_rate", &
    ae_buffer, FALSE )
ls_position = dw_1.GetItemString( al_row, "employee_position_cd", &
    ae_buffer, FALSE )
ld_start = dw_1.GetItemDate( al_row, "employee_start_dt", &
    ae_buffer, FALSE )
ls_volunteer = dw_1.GetItemString( al_row, "employee_volunteer_flg", &
    ae_buffer, FALSE )

UPDATE "person"  SET "first_name" = :ls_fname,  "last_name" = :ls_lname,
    "middle_initial" = :ls_middle, "address_one" = :ls_addr1,
    "address_two" = :ls_addr2,    "city" = :ls_city,
    "state_cd" = :ls_state, "zip_cd" = :ls_zip, "ext_zip" = :ls_extzip,
    "phone_nbr" = :ls_phone
WHERE "person"."person_id" = :ll_personid  USING sqlca ;

IF sqlca.sqlcode = 0 THEN
    UPDATE "employee"  SET "position_cd" = :ls_position,
        "start_dt" = :ld_start, "end_dt" = :ld_end,
        "volunteer_flg" = :ls_volunteer, "pay_rate" = :lc_pay,
        "pay_period_cd" = :ls_payperiod, "dept_id" = :ll_deptid
    WHERE "employee"."employee_id" = :ll_empid   ;
```

continued on next page

continued from previous page

```
    IF sqlca.sqlcode = 0 THEN
        ll_return = 1
    END IF
END IF

RETURN ll_return
```

FUNCTION SPECIFICATIONS

Function	Name	wf_update_personemp	
	Access	private	
	Returns	long	
Arguments	al_row	long	value
	ae_buffer	dwbuffer *(type in)*	value

Table 11-21 Function declaration for wf_update_personemp()

17. Save the w_employee_entry window again as a precaution.

18. To complete the basic operations, create another function called wf_insert_personemp to add new employees to the database. This function must create both the person entry and the employee entry to be complete. Use the function declaration shown in Table 11-22 along with the code that follows this paragraph.

```
long ll_empid, ll_personid, ll_deptid, ll_return=-1, ll_end
string ls_addr1, ls_addr2, ls_city, ls_extzip, ls_fname, ls_lname, ls_middle
string ls_phone, ls_state, ls_zip
string ls_payperiod, ls_position, ls_volunteer
date ld_end, ld_start
dec{2} lc_pay

ll_personid = this.wf_getpersonid()

IF ll_personid > 0 THEN
    ls_addr1 = dw_1.GetItemString( al_row, "person_address_one",ae_buffer,
&
            FALSE )
    ls_addr2 = dw_1.GetItemString( al_row,"person_address_two", ae_buffer,
&
            FALSE)
    ls_city = dw_1.GetItemString( al_row, "person_city", ae_buffer, &
            FALSE )
    ls_extzip = dw_1.GetItemString( al_row, "person_ext_zip", ae_buffer, &
            FALSE )
    ls_fname = dw_1.GetItemString( al_row, "person_first_name", ae_buffer,
&
            FALSE)
    ls_lname = dw_1.GetItemString(al_row, "person_last_name", ae_buffer, &
            FALSE)
    ls_middle = dw_1.GetItemString(al_row, "person_middle_initial", &
            ae_buffer, FALSE )
```

```
ls_phone = dw_1.GetItemString( al_row, "person_phone_nbr", ae_buffer, &
        FALSE )
ls_state = dw_1.GetItemString( al_row, "person_state_cd", ae_buffer, &
        FALSE )
ls_zip = dw_1.GetItemString( al_row, "person_zip_cd", ae_buffer, &
        FALSE)

// a check for null values where they are prohibited would be appropriate
// here, but is omitted for brevity

INSERT INTO "person"  ( "person_id", "first_name", "last_name",
        "middle_initial", "address_one", "address_two", "city",
        "state_cd", "zip_cd", "ext_zip",  "phone_nbr" )
VALUES ( :ll_personid, :ls_fname, :ls_lname, :ls_middle, :ls_addr1,
        :ls_addr2, :ls_city, :ls_state, :ls_zip, :ls_extzip,
        :ls_phone )  USING sqlca;

IF sqlca.sqlcode = 0 THEN

    ll_empid = this.wf_getemployeeid()

    IF ll_empid > 0 THEN
        ll_deptid = dw_1.GetItemNumber(al_row, "employee_dept_id", &
            ae_buffer, FALSE )
        ld_end = dw_1.GetItemDate( al_row, "employee_end_dt", &
            ae_buffer, FALSE )
        ls_payperiod = dw_1.Getitemstring( al_row, &
            "employee_pay_period_cd", ae_buffer, FALSE )
        lc_pay= dw_1.GetItemNumber( al_row, "employee_pay_rate", &
            ae_buffer, FALSE )
        ls_position = dw_1.GetItemString( al_row, &
            "employee_position_cd", ae_buffer, FALSE )
        ld_start = dw_1.GetItemDate( al_row, "employee_start_dt", &
            ae_buffer,    FALSE )
        ls_volunteer = dw_1.GetItemString( al_row, &
            "employee_volunteer_flg", ae_buffer, FALSE )

        INSERT INTO "employee"   ( "employee_id",  "person_id",
            "position_cd",  "start_dt", "volunteer_flg",  "pay_rate",
            "pay_period_cd",  "dept_id", "end_dt" )
        VALUES ( :ll_empid, :ll_personid, :ls_position, :ld_start,
            :ls_volunteer, :lc_pay, :ls_payperiod, :ll_deptid,
            :ld_end )  USING sqlca;

        // set the return code to a positive (good) value
        IF sqlca.sqlcode = 0 THEN
            // Copy the new person ID and employee ID values into the
            // DataWindow. Filter buffer items require special handling,
            // however, because SetItem only works on the primary buffer.
            // For Filter, move the row to primary, make the change, and
            // move it back
            CHOOSE CASE ae_buffer
                CASE Primary!
                    dw_1.SetItem( al_row, "person_person_id", ll_personid
)
                    dw_1.SetItem( al_row, "employee_employee_id",
ll_empid )
```

continued on next page

continued from previous page

```
                    CASE Filter!
                        ll_end = dw_1.RowCount() + 1
                        IF dw_1.RowsMove( al_row, al_row, ae_buffer, dw_1, &
                                    ll_end, Primary!) > 0 THEN
                                        dw_1.SetItem( ll_end, "person_person_id", &
                                    ll_personid )
                            dw_1.SetItem( ll_end, "employee_employee_id", &
                                ll_empid )
                            dw_1.RowsMove( ll_end, ll_end, Primary!, dw_1, &
                                al_row, Filter! )
                        END IF
                    END CHOOSE
                    ll_return = 1
                END IF
            END IF
        END IF
END IF

RETURN ll_return
```

FUNCTION SPECIFICATIONS

Function	Name	wf_insert_personemp	
	Access	private	
	Returns	long	
Arguments	al_row	long	value
	ae_buffer	dwbuffer *(type in)*	value

Table 11-22 Function declaration for wf_insert_personemp()

19. The Open event of the w_employee_entry window should establish a database connection and perform the initial DataWindow retrieve. Place the following script on the Open event of w_employee_entry to perform this function.

```
sqlca.dbms = "ODBC"
sqlca.dbparm = "DisableBind=1,ConnectString='DSN=Zoo;UID=dba;PWD=sql'"

CONNECT USING sqlca;
IF sqlca.sqlcode < 0 THEN
    MessageBox("Connection Error", &
            "Could not connect to database.", Exclamation! )
    Close( this )
ELSE
    dw_1.SetTransObject( sqlca )
    dw_1.Retrieve()
    this.wf_fixcounters()
END IF
```

20. The Close event of w_employee_entry should disconnect from the database as follows.

```
IF sqlca.dbhandle() > 0 THEN
```

```
    DISCONNECT USING sqlca;
    IF sqlca.sqlcode < 0 THEN
        MessageBox("Disconnect Error", &
            "Could not disconnect from database.", Exclamation! )
    END IF
END IF
```

21. The cb_insert CommandButton has the simple task of inserting a new row into the DataWindow. You can use the following script on the Clicked event of cb_insert.

```
long ll_new

ll_new = dw_1.InsertRow(0)
dw_1.ScrollToRow( ll_new )
dw_1.SetColumn( "person_last_name")
dw_1.SetFocus()
```

22. The cb_delete CommandButton must evaluate the row to determine whether or not to prompt the user to perform the deletion. Rows with a status of DataModified!, NotModified!, or NewModified! have data in them and should be confirmed. New! rows should be deleted without question, since no data has been entered. As the comment in the script indicates, those rows with a row status of New! or NewModified! are completely purged from memory when DeleteRow() is called; we will not accidentally delete them as a result.

```
string ls_first, ls_last, ls_middle
long ll_curr

ll_curr = dw_1.GetRow()

IF ll_curr > 0 THEN
    // Examine the row; if it's a row with data in it, prompt the user
    // Note that deleting a NewModified! row purges the row from the buffer
    // entirely; it is not copied to the Delete buffer, so we won't "delete"
    // it from the database
    CHOOSE CASE dw_1.GetItemStatus( ll_curr, 0 , Primary!)
        CASE DataModified!, NotModified!, NewModified!
            ls_first = dw_1.GetItemString( ll_curr, "person_first_name" )
            ls_last = dw_1.GetItemString( ll_curr, "person_last_name" )
            ls_middle = dw_1.GetItemString( ll_curr, "person_middle_initial"
)
            IF IsNull(ls_middle) THEN ls_middle = "" ELSE ls_middle = &
                ls_middle + ". "
            IF IsNull(ls_first) THEN ls_first = ""
            IF IsNull(ls_last) THEN ls_last = ""

            IF MessageBox( "Delete Person", &
                    "Are you sure you want to delete "+ ls_first + " " + &
                    ls_middle + ls_last + "?", Question!, YesNo! ) = 1 THEN
                dw_1.DeleteRow( ll_curr )
                dw_1.SetFocus()
            END IF
        CASE New!
```

continued on next page

continued from previous page

```
            dw_1.DeleteRow( ll_curr )
            dw_1.SetFocus()
      END CHOOSE
END IF
```

23. Save the window to preserve your work.

24. The cb_save CommandButton should examine the state of the DataWindow
buffers to determine whether or not there are any unsaved changes. This step
can be accomplished by calling DeletedCount() and ModifiedCount().
AcceptText() must be called before ModifiedCount() to ensure that
ModifiedCount() returns a correct value. If there are unsaved changes, the
script examines the delete buffer to determine the rows which need to be
deleted. It then examines the primary and filter buffers to perform inserts or
updates as appropriate. Observe the use of GetItemStatus() and row status flags
to determine whether an insert or an update operation should be performed.
The script for the Clicked event of cb_save should be entered as follows.

```
long ll_row, ll_rowcount, ll_deleted, ll_modified, ll_filteredcount
boolean lb_failed = FALSE

IF dw_1.AcceptText() < 0 THEN RETURN      // accept any pending data; abort
                                          // if it doesn't validate


ll_deleted = dw_1.DeletedCount()
ll_modified = dw_1.ModifiedCount()

IF ll_deleted + ll_modified > 0 THEN
    // Do the deletions
    ll_row = 1
    DO WHILE ll_row <= ll_deleted AND lb_failed = FALSE
        IF wf_delete_personemp( ll_row ) < 0 THEN lb_failed = TRUE
        ll_row = ll_row + 1
    LOOP

    ll_rowcount = dw_1.RowCount()

    // Do the inserts and updates, first for the primary buffer,
    // then for filter
    ll_row = 1
    DO WHILE ll_row <= ll_rowcount AND lb_failed = FALSE
        CHOOSE CASE dw_1.GetItemStatus( ll_row, 0, Primary! )
            CASE NewModified!
                IF wf_insert_personemp( ll_row, Primary! ) < 0 THEN &
                    lb_failed = TRUE
            CASE DataModified!
                IF wf_update_personemp( ll_row, Primary! ) < 0 THEN &
                    lb_failed = TRUE
            CASE New!, NotModified!
                // do nothing
        END CHOOSE
        ll_row = ll_row + 1
    LOOP

    ll_filteredcount = dw_1.FilteredCount()
```

```
    ll_row = 1
    DO WHILE ll_row <= ll_filteredcount AND lb_failed = FALSE
        CHOOSE CASE dw_1.GetItemStatus( ll_row, 0, Filter! )
            CASE NewModified!
                IF wf_insert_personemp( ll_row, Filter! ) < 0 THEN &
                    lb_failed = TRUE
            CASE DataModified!
                IF wf_update_personemp( ll_row, Filter! ) < 0 THEN &
                    lb_failed = TRUE
            CASE New!, NotModified!
                // do nothing
        END CHOOSE
        ll_row = ll_row + 1
    LOOP

    IF lb_failed = FALSE THEN // success!
        COMMIT USING sqlca;
        dw_1.ResetUpdate() // reset the status flags since we're
// successful!
    ELSE
        ROLLBACK USING sqlca;
        MessageBox( "Save", "Save failed.", Exclamation! )
    END IF

END IF
```

25. The Refresh CommandButton should remove any filter currently in place and re-retrieve the data from the database. Use the following script for the Clicked event of cb_refresh.

```
dw_1.SetFilter( "" )
dw_1.Filter()
dw_1.Retrieve()
```

26. The Apply CommandButton uses the entered last name from sle_filter to filter out rows with that name. Use the script below for the Clicked event of cb_apply.

```
string ls_filter

ls_filter = "Lower(person_last_name)<>'" + Lower(sle_filterout.text) + "'"
dw_1.SetFilter( ls_filter  )
dw_1.Filter()
```

27. The Remove CommandButton removes any filter in place. This simple script placed on the Clicked event of cb_removefilter will perform this task.

```
dw_1.SetFilter( "" )
dw_1.Filter()
```

28. The cb_exit CommandButton should simply close the window as follows. (Use the Clicked event.)

```
Close( parent )
```

29. Save the w_employee_entry window.

30. Finally, the Application object Open event should open the w_employee_entry window. Use the following script for this event.

```
Open( w_employee_entry )
```

31. Save and run the application.

How It Works

The most important part of this application is located on the Clicked event of cb_save. This script first performs an AcceptText() to ensure that the most recently entered item of information is placed in the primary buffer and marked as a change. The script then calls ModifiedCount() and DeletedCount() which, taken together, indicate the total number of new, modified, and deleted rows that are present in the DataWindow buffers. If changes have been made, the script proceeds to perform a delete operation on each row in the delete buffer. Following the deletions, the script performs inserts or updates as appropriate for each row in the primary and filter buffers. Observe the use of the dwBuffer data type in the wf_insert_personemp() and wf_update_personemp() functions to indicate which buffer contains the affected row.

When all changes have been performed, the script commits the changes in the database. Importantly, the script also resets the row flags in the DataWindow to mark all changes as having been applied and to purge all rows from the delete buffer. The ResetUpdate() function performs both of these tasks.

Comments

While native DataWindow operations are generally sufficient for most applications, some situations simply require more control than a simple DataWindow Update() can provide. Embedded SQL is one technique that can help you in these situations, as demonstrated in this How-To. However, this brief sample does not demonstrate all possibilities. For example the wf_update_personemp() function uses an update that incorporates a Where clause that references only the primary key of the existing row. This may result in lost update anomalies in your database in the event that more than one user is writing to the same row at the same time. You could improve on this script by incorporating more columns in the Where clause, much as the Key and Updateable Columns setting in the Update Characteristics window does.

You must also be mindful of the speed of execution of embedded SQL operations, due both to user-perceived delays and to a design goal of minimizing the duration of locks which are acquired during the update processing. Keep your scripts as lean and efficient as possible.

The conditional property values for protect and background.color on the employee_pay_rate and employee_pay_period columns also deserve special mention due to their simplicity. A pair of simple expressions is all it took to make those columns available or unavailable based on the employee_volunteer_flg column value. One final touch you may want to add is to code the ItemChanged event on the DataWindow control dw_1 to place null values into those fields when employee_volunteer_flg is "Y".

WORKING WITH DYNAMIC DATAWINDOWS

12

WORKING WITH DYNAMIC DATAWINDOWS

How do I...

The most dynamic component of your application is the data. Depending on who is using your application and at what time, the data displayed and the format it is displayed in can change dramatically. Dynamic DataWindows provides the ability at runtime to change what data the user sees and how he or she sees it. The examples provided will vary in enough ways to give you ideas of when and where DataWindows can be dynamically modified. You will start by learning how to create a DataWindow at runtime and associate it with an existing DataWindow control. Next you will modify the SQL of an existing DataWindow. Following this you will examine means of modifying what is displayed. You will hide and show columns based on user response or highlight a column row cell based on its value. You will modify data using the new DataWindow Object, and for reporting you will learn how to add and modify display text and graphics. Lastly, you will save your effort to a PowerBuilder library or to a database. You will come away from this chapter with a better understanding of DataWindows and how they work. Dynamic DataWindows is one of the main mechanisms to take your application *out of the box* and provide functionality that is not possible using a standard DataWindow and DataWindow control. All the examples in this chapter can be found in the PowerBuilder library DYNAMIC.PBL on the disk that comes with this book.

12.1   Create a DataWindow Object at Runtime

You do not have to set a DataWindow for a DataWindow control at design time. This How-To will examine the steps necessary for creating a DataWindow at runtime, anchoring it to an existing DataWindow control, and then retrieving data to it.

12.2   Modify the DataWindow SQL at Runtime

Chances are your DataWindows will be viewed by people who perform various jobs or have various needs. This How-To demonstrates how to modify the SQL that is the basis for your DataWindow by examining how to change the constraints (the Where clause). It demonstrates this using the PowerBuilder function SetSQLSelect.

12.3   Modify DataWindow Columns at Runtime

You may also need to modify DataWindow components at runtime, such as highlighting a column value if the value exceeds a limit, or hiding a column based on the user's permissions. This How-To demonstrates how to change column attributes.

12.4   Add and Modify DataWindow Objects at Runtime

You have probably seen examples of adding objects to a DataWindow at runtime with the use of Modify. This How-To will demonstrate how you can do this without using Modify, using the DataWindow object and other techniques.

12.5   Save and Load a DataWindow Object Definition to a PowerBuilder Library or Database

Once a user has created a DataWindow, he or she would like to be able to save it and use it again and again. This How-To explains how to save and load a DataWindow from a PowerBuilder Library and how to load and save a DataWindow from a database. You will be surprised at how easy this can be.

COMPLEXITY
BEGINNING

12.1 How do I...
Create a DataWindow object at runtime?

Problem

My application's users want the ability to perform their own ad-hoc reporting, but I can't create a new DataWindow for every table and for every person. I need to be able to create a DataWindow at runtime that will work with any table or tables the user specifies and has access to. How can I create a DataWindow dynamically, and then how do I use it to retrieve data?

Technique

PowerBuilder allows you to create a DataWindow at runtime, and either anchor it to a *blank* DataWindow control or replace an existing DataWindow. A blank DataWindow control is simply a DataWindow control that has not had a DataWindow associated with it. This How-To will explain the steps you take to define the DataWindow object, create it, and then use it in an existing window.

Steps

Access DYNAMIC.PBL from the DataWindow painter and pull up the Window named w_persinfo. This Window has two DataWindow controls, a ListBox, a CommandButton, and a GroupBox with three RadioButton controls visible as shown in Figure 12-1. Run the DYNAMIC application and select the "Personal Information" option as shown in Figure 12-2. When the window opens, the DataWindow on top has several columns with displayed data as shown in Figure 12-3. Now click on the Last Name, First Name, and City columns, and note that the column titles are displayed in the ListBox to the side as shown in Figure 12-4. Choose the Table Report style and press the Generate Report CommandButton. The second DataWindow now contains a DataWindow with the three columns you picked and in the style you picked as shown in Figure 12-5. Clicking on the top DataWindow will start the setup for a new display.

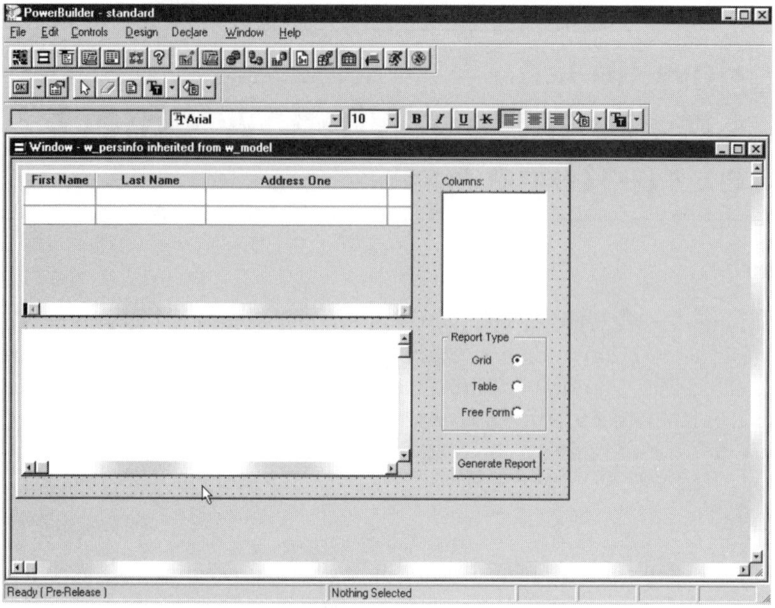

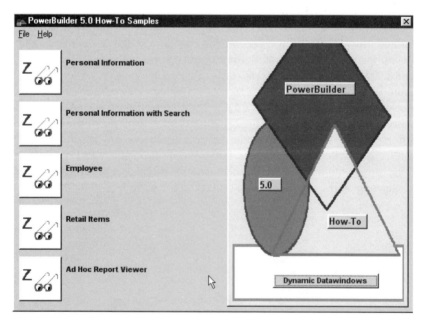

Figure 12-1 The w_persinfo window

Figure 12-2 The DYNAMIC application

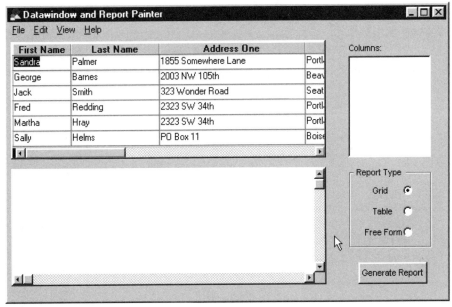

Figure 12-3 The Personal Information Window when opened

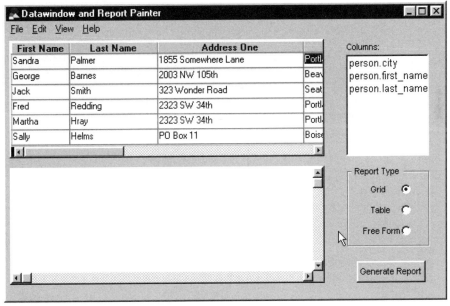

Figure 12-4 The Personal Information Window after choosing columns

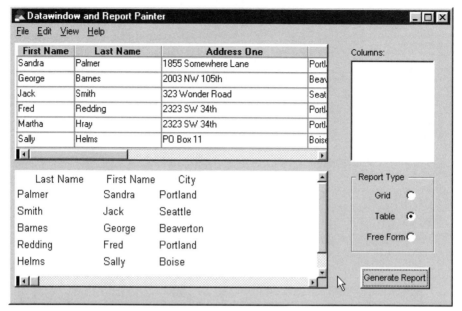

Figure 12-5 The Personal Information Window after report regeneration

To create your own ad-hoc DataWindow like the one you have just seen, follow the steps below.

1. Access the DYNAMIC.PBL library.

2. Create a new window and access the property sheet. For the window title type "Personal Information::Report". Set the window type to Main. Access the Icon tab. Set Icon Name to "book2.ICO". Close the property sheet.

3. Place a DataWindow control across the top of the window and a DataWindow control across the bottom. Label the top control dw_cols and the bottom control dw_reports as shown in Table 12-1. Select the property sheet for the top DataWindow control and choose the DataWindow "d_emp_pers_pos".

OBJECT/CONTROL NAME	ATTRIBUTE	VALUE
dw_cols	HScroll Bar	Checked
	Border	3D Raised
	H Split Scrolling	Checked
	VScroll Bar	Checked
dw_report	HScroll Bar	Checked
	VScroll Bar	Checked
	H Split Scrolling	Checked

OBJECT/CONTROL NAME	ATTRIBUTE	VALUE
	Border	3D Raised
lb_cols	Border	3D Lowered
gb_style	Border	3D Lowered
rb_grid	Checked	Checked
	Border	3D Lowered
rb_table	Border	3D Lowered
rb_form	Border	3D Lowered
cb_gen	Text	Generate Report

Table 12-1 Names and attribute settings for the runtime DataWindow creation

4. Place a ListBox control to the side of the top DataWindow control and name it lb_cols. Place a static Text control above the ListBox to label it and type "Columns" in the text field for this control. Under the ListBox place a GroupBox labeled "Report Style" and name it g_style. Within this place three RadioButtons with labels of "Grid", "Table", and "Free Form" and names of rb_grid, rb_table, and rb_form respectively.

5. The last control we will place will be for a standard CommandButton which we will label "Generate Report" and name cb_gen. This will be placed directly under the GroupBox. Your window should look similar to the one shown in Figure 12-1.

6. In the Open event of the window, set up the transaction object for dw_cols and issue a Retrieve for the data.

```
// set transaction and retrieve columns

dw_cols.SetTransObject(sqlca)
dw_cols.Retrieve()
```

7. Create an instance variable of type *string* and call it is_SqlSelect. In the Clicked event of the dw_cols DataWindow, type code that will get the column the user clicked, append the column database name to a SQL Select string, and insert the column name into the columns ListBox. The column name can be found by accessing the dwObject passed to the event in the argument list. If the dwObject is a column header the code will strip out the "_t" which should be at the end of every column header.

```
Integer      li_Column
String       ls_clickedColumn
String       ls_Column

// get clicked column
ls_column = dwo.name

// check to see if clicked column header
// if so, strip out _t
```

continued on next page

continued from previous page

```
if Right(ls_column, 2) = "_t" then
    ls_column = Left(ls_column, Len(ls_Column) - 2)
end if

// get column database name and add to listbox
ls_ClickedColumn = This.Describe(ls_column + ".dbName")
lb_cols.AddItem(ls_clickedColumn)

// if first time on select statement, set up with Select
// otherwise just append to select statement
IF IsNull(is_SqlSelect) or is_SqlSelect = "" THEN
    is_SqlSelect = "Select " + ls_clickedColumn
    dw_report.Reset()
ELSE
    is_SqlSelect = is_SqlSelect + "," + ls_clickedColumn
END IF
```

8. Next, access the Clicked event for the cb_gen button and type code that will check the report style the user has chosen from the RadioButtons; then use this and the newly created SQL statement to create the DataWindow syntax. The syntax is then used in the DataWindow Create call. Once the DataWindow has been created, the transaction object is associated with it and a Retrieve is run against the window.

```
// Access SQL from source datawindow
// parse off From and Where clause and append new select clause.
// Display report datawindow and retrieve data to it

String ls_currentSql, ls_currentFromWhere
String ls_datawindowdef, ls_err, ls_style
Integer li_pos

// check to see what style is
IF rb_grid.Checked THEN
    ls_style = "style(Type=Grid)"
ELSEIF rb_table.Checked THEN
    ls_style = "style(Type=Tabular)"
ELSE
    ls_style = "style(Type=Form)"
END IF

// get SQL from source datawindow; this allows us to capture
// any existing constraints
ls_currentSql = dw_cols.GetSQLSelect()
li_pos = Pos(Upper(ls_currentSql), "FROM ")
ls_currentFromWhere = Right(ls_currentSql, Len(ls_currentSql) - (li_pos - 1))

// append report generation select clause to newly parsed From and Where
clause
ls_currentSql = is_SqlSelect + " " + ls_currentFromWhere

// generate window syntax from generated SQL
ls_datawindowdef = sqlca.SyntaxFromSql(ls_currentSql, ls_style, ls_err)

// create datawindow
```

```
dw_report.Create(ls_datawindowdef, ls_err)

// set transaction and retrieve to datawindow
dw_report.SetTransObject(sqlca)
dw_report.Retrieve()

// reset for new report
is_SqlSelect = ""
lb_cols.Reset()
```

9. Exit from the cd_gen Clicked event and save the code just created. Without exiting your current window, from the DataWindow painter pull up the existing window, w_persinfo, and, using Save As..., rename the existing window to w_persinfo_bak. Close this window and return to the one you are currently working with. Save your new window as w_persinfo and close it. Now run the DYNAMIC application from PowerBuilder. Again, use the login of "jtower" with no password. You can see your new window by choosing the Personal Information option.

How It Works

A PowerBuilder DataWindow is really made up of two parts: the SQL used to populate the window, and the syntax that defines how the data is displayed. Creating a new DataWindow using this method requires that we create or copy the SQL that we will use to access the database, and then combine it with a specific DataWindow syntax. In our example we kept the syntax simple by specifying the DataWindow report style only, and accepting defaults for all other syntax components. For most ad-hoc reporting this is more than sufficient.

We used the From and Where clauses of the deriving DataWindow for our new Report window, changing it by adding in only the columns the user selected. The next How-To will describe how to view and modify the SQL for an existing DataWindow.

Comments

If you are feeling more adventurous, you can modify more of the syntax for the new DataWindow. For example, you could change text colors, or the color of the Detail (data) band, or the fonts. In future How-Tos to be covered in this chapter, you will see how to create a DataWindow by importing it directly from a PowerBuilder library or from a database.

COMPLEXITY

INTERMEDIATE

12.2   How do I...
Modify the DataWindow SQL at runtime?

Problem

When my users run a report, or look for data to modify, they want to be able to set the criteria that the database searches by. I can set arguments for the DataWindow for searching on specific values, but at times one person wants to search on one field and another person wants to search on another, and a third wants to search on both and add another table to the join. How can I change my SQL at runtime to fit each of their needs?

Technique

You can modify the SQL for a Select statement by using one of two methods: change the existing SQL using the SetSQLSelect statement, or modify the SQL using the DataWindow language function Modify. If your Select Statement does not have arguments and you want PowerBuilder to manage the update handling of an updateable window, you should use the SetSQLSelect function. For a faster result, or if you do not care about the update information, or you have retrieval arguments, you can use the Modify function. This How-To will demonstrate modifying SQL using the SetSQLSelect and Create functions.

Steps

Access the DYNAMIC.PBL library. From the DataWindow painter pull up the window named w_persinfo_search. This window is similar to the one created in the first How-To and was, in fact, created by copying w_persinfo_rpt and modifying it for this example. The window contains two DataWindows, one to find column names, the other to display a generated report. It also contains a ListBox for the column names, a GroupBox with three RadioButtons to choose the style of the generated report, a CommandButton to generate the report, and a SingleLineEditbox at the bottom labeled Criteria as can be seen from Figure 12-6. Run this window by running the DYNAMIC.PBL application. Choose the Reports menu and then choose the Personal Information and Search menu item. Generate a report by clicking on the first, last, and city columns in the top DataWindow, choosing a tabular report style, and pressing the Generate Report CommandButton. Now, click on the person.last_name item in the ListBox at the top and then type in any search value in the edit field at the bottom right of the window, using the case that is shown in the DataWindow if the value is a string. Notice in Figure 12-7 that when you clicked on the ListBox item, the title on the CommandButton changed from "Generate Report" to "Change Report".

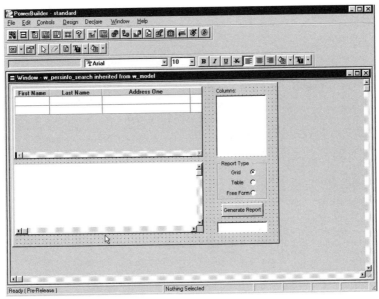

Figure 12-6 Employee reports personal information with Search window

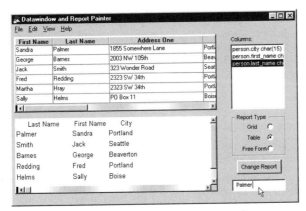

Figure 12-7 Employee reports personal information with search Window—setting criteria

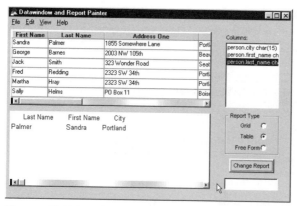

Figure 12-8 Employee reports personal
information with Search window—criteria Result

Press this CommandButton and notice that you have the columns you chose from
the previous report but now the data is limited to just those rows that match on the
criteria you specified, as shown in Figure 12-8.

To create your own Search window that allows you to modify the constraint on
one of the columns, follow the steps outlined below.

1. Access the DYNAMIC.PBL library.

2. Open the w_persinfo window and save it as w_persinfo_search. See How-
To 12.1 for steps to create w_persinfo.

3. Compress the space for the RadioButtons and the GroupBox and move
them and the CommandButton labeled cb_gen up. This will make room for
a new control you will place in the next step.

4. Place a SingleLineEditBox control just under the CommandButton and
name it "sle_criteria". Change the border on this object to 3D Lowered as
shown in Figure 12-6.

5. For the window create a new instance variable of type Boolean and call it
"ib_quoted".

6. Create a new user event for the window and call it ue_changesql. Use
pbm_custom01 as the event ID.

7. Access the Clicked event of the dw_cols DataWindow. Select the code that
exists for this event and delete it. In its place type the code listed below.
This code will access the column name and check to see if the
CommandButton is labeled "Generate Report". If so it will change the label
and reset the ListBox control and the SQL instance variable. The code will
also access the column database name and type and insert both into the
ListBox.

```
String  ls_clickedColumn
String  ls_ColType, ls_AddItem
String  ls_Column

// get clicked column
ls_column = dwo.name

// check to see if clicked column header
// if so, strip out _t
if Right(ls_column, 2) = "_t" then
    ls_column = Left(ls_column, Len(ls_Column) - 2)
end if

// setting state of button to generate new report
IF cb_gen.Text = "Change Report" THEN
    cb_gen.Text = "Generate Report"

    // reset for new report
    lb_cols.Reset()
    is_SqlSelect = ""
end if

// enable report generation button
cb_gen.enabled=TRUE

// get clicked column
ls_ClickedColumn = This.Describe(ls_Column + ".dbName")

// get clicked column datatype
ls_ColType = This.Describe("#" + String(This.GetColumn( ))  &
    + ".ColType")

// concatenate the column name and datatype, and add to listbox
ls_AddItem = ls_ClickedColumn + " " + ls_ColType
lb_cols.AddItem(ls_AddItem)


// if first time on select statement, set up with Select
IF IsNull(is_SqlSelect) or is_SqlSelect = "" THEN
    is_SqlSelect = "Select " + ls_clickedColumn
ELSE
    is_SqlSelect = is_SqlSelect + "," + ls_clickedColumn
END IF
```

8. Access the SelectionChanged event of the ListBox control lb_cols. In this event type the following code that will set the label of the cb_get CommandButton to "Change Report". Additionally, the code will access the value being selected and check its data type. If the type is "CHAR" or "DATE" then the quoted instance variable is set to TRUE.

```
// setting state of button to change existing
// report
string  ls_coltype, ls_Column
Long ll_Pos

ib_quoted = FALSE
```

continued on next page

continued from previous page

```
// enable report generation button
cb_gen.Text = "Change Report"
cb_gen.enabled=TRUE

// find the data type of selected column
ls_Column = this.SelectedItem()
ll_pos = Pos(ls_Column, " ")
ls_ColType = Right(ls_Column, Len(ls_Column) - ll_pos)
ll_pos = Pos(UPPER(ls_ColType), "CHAR")

// if CHAR or DATE, value will be quoted
IF ll_pos = 0 THEN
    ll_pos = Pos(Upper(ls_ColType), "DATE")
END IF

IF ll_pos <> 0 THEN
    ib_quoted = TRUE
END IF
```

9. Access the Clicked event of the cb_gen CommandButton control. Type code that will check to see if the CommandButton label is "Generate Report". If it is not, the code will trigger the new ue_changesql event using PostEvent and return. If the label is "Generate Report" then the type of DataWindow will be accessed from the RadioButtons. The existing SQL from the dw_cols DataWindow is accessed, and the select clause generated by clicking on columns in dw_cols is prepended to the From and Where clauses of the existing SQL. Lastly the new SQL and the style are used in a call to SyntaxFromSQL to generate new DataWindow syntax. This is used in a DataWindow Create function call.

```
// Access SQL from source datawindow
// parse off From and Where clause and append new select clause.
// Display report datawindow and retrieve data to it

String ls_currentSql, ls_currentFromWhere
String ls_datawindowdef, ls_err, ls_style
Integer li_pos

// check to see if new report or change exists
IF cb_gen.Text <> "Generate Report" THEN
    Parent.PostEvent("ue_changesql")
    return
ELSE
    this.Enabled=FALSE
END IF

// check to see what style is
IF rb_grid.Checked THEN
    ls_style = "style(Type=Grid)"
ELSEIF rb_table.Checked THEN
    ls_style = "style(Type=Tabular)"
ELSE
    ls_style = "style(Type=Form)"
END IF
```

```
// get SQL from source datawindow; this allows us to capture
// any existing constraints
ls_currentSql = dw_cols.GetSQLSelect()
li_pos = Pos(Upper(ls_currentSql), "FROM ")
ls_currentFromWhere = Right(ls_currentSql, Len(ls_currentSql) - (li_pos - 1))

// append report generation select clause to newly parsed From and Where
clause
ls_currentSql = is_SqlSelect + " " + ls_currentFromWhere

// capture existing SQL for later use
is_SqlSelect = ls_currentSql

// generate window syntax from generated SQL
ls_datawindowdef = sqlca.SyntaxFromSql(ls_currentSql, ls_style, ls_err)

// create datawindow
dw_report.Create(ls_datawindowdef, ls_err)

// set transaction and retrieve to datawindow
dw_report.SetTransObject(sqlca)
dw_report.Retrieve()
```

10. Access the ue_changesql user event for the window. Type the following code that will pull out the column database name from the ListBox and add to the existing SQL Select Where clause. Next, type code that adds in the criteria, checking to see if ib_quoted is set to TRUE. If this is so, the criteria is surrounded by quotes, in this case single quotes. The criteria edit line and ib_quoted instance variables are reset for a new report. The code listed below calls the PowerBuilder function SetSQLSelect to change the SQL statement that drives the existing DataWindow, in this case our newly generated DataWindow. As this is totally user driven, you should check for error conditions after the SetSQLSelect function call to capture potential problems and communicate them to the user. Type code to retrieve from the newly modified DataWindow, and again check results. If the new criteria results in the return of an empty selection set, notify the user accordingly and insert an empty row.

```
// Modify Where Clause and re-retrieve
String      ls_Criteria, ls_Column, ls_NewSql
Integer     li_Pos, li_rc
String      ls_rc

// get new criteria, and selected column
ls_Criteria = sle_criteria.Text
ls_Column = lb_cols.SelectedItem()
li_pos = Pos(ls_Column, " ")
ls_Column = Left(ls_column, li_pos)

// if null criteria, run report without modification
// which is original report
IF IsNull(ls_Criteria) or ls_Criteria = "" THEN
    ls_NewSql = is_SqlSelect
ELSE
```

continued on next page

continued from previous page

```
    ls_NewSql = is_SqlSelect + " AND " + ls_Column

    // if quoted datatype, add quotes
    IF ib_quoted THEN
        ls_NewSql = ls_NewSql + " = ~'" +ls_Criteria + "~' "
    ELSE
        ls_NewSql = ls_NewSql + " = " + ls_Criteria +  " "
    END IF
END IF

// reset for next criteria change, or new report
sle_criteria.Text = ""
ib_quoted = FALSE

// Set the new SQL and check for error
li_rc=dw_report.SetSQLSelect(ls_NewSql)
if li_rc = -1 then
    MessageBox(this.title, "There was a problem with the value you " + &
                "entered for the report. Please check this " + &
                "value and try again.")
    return
end if

// retrieve data and check to see if any rows returned
li_rc = dw_report.Retrieve()

IF li_rc <= 0 THEN
    MessageBox(this.title, "There were no rows matching that criteria.  " + &
                "Please re-enter with new criteria.")
    dw_report.InsertRow(0)
END IF
```

11. Save the Event script and the window and run the DYNAMIC.PBL application from PowerBuilder. Select several columns and try changing the report by searching for one of the values in one of the columns.

How It Works

As noted in the first How-To in this chapter, the DataWindow is really made up of two components, the SQL that works against the database and the syntax that defines how it displays. In this How-To we modified the existing SQL by changing the Where clause that was used to create the DataWindow and retrieving the data again based on the new results. We appended the new constraint to the end of the existing Where clause, and we added in quotes to the constraint value if necessary. With the help of the PowerBuilder-provided functionality, the SQL part of the DataWindow was modified without modification of the syntactic portion and the Retrieve function for the window was called again. The result set reflected the new criteria.

Comments

The function SetSQLSelect is capable of replacing virtually all aspects of an existing DataWindow SQL Select: from the Select result set if the new result set matches the number, type, and order of the existing DataWindow's columns; to the Where clause; and even to the table itself. However, the most common use of this is to change the Where clause to match the select needs specified by your application users. Attempting to manage all aspects of the Select statement can be cumbersome.

A typical use for changing the SQL of a DataWindow is to provide a criteria gathering window to access constraints from your users, and then to modify the SQL of the DataWindow to match these new constraints. With a more formal constraint gathering method you can build in the capability to detect when quotes are needed or when other special handling is required. Enclosing this code in an external function or non-visual user object can make this functionality available to all windows, simplifying the effort of modifying the DataWindow SQL greatly.

The changes to the DataWindow in this example could also have been accomplished by setting the visible attributes of the columns that were not selected and by using the Filter function. However, modifying the SQL before retrieving is the best alternative when the query can result in a large data set being returned.

COMPLEXITY
ADVANCED

12.3 How do I...
Modify DataWindow columns at runtime?

Problem

Not all of my users have the same data access permissions, but they all can access some of the same DataWindows. How can I modify the DataWindows columns at runtime to only show what is appropriate for the person?

Technique

How to modify a DataWindow during runtime is probably one of the most dynamic aspects of each new version of PowerBuilder. Most modifications used to occur with the user of the Modify function rather than through runtime access to attributes either directly or through new functions. With PowerBuilder 5.0 and the new DataWindow object you can, in most instances, modify the DataWindow and column attributes directly.

Steps

Access the DYNAMIC.PBL library. From the Window painter, pull up the window named w_employee. This window contains one DataWindow control, named dw_employee. Run the DYNAMIC.PBL application and access the Employee option. Login as the System Administrator "spalmer", with a password of "zoorusone1". The

Window is a simple FreeForm DataWindow as can be seen in Figure 12-9. Change one of the existing records or create a new window. Save your results. Now, login as the user "jtower" with no password required. When you pull up the window you cannot see the field Pay Rate as shown in Figure 12-10 and if you try changing any of the fields you get an error message and the field is returned to its original value. All of these behaviors are based on the user's permissions that are set from a table called APP_USER and accessed from the w_login window. The window and DataWindow test for permission during certain events and change the behavior of the columns based on these same permissions.

1. Access the DYNAMIC.PBL library.

2. From the Window painter, create a new window. Add a DataWindow control to the window, call it "dw_employee", and change the DataWindow associated with this control to d_employee.

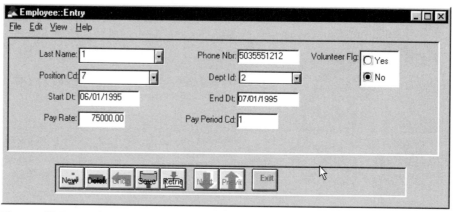

Figure 12-9 Employee window logged in as spalmer

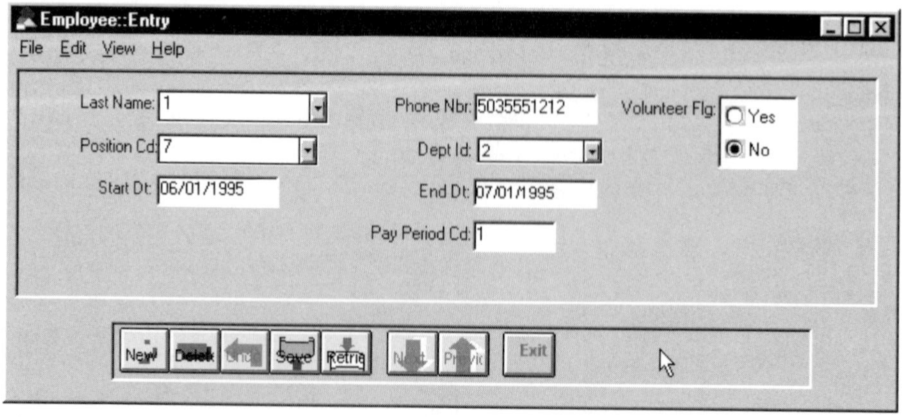

Figure 12-10 Employee window logged in as jtower

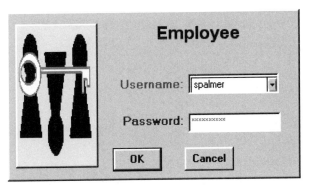

Figure 12-11 Login window

3. Modify the Border type of the DataWindow control to 3D Lowered and change the title to "Employee::Entry".

4. Access the user object from the Controls and choose "u_toolbar". Place this object directly under the DataWindow and center it.

5. Create user events for handling Insert, Delete, Retrieve, and Save for the window. These events are triggered when the user selects the appropriate buttons from the user toolbar. Use pbm_custom01 through pbm_custom04 for the events, and label the events "ue_insert", "ue_save", "ue_delete", and "ue_retrieve". Disregard other buttons from the toolbar for this example.

6. Access the ue_delete event and type code to check the user's permission and delete the row if the permissions check.

```
// delete current row
Long ll_row

if gstr_application.permission = NOCHANGE then
    MessageBox(this.title, "You do not have permission " + &
          "to delete this row.")
    return
end if

ll_row = dw_employee.GetRow()
if ll_row <= 0 then return

dw_employee.DeleteRow(ll_row)
```

7. The permission referenced is set during the login procedure as shown in Figure 12-11. The steps to create this window can be found in Chapter 3, *Application Styles*, in How-To 3.1 "How do I Create a Common Library?"

8. Access the ue_insert event and type in code to check the user's permission to insert a row.

```
// insert new row
Long ll_row
```

continued on next page

continued from previous page

```
if gstr_application.permission = NOCHANGE then
    MessageBox(this.title, "You do not have permission " + &
            "to insert a new employee record.")
    return
end if


ll_row = dw_employee.InsertRow(0)
dw_employee.ScrollToRow(ll_row)
```

9. Access the ue_retrieve event and type in code to check if the DataWindow is modified. If it is, the user will be prompted to save the results.

```
// check for changes and then retrieve
Integer li_result

if dw_employee.ModifiedCount() > 0 or &
        dw_employee.DeletedCount() > 0 then
    li_result=MessageBox(this.title, &
            "You have unsaved changes. Do you wish to save?", &
            Question!, YesNoCancel!,1)
    if li_result = 1 then
        this.TriggerEvent("ue_save")
    elseif li_result = 3 then
        return
    end if
end if


dw_employee.Retrieve()
```

10. Access the ue_save event and type in code to save the DataWindow changes, if any, and if the user's permissions allow.

```
// save any changes

if gstr_application.permission = NOCHANGE then
    MessageBox(this.title, "You do not have permission " + &
            "to save any changes.")
    return
end if

if dw_employee.Update() >= 0 then
    COMMIT;
    MessageBox(this.title, "Changes have been saved.")
else
    MessageBox(this.title, "Changes have not been saved. " + &
            sqlca.sqlerrtext)
    ROLLBACK;
end if
```

11. Access the Open event for the window and type in code that will set the transaction object for the DataWindow and retrieve data into the DataWindow control. In addition, type in code that will change the visibility of the Employee Pay Rate field and its column header.

```
// access data
dw_employee.SetTransObject(sqlca)
dw_employee.Retrieve()

// set visibility of pay rate
if gstr_application.permission = NOCHANGE then
    dw_employee.object.employee_pay_rate.Visible='0'
    dw_employee.object.employee_pay_rate_t.Visible='0'
end if
```

12. Open the ItemChanged event for dw_employee. You will be adding in script that modifies a couple of columns based on the user's permissions. Add in code that rejects the change if the user has a permission level of NOCHANGE. This value is defined as a constant in the global variables for the application.

```
String   ls_Column
Date     ldt_End, ldt_Start

// if user permission is read only, reject datavalue
// but allow focus to change
if ii_permission = NOCHANGE then
    MessageBox(parent.title, "You do not have permission to change any
values.")
    return 2
end if
```

13. Type code that will check to see if the column changed is the employee_end_dt column. If it is, the code will get the value from this column, and from the Start Date column. It will then compare the two values. If the two are equal, the code will change the background color of the column to red and issue a warning message. If the new End Date is earlier than the Start Date, the user will get an error message and the value will be rejected, and the focus will remain on the column.

```
ls_Column = dwo.name

if ls_Column = "employee_end_dt" then
    ldt_Start = GetItemDate(row, "employee_start_dt")
    ldt_End = Date(data)

    if ldt_Start = ldt_End then
        MessageBox(this.title, "You have an end date equal to the start
date.")
        this.Object.employee_end_dt.background.color=RGB(255,0,0)
    elseif ldt_Start < ldt_End then
        MessageBox(this.title, "You cannot have an end date earlier " + &
        "than the start date.", &
            Exclamation!,Ok!)
        return 1
    end if
end if
```

14. Close and save this event by selecting the next event you will be adding script to. This event is the RowFocusChanged event.

15. In the RowFocusChanged event, place code to check and see if the background color of the employee_end_dt is set to red. If it is, change it back to the standard column color, found by accessing the color of the employee_start_dt column. Use Describe to find out the existing background color.

```
//process for each row
Long ll_color

// First, check and see what the color is on end date
// if set to red, reset back to standard color
ll_color = Long(this.object.employee_end_dt.background.color)
if ll_color = 255 then
    ll_color = Long(this.object.employee_start_dt.background.color)
    this.object.employee_end_dt.background.color=ll_color
end if
```

16. Close and save the script in the RowFocusChanged event. Close and save the window. Run the DYNAMIC.PBL application and select Employee. Login as both "spalmer" with password of "zoorusone1" and "jtower" with no password and view the results.

How It Works

Modification to an existing DataWindow can be one of the easiest parts of your application or one of the most difficult. Additionally, the modification can occur via many different PowerBuilder functions. In this example we changed the tab order using SetTabOrder, and we changed the editability of a field by using SetTabOrder or by using the return value in the ItemChanged event. We use the DataWindow object to change most of the other attributes of the DataWindow column, including background color and visibility.

The DataWindow object will not work if you do not specify the column name directly when you are changing an attribute, or specify the column number when accessing the data.

Comments

In place of the DataWindow object or Modify, always use a predefined function whenever there is one. For example, SetTabOrder is a function that accesses the protect variable without using the Datawindow Object.

COMPLEXITY
ADVANCED

12.4   How do I...
Add and modify DataWindow objects at runtime?

Problem

My application has several grid reports. The data and format for each report is different but they all, by company standards, have to contain the company logo, name, page number and date. How can I modify each of the reports programmatically to do this rather than having to place these objects in each DataWindow manually?

Technique

You can use the Modify function in order to create bitmaps, computed columns, and text fields at runtime within a DataWindow. You can also do this by accessing the existing syntax of the DataWindow and appending the specifications for these objects to the end of the syntax. Then you can use the newly modified syntax to create a new DataWindow in place of the existing one in a DataWindow control. With this technique you have an alternative to the Modify function.

Steps

Access the DYNAMIC.PBL application and select the Retail Items DataWindow d_retail_items. The report is nothing more than a simple grid DataWindow as shown in Figure 12-12. Run the application and choose the Retail Items option. Notice now, as shown in Figure 12-13, the logo in the middle of the report, the zoo store name at the top, a page count at the top on one side, and the current date at the top on the other.

The steps to add this modification to an existing DataWindow follow.

1 Access the DYNAMIC.PBL library. Backup the existing w_retail_items window by opening it and saving it as w_retail_items_bak.

2. Create a new window and name it w_retail_items. Access the property sheet for the window and change the title to "Retail Items::Report" and the menu to "m_app_menu".

3 Place a DataWindow control on the window, access its property sheet, change the Datawindow Name to "d_retail_items", and change the border style to 3D Lowered.

4. Access the Function painter and create a new function called f_standard_report. Add one Argument of type string and call it "as_syntax". Set the return type of the function to string.

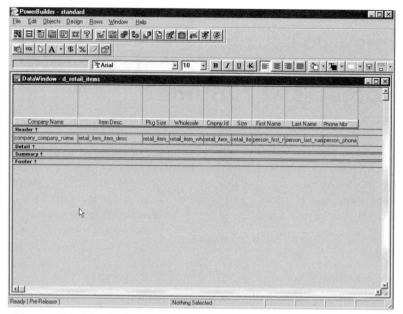

Figure 12-12 d_retail_items DataWindow from the DataWindow painter

Figure 12-13 The same DataWindow (d_retail_items) during runtime after modifications

5. Type the following code into the function. This code will append the syntax for a bitmap for the logo, a text object for the Company Title, and two computed fields for the Date and Page fields.

```
//Modify the syntax of the passed windows to add
// standard report objects
String ls_ModifyString
String ls_ExistingSyntax
```

```
ls_ExistingSyntax=as_syntax

// create the bitmap string
ls_ModifyString=' bitmap(band=background '+ &
                'filename="LOGO.BMP" '+ &
                'x="1043" y="326" height="829" '+ &
                'width="1098" border="0"  name=logo )~r~n'

ls_ExistingSyntax = ls_ExistingSyntax + ls_ModifyString

// create the title string
ls_ModifyString=' text(band=background alignment="2" '+ &
                'text="The Zoo Gift Shop "border="0" '+ &
                'color="0" x="1061" y="42" height="101"'+ &
                ' width="1427"  name=t_title  moveable=1'+ &
                '  slideleft=yes font.face="Arial" font.height="-16" '+ &
                'font.weight="700"  font.family="2" font.pitch="2" '+ &
                'font.charset="0" background.mode="1" '+ &
                'background.color="553648127" )~r~n'

ls_ExistingSyntax=ls_ExistingSyntax + ls_ModifyString

// create date computed field
ls_ModifyString=' compute(band=background alignment="0" '+ &
                'expression="today()"border="0" color="0" x="87" ' + &
                'y="118" height="53" width="513" format="[general]" '+ &
                ' name=t_date  moveable=1  font.face="MS Sans Serif" ' + &
                'font.height="-8" font.weight="400"  font.family="2" ' + &
                'font.pitch="2" font.charset="0" background.mode="1" ' + &
                'background.color="553648127" )~r~n'

ls_ExistingSyntax = ls_ExistingSyntax + ls_ModifyString

// create page computed field
ls_ModifyString=' compute(band=background alignment="0" '+ &
                'expression="~'Page ~' + page() + ~' of ~' + '+ &
                'pageCount()"border="0" color="0" x="2647" y="118" '+ &
                'height="53" width="970" format="[general]"  name=t_page'+ &
                '  moveable=1  font.face="MS Sans Serif" font.height="-8"'+ &
                ' font.weight="400"  font.family="2" font.pitch="2" ' + &
                'font.charset="0" background.mode="1"
background.color="553648127" )'

ls_ExistingSyntax = ls_ExistingSyntax + ls_ModifyString


return ls_ExistingSyntax
```

6. Close and save the new function.

7. Access the Open event for w_retail_items. Type in the following code that
will access the syntax for the DataWindow control and pass this to the new
function f_standard_report. Also, type in code that will capture the string
returned from the function, use this to create a new DataWindow for the
control, set the transaction object to it, and retrieve.

```
// retrieve to the datawindow
// modify it by calling f_standard_report
String ls_Syntax

ls_Syntax = String(dw_1.Object.Datawindow.Syntax)

// modify datawindow
ls_Syntax=f_standard_report(ls_Syntax)

dw_1.Create(ls_Syntax)
dw_1.SetTransObject(sqlca)
dw_1.Retrieve()
```

8. Access the Resize event for the window and type in the following, which will size the DataWindow control to fit the window.

```
dw_1.Resize(this.WorkSpaceWidth() - 10, this.WorkSpaceHeight() - 10)
```

9. Close and save the window.

10. To test, access DYNAMIC.PBL and run the application from PowerBuilder. Again select the Retail Items option and your new window will show.

How It Works

Previous to version 5.0, adding a bitmap, text field, or computed columns at run-time entailed using the Modify function and creating the objects. However, with the new version of PowerBuilder, you may want to make less use of Modify, and this technique is an alternative approach.

COMPLEXITY
INTERMEDIATE

12.5 How do I...
Save and load a DataWindow object definition to a PowerBuilder library or database?

Problem

I can create a DataWindow, I can modify a DataWindow, and I can add text and graphics. I can also change the SQL for the DataWindow. Now, how can I save a DataWindow so it can be brought up and run again and again?

Technique

There are actually two different ways to save a DataWindow object definition and pull it up at a later time, or even from a different location. You can save the object to a PowerBuilder library or you can save the object definition to a database. This How-To will provide the steps to save a DataWindow definition to a PowerBuilder library (.PBL) and then access it from another window. In addition, this How-To will describe how to save a DataWindow object definition to a database and then use this to run the DataWindow in another window.

Steps

Any of the windows created in this sample can provide an example of how to save a DataWindow definition to a database, and how to save the object to a PowerBuilder library. There is an event in each of the windows called ue_SaveDataWindow that calls a window that does this. As an example, run the DYNAMIC.PBL application and choose the Retail Items option. Select the Save DataWindow menu item from the Edit menu. A new window opens as shown in Figure 12-14. Select the user.PBL as the destination to save the DataWindow to and press the OK CommandButton. Close the Retail Items window and open the Report Viewer window. This window will display a saved DataWindow from either the USER.PBL library, or stored from the database as shown in Figure 12-15. Double-click on the d_retail_items entry in the Library tab and the DataWindow you just saved is displayed as shown in Figure 12-16.

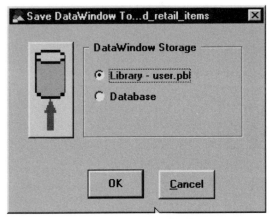

Figure 12-14 Save source Window

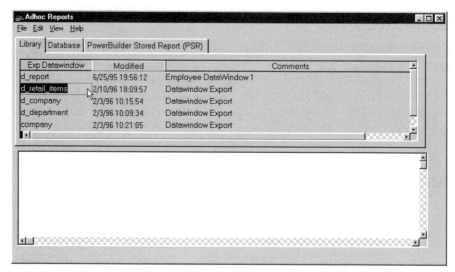

Figure 12-15 Report Viewer Datawindow display window showing new stored DataWindow

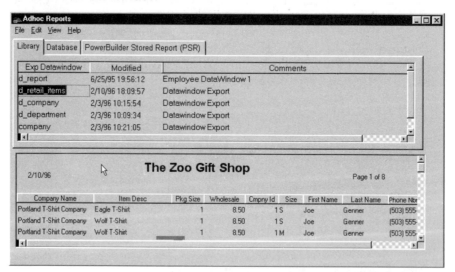

Figure 12-16 Report Viewer DataWindow displaying stored DataWindow

1. Access the DYNAMIC.PBL library.

2. Create a new window and call it w_savesource. Access the property sheet for the window and change the title to "Save DataWindow To..." and change the window type to Response. Disable the Control menu.

3. On the window place a Picture control and change the filename to "save.BMP". Next to this control place a GroupBox control. Change the text for this control to "Datawindow Storage".

4. In the GroupBox place two RadioButtons. Name the top button "rb_library" and change the text to "Library - user.pbl". Name the bottom one "rb_database" and change the text to "Database".

5. Below the GroupBox place two CommandButtons, one labeled "OK" and the other labeled "Cancel".

6. Access the Clicked event for the OK CommandButton. Type code into this event that will check and see which RadioButton is checked and save either the USER.PBL library or the database accordingly. Lastly, this code will close the window.

```
//
String ls_Syntax, ls_errors
String ls_Name, ls_File

// access datawindow syntax and name
ls_Syntax = String(idw_SaveDatawindow.Object.DataWindow.Syntax)
ls_name = idw_SaveDatawindow.DataObject

// if library import into user library
if rb_library.checked then
    ls_File = gstr_application.path + "user.pbl"
    LibraryImport(ls_File, ls_name, ImportDataWindow!,ls_Syntax, ls_errors)
    if ls_errors <> "" then
        MessageBox(parent.title, "Could not Save datawindow. " + ls_errors)
        return
    end if

// insert into database
else
    INSERT INTO datawindow_table values (:ls_Name,:ls_Syntax, :ls_name);
    if sqlca.sqlcode < 0 then
        ROLLBACK;
        MessageBox(parent.title, "Could not Save datawindow. " +
    sqlca.sqlerrtext)
        return
    else
        COMMIT;
    end if
end if

MessageBox(parent.title, "DataWindow has been saved.")

Close(parent)
```

7. Access the Clicked event for the other CommandButton and type in code to close the parent window.

```
Close(parent)
```

8. Close and save the window in the DYNAMIC.PBL library. Test the window by running the DYNAMIC.PBL application and running either of the Personal Information windows, the Employee window, or the Retail Item window. Try saving to both the USER.PBL library and the database and then running the DataWindow in the Report Viewer.

How It Works

As discussed in the other How-Tos in this chapter, a DataWindow is really made up of two components, the SQL for the data, if any, and the syntax to define how the data is displayed. Both of these components can be exported into a text form, and this text form can be stored in a PowerBuilder library, or in a database.

To use the DataWindow syntax, access it either from the library or from the database, and use the syntax to create the DataWindow.

Comments

The Report Viewer accessed in this How-To was created in Chapter 3, in How-To 3.2, "How do I build a standalone report viewer using the SDI application style?"

CHAPTER 13
WORKING WITH
OLE 2.0

13

WORKING WITH OLE 2.0

How do I...

OLE originally referred to Object Linking and Embedding and provided the ability to access and modify an object from one type of application in another application. Now, with OLE 2.0, the user has the ability to access not only the object, but functions to manipulate the object directly in the server application. With this ability, one can access a Microsoft Word object, insert data from a PowerBuilder DataWindow, and use the formatting capability of Word for printing, or use the built-in spell checking functionality. Your application will have the ability to allow your user to access and manipulate data using the tools and techniques best suited for the data and the user.

13.1   Use an OLE 2.0 Control

PowerBuilder provides you with the ability to retrieve and display data, but sometimes you will want to provide just a little more formatting than can be easily done in the tool. With an OLE 2.0 control, you can pass your data to another application to take advantage the of the features that that application can provide. In this How-To you will learn how to use your application to access and manage data while employing Microsoft Word to format and print it all, through the use of OLE 2.0.

13.2   Use an OLE 2.0 Object in Memory

You don't have to use an OLE 2.0 control to take advantage of OLE. In this How-To you will learn how to copy, in the background, data from a visible DataWindow to a Microsoft Word document.

13. 3   Use OLE 2.0 Control Activation Effectively

Using OLE 2.0 is fairly easy, but using it effectively is the toughest aspect of this technology. In the last How-To, you used an OLE 2.0 control and automation to send data from a PowerBuilder DataWindow to a Microsoft Word document. You accomplished this using OffSite activation. This How-To will demonstrate how to implement InPlace activation, including effective use of menu merging. In addition, this How-To will briefly describe the benefits of both activation techniques.

13.4   Use OLE 2.0 Custom Controls (OCX)

The Visual Basic control (VBX) that has been so common is no longer being supported by Microsoft. Instead, applications now have access to OLE 2.0 custom controls which are called OCX controls. This How-To demonstrates the steps to embed one of these controls directly into your window, and how to access one of its events.

13.5   Create a PowerBuilder OLE Automation Server to Enforce Standards

You can place common functions into a separate PowerBuilder Library (PBL) and access them in your code, but you can also place them into a completely separate application and access these functions via OLE automation. These functions will then be available for all PowerBuilder applications without having to provide the PBL. In addition, these functions can now be available for all applications that support OLE 2.0 automation.

COMPLEXITY
INTERMEDIATE

13.1 How do I...
Use an OLE 2.0 control?

Problem

I would like to access data using a DataWindow but I would like to format the results and print them with a document tool such as Microsoft Word. How can I do this?

Technique

The principle behind OLE 2.0 is for each application to provide the functionality it is best suited for and to allow all tools access to common data through this mechanism. The principle also allows for the functionality to be accessed directly in the client application, or by opening up and performing the work in the application providing the service. This How-To will provide instructions for turning your application into an OLE container application through the use of the OLE 2.0 control. In this example you will embed an object directly into a window and access the server application functionality in the server application itself. You will send the data to the server using OLE Automation, which is the ability to directly call certain functions that the application has chosen to make available to OLE Clients.

Steps

Access the OLE20.PBL library and run the application. Select the second tab, labeled Phone List Copy. This tab will access the employee phone records and open a Microsoft Word document. The data for the document is sent to the document using WordBasicfunctions which have been made available to the clients of this type of application. Once the data is in the client, you can use Word to format the data in any manner you wish, or to save or print the document. Figure 13-1 shows the results of the phone list just after it has been opened in a Word document. Figure 13-2 shows the results after formatting and adding a document header and footer. Figure 13-3 shows what the DataWindow looks like while this is occurring and Figure 13-4 shows what the DataWindow looks like when the Word application is closed and results are updated.

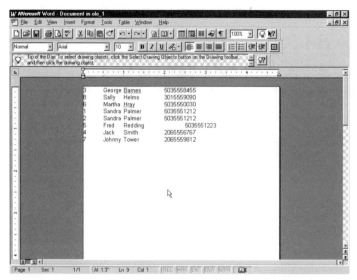

Figure 13-1 Word document just after it receives data

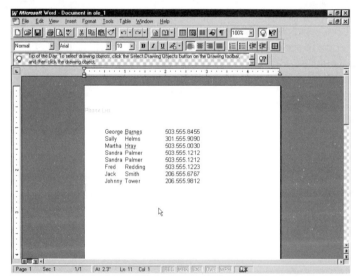

Figure 13-2 Word document after formatting

The steps to create this embedded object are below.

1. Access the OLE20.PBL library and open the w_ole window.

2. Create a tabpage on the tab by clicking with the right mouse button on the Tab control and selecting Insert TabPage. On this window place a DataWindow control and point this control to the d_phone_copy DataWindow. Name the control dw_phone and uncheck its visible attribute.

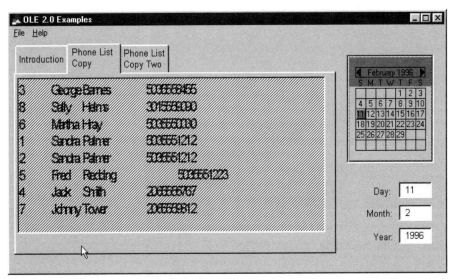

Figure 13-3 Application window while Word document is still open

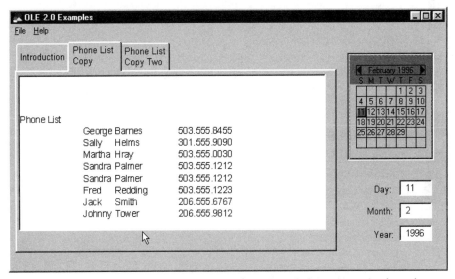

Figure 13-4 Application window just after Word document is closed

3. Place an OLE 2.0 control on the window. If it is not located in the toolbar, it can be found in the Controls menu. When you place the control on the window a dialog box will popup listing available object types defined for your desktop as shown in Figure 13-5.

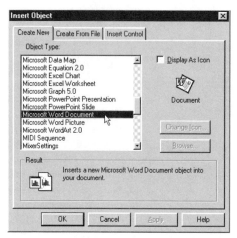

Figure 13-5 Popup dialog with OLE objects

4. Select the Microsoft Word document type and select OK. The control will resize itself and the Word application will pop open. Select Close and return to the Unnamed file option from the Word File menu. Resize the control to fit the tabpage area.

5. Double-click on the OLE control and you will see a dialog box. Make sure the visible and enabled CheckBoxes are checked, that the Embedded option is chosen from the Contents DropDownListBox, and that the Activation method is Double Click. The dialog box should look like that shown in Figure 13-6.

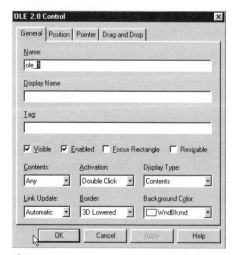

Figure 13-6 OLE 2.0 Control dialog box

6. Next you will add code to implement your OLE object. In the Constructor event for the DataWindow dw_phone, type in the following code.

```
// retrieve data into hidden datawindow
dw_phone.SetTransObject(sqlca)
dw_phone.Retrieve()
```

7. This code will retrieve the rows into the DataWindow. In the SelectionChanged event for the Tab control, type in code to call a function that will activate your OLE 2.0 control.

```
If newindex = 4 then
    wf_send_data()
end if
```

8. In the new function, type the following code that will activate the OLE 2.0 control offsite (meaning in the application) and send the records from the DataWindow to the Word document.

```
// Activate OLE 2.0 control
// Send rows from hidden DataWindow to Word document
// using Automation functions
Long        lRow, lRowCount
Integer     iEmployeeID
String  sFirstName, sLastName, sPhone
String      sText

SetPointer(HourGlass!)

lRowCount = tab_1.tabpage_4.dw_phone.RowCount()

// activate OLE control object
//tab_1.tabpage_4.ole_1.Activate(InPlace!)
tab_1.tabpage_4.ole_1.Activate(OffSite!)

sText = tab_1.tabpage_4.ole_1.ClassLongName
sText = tab_1.tabpage_4.ole_1.ClassShortName

// for each row in database insert into Word document
// in formatted manner
For lRow = 1 to lRowCount
    iEmployeeId = tab_1.tabpage_4.dw_phone.GetItemNumber(lRow, 1)
    sFirstName = tab_1.tabpage_4.dw_phone.GetItemString(lRow, 2)
    sLastName = tab_1.tabpage_4.dw_phone.GetItemString(lRow,   3)
    sText = String(iEmployeeId) + "~t" + sFirstName + "~t" + sLastName
    if Len(sLastName) > 8 then
        sText = sText + "~t"
    else
        sText = sText + "~t~t"
    end if
    sPhone = tab_1.tabpage_4.dw_phone.GetItemString(lRow, 4)
    sText = sText + sPhone + "~r~n"
    tab_1.tabpage_4.ole_1.Object.Application.WordBasic.Insert(sText)
NEXT
```

9. In the above, the OLE control is activated manually. This will override the defined activation type of Double Click. Additionally, for each row in the DataWindow, the first and last name of the employee, the employee ID, and the phone number are accessed. The fields are concatenated with tabs and a new line/carriage return is placed at end of the string. The application function to insert the text string is accessed and the string is placed into the active document.

10. Close the w_ole window, saving your work. Run w_ole from PowerBuilder and test your new tab. Notice that the Word document is activated as soon as your window starts and that you can watch the lines as they are being inserted.

11. Work with the data as you like and try printing the results. You may need to redefine the page size as you work with this. Close and return the results to your application.

12. Back in the application, double-click the control. Notice this time that the object is not activated in the Word document but is instead activated InPlace. Activation InPlace will be discussed more fully in the next How-To.

How It Works

When you created your window, you embedded an OLE container using the OLE 2.0 control. You defined the type of OLE object when you placed this object, selecting from the list of types that you were presented.

As the object you selected has also implemented OLE Automation, you were able to access functions that allowed you to directly manipulate the application, which you did by inserting text into the document you just opened.

Comments

Not all OLE servers provide OLE automation. Some may only allow you to either embed an object directly into your application and manually use their functionality, or link to them through DDE (Dynamic Data Exchange). To check to see if the server application you are interested in provides this capability, check the application's help file under OLE or OLE 2.0.

Additionally, you can make use of the registry database to check out what services an application provides. You can access this manually by running regedit.EXE, but be careful that you do not accidently change any of the entries. An excellent source of information about the registry can be found in the book *The Windows Interface Guidelines for Software Design* by Microsoft Press, published in 1995.

COMPLEXITY
ADVANCED

13.2 How do I...
Use an OLE 2.0 object in memory?

Problem

I want to be able to copy data from my DataWindow to a Microsoft Word document, but I want to be able to do this in the background. How can I do this?

Technique

You can use OLE 2.0 without having to embed an OLE 2.0 control in your window or DataWindow. PowerBuilder provides the ability to create an OLE object and manipulate it as you would a control. In order for this to be effective, your manipulation of the object must occur with automation functions provided by the OLE server.

Steps

Access the OLE20.PBL library and run the application. Select the second tab, labeled Phone List Copy Two. This tab will populate a DataWindow and open Microsoft Word, displaying an busy icon while this is occuring. When the busy icon has disappeared, select the Copy to Document button. You will not see the Microsoft Word application in your desktop at all unless you have opened it prior to running this application, as you can see from Figure 13-7. Press the Copy to Document button and again notice that there are no visual cues that Word is open and a document being written to. Close the window and the Word application appears with a dialog asking for the name to save the document with as shown in Figure 13-8.

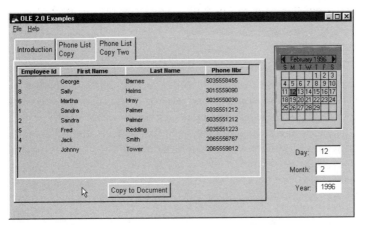

Figure 13-7 Phone List Copy window with data

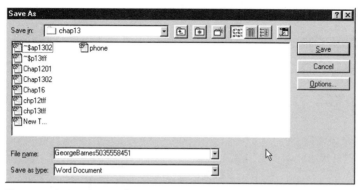

Figure 13-8 Microsoft Word common Save document dialog

The steps to create this window are below.

1. Access the OLE20.PBL library and open the w_ole window. Click on the third tab containing the existing Phone List Copy Two tab and select Cut from the popup menu. Insert a new tabpage by clicking on the Tab control with the right mouse button and selecting the Insert TabPage option.

2. On this new tabpage place a DataWindow control, name it "dw_phone_copy", and set it to d_phone_copy. Size it to fit the tabpage but leave room at the bottom. Change the text for the tab to "Phone List Copy Two".

3. Place a CommandButton just below the DataWindow control and change the text on the button to "Copy to Document". At this point your window should look like the one shown in Figure 13-7. Define an instance variable of type OLEObject and call it ole_phone.

4. Access the Constructor event for the DataWindow control and type in code to retrieve to the control.

```
this.SetTransObject(sqlca)
this.Retrieve()
```

5. Access the SelectionChanged event for the Tab control. Type in code that will check the index of the tabpage being selected. If the tab being selected is your new tab, this code will call a function that will set up your OLE object. If the selection was on your new tab and is going to another, the code will disconnect from the Word Document and destroy the OLE object.

```
// check tabpage clicked
if newindex = 2 then
    wf_send_data()
elseif newindex = 3 then
    wf_setup_ole()
end if
```

```
//
if oldindex = 3 then
    //close and save document
    ole_phone.FileClose(1)
    ole_phone.DisconnectObject()
    Destroy ole_phone
end if
```

6. Next, create the new wf_setup_ole function by creating a new window
function and typing in the following code. This code will create the OLE
object in memory, connect it to Microsoft Word, open a new document, and
go to the first line.

```
// create ole object
// connect it to Microsoft Word
// open a new document and goto first line
Integer iResult
String sFileName

SetPointer(HourGlass!)

// create object and connect
ole_phone = create OLEObject
iResult=ole_phone.ConnectToNewObject("Word.Basic")

if iResult < 0 then
    MessageBox(this.title, "Could not create OLE object for Word.")
end if

SetPointer(Arrow!)

ole_phone.FileNew()
ole_phone.editgoto("1")
```

7. Notice that the Word function is not preceeded by WordBasic as shown in the
first How-To for this chapter. This is because you established a context for the
command when you used the ConnectToNewObject PowerBuilder function.
Next you will add code to the Clicked event of your new pushbutton.

```
// For each row in the DataWindow
// access names and phone number, format and
// concatenate and send to document
Long        lRowCount
String      sText, sFirstName, sLastName, sPhone
String      sEmployeeId
Integer     iEmployeeId
Integer     iResult
Integer     lRow

lRowCount = dw_phone_copy.RowCount()
if lRowCount <= 0 then return

SetPointer(HourGlass!)

// for each row in database insert into Word Document
// in formatted manner
```

continued on next page

continued from previous page

```
For lRow = 1 to lRowCount
    iEmployeeId =        dw_phone_copy.Object.Data[lRow, 1]
    sFirstName =         String(dw_phone_copy.Object.Data[lRow, 2])
    sLastName =          String(dw_phone_copy.Object.Data[lRow, 3])

    sEmployeeId = String(iEmployeeId)
    // concatenate values with tab sep
    sText = sEmployeeId + "~t" + sFirstName + "~t" + sLastName
    if Len(sLastName) > 8 then
        sText = sText + "~t"
    else
        sText = sText + "~t~t"
    end if

    // get phone number and append
    // return and line feed
    sPhone = dw_phone_copy.Object.Data[lRow, 4]
    sText = sText + sPhone + "~r~n"

    ole_phone.insert(sText)
NEXT

SetPointer(Arrow!)



w_genapp_frame.SetMicroHelp("Ready")
```

8. The above code is very similar to that in the previous How-To except that, as noted previously, you do not have to preceed the Insert WordBasic function with the WordBasic context specifier.

9. The last change you will need to make will be to close the document you just opened. You will use the Word function FileClose with a parameter of "1" which specifies to save the document just created. This will trigger the Save dialog mentioned earlier. Lastly, you must disconnect from the Word application and you do this with the DisconnectObject function.

```
//close and save document
ole_phone.FileClose(1)

ole_phone.DisconnectObject()
Destroy ole_phone
```

10. Save your window and run the ADMIN application again.

How It Works

You do not have to have a physical element in order to take advantage of OLE 2.0 functionality. A control may hide some of the details of the implementation from you but it is not necessary for operation.

The user will not see the application unless the OLE server application needs to query for some information. Because of this, it is essential to disconnect from the object, or the server will continue running and the user will have no way of turning it off.

Comments

With new applications coming out for Windows 95, you may run into problems with getting an OLE server application to run. If a previous version was in the registry and a newer version implements a different connection based on being 32-bit, your application may look like it's accessing something, but fail when you run any of the functions. Check your registry entries for duplicates, or cases where an executable is listed in two different physical locations.

COMPLEXITY

ADVANCED

13.3 How do I...
Use OLE 2.0 control activation effectively?

Problem

When my control activates, I want to be able to activate it InPlace in my document instead of opening up and implementing it in the server application. How can I do this?

Technique

With OLE 2.0, you can embed an object in your application and when the user or your application activates it, you can choose to activate the server application InPlace. This means that you will have access to a limited set of functionality of the mail server application and you will have to merge your menus with that of the server application. However, activating the OLE control InPlace may be faster and less distracting to your clients.

Steps

Access the OLE20.PBL library and run the application. Select the second tab Phone List Copy. The window at this time activates the control OffSite, which means in the server application. Close Microsoft Word and return to OLE2.0. Double-click the OLE control. Notice that the menus and interface of your application have changed, yet you are still in your application, as shown in Figure 13-9.

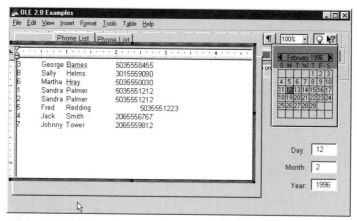

Figure 13-9 Phone List Copy document with InPlace activation

In the following steps you will modify your sheet menu to allow for negotiation between your application and the server application. In addition, you will modify your existing w_ole window to change the activation style when the window is first opened from OffSite! to InPlace!.

1. Open the m_main menu.

2. Modify the File menu item to replace the server application File menu option by selecting File from the Style dropdown list as shown in Figure 13-10.

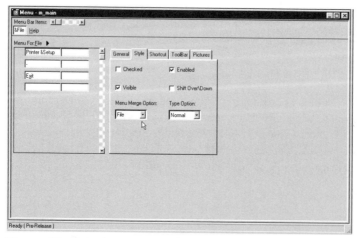

Figure 13-10 Style property sheet for m_main showing File as merge option

3. Modify the Help menu item to replace the server Help menu item by selecting Help from the list.

4. Close and save the menu.

5. Open the existing w_ole and remove the line of code listed below from the wf_send_data() function.

```
tab_1.tabpage_2.ole_1.Activate(OffSite!)
```

6. Add in the following code in place of the code you just removed.

```
tab_1.tabpage_2.ole_1.Activate(InPlace!)
```

7. Close and save the window and run the application. Now when you select the Phone List Copy tab and double-click on the control, it opens with InPlace activation. Look at the menus and notice how the server menu and your application menu have merged into one common menu.

How It Works

Microsoft Word provides for InPlace activation by providing a subset of functionality that is merged into your application. Normally the menus for the server application would completely replace the menus for your application unless you specifically included some options. Clicking anywhere else in the application would return the menu and any toolbars back to the way they are in the rest of your application.

COMPLEXITY
INTERMEDIATE

13.4 How do I...
Use OLE 2.0 custom controls (OCX)?

Problem

All of the Visual Basic Controls (VBXs) that our group used are being replaced by OLE Custom Controls (OCXs). How do I use these new controls?

Technique

The OCX is replacing the VBX in Windows 95 and you will find this an improvment in both ease of use and performance. Using an OCX is as easy as selecting the control, setting any properties, and accessing any of its publicly exposed events.

Steps

Powersoft has provided several OCX controls in its subdirectory titled Compglry. This is one of the options you could have selected when you installed PowerBuilder. If you did not install these controls, do so now. Once installed you will need to register the control if it's not already registered, and then you just drop the control on the window where you want to use it.

To use an OCX on your window follow the steps below.

1. Access the OLE20.PBL library and open w_ole. Delete the date OCX from the right side of the window.

2. Access the OLE control from the components and select the Insert Control tab. The tab displays all registered OCXs for your system as shown in Figure 13-11.

3. The control you will use will be the one labeled ctDate. If the control you wanted to use is not listed, you will need to register it.

4. To register a control you would select the Register New... button and then browse until you found the subdirectory containing the control. In this case the subdirectory is Compglry, located in the PowerBuilder directory, and the file is Ctdate32.OCX as shown in Figure 13-12.

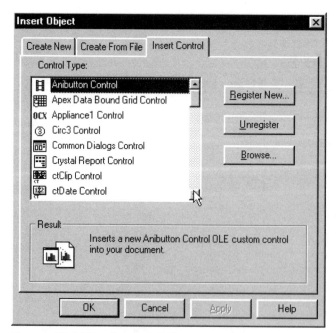

Figure 13-11 Registered OCXs

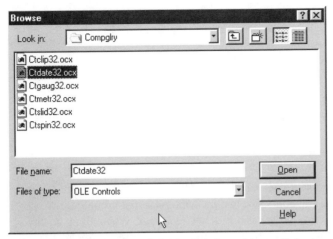

Figure 13-12 Ctdate32.OCX in Register New dialog

5. Select Open when registering this control.

6. Select the CtDate control from the list. Place it on the window where the previous control was. Size the control so that the face is easily seen.

7. This OCX will show the current date highlighted within the context of the current month and year. You will change the title color for the control by selecting OCX Properties... from the popup menu for the control.

8. The OCX properties, as shown in Figure 13-13, vary for each control and are provided by the OCX builder. Select the Colors tab.

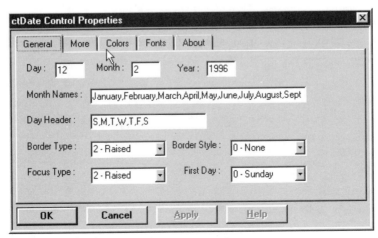

Figure 13-13 CtDate OCX property sheet

9. Select TitleColor from the DropDownListBox for Property Name and then select the bright green color from the choices on the right. Select the OK button to save your change.

10. Access the DateChanged event for the control. This event passes four integer arguments: the day of the week, the day of the month, the month, and the year. Type in code that will access the day, month, and year. Send those to the SingleLineEditBoxes that have been created just below the control.

```
sle_1.Text = String(nday)
sle_2.Text = String(nmonth)
sle_3.Text = String(nyear)
```

11. Close w_ole and save your results. Run OLE2.0 from PowerBuilder. Notice the value in the edit controls when the window is first brought up. You should see the current date as it is defined for your system. Click on any of the dates or move the month by selecting the arrow keys in the month header. Again notice the results in the edit controls.

How It Works

The VBX control was the beginning implementation of custom controls. However, OCXs go beyond what VBXs could provide by providing OLE automation as well as property and event access. This means that the OCX can provide functions for the client application to access, rather than having to create arbitrary events. In addition, OCXs can be 16 or 32-bit, meaning that they are portable, whereas VBXs are only 16-bit interfaces.

PowerBuilder 5.0 provides full OCX support, including access to any methods the OCX provides.

Comments

As the VBXs you use in your application are replaced with OCXs, you should replace them as soon as possible in your application. If the controls are converted with the same functionality, your user should see little or no difference.

COMPLEXITY
ADVANCED

13.5 How do I...
Create a PowerBuilder OLE automation server to enforce standards?

Problem

I have several functions I would like to create into one object, and then send just this one object to all the sites that need access to these functions. I don't want the sites to have access to the code, as the object creates functions to enforce standards. Additionally, not all of the sites that will need some of the functions are running applications built in PowerBuilder. How can I create this type of object?

Technique

You can create a PowerBuilder automation server contained in a Dynamic Link Library (DLL) which you can distribute to all sites that need it. To do this, you will need to create a non-visual user object to contain the functions you want to provide, and then create a registration file that exposes these functions.

Steps

The steps outline creating a new PowerBuilder library and, within this library, a non-visual custom user object is created to contain the properties and methods that are exposed for use. One function at a time is created. Then the library is compiled into a Dynamic Link Library (DLL). Next, a function is created that will generate a registry file for your new OLE automation server. Call the function and then run the registry file.

The steps in detail to create your new server follow.

1. Create a new PowerBuilder library and call it SERVER.PBL.

2. Create a new application object for the library, calling it "server_app".

3. Access the property sheet for the application object and set the library path to the COMMON.PBL library and to your new library. Save the Application object.

4. Create two global variables for the environment variable and the Application object.

```
// environment object
Environment ge_environment
```

continued on next page

continued from previous page

```
// application object
app_structure gstr_application
```

5. Type the following into the Open script for the application.

```
// get environment information
GetEnvironment(ge_environment)

// get application object
f_set_application()
```

6. Close and save the Application object.

7. Create a new non-visual user object and call it "nvo_standards_object".

8. In this user object, create a new user object function and call it "uf_standard_report".

9. The only argument for the function will be a string argument, "as_syntax", which will be passed by reference. The return type of the function is integer. This function will modify the syntax of a DataWindow report by adding in certain common standard objects, such as a title, page and date computed fields, and a logo bitmap.

10. Type the following code into the function. This code is very similar to that found in the f_standard_report user function in COMMON.PBL.

```
//Modify the syntax of the passed windows to add
// standard report objects
String ls_ModifyString
String ls_ExistingSyntax

ls_ExistingSyntax=as_syntax

// create the bitmap string
ls_ModifyString=' bitmap(band=background '+ &
                'filename="LOGO.BMP" '+ &
                'x="1043" y="326" height="829" '+ &
                'width="1098" border="0"   name=logo )~r~n'

ls_ExistingSyntax = ls_ExistingSyntax + ls_ModifyString

// create the title string
ls_ModifyString=' text(band=background alignment="2" '+ &
                'text="The Zoo Gift Shop "border="0" '+ &
                'color="0" x="1061" y="42" height="101"'+ &
                ' width="1427"  name=t_title  moveable=1'+ &
                '  slideleft=yes  font.face="Arial" font.height="-16" '+ &
                'font.weight="700"  font.family="2" font.pitch="2" '+ &
                'font.charset="0" background.mode="1" '+ &
                'background.color="553648127" )~r~n'

ls_ExistingSyntax=ls_ExistingSyntax + ls_ModifyString

// create date computed field
```

```
ls_ModifyString=' compute(band=background alignment="0" '+ &
                'expression="today()"border="0" color="0" x="87" ' + &
                'y="118" height="53" width="513" format="[general]" '+ &
                ' name=t_date  moveable=1  font.face="MS Sans Serif" ' + &
                'font.height="-8" font.weight="400"  font.family="2" ' + &
                'font.pitch="2" font.charset="0" background.mode="1" ' + &
                'background.color="553648127" )~r~n'

ls_ExistingSyntax = ls_ExistingSyntax + ls_ModifyString

// create page computed field
ls_ModifyString=' compute(band=background alignment="0" '+ &
                'expression="~'Page ~' + page() + ~' of ~' + '+ &
                'pageCount()"border="0" color="0" x="2647" y="118" '+ &
                'height="53" width="970" format="[general]"  name=t_page'+ &
                '  moveable=1  font.face="MS Sans Serif" font.height="-8"'+ &
                ' font.weight="400"  font.family="2" font.pitch="2" ' + &
                'font.charset="0" background.mode="1"
background.color="553648127" )'

ls_ExistingSyntax = ls_ExistingSyntax + ls_ModifyString

as_syntax = ls_ExistingSyntax

return 1
```

11. By default this function was created as Public. If this function were not to be exposed, you would have changed the access to Private or Protected when you created the function.

12. Close and save the function, and close and save the non-visual user object.

13. From the Library painter, select the library object for SERVER. From the Library menu, select the Build Dynamic Library option. When the Build Dynamic Library dialog opens, check the Machine Code option to create a machine code DLL. Make sure the Native executable format is selected, and the Optimization is set to Speed as shown in Figure 13-14.

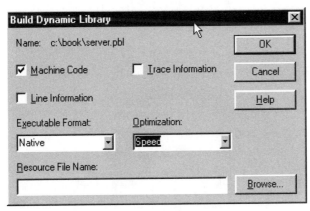

Figure 13-14 Build Dynamic Library dialog

14. You will need to create a registration file for your new object. You could use the PBGENREG.EXE that should have come with your PowerBuilder installation, or you can create your own function to create this file. To create your own file, create a function in any of your PowerBuilder libraries.

15. Name the function "create_file" and have it return [NONE] as a value.

16. Type the following into this new function. The code below will access the automation functions included with the PowerBuilder application to access the GenerateRegFile function to generate the registration file.

```
oleObject      PBObject
string         GUID
long           result

PBObject = create oleObject

// Establish a connection with PowerBuilder.Application
result = PBObject.ConnectToNewObject("PowerBuilder.Application")
if result < 0 then
   MessageBox("PowerBuilder.Application", "You could not access the " + &
               "Application object. Please check your installation.")
   return
else

   // set the library for the pbd - set to PCode
   PBObject.LibraryList = "c:\book\server.pbd"
   PBObject.MachineCode = false
   result = PBObject.GenerateGUID(REF GUID)
   if (result < 0) then
        MessageBox("Generate GUID", "You could not access the " + &
               "Generate GUID function.")

   else
     result = PBObject.GenerateRegFile(  GUID, "nvo_standards_object", &
               "nvo_standards_object",1, 0, &
                    "Report Standards Object","C:\book\standards.reg")
   end if  // GUID created successfully
end if // Connection to PowerBuilder.Application established successfully

destroy PBObject
```

17. The GenerateGUID function will generate the unique object identifier and the GenerateRegFile function will create the registry file, as shown in Figure 13-15.

18. Run the registry file by double-clicking on it. Your custom user object is now available for access by other PowerBuilder applications.

19. If you want to access this object from PowerBuilder, you can type in code to access this object any time you want to access the standard functionality. Try this by accessing DYNAMIC.PBL and opening the w_retail_items window. In the Open event, replace the existing code with the following.

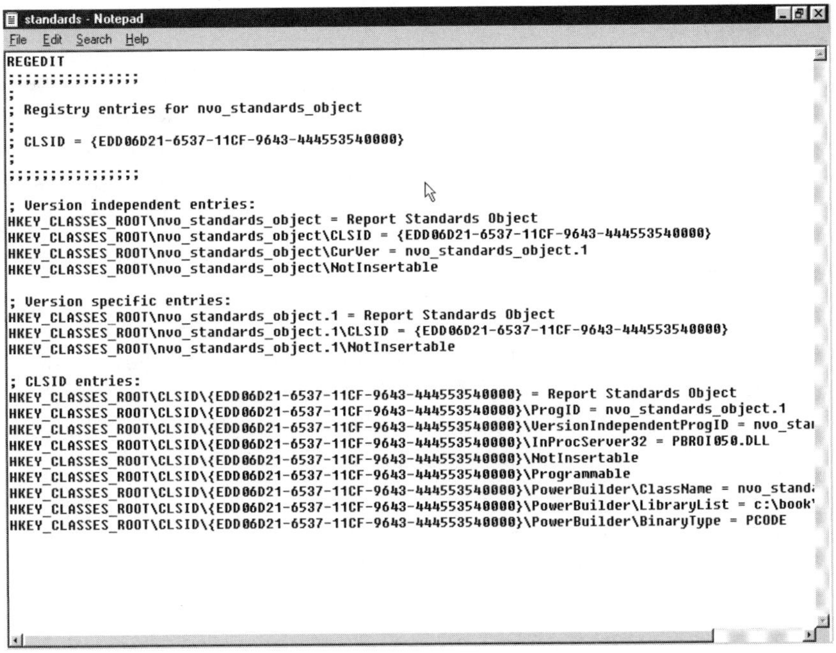

Figure 13-15 Registry file created with GenerateRegFile

```
// retrieve to the datawindow
// modify it by calling f_standard_report
String ls_Syntax
oleobject standard_object
Long ll_status

ls_Syntax = String(dw_1.Object.Datawindow.Syntax)

// modify datawindow

standard_object = create oleobject
ll_status = standard_object.ConnectToNewObject("nvo_standards_object")
if ll_status >= 0 then
    standard_object.uf_standard_report(REF ls_syntax)
    dw_1.Create(ls_Syntax)
    dw_1.SetTransObject(sqlca)
    dw_1.Retrieve()
    destroy standard_object
end if
```

20. Note the use of REF in the function call. As this user object does pass the argument by reference, you will need to use this keyword. Close the window and save the results. Run the DYNAMIC.PBL application from PowerBuilder and notice the results when you select Retail Items and the window opens.

How It Works

For the first time, you now have the ability to fully integrate your PowerBuilder applications with your other applications, and to access user-defined functions. With this you can create a function to access a database table and copy the results into something like a Microsoft Word document without manually having to run the PowerBuilder application. Use OLE automation to access the functions from Word.

Comments

The problem with using OLE objects is that they have to be created. This in itself is not a problem, but visualize the results of creating several OLE objects without destroying them.

A trick from coding Windows using C is to always code your Destroy operation just after you code your Create operation. Then place the other code in between the two operations.

CHAPTER 14
USER-DEFINED FUNCTIONS

14

USER-DEFINED FUNCTIONS

How do I...

Functions are an important part of any system development. They provide a mechanism for writing code that will be used time and again. They typically return values to the caller to indicate what happened, or give the caller some result such as an average or sum of numbers. Routines that do not return a value are referred to as *subroutines*. In PowerBuilder, as in the C language, there is no concept of a subroutine. Functions either return a value or they do not. No distinction is made based on the existence of a return value. PowerBuilder provides the developer with three types of functions — global, object level, and external. This chapter focuses on global and object level functions. External functions are covered in the next few chapters since they are exceedingly important in the Microsoft Windows environment. After reading through this chapter, you'll no doubt come up with additional functions that will be useful in all of your applications. PowerBuilder and Windows are fairly robust environments, but the need always arises to do some custom tricks. It is our hope that you will find these five functions useful and generic enough to copy right into your libraries. All the functions presented here are window level object functions. In later chapters, this will become increasingly important as you inherit from existing objects. You may eventually build your own class library of objects and functions. Class libraries are as in demand as PowerBuilder itself. When you use a class library, you enable all of your applications to look and feel like one another. But enough on that. Let's concentrate on the tasks at hand, namely building some useful user-defined functions.

14.1   Declare a Global Function

Like global variables, global functions are available to any script in the application. As a developer, you can call a global function at any time without regard to scope. Anything defined as global always stirs up a debate. Many developers claim you cannot get away from globals, while others maintain that globals are always bad, and therefore should never be used. This is a can of worms that will not be opened here. Whether or not you use global functions or variables should be evaluated on a case by case basis and is left for you to argue amongst your peers. In an object oriented environment, globals are avoided. However, PowerBuilder does not force you into object orientation. The use or exclusion of global variables and functions is a decision ultimately left to you depending on your situation. The function presented here provides for error checking and handling after the execution of an embedded SQL statement. Any time embedded SQL is executed, you must check the return codes from SQLCA. In applications where heavy use of these techniques is applied, this error code gets monotonous and hard to manage. Our global function will alleviate this problem.

14.2   Use Embedded SQL in a Function

DataWindows provide most of the power necessary for today's client/server business applications. They are truly a marvelous piece of work. Their simple existence has virtually eliminated the need for handwritten SQL. However, in their inevitable wisdom, PowerSoft provides us the ability to embed SQL right into our PowerScript code. With this ability, complete control is bestowed upon the developer. In this How-To, a simple yet powerful function allows you to populate a ListBox or DropDownListBox with the data from any column of any table. Normally, a DataWindow could be used for just such a result, but this technique gives you a jump start if you simply need a selection list for the user. Also, application size is reduced over the DataWindow technique, since no overhead for the additional DataWindow object is required.

14.3   Build a String Parser

Strings are a wonderful data type. It is not uncommon to initialize a string with a number of values, each separated by a delimiter of some type. When a specific value is needed, it can be pulled out of that string based on some key value. That is one use for a string parser. Another use is to manipulate the string in some fashion that always produces some determined value. When a user enters data into a string, it may be necessary to ensure that the value follows some rules. For example, assume your user will enter a city, and later you allow them to search for a customer by city. Capitalization and spacing play a key role in determining whether or not they can later find what they entered. In this How-To, the string parser will remove multiple spaces between words, and capitalize the first letter of each word. With this function, it is fairly safe to assume that your data will stay consistent. This function could be applied to a city column so if the user enters "los   angeles" it will be converted to its proper form of "Los Angeles".

14.4   Declare an Object Level Function

Unlike global functions, object functions are only known by a particular object, and only available when that object is open. An example of this is the DirList() function. DirList() works on ListBox controls only. If no ListBox exists on a window, DirList() cannot be called. Object level functions are one step towards object oriented programming. They encapsulate the behavior of an object. Just as scripts are written for a particular object and used only when that object is manipulated, so are object level functions. This How-To provides a window object function that performs an insert on a DataWindow.

14.5   Close All Open MDI Sheets

It is easy to close one MDI sheet. The Close() function exists for just that reason. What if you want all of the open sheets to close? This function will do it for you. You may want to allow only sheets of a certain type to close, which can be accomplished by passing an argument to control just what type of sheet it closes. This How-To demonstrates closing all sheets. Closing sheets of a particular type is left to you as an exercise.

14.6   Hide Object Level Functions

By default, any object level function is available to the outside world. This is referred to as *Public* access. If we have a window function, as presented above, any script in any object (such as a menu) is allowed to call that function, provided the window containing the function is open. However, there are times when the function must be hidden from view, allowing only the owner (or optionally its descendants) access to it. There exist two levels of protection, and both will be discussed in this How-To. Only one of these levels is incorporated however. These functions are termed *helper functions*, as they help the object, but are not available to the outside world. This How-To expands the object function in How-To 14.4. A public update function will be added, along with the ability to automatically perform a COMMIT or ROLLBACK based on the success of the DataWindow Update() function. You will add an argument to the function indicating whether or not to complete the transaction. If so, the function calls this new helper function to do the work. This new function then returns the success code (SQLCode) to the public function. This helper function clearly should be hidden, as we don't want the COMMIT or ROLLBACK performed unless the public function deems it necessary.

14.7   Build a Custom User Entry Message Box

PowerBuilder gives us the MessageBox() function to quickly and easily obtain input from the user. It is configurable to just about every need. Every need except one. What if you want the user to indicate a text based response, such as a password, zip code, or other value? For this, you would have to create your own dialog box to handle the response. Then you have to worry about the Title and StaticText in the box if you want it truly customizable. Or, you could create one dialog box for every need, clearly not a valid option. The function presented here allows you to customize a user entry message box each time the function is called.

COMPLEXITY
BEGINNING

14.1   How do I...
Declare a global function?

Problem

I have some processing that is common to all my applications. I use the same code over and over again. Each time I need a certain behavior, I code statements similar to those I've already written. This makes it difficult to maintain my application, and I always seem to do things just a little differently each time. How can I create a function that I can call whenever I need it?

Technique

User-defined functions allow you to write code once, and invoke it any time it is needed. Additionally, functions can accept arguments, allowing you to pass data to them. They usually return a value to the caller to indicate what has happened. This return value may be either a result of calculations performed, or a return code indicating success or failure. PowerBuilder provides the developer with two different types of user-defined functions—global and object functions. This How-To presents the global type, with a handy function that may be used in every application you write. A global function is stored in a PowerBuilder library as a function object. Whenever you need to call it, you use the syntax common to PowerBuilder functions such as Open(). Global functions are always available, provided the library containing the function is in your library search list.

Steps

Open and run the sample application in the file GLBLFUNC.PBL. This library contains the example function for this How-To. The user defined function is named f_CheckSQLError(). The application will attempt to connect to the database. If successful, the application should display an MDI frame window with one sheet open. An error message is displayed only if the database connection fails. This function checks the SQLCode attribute of a transaction object and optionally performs COMMIT or ROLLBACK operations. This transaction processing is not invoked here, since no data access occurs during a connect operation. However, every time you write embedded SQL in your scripts (such as CONNECT or UPDATE), good programming practice dictates that you check the success or failure of such action. If you use a lot of embedded SQL, providing such error checking can get monotonous. Using this function gives you the ability to cut down on your code, and gives your applications a common look and feel.

1. Create a new application and library for the topics of this chapter. Name the library GLBLFUNC.PBL and call the application object "userfunc". Generate an application template. By using this template, more time can be focused on the topics at hand, and less on setting up an MDI application.

2. Start the Global Function painter by clicking on the appropriate icon on the PowerBar. PowerBuilder opens the Select Function dialog box. Press New to declare a new function. All user-defined functions must be declared. This declaration tells PowerBuilder three important things. First, the function requires a name. Second, it must know what type of data to return to the caller. Third, you have the option of passing arguments on which the function will operate.

3. PowerBuilder opens the New Function dialog box. This function is called f_CheckSQLError, returns a Boolean type, and takes two arguments. Figure 14-1 shows the completed function declaration. The return value tells the caller whether or not the function was successful. The first argument is a transaction object such as SQLCA. Since PowerBuilder allows you to create your own transaction objects, this function must know which one to use. The second argument specifies whether or not to do a COMMIT or ROLLBACK as appropriate. This will usually be TRUE (do the COMMIT or ROLLBACK). When complete, press the OK button. Table 14-1 shows the attributes for this function.

ATTRIBUTE	VALUE	DATATYPE
Name	f_checksqlerror	
Returns	boolean	
Argument 1	at_trans	transaction
Argument 2	ab_commit	Boolean

Table 14-1 Attributes for global function declaration

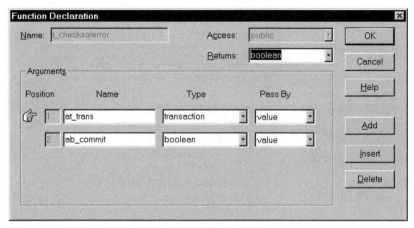

Figure 14-1 Completed function declaration

4. Place the following code in the function. The function checks the value of the SQLCode attribute of the transaction object you pass. If it is less than 0 (error), it performs a ROLLBACK if the second argument is true. It then issues an error message using the SQLErrText attribute of the transaction object. If SQLCode does not indicate an error, and the second argument is true, a COMMIT is issued. The function returns TRUE if the SQL statement was successful; otherwise it returns FALSE. Close the PowerScript editor when you are finished. If the code compiles without errors, you now have a function object in your library named f_CheckSQLError().

```
//Global function to test sql code.
//Arguments:
//at_trans is of type transaction
//ab_commit is of type Boolean - true-do commit/rollback, false-don't
Boolean lb_return = TRUE


If at_trans.SQLCode < 0 Then
//Rollback if commit/rollback flag is true
    If ab_commit Then
        Rollback Using at_trans;
    End If
    MessageBox ( "Database", "The following error occurred:~r~n" + &
                at_trans.SQLErrText)
    lb_return = FALSE
Else
//Commit if commit/rollback flag is true
    If ab_commit Then
        Commit Using at_trans;
    End If
End If


Return lb_return
```

5. Replace the script in the application Open event with the following code. This script attempts a database connection, and uses f_CheckSQLError() to check for errors. If no error occurs, the script opens the MDI frame window.

```
/* Populate sqlca for a connection */
SQLCA.DBMS      = "ODBC"
SQLCA.DBParm    = "ConnectString='DSN=zoo;UID=dba;PWD=sql'"

Connect;

//Check the error code using the global function.
If f_CheckSQLError ( SQLCA, FALSE ) Then
    /* Open MDI frame window since there was no error*/
    Open ( w_genapp_frame )
End If
```

6. Save the Application object and run the application. To test the function, you may want to comment out the first two lines of code that populate SQLCA. This will force an error, and the connection will not occur.

How It Works

Since this function is global, the calling syntax does not use dot notation. The arguments passed from the calling script end up in the variables at_trans and ab_commit. These arguments are passed by value, meaning that they are copies of the original variables. Any changes the function would make (this example does not change the variables) would have no effect on the original values. Passing arguments by reference passes the address of (a pointer to) the original variable. Therefore, changes made to the argument in the function would change the original value. The first argument is a transaction object and is provided, since you may declare multiple transaction objects and instantiate them in code. Quite often, SQLCA alone may not be sufficient for large, complex applications. The second argument to f_CheckSQLError() indicates whether or not the function should perform transaction processing (COMMIT/ROLLBACK) automatically. First, the function assumes that the most recent SQL statement was successful, so the return value (lb_return) is initialized to TRUE in the declaration. By examining the SQLCode attribute of at_trans (this is a pointer to the transaction object you pass), the function acts accordingly. From now on, you would simply call this function after every embedded SQL statement, instead of rewriting the error checking each time. The function tells you (through the return value) whether or not an error occurred, so you can handle future code appropriately. This information was used in the application Open event to determine if it was okay to open the frame window. If an error occurred during the connect, the frame will not open.

Comments

Some developers consider global functions inappropriate in today's object orient-ed programming environments. Other How-Tos in this chapter present alternatives to the global function. It is up to you to determine what type of function to create based on the intent of the function. No judgments are made here as to the appro-priateness of global functions. They are supported in PowerBuilder, and many developers successfully use them. They may execute slightly more slowly, since they may not be in memory when called, but it is doubtful that this speed difference would be per-ceptible to the user.

COMPLEXITY

INTERMEDIATE

14.2   How do I...
Use embedded SQL in a function?

Problem

Every so often, I need to populate a ListBox or DropDownListBox with data from a table. Every time I do this, I write the code necessary for the task. I would like to create a function and pass it some arguments to indicate which table and column to select from. When I try to do this, either the script won't compile, or the code just does not work. There must be a way to pass this information to a function and let the function do the work. What is that method?

Technique

PowerBuilder allows you to write embedded SQL along with PowerScript. Embedded SQL commands are sent straight to the database, and not executed by PowerBuilder. Normally, all SQL operations are handled by a DataWindow, but there are some cases where it makes sense to embed the code yourself instead. If, for exam-ple, you want to give the users a ListBox from which they will select one value, consider embedding the SQL code in a script, and populate the ListBox with the rows you want. If it is a simple list, this approach may make more sense than creating a DataWindow object, associating it with a DataWindow control, performing a SetTransObject(), and calling Retrieve(). However, when you write embedded SQL, you have to know what table and column(s) you want. This is normally known at design time. If it is not known, you have a slightly harder task in front of you. In this How-To, you will create a function that will populate a ListBox with string data. By passing the table and column(s) as arguments to the function, you can reuse this function whenever you need it.

Steps

Open and run the application in the EMBFUNC.PBL library. This opens the dialog box shown in Figure 14-2. In the Table SingleLineEdit control, type "person" (without the quote marks). Type "last_name" (again, without quotes) in the Columns SingleLineEdit control. Press the Populate button. The ListBox fills with the data from that table. You can specify multiple columns by using the column concatenation character in the Columns edit box. For Sybase SQL AnyWhere databases, this character is the double vertical bar (||). Enter "first_name || ' ' || last_name" in the Columns SingleLineEdit, check the Clear contents on load CheckBox, and press Populate. Now the ListBox contains the first and last names separated by a space. You will create the function that performs these tasks.

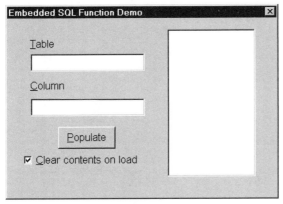

Figure 14-2 Embedded SQL Demo function dialog box

1. Create a new Application object called "embfunc" and save it in a library called EMBFUNC.PBL.

2. Create a new window object that looks like the one in Figure 14-2 above. Give this window and controls the properties shown in Table 14-2.

OBJECT/CONTROL	PROPERTY	VALUE
Window	Name	w_sql
	TitleBar	"Embedded SQL Function Demo"
	Type	Response
SingleLineEdit	Name	sle_table
	Auto HScroll	TRUE
	Accelerator	t
	Name	sle_column
	Auto HScroll	TRUE

continued on next page

continued from previous page

	Accelerator	c
ListBox	Name	lb_rows
	VScroll Bar	TRUE
CheckBox	Name	cbx_clear
	Text	"&Clear contents on load"
	Checked	TRUE
Static Text	Name	SLE_1
	Text	"&Table"
	Name	SLE_2
	Text	"&Column"
	Name	SLE_3
	Text	""
ComamndButton	Name	cb_populate
	Text	"&Populate"

Table 14-2 Attributes for SQL window

3. Create a window function. Give it the properties shown in Table 14-3. This function will populate a ListBox with the data from the table/column combination specified by the arguments. It also uses the specified transaction object for retrieval and a Boolean value to indicate whether or not to clear the ListBox prior to retrieving the data. It then returns the number of rows read from the table.

PROPERTY	VALUE	DATATYPE
Name	wf_sql	
Returns	long	
Argument 1	as_table	string
Argument 2	as_column	string
Argument 3	at_trans	transaction
Argument 4	ab_clear	Boolean
Argument 5	alb_control	ListBox

Table 14-3 Attributes for embedded SQL function

4. Place the following code in this function. In order to fill a ListBox, you must retrieve the rows one at a time. When you write embedded SQL, the result set can return only one row at a time. If you try selecting more than one row, a runtime error results. In order to populate the ListBox with numerous rows, it is necessary to use a *database cursor*. A cursor allows you to build the result set of an SQL statement (which occurs at the database when the cursor is opened), and retrieve the rows one at a time using FETCH.

This function builds the SELECT statement based on the table/column passed as arguments, declares a cursor, and fetches the rows from it. In the FETCH, the script tells the database to put the row in the program variable ls_column. The colon (:) is required in front of the variable name to indicate that it is a variable and not a column name. It then uses the AddItem() function of the ListBox to place that row into it. This loop continues until the transaction object's SQLCode indicates an error (all rows have been retrieved). Finally, it returns the number of retrieved rows back to the calling script. Save the function and the window when you are finished.

```
Long ll_rows
String ls_column, ls_select

//Build the string used for the select statement
ls_select = "Select " + as_column + " From " + as_table

//Since we don't know the input parameters, we need to declare
//a 'dynamic' cursor and prepare it for use
DECLARE lc_cur DYNAMIC CURSOR FOR SQLSA;
PREPARE SQLSA FROM :ls_select;

//Clear the listbox if user said so
If ab_clear Then alb_control.Reset()

//Open the cursor so we can get the rows one at a time
OPEN DYNAMIC lc_cur;

//Get the first row. Read in into the variable ls_column
Fetch lc_cur Into :ls_column;

//Process each row until the transaction object says it's done
Do While at_trans.SQLCode = 0
    ll_rows ++
//Add the row to the listbox and get the next row
    alb_control.AddItem ( ls_column )
    Fetch lc_cur Into :ls_column;
Loop

//Clean up so we can reuse the cursor
Close lc_cur;

Return ll_rows
```

5. Place the following code in the Clicked event of cb_populate. This script simply calls the function you created above.

```
//Retrieve the data. Simply call the function and pass the required
//arguments

long ll_rows
ll_rows = wf_SQL ( sle_table.text, sle_column.text, SQLCA, &
                        cbx_clear.checked, lb_rows )

st_3.text = String ( ll_rows ) + " rows retrieved"
```

6. Return to the Application object, and place the following code in the Open event.

```
//Open the window
Open ( w_sql )
```

7. Save all objects and run the application.

How It Works

Using embedded SQL allows you to return columns from one row into program variable(s). These variables are called *host* variables, and require the preceding colon to indicate that they are not column names. However, you can only return one row at a time, so this function declares a cursor. When a script opens the cursor, the database performs the indicated SQL statement, and produces the result set. However, the result set stays at the database until the application performs a FETCH operation. The FETCH retrieves the next row, and places the data into the host variable. The script then increments the counter variable that holds the number of rows returned, and adds the data to the ListBox. This loop continues until SQLCA.SQLCode indicates an error condition. This example is slightly more complex than you will typically use for embedded SQL. This is because the input parameters (the table name and column) are not known at design time. They are passed to the function. Therefore, the function must declare the cursor as *dynamic*, and *prepare* the cursor using PowerBuilder's dynamic staging area (SQLSA). If you know the table and column(s) at design time, you would use SQL syntax similar to the following:

```
DECLARE my_cur Cursor For SELECT visit_date FROM guests USING SQLCA;
Open my_cur;
FETCH my_cur INTO :ld_date;
etc...
```

In the above example, the table and column are explicitly used, as opposed to using variables that represent them. If the input parameters to the SQL statement are *not* known, you must declare the cursor using the "dynamic" modifier, and "prepare" the statement with SQLSA.

Comments

Cursors (or any embedded SQL) will run slightly slower than using a DataWindow, but using them is sometimes a better mechanism. DataWindows are powerful and feature rich, and therefore are sometimes overkill for the task at hand. Even though the function retrieves data into a string variable, it will work with any column type. If you were to fill the ListBox with the visit_date column from the guests table, it will all work just fine. Why? When the FETCH executes, PowerBuilder will perform a type conversion for you if it can.

COMPLEXITY
INTERMEDIATE

14.3 How do I...
Build a string parser?

Problem

My users frequently enter information such as first name and last name, or city and state, and I need to ensure that the proper spacing and capitalization are maintained. Typically, this information must be unique, and will be used for searching later. I would like to build a function that formats the strings with proper spacing and ensures that each word of the string is capitalized. How can I build a reusable function that parses and formats the strings?

Technique

This need is a good use for recursion, but recursion under Windows is dangerous. Recursion makes heavy use of the stack, and, if improperly coded, could bring the system down. This danger is not limited to Windows, but is a real hazard in any environment. The functions presented here will not use recursion, although recursion is possible with PowerBuilder. You will build two generic functions in this How-To. The first performs a search and replace, in order to remove any multiple spaces the user may enter. You could use this function any time you need to provide a search and replace capability. Next, another user-defined function performs the capitalization of each word in a string. Both of these functions lend themselves to a recursive technique, and converting them to recursive functions would be a good exercise for you.

Steps

Open and run the application in the PARSE.PBL library. When the main window opens, type "los   angeles, ca" (lots of spaces) in the SingleLineEdit control and press the Parse button. The scripts transform the string into "Los Angeles, Ca". This is a useful function for formatting proper names such as cities so they can be easily located later. This ensures that data does not end up in different formats on the database. Figure 14-3 shows the window at runtime.

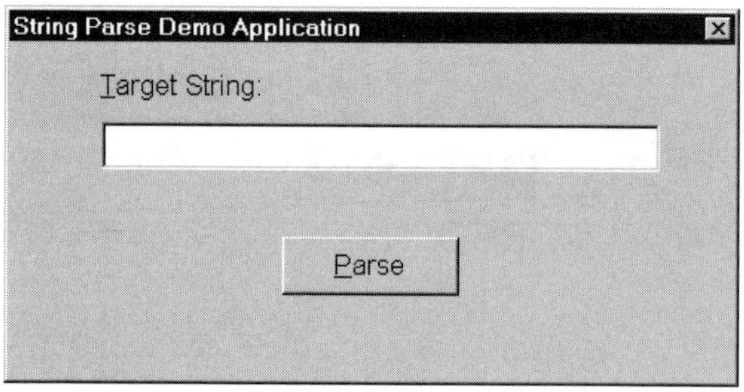

Figure 14-3 Parse window

1. Create a new Application object called "parse", and save it in a library called PARSE.PBL.

2. Create a new window object, and give it the controls and properties shown in Table 14-10 below. Use Figure 14-3 as a guide.

OBJECT / CONTROL	PROPERTY	VALUE
Window	Name	w_parse
	Title	"String Parse Demo Application"
	Type	Response
SingleLineEdit	Name	sle_target
	Auto HScroll	TRUE
	Accelerator	"t"
StaticText	Text	"&Target String:"
CommandButton	Name	cb_parse
	Text	"&Parse"

Table 14-10 Attributes for w_parse window and controls

3. Declare a new window function called wf_SearchAndReplace(). Give this function the properties shown in Table 14-11. Place the following code in this function. When you consider a search and replace operation, several data elements are required. First, you need a target string (the one on which to perform the operation). This is the first argument (as_string) to the function. It is passed by reference so the function can modify the value. The second argument indicates the string you want to replace. The function searches for this value in the target string using the PowerScript Pos() function. Pos() returns the position of a string within another string (the target in this case). Upon finding the search string, the function uses the PowerScript Replace() function. Replace() has the following declaration

```
StringVal = Replace ( SearchString, Start, Length, ReplaceString )
```

where SearchString is the string you wish to replace into, Start is the starting character position, Length is the number of characters to replace, and ReplaceString is what you want to replace with. The function returns the string in its replaced form. For example, with a target string of "Powerbuilder" and a search string of "erb", and a replace string of "erB", the call would look like:

```
Result = Replace ( "Powerbuilder", 4, "erB", 3 )
```

This user defined function iterates through the target string looking for the search string. Upon finding it, it calls Replace() to do the work.

```
Integer li_len, li_pos, li_count, li_right

//Get the length of the search string. Need this later
li_len = Len ( as_searchfor )

//Find the position of the search string in the reference argument
li_pos = Pos ( as_string, as_searchfor )

//Loop through the string, and replace all occurences
Do While li_pos > 0
    as_string = Replace ( as_string, li_pos, Len ( as_searchfor ), &
        as_replace )

//Increment the count of items replaced
    li_count++

//Get the next occurence of the search string and continue until done
    li_pos = Pos ( as_string, as_searchfor, li_pos )
Loop

//Return the count of replaced strings
Return li_count
```

PROPERTY	VALUE	DATATYPE	PASS BY
Name	wf_SearchAndReplace		
Returns	Integer		
Argument 1	as_string	string	Reference
Argument 2	as_searchfor	string	Value
Argument 3	as_replace	string	Value

Table 14-11 Attributes for wf_SearchAndReplace() function

4. Declare a new window function. Give the function the properties shown in Table 14-12. Place the following code in the function. This function capitalizes each word in the string. It gets called after the search and replace function, so you are assured that only one space separates each word. The function takes one argument, a reference string which points to the string you wish to capitalize. This function works much like the search and replace function, except the string in question gets broken into three pieces and reassembled. This is done just to demonstrate another way to manipulate strings. However, wf_Cap() parses the string based on the position of each space within the string. Upon finding a space, the code breaks the string into left, middle, and right hand strings, uses the PowerScript Upper() function to capitalize the letter stripped from the string, and reassembles the components. This operation continues until the Pos() function runs out of spaces to find.

```
Integer li_pos

//Capitalize the first character
as_string = Upper ( Mid ( as_string, 1, 1 ) ) + &
            Right ( as_string, Len ( as_string ) - 1 )

//Find the first space. Assume that the next character is the
//start of a word
li_pos = Pos ( as_string, " " )

Do While li_pos > 0
//Strip off all characters to the left, cap the next letter
//and add all characters on the right
    as_string = Left ( as_string, li_pos ) + &
                Upper ( Mid ( as_string, li_pos + 1, 1 ) ) + &
                Right ( as_string, Len ( as_string ) - li_pos - 1)

//Get the position of the next space
    li_pos = Pos ( as_string, " ", li_pos + 1 )

//Continue until done
Loop


Return
```

PROPERTY	VALUE	DATATYPE	PASS BY
Name	wf_cap		
Returns	(none)		
Argument 1	as_string	string	reference

Table 14-12 Attributes for wf_cap() function

5. Open the PowerScript painter for the Clicked event of the Parse CommandButton. Place the following code in this event. This calls the search and replace function, followed by the wf_Cap function. Finally, save the window.

```
//Since the parse functions use reference arguments, turn off the
//redraw so the user does not see the result until done
sle_target.SetRedraw ( FALSE )

//Remove all extra spaces
wf_searchandreplace ( sle_target.text, "  ", " " )
```

```
//Captitalize all first letters
wf_cap ( sle_target.text )
```

```
//Turn redraw on to show results
sle_target.SetRedraw ( TRUE )
```

6. Return to the Application painter, and place the following code in the Open event to start the application running. Save all objects and run the application.

```
//Open the parse window
Open ( w_parse )
```

How It Works

Assume you type in the string "los   angeles ". First, wf_SearchAndReplace() removes all double spaces, resulting in the string "los angeles". Then, wf_cap() parses the string, starting at position 1. The first time through the wf_Cap() function, it converts the first letter. It now starts searching for spaces. It finds the first space in position 4. It then strips off everything to the left ("Los"), the next letter, which gets converted ("A"), and finally the remainder of the string ("ngeles"). Using string concatenation, it reassembles these three pieces, and continues searching for spaces, starting at the position in which the last space was found. This continues until no more spaces are found in the string. At this point, the function has completed, and the reference argument contains the finished result.

Comments

Recursion is a powerful but dangerous technique, though it can be very useful for string parsing. Improperly coded, it can cause your memory space to become corrupt, usually due to overflowing the stack. Since a function's return address and arguments use the stack, it can eat up considerable memory. If you don't return from the function at the right time, it is possible that the function will run until the stack space runs out. Therefore, the example presented here uses an iterative approach. You will find that this approach runs slightly faster, won't corrupt stack space, and is far easier to debug and maintain. Still, with proper design, lots of testing, a little trial and error (and occasionally re-booting!), recursive functions do work just fine.

COMPLEXITY
INTERMEDIATE

14.4 How do I...
Declare an object level function?

Problem

I have written some global functions, but I would like to make my applications more object oriented. Those in the "object oriented know" seem to frown on anything labeled "global." Some of my functions are only appropriate to certain objects, and should not be available globally. These operations only make sense to one object, and I want the object to manage the details of the function. How can I create an object level function, what other benefits do object functions present, and how do I call it from other objects?

Technique

In How-To 14-1, you created a global function. Object functions are the second user-defined function type supported by PowerBuilder. The object functions that PowerBuilder supports are menu, window, and user object functions. Object functions are declared as a part of these objects, and are known only when the object is in memory. These functions are declared in the appropriate painter (such as the Window painter for a window object function), and contain code that is useful only for that object type. In this How-To, you will write an insert function for a sheet object, and call this function from the menu. This is a very common technique, as it allows the window to manage the insert, but can be called by other supporting objects.

Steps

Open the application in the OBJFUNC.PBL library. From the Edit menu, select Insert. The sheet window contains a DataWindow control into which the user can insert a new row. This clearly is a function that only makes sense to this object (the sheet), and therefore a valid reason to choose this technique. Further, the menu is allowed to call this function. When the sheet object performs the insert, some default values are provided for the DataWindow. Most of these come from the PowerBuilder repository through the extended attributes of the table, but one is provided in code. Figure 14-4 shows the application with the Edit menu open.

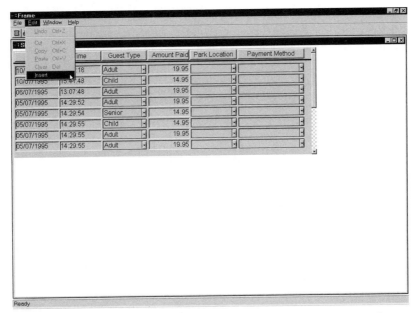

Figure 14-4 Application with Edit menu showing new menu item

1. Create a new Application object called "objfunc", and save it in a library called OBJFUNC.PBL. Have PowerBuilder generate an application template for this application.

2. Create a DataWindow object based on the guests table. This should include all rows from the table. Ensure that the tab order is non-zero, so the user will be able to edit the data. Sort the data by visit_date (descending) and visit_time (ascending). Save this in the OBJFUNC.PBL library created previously using the name d_guestlist.

3. Open the w_genapp_sheet window object. Place a DataWindow control on the window, and associate it with the DataWindow object created in step 2. Give the control the properties shown in Table 14-13.

CONTROL	PROPERTY	VALUE
DataWindow	Name	dw_guests
	VScrollBar	TRUE
	Border	None

Table 14-13 Property settings for DataWindow control

4. Place the following code in the Open event of w_genapp_sheet. This code includes the default code that PowerBuilder generated with the application template. Add only the code shown below in bold. This sets up the transaction object and retrieves the data.

```
int li_Count

dw_guests.SetTransObject ( SQLCA )
dw_guests.Retrieve ()

//Following code comes from PB application template
/* Sheet opening - reflect sheet count in title */
li_Count = w_genapp_frame.wf_getsheetcount ()
this.Title = "Sheet:" + string (li_Count)

/* Modify menu text for platform */
w_genapp_frame.wf_setmenutext (menuid)
```

5. Select Window Functions… from the Declare menu of the Window painter. PowerBuilder opens the Select Function in the Window dialog box. The list of available functions should be empty. Click New to create a new window function. The resulting New Function dialog box opens, and looks exactly like the Declare Global Function dialog. The only difference between them is the *Access* DropDownListBox has been enabled, allowing you to choose one of three access levels. Access levels dictate the *visibility* of the function (what other objects are able to call this function). Make sure to select the default of Public for this function. Declare the function as shown in Table 14-14. Place the following code in this new function. First, the function uses embedded SQL to obtain the highest guest id used so far. This is the primary key for the guests table, and therefore will be unique. If the return code from the database is fine, the script then inserts one row into the DataWindow, and the guest_id column is set to the highest id + 1. Close the PowerScript painter, and save the window.

```
Boolean lb_return
Long ll_row, ll_current_row, ll_guest

ll_current_row = dw_guests.GetRow ()

//Find the maximum guest id using embedded sql
SELECT max ( guest_id )
  INTO :ll_guest
  FROM guests
 USING SQLCA;

//Check error
If SQLCA.SQLCode < 0 Then
    lb_return = FALSE
ELSE
    ll_row = dw_guests.InsertRow ( ll_current_row + 1 )

    If ll_row < 1 Then
//Insert did not work
```

```
        lb_return = FALSE
    Else
        lb_return = TRUE
//Set some defaults for the inserted row
        dw_guests.ScrollToRow ( ll_row )
        dw_guests.SetItem ( ll_row, "guest_id", ll_guest + 1 )
    End If
End If


Return lb_return
```

PROPERTY	VALUE
Name	wf_insert
Returns	Boolean
Arguments	None

Table 14-14 Properties for Window function wf_insert

6. Open the menu m_genapp_sheet. Add an Insert item to the end of the Edit menu, and place the following code in the Clicked event of m_insert. This code first finds out which sheet is active. It needs this information in order to call the function. Since the wf_insert() function is now *encapsulated* within the window, the script needs to know which window is active, and calls the function using standard dot notation.

```
//Declare an instance of the sheet
w_genapp_sheet lw_sheet

//Find out which sheet is in the foreground so we can call the function
//inside it.
lw_sheet = ParentWindow.GetActiveSheet ()

//Check the validity of the active window since GetActiveSheet() returns
//an invalid value if an error occurred.
If IsValid ( lw_sheet ) Then
    lw_sheet.wf_Insert ()
End If
```

7. Save the menu and run the application. When the sheet opens, select Insert from the Edit menu and observe what happens.

How It Works

This object function is encapsulated within the sheet window. This is one step towards object orientation. This function clearly makes sense only to this window, and should not be a global function. You should be familiar with other object functions. One such example is the InsertRow() function of a DataWindow. When you call the InsertRow() function, you must preface it with the name of the control into which you want to insert. The standard object.function() syntax of dot notation is required to indicate *which* control gets the new row. The same holds true here. You have created a function that is a part of a window object, so it must be called using the same dot notation. In order to figure out which window function to call, the GetActiveSheet() function was used. Since there may be several sheets open at any one time, GetActiveSheet() tells you which sheet's function to use. Since this application opens instances of the w_genapp_sheet object, you must declare a variable whose data type is w_genapp_sheet, and assign the return value from GetActiveSheet() to it. If you simply declare a variable of type "window", and assign it the return value from GetActiveSheet(), a compile time error occurs. Take the following example. The compiler error occurs on the line shown in bold. The error occurs since PowerBuilder checks the *class* definition of the variable (lw_win) in order to validate that the wf_Insert() function really exists. Since normal window objects do not contain a function by this name, the compilation fails. The only class that has this function is the w_genapp_sheet class.

```
Window lw_win      //OK to do
lw_win = ParentWindow.GetActiveSheet() //This works as well since
                                       //GetActiveSheet() return a pointer to
                                       //a window

If IsValid ( lw_win ) Then    //Still OK, since the active window was found
        lw_win.wf_insert()    //Error-wf_insert not part of of standard
                              //window class
End If
```

Comments

This is one simple example of an object level function. In How-To 14-6, you will see an example of a Protected level function. Only the object (in this case w_genapp_sheet) or descendants of it can call a Protected function. This window will not save any data that you insert. That will also be the topic of How-To 14-6. In this example, the object function had an access level of Public, meaning that any other script is able to call it, provided the window is open (loaded in memory). How is this different from a global function? Global functions may be called at any time, by any script. Public functions may be called by any script, provided that the object containing them (w_genapp_sheet in this case) is loaded into memory (open). If w_genapp_sheet had never been open, a runtime error would occur when calling the function. That's just the point of using the IsValid() function — to ensure that the window is available. You may have been tempted to place the code in the Clicked event of the Insert menu item instead of a function. Though this would have worked, it is not the best place for it. Since the code operates on controls within the sheet (the DataWindow), the function clearly belongs in the window. In object oriented programming, no object should do the work of another object. One object sends a message to another (a function call in this case) to request its services.

COMPLEXITY
BEGINNING

14.5 How do I...
Close all open MDI sheets?

Problem

My MDI application has a Close menu item on the File menu that allows the user to close the active sheet. However, I want to close all open sheets, leaving the frame as the only active window. How can I do this?

Technique

PowerBuilder gives you, the developer, functions that tell you which sheet is active. If you read How-To 14.4, you saw an example of one of these functions. This How-To uses this information, along with a variable known as a *reference* variable. The script you will write in this How-To captures a reference to the active sheet, and closes it. Using a loop, the process continues until it determines that no more sheets are open.

Steps

Open and run the sample application in the CLOSEALL.PBL library. Since this application was generated using the PowerBuilder application template, it will automatically open a sheet when the MDI frame window opens. Use the New menu item in the File menu (or <CTRL>-<N>) to open several more sheets. Arrange them in a tiled configuration so all the sheets are visible. Then, from the Window menu, select Close All Sheets. After doing so, only the frame window will remain open.

1. Create a new Application object called "closeall" and save it in a library named CLOSEALL.PBL. Select Yes when PowerBuilder asks you if you want an application template.

2. Open the Window painter and load the w_genapp_frame object. Declare a window level function called wf_CloseAll for this window. This function returns an integer and takes no arguments. Place the following code in this function. Since the action of closing all of the open sheets is a job for the frame, the function is an object function of the frame object. First, it declares a variable of type window. Just as with integers, strings, and all other standard datatypes, PowerBuilder allows you to declare variables of any object type. This is called a *reference* variable, since it is used as a pointer (reference) to a particular object. This function uses the PowerScript function GetActiveSheet(), which returns a reference to the sheet that is active. Most PowerBuilder functions return a value to indicate a success or failure code, and GetActiveSheet() is no exception. A successful function call results in a pointer to a valid (open) sheet object. However, if the function fails, the return value is a reference to an invalid sheet. Because of this, wf_CloseAll() uses the IsValid() PowerScript function. IsValid() returns a TRUE if the indicated window variable points to a valid object; otherwise it returns FALSE. IsValid() works with any object type, not just window objects. Notice that this validity test is the test expression of a Do...While looping construct. If the reference is valid, it simply uses the variable to point to the window, and close it using the Close() function. The loop continues until the reference variable contains an invalid value, at which time the loop ends, and the frame window is all that remains open. In the process, it increments a counter used as the return value. This is the count of the number of sheets that closed, and is passed back to the caller.

```
Integer li_sheet_count
Window lw_win

//Get the active sheet
lw_win = this.GetActiveSheet()

//Check for the validity of the reference.
//If it is invalid, nothing is open. Continue until an invalid
//reference is found, meaning nothing is left
Do While IsValid ( lw_win )
//Increment the number of sheets found
    li_sheet_count ++
//Close the window and get the new active sheet
    Close ( lw_win )
    lw_win = this.GetActiveSheet()
Loop

Return li_sheet_count
```

3. Open the m_genapp_sheet menu and place an item labeled Close All Sheets in the Window menu. Place the following code in the Clicked event for this item. This simply calls the wf_CloseAll() function.

```
Integer li_count

//Close all the open sheets
li_count = w_genapp_frame.wf_CloseAll ()
```

4. Save the objects and run the application.

How It Works

The GetActiveSheet() function returns a pointer to a window. GetActiveSheet() tells your application which sheet object is active, and the return value is assigned to a variable of type window. This reference variable could also be of any data type whose ancestor is a window (w_genapp_sheet in this example). This is the technique used here, since w_genapp_sheet is the exact sheet type that is open. Both window and w_genapp_sheet are *class* types in object oriented terms. The object w_genapp_sheet is never opened explicitly, but is used as the class object which the application instantiates at runtime. Once this reference variable contains a valid value, it can be used just as if it were an existing window object. Therefore, wf_CloseAll() uses the syntax Close(lw_win) to close whichever active window it finds.

Comments

PowerBuilder supplies several functions that allow you to manipulate sheets, and GetActiveSheet() is just one example. Other sheet-related functions include GetNextSheet(), which returns the sheet behind the specified sheet. GetFirstSheet() returns the top sheet in the frame, which may or may not be the active sheet.

COMPLEXITY
INTERMEDIATE

14.6   How do I...
Hide object level functions?

Problem

I have created some object level functions, and they are publicly accessible. However, some of my functions are so specific to the object that I don't want them called by other objects. I don't want any other object to even know that they exist. How can I create a function that is only visible to the owning object, and cannot be accessed by others?

Technique

All functions have an *access* (or privilege) level that determines their *visibility*. If an object function's access is Public, any object can call the function. There are times when this is not desirable. Some functions must only be available to the controlling object. These types of functions are called helper functions, as they help the object accomplish some tasks only when those tasks are deemed necessary by the object. It is possible to hide functions from the outside world by changing the access level. That's just what you will learn in this How-To. The access level used for hiding functions will depend on the purpose of the function. A *Protected* function can be called by the object and any descendent objects (those objects inherited from the original class object). *Private* functions are visible to the class object itself. Even inherited objects cannot access Private functions of their ancestor. This How-To will use a Protected function.

Steps

Open and run the application stored in the HIDEFUNC.PBL library. When a sheet opens, modify an existing row of data Then, use the Update item on the Edit menu to save the changes. Open another sheet by selecting New from the File menu. Notice that the new data has been saved. In this How-To, you will create a hidden function that does basic transaction management based on some criteria which the sheet maintains. Figure 14-5 shows the application displaying the Update item on the Edit menu.

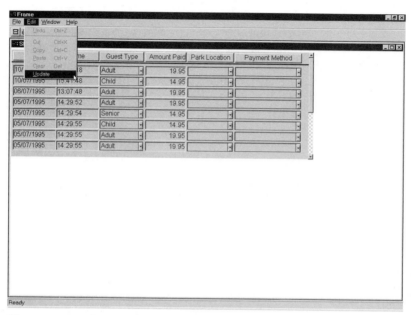

Figure 14-5 Edit menu showing Update item

1. Create a new Application object called "hidefunc" and save it in a library called HIDEFUNC.PBL. Generate an application template for this application.

2. Create a simple DataWindow object using any table you wish. Select columns from only one table, and ensure the tab order of the columns is non-zero to allow the user to edit data. Name this object "d_guestlist".

3. Start the Window painter and open w_genapp_sheet. Place a DataWindow control on the window and associate the d_guestlist object created in step 2 with this control.

4. Create a Public access function called wf_update. Table 14-13 shows the function declaration. Place the following code in the function. This performs an update on the DataWindow, based on the arguments supplied. The first argument specifies whether or not to validate the data in the column that currently has focus. The default is TRUE, but you are allowed to override this. The second argument is for coordination of multiple DataWindow updates. When a script calls the Update() function, the DataWindow resets its internal flags to indicate that all changes have been saved. If you update two or more DataWindow controls that are depending on each other, you don't want the flags updated unless all DataWindow updates succeed. This way a ROLLBACK won't leave the table and the DataWindow in inconsistent states. If both arguments are TRUE and the update succeeds, this script calls the protected function wf_transaction().

```
//Update the datawindow

Integer li_update_result

li_update_result = dw_guests.Update( ab_accepttext, ab_reset )

//Call the protected function to commit or rollback if the flags
//indicate that the processing is done. Used mainly for coordinated
//updates

If ab_accepttext AND ab_reset Then
    this.wf_transaction ( SQLCA, li_update_result )
End If

Return li_update_result
```

PROPERTY	VALUE	DATATYPE
Name	wf_update	
Access	Public	
Returns	integer	
Argument 1	ab_accepttext	Boolean
Argument 2	ab_reset	Boolean

Table 14-13 Properties for update function

5. Create another function, this time changing the access level to Protected. Give this function the properties shown in Table 14-14. Place the following code in that function. This function takes a transaction object as an argument so you are able to use transaction objects other than SQLCA. The second argument is the return code from the Update() function, and will always be 1 or -1, depending on the result of the update. If this code is 1, the function performs a COMMIT; otherwise it does a ROLLBACK.

```
//Get the value passed in the argument and perform a COMMIT or ROLLBACK
//as appropriate

If ai_code = 1 Then
    COMMIT Using at_trans;
Else
    ROLLBACK Using at_trans;
End If

Return
```

PROPERTY	VALUE	DATATYPE
Name	wf_transaction	
Access	Protected	
Returns	(None)	
Argument 1	at_trans	transaction
Argument 2	ai_code	integer

Table 14-14 Properties for protected transaction management function

6. Place the following code in the Open event for w_genapp_sheet. The code below includes the default code for the sheet that PowerBuilder generated with the template. You need only add the code shown in bold.

```
int li_Count

//Set up and retrieve the datawindow
dw_guests.SetTransObject ( SQLCA )
dw_guests.Retrieve ()

//Following code comes from PB application template
/* Sheet opening - reflect sheet count in title */
li_Count = w_genapp_frame.wf_getsheetcount ()
this.Title = "Sheet:" + string (li_Count)

/* Modify menu text for platform */
w_genapp_frame.wf_setmenutext (menuid)
```

7. Open the m_genapp_sheet menu and place an item named Update on the Edit menu. Place the following code in the Clicked event of m_update. When wf_Update() calls the DataWindow Update() function, both arguments are set to TRUE since no other DataWindow control depends on this DataWindow control. Therefore, after the update, wf_Update() calls wf_Transaction() to complete the transaction (either COMMIT or ROLLBACK).

```
//Declare an instance of the sheet
w_genapp_sheet lw_sheet

//Find out which sheet is in the foreground so we can call the function
//inside it.
lw_sheet = ParentWindow.GetActiveSheet ()

//Check the validity of the active window since GetActiveSheet() returns
//an invalid value if an error occurred.
If IsValid ( lw_sheet ) Then
    lw_sheet.wf_Update ( TRUE, TRUE )
End If
```

8. Place the following code in the Open event of the Application object. This replaces the code that PowerBuilder generated from the template.

```
/* Populate sqlca for a connection */
SQLCA.DBMS      = "ODBC"
SQLCA.DBParm    = "ConnectString='DSN=zoo;UID=dba;PWD=sql'"

Connect;

//Check the error code
If SQLCA.SQLCode = 0 Then
    /* Open MDI frame window since there was no error*/
    Open ( w_genapp_frame )
End If
```

9. Save the objects and run the application.

How It Works

The transaction management function has an access level of Protected since the sheet object should be solely responsible for its use. You would not want to allow other objects access to it. If there were outstanding transactions, other objects could corrupt the integrity of the data. If you pass FALSE to wf_Update() as the second argument, this indicates that there are other DataWindow controls that will need updating later, and therefore no transaction management will be performed. Once the update is called with both arguments TRUE, the script assumes that it is the last update, and calls the helper function if the update succeeds. Updates can be performed from a menu item, and the menu requires no knowledge of the internal workings of the functions. It simply passes arguments as appropriate for the sheet to which it is attached. Only under these certain circumstances will a COMMIT or ROLLBACK be performed, based on data internal to the sheet. An outside object will not be allowed to perform this action.

Comments

The ability to hide object functions is powerful. These functions help the object accomplish certain tasks that are not relevant to other objects, or could be detrimental if called by other objects. Private and Protected functions are similar to your ATM card. They are for you to use when appropriate, but no one else should have access unless you specify. This is one more step towards object orientation. It demonstrates the concept of encapsulation and data protection.

COMPLEXITY
INTERMEDIATE

14.7 How do I...
Build a custom user entry message box?

Problem

I have used the PowerBuilder MessageBox() function for simple user communication. However, I would like to create my own message box in which the user will enter a value, and have the message box pass the value back to my script. Ideally, this window should be reusable, so I'd like to configure the box's Titlebar and provide a custom text message at runtime. How do I create this message box-style window, and pass data to and receive data from it?

Technique

The PowerBuilder MessageBox() function is great for most applications. However, it allows for only limited user input. If you need to obtain a value from the user which the user will type in, you must create your own dialog box using a Response style window. On this window, you would need to place a SingleLineEdit control for data entry, OK and Cancel buttons, and usually some StaticText which holds the message to the user. Then, when a script opens the window, it could pass a string value to it that will become the title and message text. Passing values to and from a window is quite easy, as you will see.

Steps

Open and run the application in the ENTRYBOX.PBL library. When the window opens, enter a value and press OK. The dialog box closes and displays the value that you entered. The message box window is shown in Figure 14-6.

Figure 14-6 Custom user entry message box

1. Create a new Application object called "entrybox", and save it in a library called ENTRYBOX.PBL. Do not have PowerBuilder generate an application template.

2. Create a new window object, using Figure 14-6 as a guide. Give the window and the controls the properties shown in Table 14-15. Place the following code in the Open event of the window. This script obtains a string value from the Message object's StringParm attribute. The Message object is responsible for communication between objects. The Message object is a global object, so you must get the value from it before other objects change the values maintained by it. When the window opens (which is shown below), the calling script passes a string value to it using the Message object. You should always get the value from this object as the *first* line of executable code in a window Open event, since other scripts (or applications) may change the values in the object. This string value contains the text used for the Titlebar and the message text, which are separated by a tab (~t) character. This script parses the string to obtain each piece, and sets these properties accordingly. Since you are responsible for passing this string to the window, you have control over what the window displays. If no value is passed, or an error occurs, the window provides defaults for these values. This makes the entry box reusable.

```
String ls_message
Integer li_pos

//Get the string message sent when the window was opened
ls_message = Message.StringParm

//Find the string delimiter
li_pos = Pos ( ls_message, "~t" )

If li_pos > 0 Then
    This.Title = Left ( ls_message, li_pos - 1 )
    st_prompt.text = Right ( ls_message, Len ( ls_message ) - li_pos )
Else
//If there is no delimiter, or no value in the message object, provide
//a default title and message value
    This.Title = "Enter a value"
    st_prompt.text = "Enter a value"
End If
```

OBJECT/CONTROL	PROPERTY	VALUE
Window	Name	w_usermessage
	Type	response
CommandButton	Name	cb_ok
	Text	"OK"
	Default	TRUE
	Name	cb_cancel

continued on next page

continued from previous page

OBJECT/CONTROL	PROPERTY	VALUE
	Text	"Cancel"
	Cancel	TRUE
SingleLineEdit	Name	sle_input
	Auto H Scroll	TRUE
StaticText	Name	st_prompt

Table 14-15 Properties for window and controls for User Message Box

3. Place the following code in the Clicked event of cb_ok. This closes the window, and passes the text attribute of the SingleLineEdit back to the caller. The CloseWithReturn() function closes a window, and places the parameter in the Message object. The script that opened this dialog box will obtain the returned value, again using the Message object.

```
//Close the window and return the value in the sle
CloseWithReturn ( Parent, sle_input.text )
```

4. Place the following code in the Clicked event of cb_cancel. This closes the window and passes an empty string back to the caller.

```
//Close the window and pass back the empty string
CloseWithReturn ( Parent, "" )
```

5. Save the window using the name "w_usermessage."

6. Run the application and test the scripts.

How It Works

When a script wants to open the custom message box, it does so using the OpenWithParm() function. This function is similar to Open(), except that the Message object receives the value passed in OpenWithParm(). When PowerBuilder populates the Message object, the value can be a string, numeric, or other data type. If the argument passed is numeric, Message.DoubleParm receives the value. A string argument populates Message.StringParm. Any other data type goes in Message.PowerObjectParm. Once the Open event of the window fires, the script places the value from the StringParm attribute into a program variable. This contains a string whose value will become the Titlebar and message text in the window. Since these values are separated by a tab character, the script does some string manipulation to extract those pieces of information. It then sets the properties of the custom user message box accordingly. Once the user has entered a value and presses OK, the window closes using CloseWithReturn(). This function first puts the indicated parameter back into the Message object, so the caller may obtain the value later. If the user presses Cancel, it returns the empty string in the Message object. Notice that you won't know whether or not the user pressed Cancel, or if he or she pressed OK while the SingleLineEdit was empty. This won't cause a problem, since either way the user failed to enter data.

Comments

The Message object is a powerful object used to communicate between objects. This sample uses the StringParm attribute, but there are two others you can use as well. These are the DoubleParm, which holds any numeric value, and the PowerObjectParm which can hold anything. The functions that populate the Message object are OpenWithParm(), OpenSheetWithParm(), and CloseWithReturn(). When these functions are called, PowerBuilder automatically populates the correct attribute for you. You only have to know which one to retrieve. You can only use one of these attributes at a time, as it is not safe to manually set them. Doing so may cause other attributes of the object to change. These scripts could have passed a structure that contained fields for each of the Title and text properties for the message box. In that case, the PowerObjectParm would have been used in the Open event. Any time you pass a value that is not numeric or string, PowerObjectParm receives the value. The PowerObject is the ancestor of all PowerBuilder objects, and is capable of holding any type of data.

CHAPTER 15

INTRODUCTION TO EXTERNAL FUNCTIONS

15

INTRODUCTION TO EXTERNAL FUNCTIONS

How do I...

Chapter 14 discussed two different function types—global and object functions. There is an additional type of function supported in PowerBuilder—the external function. PowerBuilder provides a rich set of built-in functions, but you may occasionally find it necessary to venture outside of pure PowerScript. This chapter focuses on the basics of what you need to know to declare and use external functions. You'll learn how to access the Microsoft Windows Application Programming Interface (API) to directly manipulate the Windows environment. The Windows API alone contains over 1000 functions. Other examples provide you with tools to add multimedia capabilities, ODBC routines, and external functions that are not available within PowerScript. The intent here is not to teach you everything about these APIs. Rather, the goal is to familiarize you with the techniques required to communicate with Windows. Finally, some very common functions are provided that will add spice to your PowerBuilder applications.

15.1 Determine the Amount of Available Memory Using the Windows API

Windows does a pretty good job of memory management. However, users have become accustomed to having an application display the amount of available memory and system resources. Some applications put this in the status bar, others in the Titlebar, still others use an About box. Regardless of where you display the information, the technique for determining it remains the same. In this How-To, you will build an About box that displays this information.

15.2 Pass Variables to an External Function

How-To 15.2 presents three useful functions that are lacking in PowerBuilder— bitwise OR, bitwise AND, and bit shift functions. Using bitwise encoding is a powerful and efficient way to store data. For example, if you need several Boolean variables that you intend to use as flags, you must declare them as separate variables. In languages such as C or C++, one variable (such as an integer) can hold several values. This gives you the ability to use the sixteen bits of an integer for sixteen different Boolean flags. Those variables are manipulated with various bitwise operators. PowerBuilder has no such operators. Through the functions supplied here, these techniques can be added to your arsenal.

15.3 Pass a Structure to an External Function

Passing structures to an external function is no harder than passing variables of other types. However, there are some additional considerations you must be aware of. Windows uses structures extensively in working with window and mouse coordinates, as well as in drawing. However, the techniques for passing structures remain the same. In order to remain generic in this introductory material, our example calculates a payment based on a loan amount, interest rate, and number of payments. A structure holds various properties of a loan (principle, term, etc.). The function accepts this structure as an argument and returns the payment amount. This How-To examines these considerations and offers a practical example.

15.4 Start Another Application from My PowerBuilder Application

PowerBuilder provides the developer with the Run() function, used to run other applications. However, this function only works on real executable files. It does not work with files of type .DOC, .TXT or other data files. Windows allows the user to associate any file extension with any executable file, thereby permitting him or her to double-click on the data file to launch the application. Users are familiar with "running" any type of file, as long as this association has been made. This How-To emulates the same behavior as Explorer, allowing you to "run" any type of file.

15.5 Use External Subroutines

Using an external subroutine is much the same as a function, except that a subroutine does not return a value back to the caller. How-To 15.5 gives you a subroutine that automatically centers a window on the screen. By using this function, you do not have to be concerned with setting the X and Y attributes of the window at design time. If you need to center a window, simply call this subroutine in the Open event of the window. Optionally, you could call this subroutine in the Move event, in order to prevent the user from moving the window.

15.6 Use the ODBC API to Obtain Information on My Database

PowerBuilder isolates the developer from many specifics of a database. When using the DataWindow painter, PowerBuilder presents you with a list of available tables and columns. However, what do you do if you need this information at runtime? You could hard code values into your application, or create an additional table whose rows store information about the other tables. However, if the database changes, table maintenance is required. Additionally, each database must maintain its own information. The solution is to use the ODBC API functions that return information about the available data sources, tables, columns, and other ancillary information. How-To 15-6 shows you how to use the ODBC API to obtain available data sources, connect to a database, and obtain the table and column names from the database.

15.7 Determine When Another Application Is Done

Occasionally, you'll want to start an application from your PowerBuilder application, and have your application wait in the background until this secondary application has been shut down. Since Windows is a multitasking system, applications run independently of one another. There appears no way to determine when another application is complete. Or is there? With a few API calls, and some tricks, this is possible. How-To 15.7 presents the technique for this capability.

15.8 Use the Multimedia API to Play a .WAV file

Multimedia is all the rage. Users like the ability to select custom sound and graphics. With waveform audio, the boring PC beep is gone, thankfully. Even laptop computers are now equipped with sound cards. Keep in mind that when you provide any kind of sound capability, you should also allow the user to turn it off. Some people are irritated by any kind of noise no matter how technologically leading edge it is. Playing a .WAV file is probably much easier than you think. How-To 15.8 demonstrates the technique, by providing the unique scenario of a visually impaired user. This example plays a .WAV file as the user scrolls through the menu, thereby telling him or her what item is selected.

15.9 Use the Multimedia API to Play a Video Clip

Sound is not the only commonly used multimedia component. The .AVI file allows you to put full motion video into your applications. This is a powerful tool that can increase a user's productivity and enhance learning. With this technology, computers can become the surrogate instructor. Educational material can be presented and demonstrated together as a unit, which increases student interest and comprehension of new concepts. Creating .AVI files is beyond the scope of this topic. It requires special hardware and software to do so. However, if you have that capability, the potentials are limited only by your imagination. In this How-To, you will learn how to put this capability into your PowerBuilder applications. Imagine the enthusiasm of the user as you not only present text based data, but also display full motion video to support it!

COMPLEXITY
INTERMEDIATE

15.1 How do I...
Determine the amount of available memory using the Windows API?

Problem

Under Windows, the user is able to get a report of the amount of available memory, as well as a percentage of system resources. I would like to do the same thing for my applications. I would like to display this information in a standard "About" box. How do I determine the amount of free memory and resources while my application is running?

Technique

The Windows API provides two function calls for doing just this. The GetFreeSpace() function reports the amount of free memory in bytes. GetFreeSystemResources() returns a value based on an argument. This argument is the type of resource you wish to obtain. There are three different categories of resources known as User, GDI (Graphical Device Interface), and System resources. The percentage reported by Windows is the System resource value. This How-To shows the steps necessary to get the free memory and all three of the resource values.

Steps

Open and run the application in the FREEMEM.PBL library. This application displays an "About" type of dialog box showing the available free memory and system resources. This information can typically be found in the About box (under the Help menu). Therefore, this sample uses a window that resembles a common About dialog box. Figure 15-1 shows the About box in action.

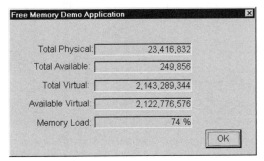

Figure 15-1 w_about window with controls for displaying free memory and resources

1. Create a new application object called "freemem", and save it in a library called FREEMEM.PBL.

2. Create a new window object. Place ten StaticText controls on the window. Give the window and controls the properties shown in Table 15-1. Use Figure 15-1 as a guide for building this window.

CONTROL	PROPERTY	VALUE
Window	Name	w_main
	Title	"Free Memory Demo Application"
StaticText	Text	"Total Physical:"
	Text	"Total Available:"
	Text	"Total Virtual:"
	Text	"Available virtual"
	Text	"Memory Load"
	Name	st_physical
	Text	blank
	Border	3D Lowered
	Name	st_totavail
	Text	blank
	Border	3D Lowered

continued on next page

continued from previous page

CONTROL	PROPERTY	VALUE
	Name	st_totalvirtual
	Text	blank
	Border	3D Lowered
	Name	st_availvirtual
	Text	blank
	Border	3D Lowered
	Name	st_memload
	Border	3D Lowered
	Text	blank

Table 15-1 Attribute settings for w_main window and controls

3. Select Window Structures... from the Declare menu. Here you will declare a structure that you will later pass to a Windows API function which is responsible for obtaining memory information. Declare eight members for this structure, as shown in Table 15-2. The function that you'll call requires a structure, which it fills with relevent memory data. Most of the fields are self explanatory. The dLength field holds the size of this structure in bytes. You will use this structure below in step 5. Save this structure using the name str_memory.

MEMBER NAME	DATATYPE	MEANING
dLength	Long	Length of the structure
dMemoryLoad	Long	Load on memory 0—none, 100—full
dTotalPhys	Long	Total physical memory installed
dAvailPhys	Long	Total available memory
dTotalPageFile	Long	Total size of the paging file
dAvailPageFile	Long	Available bytes of paging file
dTotalVirtural	Long	Total virtual memory space
dAvailVirtual	Long	Available virtual memory space

Table 15-2 Elements of str_Memory window structure

4. Declare the following local external function. You may do so by selecting Local External Functions... from the Declare menu. This function obtains eight different memory parameters, including the total memory installed, and the memory load (0 — completely free, 100 — completely full). Notice that the structure gets passed by reference, so the function (really a subroutine) can populate its elements.

```
Subroutine GlobalMemoryStatus ( ref str_Memory s_Info ) Library "Kernel32.dll"
```

5. Place the following code in the Open event of the window. The script declares an instance of the str_Memory structure, and sets its dLength element to 32. This indicates the length of the structure in bytes (eight elements, each 4 bytes long). Then it passes this structure to the GlobalMemoryStatus() function, which fills in the remaining elements with the memory configuration data. The Text property of the StaticText controls receive the information from the structure upon return.

```
Long ll_freespace
str_Memory str_MemInfo

str_MemInfo.dLength = 32
GlobalMemoryStatus ( str_MemInfo )

//Show Total Physical Memory
st_totavail.text = String ( str_MemInfo.dAvailPhys, "#,###" )

//Show Availalble Memory
st_pyhsical.text = String ( str_MemInfo.dTotalPhys, "#,###" )

//Show Total Virtual Memory
st_totalvirtual.text = String ( str_MemInfo.dTotalVirtual, "#,###" )

//Show Available Virtual Memory,
st_availvirtual.text = String ( str_MemInfo.dAvailVirtual, "#,###" )

//Show Memory Load in percent
st_memload.text = String ( str_MemInfo.dMemoryLoad  ) + " %"
```

6. Place the following code in the Open event of the Application object to start the application. Save all objects and test the scripts.

```
//Set up the application information and open the first window
Open ( w_about )
```

How It Works

As the About box opens, the script calls the GlobalMemoryStatus() function. Since this function is a part of the Windows kernel, there is no need to check for the existence of the .DLL file. (You will do this in How-To 15.4.) GlobalMemoryStatus() fills the data elements of a structure with the requested data, which you simply place in the appropriate StaticText controls.

Comments

Free memory is the area of memory available, from which programs can allocate memory. Also, this memory may not be contiguous. This How-To only used four of the seven data elements returned. (The eighth is the length of the structure, and does not return information.) When working with the Windows API, you are quite often required to pass structure by reference. The function then populates this structure with the data. You must be careful to declare the structure with the proper data types, in the proper sequence. In this example, all of the structure's data elements are long values, but this is not usually the case. Therefore, the order is critical.

COMPLEXITY
BEGINNING

15.2 How do I...
Pass variables to an external function?

Problem

I have an application that requires me to call an external function. The task that I need to accomplish is not supported in PowerScript. I need to know how to tell my application that the function is external to PowerBuilder. Additionally, this function requires me to pass variables to it. What are the necessary steps to accomplish these tasks?

Technique

PowerScript provides a rich set of functions for today's business applications. However, once in a while it is necessary to access functions that are external to PowerBuilder. These functions are available in Dynamic Link Libraries (.DLL) files. The power of .DLLs allows multiple applications to use the same functions, thereby increasing the commonality of the user interface, lowering the amount of of application code, and affording independence from application specific code. Before your applications can use these functions, they must be declared. This declaration informs PowerBuilder about details such as the return data type, the number and type of arguments passed, and the name of the Dynamic Link Library that holds the function. Once this declaration is complete, the code to call the function is no different from calling any of the standard PowerScript functions. This How-To demonstrates how to declare external functions, and how to pass information to them using PowerScript variables.

Steps

Open and run the application contained in the EXT-VAR.PBL library. Figure 15-2 shows the window at runtime, after a shift left operation. This application uses a Dynamic Link Library to offer capabilities not found in PowerBuilder. Four functions allow you to do bitwise operations such as AND, OR, shift left, and shift right. These functions work on the bit level, so a thorough understanding of these concepts is necessary. Assume you have two variables with values 15 and 36 respectively. The binary representations (base 2) are 00001111 and 00100100 respectively. An AND operation results in a 1 only when *both* bits are set, while an OR produces a 1 bit

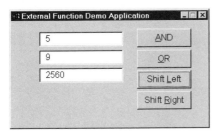

Figure 15-2 Window with AND, OR, and bit shift capabilities

if either bit is on. So, 15 AND 36 results in 4, while 15 OR 36 results in 47. See Table 15-3 below. When a value is shifted left or right, the bits simply move in the indicated direction, and any bits that "fall off" either end are lost. If 36 is shifted right by 3 bits, the result is 4. If shifted left, the value becomes 288. These examples assume that 16-bit (or greater) values are used. The included .DLL gives your applications these capabilities, and this How-To demonstrates their use.

AND	OR	SHIFT RIGHT BY 3	SHIFT LEFT BY 3
0000000000001111	0000000000001111	0000000000100100	0000000000100100
0000000000100100	0000000000100100		
0000000000000100	0000000000101111	0000000000000100	0000000100100000

Table 15-3 Results of AND, OR, and bit shift operations.

1. Create a new Application object named "extern", and save it in a .PBL named EXT-VAR.PBL.

2. Create a new window that resembles the one shown in Figure 15-2 above. Give the window and controls the properties shown in Table 15-4.

OBJECT/CONTROL	PROPERTY	VALUE
Window	Name	w_main
	TitleBar	"External Function Demo Application"
	Maximize Box	FALSE
	Control Menu	FALSE
SingleLineEdit	Name	sle_arg1
	Name	sle_arg2
	Name	sle_result

continued on next page

continued from previous page

OBJECT/CONTROL	PROPERTY	VALUE
CommandButton	Name	cb_and
	Text	"&AND"
	Name	cb_or
	Text	"&OR"
	Name	cb_shiftleft
	Text	"Shift &Left"
	Name	cb_shiftright
	Text	"Shift &Right"

Table 15-4 Properties and values for window and controls

3. Select Local External Functions... from the Declare menu. External functions are declared as either Local or Global. Just like variables, global external functions are available throughout the application. Local external functions are available only in the object for which they are declared. In this example, the functions can only be used in the window. Place the following declarations in this dialog box. Notice that the dialog has the OK button as a default, so use <CTRL>-<ENTER> to move to the next line. This declares the three functions necessary by this window. First, the syntax indicates that you are declaring a function (as opposed to a subroutine). Then you must specify the return value along with the function name. In parentheses, you indicate the arguments and data types for the function. The actual names that you give to the arguments (a1 or a2 in the example below) are irrelevent. They are used only as placeholders. Finally, the reserved word "library" followed by the name of the Dynamic Link Library file must be specified.

```
Function long band ( long a1, long a2 ) Library "extfnc32.dll"
Function long bor ( long a1, long a2 ) Library "extfnc32.dll"
Function long shift ( long a1, int a2, int dir ) Library "extfnc32.dll"
```

4. Place the following code in the Clicked event of cb_and. This uses the values entered into the SingleLineEdit controls, converts them to a long datatype, and passes them to the band() function in the Dynamic Link Library. The return value is then converted back to a string for assignment to the result SingleLineEdit.

```
Long ll_arg1, ll_arg2, ll_result

//Get the long value of each sle into a variable
ll_arg1 = Long ( sle_arg1.text )
ll_arg2 = Long ( sle_arg2.text )

//Call the AND function, passing the variables to operate on
ll_result = band ( ll_arg1, ll_arg2 )

//Place the result into the result sle
sle_result.text = String ( ll_result )
```

5. Place the following code in the Clicked event of cb_or. This script is exactly the same as the example above, except it calls the bor() function.

```
Long ll_arg1, ll_arg2, ll_result

//Get the long value of each sle into a variable
ll_arg1 = Long ( sle_arg1.text )
ll_arg2 = Long ( sle_arg2.text )

//Call the OR function, passing the variables to operate on
ll_result = bor ( ll_arg1, ll_arg2 )

//Place the result into the result sle
sle_result.text = String ( ll_result ) Long ll_arg1, ll_arg2, ll_result
```

6. Place the following code in the Clicked event of cb_shiftleft. The Shift() function takes three arguments. The first is the number to shift. The second indicates how many bits to shift by. The last argument is a 1 for a left shift, 0 for a right shift.

```
Integer li_arg1, li_arg2, li_result

//Convert the sle text into an integer value
li_arg1 = Integer ( sle_arg1.text )
li_arg2 = Integer ( sle_arg2.text )

//Call the shift function. Last argument of 1 means shift left
li_result = Shift ( li_arg1, li_arg2, 1 )

sle_result.text = String ( li_result )
```

7. Place the following code in the Clicked event for cb_shiftright. This is the same as the above code, except that the Shift() function indicates a right hand shift.

```
Integer li_arg1, li_arg2, li_result

//Convert the sle text into an integer value
li_arg1 = Integer ( sle_arg1.text )
li_arg2 = Integer ( sle_arg2.text )

//Call the shift function. Last argument of 0 means shift right
li_result = Shift ( li_arg1, li_arg2, 0 )

sle_result.text = String ( li_result )
```

8. Save the window using the name w_main. Place the following code in the Open event of the application object to open the window when the application starts.

```
//Open the window
Open ( w_main )
```

How It Works

When you declare external functions, you must decide if their scope should be global or local. Global declarations should be reserved for external functions that will be used throughout the application. Local functions are available only from scripts in the object for which the function is declared. In the declaration, you must indicate the datatype and a dummy variable name. The datatype is important, but the dummy variable name is not. This variable is not used in the function, but the name usually indicates the intended use. Once the external function has been declared, your scripts call them just like any other function. The difference is that the functions reside in a Dynamic Link Library. Upon the function call, the Dynamic Link Library gets loaded into memory, and the function executed.

Comments

The source code for the Dynamic Link Library used in this example has been included on the CD. Although it is not the intent here to teach you how to write .DLLs, you may want to review it for reference. Dynamic Link Libraries are normally written in C, as speed and portability are the main objectives with their use. Even though PowerScript is a robust language for today's business applications, it is not uncommon to use external functions during development. For example, you may be writing an image processing system that scans documents and stores them in a database. This application would require the use of a scanner, but PowerScript does not supply any functions for doing this type of work. In order to manipulate this device, it may be necessary to communicate with it in its native environment. This environment may well be a Dynamic Link Library supplied by the manufacturer. When using external libraries such as this, it is good programming practice to first ensure that the .DLL file exists. You would receive a runtime error if you tried to call a function, and the .DLL was not available to the user. This step is not required if you are simply calling Windows API functions, as Windows libraries always exist. With the help of a Windows API call, this extra step is not difficult, and How-To 15.4 shows you the technique.

COMPLEXITY
INTERMEDIATE

15.3 How do I...
Pass a structure to an external function?

Problem

I have an external function that requires a structure as an argument. I know how to declare and use external functions in general, but I don't know the details of passing structures. Are there any issues surrounding their use that I must be aware of?

Technique

External functions must be declared before they are called. The type of arguments passed to them makes little difference. When passing a structure, you must first create it in the Structure painter. This structure must match the structure that the external function expects in regards to the datatype of the individual elements, as well as the order of those elements. In this How-To, you will create a structure containing numeric data. Then, you will populate the structure with information about a simple loan. This structure gets passed to a function that calculates a loan payment based on the principle, interest rate, and number of payments.

Steps

Open and run the application in the EXT-STR.PBL library. When the window opens, enter a loan amount, interest rate (as an integer — 10 for 10%), and number of payments. Then, press the Calculate Payment button. The application calls an external function and passes the information in a structure. The function returns the payment amount, and places it in the SingleLineEdit at the bottom of the window. Figure 15-3 shows this window at runtime.

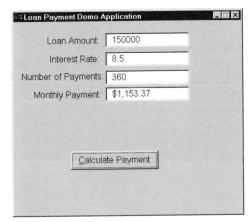

Figure 15-3 Completed Loan Payment window

1. Create a new Application object called "extern" and store it in a library called EXT_STR.PBL. Do not have PowerBuilder generate an application template. Close the Application painter for now.

2. Open the Structure painter and create a new structure. Give this structure the variable names and datatypes shown in Table 15-5. Save this structure using the name str_pay.

VARIABLE NAME	DATATYPE
principle	Double
interest	Double
periods	UnsignedInteger

Table 15-5 Variables and datatypes for the loan payment structure.

3. Create a new window object. Place four SingleLineEdit controls, four StaticText controls, and a CommandButton on the window. Use Figure 15-3 as a guideline. The properties for this window are shown in Table 15-6.

OBJECT/CONTROL	PROPERTY	VALUE
Window	Name	w_main
	TitleBar	"Loan Payment Demo Application"
	Maximize Box	FALSE
SingleLineEdit	Name	sle_loan
SingleLineEdit	Name	sle_interest
SingleLineEdit	Name	sle_numpay
SingleLineEdit	Name	sle_payment
StaticText	Text	"Loan Amount:"
StaticText	Text	"Interest Rate:
StaticText	Text	"Number of Payments:"
StaticText	Text	"Monthly Payment:"
CommandButton	Name	cb_payment
	Text	"&Calculate Payment"

Table 15-6 Attributes for Loan window and controls.

4. Select Local External Functions... from the Declare menu. Place the following declaration in this dialog box. This function takes a structure called l_struct that is of type str_pay as the argument. This is the datatype of the structure just declared in step 2. The Dynamic Link Library (EXTFUNC.DLL) must be in your path. This library can be found on the accompanying CD-ROM.

```
Function Double payment ( str_pay l_struct ) Library "extfnc32.dll"
```

5. Place the following code in the Clicked event of cb_payment. This script declares a local copy of the str_pay structure, populates its variables with the values from the SingleLineEdit controls (after converting them to the correct datatype), and calls the external function. Save the window using the name w_main.

```
//Declare structure and variables needed
str_pay lstr_loan
Double ld_result

//Load the structure with data from the singlelineedits
lstr_loan.principle = Double ( sle_loan.text )
lstr_loan.interest = Double ( sle_interest.text )
lstr_loan.periods = Integer ( sle_numpay.text )

//Call the external function
ld_result = Payment ( lstr_loan )

//Assign return value to payment singlelineedit
sle_payment.text = String ( ld_result, "$#,###.##" )
```

6. Write the code for the Open event of the Application object necessary to open the window.

```
//Open the window
Open ( w_main )
```

How It Works

This application passes a structure to an external function. If you are familiar with passing variables to functions, you can see that this example is similar. The only difference is that you must first create the structure, since structures are a user-defined, complex datatype. Many times, functions that use structures do so in order to modify some of the data in the structure. Since functions only return one value, this is a common way of allowing the function to "return" more than one value. If this is the case, the structure (as well as any data that a function modifies) must be *passed by reference*. You do not have control over what the function expects. If it requires a reference argument, you must declare it as such. This example does not use reference arguments, so a sample function declaration using a reference argument is shown below. The reference variable is indicated with the *ref* keyword, which preceeds the variable.

```
Function double payment ( ref str_pay l_struct ) Library "extfnc32.dll"
```

Comments

Structures are a powerful and useful addition to your applications. If you intend to use the Windows Application Programming Interface (API), structures will become an important issue. Many of the Windows API calls use structures for information regarding screen layout, mouse coordinates, graphic devices and so forth. If improperly declared, structures could cause the function and the system to fail. Since most external functions are written in C, you must be aware of the datatype differences between C and PowerScript. For instance, C supports the *double* datatype, as does PowerScript. However, C does not support strings. In C, strings are declared as *character arrays*. This may sound like a technicality, but be aware that the two languages do have their differences in data types. PowerScript variables of type *real* map to the

C data type *float.* The library EXTFNC32.DLL is provided on the CD, as is the C source code used to create it. If you are interested in learning more about creating your own .DLL files, you enable yourself to add power and speed to your applications.

15.4 How do I...
Start another application from my PowerBuilder application?

Problem

I would like to allow my users to start other Windows applications from my application. I have tried using the PowerScript Run() function, but it only works on executable files. Windows allows the user to "run" any type of file, such as a .DOC file, and will start the proper application based on the data file extension. How can I give this same capability to my users?

Technique

The PowerScript Run() function allows you to run any type of file that can be executed. This does not include data files. Since most users are accustomed to double-clicking on any file type and launching the application that created it, it would be nice to incorporate this functionality into PowerBuilder applications. That is just what this How-To is all about, and is accomplished with the help of the Windows API. The ShellExecute() function will execute or print any type of file. If the file is a data file, the function launches the appropriate application and loads the data file.

Steps

Run the application in the RUN.PBL library. Press the Run button, and select any file from the resulting dialog box. The file is loaded with the appropriate application. If you first click on the *Print instead of Open* CheckBox, the file will load and print. Figure 15-4 shows the application at runtime.

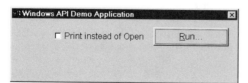

Figure 15-4 Run application window

1. Create a new Application object called "run", and save it in a library called RUN.PBL.

2. Create a new window object. Use Figure 15-4 as a guide. Add the following local external function declarations to this window. ShellExecuteA() runs an application, but since the function comes from a .DLL that may not be available to the user, this application must first ensure that it can load the library. Without this step, there would be a runtime error if the user did not have the SHELL32.DLL library. LoadLibraryA() and FreeLibrary() are two Windows API functions that perform this task for you. ShellExecuteA() takes six arguments. The first is the window handle for the owning window. A handle is a unique identifier for an object. This will be set to the handle of w_main. The second argument is the string "open" or "print" depending on what operation is desired. Argument three specifies the file to run. Then, you indicate any parameters to the executable file. This is used only if the run file is an executable, and you wish to pass a parameter to it. If the file you are "running" is a data file, this argument is not needed. Argument five specifies the directory where the file is stored. The last argument dictates the state in which to run the executable. Table 15-7 lists the values for the state argument.

```
Function UINT ShellExecuteA ( UINT hwndID, ref String op, ref string file,
ref string parms, ref string dir, UINT show) Library "shell32.dll"
Function UINT LoadLibraryA ( String as_library ) Library "kernel23.dll"
Subroutine FreeLibrary ( UINT HInstance ) Library "kernel32.dll"
```

RUN STATE	MEANING	VALUE
SW_HIDE	Hide the window	0
SW_SHOWNORMAL	Display in normal size	1
SW_SHOWMINIMIZED	Run as an icon with focus	2
SW_SHOWMAXIMIZED	Run full screen	3
SW_SHOWNOACTIVATE	Run normal without focus	4
SW_SHOW	Same as SW_SHOWNORMAL	5
SW_MINIMIZE	Same as SW_SHOWMINIMIZED	6
SW_SHOWMINNOACTIVE	Run as icon without focus	7
SW_SHOWNA	Run normal without focus	8
SW_RESTORE	Same as SW_SHOWNORMAL	9

Table 15-7 ShellExecute() Show argument value and meaning

3. Add a CheckBox and CommandButton control to the window. Give these controls the properties shown in Table 15-8.

CONTROL	PROPERTY	VALUE
CommandButton	Name	cb_run
	Text	"&Run..."
CheckBox	Name	cbx_print
	Text	"&Print instead of Open"

Table 15-8 Properties for new controls on w_main

4. Place the following code in the Clicked event for cb_run. Since the ShellExecute() function is a function in an external .DLL (not the Windows kernel), the script first checks to see if the SHELL32.DLL library exists by using the LoadLibrary() function. If LoadLibrary() returns a non-zero value, an error occurred, and it assumes the SHELL32.DLL file is not available. Otherwise, the .DLL is loaded into memory and the return value is the instance handle. After obtaining a file from the user (using the PowerScript GetFileOpenName() function), the script calls ShellExecuteA() to perform the job. If ShellExecuteA() returns a number less than 32, some error occurred. The number indicates the specific error in question. Table 15-9 shows these possible return values and their meanings. Finally, since the library was loaded with the LoadLibraryA() call, the script frees the memory taken by it using FreeLibrary(), passing the instance number returned by the load. This is only necessary if you are using a function from a library other than the Windows kernel.

```
String ls_path, ls_file, ls_parms, ls_dir, ls_command
UINT lu_return, lu_instance

//Check to see if the dll is available. Returns number < 32 if not
lu_instance = LoadLibraryA ( "shell32.dll" )
If lu_instance <> 0 Then
    MessageBox ( "Library", "Could not load SHELL32.DLL" )
Else
//Shell32.dll is there. Get a filename from the user
    GetFileOpenName ( "Run application from PowerBuilder...", &
                    ls_path, ls_file, "*", "All Files (*.*),*.*" )

    If ls_path <> "" Then
        SetPointer ( Hourglass! )
//Examine the checkbox for open or print configuration
        If cbx_print.checked Then
            ls_command = "print"
        Else
            ls_command = "open"
        End If

//Call the function. Pass the parent as the owner. Run normal.
        lu_return =  ShellExecuteA ( Handle ( Parent ), ls_command, &
                    ls_path, ls_parms, ls_file, 1 )

//Check for errors from function
        If lu_return < 32 Then
```

```
        MessageBox ( "Run", "An error occurred running~r~n" + ls_path )
    End If
End If

//Free the resources from the dll since it was loaded with the loadlibrary
//call
    FreeLibrary ( lu_instance )
End If
```

VALUE	MEANING
0	Out of memory or corrupt file
2	File not found
3	Path not found
5	Sharing or network protection error
6	Library required separate data memory segment for each task
8	Insufficient memory to start the application
10	Incorrect Windows version
11	Error in the executable file
12	Application requires different operating system
14	Unknown executable file
15	Tried to load real mode (previous version of Windows) application
16	Attempt to load a second instance of a single instance application
19	The executable file is compressed
20	Invalid DLL file
21	Application requires 32-bit extensions and was loaded in 16-bit
31	No association for the data file

Table 15-9 Return values from ShellExecute() function

5. Save and run the application.

How It Works

ShellExecuteA() is a function contained in the file SHELL32.DLL. Since this file is not part of the Windows kernel, the script first checks to see if the file is available. Assuming it is, the library file is loaded into memory. This loading of a .DLL usually happens only when you call a function, but it is unsafe to just call ShellExecuteA(), since the library may not be installed on the user's machine. You must do the error checking, and handle the errors appropriately. The GetFileOpenName() function is used to obtain the filename from the user. Since this function returns both the filename and the path, these values are passed along to ShellExecuteA(). This script does not pass any parameters to the executable file, and assumes an initial state of SW_NORMAL (1). After the ShellExecute() function finishes, you must remove the resources used by SHELL32.DLL. That's what FreeLibrary() does. FreeLibrary() does not return a value, and therefore no error checking is done.

Comments

The final argument of ShellExecute32() is the run state. The Windows API supports many more choices than PowerBuilder does. If you run an application using SW_HIDE (0), the application will not display on the desktop, nor will it be visible on the Windows taskbar. Therefore, the user has no idea that another application is running. This is useful in performing OLE automation tasks, when you want to hide the details from the user. Just be aware that since the users can't see the application, they have no way to close it. You must do that through code. This involves sending the application a command (usually [quit] but this could vary depending on the application). The only other way to shut down the application is by using a tool that displays hidden applications, or by shutting down Windows. However, if your application starts another application, it is good practice to also close it for the user. This is especially true if you start the application in a hidden state.

This example uses a simple Open type of dialog box to obtain the filename from the user. You may wish to give the user other ways, such as a SingleLineEdit, ListBox, or DataWindow from which they select the file. Also, you may wish to display a better error message to the user if ShellExecute() fails, and indicate the specific error. If you're doing this in many scripts throughout your application, this would be a good use for a user-defined function.

COMPLEXITY
BEGINNING

15.5   How do I...
Use external subroutines?

Problem

I need to call an external subroutine. Subroutines do not return values. I have used external functions before, and know they must first be declared. But I can't find anywhere to declare a subroutine. How do I do it?

Technique

Functions return values to the caller, while subroutines do processing only. They do not indicate any return value. Using subroutines is easier that using functions, since the overhead of the return value is eliminated. In this How-To you will use an external subroutine that centers a window. Any time the user resizes (or optionally moves) the window, this subroutine moves it back to the center of the user's screen. This can be useful if your applications run on systems with different screen resolutions, thereby making it impossible to center the window at design time.

Steps

Open and run the application in the EXT-SUB.PBL library. Resize the window. Notice that the window moves back to the center of the screen. Now, move the window. It stays where you move it unless you check the Center If Moved CheckBox. This window is shown in Figure 15-5.

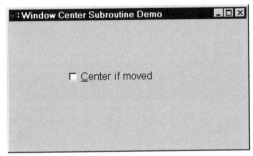

Figure 15-5 Centered window sample application

1. Create a new application called "extern" and save it in a library called EXT-SUB.PBL. Do not have PowerBuilder generate an application template. Close the Application painter for now.

2. Start the Window painter and create a new window using Figure 15-5 as a guide. The properties for this window are shown in Table 15-10. Select Local External Functions... from the Declare menu. Place the following declaration in the resulting dialog box. This function centers a window based on the window *handle*. A handle is a unique number which identifies a window object. This value comes from Windows, and PowerScript provides a function to obtain this value as you will see in a moment.

```
Subroutine center ( UINT Handle ) library "extfnc32.dll"
```

OBJECT/CONTROL	PROPERTY	VALUE
Window	Name	w_main
	TitleBar	"Window Center Subroutine Demo"
CheckBox	Name	cbx_center
	Text	"&Center if moved"

Table 15-10 Property settings for window and controls for external subroutine demo

3. Place the following code in the Resize event of w_main. Whenever the window size changes, this script will run and re-center the window. Notice that the WindowState attribute of the window is checked, and the script does not execute if the window is an icon. You may be wondering why this check is made, since the user cannot change the window size while in the iconic state (minimized on the taskbar). While this statement is true, the Resize event fires when the user minimizes the application. Without performing this check, the icon would center itself. This script is really only necessary if the window is a sheet, as minimized windows show up as buttons on the taskbar in Windows 95.

```
//The user changed the window size, so call Center function to
//Reposition it. Only do this if the window is not minimized.
//Even though the user cannot resize a minimized window, the event
//gets triggered when it's minimized.
If This.WindowState <> Minimized! Then
    Center ( Handle ( this ) )
End If
```

4. Select User Events... from the Declare menu. Map an event called "Move" and map it to the pbm_move event ID. Place the following code in this event. This script centers the window if the user moves it. Save the window using the name w_main.

```
//Check the window state. If it's minimized, don't center it as
//this would result in centering the icon.
If This.WindowState = Minimized! Then Return

//If the checkbox is checked, then center the window
If cbx_center.checked Then
    Center ( Handle ( this ) )        //Center function uses window handle
End If
```

5. Write the code for the Open event of the Application object that opens the window. Save and run the application.

```
//Open the window
Open ( w_main )
```

How It Works

The Center() subroutine takes a window handle as an argument. This handle is obtained with the PowerScript Handle() function. Each time the user resizes the window, the Resize event fires. When this occurs, the script calls the Center() subroutine, passing the window handle. The internals of this subroutine identify the window based on the handle, and obtain the current size as well as the size of the user's screen. It then changes the window's coordinates based on this information. The source code for the .DLL has been provided on the CD.

Comments

Even though subroutines do not return a value, many PowerBuilder developers refer to them as functions anyway. This is misleading as far as strict standards go, but PowerBuilder requires that the subroutine be called with parentheses at the end. Therefore, they syntactically appear as functions.

COMPLEXITY
ADVANCED

15.6 How do I...
Use the ODBC API to obtain information on my database?

Problem

I would like to give my users an ad hoc reporting capability. My application will need to connect to various data sources. The user must be allowed to connect to a variety of databases, potentially from different vendors. I would like to give them the ability to view database and table structures dynamically. How can I provide this kind of capability without getting specific as to the database vendor, and without knowing which drivers are necessary?

Technique

The Open Database Connectivity (ODBC) API provides a set of high level functions that allow you to connect, disconnect, query, and manipulate databases and tables. By using the ODBC API, your applications are capable of providing database access without knowing the details of the database specific information. In this How-To, you will learn many of the functions supported by ODBC, and how to use them to obtain information specific to the database. First, the sample application uses the API to obtain a list of available data sources. The user selects a data source from the list, and connects to that source using another API function. Once the user has successfully connected to the database, the application presents the user with a list of tables from the database. If the user selects a table from the list, the columns from that table then display.

Steps

Open and run the application in the TABLESRC.PBL library. The application populates a ListBox showing all available ODBC data sources. Click on one of the ListBox entries, and type in the appropriate userid and password, then click the Connect button. If the application successfully connects to the indicated database, the tables display in the Tables ListBox. Finally, click on a table name from the Tables ListBox. The columns and column datatype display in the Columns ListBox. Figure 15-6 shows the application's main window in action.

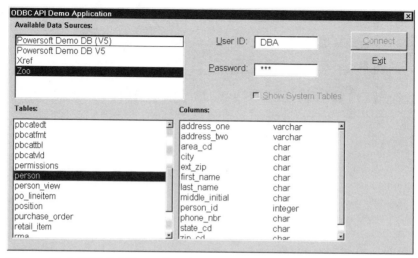

Figure 15-6 ODBC API application at runtime

1. Create a new Application object called "datasrc" and save it in a library called "TABLESRC.PBL."

2. Create a new window object. Give this object the controls and properties shown in Table 15-11. Use Figure 15-6 as a guide. Declare the following Instance variables for this window. The ODBC API functions in this example use these variables to identify the connection and various properties about any current operation. They are handles (unique identifiers).

```
Protected:
Long hEnv    //SQL Environment handle
Long hStmt   //SQL Statement handle
Long hDBC    //SQL Connection handle
```

OBJECT/CONTROL	PROPERTY	SETTING
Window	Name	w_odbc_data_sources
	Title	"ODBC API Demo Application"
	Type	Response
ListBox	Name	lb_datasources
	Name	lb_tables
	Name	lb_columns
	Tabs	20
CommandButton	Name	cb_connect
	Text	"&Connect"
	Enabled	FALSE
	Name	cb_exit

OBJECT/CONTROL	PROPERTY	SETTING
	Text	"E&xit
SingleLineEdit	Name	sle_uid
	Auto HScroll	TRUE
	Accelerator	"u"
	Name	sle_pwd
	Auto HScroll	TRUE
	Accelerator	"p"
CheckBox	Name	cbx_systemtables
	Text	"&Show System Tables"
	Enabled	FALSE
StaticText	Text	"Available Data Sources:"
	Text	"&User ID:"
	Text	"&Password:"
	Text	"Tables:"
	Text	"Columns:"

Table 15-11 Controls and properties for ODBC API sample application window

3. Declare the following Local External Functions in the window. These 14 functions provide the necessary capabilities that allow the window to connect, disconnect, and obtain database, table, and column level information. Each function will be discussed in turn when they are used in the scripts for the first time.

```
Function Integer SQLAllocEnv ( ref Long phEnv ) Library "ODBC32.DLL"
Function Integer SQLFreeEnv ( Long hEnv ) Library "ODBC32.DLL"
Function Integer SQLDataSources ( Long hEnv, Int fDirection, ref String
szDSN, Integer cbDSNMax, ref Integer pcbDSN, ref String szDescription,
Integer cbDescriptionMax, ref Integer pcbDescription ) Library "ODBC32.DLL"
Function Integer SQLAllocConnect ( Long hEnv, ref Long hdbc ) Library
"ODBC32.DLL"
Function Integer SQLConnect ( Long hstmt, ref String szDSN, Integer DSNLen,
& ref String szUID, Integer UIDLen, ref String szPWD, Integer PWDLen )
Library & "ODBC32.DLL"
Function Integer SQLDisconnect ( Long hdbc ) Library "ODBC32.DLL"
Function Integer SQLAllocStmt ( Long hdbc, ref Long hstmt ) Library &
"ODBC32.DLL"
Function Integer SQLTables ( Long hstmt, ref String szTableQualifier,
Integer  TableQualifierLen, ref String szOwner, Integer OwnerLen, ref
String szName, Integer NameLen, ref String szType, Integer TypeLen )
Library "ODBC32.DLL"
Function Integer SQLColumns ( Long hstmt, ref String szTableQualifier,
Integer TableQualifierLen, ref String szOwner, Integer OwnerLen, ref String
szName, Integer NameLen, ref String szType, Integer TypeLen ) Library
"ODBC32.DLL"
Function Integer SQLBindCol ( Long hstmt, Integer ColNum, Integer DataType,
ref String Name, Long MaxLen, ref Long ActLen ) Library "ODBC32.DLL"
Function Integer SQLFetch ( Long hstmt ) Library "ODBC32.DLL"
```

continued on next page

continued from previous page

```
Function Integer SQLError ( Long hEnv, Long hDBC, Long hStmt, ref String
SqlState, ref Long NativeError, ref String ErrorMsg, Integer ErrorMsgMax,
ref Integer ErrorMsgLen ) Library "ODBC32.DLL"
Function Integer SQLFreeStmt ( Long hStmt, Integer Options ) Library
"ODBC32.DLL"
```

4. Declare a public window function called wf_SQLError(). This function does not accept arguments, and returns "(none)". Place the following code in the function. This function reports errors that occur, and the other scripts call this function if the API function calls fail. The SQLError() API function reports the errors by populating two strings, which are passed to it by reference. Since the SQLError() function uses reference strings, this function must pre-allocate space to hold strings of the appropriate length. The first three arguments of SQLError() represent handles to the various environment data, and are discussed below when the other scripts first initialize them. The fourth argument is a string pointer that receives a string containing the SQL error identifier. This is similar to the error code, but is an alphanumeric value. Argument number five receives the error code, while the next argument receives the actual error message that occurred. The last two arguments specify the maximum number of characters the function should return, and the actual number of characters returned respectively.

```
String ls_SQLState, ls_ErrorMsg
Integer li_ErrorMsgMax, li_ret
Long ll_NativeError

//Allocate space for the returned strings
ls_ErrorMsg = Space ( 255 )
ls_SQLState = Space ( 255 )

//Call the API function that tells us what error occured
li_ret = SQLError ( hEnv, hDBC, hStmt, ls_SQLState, ll_NativeError, &
                    ls_ErrorMsg, 255, li_ErrorMsgMax )

//Display the error message to the user
MessageBox ( "ODBC: " + ls_SQLState, ls_ErrorMsg )

Return
```

5. Place the following code in the Open event of the window. This script uses several of the ODBC API calls, and the main purpose revolves around obtaining the available data sources. However, several steps are necessary prior to calling many of these API functions. You must allocate memory for the subsequent functions, so this script calls SQLAllocEnv(). The SQLAllocEnv() function takes an argument variable of type long, and passes this variable by reference. The function allocates the necessary memory, and returns a handle to the ODBC environment in the passed argument. The value contained in hEnv becomes the unique identifier used in subsequent API function calls. If memory is not available, or some other error occurs, the script calls the error handler function created above. Once the environment handle exists, the script calls the SQLDataSources() function to obtain all ODBC data sources. SQLDataSources() passes the newly acquired environment handle, and each call to this function returns one data source name. Therefore, the script repetitively calls this function until no more data sources are found. SQLDataSources() (like all of the ODBC API calls) returns a 0 or 1 on success, or a negative number upon failure. After the environment handle comes the direction flag, indicating if the function is to return the next data source name (a value of 1), the first name (value of 2), the last name (value of 3), or the prior name (value of 4). The next two arguments are the maximum data source string length to return, the actual length returned, and the pointer to the data source name. The last three arguments are maximum length, actual length, and string value of the data source description. The script calls this function as long as the return value indicates success (0), and places the returned data source name into the appropriate ListBox.

```
String ls_DSN, ls_Description
Integer li_Direction, li_DSNMax, li_DSN_Len
Integer li_DescriptionMax, li_Description_Len, li_RetVal

//Set up to get the data sources
ls_DSN = Space ( 255 )
li_DSNMax = Len ( ls_dsn )
ls_Description = Space ( 255 )
li_DescriptionMax = Len ( ls_Description )

//Allocate an environment handle
If SQLAllocEnv ( hEnv ) = - 1 Then
//could not get environment handle
    wf_SQLError()
Else
    li_Direction = 1  //forward
//Loop through and get all the data source names
    Do While SQLDataSources ( hEnv, li_Direction, ls_DSN, li_DSNMax, &
                              li_DSN_Len, ls_Description, &
                              li_DescriptionMax, li_Description_Len ) = 0
        lb_datasources.AddItem ( ls_DSN )
    Loop
End If
```

6. Place the following code in the Close event of the window. This disconnects from the database and frees the memory in use by the environment handle when the user exits the application.

```
//Disconnect from the database
SQLDisconnect ( hDBC )

//Free the memory associated with the API calls
SQLFreeEnv ( hEnv )
```

7. Place the following code in the Clicked event of cb_connect. This script connects to a data source and retrieves the table names from that database. Before establishing a connection, you must first allocate memory for it, which is the job of SQLAllocConnect(). This function returns the connection handle (hDBC) to the allocated memory, which then gets passed to the

SQLConnect() function. As with many of the other ODBC API calls seen thus far, SQLConnect() takes additional arguments which indicate the data source name and its length, the userid and its length, and the user's password and its length. These values come from the data source ListBox, and the SingleLineEdit controls on the window. Next, the script must obtain the table names from the database, but to do so requires another handle. This handle identifies all future SQL data requests, and obtaining this handle is the job of SQLAllocStmt(). SQLAllocStmt() takes two arguments. The first is the connection handle, the second is the statement handle. SQLAllocStmt() returns this statement handle in the second argument. Now that all preliminary setup work is complete, it is time to query the database for the table names.

Three steps are required in order to obtain table information. First, you must tell ODBC that you intend to retrieve the list of tables. That is what the SQLTables() function does. Using the hStmt statement handle, the function requests this information based on the values of the remaining function arguments. These arguments tell the function exactly the information to return. Following the hStmt argument are eight arguments that come in four pairs. Arguments 2, 4, 6, and 8 are strings (passed by reference) that indicate the table *qualifier*, owner, name, and type respectively. Arguments 3, 5, 7, and 9 are long values of the lengths of their respective strings. Using these arguments, the function is capable of retrieving sub-sets of tables (tables that match certain criteria). This example retrieves all tables, views, and, optionally, system tables. When SQLTables() executes, it builds the result set as a database cursor. The result set remains at the database, and is not yet passed to the calling application.

Before actually obtaining the results, the calling application must tell ODBC where to put the data created by the cursor. This is the job of the SQLBindCol() function. It binds program variables to the cursor's result set, so that when the data is obtained from the server, ODBC knows in which variables to place the data. SQLTables() makes several entities available, only one of which this script later retrieves. The possible entities are the table qualifier, owner, name, type, and remarks (table comments). Your scripts may ask for any or all of this data. This script only uses the table name, and binds the ls_Table variable to the result set. SQLBindCol() takes the arguments shown in Table 15-12. Once the program variables are bound to the result set, the script calls SQLFetch() to return one row of data. The result is the first table name in ls_Table, which subsequently gets added to the Tables ListBox. The script calls SQLFetch() until the return value of the function is non-zero (out of data). Finally, the script calls SQLFreeStmt() to release the memory used by the cursor (in effect, closing the cursor). You must close the cursor before calling other data retrieval functions.

ARGUMENT	MEANING	POSSIBLE VALUES
hStmt	SQL Statement handle	hStmt (as returned from SQLAllocStmt( ))
iCol	Result set column number	1 - 5 (Qualifier, Owner, Name, Type, Remarks)
fcType	Column data type	1 - 8, 12, 99 *See comments section
rgbValue	Storage for data	Program string variable
cbValueMax	Max length of data	varies
pcbValue	Actual returned length	varies

Table 15-12 Arguments for SQLBindCol()

```
Integer li_ret
String ls_dsn, ls_uid, ls_pwd
String ls_Qualifier, ls_Owner, ls_Name, ls_Type, ls_Table
Long ll_len


SetPointer ( Hourglass! )

//Get the information entered by the user
ls_dsn = lb_datasources.SelectedItem()
ls_uid = sle_uid.text
ls_pwd = sle_pwd.text

//Call ODBC API to allocate memory for the connection
li_ret = SQLAllocConnect ( hEnv, hDBC )
If li_ret < 0  Then
    wf_SQLError()
Else
//Attempt to connect
    li_ret = SQLConnect ( hDBC, ls_dsn, Len( ls_dsn ), ls_uid, &
             Len ( ls_uid ), ls_pwd, Len ( ls_pwd ))

    If li_ret < 0 Then
        wf_SQLError()
    Else
//allocate memory for sqlstatement
        li_ret = SQLAllocStmt ( hDBC, hStmt )
        If li_ret < 0 Then
            wf_SQLError()
        Else
//get tables and views. Include "SYSTEM TABLES" if systables are needed
            ls_Type = "'TABLE','VIEW'"

//See if user also wants system tables
            If cbx_systemtables.Checked Then
                ls_Type = ls_Type + ",'SYSTEM TABLE'"
            End If

//Create a cursor that will return table names using the ODBC API
            li_ret = SQLTables ( hStmt, ls_Qualifier, Len ( ls_Qualifier ), &
                     ls_Owner, Len ( ls_Owner ), ls_Name, Len ( ls_Name ), &
                     ls_Type, Len ( ls_Type ) )
            If li_ret < 0 Then
```

continued on next page

continued from previous page

```
                        wf_SQLError()
                Else
                    ls_Table = Space ( 255 )
                    ll_len = 255

//Tell the ODBC API which variable to put data in later. ls_table will
//hold table names once they are fetched from above defined cursor
                    SQLBindCol ( hStmt, 3, 1, ls_Table, ll_len, ll_len )

//Turn redraw of listbox off so user does not see it updated on every add
                    lb_tables.SetRedraw ( FALSE )

//Loop through the cursor to retrieve table names. SQLFetch puts the
//table name in ls_tables as defined in above call to SQLBinCol()
                    Do While SQLFetch ( hStmt ) = 0
                        lb_tables.AddItem ( ls_Table )
                    Loop

//Turn redraw of listbox on to show results
                    lb_tables.SetRedraw ( TRUE )

//Close the open cursor
                    li_ret = SQLFreeStmt ( hStmt, 0 )
                End If
            End If
        End If
End If

//Disable the button until the user selects another data source
this.Enabled = FALSE
this.Default = FALSE
cbx_systemtables.Enabled = FALSE
```

8. Place the following code in the SelectionChanged event of lb_datasources. When the user selects a data source, this script first clears the contents of the userid and password SingleLineEdit controls, then disconnects from any previous connection. The SQLDisconnect() function takes the previously established hDBC connection handle as an argument. The script does not check the return value of SQLDisconnect(), and does not report any error to the user.

```
//Clear out the user id and password edit boxes
sle_uid.text = ""
sle_pwd.text = ""

//Disconnect from the database to prepare for new connection
SQLDisconnect ( hDBC )

//Set the button to its default state
cb_connect.enabled = TRUE
cbx_systemtables.Enabled = TRUE

//Set the list boxes to default
lb_columns.Reset()
lb_tables.Reset()
```

```
//Set the focus and default button for user ease
sle_uid.SetFocus()
cb_connect.Default = TRUE
```

9. Place the following code in the SelectionChanged event of lb_tables. This
script retrieves the column names from whichever table the user selects.
This script uses the same techniques as the Connect button above, except
that it uses the SQLColumns() function instead of SQLTables(). Again, since
the functions return data in strings that are passed by reference, you must
make certain that adequate space is allocated to the strings prior to calling
the functions.

```
Integer li_ret, li_Len
String ls_Qualifier, ls_Owner, ls_Name, ls_Column, ls_ColName, ls_Type
Long ll_MaxLen

lb_columns.Reset()

//Initialize the strings passed by reference
ls_Qualifier = Space ( 255 )
ls_Owner = Space ( 255 )
ls_Column = Space ( 255 )
ls_ColName = Space ( 255 )
ls_Type = Space ( 255 )
ls_Name = Space ( 255 )

ls_Name = this.SelectedItem()

//Create the cursor that will return the column info
li_ret = SQLColumns ( hStmt, ls_Qualifier, 0, &
                             ls_Owner, 0, &
                             ls_Name, Len ( ls_Name ), &
                             ls_Column, 0 )

If li_ret < 0 Then
    wf_SQLError()
Else
//Initialize the strings that will hold the data
    ls_ColName = Space ( 255 )
    ls_Type = Space ( 255 )

//Tell the ODBC API what variables to use to put the column info into
    ll_MaxLen = 255
    SQLBindCol ( hStmt, 4, 1, ls_ColName, ll_MaxLen, ll_MaxLen )
    SQLBindCol ( hStmt, 6, 1, ls_Type, ll_MaxLen, ll_MaxLen )

//Turn redraw of listbox off so user does not see it updated on every add
    lb_columns.SetRedraw ( FALSE )

//Get the column information from the cursor created by SQLColumns()
    Do While SQLFetch ( hStmt ) = 0
//Add the column name and type to the list box
        lb_Columns.AddItem ( ls_ColName + "~t" + ls_Type )
    Loop
```

continued on next page

continued from previous page
```
//Turn redraw of listbox on to show results
    lb_columns.SetRedraw ( TRUE )

//Close the cursor
    li_ret = SQLFreeStmt ( hStmt, 0 )
End If
```

10. Place the following code in the Clicked event of cb_exit. This closes the window. Save this window using the name "w_odbc_data_sources".

```
//Close the window
Close ( Parent )
```

11. Code the Open event of the Application object as follows.

```
//Open the main window for the user
Open ( w_odbc_data_sources )
```

How It Works

It takes many API functions in order to produce the intended results. ODBC uses handles to identify various aspects of the environment. An environment handle identifies memory set aside by SQLAllocEnv(), and the ODBC driver requires this value prior to connecting to a data source. A connection handle identifies this database connection. Finally, the driver will not process any data requests without a statement handle, as returned by SQLAllocStmt(). Once these three pieces are in place, you are free to call most any function in the API. Most of the ODBC API functions return data in a result set based on cursors, and four more steps are required to obtain the desired data. First, your scripts must use the appropriate function that initializes the cursor (SQLTables() or SQLColumns() in this example). Then, you must tell the ODBC driver which data you want, and where to put this data. This is the job of SQLBindCol(). Next, the scripts repetitively call SQLFetch() to retrieve each row of data into the bound program variables. Finally, you must close the cursor using SQLFreeStmt(). This example highlights just a few of the available ODBC API calls. Many more exist, and provide a wide range of services. Table 15-13 shows some of these additional functions, as well as the job they carry out. The ODBC API is robust, and it is beyond the scope of this book to fully document it. If you are interested in further ODBC knowledge, a good reference book on the ODBC API is a must.

FUNCTION	PURPOSE
SQLDescribeCol()	Returns column descriptions for name, type and length for 1 column
SQLForeignKeys()	Returns columns that comprise the foreign keys of a table
SQLRowCount()	Returns number of rows affected by last SQL statement
SQLCancel()	Cancels processing of SQL statement
SQLExecDirect()	Executes an SQL statement
SQLGetFunctions()	Returns information on the support of a particular ODBC function
SQLPrepare()	Prepares an SQL statement for execution

FUNCTION	PURPOSE
SQLPrimaryKeys()	Returns the column names that comprise the primary key of a table
SQLTablePrivileges()	Returns list of tables and privileges for that table.
SQLTransact()	Requests a COMMIT or ROLLBACK

Table 15-13 Additional ODBC API functions

Comments

The SQLBindCol() function performs much of the processing used in the ODBC API. Many of the API functions return data as a result set, meaning that the server retrieves the data in a cursor. Your scripts must request the data one row at a time. The SQLFetch() function performs this data retrieval. However, SQLFetch() must be told where (what program variable) to use for storage of the retrieved data. This is the job of SQLBindCol(). When a script calls the SQLBindCol() function, the second argument tells the function which column of the result set to bind to which program variable. The argument contains the number of the column in question, beginning at 1, and increments up through the number of columns retrieved. The third argument tells the function the data type to which the data must be converted. SQL data types are different than C data types (remember that the API was written in C), and Table 15-14 shows these data types, their values, and how they map from SQL to the C language. Using the ODBC API provides you with a high degree of flexibility for writing portable, back-end-independent applications. However, you'll write more code using this technique. You must understand (or at least be familiar with) the C language, C calling conventions, and pointers. This is not a topic for the casual business application developer. Most developers won't understand the code that you have written, so be sure to fully document and comment your code.

SQL DATA TYPE	C DATA TYPE	VALUE USED IN SCRIPTS
BINARY	SQL_C_BINARY	-2
BIT	SQL_C_BIT	-7
CHAR, VARCHAR, DECIMAL, NUMERIC	SQL_C_CHAR	1
DATE	SQL_C_DATE	9
	SQL_C_DEFAULT	99
DOUBLE	SQL_C_DOUBLE	8
FLOAT	SQL_C_FLOAT	6
LONG	SQL_C_LONG	4
SMALLINT	SQL_C_SHORT	5
TIME	SQL_C_TIME	10

Table 15-14 Type conversions and values for SQL to C data types

15.7 How do I...
Determine when another application is done?

Problem

My application allows users to run other programs. The problem is, my application cannot continue until these others have closed. My application cannot be suspended, as the user may need to move freely between them. In one example, the user opens the Calculator, and my application needs the result which the user places on the clipboard prior to closing. How can I start another application, and receive notification when the user finishes with it?

Technique

A simple yet powerful technique will provide you with the result you want. The fact that Windows is a multitasking operating system is both a blessing and a curse in this situation. On the one hand, it is easy to allow users unlimited mobility between applications, but the problem you have described above may be important. With the help of two more Windows API functions and one PowerScript function, it is easy to get around this issue. GetActiveWindow() returns a handle to the window in the foreground. This handle is used in the IsWindow() function to test to see if the window is still there. By using a loop, you'll effectively suspend your application until the other one is complete. However, since this is an event driven architecture, you can't stop other events from occurring. This is desirable, since you want the user to have free access to all program features. Therefore, the scripts are not really suspended, but continue to process other messages in the Windows message queue.

Steps

Open and run the application in the RUNWAIT.PBL library. Click on the Run and Wait button. Select an application such as the Calculator from the dialog box. Do some processing in this application, and shut it down. You will receive a message box stating that the application ended. Additionally, run an application and return to the PowerBuilder application. Try to shut it down. You are notified that it is waiting for another program to finish, and have the ability to stop your application from closing. This window is shown in action in Figure 15-7.

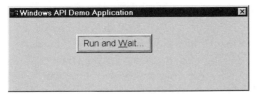

Figure 15-7 Window with new Run and Wait button.

1. Create a new Application object called "runwait" and save it in a library called RUNWAIT.PBL

2. Create a new window, using Figure 15-7 as a guide. Give this window the properties shown in Table 15-15. Declare the following local external function calls in this window.

```
Function UINT LoadLibraryA ( String as_library ) Library "kernel32.dll"
Subroutine FreeLibrary ( UINT HInstance ) Library "kernel32.dll"
Function UINT ShellExecuteA ( UINT hwnd, ref String op, ref string file, &
        ref string parms, ref string dir, UINT show) Library "shell32.dll"
Function Boolean IsWindow ( UINT HWnd ) Library "User32.dll"
Function UINT GetForegroundWindow () Library "User32.dll"
```

OBJECT/CONTROL	PROPERTY	VALUE
Window	Name	w_main
	Title	"Windows API Demo Application"
	Resizable	FALSE
CommandButton	Name	cb_runandwait
	Text	"Run and &Wait..."

Table 15-15 Properties for Run and Wait application window

3. Declare two instance variables for this window. The values for these items are shown in Table 15-16. Place the following code in the Clicked event of cb_runandwait. The script uses the Windows API function ShellExecuteA() to launch a program. You may wish to review How-To 15.3 for the specifics of this function. If the user selects a data file, ShellExecuteA() will launch the associated application. Immediately after running the application, the script calls the PowerScript Yield() function within a loop. (The upper value of this loop may have to be adjusted to fit your needs.) This gives Windows a chance to load the other application before the rest of this script runs. This is important, as the next step assumes the application has loaded. Next, the script calls the GetForegroundWindow() function, which returns the handle of the window of the newly started application's main window. This will always be the application that was just started. Using this handle in a Do...While loop, the script repetitively calls IsWindow(), which returns a Boolean value indicating whether or not the window identified by the handle argument exists. By processing the Yield() function, other applications are allowed processing time. Without the call to Yield(), your application would never relinquish control of the processor, and your PowerBuilder application would run in an endless loop. In this case, the Do…While loop would continue running, and the user could never do any further work. This results in the secondary application never becoming active, and therefore the user could not shut it down.

```
String ls_path, ls_file, ls_parms, ls_dir, ls_command
UINT lu_return, lu_handle, lu_instance

//See if the library is available
lu_instance = LoadLibraryA ( "shell32.dll" )

If lu_instance < 32 Then
//No, so issue a message
    MessageBox ( "Library", "Could not load SHELL.DLL" )
Else
    GetFileOpenName ( "Run application from PowerBuilder...", &
                      ls_path, ls_file, "*", "All Files (*.*),*.*" )

    If ls_path <> "" Then
        SetPointer ( Hourglass! )
        ls_command = "open"
//Set instance flags to indicate we're waiting. Only used by closequery
        ib_wait = TRUE
        is_file = ls_path
        lu_return =   ShellExecuteA ( Handle ( Parent ), ls_command, &
                      ls_path, ls_parms, ls_file, 3 )

//Give Windows a chance to load the application
        For lu_instance = 1 To 32768  //May need adjustment for individual
//needs
            Yield ()
        Next

//Get the handle of this new window
        lu_handle = GetForegroundWindow()
        If lu_return > 32 Then            //successful handle value
//Loop until that window is no longer there
            Do While IsWindow ( lu_handle )
                Yield ()
            Loop
            ib_wait = FALSE
//Notify user that the application finished
            MessageBox( 'Run',ls_path + "~r~nhas finished." )
            Parent.SetFocus()     //Put this application in foreground
        End If
    End If
//Free the shell.dll library
    FreeLibrary ( lu_instance )
End If
```

CONTROL/VARIABLE	PROPERTY	VALUE
Instance Variable	String	is_file
	Boolean	ib_wait

Table 15-16 New control and properties for w_main

4. Place the following code in the CloseQuery event of the window. This uses the information stored by the above script to notify the user that the application is waiting for another process to complete.

```
Integer li_yn

//See if application is waiting for another to quit
If ib_wait Then
    li_yn = MessageBox ( "Close", "This application is waiting for~r~n" + &
                is_file + "~r~nto complete. Do you want to close now?", &
                Question!, YesNo!, 2)
    If li_yn = 2 Then
//Don't close this window
        Message.ReturnValue = 1
    End If
End If
```

5. Place the following code in the Open event of the Application object to open the window for the user.

```
//Set up the application information and open the first window
Open ( w_main )
```

6. Save all objects and run the application.

How It Works

The SHELL32.DLL files defines the ShellExecuteA() function. A user may not have this file available, so this application uses the LoadLibraryA() and FreeLibrary() functions to test this condition. The two functions are a part of the Windows API, defined in the Windows kernel. LoadLibraryA() fails if SHELL32.DLL cannot be loaded, and therefore the application can test its return code. The script issues a message if the library is not available. Without this step, a runtime error results if SHELL32.DLL does not exist. FreeLibrary() unloads any function loaded with LoadLibraryA(), releasing system memory back to Windows.

Each object in the windows environment is identified by a handle. This numeric value is unique for each object that Windows maintains. As soon as another application starts, the script gets the handle for that application's main window. This handle is used in the call to IsWindow(), looping until the window identified by that handle no longer exists. This example uses the ShellExecuteA() function presented in How-To 15-3, but the PowerBuilder Run() function would work equally well, provided you intend to run an executable file. If you want to launch an application based on a data file created with it, you must use ShellExecuteA(). See How-To 15-4 for a full explanation of why.

Comments

This example only allows you to wait for one application. If you need to wait for more than one, you will need to use arrays to hold the application handle returned from GetForegroundWindow(), and test all of them with IsWindow(). The CloseQuery event that you wrote is not necessary to accomplish the result here, but you may wish to include it to notify the user that another application must first finish. If you were to shut down your application while it is processing the Yield() function, a runtime error would result. This is another reason for including this script.

COMPLEXITY
INTERMEDIATE

15.8 How do I...
Use the multimedia API to play a .WAV file?

Problem

Multimedia applications are growing in popularity, and I would like to play sounds in my applications. It seems users are accustomed to this, and even expect some level of multimedia support. How can I play sounds?

Technique

Waveform audio requires only one function as a minimum for playing sound. This function is called SndPlaySoundA(), and is a part of the multimedia API. This function takes two parameters. The first is the filename of the .WAV file you wish to play. The second argument determines how the sound plays, as discussed below. The sample application plays a different .WAV file in the Selected event for each item in a menu. This would be helpful for a user who is visually impaired. As the user moves the mouse inside an open menu, the application literally tells them which item the mouse is over. Sounds can be annoying to some users, so a mechanism should be provided to allow the user to turn sounds off.

Steps

Open and run the application in the WAV.PBL library. From the Options menu, select Enable Sounds. Use the mouse (or the arrow keys) to select various items from the File menu. The menu tells you what item is selected. The complete window with the menu is shown in Figure 15-8.

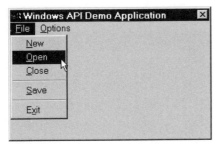

Figure 15-8 Complete window
with menu

1. Create a new Application object called "wav", and save it in a library called
WAV.PBL.

2. Create a new window, using Figure 15-8 as a guide. Save this window in
WAV.PBL using the name "w_main".

3. Create a new menu for the w_main window. Give this menu the properties
shown in Figure 15-9. Declare a Boolean instance variable called ib_play,
and place the following local external function declarations in the menu. If
you've never declared external functions, you need to select Local External
Functions... from the Declare menu. These declarations include the multimedia function for playing waveform audio, as well as two Windows API
functions for managing the loading of the .DLL.

```
Function Boolean sndPlaySoundA ( String s_file, UINT u_flags ) Library &
"WINMM.dll"
Function UINT LoadLibraryA ( String as_library ) Library "kernel32.dll"
Subroutine FreeLibrary ( UINT Hinstance ) Library "kernel32.dll"
```

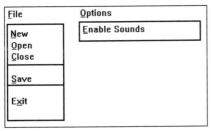

Figure 15-9 Menu for w_main

4. Declare a menu function called mf_play. This function returns no value, has
public access, and accepts a one-string argument. Place the following code
in that function. This function uses the value of ib_play to determine if the
user has turned on sounds. Then, the LoadLibraryA() function (this function checks for the existence of a .DLL) is called to verify the existence of
the multimedia library. If all is well, the sndPlaySoundA() function plays the

.WAV file passed as the argument. Finally, it calls FreeLibrary() to release the memory in use by WINMM.DLL.

```
UINT lu_instance

//Check the user settable 'sound on' flag. Only play if true
If ib_play Then
//See if the multimedia library is available
    lu_instance = LoadLibraryA ( "WINMM.dll" )
    If lu_instance = 0 Then
//Play the wave file
     sndPlaySoundA ( as_wave, 1 )
//Unload the library
        FreeLibrary ( lu_instance )
    End If
End If
Return
```

5. Place the following code in the Clicked event for m_enablesounds. This toggles the checked attribute of the menu item, sets the instance flag accordingly, and plays the appropriate sound file to tell the user which configuration is in use.

```
//Set the boolean flag for enabling or disabling sounds
this.checked = Not this.checked
ib_play = this.checked
//Tell user what configuration is in effect
If ib_play Then
    mf_play ( "sndon.wav" )
End If
```

6. The remainder of the scripts are identical, except for the .WAV file used. For each of the items in the File menu, place the following code in the Selected event, substituting the proper filename from Table 15-17. The example shown is for the New option. These scripts simply call the mf_play() function

```
//Play the appropriate file
mf_play ( "new.wav" )
```

MENU ITEM	.WAV FILENAME
File	FILE.WAV
New	NEW.WAV
Open	OPEN.WAV
Close	CLOSE.WAV
Save	SAVE.WAV
Exit	EXIT.WAV

Table 15-17 .WAV file names for each Selected event

7. Save the menu as m_wave_menu. Open the Window painter, and associate this menu with the w_main window.

8. Place the following code in the Open event of the Application object. This opens the main window for the user. Save all objects and run the application.

```
//Set up the application information and open the first window
Open ( w_main )
```

How It Works

SndPlaySoundA() is the multimedia function responsible for playing .WAV files. This function takes two arguments. The first is the name of the file. This must be in the user's path, or the fully qualified pathname must be specified. The second argument specifies options for playing the sound file. Valid values are shown in Table 15-18. The specified sound is played using asynchronous operation, allowing the user to maneuver in the application while the sound plays.

SETTING	VALUE	MEANING
SND_SYNC	0	Plays the sound, and finishes before returning
SND_ASYNC	1	Plays the sound, returns while playing
SND_NODEFAULT	2	If .WAV not found, no default sound is played
SND_MEMORY	4	Filename points to in-memory image
SND_LOOP	8	Plays in loop until sndPlaySound called with NULL value for filename
SND_NOSTOP	16	Returns FALSE if a sound is currently playing

Table 15-18 Settings for second argument to sndPlaySound() function

Comments

If the specified sound file is not found, the function plays no sound and returns FALSE. FALSE is also the return value if the SND_NOSTOP argument is specified and another sound is currently playing. Otherwise, sndPlaySoundA() returns TRUE. The multimedia API contains other functions that allow you to play music from a music CD, and provide a lower level of sound control than does SndPlaySoundA(). But for waveform audio, the technique is very straightforward.

COMPLEXITY
INTERMEDIATE

15.9 How do I...
Use the multimedia API to play a video clip?

Problem

Multimedia is all the rage. Many applications support not only sound, but video as well. I would like to incorporate video into my applications. This would be a great way to train users online, and spice up my user interface. How do I do it?

Technique

Like playing waveform audio, as presented in How-To 15.8, playing video clips (.AVI files) is as simple as calling the proper multimedia functions. Unlike the waveform example, however, there are other considerations as well. Playing video requires several functions. Adding full-motion video to your PowerBuilder application is not difficult, but it does require a thorough understanding of the functions involved, as well as the course of events that occur. The two functions involved are mciSendStringA(), responsible for sending commands to the playback device, and mdiGetErrorStringA(), which reports errors involved in the process. Additionally, mciSendStringA() requires a command string of the proper format, and must be called several times for different purposes.

Steps

Open and run the application in the AVI.PBL library. Click on the Play AVI File button. Several .AVI files are available on the accompanying CD-ROM. Select a file to play and press OK. You can stop the player any time by closing the window with the Control menu. The completed window is shown in Figure 15-10.

1. Create a new application objected called "AVI", and save it in a library called AVI.PBL.

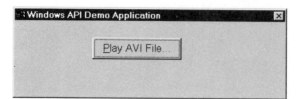

Figure 15-10 Window with Play AVI button

2. Create a simple window with one CommandButton control. Use Figure 15-10 as a guide. Add the following local external functions to this window. These include the two functions necessary for playing video, as well as two Windows API calls used to trap runtime errors in loading external functions. Save this window using the name w_main. Table 15-19 shows the properties for the window.

```
Function UINT LoadLibraryA ( String as_library ) Library "kernel32.dll"
Subroutine FreeLibrary ( UINT HInstance ) Library "kernel32.dll"
Function Boolean mciGetErrorStringA ( long error, ref string buffer, &
        int wlength ) library "winmm.dll"
Function Long mciSendString ( ref string command, ref string returnstring,
&
        int wlength, UINT wcallback ) library "winmm.dll"
```

OBJECT/CONTROL	PROPERTY	VALUE
Window	Name	w_main
	Title	"Windows API Demo Application"
	Resizable	FALSE
CommandButton	Name	cb_avi
	Text	"&Play AVI File..."

Table 15-19 Properties for AVI window and CommandButton control

3. Place the following code in the Clicked event for cb_avi. This script uses the Windows API function LoadLibraryA() to ensure the multimedia library is available. If so, it verifies that the video driver has been properly configured by looking in the registry for the AVIVideo device. The RegistryGet() function performs this task. RegistryGet() takes three arguments — the key of interest, the node within that key, and a reference string (ls_driver in the example). If the RegistryGet() function returns a 1, ls_driver contains the video playback device. If it returns -1, an error occured, and it assumes the machine is not configured for video playback. Once these preliminary checks are complete, the script obtains a video clip file from the user. Then it builds a command string to open the device. This command is then sent to the mciSendStringA() function. This command specifies the type of device (AVIVideo), and gives this file an alias (cartoon) that is used when playing the video clip. This alias name can be anything you wish, as it simply specifies a name that is used in subsequent multimedia function calls. If an error occurs while opening the device, the script calls mciGetErrorStringA() to obtain the error text. Once the device is open, the script builds a second command string which tells mciSendStringA() to play the file using the alias name. This new command string also requests *notification* (an event generated in the parent window) upon completion of playing. Once the file has run to completion (or the user closes the video clip window), the object referenced in the last argument (Handle (Parent)) receives this notification message through an event that you will declare in the next step.

```
string ls_command, ls_buffer, ls_file, ls_path, ls_driver
long ll_error
UINT lu_lib

//See if multimedia library is installed
lu_lib = loadlibraryA ( "WINMM.dll" )
If lu_lib <> 0 Then
    MessageBox ( "Path", "Could not load multimedia device library." )
Else
    FreeLibrary ( lu_lib )
    ls_buffer = "HKEY_LOCAL_MACHINE\System\CurrentControlSet\Control" + &
        "\MediaResources\MCI\AVIVideo"
    ll_error = RegistryGet ( ls_buffer, "Driver", ls_driver )
    If ll_error = -1 Then
        MessageBox ( "AVI", "No Video driver installed" )
    Else
//Get an avi file from the user
        GetFileOpenName("AVI",ls_path, ls_file, "AVI", "Video Clips
(*.avi),*.avi" )
        If ls_path <> "" Then
            ls_buffer = Fill ( char ( 0 ), 255 )
//Build the command string to open the device
            ls_command = "open "+ ls_path+ " type avivideo alias cartoon"
            ll_error = mciSendStringA ( ls_command, ls_buffer, 255, Handle (
Parent ) )
//If an error occurred, get error message text and display
            If ll_error <> 0 Then
                mciGetErrorStringA ( ll_error, ls_buffer, 255 )
                MessageBox ( "MultiMedia Error", ls_buffer )
            Else
                Yield()
                ls_command = "play cartoon notify"
//Play the file and notify the parent window upon completion
                mciSendStringA ( ls_command, ls_buffer, 255, Handle ( Parent
) )
                Yield()
            End If
        End If
    End If
End If
```

4. Declare a custom user event for w_main. Call this event ue_notify and map it to the pbm_mmmcinotify event id. This event gets triggered when the playing of the video clip is complete, regardless of what caused the video to end. The *notify* argument passed to mciSendStringA() causes the pbm_mmmcinotify event to fire. Place the following code in this event. This closes the device that you opened in the previous step, using the alias name (cartoon) created when the previous script opened the device.

```
String ls_command, ls_buffer

//Close the device
```

```
ls_command = "close cartoon"
mciSendStringA ( ls_command, ls_buffer, 255, Handle ( this ) )
Yield()
```

5. Place the following code in the Open event of the Application object to open the w_main window.

```
//Set up the application information and open the first window
Open ( w_main )
```

6. Save the window and run the application. Figure 15-11 shows an AVI file playing.

Figure 15-11 .AVI file playing at runtime

How It Works

The mciSendStringA() is a generic function used to control multimedia devices. The command string that you pass contains the operation you want carried out, along with some options. When you open the device, you send the OPEN command, followed by the filename to open, the type of the device, and an alias name. You can also specify the NOTIFY option, in which case the event mapped to pbm_mmmcinotify would be triggered. Once the device is open, another command string tells the device to play the file. The PLAY command is used here. Optionally, you could specify the WAIT option in the command string, in which case the function does not return until the video has finished. This takes control out of the users' hands, and forces them to view the entire video. They cannot close, move, or resize the window that the video plays in. Once complete, the pbm_mmmcinotify event fires, and this is where the device is closed. If you had not specified the NOTIFY option in the command string, the pbm_mmmcinotify event would not occur, and you would have no way of knowing when the video had finished. Therefore, you could not close the device, and an error would occur the next time you tried to open it. If an error occurs, the return value is non-zero.

The second argument to mciSendStringA() is a buffer where an error message is placed. This string cannot be used directly in a MessageBox() function, and must be converted to the actual message. The mciGetErrorStringA() function does this for you using the return value and the error buffer from mciSendStringA(). The third argument specifies how large the error buffer is, and argument four is the handle to the object that receives any notification.

Comments

This example allows the user only to play one video clip at a time. This is not a problem, since videos take up a great deal of processor time and disk access. If you wanted to play more than one at a time, you would have to create a unique alias name each time, and store it in an instance variable array. This could be accomplished by generating a name based on the system time with the statement :

```
is_alias [ ii_video_count ] = String ( Now () )
```

where ii_video_count is the index (the number of currently playing clips plus 1) into the string array is_alias. You would also have to keep track of which video finished playing so the appropriate alias name could be used when the device is closed. Notice that the mci functions automatically create a window in which to display the video clip. The multimedia API is fairly robust and easy to use, once you understand all of the intricacies of it.

CHAPTER 16
USER OBJECTS

16

USER OBJECTS

How do I...

User objects are among the most flexible objects in PowerBuilder development. With them, you are able to customize the standard controls, create your own controls, incorporate custom controls from other vendors, and take advantage of the Visual Basic .VBX control format. The first part of this chapter focuses on these *visual* user objects. Visual user objects provide you the extendibility you need to create custom, professional applications with a consistent interface. It also reduces the coding required in the long run by extending or creating functionality common to all applications. This is yet another step towards reusability and object orientation. This chapter by no means exhausts the limits of user objects. It will give you a starting point from which your creativity can flow. The remainder of the chapter deals with *non-visual* objects. These are called *class* user objects. Class user objects come in two varieties, *custom* and *standard*. Custom class objects are a repository for functions. They contain no graphical component and are used heavily to incorporate business logic. Standard objects are SQLCA, ERROR, and MESSAGE just to name a few. These are the global objects that PowerBuilder lets you customize if necessary. Class objects give applications the power of object orientation, without the overhead of the visual components. It is possible to encapsulate code and data specific to a particular task with these objects. The standard class objects are typically available throughout the application, as they can (but do not have to) replace the default global objects such as SQLCA, ERROR, or MESSAGE. Although there are many non-visual objects available, we'll concentrate on four specific, commonly used ones.

16.1   Build a Standard User Object

Building a standard user object allows you to extend the behavior of the standard controls. DataWindows, CommandButtons, ListBoxes and the like all provide certain behaviors. However, creating standard user objects based on these controls, coding common functionality into them, and using these objects in place of standard controls provides limitless power. In this How-To, you will learn how to create a standard DataWindow object. You will write a custom function called Undelete() that will give users the ability to undelete rows provided the table has not yet been updated. Normally, once a user deletes rows from a DataWindow, it appears that they are gone forever. This is not the case. When the user deletes a row from a DataWindow control, PowerBuilder moves the row from the *primary* buffer to the *delete* buffer. How-To 16.1 provides the ability for you to incorporate a DataWindow "undelete" function into your applications. From this point forward, you place this standard object on a window surface, instead of a standard DataWindow control.

16.2   Build a Custom User Object

Custom user objects have numerous advantages. For example, you could create an object containing OK and Cancel buttons that would close and save or close and roll back any dialog box action. By creating this style of object once, you would then drop the object on any window for immediate use. No additional coding would be required. Also, custom user objects allow you to create a custom control that is not otherwise available in PowerBuilder. Examples of custom user objects include simple calendars or outline controls, as well as complex, multi-control objects such as a list manager. This How-To shows you how to build a progress meter that is common in today's applications.

16.3   Add User Events to a User Object

Once you have built a user object, you customize it with code. Typically, object functions provide this interface. How-To 16.3 shows you how to create a "slider" control, similar to those used in electronic equipment such as a graphic equalizer. The slider contains a movable bar that changes the current value of the custom control. As the user moves the slider, the control notifies you of this change through a custom user event.

16.4   Use an .OCX Custom Control

PowerBuilder provides support for custom controls with an .OCX extension. Files of this type are designed for the Visual Basic environment. With the popularity of Visual Basic, these controls cannot be ignored. Although most of the standard controls available with VB are already supported by PowerBuilder, many vendors supply additional controls for Visual Basic. We will not assume that you have any of these third party controls, except those that ship with PowerBuilder. PowerBuilder comes with several good .OCX controls. How-To 16.4 uses a calendar control to add a graphical twist to editing date columns in a DataWindow.

16.5   Build a Custom Class User Object

The class user object is not placed directly on a window as are other user objects or controls. Class user objects contain functions and properties only—no visual component exists. With these objects, your application is able to implement business rules, or any set of functions specific to a task. In this How-To, you will build a custom class object that works in conjunction with a menu. This object will determine whether or not the Undo, Cut, Copy, and Paste options should be enabled on the menu. The menu then turns the enabled attribute on or off appropriately. This object will be instantiated in the script for the menu. This keeps memory resources low, and reusability high. Instead of writing a menu function, this object provides reuse with any menu object.

16.6   Customize the Error Object

When a runtime error occurs, the Application object fires the SystemError event. At this point, PowerBuilder populates the ERROR object with information relative to the error. This information includes the object, event, and line number of the error, just to name a few. Using the SystemError event gives the application a chance to gracefully handle errors. Without an error handler in this event, PowerBuilder displays a default error message and exits the application. This How-To customizes the existing ERROR object, adding Save() and SaveSetUp() functions. The application's Open event calls SaveSetup() in order to initialize the object. This is done to indicate where to later save an error log. In the SystemError event, the application calls Save() to write the error data out to the defined log file. This way, you'll always have a reference to all runtime errors that occur, even if you are not present to witness them.

16.7   Customize the Message Object

The Message object is a global system variable—all applications use it. The two jobs of the Message object are to notify applications about events, and to pass data to these events. Most often, PowerBuilder developers use it to pass information from one window object to another. This is accomplished with the OpenWithParm(), OpenSheetWithParm(), or CloseWithReturn() functions. One of its problems involves the fact that it is global system-wide. If you fail to get the data from its properties at the first possible opportunity, another process can change the values. This How-To fixes this shortcoming by customizing the standard Message object. You will add several instance variables and four functions to it. This combination of variables and functions allows the new Message object to save its current state. This way, you can get the data out whenever it is convenient to do so. You will implement this by adding a call to one of these new functions in an ancestor sheet. Using this technique provides data protection from other objects or applications.

16.8   Build a Custom Transaction Object

The built-in transaction object, SQLCA, is adequate for small applications. However, in order to manage many concurrent transactions, additional transaction objects may be necessary. PowerBuilder makes SQLCA available as a default. It is up to the developer to declare and instantiate additional ones if necessary. After creating this additional object, you must write the code responsible for populating and connecting to the database. You must also perform the necessary error checking after processing any SQL statement. In this How-To, you will customize the transaction object so that these necessary but mundane tasks are accomplished through custom functions. By extending the default transaction object, you provide an automated, consistent, easy-to-use, and reusable object, from which all applications benefit.

COMPLEXITY
INTERMEDIATE

16.1   How do I...
Build a standard user object?

Problem

I know that user objects provide a lot of power. I also know that there are many types of user objects. I have never ventured into this realm of PowerBuilder. Standard user objects look just like regular controls, and I would like to build a standard DataWindow control that allows the user to undelete rows that the user previously deleted. How can I create a standard user object, write a function like this undelete function, and reuse this control in all of my applications?

Technique

Many PowerBuilder applications do not use standard controls such as CommandButtons and DataWindows. Instead, developers create standard user objects and add event scripts and functions to them. The application then uses these custom user objects, instead of standard controls. This provides several benefits. First, it is not uncom-

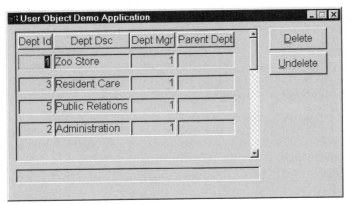

Figure 16-1 Window with standard DataWindow object

mon to extend the capabilities of standard controls. Second, when corporate-wide changes occur, all applications continue to behave the same way. By changing only the user object, one change propagates throughout your entire suite of applications. A recompilation completes the change(s) for the entire application. This How-To shows you how to create a standard DataWindow control with a built-in function that restores previously deleted rows. Once you have this user object, it replaces the standard DataWindow control. Now all of your applications can support an undelete operation with little additional code on your part.

Steps

Open and run the application in the STANDUO.PBL library. Once the application starts, press the Delete button several times to delete rows from the DataWindow. Then press Undelete. All the previously deleted rows come back, and the StaticText control (at the bottom of the window) shows the number of restored rows. Figure 16-1 shows the window at runtime.

1. Start by creating a new Application object called "standard", and store it a library called STANDUO.PBL. Do not have PowerBuilder generate an application template. Do not place any code in this object yet. You'll come back and do this after you create the initial window object.

2. Start the User Object painter by clicking its icon from the PowerBar. From the Select User Object dialog box, click New. PowerBuilder displays the New User Object dialog. From here you chose the type of user object you wish to create. User objects are divided into two groups. Class user objects are invisible to the user, and get instantiated at runtime. Visual user objects can be seen by the user. Click the icon labeled "Standard" in the "Visual" GroupBox and press OK. Now PowerBuilder wants to know what type of standard user object to create. Click on "datawindow" and press OK. PowerBuilder now displays a generic DataWindow control object in the User Object painter.

3. Select User Object Functions… from the Declare menu. This is where you create the undelete function for this DataWindow control. Give this new function the properties shown in Table 16-1. Place the following code in the function. First, the function needs to know how many rows have been deleted. The DeletedCount() function provides this information. Then, using the DataWindow function RowsMove(), it moves these rows from the Deleted buffer to the Primary buffer. DataWindow buffers are explained fully below, but briefly, the Delete buffer is where PowerBuilder stores rows targeted for deletion. The Primary buffer is where all user modifications and insertions occur. Finally, if RowsMove() returns an error (-1), the function's return value is set to 0. Otherwise, it indicates the number of rows that had originally been deleted. This value is returned to the caller.

```
Long ll_rows
Integer li_ret

//Get the count of the number of deleted rows
ll_rows = this.DeletedCount()

//Move the deleted rows from the delete buffer to the primary buffer
li_ret = this.RowsMove ( 1, ll_rows, Delete!, this, 1, Primary! )

//See if an error occurred and handle the return code appropriately
If li_ret = -1 Then ll_rows = 0

Return ll_rows
```

PROPERTY	VALUE
Name	UnDelete
Returns	Long

Table 16-1 Properties for UnDelete() function declaration

4. Save this object using the name suo_dw_with_undelete and close the User Object painter.

5. Create a simple DataWindow object. The data source and presentation style are left for you to select as you desire. If your DataWindow joins multiple tables, ensure that the tab order of each column has a non-zero value, since you will be deleting rows from this DataWindow at runtime. Save this object using the name d_undelete.

6. Create a new window object. Place two CommandButtons and one StaticText control on the window. Use the window shown in Figure 16-1 as a guide.

7. You now need a DataWindow control in which to display the data. Instead of choosing a regular DataWindow control from the Controls DropDown, select the UserObject button instead. Notice that both the Controls

DropDown and the PowerBar have UserObject icons on them. From the resulting dialog box, select the suo_dw_with_undelete object and press OK. Drop this object onto the window surface. Give the window and all controls the properties shown in Table 16-2.

OBJECT/CONTROL	PROPERTY	VALUE
Window	Name	w_dw_undelete
	TitleBar	"User Object Demo Application"
	Resizable	FALSE
	Maximize Box	FALSE
CommandButton	Name	cb_delete
	Text	"&Delete"
	Name	cb_undelete
	Text	"&Undelete"
DataWindow	Name	dw_undelete
	VScroll Bar	TRUE
	DataObject	d_undelete
StaticText	Name	st_undeleted_rows
	Text	*blank*

Table 16-2 Properties for window and controls

8. Place the following code in the Open event for the window. This establishes the relationship between the DataWindow control and the transaction object. Notice that even though the DataWindow is a user object, it looks and behaves like a standard DataWindow control.

```
//Set up the datawindow
dw_undelete.SetTransObject ( SQLCA )
dw_undelete.Retrieve ()
```

9. Place the following code in the Clicked event for cb_delete. This deletes the current row from the DataWindow so you can later test the undelete function.

```
//Delete a row
dw_undelete.DeleteRow ( 0 )
dw_undelete.SetFocus ()
```

10. Place the following code in the Clicked event of cb_undelete. This calls the DataWindow undelete function created in step 2. Notice that since the function is encapsulated within the object, you must preface the function call with the DataWindow control name, just as you do for any built-in function such as InsertRow(). After calling UnDelete(), this script sets the Text property of the StaticText control to show the user how many rows

were recovered. Save the window using the name w_dw_undelete when
you are finished.

```
Long ll_rows

//Call the undelete function of the datawindow.
//Display the number of undeleted rows in the static text

ll_rows = dw_undelete.Undelete()
st_undeleted_rows.Text = String ( ll_rows ) + " rows undeleted"
```

11. Return to the Application painter and place the following code in the Open
event. This connects the application to the zoo database distributed on the
accompanying CD.

```
//Set up SQLCA for a connection
SQLCA.DBMS = "odbc"
SQLCA.DBPARM = "ConnectString='dsn=zoo;uid=dba;pwd=sql'"

Connect Using SQLCA;
If SQLCA.SQLCode < 0 Then
    MessageBox ( "Database", "Could not connect to database.~r~n" + &
                 SQLCA.SQLErrText )
    Halt Close
End If

//Open the window
Open ( w_dw_undelete )
```

12. Save the Application object, run the application, and test your new standard user object.

How It Works

Standard visual user objects look and behave just like standard controls. By creating this type of user object, you enable your applications to support extended services.
Such services may include this undelete function, as well as functions for custom
sorting, filtering, or even providing a popup calendar if the user right mouse clicks
on a date column. By placing these functions in, and using a standard visual user
object, your applications take on a standard, predictable, and custom look and feel.
Your applications gain this power automatically as you extend a control's capabilities.

DataWindow controls are made up of four *buffers*. These buffers are the *Primary*,
Delete, *Filter*, and *Original* buffers. The Primary buffer contains the data displayed
by the control, and is the only buffer the user works with directly. The Original buffer
contains the rows with values at the time of retrieval. Its job is to provide information
used in updating the table, as well as replacing a column's data if the user presses
<ESC> while editing a column. The Filter buffer contains all rows filtered out through
the SetFilter() and Filter() functions. The Delete buffer contains all rows targeted for
deletion. Any time the user deletes a row, PowerBuilder simply moves the row from
the Primary buffer to the Delete buffer. When a script calls the DataWindow

undelete function, the object simply moves any rows from the Delete buffer into the Primary buffer. This DataWindow user object control is based on the definition of a standard DataWindow control. The object now contains the behavior you wrote through its function interface.

Comments

Standard user objects allow you to *subclass* controls. Subclassing is a technique whereby the object definition comes from a higher level object. Subclassing and inheritance are synonymous terms. In this case, you sub-classed a DataWindow control and created a new user object based on that control's original definition. In PowerBuilder, all controls are sub-classed from a *graphic object*, which in turn is sub-classed from yet a higher ancestor. So creating user objects from standard controls is a very natural extension of the inheritance chain already in place. It is very common to create standard user objects for all of the controls, and place these user objects on a window instead of using the standard controls. This way, you are able to customize the controls for your specific needs or business. Since these "controls" are user objects, any application using them reflects changes made to them simply by recompiling. Many other possibilities exist for extending control behavior. For example, the DataWindow user object could support the right mouse button. When the rbuttondown event fires, the script could determine the datatype of the column under the mouse. If it is a date column, it might open a calendar to allow the user graphical selection of a date. If the column is numeric, it may open a Calculator and paste the current column value into the Calculator's display. Other ideas include sorting or filtering capabilities, depending on where in the control the user clicks. Think of the reduction of code, and the increase in functionality, as you incorporate user objects in place of standard controls. As you work with controls, try to envision additional behavior, and create standard user objects to provide these capabilities. If you start out development with all standard user objects, these capabilities may easily be added and incorporated any time down the road.

COMPLEXITY

INTERMEDIATE

16.2 How do I...
Build a custom user object?

Problem

Progress meters give users a visual indication of the completed percentage of a lengthy operation. I have seen many applications that use progress meters, and I would like to give the same feedback to my users. Although I could purchase a custom control in the form of a .DLL, I would like to build my own. However, I don't want to have to learn C or C++ in order to do this. How can I build my own progress meter in PowerBuilder using a custom user object?

Technique

Custom visual user objects allow you to build components that look and work like any other control, even controls that are not a part of the PowerBuilder environment. The only limit is that of your imagination. For example, you might create a custom user object that works like the progress meter you mentioned above. In this How-To, you will learn how to build just such a progress meter. This is accomplished through the use of two overlapping StaticText controls. One starts off at a default width, showing the full width of the current process. This control has a lowered style border. The second control starts off with a width of 0, and gradually increases its width to overlay the first StaticText control. This overlaid control has a raised border, and a different color. The visual effect to the user is that the meter appears to slide from left to right. This new control provides functions that set the upper limit value, as well as the current progress percentage, and the color of the slider bar.

Steps

Open and run the application in the CUSTOMUO.PBL library. When the window opens, press the Progress button. The window simulates a lengthy process that runs from 0 through 100 percent. Figure 16-2 shows the progress meter at runtime, midway through a long operation.

1. Create a new application called "custom", and save it in a library named CUSTOMUO.PBL.

2. Open the User Object painter. Create a new object and select Custom from the New User Object dialog box. PowerBuilder displays a blank work surface similar to a window surface. Place three StaticText controls on the window. Don't worry about the size or position of any of the controls, as your code will set them appropriately.

3. The following code, which goes in the Constructor event of the object, takes care of sizing the controls dynamically. The Constructor event fires when the window paints the control on its surface at runtime. (You'll drop this object on a window surface later.) Constructor events are to user objects what the Open event is to a window object. This script aligns the StaticText controls, and sets their widths and border styles. Table 16-3 shows the properties for the controls, while Figure 16-3 shows the user object in the painter at design time.

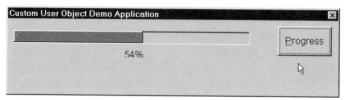

Figure 16-2 Progress meter in action

Figure 16-3 Progress meter control object at design time in the User Object painter

```
//Set the height and width of the statictext
st_foreground.height = st_background.height
st_foreground.width = 0

//Set the position of the controls within the object
st_background.x = 0
st_background.y = 0
st_foreground.x = 0
st_foreground.y = 0

//Set the borderstyle for each
st_background.BorderStyle = StyleLowered!
st_foreground.BorderStyle = StyleRaised!

//Position the text control that displays the percentage text
st_percent.y = 100

//Size the object
this.height = st_foreground.height + st_percent.height + 10
```

CONTROL	PROPERTY	VALUE
StaticText	Name	st_foreground
	Name	st_background
	Name	st_percent
	Text	blank

Table 16-3 Properties of controls on the custom progress meter

4. Declare the following instance variable. This variable should have a *Protected* access level. Protected instance variables are not accessible by the other objects. They are only changeable through User Object Event scripts or functions. This is a standard object oriented approach, allowing an object to protect data that it considers important. You must provide functions or Event scripts that manipulate the value. This approach allows the user object code to possibly verify values prior to changing them. With direct manipulation of a property (such as sle_name.Text="Smith"), the object has no control over the value of the property. Other objects need not know the name of this variable, or the implementation details. All that is necessary is the knowledge of the appropriate function name. Consider the DataWindow function InsertRow(). You don't care how the control does the

work. All that interests you is the fact that the DataWindow inserts a new
row at the specified location.

```
Protected:
    Long il_limit
```

5. Declare an object function called SetProgress() by selecting User Object
Functions… from the Declare menu. Table 16-4 shows the properties of the
function. Place the following code in this function. Its purpose is to set the
width of the foreground StaticText control (the one whose width "grows")
to the appropriate width, indicating the percent complete. Other objects
call this function, which is responsible for changing the visual action of the
meter.

```
Integer li_percent, li_width

//Set the widths of the foreground static text control, and indicate
//the percentage complete with st_percent
li_width = st_background.width / il_limit * ai_value
st_foreground.width = li_width
li_percent = st_foreground.width / st_background.width * 100
st_percent.text = String ( li_percent ) + "%"
Return
```

PROPERTY	VALUE	DATATYPE
Name	SetProgress	
Returns	(None)	
Argument 1	ai_value	Integer

Table 16-4 Properties for SetProgress() function

6. This object allows you to set the color of the meter's sliding bar at runtime
and is accomplished with the following function. Declare another function
called SetColor().Table 16-5 shows the function declaration, and the following code makes up the function.

```
//Set the color of the foreground control

st_foreground.BackColor = al_color
Return
```

PROPERTY	VALUE	
Name	SetColor	
Returns	(None)	
Argument 1	al_color	Long

Table 16-5 Properties for SetColor() function declaration

7. The object requires one last function before the meter is complete. Name this function SetLimit(). It sets the instance variable (declared in step 4 above) to the desired upper limit of the object. Its value is used in calculating the percentage complete. Table 16-6 shows the declaration. Place the following code in this function. SetProgress() reads this value to determine how wide to make the sliding portion of the meter.

```
//Set the upper limit of the control

il_limit = al_value
Return
```

PROPERTY	VALUE	DATATYPE
Name	SetLimit	
Returns	None	
Argument 1	al_value	Long

Table 16-6 Properties for the SetLimit() function declaration

8. Save this object using the name cuo_progress.

9. Create a new window object. From the Controls DropDown list, select the UserObject button, and place an instance of the cuo_progress object on the window surface. Name this control cuo_progress. Next, place a CommandButton on the window. Table 16-7 shows the properties for the window and both controls, while Figure 16-4 shows the completed window.

CONTROL	PROPERTY	VALUE
Window	Name	w_progress
	TitleBar	"Custom User Object Demo Application"
	Window Type	Response
UserObject	Name	uo_progress
	Border	FALSE
CommandButton	Name	cb_progress
	Text	"&Progress"

Table 16-7 Properties of window associated controls

10. Declare two instance variables, ii_x and ii_y, both integers.

```
Public:
    Integer ii_x, ii_y
```

11. Place the following code in the Clicked event of cb_progress. The script sets the color of the slider to red, using the RGB() function. RGB() takes three

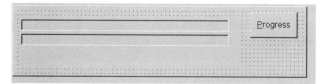

Figure 16-4 Complete window with Meter object

arguments which specify the red, green, and blue components respectively. Each argument ranges from 0 (no value) through 255 (full saturation). It then sets the upper limit of the object to 100. This number can be anything you want, as it sets the relative percentage of the control. For example, if you were using the meter to show the progress of a copy operation where you were copying 40 files, you might set this value to 40. Then, using a simple For...Next loop, the script might increment the meter by 1 for each file copied. The SetProgress() function (created earlier) changes the value of the meter. Once you have completed this script, close the PowerScript painter and save the window.

```
//Indicate a long process in progress

//Set the color of the slider bar to red
uo_progress.SetColor ( RGB ( 255, 0, 0 ) )
//Set the upper limit to 100
uo_progress.SetLimit ( 100 )
//Empty loop to simulate the progress
For ii_x = 1 to 100
    For ii_y = 1 to 1000
    Next
    uo_progress.SetProgress ( ii_x )
Next
```

12. Code the Open event of the Application object to open the window.

```
//Open the window
Open ( w_progress )
```

How It Works

This meter uses two StaticText controls. One has a lowered border and shows the unprocessed portion of the operation. The second StaticText control has a raised border whose width starts at zero, and increases horizontally to overlay the first. An instance variable holds the value of the upper bound of the control. The object protects the instance variable (since you declared it as protected), and does not allow other objects to directly modify the value. The object's member function provides indirect access to the property (instance variable). The Constructor event fires when Windows paints the object on the window. This event gives the object the opportunity to do some setup work, much as you do in the Open event of a window. In this example, the Constructor aligns the two StaticText controls, sets their initial sizes, and changes the border style of the controls. Three member functions control the behavior of the object. SetProgress() is the main workhorse of the object. Notice that once you place the object on a window, you do not have access to its internals. For example, you cannot see the code for the functions, see the instance variables, or modify the static text controls within it. You don't even have access to the object's Constructor, except at the descendent level. By placing this control on a window surface, you're really inheriting from the class cuo_progress. Therefore, the Constructor event you wrote earlier is really an ancestor script. All work that the object performs occurs through the defined interface (the functions and internal events).

Comments

Although this example does not make use of the fact that the instance variable is protected, you might want to put some logic in the function to validate the upper bound, ensuring that it is never set to a negative number. A negative value would clearly violate the integrity of the object, and the SetLimit() function could verify the value before setting the internal property. As an enhancement to this object, you may consider writing other functions that let the meter grow vertically instead of horizontally. With custom visual user objects, you have complete control over the interface of your applications. One thing to keep in mind, however, is the count of the controls that eventually get placed on a window. Each control takes precious system resources, and increases memory overhead. You should always attempt to keep the control count as low as possible. Even though the progress meter is one object, it really counts as four as far as Windows is concerned—one for each control (there are three StaticText controls), and one for the entire object itself. Keep this in mind when designing your own objects.

COMPLEXITY
ADVANCED

16.3   How do I...
Add user events to a user object?

Problem

I have created a user object, and now I want to add some user events to it. I would like my user object to provide notification as the user performs certain actions with it. I have a complex object, and have created it in order to emulate a control that does not exist in PowerBuilder. As the user manipulates this new control, other scripts must be aware of the actions. How can I provide object notification through custom user events?

Technique

Just as you can declare user events for other objects (such as windows or CommandButtons), you can also do so for user objects. In this How-To, you will provide just such notification as is described above. You'll declare three custom events within the user object, and map them to custom event IDs which the object triggers as certain actions occur. This new control emulates a Slider control, found on electronic devices such as graphic equalizers. The object uses a sliding bar that the user moves to "adjust" the control, and the control provides notification so other scripts will know when the user moves the control's slider.

Steps

Open and run the application in the ADDEVENT.PBL library. The window contains three Slider controls. To change a slider, click and hold the mouse button on one of the slider's "handles", and drag it to a new location. The value of each control modifies the red, green, and blue components of the window color. Notice that you cannot move the mouse horizontally, and that the associated SingleLineEdit control reflects the value of the Slider control. Type a value into one of the SingleLineEdit controls, and press TAB. The associated slider changes to the correct position. If you enter a value higher than the valid range, the handle moves to the top of the slider. Similarly, entering a negative number results in the handle moving to the bottom of the slider. Custom user events control the entire operation. How-To 16.3 describes the creation of this object. Figure 16-5 shows the completed application at runtime.

1. Create a new application object called "addevent", and save it in a library called ADDEVENT.PBL.

2. Start the Structure painter. Create a new structure, giving it the properties shown in Table 16-8. You'll use this structure in the next step to specify

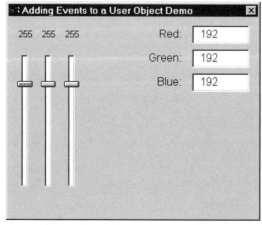

Figure 16-5 Window object at runtime

mouse coordinates for the Slider control. It is critical that you define the variables of the structure in the order shown. In the next step you will call a Windows API function that expects these variables in the order shown. Save this structure using the name s_mouse.

VARIABLE NAME	DATA TYPE
Left	Long
Top	Long
Right	Long
Bottom	Long

Table 16-8 Details for s_mouse structure

3. Start the UserObject painter, and create a new custom visual user object. The Slider control consists of three separate standard controls to provide the visual effects. Place two StaticText controls and one PictureButton on the surface of the user object. Figure 16-6 shows the Slider control object in the UserObject painter. Use Figure 16-6 as a guide in placing the controls, but don't be overly concerned with the details. The Constructor event of the object handles many of the details for you, such as setting the control's sizes and positions. Make your object as close to the above figure as possible. Table 16-9 shows the properties for the various controls.

Figure 16-6 Slider control in the UserObject painter

CONTROL	PROPERTY	VALUE
StaticText	X	225
	Y	193
	Height	545
	Width	42
	Name	st_slider
	Border	3DLowered
	Enabled	TRUE
	Text	*blank*
	X	69
	Y	65
	Height	73
	Width	174
	Name	st_scale
	Text	*blank*
PictureButton	X	10
	Y	253
	Height	137
	Width	211
	Name	pb_handle
	Text	*blank*

Table 16-9 Properties for controls of slider user object

4. Declare the following local external function. You will use this function in steps 14 and 15 to restrict mouse movement to a particular area of the screen.

```
Subroutine ClipCursor ( s_mouse str_pos ) Library "User32"
```

5. Declare the following instance variables for the object. These variables control various aspects of the object. For example, ib_showscale controls whether or not the object provides the user with the label at the top of the control, which displays its upper limit. You'll see the use of the other variables in the steps that follow.

```
Public:
    Boolean ib_showscale    //show max value

Private:
    Boolean ib_mousedown    //if button down
    Long il_max = 100       //max for control
    Window iw_parent        //ptr to parent win
```

6. Declare two custom user events for the user object by selecting User Events... from the Declare menu. Table 16-10 shows the event names and

IDs. The Paint event fires each time the control changes any visual aspect of the control. This object uses this event to set up some details of the object. The Change event will fire each time the user moves the Slider control to a new relative value.

EVENT NAME	EVENT ID
paint	pbm_paint
change	pbm_custom01

Table 16-10 Custom user events for the Slider control

7. Place the following code in the Constructor event of the user object. This script sets the width, height, and position of the three controls, based on the size of the object on the window. (You'll place and size this object on a window later.) First, it sets the height of the "handle." The handle is the PictureButton that the user slides. The value of 30 is somewhat arbitrary, but changing it requires changing the sizes of the other controls. The Slider control uses the size of these controls to determine the "value" of the current position of the handle. The value of 30 was obtained through trial and error. Then it sets the height of the slider portion (the area in which the handle can move). Then the controls are centered within the object. Finally, iw_window receives a pointer to the parent window. You'll use iw_window later to calculate some information on the parent window.

```
//Size all controls on this object based on size the developer
//set the object size on the window

pb_handle.height = 30
st_slider.height = this.height - pb_handle.height - st_scale.height*2

//Keep the slider centered
st_slider.y = this.height - st_slider.height - pb_handle.height
st_slider.x = ( this.width / 2 ) - ( st_slider.width / 2 )

//Keep the handle centered
pb_handle.width = this.width - 20
pb_handle.x = (this.width / 2 ) - ( pb_handle.width / 2 )
pb_handle.y = this.height - pb_handle.height

//Keep the scale indicator centered
st_scale.x = ( this.width / 2 ) - ( st_scale.width / 2 )
st_scale.y = st_slider.y - st_scale.height * 1.75

//Set the instance flag so the scripts can access the window later
//This is used in moving the handle (mouseup, mousedown, mousemove events)
iw_parent = Parent
```

8. Place the following code in the Paint event of the user object. As mentioned above, ib_showscale determines whether or not the object displays the upper limit of the control. This script sets the text property of st_scale, provided that the user wants to see it. This code must go in the Paint event as opposed to the Constructor, since the Constructor event fires prior to you setting a value for ib_showscale. Finally, this event triggers the Change event, which notifies the object that the user changed the control. Using this event, other scripts can obtain the value of the slider when the control first paints on the window.

```
Integer li_width

//Set the scale indicator if user wants to show it
If ib_ShowScale Then
    st_scale.Text = String ( il_max )
End If

//Post a change message so the control reports its
//position upon instantiation
this.PostEvent ( "change" )
```

9. Declare a user object function named GetValue(). Table 16-11 shows the function declaration. Place the following code in the function. GetValue() returns the value of the control back to the caller. The control calculates the value based on the height and position of the slider, compared with the height and position of the handle. The result is the ratio of the handle's position. This ratio gets multiplied by the upper bound of the control to obtain the final value.

```
Double ld_s1, ld_s2, ld_result
Long ll_value

//Find the 'approximate' value of the control
//This will be slightly inaccurate for sliders with LARGE upper bounds

//Get bottom coordinate of the slider
ld_s1 = st_slider.y + st_slider.height

//Get bottom coordinate of the handle
ld_s2 = pb_handle.y + pb_handle.height

//Get value based on the positions and the upper value of the control
ll_value = ( ( ld_s1 - ld_s2 ) / st_slider.height ) * il_max

//Return the value to the caller
Return Max ( ll_value, 0 )
```

PROPERTY	VALUE
Name	GetValue
Returns	long

Table 16-11 Function declaration for GetValue() function

10. Declare another user object function named SetMax(). Table 16-12 shows the declaration. Place the following code in this function. SetMax() sets the upper limit of the control, which the control stores in the protected instance variable named il_max.

```
//Set the private instance variable to the upper value of the control
//that the user has passed
il_max = al_value

Return
```

PROPERTY	VALUE	DATATYPE
Name	SetMax	
Returns	(none)	
Argument 1	al_value	Long

Table 16-12 Function declaration for SetMax() function

11. Declare one more user object function named SetValue(). Table 16-13 shows the details for this declaration. Place the following code in this function. The object uses this function to allow the user to set the value of the control manually (without moving the slider handle).

```
Double ld_percent

//Make sure the value passed is not too large (higher than il_max)
al_value = Min ( al_value, (  il_max ) )

//Make sure the value is not less than zero
al_value = Max ( al_value, 0 )

//Get the percentage value of where the handle should be in relation
//to the height of the slider
ld_percent = al_value / ( il_max )
ld_percent = st_slider.height * ld_percent

//Move the handle to this new position
pb_handle.y = ( st_slider.y + st_slider.height ) - &
              ld_percent - pb_handle.height

Return
```

PROPERTY	VALUE	DATATYPE
Name	SetValue	
Return	(none)	
Argument 1	al_value	Long

Table 16-13 Function declaration for SetValue() function

12. Declare three user events for pb_handle. Table 16-14 shows the event names and IDs. These events fire when the user moves the mouse, presses the left mouse button, or releases the left mouse button, respectively. The

PictureButton requires these events, as the clicked event does not supply adequate information.

EVENT NAME	EVENT ID
MouseMove	pbm_mousemove
MouseDown	pbm_lbuttondown
MouseUp	pbm_lbuttonup

Table 16-14 User event mapping for pb_handle control

13. Place the following code in the MouseMove event of pb_handle. It is the responsibility of this script to move the handle as the user slides it up or down. This script then triggers the Change event of the user object. By triggering this event, the control reports every change to the parent object (the user object). Later, you'll take advantage of this automatic event trigger. This event completes the main focus of How-To 16.3, as it meets the goal of adding automatic events to an object.

```
//Only move the slider handle if the mouse is down
If ib_mousedown Then

//Turn off drawing of the slider
    st_slider.SetRedraw ( FALSE )

//Move the handle to its new position
    this.Move ( this.x , Parent.PointerY() - this.Height / 2 )

//Turn drawing back on and bring the handle to the top so it does
//not get cut off
    st_slider.SetRedraw ( TRUE )
    this.BringToTop = TRUE

//Trigger the change event so each instance can do some work
    Parent.TriggerEvent ( "change" )
End If
```

14. Place the following code in the MouseDown event of pb_handle. This script is the most complex of the entire object. If you remember from the sample application, the mouse will not move horizontally, and it stays within the confines of the slider as the user moves the slider handle. This script assures that behavior, which is accomplished with the Windows ClipCursor() API function. ClipCursor() allows you to define a rectangle (identified by the left, top, bottom, and right coordinates). ClipCursor() expects these coordinates in units of pixels. PowerBuilder uses PowerBuilder units, so this script calls the PowerScript UnitsToPixels() function. UnitsToPixels() converts PowerBuilder units to pixels and vice versa, depending on the last argument passed to it. This script calculates the center position of the slider, as well as the position of the top and bottom of the slider. Notice that the left and right coordinates are set to the same value, resulting in restriction of horizontal movement. This coordinate is fairly straightforward, but the top and bottom are not. The top value can be found by examining the Y property of the parent window, and adding the Y property of the control object, followed by the Y property of the slider. It then subtracts the height of the Handle control (so the handle won't slide above the top of the slider), and adds the height of the window's Titlebar and menu (if any). The calculation of the bottom property takes the top's value, and adds the height of the slider portion. ClipCursor() works with pixels, and expects these coordinates in relation to the entire screen, not the window in which you want to clip the mouse. Finally, the script sets the ib_mousedown attribute to TRUE, so other scripts know that the user is moving the slider handle.

```
s_mouse str_pos

//Need to keep the mouse in the boundaries of the slider
//so as the user moves the mouse, it cannot move horizontally
//and only goes to the top and bottom of the slider. The Windows API
//function uses pixels (in a structure), so convert from PowerBuilder
//Units to pixels

//Find the left edge of the new rectangle
str_pos.left = UnitsToPixels ( iw_parent.x + Parent.x + st_slider.x + &
                        st_slider.width, XUnitsToPixels! )

//Add the width of the window to the left edge
str_pos.left += UnitsToPixels ( iw_parent.width - &
            iw_parent.WorkSpaceWidth(), XUnitsToPixels! ) / 2

//Right edge is the same to force vertical movement only
str_pos.right = str_pos.left

//Find the upper boundary. This is the y position of the window +
//the y position of the parent object +
//the y position of the slider portion +
//the height of the handle portion (so it slides all the way up) +
//the height of the window titlebar and menu if any +
str_pos.top = UnitsToPixels ( iw_parent.y, YUnitsToPixels! )
str_pos.top += UnitsToPixels ( Parent.y, YUnitsToPixels! )
str_pos.top += UnitsToPixels ( st_slider.y, YUnitsToPixels! )
str_pos.top -= UnitsToPixels ( this.height, YUnitsToPixels! ) / 1.1
str_pos.top += UnitsToPixels ( iw_parent.height - &
                        iw_parent.WorkSpaceHeight(), YUnitsToPixels! )

//Bottom edge is top edge + slider object height + 1/2 handle
str_pos.bottom = str_pos.top + &
  UnitsToPixels ( st_slider.height + this.height / 2 , YUnitsToPixels! )

//Call Windows API to keep the mouse in these coordinates
ClipCursor ( str_pos )

//Set flag to show the mouse button is down
ib_mousedown = TRUE
```

15. Place the following code in the MouseUp event of pb_handle. The script calls GetEnvironment() to determine the size of the user's screen. This is necessary in order to once again allow the mouse free movement across the entire screen. The MouseUp event instantiates another instance of the s_mouse structure, and sets the top and left attributes to zero. The screen height and width information from GetEnvironment() populates the bottom and right attributes, respectively. One more call to ClipCursor() with this new setting allows the mouse free movement around the screen. After resetting the mouse, the script checks to ensure that the handle has not inadvertently moved to an invalid position. If too high, the script sets it to the maximum position. If too low, the handle moves to zero. Finally, the slider SingleLineEdit control receives focus. This is to aid in the proper drawing of the object. Without it, the vertical borders of the slider are visible on top of the handle.

```
s_mouse str_pos
environment l_env

//Get environment information so we can set the mouse movement back
//to the entire screen
GetEnvironment ( l_env )

//Reset the button flag, showing that it is up
ib_mousedown = FALSE

//Set the structure to the coordinates of the screen
str_pos.left = 0
str_pos.top = 0
str_pos.right = l_env.ScreenWidth
str_pos.bottom = l_env.ScreenHeight

//Call Windows API to reset mouse movement
ClipCursor ( str_pos )

//Due to rounding errors caused by using pixels, reset the handle
//to only valid coordinates. This is necessary in order to keep the
//handle within the bounds of the slider

//If it is too low
If this.y + this.height > st_slider.y + st_slider.height Then
    this.y = st_slider.y + st_slider.height - this.height
End If

//If it is too high
If this.y + this.height < st_slider.y Then
    this.y = st_slider.y - this.height
End If

st_slider.SetFocus ()
```

16. Save this object using the name suo_slider, and close the User Object painter.

17. Create a new window object. Place three instances of suo_slider, along with three SingleLineEdit controls and three StaticText controls on this window. Size the slider objects to any size that you wish. Notice that the object does not repaint on the window, but will at runtime. Give this window and the controls the properties shown in Table 16-15. Figure 16-7 shows the window in the Window painter.

OBJECT/CONTROL	PROPERTY	VALUE
Window	Name	w_slider
	Title	"Adding Events to a User Object Demo"
	Maximize Box	FALSE
	Minimize Box	FALSE
User Object	Name	uo_Red
	Name	uo_Green
	Name	uo_Blue
SingleLineEdit	Name	sle_Red
	Name	sle_Green
	Name	sle_Blue
StaticText	Text	"Red"
	Text	"Green"
	Text	"Blue"

Table 16-15 Properties of window object and controls

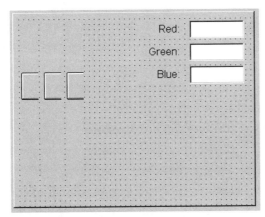

Figure 16-7 New window with Slider control at design time

18. Place the following code in the Open event of the window. This sets the upper bound of the controls to 255, the range of each of the color components. It then sets the initial value of each control to 192, resulting in a light gray color. Finally, it turns on the scale indicator for each.

```
//Set the values for the upper bounds of all the slider controls
uo_red.SetMax ( 255 )
uo_green.SetMax ( 255 )
uo_blue.SetMax ( 255 )

//Set an initial value for each control
uo_Red.SetValue ( 192 )
uo_Green.SetValue ( 192 )
uo_Blue.SetValue ( 192 )

//Turn on the display of the scale for all sliders
uo_red.ib_ShowScale = TRUE
uo_green.ib_ShowScale = TRUE
uo_blue.ib_ShowScale = TRUE
```

19. Place the following code in the Change event of uo_Red. The control sets the appropriate SingleLineEdit control to indicate the current value, and then changes the color of the window. When using this control in a real business application, you might set other properties, depending on what function the control provides. Steps 20 and 21 below contain similar scripts, so no further explanation will be provided.

```
//Set the SingleLineEdit control to the value of this slider
//and set the window color appropriately

sle_red.text = String ( this.GetValue() )
Parent.BackColor = ( uo_blue.GetValue() * 256^2 ) + &
                   ( uo_green.GetValue() * 256 ) + this.GetValue()
```

20. Place the following code in the Change event of uo_Green.

```
//Set the SingleLineEdit control to the value of this slider
//and set the window color appropriately

sle_Green.text = String ( this.GetValue() )
Parent.BackColor = ( uo_blue.GetValue() * 256^2 ) + &
                   ( this.GetValue() * 256 ) + uo_red.GetValue()
```

21. Place the following code in the Change event of uo_Blue.

```
//Set the SingleLineEdit control to the value of this slider
//and set the window color appropriately

sle_Blue.text = String ( this.GetValue() )
Parent.BackColor = ( this.GetValue() * 256^2 ) + &
                   ( uo_green.GetValue() * 256 ) + uo_Red.GetValue()
```

22. Place the following code in the Modified event of sle_Red. This changes the value of the Slider control if the user enters a new value. Steps 23 and 24 contain the same code (except for the names of the controls used).

```
//Set the slider to the indicated value

uo_Red.SetValue ( Long ( this.text ) )
```

23. Place the following code in the Modified event of sle_Green.

```
//Set the slider to the indicated value

uo_Green.SetValue ( Long ( this.text ) )
```

24. Place the following code in the Modified event of sle_Blue.

```
//Set the slider to the indicated value

uo_Blue.SetValue ( Long ( this.text ) )
```

25. Place the following code in the Open event of the Application object used to open the window. Save all objects and run the application.

```
//Open the window
Open ( w_slider )
```

How It Works

The user presses the mouse button while over the handle of the slider. At that time, the MouseDown event of the control fires. This is a custom user event, as are the MouseUp and MouseMove events. The object must know when these events occur, as specific processing must transpire at these times. When the user presses the left mouse button while over the handle, the script calculates the rectangular coordinates of the slider, and restricts the mouse to the boundaries of this rectangle. The control then sets a private instance variable that indicates that the mouse is down. The MouseMove event examines this instance variable, and if the value is TRUE, it moves the handle appropriately. The MouseMove event is paramount to this control, as this is where the control fires its Change event. You'll notice that the slider object does not do processing in the Change event, but instead provides it as the interface to the individually instantiated objects.

Comments

Events are one simple way for object communication. Since the Slider control object automatically triggers the Change event at the appropriate time, your code can respond as necessary. The GetValue() and SetValue() functions may not be completely accurate, due to the fact that the control derives the value based on pixels. With large values, some rounding errors may appear. There are other functions you may consider including with this object. For example, how about allowing the user to click on the slider, and moving the handle to that location? With some thought, you will come up with some ideas of your own. These are left for you as an exercise.

16.4   How do I...
Use an .OCX custom control?

Problem

My company has many .OCX files from Visual Basic applications. Additionally, PowerBuilder ships with several that I would like to use. I know that .OCX files are custom controls for Visual Basic, and I want to use these controls in PowerBuilder. This will provide my application with a look and feel similar to existing applications. I know PowerBuilder supports this, but I have never done it. How does an .OCX control work with PowerBuilder?

Technique

Files with an .OCX extension are similar to custom controls in .DLL files. However, they have a different interface and internal structure than that of a Dynamic Link Library. The techniques used for .OCX files parallel the old Windows 3.1x technique of using .DLLs somewhat, except that you code event scripts instead of sending messages to the control. In Visual Basic, controls respond to *event procedures*, which are basically the same as PowerBuilder events. Like PowerBuilder, Visual Basic also supplies parameters (arguments) to the event procedures. PowerBuilder allows you to obtain the parameters sent to an .OCX event procedure, just as you can from any native PowerBuilder event. In order to use an .OCX control, you must place an OLE control on the window, set the properties, and write code for the proper events. The only differences between PowerBuilder events and Visual Basic events are the event names themselves, and handling any event parameters supported by the .OCX control.

Steps

Open and run the application in the OCX.PBL library. The control used in this example ships with PowerBuilder, and you are free to use and distribute it as you like. The control is a calendar object. This example provides graphical date editing within a DataWindow control. Once the application starts, double-click on any date in the DataWindow. A calendar displays, allowing you to select any date you like. The arrow button in the upper corners of the control provides for forward and backward month scrolling. Once you set focus to the control, you may also use the keyboard for navigation. The up, down, left, and right arrow keys provide scrolling for day and month, and the PGUP and PGDN keys scroll the year. You may double-click on any date (or press ENTER), in order to populate the column of the DataWindow. Pressing ESC closes the calendar without changing the date. Figure 16-8 shows the application with the calendar visible.

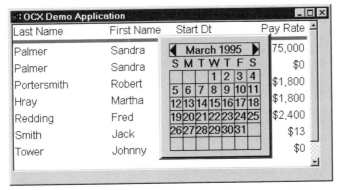

Figure 16-8 Custom calendar object from an .OCX control

1. In order to use .OCX controls, they must have previously been installed. If they have not yet been installed, you must do this from the original PowerBuilder CD. You will need to install the "*Component Gallery*" option.

2. Create a new Application object called "ocx" and save it in a library called OCX.PBL.

3. Start the DataWindow painter, and create a simple DataWindow object. Choose any data source you wish, as long as you select at least one date column. The Tabular presentation style works best. The sample application uses employee information. Save the DataWindow using the name "d_employee."

4. Create a new window object. Place a DataWindow on the window, and associate it with the d_employee DataWindow object created in step 3. From the Controls menu, select OLE 2.0. Once the Insert Object dialog box appears, click on the Insert Control tab. If the Control Type ListBox shows the ctDate control, procede to step 5. Click on the Register New... button, and select the file Ctdate32.OCX. (This will be in your PB5I32\Compglry folder.) Press Open.

5. Click on the ctDate Control option in the Insert Object dialog box and press OK. Drop this object on the window surface, and size it appropriately. Give this window and controls the properties shown in Table 16-16.

OBJECT/CONTROL	PROPERTY	VALUE
Window	Name	w_vbx
	Title	"OCX Demo Application"
DataWindow	Name	dw_employee
	DataObject	"d_employee"
	VScroll Bar	TRUE

continued on next page

continued from previous page

OBJECT/CONTROL	PROPERTY	VALUE
OLE	Name	OLE_Calendar
	Border	3D Raised
	Visible	FALSE

Table 16-16 Property settings for OCX window and controls

6. Since you just set the Visible property of the calendar to FALSE, PowerBuilder has hidden it from view. In order to work with the control in the painter, select Options... from the Design menu. Turn the Show Invisibles CheckBox to TRUE.

7. Place the following code in the DoubleClicked event of dw_employee. This code first determines the current column name, and passes this information to Describe() to determine if the column is a date. If so, it gets the current value from the column, and sets the properties of the calendar to reflect the existing date. Notice the syntax to access the properties of the .OCX control. Setting the MonthButtons property to TRUE causes the directional arrows to appear in the upper corners of the calendar. Finally, it makes the calendar visible for the user.

```
String ls_Col, ls_Type
Integer li_Tab
Date ld_Date

//See what column we're over
ls_Col = This.GetColumnName()


//If it is a date, display the calendar
ls_Type = This.Describe ( ls_Col + ".ColType" )

//See if we have a date column
If Left ( Upper ( ls_Type ), 4 ) = "DATE" Then
    ld_Date = This.GetItemDate ( Row, ls_Col )
    //Set the date
    ole_Calendar.Object.MonthButtons = TRUE
    ole_Calendar.Object.Day = Day ( ld_Date )
    ole_Calendar.Object.Month = Month ( ld_Date )
    ole_Calendar.Object.Year = Year ( ld_Date )
    ole_Calendar.Visible = TRUE
End If
```

8. Place the following code in the DblClick event of the calendar control. This gets the value of the currently selected date, and populates the DataWindow with it.

```
Date ld_Date

//Set the date in the datawindow, and make the calendar invisible.
ld_Date = Date ( This.Object.Year, This.Object.Month, This.Object.Day )
dw_employee.SetItem ( dw_employee.GetRow(), dw_employee.GetColumnName(),
```

```
ld_Date )
This.Visible = FALSE
```

9. This control comes with a keyboard interface for changing the day, but does not provide facilities for easily changing the month or year. (Scrolling to the end of a month causes the next month to display.) In order to provide this interface, place the following code in the KeyDown event of the calendar. This event supplies two arguments — the ASCII keycode, and a shift value (to determine if SHIFT, CTRL, or ALT keys are down). Using the KeyCode argument, this script calls the appropriate functions to change the displayed date, select a date, or cancel the calendar. Again, notice the syntax of the function calls. Once the user selects a date or cancels, the script hides the control from the user's view.

```
Date ld_Date

//Handle the keys appropriately
Choose Case KeyCode
    Case 37              //Left Arrow
        This.Object.LastMonth()
    Case 39              //Right Arrow
        This.Object.NextMonth()
    Case 33              //Page Up
        This.Object.LastYear()
    Case 34              //Page Down
        This.Object.NextYear()
    Case 13              //Enter
        ld_Date = Date ( This.Object.Year, This.Object.Month,
This.Object.Day )
        dw_employee.SetItem ( dw_employee.GetRow(),
dw_employee.GetColumnName(), ld_Date )
        This.Visible = FALSE
    Case 27              //Escape
        This.Visible = FALSE
        dw_employee.SetFocus()
End Choose
```

10. Place the following code in the Open event of the window, in order to populate the DataWindow. Save the window using the name "w_main", and close the Window painter.

```
//Set the details for the datawindow
dw_employee.SetTransObject ( SQLCA )
dw_employee.Retrieve()
```

11. Place the following code in the Open event of the Application object. This connects to the database, and opens the window upon a successful database connection. Save all objects and run the application.

```
//Set up SQLCA for a connection
SQLCA.DBMS = "odbc"
SQLCA.DBPARM = "ConnectString='dsn=zoo;uid=dba;pwd=sql'"
```

continued on next page

continued from previous page

```
Connect Using SQLCA;
If SQLCA.SQLCode < 0 Then
    MessageBox ( "Database", SQLCA.SQLErrText )
Else
    Open ( w_main )
End If
```

How It Works

The calendar is really an OLE server object. OLE servers make services available to your application. This control remains invisible until the user double-clicks on a date column. (You might decide to use the RbuttonDown event instead of the DoubleClicked event.) At this time, it determines the current column, and obtains the column data type using the Describe() function. If the column is indeed a date, it makes the calendar visible. Once the calendar displays, the user can navigate through the dates using the month buttons, or the keyboard. Once they select a date, the control changes the date in the DataWindow. Notice that there is no mouse interface for canceling the calendar. You would probably want to provide this to your users as well.

Comments

PowerBuilder makes it easy to incorporate custom controls from external sources. Using an .OCX control is no more difficult that a standard PowerBuilder control. The main difference is that any .OCX control must first be registered. The Visual Basic .OCX controls are particularly easy, as the two environments handle events in a similar manner. PowerBuilder and Visual Basic both allow you to change the characteristics of controls. You can use these controls even without documentation. How? The answer lies in the Object Browser. This PowerBuilder tool shows you all of the properties, events, and methods (functions) of any type of object. You can start the Object Browser in one of two ways. From the Library painter, select Browse Objects... from the Utility menu. Or, if you have the PowerScript painter open, select Browse Object... from the Edit menu. Once PowerBuilder displays the browser, click on the OLE tab, and double-click OLE Custom Controls. The item expands, showing you the various .OCX controls available. Again, double-click on the control of interest. From here, you can double-click on the Methods, Events, or Properties items to obtain information about each area. Figure 16-9 shows the Object Browser. Once you find an item that interests you, select it and press Paste (if you opened the browser from a code window). PowerBuilder pastes the item into your script. All you need do is change the name of the control. (PowerBuilder supplies you with the name "OLECustomControl" prefixing the resulting code.)

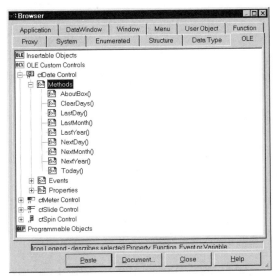

Figure 16-9 Object Browser showing information about the ctDate Control

COMPLEXITY
INTERMEDIATE

16.5 How do I...
Build a custom class user object?

Problem

I have heard other developers talk about custom class user objects. I know they provide functions but have no graphical component to them. It sounds like they would be a good place to encapsulate business logic, or routines that are generic to an object. It seems that they provide a high level of reuse across objects. Therefore, I would like to create a custom class object that helps me control the menu of my application. How do I do it?

Technique

You're right. Custom class user objects enable you to perform processing that contains no graphical elements. Class user objects define any number of user-defined functions. Usually, these functions are specific to an object type, but not to any one particular object. Custom class user objects are quite frequently referred to as NVOs. This acronym stands for *Non-Visual Object*. Using NVOs reduces memory requirements, and therefore application overhead since the graphical component of an object consumes much memory. Any time you reduce the memory overhead, you increase performance in the application. In this How-To, you will create a custom class user object that works with a menu. The object contains one function, but, with a little

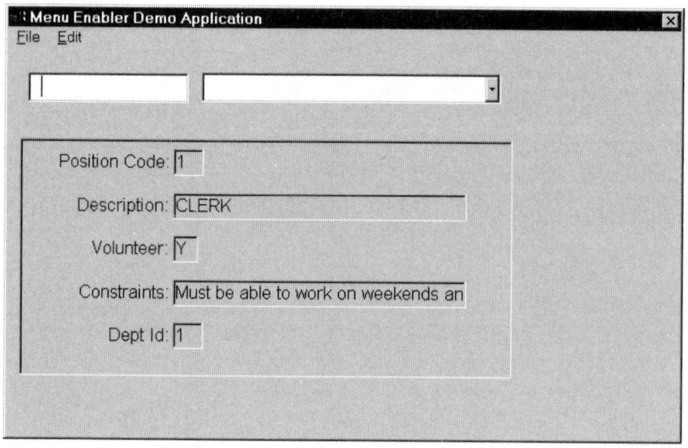

Figure 16-10 Window object that uses the custom class object

thought, other useful functions for this object may come to mind. The function presented determines whether or not various menu items should be available to an application, and sets the enabled property accordingly when the user opens the associated menu.

Steps

Open and run the application stored in the CLASSUO.PBL library. First, click on the Edit menu. All of the menu items are grayed out. Next, type some text into the SingleLineEdit control and again click on the Edit menu. The Undo option has been enabled. Highlight the text you just entered and open the Edit menu one more time. Cut and Copy are now enabled. Finally, press (CTRL)-(C) to copy the text to the clipboard. The Paste item on the Edit menu should now be available. When the user clicks on the Edit menu, the NVO function determines what control has focus, and whether or not the options in that menu need to be made available. Figure 16-10 shows the application in action.

1. Start the Application painter and create a new Application object called "classuo". Save it in a library named CLASSUO.PBL. Do not generate an application template for this sample.

2. Start the User Object painter and create a new object. When prompted, select Custom from the Class GroupBox. PowerBuilder displays a blank workspace. Notice that this workspace looks much like a window surface. However, you cannot place controls on it. Select User Object Functions... from the Design menu. Create a new function called uf_EditEnable(), giving it the properties shown in Table 16-17. Place the following script in this function. The function determines which control has focus. It then looks at the passed argument to determine if an Undo, Cut, Copy, or Paste operation has been requested. By determining the type of control in focus, it assigns the reference the correct control type. This needs to be done so that the calls to the control level function (such as CanUndo() and SelectedLength()) won't cause a compiler error. Only certain controls support these functions, and you must call the function for the appropriate control type. Save this object using the name ccuo_menucheck.

```
//This function determines whether or not the undo, cut, copy, and
//paste options on a menu should be enabled. It returns a true/false
//value based on the parameters passed


//Declare local object references to the various controls that support
//undo, cut, copy and paste
SingleLineEdit lsle_which            //reference to SingleLineEdit
MultiLineEdit lmle_which             //and to MultiLineEdit
DataWindow ldw_which                 //and DataWindow
Boolean lb_return                    //function return value
Integer li_len                       //Length of selected text, if any
GraphicObject lg_control             //Control that has focus

//Set return code to a default value
lb_return = FALSE

//Get the control that currently has focus
lg_control = GetFocus()

Choose Case Upper ( as_type )

    Case "UNDO"
//Find out what type of control it is, and call that control's canundo
//Function
        Choose Case lg_control.TypeOf ( )
            Case SingleLineEdit!
                lsle_which = lg_control
                lb_return = lsle_which.CanUndo ()
            Case MultiLineEdit!
                lmle_which = lg_control
                lb_return = lmle_which.CanUndo ()
            Case DataWindow!
                ldw_which = lg_control
                lb_return = ldw_which.CanUndo ()
            Case Else
                lb_return = FALSE
        End Choose

    Case "CUT", "COPY"
//Find out what type of control it is, and call that control's
//selectedlength to see if text has been selected
        Choose Case lg_control.TypeOf ( )
            Case SingleLineEdit!
                lsle_which = lg_control
                li_len = lsle_which.SelectedLength ()
            Case MultiLineEdit!
                lmle_which = lg_control
                li_len= lmle_which.SelectedLength ()
            Case DataWindow!
```

continued on next page

continued from previous page

```
                    ldw_which = lg_control
                    li_len= ldw_which.SelectedLength ()
            End Choose
//Set the return value based on the selected length
            If li_len > 0 Then lb_return = TRUE


    Case "PASTE"
//See if the current control is an edit control
        Choose Case lg_control.TypeOf()
            Case SingleLineEdit!, MultiLineEdit!, DataWindow!

//Yes, so see if there is text available on the clipboard
                If ClipBoard() <> "" Then
                    lb_return = TRUE
                Else
                    lb_return = FALSE
                End If
        End Choose
End Choose


Return lb_return
```

PROPERTY	VALUE	
Name	uf_editenable	
Returns	Boolean	
Argument 1	as_type	String

Table 16-17 Function declaration for ue_EditEnable()

3. Create a simple DataWindow object using any presentation style. The data source is not important. Make sure that the tab order of the columns is non-zero. Save the DataWindow object using the name d_data.

4. Create a new menu. The structure of the menu is not important, but should include an Edit menu with Undo, Cut, Copy, and Paste items. Place the following code in the Selected event of m_edit. When you use functions from class user objects, the object must be *instantiated* in code. Instantiation creates a runtime copy of the object with which you work. Class user objects cannot be dropped onto a window surface as can visual user objects. You must instantiate them in code. After instantiation, the script calls the object's function four times, using the return value as the new value of the associated menu item property. When you no longer need an object, it must be destroyed. That is what happens at the end of the following script. Save this menu using the name m_menu.

```
//Declare an instance of the custom class user object
ccuo_MenuCheck lcuo_MenuCheck

//Instantiate the object
lcuo_MenuCheck = Create ccuo_MenuCheck
```

```
//Call the function for each item in the menu, using
//the return value as the new attribute setting
This.m_undo.enabled = lcuo_MenuCheck.uf_EditEnable ( "undo" )
This.m_cut.enabled = lcuo_MenuCheck.uf_EditEnable ( "cut" )
This.m_copy.enabled = lcuo_MenuCheck.uf_EditEnable ( "copy" )
This.m_paste.enabled = lcuo_MenuCheck.uf_EditEnable ( "paste" )

//Release memory resources for the object
Destroy lcuo_MenuCheck
```

5. Create a new window object using Figure 16-10 as a guide. Place a DataWindow control on the window, and associate the control with the d_data object. Place a SingleLineEdit and DropDownListBox on the surface. Table 16-18 shows the properties for the window and the controls. Place the following code in the Open event of this window.

```
//Set up the datawindow for retrieval
//No error checking done here, although you would in a typical application
dw_list.SetTransObject ( SQLCA )
dw_list.Retrieve ()
```

OBJECT/CONTROL	PROPERTY	VALUE
Window	Name	w_menudemo
	TitleBar	"Menu Enabler Demo Application"
	Menu	m_menu
	Minimize box	FALSE
	Maximize box	FALSE
	Resizable	FALSE
DataWindow	Name	dw_list
SingleLineEdit	Name	sle_name
DropDownListBox	Name	ddlb_items

Table 16-18 Properties for the window object

6. Place the following code in the Open event of the Application object. After connecting to the database, it clears the contents of the clipboard so the demo works as described. If it did not clear the clipboard, and existing data resided there, the NVO you created would turn on the Paste option. Note that this is probably the behavior you would desire, but not for this example. It then opens the window.

```
//Open the window
SQLCA.DBMS = "odbc"
SQLCA.DBPARM = "ConnectString='dsn=zoo;uid=dba;pwd=sql'"

Connect Using SQLCA;
If SQLCA.SQLCode < 0 Then
    MessageBox ( "Connect", "Could not connect to database." + &
            SQLCA.SQLErrText )
```

continued on next page

continued from previous page

```
    Halt Close
End If

//The following line of script is for demo purposes only. It ensures
//that no text is available on the clipboard
ClipBoard ( "" )

Open ( w_menudemo )
```

How It Works

When building a custom class user object, the "size" of the design surface in the painter is irrelevant. NVOs are merely function and data repositories. The difference with NVOs is that the objects must be instantiated in scripts before they are used. The function created here obtains the current control using the GetFocus() function. This PowerScript function returns a *GraphicObject* data type. All PowerBuilder controls are descendants of the GraphicObject. After obtaining the current control, the function determines whether Undo, Cut, Copy, and Paste are valid options. The CanUndo() function tells the script if the last edit is reversible. Similarly, SelectedLength() returns the length of any selected text. If this value is positive, it's safe to assume that the user selected text, and therefore Cut and Copy are valid. The problem is, not all controls support CanUndo() and SelectedLength(). The TypeOf() function indicates which *type* of control has focus. If the current control supports these functions, the script calls them as appropriate.

You may be tempted to write a menu object function, or even use this script directly in the Selected event of the menu. Although these techniques would certainly work, the code would not be reusable by other menus. By encapsulating the function into an NVO, it is available to any menu that needs it.

Comments

You may be wondering why NVOs are popular, since global functions provide the same benefit. Well, they really don't. Custom class user objects allow you to construct functions that support Public, Private, or Protected access. As application development moves towards object orientation, global functions become less of an option. Since global functions make themselves available to every script in an application, they are incapable of protecting data (encapsulation). A global function is not an object. An object must contain both properties (data) and code (functions or scripts). For this reason, global functions do not provide the level of flexibility required for data hiding and abstraction. Data integrity depends heavily on the ability to hide (and thereby protect) local data.

COMPLEXITY
INTERMEDIATE

16.6 How do I...
Customize the error object?

Problem

When my application reaches the beta test stage, I want to trap every runtime error that occurs, and store them in a file. This way, I can review the error log and get the specific information I need to correct the problems, even if I am not present to witness them. I know that the error object contains information specific to the most recent error, and I want to centralize all error handling into an error object function. Although I could write code for the Application object's SystemError event and produce these results, I need a reusable object for all of my applications. This way, my error handling looks and works the same, and I don't have to rewrite the error handler each time I create a new program. How can I customize the ERROR object to provide these results?

Technique

The ERROR object is a non-visual, system level object that contains all pertinent information about runtime errors. When a runtime error occurs in a PowerBuilder application, the Application object fires its SystemError event. This event performs runtime error handling. In this How-To, you will customize the standard PowerBuilder error object and provide an error handling function that performs basic file I/O. This function writes the error information to a log file. The SystemError event calls this function automatically whenever a runtime error occurs. Then you'll do something you normally don't have the luxury of doing in your job—purposely write code that generates nothing but errors!

Steps

Open and run the application stored in the ERRORUO.PBL library. When the application starts, click each of the CommandButtons. Both cause runtime errors that get logged to a file. Additionally, the error handler presents the user with a message box that displays the error, and gives the user the option of continuing or exiting the application. Without code in the SystemError event, PowerBuilder automatically terminates your application upon a runtime error. The function you'll write in this How-To warns the user that continuing could cause future runtime errors. Figure 16-11 shows the error prone window. Use WordPad (or another text editor) to view the error log. The name of the file is ERROR.LOG, located in the root directory of drive C:.

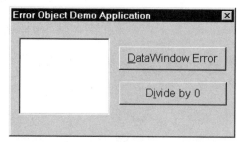

Figure 16-11 The error prone window at runtime

1. Create a new application object called "erroruo" and store it in a library called ERRORUO.PBL.

2. Start the Window painter and create a window using Figure 16-11 as a guide. Give the window and the controls the properties shown in Table 16-19.

OBJECT/CONTROL	PROPERTY	VALUE
Window	Name	w_errorprone
	Title	"Error Object Demo Application"
	Type	Response
DataWindow	Name	dw_error
CommandButton	Name	cb_error
	Text	"&DataWindow Error"
	Name	cb_dividebyzero
	Text	"D&ivide By Zero"

Table 16-19 Properties for window and controls for the error prone window.

3. Place the following code in the Clicked event of cb_error. This script attempts to get some data from the DataWindow. Since no rows exist in the control, an error occurs.

```
//Generate a dw error. There are no rows or columns in the control
dw_error.GetItemNumber ( 1, "error" )
```

4. Place the following code in cb_dividebyzero. This generates a divide by 0 error. Save the window using the name w_errorprone.

```
//Generate a divide by zero error
int li_x

li_x = li_x / 0
```

5. Start the User Object painter. Create a new user object, and select Standard from the Class GroupBox. From the Select Standard Class Type dialog box, select "error" and press OK. Declare the following instance variable after the painter appears. This string variable holds the name of the file to which the object will write the error information.

```
Private:
String is_file
```

6. Declare a User Object function, using Table 16-20 to set the properties. This function sets the instance variable to the name of the error log. You will call this function from the Open event of the Application object. Place the following code in this function.

```
//Set the error log file to the argument passed. Used later in the
//Save function
is_file = as_file
Return
```

PROPERTY	VALUE	DATATYPE
Name	SaveSetUp	
Returns	(None)	
Argument 1	as_file	String

Table 16-20 Properties for uo_setfile function.

7. Create one more User Object function. This function performs the file I/O when an error occurs. Give this function the properties shown in Table 16-21, and place the following code in the function. The first thing the function does is verify the validity of the instance variable holding the name of the error file. If not valid, it uses C:\ERROR.LOG as the default. It then builds a tab delimited string containing all attributes of the error object. The function then adds the date and time to this string. Using the name set for the error log, the function opens the file, writes the error string to it, and closes the log. It then presents the user with a dialog box, giving him or her the ability to continue or exit the program. Save this object using the name suo_error.

```
String ls_error          //used to build error string to write to file
Integer li_handle, li_yn //error file handle, message return value

//if_file is a shared string that holds the file name of the error log
//See if error file has been set. If not, create a default
If is_file = "" Then
    is_file = "C:\ERROR.LOG"
End If

//Use the attributes of the object to build a single error string
//Add date and time of error as well
ls_error = String ( this.Line ) + "~t" + String ( this.Number ) + &
```

continued on next page

continued from previous page

```
    "~t" + this.Object + "~t" + this.ObjectEvent + "~t" + this.Text + &
    "~t" + this.WindowMenu + "~t" + String ( Today() ) + "~t" + &
    String ( Now() ) +   Char ( 13 )

//Open the error file
li_handle = FileOpen ( is_file, LineMode!, Write!, Shared!, Append! )

//If successful, write the error out and close the file
If li_handle > 0 Then
    FileWrite ( li_handle, ls_error )
    FileClose ( li_handle )
End If

//Show error message to user. Ask if they want to continue
li_yn = MessageBox ( "Runtime Error", "The following error has occurred:"
+&
    "~r~n" + this.Text + &
    "~r~nDo you want to continue (risking further errors)?",&
    Question!, YesNo!, 2 )

//Check user response. If they choose NO, (return value = 2) then halt app
If li_yn = 2 Then
    Halt Close
End If

//Exit the error function
Return
```

PROPERTY	VALUE
Name	Save
Returns	(None)

Table 16-21 Function declaration for uo_WriteError

8. Place the following code in the Open event of the Application object. This sets the name of the error log and opens the window. Close the PowerScript painter, but leave the Application painter open.

```
//Set the default name for the error log using the new error
//object member function
error.uo_SetFile ( "c:\error.log" )

//open the errorprone window
Open ( w_errorprone )
```

9. Place the following code in the SystemError event of the Application object. This event fires only when a runtime error occurs, so it calls the custom error object function.

```
//An error has occurred. Call the custom error handler that writes
//the error to the log file
error.uo_WriteError ()
```

10. Select Properties... from the Edit menu of the Application painter, and select the Variable Types tab. Replace the default error object with suo_error, and press Apply, followed by OK.

11. Save all objects, run the application, and hope for some errors! Verify that the ERROR.LOG file contains the errors that the application produces.

How It Works

The error object contains six properties that PowerBuilder populates with information relative to all runtime errors. Table 16-22 shows these properties, their datatypes, and the meaning of each. When an error occurs, the error object's properties are automatically populated. These properties and their meanings are shown below. Once you create a sub-classed object (in this case you called it suo_error), you replace the default global error object with your own. Notice, however, that the PowerBuilder name for the error object is "ERROR," and you continue to refer to this object using this name, even when you replace the object with your own custom object. Therefore, your existing code will still work. You need only add the calls to the specific functions where they are appropriate.

PROPERTY	DATA TYPE	MEANING
Line	Integer	Line number where error occurred.
Number	Integer	PowerBuilder error number.
Object	String	Name of the object that the error occurred in.
ObjectEvent	String	Event name in which the error occurred.
Text	String	Description of the error.
WindowMenu	String	Name of the Window or Menu object where the error occurred.

Table 16-22 ERROR object properties, datatypes, and meaning

Comments

You could write code for the SystemError event that handles the error directly, instead of creating a new object with a custom function. However, for future applications, you would be forced to either copy that script, or rewrite it. Since you encapsulated the Save() function into a user object, any application can use it by including the object's library in the library search path. You may consider moving this object to a common library that stores only custom objects, and use these custom objects as the ancestor for all application objects.

Runtime errors are going to occur, and are typically not difficult to correct. What makes these fixes difficult is that you cannot always be a witness to them. A user may call the help desk and say, "I had an error occur in the so-and-so application. It said something about a problem regarding some object. I really don't remember what it said or what I was doing at the time." This information is not helpful. Certainly, the average user cannot be responsible for accurately reporting errors, as errors may be very technical in nature. The average business user is not always computer literate. Logging all runtime errors to a file gives you the chance to review exactly what happened, in what script it occurred, and approximately what the user may have been doing at the time.

COMPLEXITY
INTERMEDIATE

16.7   How do I...
Customize the Message object?

Problem

When I use the Message object to pass data between objects, I must be concerned with the data type passed. Even though PowerBuilder places the data in the correct property of the Message object for me, I have to know which property contains that data. Also, since the Message object is global to all running processes on a computer, it is quite possible that the information may get changed by another process before my scripts process it. I have to get the data from the Message object at the first possible opportunity. And, I can only pass one thing at a time. Even though the Message object will handle structures using the PowerObjectParm, this requires that I first create the structure, declare it in my scripts, and finally write code to manipulate the various properties of these structures. I don't want to be concerned with these details. I need to pass multiple values to other objects, and always want assurance that the data won't change until I change them. How can I customize the Message object and gain all of these desired traits?

Technique

The Message object is global to the system, and therefore shared by all running applications. Windows applications use this communication mechanism, which allows them to communicate with each other. The Message object contains properties that your application passes to other objects within the application. When a script calls OpenWithParm(), OpenSheetWithParm(), or CloseWithReturn(), PowerBuilder populates one of three properties with the value passed by these functions. Other objects obtain these Message object properties at the appropriate time, usually as a window opens, or after a dialog box (response window) closes. This way, objects are able to communicate with each other. The three properties are Message.DoubleParm (for numeric values), Message.StringParm (for string values), or Message.PowerObjectParm (for any other datatype). The problem is, since all applications share the Message object, one process can overwrite a value before the destination object gets hold of it. To alleviate this problem, your scripts must retrieve the appropriate message property at the first possible instant. One other problem with the Message object is that only one value may be passed at a time. If you need to pass several values, you must declare a structure, and pass the structure in the PowerObjectParm. This How-To solves all of these problems.

Steps

Open and run the application in the MSGUO.PBL library. After the application starts, open several sheets using the New option on the File menu (or the toolbar item). Use the Window menu to arrange the sheets in a tiled configuration. Finally, click on each sheet in turn, and note the change in the Titlebar. As each sheet opens, the custom Message object passes several pieces of data—a string ("New Sheet"), as well as the date and time the most recent sheet opened. This application does not use a structure to pass various data elements, as is typical in many PowerBuilder applications. When you click on the window, the window retrieves all of this information and displays it in the Titlebar. Notice that the custom Message object makes this data available any time after the sheet opens. No potential exists for other processes to inadvertently change these values. Since the Message object is global, each sheet does overwrite previous data. However, other applications cannot modify them. This new object holds any number of attributes. You are not restricted to the problems associated with structures. Figure 16-12 shows the application in action.

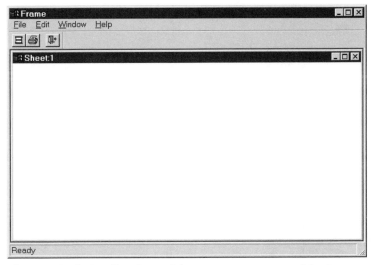

Figure 16-12 Application with custom message object

1. Create a new application object called "msguo" and save it in a library called MSGUO.PBL. Generate an application template for this application.

2. Start the User Object painter and create a new object. When PowerBuilder displays the New User Object dialog box, double-click on the "Standard" icon in the Class GroupBox. PowerBuilder displays the Select Standard Class Type dialog. Select "message" and press OK.

3. Declare the following instance variable for this object. This is a private array of type *Any*. Using a variable whose type is Any allows you to store any data type in the variable. It uses type Any, since the object does not know what data type other objects will send to it. It is declared Private to ensure that no other object has direct access to it.

```
private:
Any ia_parm[]
```

4. Declare a new function for the object. Give the function the properties shown in Table 16-23. Place the following code in the function. This function returns a value to the caller, based on the array index requested.

```
//Send the value of the private array back to the caller
//using the array element they provide
String ls_return

//Check the data type of the array element
//Need to convert it to a string if it's not already
If ClassName ( ia_parm [ ai_index ] ) = "string" Then
    ls_return = ia_parm [ ai_index ]
Else
    ls_return = String ( ia_parm [ ai_index ] )
End If

Return ls_return
```

PROPERTY	VALUE	DATATYPE
Name	GetMessageParm	
Returns	String	
Argument 1	ai_index	Integer

Table 16-23 Function declaration for GetMessageParm()

5. Declare one more function for the object. Give this function the properties shown in Table 16-24. This function sets an element in the private array, using the value and array index passed to the function.

```
//Set the private attribute to the passed value, using the index
//indicated by the caller

ia_parm [ ai_index ] = aa_parm
return
```

PROPERTY	VALUE	DATATYPE
Name	SetMessageParm	
Returns	(None)	
Argument 1	aa_parm	Any
Argument 2	ai_index	Integer

Table 16-24 Properties for SetMessageParm() function

6. The MDI frame generated by PowerBuilder contains a function named NewSheet(). Place the following code in that function. The following listing shows the entire function. You must add only the code shown in bold. This function opens a sheet generated by the PowerBuilder application template. You add just the calls to the new Message object that passes the data.

```
w_genapp_sheet lw_Sheet

//Pass some stuff in the new message object
Message.SetMessageParm ( Now(), 1 )
Message.SetMessageParm ( Today(), 2 )
Message.SetMessageParm ( "New Title", 3 )

/* Enable printing */
wf_enableprint (true)

/* Open a new instance of a sheet */
return OpenSheet (lw_Sheet, this, 3, layered!)
```

7. Open the Application painter. Select Properties... from the Edit menu, and select the Variables Type tab. Replace the default error object with your new scou_error object. Figure 16-13 shows this dialog box. Run the application and test the scripts.

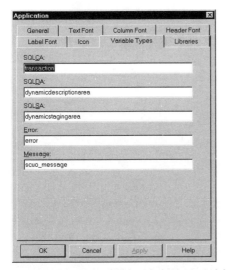

Figure 16-13 Default Global Variable Types dialog box

How It Works

The properties of the Message object (DoubleParm, StringParm, and PowerObjectParm) are available to all PowerBuilder applications. For this reason, it is unsafe to assume that values placed in these properties contain the values your application set previously. Since the Message object is a global variable, caution must be exercised in its use. The custom Message object presented here provides an instance variable with private visibility, support for any data type, and any number of elements. To pass a value in the Message object, your script calls SetMessageParm() indicating the parameter you wish to pass, along with the index of the array element in which to store this value. Then you call any of the OpenSheet(), Open(), or Close() functions. You no longer need to use OpenSheetWithParm(), OpenWithParm(), or CloseWithReturn(). From that point forward, the Message object contains the data you set, until you change it. No longer will Windows overwrite the value. By using the Any data type, you need not be concerned with the actual, underlying data type.

Comments

The PowerBuilder default Message object only supports passing one property at a time. Therefore, passing several data elements requires the use of a structure in conjunction with the PowerObjectParm property. Using a structure not only requires more work on your part (to create and maintain the structure), but also adds an additional object to your library. Structures are not object oriented, as they do not contain events or functions. If you use structures, your applications cannot fully exploit object oriented technology.

COMPLEXITY
ADVANCED

16.8 How do I...
Build a custom transaction object?

Problem

I am writing a Multiple Document Interface (MDI) application, and the user could have many sheets open at one time. I am having a problem committing and rolling back transactions throughout the application. If a user has multiple sheets open and I perform a rollback, the rollback occurs for every DataWindow on every open sheet. Therefore, my DataWindows get out of sync with the tables. This results in lost data. The user thinks he or she saved the data, but since a rollback occurred, every DataWindow is affected. I can't seem to perform a rollback in one sheet and commit my changes in another. There must be a way to do this. What's the answer?

Technique

The problem you are describing comes from the fact that SQLCA is a global variable. Transaction processing occurs based on a transaction object (such as SQLCA), and any time you perform a commit or rollback, the operation occurs for every transaction handled by the transaction object. For example, if you issue "Rollback Using SQLCA", all outstanding transactions handled by SQLCA roll back. If SQLCA is the only transaction object used by the application, all outstanding transactions are affected. You must define multiple transaction objects for each separate transaction. This could be expensive in terms of database resources, but the alternative could result in lost data. In this How-To, you will customize the standard transaction object, adding a function that provides automatic login capabilities. For each MDI sheet, you declare an instance of this new transaction object. When a sheet opens, the Open event uses this instance transaction object to connect to the database. In all future work, the sheet uses this instance variable instead of SQLCA. Now you have the ability to perform a commit in one sheet, and rollback in another.

Steps

Open and run the application in the TRANSUO.PBL library. When the application opens, it opens a sheet for you. Notice the Titlebar of this sheet. The sheet instantiates a new transaction object each time it opens. Open another sheet by selecting New from the File menu. A new sheet displays, and a new transaction object gets created. Any DataWindow control that you place on the sheet would use this instantiated transaction object for calls to SetTransObject(), or for embedded SQL. Figure 16-14 shows the application at runtime.

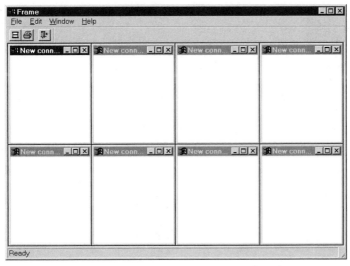

Figure 16-14 The custom transaction application

1. Create a new Application object called "transuo" and store it in a library called TRANSUO.PBL. When prompted, select Yes to generate an application template, since this example uses the Multiple Document Interface. The application template generated by PowerBuilder is an MDI application.

2. Start the User Object painter and create a new object. When prompted, select Standard from the Class GroupBox. PowerBuilder displays the Select Standard Class Type dialog box. PowerBuilder allows you to *sub-class* any of the standard global variable types. Select Transaction and press OK. PowerBuilder now displays a blank work surface. This is a *virtual* surface only. A transaction object is a non-visual object, and you are not allowed to (nor would you want to) place controls on this surface.

3. Select User Object Functions... from the Declare menu. Use Table 16-25 to set the properties for the function. Place the following code in the function. This script uses the global SQLCA transaction object as a template to copy its properties and connect to the database. The argument ab_showerror is a Boolean value that determines whether or not this function handles error messages, or if you'll display the error based on the return code from the function. The uo_Login() function returns the SQLCode property, so the calling script can handle any runtime errors that may occur. The first thing the script does is to declare a local copy of a transaction object. PowerBuilder does not allow the statement *Connect Using This*, so a local instance of type transaction must be used. Your application should initially connect to the database using SQLCA. Then the Open event of a sheet instantiates a transaction object using an instance variable, and connects again using this function. As mentioned previously, having one transaction object connected per open sheet can be expensive in terms of database resources. Use this technique only when separate physical transactions become necessary.

```
//Declare a local instance of a transaction object
//We need this since the statement 'connect using this' is illegal
transaction lt_trans

//Copy all of the attributes of the passed transaction object
this.DBMS = at_trans.DBMS
this.DataBase = at_trans.DataBase
this.ServerName = at_trans.ServerName
this.UserID = at_trans.UserID
this.DBPass = at_trans.DBPass
this.LogID = at_trans.LogID
this.LogPass = at_trans.LogPass
this.AutoCommit = at_trans.AutoCommit
this.DBParm = at_trans.DBParm
this.Lock = at_trans.Lock

//Get a local reference to the object and connect
lt_trans = this
Connect Using lt_trans;            //Connect Using This; is INVALID statement
```

```
//Check the error code
If this.SQLCode = - 1 Then
//Display error only if specified in the function call
    If ab_ShowError Then
        MessageBox ( "Connect", "Could not connect to database:~r~n" + &
                    this.SQLErrText )
    End If
End If

//Return the error code in case the caller wants it
Return this.SQLCode
```

PROPERTY	VALUE	DATATYPE
Name	uo_login	
Returns	Integer	
Argument 1	at_trans	transaction
Argument 2	ab_showerror	Boolean

Table 16-25 Properties for transaction object login function

4. Open w_genapp_sheet. PowerBuilder created this object when you generated the application template. Select Instance Variables... from the Declare menu. Place the following declaration in the Declare Instance Variables dialog box.

```
protected:
suo_transaction it_trans
```

5. Place the following code in the Open event of w_genapp_sheet. Some of this code already exists in the script, so you need only add the portion shown in bold. The uo_Login() function of the transaction object takes two parameters. The first is the transaction object that is used as the basis for the connection. The application uses SQLCA to initially connect, and this connection exists through the life of the application. This enables you to use SQLCA for all general purpose transaction processing. When the uo_Login() function executes, uo_Login() copies each attribute from SQLCA to the sheet's instance transaction variable. Don't simply code *it_trans = SQLCA*, as this causes it_trans to point to the same memory space as SQLCA, resulting in two variables that are identical. The second argument, a Boolean value, indicates whether the function handles the display of error messages internally. Setting it to FALSE indicates that the caller (as opposed to the function) handles any errors that occur.

```
int li_Count
int li_Success

    /* Sheet opening - reflect sheet count in title */
    li_Count = w_genapp_frame.wf_getsheetcount ()

    /* Modify menu text for platform */
```

continued on next page

continued from previous page

```
        w_genapp_frame.wf_setmenutext (menuid)


//Instantiate the new transaction object
it_trans = Create suo_transaction

//Set up the new transaction and log in
li_Success = it_trans.uo_LogIn ( SQLCA, FALSE )

//See if the connection was successful. If not, close the window
//since no transaction object is available
If li_Success = 0 Then
    this.Title = "New connection established - #" + String ( li_Count )
Else
    MessageBox ( "Transaction", "Could not login to database:~r~n" + &
                 it_trans.SQLErrText )
    Close ( this )
End If
```

6. Place the following code in the Close event of w_genapp_sheet. Some of this code already exists. You need to add only the code shown in bold. This disconnects the sheet from the database, and destroys the instance variable used as the transaction object.

```
/* Disable printing if last sheet */
if w_genapp_frame.wf_getsheetcount () = 1 then
    w_genapp_frame.wf_enableprint (false)
end if

//Disconnect the transaction from the database
//Don't do error checking since failure to disconnect usually means that
//there was a failure to connect. Don't want user seeing two errors
Disconnect Using it_trans;

//Destroy the transaction object
Destroy it_trans
```

7. Run the application. As you open sheets, note the Titlebar. The title changes to indicate a successful connection to the database. Continue opening new sheets until you receive an error message. Take note of this error. A discussion of this error situation follows.

How It Works

The uo_Login() function copies each of the properties of the transaction object argument to the attributes of the instance transaction. It is not valid to simply code *it_trans* = *SQLCA*. Doing so causes it_trans and SQLCA to point to the same variable, instead of creating two separate copies. In order to establish a second copy, each property must be copied individually. The transaction object now takes care of connecting to the database. And the sheet automatically creates one for you. When you place DataWindow controls on the sheet, you'll use it_trans instead of SQLCA for any embedded SQL or in calls to SetTransObject().

Comments

The ability to sub-class the standard class object is a powerful technique that gives your applications reusability. Transaction processing is, however, a touchy topic. Without a separate transaction object for each database transaction, you cannot perform separate commit and rollback operations concurrently. This is why each sheet in this How-To incorporates the techniques presented. However, each transaction object connected to a database uses precious resources, not only on the client, but on the server as well. It is up to you to strike a balance between these two techniques. As additional transaction objects connect to the database, you use an additional connection on the server. This may result in running out of available database connections, thereby preventing other users from getting their work done. If you must use separate objects for different transactions, you should release the connection at the earliest possible opportunity. If you use the techniques presented here, you may wish to limit the number of allowable open sheets. This saves resources both at the server and on the client. Another way to alleviate resource bottlenecks involves performing frequent commits. This releases locks held at the database.

EVENT DRIVEN PROGRAMMING

EVENT DRIVEN PROGRAMMING

How do I...

17.1   Trigger and post events in a window?

17.2   Send parameters while triggering an event?

17.3   Pass event parameters using arguments?

Events are the mechanisms used to notify your program of some occurrence in the system. They play a significant role in any PowerBuilder application. Some of the events your program might receive are user-related, such as a Clicked event when the user clicks a CommandButton. Others may be system-related, such as the Open event that occurs immediately before a window is drawn for the first time.

You may also define your own events, called *custom user events*, which can have parameters much like functions do. Defining user events in your program is one technique that can be used to create objects that are more easily reused. Rather than manipulating object attributes and variables directly, your program components can invoke user events on each other and thus isolate each other from their internal structure, including control and variable names. The techniques presented in this chapter will apply primarily to these custom user events, although there is nothing to prevent most of these techniques from being used with the other types. Mastering the event mechanism is central to becoming an effective PowerBuilder developer.

Several fundamental changes have been made in the event capabilities of PowerBuilder in version 5.0. The ability to send parameters with an event and the ability to post a function have resulted in function and event capabilities converging somewhat. This change is especially highlighted in the comments accompanying How-To 17.3.

This chapter includes coverage of all of the fundamental event techniques. You will learn how to *trigger* and *post* events, and you will gain an understanding of the difference between the two methods. You will also learn how to send parameters with an event using both the traditional and new 5.0 techniques. All of these methods will serve you well as you create your own PowerBuilder applications.

17.1   Trigger and Post Events in a Window

The most basic form of sending an event to an object is to trigger that event, which executes that event immediately by transferring control to that triggered event's script. In order to allow other processing to complete, you may want the program to delay processing of the event being sent. You can implement this behavior by posting the event rather than triggering it. This How-To provides a simple example to examine some of the differences between triggering and posting an event. It also demonstrates the utility of posting an event while opening a window in order to improve performance.

17.2   Send Parameters While Triggering an Event

One way to pass parameters with an event is to use the Message object. While this method is not as flexible as the full event parameters discussed in How-To 17.3, it works well in a variety of situations and is compatible with pre-5.0 versions of PowerBuilder. This How-To demonstrates this parameter passing technique.

17.3   Pass Event Parameters Using Arguments

PowerBuilder 5.0 introduces an exciting new ability to pass an arbitrary number of parameters of any data type when invoking an event. This capability greatly expands the usefulness of events for intraapplication communication. This How-To demonstrates this new technique.

COMPLEXITY

BEGINNING

17.1   How do I...
Trigger and post events in a window?

Problem

I have an event script that I would like to invoke from more than one location, but I don't know how to tell PowerBuilder to execute that script. Additionally, I am experiencing a performance problem in my PowerBuilder application when I open a window that contains a long-running Open event script. Is there any way to activate an event programmatically? Is there any solution to my performance problem?

Technique

PowerBuilder offers two functions, TriggerEvent() and PostEvent(), that you can use to invoke events programmatically (i.e., without user actions). The functions are similar in that both of them execute the requested script. The difference between these two functions is *when* the requested event occurs following the function call. TriggerEvent() results in a transfer of control to the target event immediately, while PostEvent() places the event at the end of the *event queue*, allowing other scripts to complete before the requested script is executed. This How-To will explore the differences in these two functions.

Steps

The application for this How-To can be found in TRIGPOST.PBL on the included CD-ROM. Run the application. Once the initial window, w_startup, opens as shown in Figure 17-1, click on the first CommandButton, which opens a window instructing it to use the TriggerEvent() function in its processing. Observe that the second window, pictured in Figure 17-2, takes several seconds to appear with a list of numbers displayed in the MultiLineEdit control (depending on the speed of your computer). Return to the initial window again and click on the second command, which opens a second copy of w_trigpost, telling it to use PostEvent(). Observe that the second copy of w_trigpost opens significantly faster than the first copy, although there is a brief delay before the contents of the MultiLineEdit appear. To build this application, follow the steps below.

1. Create a new PBL and Application object called TRIGPOST.PBL and a_trigpost, respectively, using the Application painter. Answer "No" when prompted to create an application template.

2. Create a new window called w_trigpost using the settings presented in Table 17-1. This window is shown in Figure 17-2.

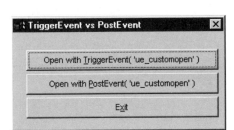

Figure 17-1 The w_startup window

Figure 17-2 The w_trigpost window using TriggerEvent()

WINDOW/CONTROL NAME	PROPERTY	VALUE
Window		
w_trigpost	Window Type	Popup
	Maximize Box	FALSE
	Minimize Box	FALSE
	Resizable	FALSE
MultiLineEdit	Name	mle_1
	VScroll Bar	TRUE
CommandButton	Name	cb_close
	Text	"&Close"
	Cancel	TRUE

Table 17-1 The w_trigpost window

3. Single-click on the window surface, then use the Declare/User Events...
menu item to declare a new event with an event name of ue_customopen
mapped to Event ID pbm_custom01 (see Figure 17-3). Be sure that the
Events window indicates you are working on w_trigpost and not on one of
the controls on the window. If it does not, click Cancel to close the Events
window, and then click on the surface of w_trigpost before defining the
event. This process creates a new custom event that you can use in your
scripts without being concerned about conflicting with a standard event.
You have 75 event IDs (pbm_custom01 through pbm_custom75) available
for your use.

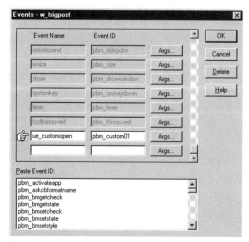

Figure 17-3 Creating a user event
ue_customopen mapped to event ID
pbm_custom01

4. Enter the Script painter for w_startup and place the following script in the Open event. This script activates the custom event ue_customopen using TriggerEvent() or PostEvent() based on an incoming parameter. For more information on passing parameters to a window, see How-To 2.5.

```
// Based on the incoming parameter, use TriggerEvent() or
// PostEvent() to activate the ue_customopen event
integer li_parm
li_parm = Message.DoubleParm

SetPointer( Hourglass! )

IF li_parm = 1 THEN
    this.title = "TriggerEvent"
    this.TriggerEvent( "ue_customopen" )
ELSE
    this.title = "PostEvent"
    this.PostEvent( "ue_customopen" )
END IF
```

5. Without leaving the Script painter, use the Select Events DropDownListBox at the top of the painter to switch to the ue_customopen event that you defined earlier. This script will create a string containing a sequence of numbers. This script should take a little while to execute to demonstrate the difference between PostEvent() and TriggerEvent(). Use the following code for the ue_customopen event.

```
// Create a string containing a list of numbers up to a limit.
// You may adjust the upper limit below to observe the effect on
// the application's performance. Values over 2000 are
// not recommended due to long running times.

integer li_index
string ls_mlecontents

FOR li_index = 1 TO 200
    ls_mlecontents = ls_mlecontents + string( li_index ) + "~r~n"
NEXT

mle_1.text = ls_mlecontents
```

6. Place the following script on the Clicked event of cb_close.

```
Close( parent )
```

7. Save the w_trigpost window.

8. Using the Window painter, create a new window called w_startup using the specifications shown in Table 17-2. This window is shown in Figure 17-1.

WINDOW/CONTROL NAME	PROPERTY	VALUE
Window		
w_startup	Title	"TriggerEvent vs PostEvent"

continued on next page

continued from previous page

WINDOW/CONTROL NAME	PROPERTY	VALUE
	Maximize Box	FALSE
	Minimize Box	FALSE
	Resizable	FALSE
CommandButton	Name	cb_trigger
	Text	"Open with &TriggerEvent('ue_customopen')"
CommandButton	Name	cb_post
	Text	"Open with &PostEvent('ue_customopen')"
CommandButton	Name	cb_exit
	Text	"E&xit"
	Cancel	TRUE

Table 17-2 The w_startup window

9. Place the following code on the Clicked event of cb_trigger. This script opens the w_trigpost window, sending it a parameter indicating it should use TriggerEvent() when the window opens.

```
w_trigpost lw_temp

// Open an instance of w_trigpost, telling it to use
// TriggerEvent() within its Open event
OpenWithParm( lw_temp, 1 )
```

10. Place a script on the Clicked event of cb_post as follows. The only difference between this code and the script in step 9 is the parameter value.

```
w_trigpost lw_temp

// Open an instance of w_trigpost, telling it to use
// PostEvent() within its Open event
OpenWithParm( lw_temp, 0 )
```

11. Code the following script in the Clicked event of cb_exit.

```
Close( parent )
```

12. Save the w_startup window.

13. Using the Application painter, place the following script in the application Open event.

```
Open( w_startup )
```

14. Save and run the application.

How It Works

When the w_trigpost window is opened by one of the buttons on w_startup, it receives an Open event allowing it to initialize itself *before the window is drawn*. Depending on the button you used to open the window, the Open event script uses either TriggerEvent() or PostEvent() to invoke the code contained in the ue_customopen event you created in steps 3 and 4. If TriggerEvent() is called, PowerBuilder immediately transfers control to the named event, ue_customopen in this case. However, the window has not yet been drawn on the screen, and it will not be drawn until the ue_customopen and Open events end. If the processing performed by the Open event (including ue_customopen) is lengthy, there will be a noticeable delay between clicking cb_trigger on w_startup and seeing w_trigpost.

If PostEvent() is called, PowerBuilder adds the specified event to the end of the event queue and continues executing the original script. When the Open event ends, the window is drawn on the display. However, when all other events in the queue have been processed, PowerBuilder will finally receive and process the ue_customopen event placed in the event queue by PostEvent(). The result of the PostEvent() method is that the window is drawn sooner (making the program feel faster) at the expense of a delay once the window has been drawn.

To summarize, the TriggerEvent() function activates an event *synchronously* by immediately transferring control to it while PostEvent() activates an event *asynchronously* by placing it at the end of the event queue.

Comments

The PostEvent() technique presented in this How-To is extremely useful when you have a window that has extensive initialization to perform. By posting to a custom event from the Open event, the window is drawn quickly, giving the user the illusion that the program is quicker than it really is. There is a chance, however, that the user will be able to invoke controls on the window before the window has completed its initialization, especially on slower machines. This may cause unpredictable errors in your program. You may want to consider disabling all of the window controls by default, enabling them only at the conclusion of the posted event to avoid this problem.

COMPLEXITY
BEGINNING

17.2 How do I...
Send parameters while triggering an event?

Problem

I have encountered a situation where I want to use an event mechanism in my program, but I need to be able to pass parameters to the event scripts. I have been successful in calling functions when I want to pass parameters to a script, but I can't figure out how to pass parameters when triggering or posting events. Can I do this in PowerBuilder?

Technique

PowerBuilder allows you to specify up to two parameters when calling the TriggerEvent() or PostEvent() functions. You may pass two long integer values or a long integer value and a string. This How-To consists of a simple application demonstrating the code required to pass parameters to an event.

Steps

The application for this How-To can be found in TRIGPARM.PBL in the accompanying CD-ROM. Run the application, and you will see the TriggerEvent with Parameters window shown in Figure 17-4. Try typing an integer into the Number EditMask and a string into the String SingleLineEdit. Click the Trigger CommandButton and observe the response window echoing the values you entered as shown in Figure 17-5. The script displaying the response window had the two values sent to it from the TriggerEvent() function. To construct this application use the following steps.

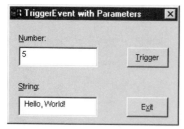

Figure 17-4 The Trigparm application

Figure 17-5 The response window displaying the parameter values

1. Create a new PBL and Application object called TRIGPARM.PBL and a_trig-parm, respectively, using the Application painter. You will not need an application template for this sample.

2. Using the Window painter, create a new window called w_trigparm using the settings shown in Table 17-3. This window is shown in Figure 17-4.

WINDOW/CONTROL NAME	PROPERTY	VALUE
Window		
w_trigparm	Title	"TriggerEvent with Parameters"
	Maximize Box	FALSE
	Minimize Box	FALSE
	Resizable	FALSE
StaticText	Name	st_number
	Text	"&Number:"
	Alignment	Left
StaticText	Name	st_string
	Text	"&String:"
	Alignment	Left
EditMask	Name	em_number
	Mask	"#####"
	Accelerator	"n"
SingleLineEdit	Name	sle_string
	Auto HScroll	TRUE
	Accelerator	"s"
CommandButton	Name	cb_trigger
	Text	"&Trigger"
CommandButton	Name	cb_exit
	Text	"E&xit"
	Cancel	TRUE

Table 17-3 The w_trigparm window

3. Using the Declare/User Events... menu item, declare a user event called ue_testevent mapped to event ID pbm_custom01. Be sure to single-click on the window surface before defining the event to ensure that the event you define is for the window and not for a control on the window.

4. Place the following script on the Clicked event for cb_trigger. Notice that the GetData() function returns a double, when the program requires a long integer. The script does an assignment of a double, ldb_word, into a long integer, ll_word, to perform this conversion. Also note the use of the second and third parameters to the TriggerEvent() function.

```
double ldb_word
long ll_word
string ls_temp

// get the long integer contents of em_number (as a double)
// and convert it to a long integer
em_number.GetData( ldb_word )
ll_word =  ldb_word

ls_temp = sle_string.text

// trigger ue_testevent, sending the two items of data along
Parent.TriggerEvent( "ue_testevent", ll_word, ls_temp )
```

5. Single-click on the window surface and code a script for the ue_testevent event as follows. This script accepts the incoming data items and performs the conversion required to access the string.

```
string ls_temp
long ll_word, ll_long

// get the incoming data
ll_word = Message.WordParm
ll_long = Message.LongParm

// interpret ll_long as a string address and place the string
// into a variable
ls_temp = String( ll_long, "address" )

MessageBox( "ue_testevent", "Number: " + String( ll_word ) + &
            "~rString: " + ls_temp )
```

6. Place the following script in the Clicked event of cb_exit.

```
Close( parent )
```

7. Save the window.

8. Using the Application painter, code the Application object Open event as follows.

```
Open( w_trigparm )
```

9. Save and run the application.

How It Works

Even though this sample only demonstrates TriggerEvent(), both TriggerEvent() and PostEvent() have the capability to send parameters when calling an event. When the second and third parameters to these functions are specified, PowerBuilder copies the data items to the WordParm and LongParm properties of the Message object. The receiving script can extract these properties into variables via a simple assignment, as was done in the ue_testevent script in this application.

As mentioned in the Techniques section of this How-To, your application can pass a pair of long integers or a long integer and a string. To send a pair of long integers, simply access WordParm and LongParm normally. When sending a string, the receiving script must dereference the string address contained in the LongParm property. This can be done by calling the String() function using "address" as the format (second) parameter:

```
string ls_parm
ls_parm = String( Message.LongParm, "address" )
```

Note that when passing parameters in multiple PostEvent() calls there is no danger of corrupted information in the receiving event. PowerBuilder preserves the contents of the WordParm and LongParm properties so that multiple scripts may pass parameters at any given time.

Comments

Passing parameters when using TriggerEvent() and PostEvent() is preferable to setting global variables to communicate the same information.

COMPLEXITY
INTERMEDIATE

17.3 How do I...
Pass event parameters using arguments?

Problem

I have an application with a menu that needs to convey sorting information to its parent window, and I want to trigger an event from the menu to perform this task. However, the menu must pass more than one string value to the parent window, and the TriggerEvent() and PostEvent() functions will only allow me to pass a single string value plus a long integer. I know that PowerBuilder 5.0 has added the capability of defining any number of parameters for an event. How can I pass event parameters using arguments?

Figure 17-6 The
Parms application

Technique

As mentioned in the problem, PowerBuilder 5.0 has the ability to trigger and post events that have more than the limited two parameters allowed by PostEvent() and TriggerEvent(). To create an event that uses parameters, we will use the normal Declare/User Events... menu item in the Object painters, but we will not map the event to a standard PowerBuilder event as was done in How-To 17.2. We can then define arguments for this event. To invoke the event, your program will use the new event syntax in PowerBuilder 5.0, passing the desired values for the parameters.

Steps

The sample program for this How-To can be found in the PARMS.EXE program, with the source code located in PARMS.PBL. Run the Parms program, and a window listing the Zoo departments will appear as shown in Figure 17-6. Choosing any of the sorting options under the Sort menu will sort the department listing as appropriate. The sorting information is being communicated from the menu to the window using the event parameter mechanism. To construct this application, follow the steps below.

1. Using the Application painter, create a new PBL and Application object called PARMS.PBL and a_parms, respectively. Answer "No" when prompted to build an application template.

2. Use the DataWindow painter to create a department listing DataWindow object called d_dept_list as shown in Figure 17-7. The specifications for this DataWindow object are summarized in Table 17-4.

WINDOW	OPTION	VALUE
New DataWindow		
	Data Source	Quick Select
	Presentation Style	Tabular
	Generation Options	Background color: white
		Text border: none
		Text color: WndText
		Column border: none
		Column color: WndText
Quick Select		
	Table	department
	Columns	dept_id, dept_dsc
Design		
	Column	dept_id
	Tab order	0
	Column	dept_dsc
	Tab order	0

Table 17-4 Specifications for the d_person_entry DataWindow object

3. Create a new window called w_parms using the Window painter. The specifications for this window are listed in Table 17-5. The window is shown in Figure 17-6 at the start of this How-To.

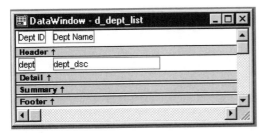

Figure 17-7 Layout of the d_dept_list DataWindow object

WINDOW/CONTROL NAME	PROPERTY	VALUE
Window		
w_parms	Title	"Event Parameters"
	WindowType	Main
	Maximize Box	FALSE
	Resizable	FALSE
DataWindow control	Name	dw_1
	DataWindow Object name	"d_dept_list"
	HScrollBar	TRUE
	VScrollBar	TRUE
	Border	3D Lowered

Table 17-5 The w_parms window specifications

4. When the window opens, it should connect to the database and perform the initial retrieve for the DataWindow. Place the following code in the Open event of w_parms to perform this task.

```
sqlca.dbms = "ODBC"
sqlca.dbparm = "ConnectString='DSN=Zoo;UID=dba;PWD=sql',DisableBind=1"

CONNECT USING sqlca;
IF sqlca.sqlcode <> 0 THEN
    MessageBox("Connect", "Could not connect.~r~n"+&
          sqlca.sqlerrtext, Exclamation! )
END IF


dw_1.SetTransObject( sqlca )
dw_1.Retrieve()
```

5. When the window closes, it should disconnect from the database. Perform the disconnect in the Close event of w_parms as follows.

```
IF sqlca.dbhandle() <> 0 THEN
    DISCONNECT USING sqlca;
END IF
```

6. You should now declare the user event required to perform the sorting. From within the Script painter for the Close event of w_parms, or after clicking the window surface, choose the Declare/User Events... menu item. Scroll to the bottom of the event list and add an event called ue_sort. However, do *not* specify an Event ID for this new event. (If you do, you can't add event parameters.) Click the Args... CommandButton for the ue_sort event and define the event parameters listed in Table 17-6. When done, click OK to close the Event Declaration window and click OK to close the User Events window.

EVENT SPECIFICATIONS

Event	Name	ue_sort	
	Returns	(None)	
Arguments	as_col	string	value
	as_sort	string	value

Table 17-6 Specifications for the ue_sort event

7. Place the following script inside the ue_sort event you just declared. This simple script accepts an incoming column expression and sort specification and instructs the DataWindow to sort accordingly.

```
IF as_col <> "" AND as_sort <> "" THEN
    dw_1.SetSort( as_col + " " + as_sort )
    dw_1.Sort()
END IF
```

8. Return to the window surface and save the w_parms window.

9. You should now create the m_parms menu from the Menu painter. This is a simple menu; its structure is listed in Table 17-7.

TOP-LEVEL MENU ITEM TEXT	SUB-MENU ITEM TEXT	PROPERTY	VALUE
"&Sort"		Name	m_sort
	"ID &Ascending"	Name	m_idascending
	"ID &Descending"	Name	m_iddescending
	"&Name Ascending"	Name	m_nameascending
	"Name D&escending"	Name	m_namedescending
	"_"	Name	m_-
	"E&xit"	Name	m_exit

Table 17-7 Structure for the m_parms menu

10. Each of the sort menu items should invoke the ue_sort event on the w_parms window to perform the appropriate sorting action. To begin, place the following script on the Clicked event of m_idascending.

```
ParentWindow.event dynamic trigger ue_sort( "Long(dept_id)", "a" )
```

11. Copy the script from the Clicked event of m_idascending and place it on m_iddescending, changing the second parameter so that the line looks as follows.

```
ParentWindow.event dynamic trigger ue_sort( "Long(dept_id)", "d" )
```

12. Enter the line of code below for the Clicked event of m_nameascending.

```
ParentWindow.event dynamic trigger ue_sort( "dept_dsc", "a" )
```

13. Copy the code from step 12 and place it on the Clicked event of m_namedescending again, modifying the second parameter as shown below.

```
ParentWindow.event dynamic trigger ue_sort( "dept_dsc", "d" )
```

14. The m_exit menu item should end the application. To do so, use the code listed below for the Clicked event of m_exit. Save the m_parms menu when done.

```
Close( ParentWindow )
```

15. Return to the Window painter, and access the properties for w_parms. Set its menu name to m_parms and then save the window.

16. Write the script below for the Open event of the Application object.

```
Open( w_parms )
```

17. Save and run the application.

How It Works

The two basic techniques in use in this application are the ability to declare an event that has an arbitrary number of events and then to invoke that event passing those parameters. To perform the event definition, you used the Declare/User Events... menu item in step 6. Specifically, by not specifying a PowerBuilder event ID for the new event, you are permitted to declare your own parameters for this event. (Had you specified an event ID, you would have been limited to the standard two parameters explored in How-To 17.2.)

To invoke the event, you used the strange-looking syntax shown below.
```
ParentWindow.event dynamic trigger ue_sort( "dept_dsc", "d" )
```
You should examine this line of script in detail. Beginning with the "event" keyword, you are telling PowerBuilder to activate an event. Specifying "dynamic" (instead of "static") tells PowerBuilder to defer checking the validity of this event until runtime. This is important here, because the ue_sort cannot be verified to exist against the parent window pronoun, which could refer to any window regardless of whether or not it has a ue_sort event. "Trigger" (instead of "post") tells PowerBuilder to activate the event synchronously. (Triggering versus posting is explored in How-To 17.1.) Finally, note the use of the event parameters specified following the event; the syntax resembles that of a function call.

Comments

One of the big questions developers have about this event parameter mechanism is, "What's the difference between using a function and using an event?" Clearly, the event and function mechanisms in PowerBuilder are converging somewhat in version 5.0. However, there are still some key differences. Specifically, events cannot be overloaded as functions can; that is, you cannot declare the same event name twice on the same object class in order to specify different versions of that event. (For more information on function overloading, see How-To 18.2.) On the other hand, events can be extended when inheritance is used, while functions cannot be. If an event is declared on an ancestor object and coded on both the ancestor and a descendant, it is possible for both the ancestor and descendant scripts for that event to execute. Functions, in contrast, *replace* the ancestor functionality when they are re-declared on a descendant.

INTRODUCTION TO OBJECT-ORIENTED PROGRAMMING

18

INTRODUCTION TO OBJECT-ORIENTED PROGRAMMING

How do I...

This chapter is filled with exciting and powerful techniques that will "object orient" your applications. Object orientation is becoming more and more the standard. There is object oriented analysis, design, and programming. And it is not just limited to application development. These techniques apply to database design, business re-engineering, and many other areas. Object orientation (OO) is a way of thinking, not just coding. It seems that everyone is talking OO, but all have their own definitions of what OO is. And, since it is one of the current buzzwords of our industry, even those who have no idea what OO is all about are jumping on the bandwagon. This chapter is designed to clear up the mystery concerning objects and object orientation. These techniques will allow you to complete the class library needed for your applications (although, like a good program, a good class library is never complete!). Object orientation involves four areas — abstraction, inheritance, polymorphism, and encapsulation. The How-To's presented here cover each area, and specifically how they are supported and used in PowerBuilder.

18.1   Hide Properties of an Object

When properties are modified using standard dot notation (such as w_main.Title = "Main Window" to change the Titlebar of a window), we are directly manipulating the Title property. While this is fine at times, there are some instances where it is not desirable. Under certain circumstances, the owning object should be the only object allowed to modify the property. The property itself is hidden from all other objects. How then, do you access it? The answer lies in creating object functions responsible for getting and setting the property. One object then calls these functions to obtain or set the property. Now the property is protected from the outside world. This How-To uses a SingleLineEdit control that maintains a custom help context id. If the user presses F1 while the control has focus, a specific help page displays. This allows you to write applications with context-sensitive help. If the developer accidentally sets the HelpContext to an invalid number, the Windows help engine will complain (at runtime). This is not acceptable behavior from the user's perspective. To fix this potential problem, a function validates the HelpContext before setting it. This ensures that the help engine never has a problem accessing a help topic.

18.2   Overload Object Functions

Overloading functions is a powerful object oriented technique, the result of which you have used many times. Take for example the PowerScript MessageBox() function. This function takes five arguments, only two of which are required. The arguments specifying the icon, button style, and default button are optional. This was accomplished by overloading the function. Function overloading is so common in today's development environments that nobody gives it a second thought. That is, until you want to create your own overloaded functions. This How-To shows you how you can overload your own functions, thereby providing default values for the optional parameters, or creating functions that take arguments of varying data types. How-To 18.2 demonstrates the techniques of creating several functions with differing argument types, and optional arguments.

18.3   Send Messages to an Object

One problem we face in PowerBuilder development is in using functions. Functions cannot be called if they don't exist. This makes sense. Object functions cannot be called unless the object has been loaded into memory. However, in building reusable objects or class libraries, nothing can be assumed. Let's assume that you are responsible for designing menu items and writing the scripts. A co-worker is doing the same for window objects. Your menu needs to delete a row in the DataWindow of the active window, through a window function called wf_DeleteRow(). When writing your menu scripts, the window function must exist before your script will compile. So, what if the other developer has not completed writing the function? You cannot test your system until the function is complete. The answer lies in message passing instead of calling functions. In this How-To, you will learn how to implement a message passing architecture.

Functions allow us to pass parameters to them, but did you know that you can also pass parameters to an event? The TriggerEvent() function has two optional arguments that you can utilize to communicate between events. This How-To provides a mechanism for sending messages, as well as arguments, to an object. Specifically, this example indicates whether or not to verify the deletion with the user, based on the setting of a menu item. Since the menu maintains this setting, you need to pass that information along with the message.

18.4   Share Variables Across Instances of a Class

Instance variables provide an easy way to store object specific data. But what about class specific data? This is where the shared variable comes into play. Shared variables behave similarly to, yet differently from, instance variables. This How-To presents the shared variable, explains its use, and covers some important differences between it and the instance variable. Here, the example uses a sheet window that maintains a shared array of long values. This array is populated with the key value of the current data, and prevents a user from opening the sheet with the same data twice. It also incorporates an instance variable to point to the array index so the value can be reset upon closing.

18.5   Write a Script to Look for Unsaved Changes in All Windows and Save Those It Finds

PowerBuilder provides the GetActiveSheet() function that tells your scripts what sheet is in the foreground. You can use this information to call a function in that sheet. Calling a function in a window is easy, but you need to know the window class, and declare a variable of that type. What if you don't know the class? Or, what if you want to call the function in a non-sheet window? GetActiveSheet() will not help you for windows you have opened with Open() or OpenWithParm(). In this How-To, we will revisit several topics covered up to this point, such as class user objects, shared variables, and the TriggerEvent() function, that will allow your application to save changes in a window regardless of the window class.

18.6   Use Custom Class User Objects to Implement Business Rules

Custom class user objects are multifaceted. You can use them to perform a wide variety of tasks, anywhere from simple function repositories, to object orientation. However, custom class user objects very commonly fill one particular task — encapsulating business rules. What exactly does this mean, and what does it buy you? By placing business related rules in a custom class user object, you are able to perform data validation about your business. By doing so, you leverage one aspect of object orientation. When (not if!) the business changes, all that is required is a simple modification in the object that contains the function(s). So, how is this better than using a global function for the same result? First, since the functions exist in a user object, one can inherit from them to tailor the function to the task at hand. Also, custom class user object functions benefit from function overloading. These concepts are not supported in a global function. How-To 18.6 examines the techniques and theory behind data encapsulation and validation.

COMPLEXITY
BEGINNING

18.1   How do I...
Hide properties of an object?

Problem

I have added several properties to my objects, but I don't want other objects to have direct access to them. I want the owning class object to maintain control over its own properties. The values these properties maintain are critical to the integrity of the application. Other objects must have access to the values of these properties, but the class object must be responsible for changing them based on some criteria. How can I hide properties from other objects, still providing a way for other objects to gain limited access to them?

Technique

Properties are really nothing more that instance variables. Hiding properties involves assigning an *access* level to the instance variable. Access levels dictate the *visibility* of a property or function, and specify which objects are capable of manipulating property values (or call functions). PowerBuilder provides three levels for instance variables and object functions. These access levels are *Public*, *Private*, and *Protected*. Public access indicates that any script in any object may access and modify the variable, provided that the object containing the instance variable resides in memory. Private access limits the variable's use to the owning object only. Other objects may not use them. This exclusion includes even descendant objects. Therefore, Private properties are available only to the class. Protected properties may be used by the owning object class, and any descendants of that class. You must assign an access level when you declare instance variables. By default, all instance variables are Public unless you specify otherwise. In this How-To, you will declare a Private property for a SingleLineEdit control. This limits its use, thereby hiding access to the property from the outside world. The SingleLineEdit control maintains a *helpcontext* id, which specifies the particular help topic to open if the user presses F1 while the control has focus. This helpcontext value is an integer value that a script initializes, depending on the specific purpose of the individual control. This example uses a Private property, along with a member function. It is the responsibility of the member function to set the initial value of the custom property. Using this technique allows the object (the SingleLineEdit control) to validate the property.

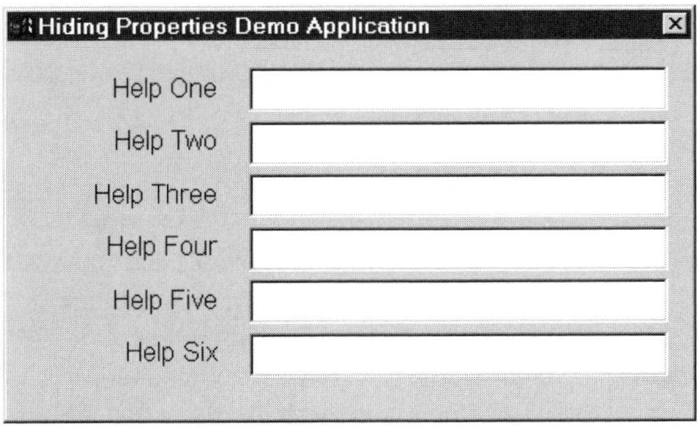

Figure 18-1 Main window of the Hiding properties How-To

Steps

Open and run the application in the HIDEPROP.PBL library. You will receive an error message when the application loads. This error simply demonstrates how the object could report an error condition, and would not normally perform this way in a real business application. Figure 18-1 shows this window at runtime. When the window opens, press the [F1] key. The application opens a help page based on the value of its helpcontext property. Close this help page and press [TAB]. Again, press [F1]. A different help page opens. Each SingleLineEdit control specifies a different help page.

1. Create a new application object named "hideprop" and save it in a library named HIDEPROP.PBL. Do not generate an application template for this application.

2. Start the User Object painter, and create a new object. This object should be a Standard Visual object. When PowerBuilder displays the Select Standard Visual Type dialog box, select SingleLineEdit, and press OK. Add the following property to the object, by declaring an instance variable. This declares the instance variable as having private visibility, so no other object may directly touch this value.

```
Private:
Integer ii_HelpContext
```

3. Select User Events... from the Declare menu and create a custom user event. Map this event to the pbm_keydown Event ID. Place the following code in this event. This script detects the [F1] key, and opens a help file using the instance variable as the help context pointer into the file. Save this object using the name suo_sle.

```
//This event fires each time the user press a key
//Check to see if the F1 key is down
```

continued on next page

continued from previous page

```
If KeyDown ( KeyF1! ) Then
//The F1 key has been detected, so open the the help file.
//This example uses the PowerBuilder help file, but you would change
//the function call to use one from your application
    ShowHelp ( "pbhlp050.hlp", Topic!, this.ii_HelpContext )
End If
```

4. Since the variable is private, you may be wondering how other scripts can use it. This is accomplished through a user object function. Declare a new User Object function for this object by selecting User Object Functions... from the Declare menu. The object encapsulates this function; therefore it has the authority to change the value of the property. Give the function the properties shown in Table 18-1. Place the following code in this function. Additionally, the function performs some range checking to verify that the requested value falls within the range that is valid for this application. Save the object, and close the User Object painter.

```
//This function allows other objects to set the property once.
//Once the property contains a valid value, it may not be changed.
//The function returns TRUE if the property was successfully modified
//otherwise it returns FALSE
Boolean lb_return

//See if the property has been previously set. If so, do not allow
//modification to it.
If ii_helpcontext <> 0 Then
    lb_return = FALSE

//Ensure that the value passed by the caller is valid for this context
ElseIf ai_help < 100 Then
    ii_helpcontext = ai_help
    lb_return = TRUE

Else
//Invalid value specified. Set it to something safe
    ii_helpcontext = 1
    lb_return = FALSE
End If

//Tell the caller what happened
Return lb_return
```

PROPERTY	VALUE	DATATYPE
Name	uo_SetHelpContext	
Returns	Boolean	
Argument 1	ai_help	integer

Table 18-1 Property settings for uo_SetHelpContext user object function.

5. Create a new window object, using the example in Figure 18-1 as a guide. Instead of placing SingleLineEdit controls on the window, select User Object... from the Controls DropDown. Place six copies of the suo_sle object created in step 2. Give this window and the controls the properties shown in Table 18-2.

OBJECT/CONTROL	PROPERTY	VALUE
Window	Name	w_help
	TitleBar	"Custom Property Help Demo"
UserObject	Name	sle_one
	Accelerator	"o"
	Name	sle_two
	Accelerator	"t"
	Name	sle_three
	Accelerator	"h"
	Name	sle_four
	Accelerator	"f"
	Name	sle_five
	Accelerator	"i"
	Name	sle_six
	Accelerator	"s"
StaticText	Name	st_one
	Text	"Help &One"
	Name	st_two
	Text	"Help &Two"
	Name	st_three
	Text	"Help T&hree"
	Name	st_four
	Text	"Help &Four"
	Name	st_five
	Text	"Help F&ive"
	Name	st_six
	Text	"Help &Six"

Table 18-2 Properties for w_help window and controls

6. Place the following code in the Open event of the window. This script uses the object's public function in order to set the private property. The last function call in this script attempts to set the help context to an invalid value. The object function notifies the script (and the user in this case) of this situation. When this happens, the object function therefore sets this property to a valid value. It is for this reason that a private property and public interface function are used. Finally, save the window using the name w_help.

```
//Set the help context using the public function
sle_one.uo_SetHelpContext ( 1 )
sle_two.uo_SetHelpContext ( 2 )
sle_three.uo_SetHelpContext ( 3 )
sle_four.uo_SetHelpContext ( 4 )
sle_five.uo_SetHelpContext ( 5 )
//Test the return value of this one function call only.
//Normally this would be done on each function call
If Not sle_six.uo_SetHelpContext ( 12345 ) Then
    MessageBox ( "Help Context", "Invalid value set. Using default of 1." )
End If
```

7. Place the following code in the Open event of the window.

```
//Open the main window for the user

Open ( w_help )
```

How It Works

The help context property is Private. Other objects are not allowed to directly manipulate the value. In order to set the value, this example provides a Public access level user object function. This technique allows the function to first verify the value of the passed argument, and determine whether or not it is appropriate or valid to change the property's value. Notice that the object itself reads the value, and acts upon it. In this sample application, other objects do not need to know the value of the Private property. This is not always the case, however. If other objects require the current value, you would create another Public access function that simply returns the value. An example of this function follows.

```
//GetHelpContext() function.
//This function returns the value of the private property back to the
//caller.

Return ii_HelpContext
```

Comments

While declaring this function, you may have noticed that user object functions have access levels as well. These access levels are the same as those for instance variables. Most instance variables should be marked as either Private or Protected, while the object provides Public functions used to manipulate their values. Most object level functions are Public. Only under certain circumstances would you declare one otherwise. You would create a Private or Protected function only if the function helps the object do work specific to the object. See How-To 18.6 for an example of this type of function. Normally, when working with Private or Protected properties, the object provides a pair of functions for manipulating these values. Quite often, these function names begin with Set or Get (such as SetHelpContext() and GetHelpContext()).

18.2 How do I...
Overload object functions?

Problem

PowerScript provides many functions that have optional arguments. MessageBox() is one such example. Additionally, some functions accept arguments with varying data types, such as Print(). Can I provide the same type of flexibility with my own functions?

Technique

Yes, you can, but don't let the complexity rating of "intermediate" scare you if you're new to PowerBuilder. The technique is known as *function overloading*. Overloading a function is as simple as declaring multiple functions that all share the same name, but have differing function signatures. PowerBuilder allows you to create functions with optional parameters, or that accept different data types in the argument list. Prior to PowerBuilder 5.0, the technique required you to write an object function, inherit from that object, and create the function again with different parameters. This type of polymorphism extended across class boundaries — in other words, each class provided its own implementation of the function. PowerBuilder 5.0 allows you to overload functions within a class. When you declare a function, you indicate the data type of the return value, along with an argument list accepted by the function. The combination of these function properties is known as the *function signature*, and uniquely identifies the function. Overloading involves declaring multiple functions, each with the same name but having different function signatures. This example presents a search and replace function for a DataWindow.

Steps

Run the application in the OVERLOAD.PBL library. Figure 18-2 shows the application at runtime. Once the application starts, try it out using the values from Table 18-3. Enter in a column, search criteria, and replace criteria. Once complete, press [ENTER] or click OK. The DataWindow replaces the data it finds. Since the various column values have differing datatypes (string, number, and date with this example), an overloaded function provides the interface to accomplish the task.

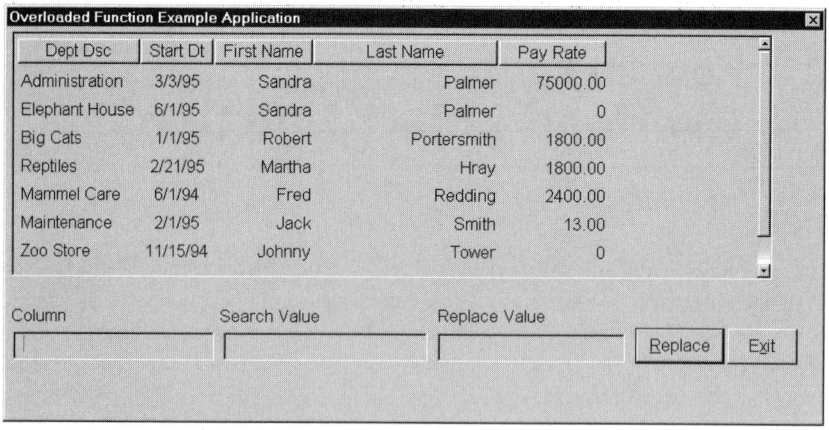

Figure 18-2 Overloaded Function Demo at runtime

COLUMN	SEARCH	REPLACE
person_first_name	"Sandra"	"Debbie"
employee_pay_rate	1800	2650
employee_start_dt	6/1/94	1/1/90

Table 18-3 Values for SingleLineEdit controls for overloaded function demo

1. Create a new Application object called "overload", and store it in a library called OVERLOAD.PBL. Do not generate an application template.

2. Start the DataWindow painter and create a new DataWindow object. The sample application used the person and employee tables, but you can use any tables you like. Just make sure that you include at least one string, one numeric, and one date column. You'll probably want to use a Tabular presentation style, thus making it easier to observe the results of the search and replace function at runtime. Save the DataWindow using the name "d_person".

3. Since the search and replace function works with DataWindows only, you will want to create the functions as a part of a DataWindow. If you already know how to create a standard DataWindow user object, you can skip to step 4 at this point. Start the User Object painter. Click the New button from the Select User Object dialog box. Once the New User Object dialog box opens, select Standard from the Visual GroupBox, and click OK. PowerBuilder now displays the Select Standard Type dialog box. From here, select DataWindow and click OK.

4. PowerBuilder displays a new DataWindow control in the User Object painter. Let's create the first function, which performs the search and replace for string type columns. Select User Object Functions... from the

Delare menu. Give this function the properties shown in Table 18-4. Once you have completed the function declaration, place the following code in the body of the function. The heart of this function is the Find() function, which locates a row in a DataWindow based on an expression. Here, you pass a column name (where to search), values indicating what to search for, and the value to replace it with. The Find() function takes three arguments. The first is the expression used to locate data, and this expression must match the data type for the column in question. This script builds this expression by adding the search value to the column name. Then it uses this expression to find the first matching row. Since Find() requires a starting and ending row on which to search, these values are first obtained. Take note of the last argument to your SearchAndReplace() function (ab_start). This Boolean value indicates whether to start the search at row 1 (a value of TRUE) or at the current row (a value of FALSE). Find() returns the row on which the requested value was found. This value is subsequently used in the SetItem() function, used to replace the value. As long as Find() locates a row, the script loops to find the next row, each time using the previous row number plus 1 as the new starting row. Each time the loop executes, it increments ll_Count, used to return the number of replacements made. When you have finished, close the User Object Function painter.

```
String ls_SearchString
Long ll_FoundRow, ll_Start, ll_End, ll_Count

//Find out how many rows are in this datawindow
ll_End = This.RowCount()

//Figure out where to start from
If ab_Start Then ll_Start = 1 Else ll_Start = This.GetRow ()

//Search the datawindow and replace values
ls_SearchString = as_Col + " = '" + as_SearchValue + "'"
ll_FoundRow = This.Find ( ls_SearchString, ll_Start, ll_End )
Do While ll_FoundRow > 0
    //Increment the number of replacements made
    ll_Count++
    This.SetItem ( ll_FoundRow, as_Col, as_ReplaceValue )
    //Get the next starting row
    ll_Start = ll_FoundRow + 1
    ll_FoundRow = This.Find ( ls_SearchString, ll_Start, ll_End )
Loop

Return ll_Count
```

PROPERTY	VALUE	DATATYPE
Name	searchandreplace	
Returns	long	
Argument 1	as_col	string
Argument 2	as_searchvalue	string

continued on next page

continued from previous page

PROPERTY	VALUE	DATATYPE
Argument 3	as_replacevalue	string
Argument 4	as_start	Boolean

Table 18-4 Function declaration for Search and Replace function—string style

5. Now let's create another version of SearchAndReplace(). This version will handle columns with a numeric data type. Select User Object Functions... from the Declare menu. Use Table 18-5 to declare this function. Here, the function name is a duplication of the previous function, but the function signature is different. The script for this function follows. The main difference between this code and the previous code is the way in which it builds the search criteria. Since this function handles numeric data, the search expression is slightly different.

```
String ls_SearchString
Long ll_FoundRow, ll_Start, ll_End, ll_Count

//Find out how many rows are in this datawindow
ll_End = This.RowCount()

//Figure out where to start from
If ab_Start Then ll_Start = 1 Else ll_Start = This.GetRow ()

//Search the datawindow and replace values
ls_SearchString = as_Col + " = " + String ( al_SearchValue )
ll_FoundRow = This.Find ( ls_SearchString, ll_Start, ll_End )
Do While ll_FoundRow > 0
    //Increment the number of replacements made
    ll_Count++
    This.SetItem ( ll_FoundRow, as_Col, al_ReplaceValue )
    //Get the next starting row
    ll_Start = ll_FoundRow + 1
    ll_FoundRow = This.Find ( ls_SearchString, ll_Start, ll_End )
Loop

Return ll_Count
```

PROPERTY	VALUE	DATATYPE
Name	searchandreplace	
Returns	Long	
Argument 1	as_col	string
Argument 2	al_searchvalue	song
Argument 3	al_replacevalue	long
Argument 4	ab_start	Boolean

Table 18-5 Declaration for SearchAndReplace() function—numeric style

6. The next verion of SearchAndReplace() handles date type data. Create
another function for this user object, using Table 18-6 for the function
properties. The following code does the job. Again, the main difference
between this verion and the other two is the way in which it builds the
expression used in the Find() function.

```
String ls_SearchString
Long ll_FoundRow, ll_Start, ll_End, ll_Count

//Find out how many rows are in this datawindow
ll_End = This.RowCount()

//Figure out where to start from
If ab_Start Then ll_Start = 1 Else ll_Start = This.GetRow ()

//Search the datawindow and replace values
ls_SearchString = "String (" + as_Col + ") = '" &
    + String ( ad_SearchValue ) + "'"
ll_FoundRow = This.Find ( ls_SearchString, ll_Start, ll_End )
Do While ll_FoundRow > 0
    //Increment the number of replacements made
    ll_Count++
    This.SetItem ( ll_FoundRow, as_Col, ad_ReplaceValue )
    //Get the next starting row
    ll_Start = ll_FoundRow + 1
    ll_FoundRow = This.Find ( ls_SearchString, ll_Start, ll_End )
Loop

Return ll_Count
```

PROPERTY	VALUE	DATATYPE
Name	searchandreplace	
Returns	Long	
Argument 1	as_col	string
Argument 2	ad_searchvalue	date
Argument 3	ad_replacevalue	date
Argument 4	ab_start	Boolean

Table 18-6 Declaration for SearchAndReplace() function—date style

7. One last function completes this user object. Up until now, the variations of
SearchAndReplace() have used four arguments, with differing datatypes.
Passing differing data types is only one style of overloading. The other
method involves functions with optional arguments. MessageBox() is one
such function. MessageBox() provides up to five arguments, only two of
which are required. The last three arguments are optional. This next function provides just such an example. This version makes the last argument
(ab_start) optional for the string version of the function. If not provided, a
value of TRUE (search the whole DataWindow) is assumed. Declare one last

version of SearchAndReplace(), using Table 18-7 for the declaration. The following code does the job. Since this code is just slightly different from the original string version, you may wish to use Copy and Paste, as opposed to completely recoding.

```
String ls_SearchString
Long ll_FoundRow, ll_End, ll_Count
Long ll_Start = 1                                    //Starting Row

//Find out how many rows are in this datawindow
ll_End = This.RowCount()

//Search the datawindow and replace values
ls_SearchString = as_Col + " = '" + as_SearchValue + "'"
ll_FoundRow = This.Find ( ls_SearchString, ll_Start, ll_End )
Do While ll_FoundRow > 0
    //Increment the number of replacements made
    ll_Count++
    This.SetItem ( ll_FoundRow, as_Col, as_ReplaceValue )
    //Get the next starting row
    ll_Start = ll_FoundRow + 1
    ll_FoundRow = This.Find ( ls_SearchString, ll_Start, ll_End )
Loop

Return ll_Count
```

PROPERTY	VALUE	DATATYPE
Name	searchandreplace	
Returns	Long	
Argument 1	as_col	string
Argument 2	as_searchvalue	string
Argument 3	as_replacevalue	string

Table 18-7 Declaration for SearchAndReplace() function — string style with optional argument

8. Save this user object using the name suo_dw, and close the UserObject painter.

9. Create a new window. Place one instance of the suo_dw object, three SingleLineEdit controls, two CommandButton controls, and three StaticText controls on the window surface. Use Figure 18-2 as a guide, and give the window and each of its controls the properties shown in Table 18-8.

OBJECT/CONTROL	PROPERTY	VALUE
Window	Name	w_overload
	Title	"Overloaded Function Example Application"
	Type	Response!
DataWindow	Name	dw_person
	DataWindow Object	d_person
	HScroll Bar	TRUE
	VScroll Bar	TRUE
	Border	3D Lowered
SingleLineEdit	Name	sle_column
	Text	(blank)
	Border	3D Lowered
	Name	sle_Value
	Text	(blank)
	Border	3D Lowered
	Name	sle_replace
	Text	(blank)
	Border	3d Lowered
StaticText	Name	st_Column
	Text	"Column"
	Name	st_Value
	Text	"Search Value"
	Name	st_replace
	Text	"Replace Value"
CommandButton	Name	cb_Replace
	Text	"&Replace"
	Default	TRUE
	Name	cb_Exit
	Text	"E&xit"

Table 18-8 Properties for the w_overload window

10. Place the following code in the Open event of the window, in order to retrieve the data into the DataWindow.

```
//Get the data...

dw_Person.SetTransObject ( SQLCA )
dw_Person.Retrieve ()
```

11. The following script is for the Clicked event of cb_replace. This script gets the data from the SingleLineEdit controls, and figures out what data type it is. This conversion is only necessary since the data comes from SingleLineEdit controls, which only provide a text property. When using an overloaded function in a script, you really don't worry about the data type. That's one of the benefits of such functions.

```
Long ll_Count

//Since the data is in an SLE, we must determine the data type
//This is for example only. Normally, we know what we're replacing
If IsDate ( sle_Value.Text ) Then
    ll_Count = dw_Person.SearchAndReplace &
        ( sle_Column.Text, Date ( sle_Value.Text ), &
            Date ( sle_Replace.Text ), TRUE )
ElseIf IsNumber ( sle_Value.Text ) Then
    ll_Count = dw_Person.SearchAndReplace &
        ( sle_Column.Text, Long ( sle_Value.Text ), &
        Long ( sle_Replace.Text ), FALSE )
Else
    ll_Count = dw_Person.SearchAndReplace &
        ( sle_Column.Text, sle_Value.Text, sle_Replace.Text )
End If

//Notify the user of the number of replacements made
MessageBox ( 'Search And Replace', String ( ll_Count ) + &
        ' Replacements made.' )
```

12. Code the Clicked event of cb_exit as follows, allowing the user to shut the application down. When you are through, close the Window painter, and save this window using the name w_overload.

```
//Shut down the application

Disconnect Using SQLCA;
Close ( Parent )
```

13. Finally, code the Open event of the Application object to connect to the database and open w_overload.

```
//Connect to the database

SQLCA.DBMS = "ODBC"
SQLCA.DBParm = "ConnectString='DSN=zoo;UID=dba;PWD=sql'"

Connect Using SQLCA;

If SQLCA.SQLCode = 0 Then
    Open ( w_OverLoad )
End If
```

14. Save all objects and run the application.

How It Works

Normally, you identify a function by its name, but this is not the case in an object oriented world. Functions are really identified by their name *and* their signatures. When you call a function, PowerBuilder executes the one whose argument types match that of the function call. Therefore, you don't worry about the argument types. The Clicked event of cb_replace was a little more complex than necessary. The reason for this was that SingleLineEdit controls only provide the Text property. Everything you enter into them becomes a string. In order to provide the example, and let you enter new values, a conversion to the proper data type was necessary.

Comments

Function overloading involves declaring multiple functions, all sharing the same name. It's the function's signature, made up of the arguments and return type, that uniquely identifies it. Through overloading, you provide the ability for objects to maintain a consistent development interface. No longer do you have to worry about function names that are dependent on the values on which it operates. Additionally, function overloading allows you to create functions with optional arguments. In order to make the SearchAndReplace() function more flexible, you'll no doubt want to add additional functions. How about one that operates on datetime, or time values? You may also want to make the last argument (ab_start) optional for all versions, not just the string version. Take the MessageBox() function mentioned above. The actual declarations for it are given below. You'll notice that the optional arguments always fall at the end of the argument list. You cannot overload a function, making the first argument optional but the second one required. You must structure your declaration so the optional arguments come last.

- messagebox (string c, boolean t) returns integer
- messagebox (string c, boolean t, icon i) returns integer
- messagebox (string c, boolean t, icon i, button b) returns integer
- messagebox (string c, boolean t, icon i, button b, integer d) returns integer
- messagebox (string c, double t) returns integer
- messagebox (string c, double t, icon i) returns integer
- messagebox (string c, double t, icon i, button b) returns integer
- messagebox (string c, double t, icon i, button b, integer d) returns integer
- messagebox (string c, string t) returns integer
- messagebox (string c, string t, icon i) returns integer
- messagebox (string c, string t, icon i, button b) returns integer
- messagebox (string c, string t, icon i, button b, integer d) returns integer

COMPLEXITY
INTERMEDIATE

18.3 How do I...
Send messages to an object?

Problem

I am having trouble managing my application. I have to write some menus, while a co-worker creates the window objects. The window objects contain functions that my menu scripts call. However, I am unable to complete the menu scripts until my co-worker completely writes the functions and saves the window object. My scripts won't compile since the functions I am trying to call do not yet exist. My objects contain user-defined functions, and respond to standard events. I would like to use message passing in order to maintain a more object oriented approach, and so that my objects are reusable. I like this technique, since I can write scripts without regard to whether the message will be received by the destination object. Sometimes I need to pass arguments to another object, and I therefore use functions. I'd rather use messages. How can I pass parameters with a message and reduce the use of custom user-defined functions? Is there a solution to this dilemma?

Technique

The answer to this problem involves sending messages to an object. In object oriented programming, one object should never do the work of another. Therefore, one option is to call an object level function. You're on the right track by calling a function as opposed to writing the code as a part of the menu. However, using this approach leads to the problem that you have encountered — the function you're attempting to call must exist as a part of the object. Microsoft Windows uses a message passing architecture in order to communicate between objects. The answer lies in triggering events instead of calling functions. However, the use of functions gives your scripts the ability to pass parameters. Well, rest easy. You can pass arguments with messages as well. This How-To demonstrates these techniques. Although the number of available parameters is somewhat limited, they should serve many applications. With the standard messaging technique, your scripts can pass a numeric value, a string value, or a combination of the two.

Steps

Open and run the application in the SENDPARM.PBL library. Select Delete... from the Edit menu. The application confirms the deletion of the DataWindow control's current row, provided the user sets the Confirm Delete menu item. This is the default value. The menu sends a message to the parent window, and passes two arguments with the message. The first argument constitutes a numeric value based on the state of the Confirm Delete menu item; the second is a string value used by the associated MessageBox() function. Figure 18-3 shows the application at runtime.

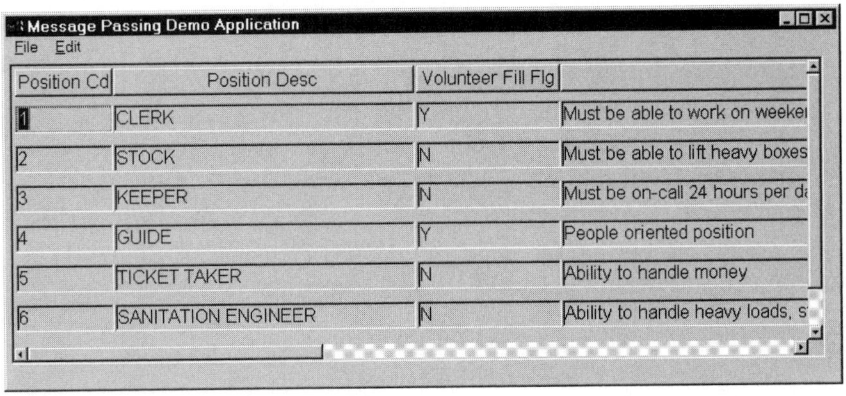

Figure 18-3 Sending messages to an object demo at runtime

1. Create a new Application object called "sendmsg" and store it in a library called SENDPARM.PBL. Close the Application painter and save changes for now.

2. Create a DataWindow object for the application. This should be a simple, one-table DataWindow. Use any table from the Zoo database. Ensure that the tab order of the columns is non-zero so you can interact with the DataWindow later. Save this object using the name d_data.

3. Create a new menu object for use by the application. The menu bar should contain a File and an Edit menu, with Exit in the File menu, and Confirm Delete and Delete as the Edit menu items. Ensure that you set the checked property of the Confirm Delete option to TRUE. Use the menu from the sample application as a guide. Declare the following instance variable in the menu. The value of this variable indicates the current status of the checked properties of the Delete option on the menu. Later, you will pass this value with the message. Since PowerBuilder does not allow you to pass Boolean values, the scripts maintain this integer to represent the value of the checked property.

```
Protected:
Integer ii_confirm = 1
```

4. Place the following code in the Clicked event of m_exit. This script sends the ue_exit message to the parent window. This message is a custom user event that you will declare in the window object later. PowerBuilder will not balk during compile time, even though this object and event do not yet exist.

```
//Send a message to the parent window telling it to close
ParentWindow.TriggerEvent ( "ue_exit" )
```

5. Place the following code in the Clicked event of m_delete. The TriggerEvent() function supports two additional arguments, known as the

WordParm and LongParm, respectively. WordParm represents a 16-bit value, while LongParm contains 32 bits. (PowerBuilder actually implements them both as 32-bit values according to the help library.) Windows uses this mechanism in communicating with objects. When an event occurs, Windows notifies the application by sending it a message to indicate which event happened. Along with this message, Windows may pass additional information in these two properties of the message object. This script passes the value of ii_confirm, so the window object knows whether to first confirm the deletion with the user. Then, it passes the address of a string in the LongParm property. The window uses this information upon receipt of the message. Save the object and close the Menu painter.

```
//Send a message telling the parent window to delete a row
Integer li_confirm

//Send the instance variable, as well as a string with the message
ParentWindow.TriggerEvent ( "ue_delete", ii_confirm, &
                    "Really delete this row?" )
```

6. Place the following code in the Clicked event of m_confirmdeletes. This toggles the Checked property, and synchronizes ii_confirm with the current checked state.

```
//Change the checked property to whatever it isn't and change
//the property to reflect its value

//Set the instance variable to 1 for confirm, 0 for no confirm
ii_confirm = 1 - ii_confirm
this.Checked = Not this.Checked
```

7. Create a new window object. Place a DataWindow control on the surface. Give the window and the DataWindow control the properties shown in Table 18-9. Declare two custom user events as shown in Table 18-10.

OBJECT/CONTROL	PROPERTY	VALUE
Window	Name	w_main
	Title	"Message Passing Demo Application"
DataWindow	Name	dw_datalist
	Dataobject	d_data
	HScroll Bar	TRUE
	VScroll Bar	TRUE

Table 18-9 Properties for window and DataWindow control

EVENT NAME	EVENT ID
ue_delete	pbm_custom01
ue_exit	pbm_custom02

Table 18-10 Custom user events for w_main

8. The Clicked event of the Delete... menu item passes two arguments. These indicate whether or not to confirm the deletion with the user, and a string value used as the prompt. The "prompt" value exists in the WordParm of the Message object. The string resides as an address in the LongParm of the Message object. This script converts the value in Message.LongParm to a pointer to the string, and passes this string to the MessageBox() function. Place this code in the ue_delete event.

```
//This message sent by the menu. Delete the current row
//of the datawindow. Set the initial value of li_yn to 1 to indicate a
//default of "yes" for the delete. Only change this if the user says "no"
Integer li_yn = 1

//Expecting a value in the WordParm property. A value of 1 means
//to prompt the user before deleting a row
If Message.WordParm = 1 Then

//A string address expected in the LongParm. Get the value and
//convert it to a string
    li_yn = MessageBox ( "Delete", String ( Message.LongParm, "address" ), &
            Question!, YesNo! )
End If

If li_yn = 1 Then
    dw_datalist.DeleteRow ( 0 )
End If
```

9. Place the following code in the Open event of the Application object.

```
//Connect to the database and open the frame
SQLCA.DBMS = "odbc"
SQLCA.DBParm = "ConnectString='dsn=zoo;uid=dba;pwd=sql'"

Connect Using SQLCA;
If SQLCA.SQLCode < 0 Then
    MessageBox ( "Database", "Could not connect to database." )
    Halt Close
End If

Open ( w_main )
```

10. Finish this window object by coding the ue_exit event. The menu triggers this event when you select Exit from the File menu.

```
//This event fires when the menu sends it the ue_exit message
//Close this window (and therefore the application)

Close ( This )
```

11. Save all objects and run the application.

How It Works

When the user clicks on the desired menu item, the clicked event of the menu sends a message to the window object using the TriggerEvent() function. The window object receives this message, and acts upon it as it sees fit. How does this help you? Well, if the event does not yet exist, the message is simply ignored. Therefore, you are able to create the menus (or other objects), and use a message passing architecture to communicate. This is far better than attempting to call a function in the other object. PowerBuilder performs syntax checking at compile time, so if the function does not yet exist, the script will not compile. Using TriggerEvent() alleviates this problem, since PowerBuilder does not check for the existence of the desired event at compile time (or runtime). It simply sends this message to the target object. It is the job of this target object to receive and act upon the message.

In Windows, messages are identified by numeric values. PowerBuilder abstracts this detail from you, by giving these messages *event names*. By design, Windows uses a message passing architecture. When an event occurs in an application, the application is really receiving a message. A message is comprised of four components. The first is the object that the message is destined for. The second is the message itself, which identifies what action the object is to take. The last two components are "additional information" used by the message. Windows programmers familiar with C or C++ know these parameters as the wParam and lParam (word and long parameter, respectively). When you call the TriggerEvent() function, you are really sending a message to an object. TriggerEvent() supports two optional parameters, namely the wParam and lParam. PowerBuilder places these values in the WordParm and LongParm properties of the Message object. In the example presented here, WordParam contains a 1 or 0, indicating whether or not to confirm the deletion with the user. When passing a string, the LongParm actually contains a pointer (the address) to the string value. If the object expects a string in the LongParm property, the value of this property must be converted to a string, as you did in the custom user event of the w_main window object.

Comments

Instead of calling functions from another object, consider triggering an event in the object instead. This way, the scripts will compile, and your applications move closer to object orientation. If the requested event does not exist, the message is simply ignored. This is far better than causing a runtime error. This also makes your objects totally reusable. With this technique, you could create a standard menu for your MDI frame and sheet window objects, place the menu in a common library, and simply attach the menu to new window objects as you create them. You declare the custom user events in these window objects, and place the object-specific code in these events. In an object-oriented system, no object should ever do the work of another object. So, the menu simply makes a request of the window to perform a specific action. Consider this: How many programmers does it take to change a light bulb? Answer: None, since, if the lighting system is object oriented, the light bulb will change itself!

Message passing is central to Microsoft Windows. The Message object contains the message itself, as well as the wParam and lParam values. The PowerBuilder Message object contains additional properties such as StringParm, DoubleParm, and PowerObjectParm. These are custom properties defined by PowerBuilder. If you need to pass additional information in these properties, set them prior to calling TriggerEvent(). Be careful doing so, however, since the Message object is a system wide variable (global to all applications), and directly changing the values of these properties may cause the Message object to become corrupt (not containing the data you expect). If you do pass additional values, set the properties of the Message object *immediately* prior to sending the message, and retrieve the value(s) as the *first line* of executable code (not including variable declarations) in the event receiving the message.

COMPLEXITY
INTERMEDIATE

18.4 How do I...
Share variables across instances of a class?

Problem

I'm writing an MDI application. When the application first opens, it presents the user with an initial sheet that displays items from which the user may select. This sheet contains a DataWindow control, and the user double-clicks a row in order to display additional detail information about the selected row. Since the application uses MDI, the user can have multiple detail sheets open at any time. However, each summary row should display a maximum of one instance of the detail sheet. If the user attempts to open multiple instances of the same detail row, the application should disallow it. How can I accomplish this without creating multiple detail classes?

Technique

A shared variable will solve the problem. Assume you have one sheet called w_summary from which the user selects a row. Upon double-clicking on the desired row, the application opens an instance of w_detail_sheet. Since the application uses MDI, the user could open multiple instances of w_detail_sheet, each displaying the same information. In this How-To, you'll create a shared array variable for the detail window, and populate it with the key value of the data. Upon instantiation, the sheet checks to see if the requested data already exists in this array. The array is shared between instances of the class, so each class member can see

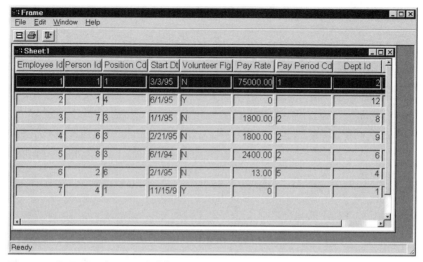

Figure 18-4 Sharing variables within a class demo at runtime

and manipulate its contents. If a previous copy of the data exists, the sheet notifies the user of this condition, and gracefully closes.

Steps

Run the application in the SHARE.PBL library. When the first sheet displays, double-click a row of the DataWindow control. Another sheet opens, showing detail information about the selected row. Leave this detail sheet open, and click on Sheet 1 to display the initial employee list. Double-click on the same row. The application displays an error message, and denies the request. Click on the Person Listing sheet and close it. Again, double-click on the same row. This time, the sheet opens and displays the information. Open multiple instances of the Person Listing sheet, using different employees for each. The application allows multiple instances of the Person Listing sheet, but denies multiple instances of the same person. Figure 18-4 shows the application at runtime.

1. Create a new Application object called "share," and save it in a library called "SHARE.PBL". Go ahead and generate an application template.

2. Create a tabular DataWindow object. Use the employee table as the data source, and include every column in the SQL Select statement. Select Tab Order from the Design menu, and set the tab order to 0 for every column. The user will not modify this data. Don't be concerned with the layout of this DataWindow. Save it using the name d_emp_list.

3. Create another new DataWindow object. Use FreeForm as the presentation style, and select all columns from the person table. While in the SQL painter, select Retrieval Arguments... from the Objects menu. Declare one argument of type number called person_id. Set the Where clause of the

DataWindow to include only the rows where the person.person_id = :person_id. Save this DataWindow using the name d_person_list, and close the DataWindow painter.

4. Create a new window object. This sheet opens to display detail information about the selected employee. Place one DataWindow control on the window surface. Set the properties for this window using Table 18-11.

OBJECT/CONTROL	PROPERTY	VALUE
Window	Name	w_person
	Title	"Person Listing"
DataWindow	Name	dw_person
	DataObject	d_person_list

Table 18-11 Properties for w_person sheet

5. Select Shared Variables… from the Declare menu. Place the following declaration in the Shared Variables dialog box. This is an unbounded shared array. As the sheet opens, this variable receives the id number of the requested data.

```
Integer si_id[]            //Shared variable to hold person id.
```

6. Place the following code in the Open event of the window. You will open this sheet using the OpenSheetWithParm() function later. This script obtains the parameter from the message object, in order to determine which person the user requested. It then loops through the shared array, looking for this number. If it finds a match, the script knows that the requested person record exists in another instance of this sheet. It therefore issues a message to the user, and closes itself. Assuming no match was found, the script inserts this new person id into the shared variable, and retrieves the data for that person.

```
Integer li_id, li_index, li_count

//Get the id passed from the first sheet
li_id = Message.DoubleParm

//Find out how many sheets are open. The upperbound of the shared
//array tells us this since one entry exists for each open sheet
li_count = UpperBound ( si_id[] )

//Loop through each entry in the array, looking for the requested data
For li_index = 1 to li_count

//If the id exists in the array, the sheet was opened previously with
//this data
    If si_id [ li_index ] = li_id Then
        MessageBox ( this.Title, "That employee has already been opened." )
        Close ( this )
```

continued on next page

continued from previous page

```
//The RETURN statement is necessary to prevent the remainder of the script
//from executing
        Return
    End If
Next

//Employee has not been opened previously, set the array with the
//employee id

//First, increment the counter that holds the array index
li_count++

//Set the shared array to indicate this employee has been loaded
si_id [ li_count ] = li_id

//Set the custom property that holds the upper bound of the array
ii_index = li_count

//Set the transaction object and retrieve the data
dw_person.SetTransObject ( SQLCA )
dw_person.Retrieve ( li_id )
```

7. Place the following code in the Close event for the window. When the sheet closes, the instance must be responsible for cleaning up the array. This ensures that a match on the current person will not be found later. Close the Script painter and save the window using the name w_person.

```
//Set the array element to 0 so the person information
//can be opened again later.

If ii_index <> 0 Then
    si_id [ ii_index ] = 0
End If
```

8. Select Open from the File menu of the Window painter, and open w_genapp_sheet. PowerBuilder generated this window object as a part of the application template. Place a DataWindow control on this sheet, associating it with the d_emp_list DataWindow object. Give this control the properties shown in Table 18-12.

CONTROL	PROPERTY	VALUE
DataWindow	Name	dw_employee
	HScroll Bar	TRUE
	VScroll Bar	TRUE
	X	0
	Y	0

Table 18-12 Properties for DataWindow control on w_genapp_sheet

9. Place the following code in the Open event of w_genapp_sheet. PowerBuilder generated much of this script for you. You need add only the script shown in bold. This performs the retrieval of the employee data.

```
int li_Count

    /* Sheet opening - reflect sheet count in title */
    li_Count = w_genapp_frame.wf_getsheetcount ()
    this.Title = "Sheet:" + string (li_Count)

    /* Modify menu text for platform */
    w_genapp_frame.wf_setmenutext (menuid)

//Set the transaction and retrieve the data
dw_employee.SetTransObject ( SQLCA )
dw_employee.Retrieve()

//Highlight the first employee
dw_employee.SelectRow ( 1, TRUE )
```

10. Place the following code in the Resize event for the window. This script sizes the DataWindow control to the size of the sheet. This way, the entire DataWindow is visible if the user changes the size of the sheet.

```
//Size the datawindow. Take into account the size of the scroll bars
//and the title bar

dw_employee.height = this.height - 100
dw_employee.width = this.width - 40
```

11. Place the following code in the Doubleclicked event of the DataWindow control. The script obtains the id of the requested employee, and opens the detail sheet, passing the person id in the message object.

```
Integer li_id
Long ll_row
w_person lw_person

//Get the current row of the datawindow
ll_row = this.GetRow ()

//Find the id of that person
li_id = this.GetItemNumber ( ll_row, "person_id" )

//Open the sheet, and pass that person id using the message object
OpenSheetWithParm ( lw_person, li_id, w_genapp_frame, 0, Original! )
```

12. Place the following code in the RowFocusChanged event of the DataWindow control. This script highlights the current row of the DataWindow, after turning off all previously highlighted rows.

```
Long ll_row

//Find the current row
ll_row = this.GetRow ()
```

continued on next page

continued from previous page

```
//Turn off all existing highlights on the datawindow
this.SelectRow ( 0, FALSE )

//Highlight just the requested row
this.SelectRow ( ll_row, TRUE )
```

13. Save all scripts and run the application.

How It Works

Shared variables are in scope (available for use) any time the containing class exists in memory. As each instance opens, the Open event scans the values stored in the shared variable, looking for the key value used in the retrieval. Using a shared variable allows the class to communicate between individual instances of that class. If the script determines that the requested data exists in another sheet (of the same class), it denies the retrieval and closes itself. You may have been tempted to declare an instance array in w_genapp_sheet instead, and check the values in this array prior to opening the detail sheet. This, however, would not work. The reason is simple. The shared array must contain only information pertinent to open detail sheets. Once a detail sheet closes, the information must be removed. Otherwise, the Open event of the detail sheet always thinks the requested data exists on another instance. Therefore, the Close event of this sheet must "clean up" after itself, and remove its reference from the shared array. The detail sheet could communicate with the summary sheet, but if the user closes the summary sheet, the communication mechanism falls apart.

Comments

Unlike other variable scopes, the value of a shared variable does not get destroyed when the associated class closes. This little known trick allows objects to maintain values between instances of a class, even when the class does not reside in memory. In short, shared variables behave much like static variables in the C language. For another look at shared variables and their use, read the following How-To.

COMPLEXITY
ADVANCED

18.5 How do I...
Write a script to look for unsaved changes in all windows and save those it finds?

Problem

I need to ensure that my application saves all modified data on all open windows. When the user closes the application, I'd like a simple way to update all DataWindows. Although I could create a base class, and save specific data in the Close or CloseQuery events, I need this function to work independently from the class object. Many of my sheets do not come from a base class, and I don't want to rewrite them. I could use the GetActiveSheet() and GetNextSheet() functions, but this would only work in MDI applications. Single Document Interface applications, as well as non-sheet windows in my MDI application, would not benefit from the use of these sheet functions. How can I write one script that saves all unsaved data in any open window, regardless of the window class?

Technique

Normally, a window or sheet manages all saving, through code inherited from the class. However, many window objects have no user-defined class, and are direct descendants of the standard window class. This makes it difficult to provide common functionality. If your application uses MDI sheets exclusively, the GetActiveSheet() and GetNextSheet() provide some help. However, these two functions only return instances of sheets. If your application contains popup, main, or child windows, you must resort to other mechanisms. In this How-To, you will build a custom class user object that manages all open windows, regardless of their type. Before opening a window, your scripts *register* the window with this object. This way, the custom class object always knows which windows are open, and can communicate with them directly.

Steps

Open and run the application in the SAVEALL.PBL library. Open several sheets, and change some values in the DataWindow controls. Ensure that you don't modify the same row in different instances. Finally, select Exit from the File menu, and restart the application. The application has saved all previous changes. Figure 18-5 shows this application at runtime.

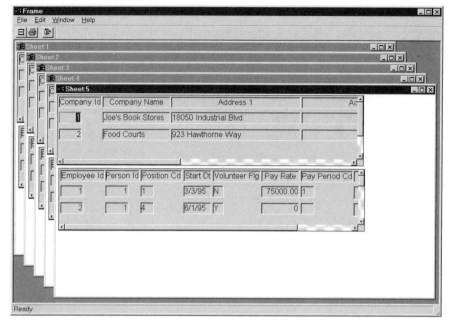

Figure 18-5 Save all open window applications at runtime

1. Create a new Application object called "saveall", and save it in a library named SAVEALL.PBL. Have PowerBuilder generate an application template for you.

2. Start the User Object painter and create a new custom class object. This object maintains all necessary information about any currently opened window objects. Select Shared Variables… from the Declare menu, and place the following declaration in the resulting dialog box. This shared array holds a pointer to each open window. You'll use this information later when you register instances or windows and when you save data.

```
window sw_window[] //array for open window objects
```

3. Declare a User Object function named RegisterInstance(). Give this function the properties shown in Table 18-13. Place the following code in this function. You'll call this function each time you open an instance of a window. RegisterInstance() receives a pointer to the window, and places that pointer in the array declared in step 2. To do so, this function steps through each array element, looking for a null value. (Later, you'll remove this pointer by setting its array element to null.) If it does not find a null entry, RegisterInstance() creates a new array element for the instance. This scanning ensures that previously used elements are reused, therefore lowering memory requirements.

```
Long ll_count, ll_index

//Find out how many instances have been registered
ll_count = UpperBound ( sw_window [] )

//Loop through each one, looking for a slot to reuse
For ll_index = 1 to ll_count
    If IsNull ( sw_window [ ll_index ] ) Then
//Found one, so end the loop
        Exit
    End If
Next

//ll_index is either an old position, or one higher than max, so use this
//array element for the new instance
sw_window [ ll_index ] = aw_win

Return
```

PROPERTY	VALUE	DATATYPE
Name	RegisterClass	
Returns	(none)	
Argument 1	aw_win	window

Table 18-13 Properties for the RegisterInstance() function

4. Declare another user object function called DestroyInstance(). Table 18-14 shows the declaration. Place the following code in this function. This function removes a window instance from the shared array of the class user object. The Close event of a window calls this function. If a window closes, but leaves the associated pointer in the array, a runtime error results when parsing the array. (You will do this in the next step.) The shared array must contain pointers only to currently open window objects. This function accepts a window as an argument, and searches the array looking for a matching pointer. Upon finding a match, the function sets the associated array element to null so other calls to RegisterInstance() can reuse that particular array element.

```
Integer li_count, li_index

//Find the number of instances registered
li_count = UpperBound ( sw_window [] )

//Loop through each instance, and see if it is the one passed in the func-
tion
For li_index = 1 to li_count
    If sw_window [ li_index ] = aw_window Then

//Yes, so set the array element null for future re-use
        SetNull ( sw_window [ li_index ] )

//Exit the loop, since we don't need to check anymore
```

continued on next page

continued from previous page

```
        Exit
    End If
Next

Return
```

PROPERTY	VALUE	DATATYPE
Name	DestroyInstance	
Returns	(none)	
Argument 1	aw_window	window

Table 18-14 Declaration of DestroyInstance() function

5. Declare one last function for this user object. Table 18-15 shows the declaration. Place the following code in the function. This function loops through the shared array looking for DataWindow controls on each of the previously registered window objects. It then saves any *dirty* DataWindows it finds. The return value indicates the number of DataWindows subsequently saved, or -1 if an error occurs. The UpperBound() function tells SaveAll() how many windows have been registered. SaveAll() then begins a For…Next loop to point to each window object in turn. The IsValid() function ensures that the window to which the function points is indeed valid. If the current array element points to a non-existent window, you don't want to process the invalid window. SaveAll() then begins another For…Next loop. This loop examines each control on the associated window and determines if the control is a DataWindow. If SaveAll() finds a DataWindow, it must determine whether or not the DataWindow has update capabilities. You wouldn't want to attempt to update a DataWindow that was designed as not updatable. It therefore calls the Describe() function, requesting the table name. Describe() returns the name of the table used in the update, or "?" if the DataWindow does not have update capabilities. Assuming that updating is allowed, the function calls AcceptText() to validate the DataWindow's edit control, and checks to see if outstanding edits exist. This ensures that a *clean* DataWindow never calls Update(). Calling Update() on an unmodified DataWindow does not pose a problem, but the return value of the function indicates the number of DataWindows found to be dirty. This function then calls Update() and sets the return code appropriately, based on the success or failure of the update.

```
Long ll_index, ll_count
Integer li_ControlCount, li_Index, li_return
DataWindow ldw_dwc

ll_count = UpperBound ( sw_window [] )
For ll_index = 1 to ll_count

    If IsValid ( sw_window [ ll_index ] ) Then
//Look at each registered window
        li_ControlCount = UpperBound ( sw_window [ ll_index ].Control [ ] )
```

```
//Loop through all controls and see if the control is a datawindow
        For li_Index = 1 to li_ControlCount

//Check the validity of the window object
        If IsValid ( sw_window [ ll_index ] ) Then
//If the control is a datawindow, assign to a variable so we
//can call the update() function
                If sw_window [ ll_index ].Control [ li_index ].TypeOf() &
                                        = DataWindow! Then
                    ldw_dwc = sw_window [ ll_index ].Control [ li_index ]

//See if the table can be modified, and if so update it
                If ldw_dwc.Describe ( "DataWindow.Table.UpdateTable" ) <> "?"
Then

//Make sure the last edit has been validated
                    ldw_dwc.AcceptText ()

//See if any updates are necessary. Used by the return code
//If no updates are necessary, the return value indicates that the
//datawindow was updated
                    If ldw_dwc.ModifiedCount() > 0 Or &
                            ldw_dwc.DeletedCount() > 0 Then

//If the update fails the first time, set the error code
//Otherwise increment the current save count for return to caller
                        If ldw_dwc.Update () < 0 And li_return <> -1 Then
                            li_return = -1
                        Else
                            li_return ++
                        End If
                    End If
                End If
            End If
        Next
    End If
Next

Return li_return
```

PROPERTY	VALUE
Name	SaveAll
Returns	Integer

Table 18-15 Declaration for SaveAll() function

6. Save this user object using the name ccuo_dw, and close the painter.

7. Create a DataWindow object. Use a Tabular presentation style, based on a the company table. Don't be concerned with the aesthetics of the object. Use the Update… option from the Rows menu to set the update characteristics. Allow updates for this DataWindow. Preview the DataWindow and ensure that the tab order is non-zero so that you can make edits at runtime. Save this object using the name d_company.

8. Create one more DataWindow, again using the Tabular presentation style. Select all columns from the employee table. This time, use the Update... option from the Rows menu to disallow updates. Save this object using the name d_employee and close the DataWindow painter.

9. Start the Window painter, and load w_genapp_sheet. PowerBuilder generated this object as part of the application template. Place two DataWindow controls on the sheet, and set the properties as shown in Table 18-16.

CONTROL	PROPERTY	VALUE
DataWindow	Name	dw_company
	HScroll Bar	TRUE
	VScroll Bar	TRUE
	DataObject	"d_company"
	Name	dw_employee
	HScroll Bar	TRUE
	VScroll Bar	TRUE
	DataObject	d_employee

Table 18-16 Properties for new DataWindow controls on w_genapp_sheet

10. Place the following code in the Open event of the sheet. PowerBuilder generated some of this script for you, so just add the code in bold. When the sheet opens, it first creates an instance of the user object created above, and registers this instance with that object. It then destroys the object since the instance is no longer necessary. The script then sets the transaction object for both DataWindows, and retrieves the data.

```
int li_Count
ccuo_dw lcuo_dw

//Create an instance of the custom class uo
lcuo_dw = Create ccuo_dw

//Register this window with the object
lcuo_dw.RegisterInstance ( this )

//Destroy the instance, since it is no longer needed
Destroy lcuo_dw

    /* Sheet opening - reflect sheet count in title */
    li_Count = w_genapp_frame.wf_getsheetcount ()
    this.Title = "Sheet:" + string (li_Count)

    /* Modify menu text for platform */
    w_genapp_frame.wf_setmenutext (menuid)
```

```
dw_company.SetTransObject ( SQLCA )
dw_company.Retrieve()
dw_employee.SetTransObject ( SQLCA )
dw_employee.Retrieve ()
```

11. Place the following code in the Close event of the sheet. This script instantiates the user object once again, calls the SaveAll() function, removes the sheet from the user object and destroys the object's instance. Again, only add the code shown in bold, since the remainder already exists.

```
ccuo_dw lcuo_dw

//Create a local instance of the save object
lcuo_dw = Create ccuo_dw

//Save all the datawindows in open window objects
lcuo_dw.SaveAll ()

//Destroy this instance, since it s closing
lcuo_dw.DestroyInstance ( this )

//Destroy the save object
Destroy lcuo_dw

/* Disable printing if last sheet */
if w_genapp_frame.wf_getsheetcount () = 1 then
    w_genapp_frame.wf_enableprint (false)
end if
```

12. Save the sheet and run the application.

How It Works

The custom class user object contains a shared array that holds pointers to window objects. As you open windows, you instantiate this object, and register the window with it. The object places a pointer to the window in this array. You then destroy the object. Since the array has a visibility of shared, its contents are not destroyed when the object itself goes out of scope. This is a little known trick with shared variables. When you want to save all DataWindow controls on all open windows, you again create an instance of the custom class object and call the SaveAll() function. The contents of the shared array still exist, so the function can loop through each of these previously registered windows. Each window contains an array, maintained by PowerBuilder, with pointers to each of the controls on that window. The SaveAll() function uses this information to search for DataWindows on that window. Upon finding a DataWindow control, SaveAll() invokes several DataWindow functions to determine if the DataWindow has update capabilities, and if the data in the DataWindow buffers is dirty. If both of these conditions hold, SaveAll() calls the DataWindow Update() function, and handles the return codes appropriately. The Close event of each window destroys the pointer held by the shared array, since the window is no longer valid. Since shared variables do not re-initialize each time they are created, RegisterInstance() searches the array looking for a pointer whose value is null. Any new registered windows reuse these null array elements in order to reduce memory overhead. Otherwise, the array would continue to grow as RegisterInstance() registers new windows. All window classes benefit from this custom class object. You must call RegisterInstance() when opening windows, and DestroyInstance() when closing windows. Any time you need to update all open windows, instantiate the user object and call its SaveAll() function.

Comments

You may have been tempted to create a global function that does the job provided by SaveAll(). While this would work, your function still needs to maintain pointers to all open windows. Therefore, you would need to create a global variable to hold this information. Doing so could violate the integrity of the window pointers, as well as ignore the power of object orientation. Shared variables are protected. Notice that scripts do not have access to the pointers, and therefore cannot modify them or gain access to the windows they point to. With a global array, any script could change the data, or use it for other purposes. Protecting (or hiding) data guarantees data integrity, and keeps the data under the authority of the owning object.

COMPLEXITY
ADVANCED

18.6   How do I...
Use custom class user objects to implement business rules?

Problem

I am tired of rewriting complex windows every time my business rules or my user interface requirements change. I would like to be able to create my application so that the user interface is completely separate from the processing, so that it is possible to change or replace either one without major modifications. How do I use custom class user objects to implement business rules?

Technique

This How-To presents the usage of a custom class user object to add, save, and look up persons in the Zoo database. A custom class user object (CCUO) is a *non-visual* user object; that is, unlike a window, the CCUO has absolutely no visual representation. A CCUO's primary purpose is to give you a way to create application logic in an easily reusable and *inheritable* component (which means additional logic can be derived from your original).

This How-To consists primarily of a CCUO that offers a mix of public functions your window can call to accomplish the person tasks defined above. Because all of the real functionality is encapsulated within the person user object, the window used to provide the interface has very little code on it.

As you work through this How-To, think about why certain user object functions are declared as Private (inaccessible outside the user object) versus Public. These distinctions are made to support the interface of the user object. The selection of this user object interface is a critical design decision.

Steps

The solution for this How-To may be tested by running BUSRULE.PBL or BUSRULE.EXE from PowerBuilder or Windows, respectively. Once the program is running, observe that the person information area of the window is empty as shown in Figure 18-6. Enter "2" as a person ID in the EditMask in the upper right corner and click Look Up. Notice that the person's information appears in the information area. Change the address of person 2 (Jack Smith) to be "323 Wonder Drive". Click Save to write that change to the database. Choose New to enter a new person; the information area will clear. Enter all of the details for a particular person (except for person ID, which is system-generated). Click Save again and notice that a new person ID was assigned to this new person during the save. The program is structured in such a way that will prevent two users from obtaining the same person ID.

All of the functionality provided by the CommandButtons has been placed in a custom class user object. To construct this application follow the detailed steps below.

1. Using the Application painter create a new PBL and Application object called BUSRULE.PBL and a_busrule, respectively. You will not require an application template for this How-To.

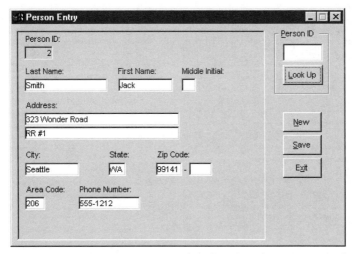

Figure 18-6 The Person Entry application (BUSRULE.PBL)

2. Using the DataWindow painter, create a DataWindow object called d_person_entry using the specifications listed in Table 18-17. The DataWindow object is shown in layout mode in Figure 18-7.

WINDOW	OPTION	VALUE	
New DataWindow			
	Data Source	SQL Select	
	Presentation Style	Freeform	
	Generation Options	Background color: Silver	
		Text border: none	
		Text color: WndText	
		Column border: 3DLowered	
		Column color: WndText	
SQL Select	Tables	person	
	Columns	*all*	
	Retrieval Arguments	an_person_id	Number
	Where	person.person_id = :an_person_id	

Table 18-17 Specifications for the d_person_entry DataWindow object

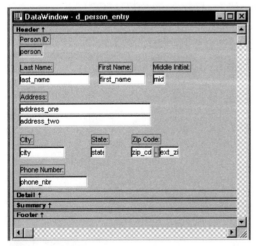

Figure 18-7 The d_person_entry DataWindow object

3. Create a new user object by choosing the User Object button from the PowerBar. Choose Custom Class as the user object type when prompted. Save this user object as u_person.

4. The user object will need instance variables to store the transaction object to use for database communication, the DataWindow control it references, and a flag to indicate whether or not the object has been initialized. Using the Declare/Instance Variables... menu item, make the following instance variable declarations.

```
transaction ito_1
datawindow  idw_1
boolean     ib_initialized = FALSE
```

5. Save the user object.

6. This user object will need to be initialized before a program can use it. You need to code a function called uf_init that allows the program to establish the transaction object and DataWindow control to be used by the u_person user object. Create uf_init by choosing the Declare/User Object Functions... menu item and clicking the New button. The specifications for this function are shown in Table 18-18. Use the following code for the body of the function.

```
// initialize the user object by establishing the transaction object
// to be used and the DWC to be used
integer li_return

ito_1 = ato_1

// check that the transobject is connected; if it is, proceed
IF ito_1.dbhandle() > 0 THEN
    idw_1 = adw_1
    IF idw_1.SetTransObject( ito_1 ) > 0 THEN
        li_return = 1
        ib_initialized = TRUE
    ELSE
        li_return = -2
    END IF
ELSE
    li_return = -1
END IF

RETURN li_return
```

FUNCTION SPECIFICATIONS

Function	Name	uf_init	
	Access	Public	
	Returns	integer	
Arguments	ato_1	Transaction	Value
	adw_1	Datawindow	Value

Table 18-18 Function specifications for uf_init()

7. The u_person user object provides the capability to assign unique, incrementing IDs to new persons in the database. To do this properly the user object depends on a counters table in the Zoo database to provide the *last used* person ID. If a user (or you!) were to add persons without updating the counters table to reflect that change, this program might not work. You will add a function called uf_fixcounters() that your program can call to ensure that the counters are correct before you use the object. Use the Declare/User Object Functions... menu item to declare a function called uf_fixcounters using the specifications in Table 18-19. The body of the function is given below.

```
// script ensures that the counter table has correct values so that
//attempts to use uf_getpersonid() do not cause problems

IF ib_initialized THEN

UPDATE counter SET employee_id = (SELECT MAX( employee_id ) FROM employee
),
                    person_id = (SELECT MAX (person_id ) FROM person )
    USING sqlca;

IF sqlca.sqlcode = 0 THEN
    COMMIT USING sqlca;
    IF sqlca.sqlcode = 0 THEN
        RETURN 1
    ELSE
        MessageBox("Database Error", "Could not fix counters.~r~n"+&
                sqlca.sqlerrtext, Exclamation! )
        RETURN -1
    END IF
ELSE
    ROLLBACK USING sqlca;
    MessageBox("Database Error", "Could not fix counters.~r~n"+&
            sqlca.sqlerrtext, Exclamation! )
    RETURN -1
END IF

END IF

RETURN -2
```

FUNCTION SPECIFICATIONS

Function	Name	uf_fixcounters
	Access	Public
	Returns	integer
Arguments	*(none)*	

Table 18-19 Function specifications for uf_init()

8. Save the user object.

9. The user object now needs a function called uf_getpersonid() to obtain a new, unique person ID value from the counters table in the Zoo database. The order of the SQL operations in this function is very important. The function should increment the ID value *first*, before obtaining the value. Doing so will cause most databases to grant you an exclusive lock, which prevents other users from getting a duplicate ID value. This method also prevents deadlock situations on the database server. Create uf_getpersonid by choosing the Declare/User Object Functions... menu item and using the specifications shown in Table 18-20. The script below is the body of the function.

```
// this function requests the next available person_id value
// from the database and will prevent two users from
// getting the same person_id.

long ll_personid

IF ib_initialized THEN
     UPDATE "counter"
    SET "person_id" = person_id + 1 USING ito_1 ;

    IF ito_1.sqlcode = 0 THEN
        SELECT "counter"."person_id"
               INTO :ll_personid  FROM "counter"  USING ito_1;
        IF ito_1.sqlcode = 0 THEN RETURN ll_personid
    ELSE
    // error handler
    END IF
END IF

RETURN -1
```

FUNCTION SPECIFICATIONS		
Function	Name	uf_getpersonid
	Access	Public
	Returns	long
Arguments	*(none)*	

Table 18-20 Function specifications for uf_getpersonid()

10. The u_person user object also needs a function to verify that a person ID is valid (exists in the person table). Create a function (using the Declare/User Object Functions... menu item) called uf_personexists() using the specifcations listed in Table 18-21. The following script should be used as the body of the function.

```
// simple function to determine if a person ID exists in the database.
// Yes it does = TRUE, No it doesn't = FALSE
```

continued on next page

continued from previous page

```
integer li_count
boolean lb_return = FALSE


IF ib_initialized THEN
   SELECT COUNT( * )
     INTO :li_count
     FROM "person"
    WHERE "person"."person_id" = :al_personid    ;

        IF li_count > 0 THEN lb_return = TRUE
END IF

RETURN lb_return
```

FUNCTION SPECIFICATIONS

Function	Name	uf_personexists	
	Access	Private	
	Returns	Boolean	
Arguments	al_personid	long	by value

Table 18-21 Function specifications for uf_personexists()

11. Save the user object.

12. The user object must be able to save a person record. You should create a function called uf_update() that updates the database. This function must distinguish between existing persons with changes versus new persons. New persons must be assigned a person ID. Create the uf_update functions by choosing Declare/User Object Functions... from the menu and declaring it as shown in Table 18-22. The code for the function is shown below.

```
// Function saves the current person record

integer li_return = -1
long ll_row, ll_personid
dwitemstatus le_status

IF ib_initialized THEN
        // determine the current row (there is only one row in the DW,
        // so this will be the one that's visible
        ll_row = idw_1.GetRow()
        IF ll_row > 0 THEN
            // if the row has been newly inserted, it will require a
            // person ID assigned to it
            le_status = idw_1.GetItemStatus( ll_row, 0, Primary! )
            IF le_status = NewModified! THEN
                ll_personid = this.uf_getpersonid()
                idw_1.SetItem( ll_row, "person_id", ll_personid )
            END IF
            IF idw_1.Update( ) > 0 THEN
                COMMIT USING ito_1;
```

```
                  IF sqlca.sqlcode = 0 THEN li_return = 1
            ELSE
                  ROLLBACK USING ito_1;
            END IF
      END IF
ELSE
      li_return = -2
END IF

RETURN li_return
```

FUNCTION SPECIFICATIONS

Function	Name	uf_update
	Access	Public
	Returns	integer
Arguments	*(none)*	

Table 18-22 Function specifications for uf_update()

13. A lookup capability that allows a complete person record to be retrieved when the person ID is known would be a nice feature. Create a function called uf_lookup() using the declaration listed in Table 18-23 and the code shown below.

```
// function verifies that a person exists in the database, and, if they do,
// retrieves the person record
boolean lb_exists=FALSE

IF this.uf_personexists( al_personid ) THEN
    idw_1.Retrieve( al_personid )
    lb_exists = TRUE
END IF

RETURN lb_exists
```

FUNCTION SPECIFICATIONS

Function	Name	uf_lookup	
	Access	Public	
	Returns	Boolean	
Arguments	al_personid	long	by value

Table 18-23 Function specifications for uf_lookup()

14. Another function should check that a person row in the DataWindow has been modified or not. Create a function called uf_modified() using the information in Table 18-24 and the code shown below.

```
// function determines if there are unsaved changes
```

continued on next page

continued from previous page

```
// Changes found = 1, no changes = 0, Error = -1
integer li_return = -1

IF idw_1.AcceptText() > 0 THEN
    IF idw_1.ModifiedCount() + idw_1.DeletedCount() > 0 THEN
        li_return = 1
    ELSE
        li_return = 0
    END IF
END IF


RETURN li_return
```

FUNCTION SPECIFICATIONS

Function	Name	uf_modified
	Access	Private
	Returns	integer
Arguments	*(none)*	

Table 18-24 Function specifications for uf_modified()

15. Finally, the user object should be able to add a new person to the database. Create a function called uf_new() to perform this capability. The specifications are shown in Table 18-25, and the code is shown below. This function first saves any pending changes and then creates the new row in the DataWindow.

```
// Function adds a new person record to the DataWindow
// It first saves any pending modifications
long ll_new
integer li_return = -1
boolean lb_do_a_new = TRUE

IF ib_initialized THEN
    IF this.uf_modified() > 0 THEN
        IF this.uf_update() < 0 THEN
            lb_do_a_new = FALSE
        END IF
    END IF

    IF lb_do_a_new THEN
        idw_1.Reset()
        ll_new = idw_1.InsertRow( 0 )
        idw_1.ScrollToRow( ll_new )
        idw_1.SetColumn( "last_name" )
        idw_1.SetFocus()
        li_return = 1
    END IF

END IF

RETURN li_return
```

FUNCTION SPECIFICATIONS

Function	Name	uf_new
	Access	Public
	Returns	integer
Arguments	*(none)*	

Table 18-25 Function specifications for uf_new()

16. Save the user object and close the User Object painter. This will complete the u_person user object. The remainder of the How-To focuses on the construction of the window that utilizes this user object.

17. Using the Window painter, create a window called w_business to serve as the graphical interface for adding a person. Use the settings listed in Table 18-26. The window is shown in Figure 18-6.

WINDOW/CONTROL NAME	PROPERTY	VALUE
Window		
w_business	Title	"Person Entry"
	WindowType	Main
	MaximizeBox	FALSE
	Resizable	FALSE
DataWindow control	Name	dw_1
	DataWindow object name	"d_person_entry"
	HScrollBar	FALSE
	VScrollBar	FALSE
	Border	3DLowered
EditMask	Name	em_lookupid
	Type	Number
	Mask	"####"
CommandButton	Name	cb_lookup
	Text	"Look Up"
CommandButton	Name	cb_new
	Text	"&New"

continued on next page

continued from previous page

CommandButton	Name	cb_save
	Text	"&Save"
CommandButton	Name	cb_exit
	Text	"E&xit"
GroupBox	Name	gb_1
	Text	"Person ID"

Table 18-26 The window and control settings for w_business

18. The w_business window will use user events created at the window level to invoke the processing inside u_person. By placing this code in the user events, you allow this window to be controlled from menu items (if you have a menu) as well as from the CommandButtons used here. Click on the background of the window (to make it the current object), and use the Declare/User Events... menu item to declare three user events: ue_new mapped to pbm_custom01, ue_lookup mapped to pbm_custom02, and ue_save mapped to pbm_custom03.

19. Save the w_business window to preserve your work.

20. Place the following script in the Clicked event of cb_lookup. This script invokes the ue_lookup user event created in step 18.

```
parent.PostEvent( 'ue_lookup' )
```

21. The cb_new CommandButton should invoke the ue_new user event created in step 18. Place a script to perform this action on the Clicked event of cb_new as follows.

```
parent.PostEvent( 'ue_new' )
```

22. As with the other CommandButtons, cb_save should invoke a user event, ue_save, on the window. Place the following code on the Clicked event of cb_save to do so.

```
parent.PostEvent( 'ue_save' )
```

23. Code the cb_exit CommandButton so that it will terminate the program using the script below.

```
Close( parent )
```

24. Save the window to preserve your work.

25. In order to use the u_person user object, we must first declare an instance of that object on the window. Click once on the background of the window surface (to make the window the current object) and choose Declare/Instance Variables... from the menu to make the following declaration.

```
u_person      iuo_person
```

26. The window must also instantiate (create) and initialize the object at run-time. To perform this processing, add a script for the Open event of w_business as indicated here.

```
long ll_new

// create an instance of our person business object
iuo_person = CREATE u_person

// if it got created OK, then proceed.
IF IsValid( iuo_person ) THEN
    // initialize the UO (nothing works without this step )
    iuo_person.uf_init( sqlca, dw_1 )

    // the following call would not need to be performed if *all* person
    // adds were handled by this UO. However, in our context, let's make
    // sure the counters are good
    iuo_person.uf_fixcounters()

    // start out with an empty person displayed
    iuo_person.uf_new()
ELSE
    MessageBox("Error", "Unable to create person object.", Exclamation!)
    Close( this )
END IF
```

27. To actually perform a lookup operation, a script must be coded on the ue_lookup event on the w_business window. This script contains little functionality of its own; it uses the logic contained in the instance of u_person referenced by iuo_person. Place the following script on ue_lookup to invoke this capability.

```
// script looks up the person referenced by the ID in em_lookupid
long ll_personid

ll_personid = Long (em_lookupid.text )

IF iuo_person.uf_lookup( ll_personid )  = FALSE THEN
    MessageBox( "Lookup", "Person does not exist." )
END IF

em_lookupid.text = ""
```

28. To perform a save operation, the ue_save event on the window should call the uf_update() function on the instance of iuo_person created previously. Place the following code on the ue_save event of w_business to perform a save.

```
// save the person
iuo_person.uf_update()
```

29. To add a new person, code the ue_new event of the w_business window to access the uf_new() function on iuo_person. Place the following script on the ue_new event to do so.

```
// create a new person
iuo_person.uf_new()
```

30. Finally, the program window should destroy any instances of objects it has created. This can be performed by the Close event of w_business by executing the following script.

```
// if the iuo_person object got instantiated when the window
// opened, go ahead and destroy it now

IF IsValid( iuo_person ) THEN
    DESTROY iuo_person
END IF
```

31. Save the w_business window.

32. Using the Application painter, code a script to connect to the database and open the w_business window. Enter the script below for the Open event of the Application object.

```
sqlca.dbms = 'ODBC'
sqlca.dbparm = "ConnectString='DSN=Zoo;UID=dba;PWD=sql'"

CONNECT USING sqlca;
// a check for Sqlca.Sqlcode would be a good idea here...
Open( w_business )
```

33. Disconnect from the database by entering the script below for the Close event of the Application object.

```
DISCONNECT USING sqlca;
```

34. Save and run the application.

How It Works

The u_person object is the centerpiece of this program. All of the logic that directly relates to looking up, adding, and saving persons is contained in the custom class user object u_person. The window w_business becomes a simple front end onto a complex object. (Look at the number of functions!) In this How-To, you created a window with custom user events that served as hooks to access the iuo_person instance of u_person. When the user clicks a button, such as New, the button immediately transfers control to the hook events that invoke the logic contained in the u_person user object.

With this structure, it is a simple matter to replace w_business with another window because so little code exists on w_business. Any replacement simply calls the needed functions for u_person. This u_person object also has the capability of being instantiated in multiple places (to support multiple person entry windows) and in different programs (by adding the object's library to the application search path). Changes made in the code of the u_person user object will automatically affect any application that uses it, which adds a great deal of consistency to any system.

Comments

The u_person user object presented here offers minimal functionality. (It has to fit in the book!) Some extensions you could consider adding include deletion of persons and validation of fields (such as state or zip code). Additionally user objects are *inheritable*. This means it is possible to inherit from u_person to create u_employee, which would share the same basic capabilities, along with the ability to do "employee things" such as receiving pay raises, getting hired, getting fired, and moving.

DEPLOYMENT INFORMATION

19

DEPLOYMENT INFORMATION

How do I...

The most significant change to PowerBuilder with version 5.0 is the ability to compile machine code level applications in addition to the Psuedo Code (pCode) level applications we have had prior to this. Additionally, PowerBuilder has provided functions to allow full access to the registry, a database that stores information about the application and that replaces the .INI files we were used to. This chapter covers how to work with both functions.

19.1   Compile a PowerBuilder Application

When building your application, you now have the ability to specify whether you would like PowerBuilder to generate C code and create a machine level application or to have it build the executable using pCode. Additionally, when you do build a machine code level application, you can have PowerBuilder optimize it for speed or for size. This How-To provides steps for building both types of executables.

19.2   Create a Dynamic Link Library

You can generate your dynamic libraries into the pCode version with a file extension of .PBD or you can have PowerBuilder generate a machine code level Dynamic Link Library with an extension of .DLL. This How-To provides steps for the Dynamic Link Library option.

19.3   Use the Registry to Install an Application

The registry is a database, which can be local to your machine and/or installed on your network, that allows storage of application information. With this you no longer need to depend on .INI files nor try to place all of your applications on a small and highly limited path in your autoexec.BAT file. This How-To describes the areas of the registry and how you can use PowerBuilder's new registry functions to set and access registry information, including the key that needs to be set in order to uninstall your application cleanly.

COMPLEXITY
BEGINNING

19.1   How do I...
Compile a PowerBuilder application?

Problem

I have built my application and I now want to create an executable. Which approach (machine code or pCode) is the best and how do I use each one?

Technique

Beginning with PowerBuilder 5.0 you can create a machine code executable and increase the performance of your application. You can also continue to build pCode executables which may be faster to create for quicker prototyping and testing. With machine level code generation you can generate 16-bit or 32-bit executables and you can optimize for speed or for space.

Steps

In this How-To you will create a new PowerBuilder project and use this to first create a traditional PowerBuilder executable using pCode, and then to create a machine code executable that is optimized for speed. You will create a new project for the SINGLE.PBL library that came with the CD-ROM for this book.

The steps to use the Project object follow.

1. Access the SINGLE.PBL library and set the Application object to be your default Application object. Delete the project that is included with it.

2. Create a new Project object by selecting the Project option from the Power Bar.

3. At the top of the Project, type in the name for your executable, "viewer.EXE".

4. Underneath the place to type the resource file you will find three options: whether you will be prompted when PowerBuilder is about to overwrite a file; whether PowerBuilder should regenerate the included PowerBuilder libraries; and whether to prepare this executable as an Open Server Executable. Choose the prompts to overwrite and regenerate options. This executable will be run in a Windows environment only, so you do not need to check for the Open Server option.

5. The next set of options will determine if you will be creating a machine code executable or the traditional pCode executable. You are creating a pCode executable so leave this option unchecked.

6. The next set of options, for tracking and line information and optimization, are for machine code executables only so these will be disabled.

7. Below the options is a list of PowerBuilder libraries that provide one or more objects to the application. You can choose to have a PowerBuilder Dynamic Link Library built for each library or you can choose to have the objects used compiled into your executable. Note that if you use dynamic assignment of DataWindows you will want to create a .PBD file for the library containing the DataWindow, or you will need to include this in your .PBR file.

8. There is a .PBR (PowerBuilder Resource file) for this application. This file contains references for the graphic objects that are referenced dynamically in the code. An example of dynamic assignment of a graphic object is given in the listing below.

```
// assign picture to picture control
p_1.FileName = "logoc.bmp"
```

9. Type the name of the .PBR file, "single.pbr", into the Resource filename for the SINGLE.PBL library.

10. Choose to create a .PBD file for the application main library, SINGLE.PBL, and have the COMMON.PBL objects built into the executable as shown in Figure 19-1. You are now ready to create your executable.

11. There is only one option on the Painter bar for a Project object and this will create the executable. Press the toolbar item to create the executable.

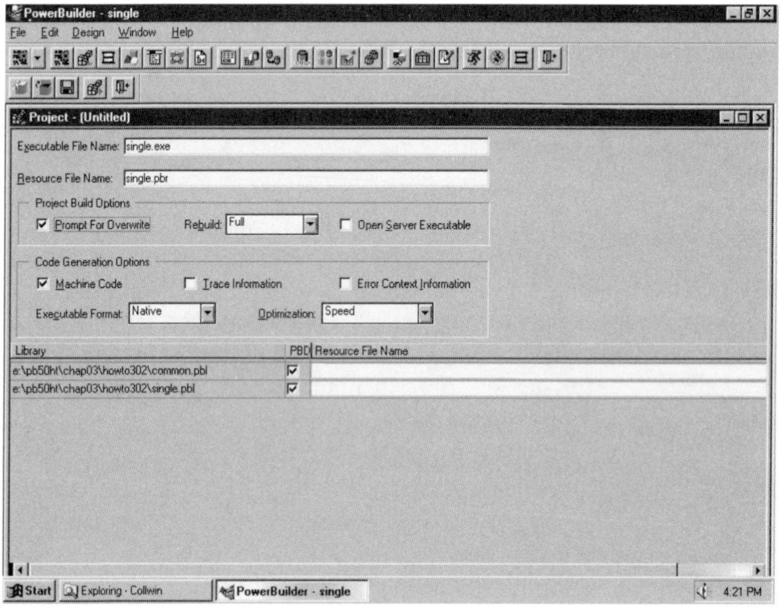

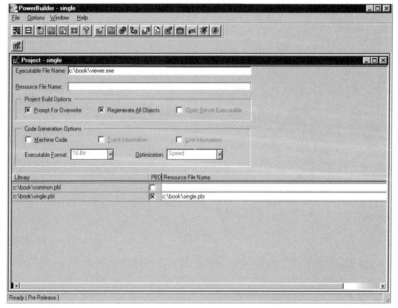

Figure 19-1 Project after all options and choices

Figure 19-2 Project object with options selected

12. Once PowerBuilder has created your executable, copy the executable file and .PBD files to another directory.

13. You will adjust the Project object to create a machine code executable next. Check the Machine Code option and then choose the 32-bit option for the Executable Format, and Speed for the Optimization. Leave the Trace Information and Line Information options unchecked as shown in Figure 19-2.

14. Again, select the toolbar option to create the executable.

15. Run both of the applications, test the results, and examine the files to see differences in sizes.

How It Works

With PowerBuilder 5.0 you now have the option of creating a machine code executable or a pCode (Pseudo Code) version. A pCode executable requires a runtime engine in order to run; the executable does not. The machine code application will be larger in size but should be much faster than the pCode application. The machine code executable will also take longer to compile.

You can look at the C code that PowerBuilder generates, which might be of interest, but don't expect it to be too readable as this is meant for compilation only. If the tool deletes the C files, use your undelete utilities to reinstate.

The code is compiled with the Watcom C/C++ compiler.

Comments

You might be tempted to try modifications to the generated C code in order to do a little customization. We recommend that you refrain from this type of activity as this will only create a maintenance nightmare.

Note that you are not creating a standalone executable when you use the machine code option. With a PowerBuilder application you will still need the PowerBuilder runtime environment.

COMPLEXITY
BEGINNING

19.2   How do I...
Create a Dynamic Link Library?

Problem

I would like to use some of the functionality of my PowerBuilder application from other applications written in C++. How can I generate a Dynamic Link Library and how can I use this with other applications?

Technique

You can create a Dynamic Link Library with PowerBuilder but you cannot use this with other applications. This How-To will demonstrate how to create this type of file and present a workaround in the Comments section for accessing PowerBuilder functionality from other applications.

Steps

You will create a Dynamic Link Library (DLL) of the COMMON.PBL library. This library is used by several different PowerBuilder applications. Creating a .DLL file from this library will allow each of the applications to have access to it, yet Windows only has to load one copy of the library into memory.

To create a Dynamic Link Library follow the steps below.

1. From the Library painter click on the COMMON.PBL library object.

2. Select the Build Dynamic Library menu item from the Library main menu.

3. Check the Machine Code option without the Trace Information or Line Information options.

4. Change the Executable Format to Native and the Optimization to Speed, which means that the machine code will match the current environment (in this case with Windows 95 or NT, 32-bit), and the code will be optimized for speed.

5. There is no PBR file for this library. The Build Dynamic Library should look like that shown in Figure 19-3.

6. When you press the OK button, the Dynamic Link Library will be created.

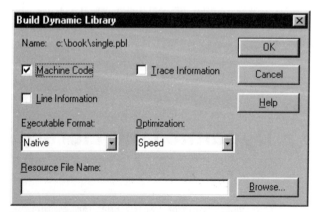

Figure 19-3 Build Dynamic Library dialog after options have been selected

How It Works

PowerBuilder can create a machine code or pCode version of a Dynamic Link Library. With machine code generation, you can include line and trace information and optimize and change the format of the file.

Comments

As stated in the Techniques section, the PowerBuilder DLLs will not contain functions that are callable by non-related applications. However, you can create OLE 2.0 Automation Server functions (see Chapter 13) and use these from other application tools such as Visual Basic, Delphi, Excel, Word, etc.

COMPLEXITY
INTERMEDIATE

19.3 How do I...
Use the registry to install an application?

Problem

I am creating an installation program for my application that will work on Windows 95 and Windows NT. I want my application to be Windows 95 compliant, which means I will need to work with the registry. How can I set and get information from the registry?

Technique

The registry is actually quite simple to work with, once you understand the key structure, which may not be as simple. This How-To will use the built-in PowerBuilder functions to write to and read from the registry as well as demonstrate how to create a .REG file (registry) file to install your application keys.

Steps

This How-To will describe specific keys in the registry, why they are important, and how to use the PowerBuilder functions to set or get the key(s) and their associated value(s). This How-To will also demonstrate how to use the Export functionality of the registry to create a .REG file that you can use as a template to create your own registry file. The steps are for an application that has never been installed before. Check the Comments section about steps you will need to follow when installing a newer version.

Follow the steps below to gain more understanding of the registry.

1. When you install your application, you will want to put your executable and any support files into a subdirectory that you create. You can access the registry to get the Program Files subdirectory and create your subdirectory there, or at least provide this option to your application user.

2. The location of the Program Files subdirectory and the associated PowerBuilder function call is listed below.

```
String ls_Database_key, ls_Directory

ls_Database_key = &
"HKEY_LOCAL_MACHINE\SOFTWARE\Microsoft\Windows\CurrentVersion\"

// access directory
registryGet(ls_Database_Key, "ProgramFilesDir", ls_Directory)
```

3. Once you have the Program Files directory, and your user has specified that he or she wishes the application installed in a subdirectory under Program Files, you will create the subdirectory and a related Systems subdirectory for any related .DLL or .PBD files.

4. Once you have created your new subdirectory, you will want to register your path. The best way to do this is to place the values in a registry file, which is a file with a "REG" extension that contains keys and their associated values, preceded by the REGEDIT command.

5. A trick to knowing what to place in the file is to find an entry in the registry that is close to what you want and to export it to a registry file. Then edit it to show what you want, as in the listing below.

```
REGEDIT4

[HKEY_LOCAL_MACHINE\SOFTWARE\Microsoft\Windows\CurrentVersion\App
Paths\viewer.exe]
"Path"="C:\\Program Files\\Viewer"
```

6. You can use this same trick or use the PowerBuilder function RegistrySet to enter the database parameters into the registry.

```
String ls_Database_key

// set key
ls_Database_key = &
"HKEY_LOCAL_MACHINE\SOFTWARE\HOWTO\CurrentVersion\Database"

// set registry values
RegistrySet(ls_Database_Key, "Database", "Zooadmn")
RegistrySet(ls_Database_Key, "DBMS", "ODBC")
RegistrySet(ls_Database_Key, "PARM", "ConnectString='DSN=Zooadmn'")
RegistrySet(ls_Database_Key, "UID", "dba")
RegistrySet(ls_Database_Key, "PWD","sql")
```

7. You can register your application icon, which will enable Windows to know what icon to display with what file type. This will only be meaningful if you are working with files and a standardized file extension. You should also use caution with the file extension you claim for your application.

```
String ls_key

ls_key = "HKEY_CLASSES_ROOT\.ing"

RegistrySet(ls_key, "DefaultIcon","myapp.ico")
```

8. A last important registry entry you will examine will be the uninstall key value. Windows 95 and up requires that an application provide the ability to uninstall itself cleanly from the system. The program that sets up the application will usually uninstall it if a flag is given. The uninstall command must be registered in a specific key path as the listing below shows.

```
string ls_key

ls_key = "HKEY_LOCAL_MACHINE\SOFTWARE\Microsoft\" + &
            "Windows\CurrentVersion\Uninstall\myapp"

// register values
RegistrySet(ls_key, "DisplayName", "my application")
RegistrySet(ls_key, "UninstallString", "myapp.exe -u")
```

9. The DisplayName is the name that will display in the Install/Remove utility. The string provides the executable and flag that will trigger the uninstall program.

How It Works

This How-To provided a sampling of helpful registry values and how to set or get them using two PowerBuilder functions: RegistryGet and RegistrySet. Less common registry keys can set Shell extensions (such as what displays on the popup menu for your file icon), autorun (for an application installing from a CD-ROM), user-specific information, ODBC driver information, etc. The functions defined in these steps can be accessed in REGISTRY.PBL.

The HKEY_LOCAL_MACHINE major key contains references to information relative to the machine the registry file is located on. The HKEY_CURRENT_USER key contains information about application state for the individual user. The HKEY_CURRENT_USERS key contains general application state information. The HKEY_CLASSES_ROOT key contains information defining automation servers, Shell extensions, and registration of class IDs and icons.

Comments

An invaluable resource on the registry and other integration issues is *The Windows Interface Guidelines for Software Design* published by Microsoft Press.

INDEX

Go for the end zone
with full-contact
PowerBuilder 5.0 training.

Interactive courses let you train right at your desktop!

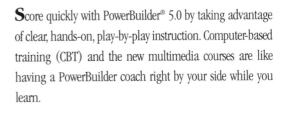

Score quickly with PowerBuilder® 5.0 by taking advantage of clear, hands-on, play-by-play instruction. Computer-based training (CBT) and the new multimedia courses are like having a PowerBuilder coach right by your side while you learn.

Each CBT lesson includes interactive, graphical exercises that walk you through the application development process. Multimedia courses combine sight and sound in "video" demos and instruction for a highly effective training program.

Best of all, you learn at your own pace — anytime, anywhere.

So before you tackle your next development project, order these self-paced training courses and take 15% off with this ad! See reverse for course topics and order form or call **800-395-3525** today.

Discount is valid only on purchases made through Powersoft from Jan. 1 - Dec. 31, 1996.

Save 15% on any PowerBuilder 5.0 self-paced training course.

Save 15% on PowerBuilder 5.0 Self-Paced Training (with this ad.)

Get up to speed quickly on the latest PowerBuilder® release with any of these highly effective, self-paced training courses. And be sure to check out the Powersoft® home page on the World Wide Web for full course descriptions, plus new video, multimedia, and CBT course offerings. Visit us at *www.powersoft.com* today.

Name

Title

Company

Address

City

State/Province   Zip/Postal Code

Phone   FAX

Qty	Course	Item #	Price Save 15%!	Total
	Making the Most of PowerBuilder 5.0 CBT	50300	~~$249~~ $212	
	Introduction to PowerBuilder CBT Series			
	• PowerBuilder: The Basics	50303	~~$249~~ $212	
	• DataWindow Concepts	50306	~~$249~~ $212	
	• Implementing a User Interface	50309	~~$249~~ $212	
	• Object-Oriented Essentials in PowerBuilder	50312	~~$249~~ $212	
	• All four Introduction to PowerBuilder CBT modules	50320	~~$695~~ $591	
	Fast Track to PowerBuilder 5.0 Multimedia CD	50323	~~$649~~ $552	
	This series includes the following course topics: • Preparing for Distributed Computing • Developing PowerBuilder Applications in Windows 95™ • Extending PowerBuilder: Exploiting OLE and OCX • Leveraging PowerBuilder 5.0 Object-Oriented Language Features • Accelerating Development Using PowerBuilder Foundation Classes	*Available May, 1996*		

Note: All pricing is in U.S. dollars. *To receive pricing and ordering information for countries within Europe, the Middle East, and Africa, please contact PW direct at tel: + 494 55 5599 or email: pwdsales@powersoft.com.*
For all other countries, please contact your local Powersoft office or representative.

Subtotal

Applicable Sales Tax

Shipping ($8.50 per product)

TOTAL

ATR 40F6HT

Method of Payment:

Make checks payable in U.S. dollars to **Powersoft** and include payment with order. Please do not send cash.

❑ Check   ❑ Purchase Order   ❑ MasterCard   ❑ Visa   ❑ American Express

Credit Card number, Purchase Order number, or Check number   *Expiration date*

Name on Credit Card

Cardholder's Signature

THREE EASY WAYS TO ORDER!

#1 **CALL** Powersoft at **800-395-3525**.

#2 **FAX** this order form to **617-389-1080**.

#3 Or **MAIL** this order form along with payment to Powersoft, P.O. Box 9116, Everett, MA 02149.

NOTES

NOTES

NOTES

NOTES

NOTES

NOTES

NOTES

NOTES

NOTES

NOTES

NOTES

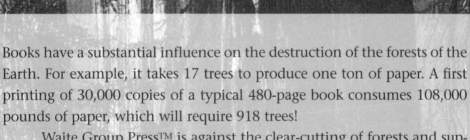

Books have a substantial influence on the destruction of the forests of the Earth. For example, it takes 17 trees to produce one ton of paper. A first printing of 30,000 copies of a typical 480-page book consumes 108,000 pounds of paper, which will require 918 trees!

Waite Group Press™ is against the clear-cutting of forests and supports reforestation of the Pacific Northwest of the United States and Canada, where most of this paper comes from. As a publisher with several hundred thousand books sold each year, we feel an obligation to give back to the planet. We will therefore support organizations which seek to preserve the forests of planet Earth.

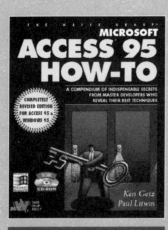

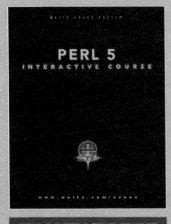

This is a legal agreement between you, the end user and purchaser, and The Waite Group®, Inc., and the authors of the programs contained in the disk. By opening the sealed disk package, you are agreeing to be bound by the terms of this Agreement. If you do not agree with the terms of this Agreement, promptly return the unopened disk package and the accompanying items (including the related book and other written material) to the place you obtained them for a refund.

SOFTWARE LICENSE

1. The Waite Group, Inc. grants you the right to use one copy of the enclosed software programs (the programs) on a single computer system (whether a single CPU, part of a licensed network, or a terminal connected to a single CPU). Each concurrent user of the program must have exclusive use of the related Waite Group, Inc. written materials.

2. The program, including the copyrights in each program, is owned by the respective author and the copyright in the entire work is owned by The Waite Group, Inc. and they are therefore protected under the copyright laws of the United States and other nations, under international treaties. You may make only one copy of the disk containing the programs exclusively for backup or archival purposes, or you may transfer the programs to one hard disk drive, using the original for backup or archival purposes. You may make no other copies of the programs, and you may make no copies of all or any part of the related Waite Group, Inc. written materials.

3. You may not rent or lease the programs, but you may transfer ownership of the programs and related written materials (including any and all updates and earlier versions) if you keep no copies of either, and if you make sure the transferee agrees to the terms of this license.

4. You may not decompile, reverse engineer, disassemble, copy, create a derivative work, or otherwise use the programs except as stated in this Agreement.

GOVERNING LAW

This Agreement is governed by the laws of the State of California.

SOFTWARE LICENSE AGREEMENT